# Religion, Supernaturalism, the Paranormal, and Pseudoscience

# Religion, Supernaturalism, the Paranormal, and Pseudoscience

## An Anthropological Critique

H. Sidky

ANTHEM PRESS

Anthem Press
An imprint of Wimbledon Publishing Company
*www.anthempress.com*

This edition first published in UK and USA 2020
by ANTHEM PRESS
75–76 Blackfriars Road, London SE1 8HA, UK
or PO Box 9779, London SW19 7ZG, UK
and
244 Madison Ave #116, New York, NY 10016, USA



*British Library Cataloguing-in-Publication Data*
A catalogue record for this book is available from the British Library.

ISBN-13: 978-1-78527-162-5 (Hbk)
ISBN-10: 1-78527-162-8 (Hbk)

This title is also available as an e-book.

For Kathryn Lea. Thank you for being my *advocatus diaboli* in Venice, Italy and helping me shape many of the ideas expressed here.

# CONTENTS

# ACKNOWLEDGMENTS

My thanks go to several people for their contributions to this project. First, I would like to thank my colleagues at the Department of Anthropology, Miami University, whose debates about the state and direction of the field of anthropology shaped many of the ideas expressed here. Special thanks also go out to the three reviewers—all anonymous, so I cannot thank them by name—each of whom made different but valuable critical comments that helped me improve the final draft of the manuscript. I alone assume responsibility for any errors and the views expressed in this manuscript.

# INTRODUCTION

*When governments and societies lose the capacity for critical thinking, the results can be catastrophic—however sympathetic we may be to those who have bought the baloney.*

—Carl Sagan, *The Demon-Haunted World* (1995)

*There [. . .] is a price we pay when we tolerate flawed thinking and superstitious beliefs. [. . .] Thinking straight about the world is a precious and difficult process that must be carefully nurtured. By attempting to turn our critical intelligence off and on at will, we risk losing it altogether, and thus jeopardize our ability to see the world clearly. Furthermore, by failing to develop our critical faculties, we become susceptible to the arguments and exhortations of those with other than benign intentions.*

—Thomas Gilovich, *How We Know What Isn't So* (1991)

At the end of the second decade of the twenty-first century, a large proportion of the American public does not know that the earth orbits the sun in a year-long cycle. Over half of the people are unaware that dinosaurs died before the appearance of humans, and about as many affirm that the earth was created during the Bronze Age (Otto 2016: 224). Astonishingly, an equal number of our citizens believe in the existence of ghosts, extraterrestrial beings, paranormal monsters, alien abductions, Bigfoot, hauntings, demonic possession, angels, miracles, and so forth (Chapman University Survey of American Fears 2018; Smith 2010: 22–23). This mostly scientifically illiterate public seems to lack the rudimentary skills to distinguish between contending claims to knowledge. We now live in a scary and confusing "post-truth" era of disinformation, "fake news," "counter-knowledge," "weaponized lies," conspiracy theories, magical thinking, and sheer irrationalism (Sidky 2018).

Even the paragons of our political system are unashamedly declaring that it is impossible to distinguish between fact and opinion, that for every fact there is "an alternative fact," that truth is whatever people want it to be, and that science is just another story (Otto 2016: 175–76; Sidky 2004: 394–412, 2007a). These political doyens have normalized anti-science rhetoric and irrationalism in US politics. Their main objective is to circumvent input from scientific experts and exclude scientific studies from the policymaking process, thereby jeopardizing the ability of the United States to cope with current and future public health and environmental problems (Carter et al. 2019; Otto 2016: 29).

Profit-hungry energy extraction and agrochemical corporations are overjoyed by these developments. Seeking to dodge environmental and safety regulations and undermine policymaking based on scientific evidence, they have formed an "unholy alliance" with evangelical churches to present a unified front against science and rationality (Sidky

2018). This could be considered one of the dividends of the extensive efforts of "corporate America" to create a fundamentalist "Christian America" (Kruse 2015).

The current intellectual climate has enabled a proliferation of clairvoyants, spirit-channelers, ghost-finders, exorcists, and New Age messiahs whose ideas are daily an affront to the intelligence and sensibilities of rational people. A resurgence of reinvigorated, intolerant, and politically empowered religious extremism that has accompanied these developments along with a profusion of home-grown evangelical ayatollahs, prophets, and self-proclaimed ambassadors of heaven is particularly troublesome and frightening. These purveyors of archaic and medieval credulities are in unison announcing with bluster and hubris that science is now defunct and rationality is obsolete, and they are offering their own "truths" and "ways of knowing" as better substitutes. Anti-science, anti-intellectualism, and irrational thinking seem to be the order of the day.

History has recurrently demonstrated that tolerating irrationalism and superstitious beliefs poses many dangers. First, it is dangerous to individual well-being. In our time, numerous people have died because of their trust in sham alternative medical cures and supernatural remedies, and many others have lost their life savings by believing in pretended psychics, diviners, and miracle workers. Second, acquiescence to irrationalism is inimical to a free society and threatens the well-being of our democracy (see Thompson and Smulewicz-Zucker 2018). As philosophers Theodore Schick and Lewis Vaughn (2014: 13) observe,

> A democratic society depends on the ability of its members to make rational choices. But rational choices must be based on rational beliefs. If we can't tell the difference between reasonable and unreasonable claims, we become susceptible to the claims of charlatans, scoundrels, and mountebanks.

Along the same lines, the historian of religion Leonardo Ambasciano (2018: 172) has astutely pointed out that "science and democracy are intertwined." They both empower people and encourage critical thinking. This is why, he adds, right-wing reactionaries and conservative forces exert enormous amounts of effort and resources to "delegitimize science" and its significance in human life.

This book is written with these particular predicaments and concerns in mind. It is an effort to subject the entire range of contemporary supernatural and paranormal "truths" and religionist postulates on offer to unremitting critical scrutiny and skeptical analysis *as comprehensively as possible* from the perspective of science and scientific anthropology. The present study differs from other critical works on religion and the paranormal in several respects. Many researchers consider paranormal beliefs and religious precepts as separate manifestations. In this study, religious, supernatural, and paranormal beliefs, including pseudoscientific theories based upon the latter, are all treated as interrelated and mutually supporting phenomena. In other words, every practice and belief that may be labeled supernatural or paranormal, whether mediated by priests, shamans, mullahs, *ayatollahs*, rabbis, monks, *rimboches*, clairvoyants, vatics, prophets, psychics, or New Age messiahs fall within the scope of the present study. As such, this study addresses paranormalism and religiosity more comprehensively than has been accomplished by others and is not merely an argument for atheism.

Throughout this work, I rely upon my scientific anthropological background and ethnographic field research of supernatural and paranormal beliefs and practices during the last 30 years, an effort that has taken me to various locations and cultural settings around the world and encounters with many religious communities and supernatural practitioners. The overall approach is anthropological. However, this book brings together *in one place* materials from a variety of fields. These include the most relevant skeptical philosophical arguments; ideas presented by certain theologians; the findings by evolutionary, cognitive, experimental, and anomalistic psychologists, evolutionary and cognitive anthropologists; as well as ideas forwarded by scientific cultural anthropologists.

# Chapter One

# THE PROBLEM WITH RELIGION: PRELIMINARY ISSUES

*Too absurd for belief, too impossible to convince, and too inconsistent for practice, [religion] renders the heart torpid, or produces only atheists and fanatics. As an engine of power, it serves the purpose of despotism; and as a means of wealth, the avarice of priests; but so far as respects the good of [humans] in general, it leads to nothing here or hereafter.*

—Thomas Paine, *The Age of Reason* (1795)

*That which is absurd and impossible, that which in any other history would be called falsehood, deception, outrage, and cruelty, cannot be made reasonable, righteous, and true by the added words: Thus saith the Lord.*

—Hermann Reimarus, *Fragments from* Reimarus (1879)

*A good world needs knowledge, kindness, and courage; it does not need a regretful hankering after the past or a fettering of the free intelligence by the words uttered long ago by ignorant men.*

—Bertrand Russell, *Why I Am Not a* Christian (1957)

*More wars have been waged, more people killed, and these days more evil perpetrated in the name of religion than by any other institutional force in human history.*

—Charles Kimball, *When Religion Becomes Evil* (2008)

In the second decade of the twenty-first century, religion has become one of the most powerful and dangerous forces in the world. For an overwhelming number of devout believers, faith and the triumph of their respective religions outweigh the sanctity of human life as well as all other concerns, including peace on earth, human rights, secularism, democracy, and the fate of this planet (cf., Dennett 2006: 15–16). Religious hatreds, violence, and warfare in the name of one vicious god or another have obliterated whole generations and torn apart entire societies. I have personally lived through and witnessed such tragic events during my travels and field research around the world during the last 30 years.

These are harsh words, and indignant believers will present the standard objections that religion is indispensable because it provides psychological solace, meaning, a sense of community, and, above all, that it ensures moral behavior (Konner 2019: 175–76). In his book *The End of Materialism: How Evidence of the Paranormal Is Bringing Science and Spirit*

*Together* (2009), paranormalist Charles Tart (2009: 35) expresses such sentiments in the context of his diatribe about the inadequacies of science:

> Our ethics and morality, our highest values, come from religion. Won't we be on the same level as the savage beast, "red in tooth and claw," if we completely reject religion? And is everything in religion factually false?

Unfortunately, Tart is wrong on all these points. It is true that through authoritative sacred texts purportedly authored by God, or the gods, and from the mouths of self-proclaimed "ambassadors from heaven," religions provide codes of conduct. However, these directives were the brainchild of superstitious, ignorant, and violent tribal people who lived and died thousands of years ago. It is for this reason that the holy books on offer are full of horrors, incineration, torture, mutilation, intimidation, and terrorism interspersed with declarations about mercy, love, and compassion, and read almost like handbooks or catalogs of psychopathology.

There is very little evidence that religious believers lead more moral and law-abiding lives than nonbelievers; otherwise the more than two million people housed in the numerous penitentiaries in the United States and the close to five million more who are on probation or parole would consist only of atheists (cf., Bondi 2003: 148: Dennett 2006: 279). Moreover, cross-cultural comparative studies indicate that mostly secular societies with large numbers of atheists, such as Denmark and Sweden, have significantly lower murder and suicide rates; fewer rapes, teen pregnancies, abortions; and lesser frequencies of sexually transmitted disease than the highly religious and "moral" United States (Bloom 2012: 189, 192). These findings, some have argued, contradict assertions that religion is necessary for a moral society (Bloom 2012: 189; Paul 2005; Zuckerman 2008).

The fact is that purported moral and ethical religious people have committed great atrocities across space and throughout time. Religion incites hostility, prejudice, misogyny, racism, and violence toward others. Anthropological and psychological studies suggest as much, but the weight of history is alone sufficient to demonstrate the horrific dark side of faith-based beliefs (Bloom 2012; Ganges et al. 2009; Hall et al. 2010). Also, people have had religion for millennia, yet immoral behavior, war, crime, and other villanies and acts of inhumanity have not only flourished but in many cases been instigated and exacerbated for religious reasons. In actuality, much of the violence taking place on this planet today stem from ancient religious hatreds. Moreover, contra Tart's assertion, religion is factually wrong because its central premises are illogical, nonsensical, contradictory, and unequivocally false. Nonetheless, the minds of nearly all of the eight billion people who live on earth today are fettered by archaic and medieval theistic religious credulities that we have inherited from a benighted time of ignorance, cruelty, and violence.

Apologists may also point out that it is the "extremists" who are responsible for the horrible things done in the name of religion, hence the suggestion that we should balance the good with the bad. Those who make this suggestion assume that the horrors and dark deeds perpetrated by true believers, such as the crusades, *auto-de-fés*, inquisitions, pogroms, religious ritual murders in the form of witch-hunting, *jihads*, ethnic cleansings, suicide bombings, amputations, beheadings, and other monstrous acts are mere perversions of religion. However, this view collapses the instance one looks at the track record of religion across space and time.

Religion indoctrinates believers to treat its supernatural and paranormal precepts as being more important than human life and the secular virtues of human rights, social equality, tolerance, empathy, rationality, and peace on earth (Weinberg 1993: 258). These are not peripheral symptoms of religious beliefs but are indispensable parts of their central tenets. As the philosopher John Hick (1993: 81) has put it,

> The history of every major religious tradition includes great moral evils committed by its adherents. Sometimes these have not only been justified on prudential grounds by those who committed or acquiesced in them but have been validated by appeal to the official teaching of the traditions itself.

Hick goes on to say, however, that the problem is not religious beliefs but rather the fact that such views are inherently liable to dangerous misuse due to shortcomings of human nature. This assertion is not very convincing. The violent militants who commit evils paradoxically in the name of their merciful and benevolent gods rely on the same sacred texts and the same doctrines as "good" believers, or the so-called peace-loving moderates (cf., Harris 2004: 29–31). The same biblical texts used by peaceful believers, for example, have inspired the development of cults and sects, such as Peoples Temple and the Branch Davidians whose members came to violent ends (Percy 2001: 30). As the professor of religious studies Charles Kimball (2008, 2011) points out, history shows that religion is directly linked to the worst types of human behavior. Religion, he adds, has incited more wars, more deaths, and greater evil than any other institutional force in human history (Kimball 2008: 1).

Many others also see religion as a dark and uncontrollable force, an actor in its own right and not a surrogate for some grievance, that causes irrational behavior, violence, and terrorism (McTernan 2003: x). Investigative author and skeptic James Haught describes what I have encountered repeatedly during field research. He states that whenever and wherever religion becomes the ruling force in society, the result is horror. The strength of the supernatural beliefs is proportionate to the intensity of the inhumanity. Cultures that dominate by intense faith are invariably cruel to those who do not share the beliefs and also to many that do (Haught 1990: 14).

Even so-called religions of peace, such as Buddhism, have demonstrated this dark side. Attesting to this is the role of the Buddhist monk Ashin Wirathu in inciting genocidal attacks against the non-Buddhist Rohingya in Myanmar. Apologists such as the Dalai Lama offering the usual religionist excuse that such individuals are not true believers are not convincing. Such horrors occur too often to be explained away as the handiwork of wayward fanatics. For reasons I shall discuss, violence seems to be an embedded feature or subroutine of all religious programs. It is not wicked people who do bad things in the name of religion, but rather it is ordinary people who are religious who engage in atrocities and violence. This propensity led social psychologist C. Daniel Batson to call religion a "double agent" because, while it seeks to make "all men brothers" it produces Crusades, the Inquisition, and relentless witch hunts. He adds that virtually every religion has been an excuse for or the cause of violent, inhuman, and antisocial behavior (Batson 1976: 30). For these reasons, it is impossible to accept claims by religious sympathizers and proponents of interfaith dialogue, such as Karen Armstrong (2014). She asserts that religion has many different attributes, stresses that violence is not one of those attributes, and ascribes faith-based malevolence and the all too common enthusiastic slaughter and destruction in which believers avidly partake to other factors and forces, such as colonialism, modernity, and so forth.

In his book *Believers: Faith in Human Nature* (2019), the anthropologist Melvin Konner adopts a similar deferential if not apologetic stance toward religion. After listing a litany of horrors perpetrated by believers across the globe, he argues that the good done by religion outweighs the evils it has caused. By this, he is referring to the standard list of things such as religion offering psychological solace, a sense of identity and community, meaning, a way to deal with the uncertainties of life, and so on. Moreover, he expresses admiration for the fact that religious thinkers from all faiths have repudiated rationalist critiques "*without* abandoning their faith, or even while embracing it more strongly" (Konner 2019: xxv). Furthermore, he considers faith (i.e., belief in things for which there is no evidence) as something praiseworthy and desirable that deserves respect. Konner is wrong on all these points.

Long ago, the anthropologists Bronislaw Malinowski argued that religion and magic have a positive function that addresses anxieties arising from aspects of life over which people lack control. Hence, what Konner says is neither a new idea nor a very convincing one. What he overlooks is that religion also *causes* anxiety, guilt, stress, and fear: fear of vengeful ancestral ghosts, spirits, and gods; fear of damnation and eternal combustion; and so forth. Religion for all the purported good ascribed to it creates fanatics, sectarians, bigots, terrorists, and mass murderers.

As the noted American skeptic Robert Ingersoll (1907: 792) put it,

> In every land, where [God's holy text has] been read, the children to whom and for whom it was written have been filled with hatred and malice. They have imprisoned and murdered each other, and the wives and children of each other. In the name of God every possible crime has been committed, every conceivable outrage perpetrated.

Also, religion enables not so pious megalomaniacal self-appointed representatives of some purported god to delude the faithful into accepting whatever outlandish beliefs they are peddling. For this reason, religion has and continues to serve the interests of those in power. It is one of the most effective means of social and thought control that has deluded the faithful for millennia.

As for religious devotees retaining their beliefs in the face of skeptical critique, Konner is, in reality, expressing admiration for two specific human cognitive defects or shortcomings. These are the *confirmation bias* and the "backfire effect" (McIntyre 2018: 36–58). The confirmation bias entails the human proclivity to selectively use facts that prop baseless beliefs and the peremptory rejection of those that do not. The backfire effect refers to the fact that when people confront evidence that their deeply held beliefs are wrong, they reject the evidence and double down on their erroneous beliefs and embrace them with greater enthusiasm. These biases are at the center of today's post-truth cultural climate and have contributed to rampant anti-intellectualism and the proliferation of conspiracy theories, and superstitious and pseudoscientific nonsense. These are hardly admirable human traits or qualities.

Finally, Konner seems to conflate people's right to their own opinions, which should be inalienable, and the *rightness* of those opinions, which is always subject to contestation. Indeed, as the scientific anthropologist James Lett (1997: 113–14) observes, people who are compelled through ignorance, fear, or cowardice to accept erroneous beliefs while perhaps eligible for sympathy never deserve respect or admiration. Anyone who has honestly looked at the contents of the purported sacred texts on offer and has examined the dark, bloody, and disturbing behavior across time and space inspired by the words of God, or the gods, contained in those books will find it difficult to accept Armstrong's apologetics and Konner's deference.

As to the solace that people are said to obtain from religion, this is ephemeral and has come at substantial costs. In his book, *The Age of Reason* (1794–1807), Thomas Paine, the American hero, politician, philosopher, and one of the first courageous Bible demythologizer, offered profound insights about theistic religion that are worth heeding today. In his words,

> The most detestable wickedness, the most horrid cruelties, and the greatest miseries that have afflicted the human race have had their origin in this thing called revelation, or revealed religion. (Paine 1880 [1795]: 142)

Paine (1880 [1794]: 147) accurately saw religion as a human invention, rather than a cosmic miracle, devised to terrify and enslave humankind and monopolize power and profit:

> Too absurd for belief, too impossible to convince, and too inconsistent for practice, it renders the heart torpid, or produces only atheists and fanatics. As an engine of power it serves the purpose of despotism; and as a means of wealth, the avarice of priests; but so far as respects the good of [humankind] in general, it leads to nothing here or hereafter.

The philosopher and logician Bertrand Russell held similar views:

> the more intense has been the religion of any period and the more profound has been the dogmatic belief, the greater has been the cruelty, and the worse has been the state of affairs. In the so-called ages of faith [...] there was the Inquisition, with its tortures; there were millions of unfortunate women burned as witches; and there was every kind of cruelty practiced upon all sort of people in the name of religion. [...] A good world needs knowledge, kindness, and courage; it does not need a regretful hankering after the past, or a fettering of the free intelligence by the words uttered long ago by ignorant men. [...] The whole contention that Christianity has had an elevating moral influence can only be maintained by wholesale ignoring or falsification of the historical evidence. (Russell 1957: 19, 20, 23, 202)

What Russell said about Christianity applies equally to any of the other religions. The frightening thought is that during the twenty-first century, we are entering a new age of faith and a time of reinvigorated fundamentalisms and dogmatic beliefs along with all of their associated horrors and cruelties.

If religion, any religion, had any elevating moral influences, we would not be living in the kind of world we have. Here three billion people barely make a living, close to one and a half billion are suffering extreme poverty and near starvation, and where inhumanity, war, crime, injustice, inequality, oppression, slavery, the abuse of women and children, and cruelty to nonhuman life forms are daily facts of life. So, what happened to our highest moral values, charity, empathy, tolerance, and love that religion supposedly provides? Where are the handprints in this terrible world of the merciful, compassionate, and benevolent authors of these religions? Our revered religions have had thousands of years to put such things into place. Why are there no signs of the promised charity, kindness, tolerance, and love? No form of apologetics and special pleading can explain away this glaring and embarrassing incongruity. If religion is the best solution for the salvation of humanity, it has failed terribly.

## Why Are Believers Incensed by Criticism?

Despite religion's dark history and the untold misery, fear, and oppression it has caused, in many places religious believers receive a degree of respect, deference, and even public and governmental support that is difficult to understand. Indeed, there is a widespread view that religion is a good thing and peoples' religious beliefs fall into a special privileged category that deserves particular respect and exemption from critical scrutiny (Bondi 2003: 147; Dawkins 2006: 20–21, 2003: 154). Such deference is requisite because religious people are said to be extremely sensitive to criticism. One can compare this to an almost "religious" conviction or taboo that says, "thou shalt not question religious truths." In other words, the truth and falsity of religious beliefs are not topics of discussion in public or scholarly discourses on religion. Instead, the demand is for deference.

The question to ask is: Why are the faithful so horrified and outraged by criticism? Why the vehement indignation and sense of sacrilege? After all, aren't their supernatural beliefs divinely ordained and communicated by no less an authority than the Creator of the universe? Shouldn't such creeds be inherently beyond reproach? Shouldn't directives and truths conveyed by such an omnipotent, omniscient being—characteristics that believers everywhere attribute to their purported gods—be self-evidently valid without the necessity to be defended by puny human beings? The sense of sacrilege evoked by criticism suggests that perhaps things are not as they seem and that the faithful lack confidence and are fearful that their beliefs may be shown to be banal, fallacious, and delusional.

The tendentious Christian apologist Alvin Plantinga (2000) argues that religious beliefs—specifically Christian beliefs—are "basic beliefs," a kind of knowledge that requires no inferential justification. In other words, religious truths are self-certifying, self-evident, and acceptable without question. This argument is unconvincing. It is merely a duplicitous attempt to immunize religion from evidentiary challenges, which is the primary objective of all such apologetics. What it does, however, as the philosopher Herman Philipse (2014: 42) points out, is to reinforce "religious dogmatists in their dogmatism, and [...] bolsters up bigots in their bigotry."

If religious truths are self-evident, as apologists say, then why do all religions exert massive efforts to ensure that the faithful do not deviate, or "god forbid" become apostates and heretics, by bringing to bear extensive thought control and thought monitoring arsenals? These include childhood indoctrination, Bible camps, *madrassas*, Sunday schools, creation museums, Ark exhibits, Bible amusement parks, careful management of group dynamics, ritual regimentation, peer pressure, *fatwas*, papal bulls, coercion, sheer violence, and even the death penalty. Also, why do all religions maintain cadres of thought control specialists and enforcers—the keepers of the truth and guardians of the mysteries—called popes, cardinals, priests, reverends, rabbis, ayatollahs, mullahs, lamas, geshes, monks, goswamis, shamans, inquisitors, and other enforcers? The answer is simple. Such things are in use because they are necessary. Added to this are the huge investments into monumental religious architecture, such as pyramids, temples, cathedrals, and mosques, to be found across the planet, which continually broadcast the formidability, invincibility, and awesomeness of the gods and their earthly representatives (Harris 1971: 407; Sidky 2015: 138).

Moreover, if the central precepts of religion genuinely emanate from a divine source, as religionists claim, then why have those professing other faiths not abandoned their beliefs and accepted the self-evident truths proposed? The presence of thousands of religions, denominations, sects, and cults attests to the fact that the divine messages are not self-evident. As the noted American skeptic Robert Ingersoll (1907: 791) put it about Christianity,

> Every sect is a certificate that God has not plainly revealed His will to man. To each reader, the Bible conveys a different meaning. About the meaning of this book called a revelation, there have been ages of war and centuries of swords and flame. If written by an infinite God, He must have known that these results must follow; and thus knowingly, He must be responsible for all.

Along the same lines, Paine (1880 [1795]: 57) perspicaciously observed regarding the Bible,

> It has been the practice of all Christian commentators on the Bible, and of all Christian priests and preachers, to impose the Bible on the world as a mass of truth and as the word of God; they have disputed and wrangled, and anathematized each other about the supposed meaning of particular parts and passages therein; one has said and insisted that such a passage meant such a thing; another that it meant directly the contrary; and a third, that it meant neither one nor the other, but something different; and this they call understanding the Bible.

Religion, of course, has a readily available response to epistemic challenges, not by marshaling irrefutable evidence of the divine infallibility of its precepts—such evidence does not exist—but by the suppression or physical elimination of its opponents. One of the main reasons these antiquated belief systems have persisted is that they have incessantly ostracized or condemned critics as heretics and apostates (Hitchens 2007: 17; Kurtz 2003a: 277).

## Religion as a Mind Virus

Some scientists have used the metaphor of "intellectual infection" or "mind virus" to describe the spread, proliferation, and effects of religious beliefs. The basis of this perspective is the concept of memes proposed by the evolutionary biologist Richard Dawkins in his book *The Selfish Gene* (1976). Memes, according to Dawkins, are "units of cultural inheritance" that offer a way of conceptualizing the transmission and evolution of cultural traditions. Several books have been published that elaborate upon these ideas. These include: *Thought Contagion* (1996) by the mathematician and philosopher, the late Aaron Lynch; *Virus of the Mind* (2009) by the computer scientist Richard Brodie; *The God Virus* (2009) by psychologist Darrel Ray; and *The Meme Machine* (1999) by the skeptic Susan Blackmore. The concept of meme also plays a central role in the theory of consciousness promulgated by the cognitive scientist and philosopher Daniel Dennett in his books *Consciousness Explained* (1991) and *Darwin's Dangerous Idea* (1995).

Memes are "copy-me" programs, or nongenetic replicating coded pieces of information, comparable to genes and computer viruses (Boyer 2001: 35; Dennett 2006: 346). They invade our evolved cognitive apparatus and perceptual system, which unlike many computers these days do not come with a firewall, antivirus protection, or antispyware software. Our brains are therefore open to such self-replicating programs that can infect vulnerable neural networks and gain administrative control, sneaking in the same way that computer viruses gain access to our laptops or home computers when we open what appears to be an innocuous music file or spam email with a hidden "copy-me" program. These bits of copy-me information can act like "resident viruses" that are installed but difficult to identify, or they can overwrite and corrupt preexisting information files. Thus, like computer viruses, brain infections gain control over stored data, reformat thoughts and beliefs, and affect behavior. As soon as they gain access, these viruses begin self-replication, such as when the infected person gets the urge to share his or her new "spiritual wisdom" and "sublime truths" with others. Sometimes, the brain virus may remain dormant until activated by some external trigger. For example, the idea of martyrdom, or dying for God, may be part of the program but may remain dormant until set into motion by sponsors and enablers.

In humans, aside from childhood indoctrination, such infections happen with exposure to ideas and beliefs that resonate and are intuitively appealing. These enter the mind when a person listens to a sermon of salvation, reads a proselytizing propaganda pamphlet sent by a cult or new religious group promising solutions to all of the riddles of life, or attends a free lecture that claims to make him or her a better, wiser, and more enlightened person. Who does not want these things? These infectious beliefs may resonate with someone because of their particular existential and emotional circumstances at that moment. They exploit the human cognitive propensity to soak up specific types of fantasies, our tendency to trust what authority figures tell us, our proclivity for teleological thinking, and our hyperactive proclivity that lead us to believe that we are sensing incorporeal agents all around (see Chapter 6). Some ideas are particularly attractive, such as the assertion that people are more than piles of flesh and bones and possess "special" and miraculous spiritual aspects that outlast the demise of their physical bodies (Stewart-Williams 2015).

Memes are discrete memorable ideas, such as tunes, catchphrases, jokes, clothing fashions, methods for constructing a wheel, how to make pots, how to build arches, calendars, chess, right triangles, the song "Greensleeves," urban legends, certain conspiracy theories, and so forth (Dennett 1995: 344). Putting it differently, these ideas are "sticky" and easily take hold (Heath and Heath 2007). As pieces of information or sets of instructions for particular types of behavior, memes "propagate themselves in meme pools by leaping from brain to brain" through the process of imitation and learning (Dawkins 1976: 206). Certain memes catch on particularly fast and proliferate widely irrespective of whether they are neutral, useful, or deleterious to the hosts (Blackmore 1999: 4, 7). Anything transmitted in this fashion from person to person is a meme. Other examples include the vocabularies people use, songs they sing, stories they tell, skills and habits they acquire from others, games they play, and rules they follow (Blackmore 1999: 7). Every one of these memes is the product of its unique evolutionary trajectory and history, and each one utilizes human behavior to get itself replicated (Blackmore 1999: 7).

Memes may be viewed as a new kind of replicating entity, or "new replicator," that appeared in the course of human evolution alongside genes, but in different transmission media, such as spoken language and later written language that helped create the "infosphere" in which cultural evolution happens (Dennett 1995: 347). If we adopt an abstract definition of evolution to mean "differential survival of replicating entities," then we can talk about memetic evolution in the same way as we do about genes (Dawkins 1976: 206). Memes undergo their individual evolutionary development and trajectory unconnected to their effects on genes (Dawkins 1976: 193–94). Like genes, however, they evolve through differential survival during competition with alternative memes (Dawkins 2006: 192). Better copy-me programs become more widespread in the meme pool at the expense of replicators that do not get copied well and dissipate. Memes spread longitudinally down generations, from parents to children, and horizontally, from person to person, like viruses during an epidemic (Dawkins 1999: ix).

Similar to genes, memes are invisible, and their transmission is via various meme vehicles, such as human brains, books, photos, symbols, signs, computer chips, electronic signals, and other media. They can also bounce from one medium to another, such as going from spoken words to written form, to video, and so forth. Memes enter into human minds through the eyes and ears in a manner analogous to the way parasites enter human bodies through the mouth, nose, or skin. Some memes are valuable from the standpoint of the human hosts, such as the memes for cooperation, writing, arms control, and so on (Dennett 1991: 203). However, others are pernicious and deleterious and very difficult to eliminate, such as the memes for anti-Semitism, xenophobia, racism, school shootings, conspiracy theories and the meme for "faith" that disables critical judgment. These malignant memes are like viral pathogens that exploit their hosts to propagate themselves in a manner only advantageous to themselves, irrespective of their adverse effects on the hosts. They clutter our minds and derange our critical thinking. Dawkins gives the example of the suicide meme that can proliferate when a dramatic and publicized martyrdom by one suicide bomber inspires others to strap on explosive vests and kill themselves for a cherished cause, and this, in turn, encourages others to kill themselves and those around them (Dawkins 1982: 111).

Memes, therefore, possess their own individual fitness as replicating coded pieces of information that is distinct from any contributions they may or may not make to the genetic fitness of their hosts, the human vectors (Dawkins 1976: 214; Dennett 2006: 350). They exploit their hosts and attempt to replicate and infest as many minds as possible. These characteristics are why memes are comparable to viruses, and religion is conceptualized as a kind of thought epidemic.

According to Dawkins (1991) thought epidemics, or "crazes," follow patterns similar to an outbreak of measles that sweeps through a group and even leaps from one community to another. One innocuous example of this kind of psychogenic epidemic was the mania associated with the hip-swiveling toy called the hula-hoop that spread across the United States starting in 1958. People purchased an estimated 25 million hula-hoops in the first few months after their introduction. Another example is the spread of the habit in the United States of wearing backward baseball caps. Included here are also the not so innocuous epidemics of witch hunting that proliferate and grip whole communities, such as the "witch craze" in early-modern Europe that I have investigated historically and the kinds of witch panics I encountered during fieldwork in places such as Nepal (Sidky 1997; 2008: 135–46). Numerous other examples of such thought or psychogenic contagions, including the medieval dance manias, the Dutch Tulip craze, and other mass panics are to be found in Charles Mackay's book *Extraordinary Popular Delusions and the Madness of Crowds* (1841) and Robert Bartholomew's *Little Green Men, Meowing Nuns, and Head-Hunting Panics* (2001). These phenomena indicate that human minds are susceptible to informational parasites and are typically quickly and massively infected.

Effective mind-parasites tend to cluster into mutually supporting groups, or memeplexes, that diffuse as bundles from one brain to another. Some of these meme clusters become stable enough to be given collective names, such as Islam, Judaism, Roman Catholicism, Mormonism, Voodoo, Santeria, or Scientology. Another example is the alien abduction memeplex that is prevalent in the US and other Western cultures (Blackmore 1999: 176).

Some religious memes survive because of their universal psychological appeal and others proliferate because they are compatible with other already abundant memes in the meme pool (Dawkins 2006: 199, 201). An excellent example of a meme that has psychological appeal is, You will survive after death (Dawkins 1991; Stewart-Williams 2015). The idea of life after death is highly appealing to humans and was one of the reasons for the success of Christianity in the Roman world.

Memes have phenotypic expressions that make their replication more likely and counteract environmental forces that would eliminate them. For example, the conspiracy theory meme has a built-in defense against the objection that there is no evidence for the conspiracy—"Yes, that is how extensive the conspiracy is!" (Dennett 1995: 349). In religion, the meme for "faith," which is the platform on which various superstitious ideas piggyback, does the same thing by discouraging the exercise of critical judgment that might lead to the thought that faith-based beliefs are dangerous (Dennett 1995: 349). Indeed, religious faith is expressed as a virtue—the more a belief defies evidence, the more virtuous the believer and the greater the heavenly or divine rewards. Similarly, the martyrdom meme associated with the religious war meme is replicated with the idea that death in the cause of religion is an automatic ticket to paradise and heavenly largess (Lynch 1996: 127). The meme for counterintuitive religious phenomena, such as a virgin giving birth to God or that there is an afterlife, includes the countermeasure that these are divine mysteries not meant to be questioned or comprehended (Edis 2008: 172).

Successful religions have some or all of the following: the God meme associated with reward and eternal salvation for believer and eternal damnation for the disbelievers; the heaven and hell memes, which work against non-receptivity by uninfected hosts; the evils of apostasy meme that confers immunity and encourages aggression against apostates and nonbelievers; the life after death meme that promises rewards in some transcendental location (Lynch 1996: 97–133). The pay-offs or benefits to the hosts in these cases are unequal to the high costs associated with what is demanded, such as personal social and economic commitments, missionary work, crusades, martyrdoms, and *jihads* against nonbelievers instigated by such memes (Edis 2008: 172). However, from the perspective of the meme, such activities are invaluable for its proliferation.

The concept of memes is not without its critics. Anthropologist Scott Atran and psychologist Ara Norenzayan (2004: 718) object to memetics because the approach is "'mind-blind' to the cognitive constraints on religious beliefs." Anthropologist Pascal Boyer (2001: 37–40) raises a similar point. For example, memetics does not tell us why some memes are "sticky" and so highly contagious that they are readily absorbed and passed on unchanged, while others undergo mutations or even disappear. Alternatively, why are the memes for only specific types of supernatural agent concepts prevalent in religious thinking?

Moreover, just what exactly is the universal psychological appeal of specific memes dealing with the supernatural and the paranormal? These questions seem to be outside the scope of the memetic perspective. However, these two approaches are not necessarily irreconcilable as they address somewhat different phenomena. The cognitive perspective, for example, does not specify precisely how once a counterintuitive concept develops it is then copied, catches on, jumps from one brain to another, spreads, and is transmitted across generations (i.e., becomes part of a cultural tradition). In this area, the memetic approach, which deals with the evolution of nongenetic cultural information, may well make a supporting contribution to cognitive perspectives.

Also, an unresolved question is whether the evolution of memes does indeed follow the rules of natural selection or whether it merely operates in a way only superficially analogous to genetic evolution. In other words, do memes go through the same type of evolutionary algorithms that occurs in the case of gene transmission? Also, some critics have raised the question as to whether memes even exist (Dennett 2006: 349). Genes exist, and we know they are organized from DNA, but what is the composition of memes? However, one can say the same thing about spoken words, and yet no one would doubt their existence. Finally, another objection is that the concept of memes cannot be operationalized, although one could raise a similar objection to the concept of culture.

Despite these issues, the memetic approach is a novel way of thinking *metaphorically* about ideas and their transmission and their relationship to cultural evolutionary processes. In other words, figuratively describing the spread of "units of cultural inheritance" in the lexicon of genetic evolution provides an innovative way of conceptualizing how items in culture affect people and each other (Dennett 1991: 202). These features are why the metaphor of the *mind virus* is used here as a way of discussing certain attributes of religion. While this idea requires that we proceed using analogies and has limitations, the metaphor of religion as a virus or parasite that infects the human brain, takes over perceptions, and shuts down critical thinking skills is an apt description of what happens to the religiously indoctrinated. Years ago, the historian and philosopher of science Michael Scriven (1966: 164) referred to this phenomenon as the "intellectual infection of the theistic myth."

There are many examples of viruses and other parasites that take over and control parts of the brains of their hosts and reprograms them for their own benefit. In his book *Breaking the Spell* (2006), Dennett uses the metaphor of mind infection to describe specific attributes of religion. He mentions the example of the tiny lancet fluke (*Dicrocoelium dendriticum*) that infects the brains of ants, making them behave in ways advantageous to the parasite (Dennett 2006: 3–6). The infected ant is compelled to climb to the top of a blade of grass where a cow ingests it, allowing the fluke to lay its eggs inside the cow's digestive system. Similar to the way that the parasite commandeers the perceptions of the ant, religion (as a set of parasitic, self-replicating ideas) seems to take over the perceptions of those it infects. Parasites operate within biological systems, while mind viruses operate within cognitive and social networks.

The idea of a virus-like "takeover" of the mind, or "intellectual infection," seems to kick in like a computer program or subroutine the moment one engages a true believer in a critical conversation about his or her religion. During my years of fieldwork, I found that the emotional reaction and behavior elicited by such interactions is always the same whether one is conversing with an evangelical Christian, a radical Muslim cleric, a Taliban foot soldier, an orthodox Jew, a Sikh, a member of the Hindutva movement, or a Buddhist monk. Even the possibility of contemplating critical thoughts sets off in the believer's mind various built-in mental alarm bells about sacrilege and blasphemy and the fear of sanctions from on high or from the earthly guardians and enforcers of the faith. Refusal to continue the conversation, rejection, and rage follow (Ray 2009: 20).

Brodie (2009: 182, 196) points out that such memes are programmed to drive involuntary reactions, and this is what makes them scary. He adds that someone programmed with the dogma-as-truth meme behaves very differently from those who see the same information as parables or myths. Blackmore (1999: 176, 188) notes that to the uninfected such beliefs will appear extremely strange and bizarre. The uninfected would ask: How can anyone believe two-thousand-year-old stories about a virgin-birth and a corpse that came back to life? Alternatively, how could anyone think that there is an all-knowing invisible Being up in the sky who communicates with certain people? Then again why would anyone believe that such an entity watches people around the clock, has an unending demand for praise, and is concerned about the tiniest aspects of human behavior, including what they eat and drink, how many times they prostrate themselves, the length of their hair, and even whose spouse they covet? The infected, however, perceive such ideas and beliefs as perfectly natural, reasonable, and indispensable.

In sum, religion is an ancient viral intellectual infection that is powerful and tenacious. It operates in ways analogous to a computer virus program that mystifies, mesmerizes, and pacifies. It tends to generate fanatical automatons with a built-in and hair-triggered self-defense subroutine that evokes a sense of anger and sacrilege and is primed for violence whenever those carrying this program encounter doubters or opposition.

The metaphor of a virus-like computer program that "takes over" is further supported by the fact that the contagion does not easily relent. There are innumerable historical instances when experience and empirical evidence have definitively disconfirmed sets of deeply held religious beliefs, such as when prophecies and pivotal predictions fail (see Chapter 16). Nevertheless, the infected are unable to give up those demonstrably falsified beliefs in the same way that a victim of an actual virus is unable to shake off a severe infection without medical intervention.

Dawkins (1991) points out that successful mind viruses are difficult to detect by the infected victims. However, some of the telltale signs of infection would include:

> Being impelled by powerful inner convictions that something is true and virtuous in the absence of any evidence.
>
> Thinking that the less evidence there is for a belief, the higher the virtue of believing it.
>
> Intolerance and even violence toward apostates, heretics, and those who subscribe to other modes of thought.
>
> The presence of specific methods to replicate the virus. Replication is achieved by passing on the virus to the host's children via rituals, such as first communion, Baptism, Bar Mitzvah, confirmation, daily prayers, Bible reading, and confession.
>
> The existence of methods to spread the viral infection horizontally across space. This is done via carriers or vectors in the form of priests, ministers, deacons, nuns, imams, mullahs, rabbis, popes, televangelists, shamans, lamas, gurus, apostles, Bible professors, Sunday school teachers, and elders. (Ray 2009: 26)

The targets of indoctrination are children who, as Dawkins observes, are like immune-deficient patients "wide open to mental infections." Religious memes exploit the programmed-in gullibility of children that is essential to learning language and traditional wisdom but is easily sabotaged by various purveyors of supernaturalism. Children do not choose their religion but acquire it through indoctrination in the religious beliefs of their parents. Indeed, the most significant factor in determining a person's religion is the accident of birth. Theistic theologians provide lengthy and perfidious discourses about how God gives humans the freedom to decide whether to believe or not (e.g., Swinburne 2004: 119, 238). However, there is no such thing as freedom of choice in religion. The brain viruses of their parents have infected the majority of believers. Religion thus succeeds because it relies upon the indoctrination of receptive brains in early childhood. This process entails commandeering an evolutionary characteristic of our species, which is for children to accept the authority of their elders that once enhanced survival among our ancestors. The young were taught to adopt the ideas and trust the experiences of adults, which eliminated the need for them to engage in dangerous trial-and-error approaches to various tasks that others in their groups had already discovered and mastered (Coyne 2015: 89).

## Immunizing the Mind Virus

Once religious beliefs are in place, the indoctrinated require immunization against other infectious beliefs. This measure is also needed to prevent the delusion-producing spell that binds the believer from being broken through critical thinking and demand for evidence operative in other aspects of life. Massive investments and substantial hard-to-fake and easily monitored indicators of allegiance are demanded of the believers to keep them engaged, involved, entranced, engrossed, and mystified. The faithful must devote considerable amounts of time, effort, and money to religious activities, such as praying individually and in groups according to timetables, taking vows of celibacy, attending mandatory ceremonies, conducting rituals, going to church, temple, or mosque, and paying to support religious personnel and for the construction of churches, mosques, temples, monasteries, and other structures. Other costs include emotional exertion in the form of fears, anxieties, hopes, and wishes as well as the cognitive burden of having to uphold counterintuitive beliefs and conflicting models about how the world works (Atran and Henrich 2010: 2).

Moreover, believers must undergo scarification, genital mutilation, the extraction of teeth, amputation of fingers, piercing with sharp objects, and whipping with chains and leather straps, among other such requirements. Finally, the faithful are obliged to observe many interdictions and taboos that are designed to set them apart from those infected by other mind viruses. These entail precise rules about what to eat, what to wear, how to cut one's hair, the dimensions of men's beards, the length of women's skirts, whom to marry, with whom to interact and not interact, and which beliefs not to tolerate.

Religion is therefore a powerful mechanism of "othering," of separating people into "us" and "them," or differentiating between the righteous and the iniquitous, between those who are in God's grace and the loathsome who will suffer the torments of hell (Bloom 2012: 191, 196; Hall et al., 2010; Ginges et al. 2010). The charity, compassion, and sisterly and brotherly love that religionists use to describe their moral behavior rarely extend to outsiders (Graham and Haidt 2010).

The insulation of religious beliefs against inimical ideas and outside influences is also achieved through the inbuilt mechanism of fear, using scary concepts such as "blasphemy," "sin," and eternal "hell fire" (cf., Bivins 2008). Anthropologists and sociologists have shown how various organizations use fear as an extraordinarily powerful means of thought control and social and political manipulation (Glassner 1999; Harris 1971: 407; Sidky 2015: 132–39). Purveyors of supernaturalism discovered this fact long ago. But the best of all is the use of what Dennett (2006: 207) calls "the diabolical lie," that is, that everything critics say is inspired by Satan, "the Father of Lies," to steer you down the path to perdition. These fear concepts comprise potent forms of ideological terrorism to keep the hapless faithful intimidated and in line because of God's love for them.

The doctrine of eternal combustion in the depths of hell, in particular, requires a comment. It represents, as the philosopher Keith Parsons (2011: 253–54) points out, "an eternal glorification of vindictiveness." Parsons explains why an institution that lauds itself as "the Light of the World" rests on obedience and fear of hell: "A doctrine that can frighten people into belief and obedience but that can even squelch doubts is a zealot's dream come true." Without the doctrine of hell to scare and intimidate people into belief, he adds, Christianity would have a hard time selling itself "on its merits in the marketplace of ideas," and its stock will plummet. Along the same line, Thomas Paine (1797a) caustically remarked:

> Of all the tyrannies that afflict [humankind], tyranny in religion is the worst. Every other species of tyranny is limited to the world we live in, but this attempts a stride beyond the grave and seeks to pursue us into eternity.

## Faith Is Superstition

Religious indoctrination demands faith and effectively disables critical thinking, reason, common sense, the spirit of inquiry, and the demand for evidence that are operational in other facets of daily human life. Faith is a perfect description of the condition of being infected by the mind virus of religion. As Russell (1957: vi) pointed out, "It is thought virtuous to have Faith—that is to say, to have a conviction which cannot be shaken by contrary evidence. Alternatively, if contrary evidence might induce doubt, it is held that contrary evidence must be suppressed."

When confronted with opposing evidence or absence of evidence for the supernatural, religious believers will unvaryingly insist that they believe on *faith*, and evidence is irrelevant. Once this epistemological license is admitted, beliefs become immune to scientific appraisal because they become classified as phenomena for which no substantiation is necessary. However, if this is the case, then as the neuroscientist Yonatan Fishman (2009: 825) has put it, "One is not only permitted to believe in a countless number of absurdities, but one is logically compelled to do so." So why not also believe in extraterrestrial aliens (ancient and the rapacious contemporary types), goblins, zombies, demons, ancestral spirits, astral intelligences, fairies, and the whole array of obsolete gods, such as Zeus, Athena, Baal, Enlil, Enki, Inanna, and so forth?

Aside from opening the possibilities of all sorts of credulities, faith is self-defeating and leads us into error. As historian and philosopher Richard Carrier (2005a: 6) observes:

> The number of false beliefs always vastly outnumber the true. It follows that any arbitrary method of selection will be maximally successful at selecting false beliefs. So, the probability is always very high that a belief based on mere faith will be false.

All religions require unquestioned acceptance or "blind faith." The correct label for blind faith, as biblical historian Roy Hoover (2008: 89) points out, is "superstition." The skeptic David Mcafee (2017: 44–63) aptly refers to religion as "organized superstition." And theologian David Taylor (1992: 55) describes faith and the implications of holding beliefs on faith as follows:

> "Faith" […] looks rather like a fraud word meaning simply, "We insist on the truth of these claims, though we have no demonstrable or examinable grounds for making them." Provided everyone remains agreed on what "faith" is to consist of, the practical difficulties can be

> contained. But when the day comes (and history shows it is never delayed for very long) that people start to disagree about faith, the resulting quarrel is inordinately fanatical for the very reasons that there is no calm and rational way of deciding it; sadly also in a totally unreasonable quarrel, the least reasonable opponent is generally the victor. The history of the Christian church is perhaps the best illustration of all time of this sobering truth.

Taylor highlights a very significant point here, namely that because faith-based beliefs have no evidentiary foundations, disputes can never be resolved rationally by independent evidence and the systematic investigations of facts. Believers of different faiths make equal claims to sole ownership of the absolute truth. The inevitable outcome when absolute truths collide is that the devout resort to force, intimidation, suppression, violence, and extermination to establish the veracity of their supernatural beliefs. It is not just the Christian church that has such an appalling record. The history of nearly all other faith-based religions is the same.

## Faith Promotes Unreason

Religious demagogues discovered long ago that the antidote for religious programming is rationality and the demand for evidence. It is challenging to keep minds infected if believers are allowed to be inquisitive about the virus and its effects on them. As the Greek philosopher and one of the first perceptive Bible demythologizers Celsus (1987: 54, 75), writing nearly two thousand years ago, pointed out, Christians have stressed faith over reason and knowledge from the very start of their cult:

> Their favorite expressions are "Do not ask questions, just believe!" and: "Your faith will save you!" "The wisdom of this world," they say, "is evil; to be simple is good." [They say] make sure none of you ever obtains knowledge, for too much learning is a dangerous thing: knowledge is a disease for the soul, and the soul that acquires knowledge will perish.

The strategy to preserve the virus is to convince the infected that the more impossible and implausible a belief, the greater the virtue of believing it and the more prodigious the heavenly rewards for doing so. This idea is expressed perfectly in the Gospel of John 20:29 which states: "Then Jesus told him, 'Because you have seen me, you have believed; blessed are those who have not seen and yet have believed.'" For the believer, this is a powerful, or perhaps the ultimate, demonstration of their commitment to the virus. This blasphemy of reason finds expression in the Christian polemicist Tertullian's phrase "*Credo quia absurdum*," which means "I believe because it is absurd," stated as justification for his faith-based conviction that a corpse came back to life (*De Carne Christi*, ca. 203–6 CE).

While someone like Konner (2019: xxv) may see faith as an admirable human quality or a quest for "spirituality," faith is conducive to rabid fanaticism. Amidst every religion, we find potent mechanisms operating to promote fanatical unreason. Without this, the virus, the intellectual infection, cannot be maintained. Of course, the definition of belief without the exercise of reason and the demand for evidence is *irrationality*. As the evolutionary biologist Jerry Coyne puts it in his book *Faith versus Fact* (2015), religious beliefs are irrational because they are not based on reason or any sort of systematic investigation, but on faith. In his words, faith is "belief in matters for which there's no convincing evidence, but which are seen as true simply because people *want* them to be true, or were *taught* that they were true" (Coyne 2015: 259). Similarly, Russell (1957: 30, 204) observed:

> The most dangerous feature of [religion] consists of fanatical acceptance of doctrines embodied in a sacred book, unwillingness to examine these doctrines critically, and savage persecution of those who reject them. [Religion teaches] that one ought to believe such a proposition independently of the question whether there is evidence in its favor […] an attitude which produces hostility to evidence and causes us to close our minds to every fact that does not suit our prejudices.

This unwillingness to ask for evidence is the reason why noxious, arcane and absurd beliefs from a benighted time of cruelty and barbarism have been retained as sacrosanct truths into the twenty-first century while other aspects of the archaic belief systems of which they were a part have long since been discarded. These ancient superstitions that are the foundations of all faith-based beliefs make religion dangerous (Hitchens 2007: 56; Russell 1957: 30).

For rational thinkers, free of this intellectual virus, believing in things for which there is no evidence is to abrogate one's moral and ethical responsibilities as a human being. This view was expressed long ago by the British mathematician and philosopher William Kingdon Clifford (1999: 77) in a lecture delivered to the Metaphysical Society in London in 1876: "It is wrong always, everywhere, and for anyone, to believe anything upon insufficient evidence." He added that such a person who purposefully avoids evidence that calls his or her baseless beliefs into question commits an affront against humankind.

The faithful, however, are programmed to revel in their virulent irrationality, and they are happy and willing and sanction by transcendental powers from above to hurt, maim, kill, and even die to preserve their viral infections. In the words of the seventeenth-century philosopher and mathematician Blaise Pascal (1958: 265), "Men never do evil so completely and cheerfully as when they do it from a religious conviction." These attributes of religion become a scary proposition once we realize that there are billions of people carrying this perverse ancient brain contagion.

## Why Believers Are Dangerous

Religious believers are indoctrinated to make massive emotional investments in their purported absolute truths. They are therefore profoundly intolerant of criticism and are conditioned to react vehemently and violently, and even advocate the death of detractors. The detractors do not need to be outsiders. Christians, for example, have committed more atrocities against each other than outsiders have inflicted upon them. As Russell (1957: 36) said, "From the age of Constantine to the end of the seventeenth century,

Christians were far more fiercely persecuted by other Christians than they ever were by the Roman emperors."

One merely has to recall the Cistercian Inquisitor Arnoldus Amalricus infamous declaration in 1209, "Kill them all, God knows his own," when his crusaders raised concerns about Catholic casualties during an attack on the Cathar stronghold of Béziers, in southern France. The result was the indiscriminate and wholesale slaughter of the inhabitants of the entire city, a terrifying event that became known as the "massacre at Béziers." Alternatively, to use an example from another religion, the Taliban and ISIS militants have happily killed more Muslims than those they consider infidels and enemies of their God.

For these reasons, various critics advocate that people should not tolerate faith-based dogmas anywhere. As the author, skeptic, and humanist the late Arthur C. Clarke (2003: 186) stressed, faith-based dogmas have repeatedly turned out to be wrong, sometimes "worse than wrong," and must be resisted. What has been worse are the horrors that have befallen humankind when people convinced of the unassailable truths of their beliefs have acquired political power. Consider Afghanistan, where today the United States is involved in one of the longest wars in its history. Involvement there by the "In God We Trust" United States intent on destroying communist-atheists, in reality, began on July 3, 1979, six months before the Soviet invasion on December 25, 1979. The specific objective of this intervention was to incite a Soviet military response "to give the USSR its own Vietnam" (Sidky 2007b). Altogether, the United States and the "pious" Middle Eastern Islamic confederates it recruited (Saudi Arabia, Egypt, the Gulf States, and others) funneled around 5 billion dollars to fund the so-called Afghan *Jihad*. The number of conventional weapons (including Stinger missiles) the holy war sponsors sent exclusively to extremist Islamic groups made Afghanistan the most heavily armed country on earth during the second half of the twentieth century. Also, the United States facilitated the recruiting and training of the most radical religious militants from the Middle East and across the globe and transported them to Afghanistan. The underlying premise of this policy was the ludicrous idea that "the enemy of my enemy is my friend."

The sponsors of the Afghan anti-Soviet resistance deliberately cast the war as a *jihad*, or religious war, and denied aid to the secular nationalist and royalist groups (Sidky 2007b). The recipients of this largesse, god-fearing believers then began systematic and indiscriminate slaughter, enthusiastically butchering their fellow citizens and destroying their wretched country in the name of Allah the merciful and compassionate. Over a million and a half people died in that grotesque and bloody religious war (Sidky 2007b, 2006).

After the Soviet withdrawal in 1989, others appeared on the scene in that unhappy place, again with massive funding from ultra-religionists in Pakistan, Saudi Arabian princes, and the wealthy donors in the Gulf States. These self-proclaimed "genuine" believers, who in their role as the "real" possessors of the truth and the emissaries of heaven, intend to establish Allah's Caliphate on earth. The virtues of these pious homicidal moralists include acts of ethnic cleansing, the persecution, torture, and murder of religious minorities, heretics, and blasphemers, public execution of schoolteachers, the wholesale massacre of civilians, joyfully sending brainwashed children on suicide bombing missions, and terrorizing defenseless women and girls for the sake of Allah's compassion.

Circumstances such as these are what have made believers of absolute truths the bane of humanity. It cannot be stated better than by Thomas Paine (1880 [1794]: 12) who wrote that the history of religion is "a history of wickedness" that has served "to corrupt and brutalize" humankind. Historically across space and time, religion has kept tyrants and despots in power and the masses ignorant and in poverty. Paine (1880 [1795]: 143) added:

> Whence arose all the horrid assassinations of whole nations of men, women, and infants, with which the Bible is filled, and the bloody persecutions and tortures unto death, and religious wars, that since that time have laid Europe in blood and ashes—whence rose they but from this impious thing called revealed religion, and the monstrous belief that God has spoken to man?

The examples provided by James Haught in his delightful little book *Holy Horrors* (1990) and the catalog of religiously inspired violence supplied by Sam Harris in his book *End of Faith* (2004) merely scratch the surface.

Well-meaning writers such as Konner (2019: xxv, 179) express respect and admiration for people of faith. Yet what they overlook is the sad fact that faith-based ideological perspectives are dangerous because they render believers vulnerable to not so virtuous ideologues, scoundrels, mountebanks, hacks, and cranks, who have for millennia thrived on bamboozling the gullible and the defenseless. When people are habituated to accept without evidence, any absurdity becomes a plausibility. Believers are thus easy marks for conmen, political opportunists, and unscrupulous ideologues who exploit people's hopes, psychological insecurities, and fears to promote all sorts of perverted private self-serving and unholy agendas.

Such opportunist ideologues include Osama bin Laden and the ISIS suicide-bombing orchestrators following in his footsteps now operating in Afghanistan. These reverent men forward their iniquitous agendas by preying upon the naivety and religious sentiments of susceptible young children to blow themselves up for Allah on the promise of eternal glory and residence in Paradise and some cash for their impoverished families. The predacious martyr-operation architects and feigned holy warriors who, like bin Laden the innovator and mastermind of this strategy, never martyr themselves use the suicide operations to vie for more cash and esteem from their fanatical religious sponsors around the globe. The anthropologist David Edwards describes the dark deeds of these martyrdom enablers in his book *Caravan of Martyrs: Sacrifice and Suicide Bombing in Afghanistan* (2017; see also Sidky 2017a).

Dawkins (1991) provides a different, more commonplace, and unfortunate example of contemporary American televangelists who con the faithful into parting with their meager savings proclaiming that "God really appreciates a donation [...] when that donation is so large that it hurts." At least mainstream churches bilk their parishioners only to the extent of having them pay for the religious infrastructure and the maintenance of their heavenly representatives. American televangelists are the most despicable kind of religionists. These self-styled Jesus aspirants, with their electronic churches, Hollywood special effects, and soundtracks, fill their bank accounts with the life savings of sad old people in desperate need of any solace in their final miserable days on this ugly, brutish, and callous world. The catchphrase of these pious charlatans is that the more burdensome the donations, the happier is the Lord. Where did God's mercy and compassion go? Where are Jesus's love and religious benevolence? The fact that these despicable con-artists and pretended envoys of the Lord are not struck down in some Old Testament–style divine display of fire and lighting suggests that the benevolent Creator is either absent or simply does not care.

## Religion as an Evolutionary By-Product

Defenders and apologists maintain that if religion is not good, useful, and adaptive from an evolutionary standpoint, it would not exist and be so widespread (Konner 2019: xvi, 176). However, the fact that supernatural and paranormal ideation has an evolutionary foundation does not mean that they are *naturally good*, desirable, or unfailing. As Ambasciano (2018: xv) observes, heart attacks are also the natural outcome of the evolutionary propensity for humans to eat high-calorie foods, but that does not mean that heart attacks are useful or desirable. It is true to say that the stuff of religion, such as teleological thinking, anthropomorphic projections, and notions about noncorporeal superhuman agents and transcendental realities, has deep evolutionary cognitive roots and has powerful species-wide intuitive appeal. Their downside is that they are incompatible with, disable, and overwrite rational and scientific modes of thought and have recurrently led people down the path to perdition (see Chapter 6).

There is growing scientific evidence that religious beliefs, specifically ideas relating to supernatural agents, creationism, miracles, and the notion of souls, were an evolutionary by-product of particular cognitive capacities that evolved for dealing with the natural and social worlds (Bloom 2012: 185). In other words, to use a term coined by the evolutionary biologists Stephen Jay Gould and Richard Lewontin (1979), religion is a *spandrel.* This means that religion was a derivative of attributes of the human mind that evolved *for reasons other than religion*, such as the need to continually seek out and be wary of dangerous predators in the environment and the capacity to decipher the minds of deceptive and treacherous human beings. The by-product perspective on religion is the topic of Chapter 6.

There are various other types of evolutionary by-products alongside religion. One example to clarify this idea is our craving for junk food that stems from our adaptive needs to desire fat, salt, and sugar. The fast-food industry has capitalized upon this by producing inordinate amounts of fatty, salty, and sugary foods and beverages. One consequence of this enterprise has been the increasing prevalence of early-onset type 2 diabetes mellitus (T2DM) in the United States and elsewhere (Cowie et al. 2009). A host of other health issues are related to such practices by the commercial food industry.

If the by-product view of religion is correct, and there is a great deal of evidence that it is, then the species-wide delusion that ghosts, demons, spirits, gods, or God haunt or populate the world—all the stuff of religion—is an evolutionary derivative of the cognitive and perceptual apparatus intrinsic to human brains. In other words, contra to Konner (2019: 176) who says that "in evolution, religion must have been adaptive or it would not be here," religion was not adaptive. The descriptor "delusion" is apt because supernatural beliefs lack evidentiary justification and have historically and across cultures come at enormous psychological and physical costs to humankind. Just because lots of people share the delusion does not alter its ontological standing.

Finally, others have maintained that religious beliefs are not merely an evolutionary spandrel, but are deleterious to their carriers because they are not anchored in reality and stem from superstitious precepts found in contradictory ancient and sacred texts (Dawkins 2006; Ginges et al. 2009; Harris 2004; Hitchens 2007). The view of religion as a pathogenic mind infection or parasite has already been addressed.

## The Flaws in the Scholarly Studies of Religion

Among researchers in disciplines such as anthropology, religious studies, comparative religion, sociology, and related fields, who are well situated to tell us why humankind remains shackled to antiquated, destructive, and nonsensical beliefs, there is a hands-off policy when it comes to assessing the ontological status of religious ideologies, which means a refusal to evaluate their truth and falsity. This deferential perspective stems from the common belief that religion is something valuable to be cherished and deserves exceptional respect and tolerance. Thus, instead of analyzing religious beliefs in terms of scientifically meaningful categories in accordance with the tradition of systematic skepticism, many of those studying religion adopt the perspective of the believer and have become overt or covert advocates and endorsers of supernaturalism (Segal 1983: 111; Wiebe 1984a: 158; see also Martin and Weibe 2012, 2016). Dennett (2006: 258–64) refers to this as "the academic smokescreen" that has served to impede the scientific analysis of religion.

If there were an iota of evidence for the existence of transcendental realities and supernatural beings and forces at the core of nearly all religions, then there would be no need to address the truth or falsity of religious beliefs as these would be self-evident and perfectly understandable. However, although diligent efforts by scientists have been made to detect such evidence, it is just not there (see Chapter 3). Therefore researchers who opt to leave religious truths alone are overlooking the very question that demands an answer: Why do people believe in premises for which there is either no evidence or are demonstrably false? For this reason, it is problematic to delink causal explanations for religious behavior from the truth or falsity of religious beliefs.

In anthropology, the hands-off stance is justified by proclaiming "methodological agnosticism," which entails bracketing out the question of the truth and falsity of religious beliefs (Sidky 2015: 2). In other words, the ontological status of religious claims is considered to be outside the scope of analysis and irrelevant for the anthropological explanation of religious phenomena (Lett 1997a: 103). Thus, as the noted British anthropologist Edward Evans-Pritchard (1965: 17) puts it in his book *Theories of Primitive Religion* (1965),

> [The anthropologist] is not concerned, *qua* anthropologist, with the truth or falsity of religious thought. As I understand the matter, there is no possibility of his knowing whether the spiritual beings of primitive religions or of any others have any existence or not, and since that is the case, he cannot take the question into consideration. The beliefs are for him sociological facts, not theological facts, and his sole concern is with their relation to each other and to other social facts. (Evans-Pritchard 1965: 17)

The esteemed American anthropologist Anthony Wallace (1966: 5) also expressed this "hands-off" approach to religion in his influential book *Religion: An Anthropological View* (1966):

> we shall ignore the extremes of fundamental piety or anticlerical iconoclasm. Thus, for us, religion will be neither a path to truth nor a thicket of superstition, but simply a kind of human behavior: specifically, that kind of behavior which can be classified as belief and ritual concerned with supernatural beings, powers, and forces. (Wallace 1966: 5)

In other words, it is the secondary effects of religious beliefs that are of concern for these researchers. This perspective is still widely held. As anthropologist Brian Morris (2006: 9–10) states,

> Anthropologists [...] are not concerned with the truth status or morality of specific religious concepts or beliefs, nor with the authenticity of the personal experiences that are often attributed to religious devotees or prophets. [...] Anthropologists as social scientists have thus, following their vocation, been neither for nor against religion, neither engaged in theology, apologetics, or advocacy, nor in explicitly attacking or dismissing religion as meaningless or irrational.

Similarly, anthropologist Jack Eller (2009: 2) notes that:

> Anthropology does not approach religion to falsify it nor to verify it nor even to judge it. Anthropology is not the seminary, intending to indoctrinate the student into any one particular religion. It is not apologetics, attempting to prove or justify some religion; neither is it an exercise in debunking any or all religion.

Others add to this by insisting that the scientific appraisal of religious claims is inappropriate and unethical. For example, here is what anthropologist Richley Crapo says in his book *Anthropology of Religion* (2003):

> If we resort to simply deciding that belief in things that are not accepted by the contemporary scientific community as "real" should be called "supernatural beliefs," then we adopt a truly

ethnocentric method, one that amounts in essence to equating "supernatural" with "(scientifically) false." (Crapo 2003: 8–9)

This perspective is shared by many in the social sciences. Consider the work of the sociologists of religion Rodney Stark and Roger Finke (2000: 21), who are not averse to using social-scientific methods to investigate religious behavior, but reject any such efforts to assess the authenticity or truth or falsity of religious experiences, which they consider to be genuine supernatural transmissions of divine origins.

As religious studies scholar Robert Segal (1980: 404) observed long ago, there are two perspectives for assessing religious beliefs: (1) those that evaluate the truth of the beliefs themselves, which is in the domain of philosophy and the natural sciences; (2) those that assess the holders of the religious beliefs, which is the domain of the social sciences. The conventional view in the social sciences, he adds, is that social-scientific explanations do not offer positive or negative affirmation about the ultimate ontological status of religious beliefs (Segal 1980: 406). In other words, such explanations for religious beliefs have no bearing on the truth of those beliefs. A perspective such as this is not unlike that adopted in cultural anthropology (Lett 1997a). However, is this really justified?

Segal points out further that whether or not such explanations presuppose the falsity of religious beliefs, in practice they invariably do so. The reason for this is that such explanations rely on the premise that things are not the way they seem, that this is not "the whole truth," that there is more than meets the eye, and that something additional is at work than what the believer can furnish. Years ago, the sociologist Ian Hamnett (1973: 2) made a relevant observation about the sociology of religion that also applies to anthropological studies. He observed that the "problem" that launches a sociological inquiry, to begin with, is the question: "How can people possibly believe *that*?" In other words, there would be no need to provide an explanation if the phenomenon in question is deemed self-evidently and unmistakably true. Indeed, explanatory theories are not offered for "nonproblems." "The whole enterprise of the sociology of religion," Hamnett adds, "thus carries within itself the assumption that religion is something that calls for an explanation outside itself." This perspective, he observes, can be characterized as the "sociology of error," or the effort to find explanations for "erroneous forms of beliefs."

Despite lip service to methodological agnosticism, anthropological and sociological explanations of religion are in fact about "erroneous beliefs." Moreover, there is nothing in principle to prevent such explanations from explicitly weighing in on the truth and falsity of those beliefs whenever the supernatural is used to justify those beliefs. A sufficient socioscientific explanation for a religious belief, that is, one that can account for all aspects of that belief, according to the principle of parsimony, or Ockham's razor, renders supernatural perspectives superfluous (Segal 1980: 407). A comprehensive explanation of this kind would refute a supernatural one in the same way that science challenges such beliefs by explaining the empirical world without postulating the involvement of transcendental powers and beings, miracles, revelations, religious experiences, or the existence of God or gods. Such sociological explanations of religious beliefs, like scientific explanations of the physical world, are more straightforward because they do not postulate supernatural entities in addition to all the empirical ones already known because interjecting God complicates things incalculably (Segal 1980: 407). Also, this kind of social-scientific explanation of religious beliefs has higher prior probability than a supernatural explanation because of its naturalist framework that is also the basis of the compelling explanations of the physical world offered by science. Explaining religious beliefs in these terms undermines the common supernatural justification offered for the truths of those beliefs (Segal 1980: 410).

A related problem in the study of religion is the implicit or explicit assumption on the part of researchers that religion is somehow different from all other human phenomena. Russell McCutcheon, in his book *Critics Not Caretakers* (2001), has cogently analyzed this issue concerning his discipline of religious studies (see also McCutcheon 1997). While McCutcheon's perspective may be in the minority and what he speaks to may not reflect current trends in that field of study, the issues he raises are directly relevant to anthropological studies of religion. It is for this reason that a brief discussion of his views is necessary.

We may begin with the problematic underlying supposition that religion encompasses a mysterious, non-quantifiable, inscrutable, and non-falsifiable inner world. Religion, in this view, is a subjective experience, or a pure inner impulse, that the outsider is at best able to describe, empathize with, "respect," appreciate, and "take seriously" and nothing more (cf., McCutcheon 2001: 4–5). Religious and spiritual consciousness thus become autonomous self-generating independent variables that have sociopolitical effects, but themselves have no causes (McCutcheon 2001: 85). Clifford Geertz (1973) and his emulators have promoted a similar perspective within anthropology (cf., Frankenberry and Penner 1999).

A variation of this view appears in the premise that religion is sui generis (self-generated), espoused by the noted French sociologists Émile Durkheim, and his idea that religion is irreducible to any other phenomena. The highly influential Romanian philosopher and historian of religion Mircea Eliade was the champion of a similar outlook. He asserted that religion is understandable in its own terms alone rather than in psychological, anthropological, biological, or sociopolitical terms, which he dismissed as reductionistic (Segal 1983: 98). The terms "reductionist" and "reductionism" have since become catchphrases among religious studies researchers who use them to dismiss perspectives that depart from their deferential treatment of religious phenomena as things explicable solely in their own terms. In Eliade's (1963b: xiii) words,

> A religious phenomenon will only be recognized as such if it is grasped at its own level, that is to say, if it is studied *as* something religious. To try to grasp the essence of such a phenomenon by means of physiology, psychology, sociology, economics, linguistics, art or any other study is false; it misses the one unique and irreducible element in it—the element of the sacred.

Eliade (1969: 70) was a mystic of sorts enthralled with "cosmic sacrality." For him, the meaning of the sacred was trans-human and outside time and place. For this reason, he contemptuously dismissed what he termed "reductionistic" interpretations as irrelevant because they overlook this irreducibly "religious" meaning of religion. Eliade's influence on the study of religion across disciplines has been massive, including the study of shamanism (for a critique of his views on shamanism, one of my specialties, see Sidky 2008: 1–24). Many following in Eliade's footsteps continue to construe religion as a unique and self-evidently meaningful, apolitical phenomenon "that causes other things to happen but is itself uncaused since it is an indescribable impulse and personal conviction" (McCutcheon 2001: 17). Such a singularity is amenable only to the nuanced description and "sympathetic appreciation," "respectful" treatment, and as something to be taken "seriously" but not open to critical analysis. Ambasciano (2018: 176) calls this methodology the "unnatural history of religion," which is characterized by a subjective approach and an antiscientific and fideistic partiality, that is, a perspective that construes faith as something independent of reason or rationality.

However, an important question here is, How can an outsider/nonbeliever sympathetically appreciate the reality of such sublime indescribable impulses and convictions, or grasp the insider's perspective, without considering the source of those impulses, or the divine, as real for themselves? As Segal (1983: 100) says, "What else can appreciating the reality of the divine mean except accepting it?" One cannot take seriously, respect, and appreciate what one cannot accept. To accept the mythical and archaic worldview that religion encompasses in this fashion requires a nonbeliever to become a kind of believer. In other words, some form of "conversion is a prerequisite." However, is it indeed possible to apprehend religion in this manner? To say yes, Segal (1983: 110) adds, entails self-deception because modern science and scholarship pose considerable difficulties upon efforts to honestly accept as truth any archaic religious mythology and its patently false premises about the world and universe.

The self-delusion that such a move involves was addressed long ago by the theologian Rudolf Bultmann concerning the literal acceptance of the mythology contained in the Bible, which he described as "the cosmology of a prescientific age" (Segal 1983: 110). Bultmann advocated accommodating the Bible to modern culture by jettisoning its supernaturalism without abandoning its central message, or the kerygma. Accepting the Bible literally, Bultmann (1978: 668) wrote,

> would involve a sacrifice of intellect which could only have one result—a curious form of schizophrenia and insincerity. It would mean accepting a view of the world in our faith and religion, which we should deny in our everyday life. Modern thought as we have inherited it brings with it criticism of the New Testament view of the world.

Treating religion as a unique self-evidently meaningful and transcendent set of values and feelings in effect valorizes the subjective, personal, and private. Moreover, it avoids risking the disclosure, as McCutcheon (2001: 14) puts it "that religion—like all other aspects of human social life—may well turn out to be all too ordinary." One can add that this also shields religious beliefs from evidentiary challenges because of the insistence that they are non-quantifiable and non-falsifiable. Eliade's doggedness about a "non-reductionist" approach to religion was not because the subject matter demands it, scientific methods are perfectly adequate for the task (see Chapter 3), but because of his fear that "reductionist" perspectives would "reduce God to a delusion" (Segal 1983: 114–15).

What Eliade and his followers advocate amounts to taking "the stance of the devotee as over against the skeptic on metaphysical issues" and entails nothing less than "understanding of religion with endorsement" (Wiebe 1984a: 158).

However, as McCutcheon (2001: 10) rightly asks, are any aspects of human behavior or experience really unique and can exist apart from historical forces, social influences, the effects of culture, and even human biology? The answer is an obvious no. Most scientific anthropologists would concur with this point. While wishful thinking religionists construe their faith as miraculous, cosmically significant, and even above and beyond empirical constraints, there are no human phenomena, including religion, that exist apart from or outside of historical and cultural forces and influences.

Moreover, the emphasis on the insider's perspective is of limited analytical and explanatory utility. This limitation is because believers do not have automatic, privileged access to the true nature of their own beliefs and behaviors (Segal 1983: 114). Scientific anthropologists have adequately demonstrated that the emic (insider's) perspective alone seldom provides adequate explanations for sociocultural phenomena (see Sidky 2004: 360–61).

An excellent demonstration of the problematic nature or the insider's points of view occurs in the findings of the archaeologist William Rathje (1992) on consumption patterns in American households. Rathje collected two types of information, accounts from household members obtained through interviews and informant reports (insider accounts); and information obtained through the analysis of the garbage from these households (outsider's description). Rathje found significant discrepancies between what people said about their consumption patterns and what the physical evidence revealed. For instance, there were differences between the amount of beer reported to have been consumed during a given period and the actual number of beer cans retrieved by the archaeologists sifting through their garbage.

Numerous other examples of this appear in the anthropological literature (see Sidky 2015: 140–58). Such findings are the reason why scientific anthropologists insist that the insider's perspective alone is insufficient for understanding sociocultural phenomena (Murphy and Margolis 1995: 4).

In my ethnographic research, I regularly encountered discrepancies between what people conveyed during surveys and interviews and what actual empirical observations revealed. These included reports about the number of individuals in households, the figures provided for the head of livestock owned, the number of times family members prayed, and other such information. Scholars in other fields have also noted the problems of attaining the insider's view. As the philosopher Graham Oppy (2018: 33) correctly points out, no one is so well-placed as to be able to assess the insider's perspective precisely. In the words of anthropologist William Klausner (1994: 18),

> There are limitations to culture conversion, no matter how close one's identification, engagement, attachment, and empathy. As in religious conversion, one often becomes more Papal than the Pope and loses one's perspective and objectivity. However, loss of detachment and objectivity does not mean one has actually assumed the essence, as well as the form, of a new cultural identity. One can study and grasp the intellectual meaning of a country's literature

> and history; of its language; its proverbs; its fairy tales; its religion and worldview. However, unlike a child's enculturation process wherein literature, language, history, morality and appropriate behavior are learned, largely uncritically, and impressed on a veritable cultural tabula rasa, the alien anthropologist, at a later stage in life, inevitably studies and learns through the lens of his or her own cultural and intellectual background; often rather heavy baggage.

The problem, of course, goes beyond the impossibility of genuinely attaining an insider's perspective. An additional hindrance is the persistent avoidance or disdain for subjecting religious beliefs to critical ontological examination and analysis. Konner (2019: xv), for example, describes his approach to various religions as always respectful and nonjudgmental so as to learn about their commonalities and differences. Those who take such a stance seek to justify their viewpoint by declaring that they are in the business of "taking religion seriously," which is a phrase one also repeatedly encounters in the contemporary anthropological discourse on religion. But, as McCutcheon (2001: 73) rightly queries, what does that really mean? The answer can only be "understanding of religion with endorsement" (Wiebe 1984a: 158). By taking this stance, however, these scholars in effect suspend "their own critical faculties and their capacity for disbelief" and sidestep rational argumentation (McCutcheon 1997: 445). Thus, the study of religion becomes merely "a reporter repeating the insider's unsubstantiated claims," an enterprise justified by invoking methodological agnosticism (McCutcheon 1997: 449). In anthropology, methodological agnosticism as a starting point has oddly directed some "respectful" researchers toward a very non-agnostic trajectory by transforming them into believing advocates of indigenous spirituality and superstition (see Chapter 5).

Research conducted within such parameters can offer little, apart from descriptive accounts, with little explanatory value or utility for public policy. Such expert voices, however, are critical given the power religion has acquired today as a means through which believers negotiate the social and political world, monitor social cohesion and identity, and defend and contest power and privilege (McCutcheon 2001: 134). In McCutcheon's (1997: 449) words,

> When it comes to deciding whether and to what extent religious positions that claim ahistorical authority, wisdom, and direction are useful in charting the course of a public-school curriculum, a welfare agency, or even a policy for war, such translators have no voice and little, if anything, to add.

McCutcheon's view may be in the minority, and it is likely that some or perhaps even all scholars in fields like religious studies and anthropology may feel that the study of religion is not about input into public policy. In their minds, adopting such a stance is admissible because they are "taking religion seriously" and subjecting religious beliefs to critical ontological examination is not their business. However, when researchers who are best situated to tell us why humankind remains fettered to harmful and nonsensical creeds fail to provide reliable information for public policy, then their hermeneutical intellectual enterprise, no matter how erudite and sophisticated they may be, becomes irrelevant. Such a failure is particularly lamentable given the fact that in our time we are confronted with the resurgence of religious fundamentalisms and militancy and proliferation of archaic delusions among empowered believers intent on imposing their supernaturalism on others by force if necessary.

Long ago the philosopher of religion Donald Wiebe (1984b) referred to this as a "failure of nerve" because the scholars in question have renounced critical ontological investigation and analysis in favor of phenomenologically and hermeneutically based approaches (McCutcheon 1997: 448). Again, researchers committed to such hermeneutical perspectives may object, pointing out that taking religion seriously and their interpretive stance *does* entail critique from the scholar. Such arguments are not very convincing. Given the urgent need to figure out why humans continue to tout irrational supernatural beliefs at this historical juncture, this type of critique is next to useless. As I see it, scholars in the field of religious studies and comparative religion and anthropologists studying religion have overtly or covertly operated primarily to legitimize, valorize, and validate supernatural beliefs.

Given the circumstance in which we find ourselves today, privileging religion is no longer tenable. Nor are there theoretical, methodological, or evidentiary reasons for doing so. The sad fact is, contrary to what scholars such as Crapo maintain, all things supernatural, paranormal, religious, transcendental, or any other label one wishes to use are indeed scientifically false as the anthropologist James Lett (1997a: 111) cogently pointed out years ago. Only a failure of nerve has prevented scholars of religion and many anthropologists from admitting that they are studying erroneous beliefs. What Crapo and those who think like him fail to grasp is that the problematic epistemic status of religious beliefs does not change just because this or that culture has dignified and attached cosmic significance to them (cf., Slezak 2012: 405). History is replete with dignified and cosmically significant belief systems that have led their believers into the abyss. As the critical philosopher of religion Hermann Reimarus (1879: 6) put it more than a century ago,

> That which is absurd and impossible, that which in any other history would be called falsehood, deception, outrage, and cruelty, cannot be made reasonable, righteous, and true by the added words: Thus saith the Lord.

In sum, it is intellectually dishonest to withhold judging irrational and egregious propositions critically just because such dogmata have a culturally exalted status in a particular society. Crapo and Konner are in the company of those who are content to bracket out questions of truth and falsity of supernatural beliefs and allow room for epistemological compromise, rather than scrutinizing such beliefs in accordance with the tradition of systematic skepticism. Yet, this is the kind of scrutiny that is now required at this critical historical juncture as irrationalism and religious fanaticism are erupting all around (Sidky 2018).

Except for a few honest and courageous individuals who have followed where the evidence has taken them, in general, anthropologists have seldom challenged religion's privileged status but have instead supported it. Consider, for example, the anthropological treatment of the Creation Museum in Petersburg, Kentucky, and its multi-million-dollar Ark amusement park in Williamstown, Kentucky, a little over seventy miles from my university in Ohio. A brief description of this exhibit is in order before a discussion of the anthropological study. The Ark exhibit and the museum, which are carefully designed to instill the Bible creation myth, may more accurately be described as a funfair intended to bamboozle the gullible faithful who visit in large numbers and devoutly pay $40 per person for adults, $31 for seniors, and $28 for children. The centerpiece of this exhibit is a large boat, purportedly a recreation of Noah's Ark.

The story of the Ark found in The Book of Genesis (chapters 6–9), it should be noted, was plagiarized from an ancient Sumerian flood myth dating to the third millennium BCE, or one of its several later variants. The protagonist in one version of this story is Ziusudra, the Sumerian king of the city of Šuruppak in lower Mesopotamia. Ziusudra discovers through a vision that the gods are planning to unleash a storm to cleanse the world of humans. A message from the god Enki confirms his vision. Enki tells him that the solution is to build a boat. Ziusudra commandeers a ferry and loads it with some livestock and thus weathers the storm and the waters. In the Bible story, this becomes hauling two of every species of animal life on earth in a wooden barge.

The calamitous event was a sizeable localized storm that flooded the Euphrates River and inundated a few cities in southern Sumer. This area is susceptible to regional flooding, and it is no surprise that stories about devastating rains and inundations were part of the lore of those ancient local cultures. Such stories are typically found among cultures in environments prone to flooding but are absent in ones not susceptible to such devastating torrents (Shermer 2002: 130). The Babylonian variants of this myth appear in the epic of king Atra-Hasīs, dating to 1654–1626 BCE, and in the Epic of Gilgamesh, which was inscribed around 1100 BCE (see Best 1999; Dalley 2000; Lambert and Millard 1969). In the Gilgamesh saga, the flood hero is a man named Ut-napištim who builds a boat and saves his kinfolk and some animals from a massive flood.

What are we to make of such tales? Could they have involved actual historical events on a global scale? Did water cover the entire planet and then magically recede and evaporate into outer space? Did some ancient personality manage to fit two each of the millions of species of animals on a wooden ferry or barge? No, not really. These are absurd notions. As the noted expert on Sumerian culture Samuel Kramer put it in his book, *History Begins at Sumer* (1981), regarding the scribes or mythographers who wrote these stories,

> Their main literary tools [...] were not logic and reason, but imagination and fantasy. In telling their story, these poets did not hesitate to invent motives and incidents patterned on human action.

It is these imagined yarns that are the sources of the account of a global deluge in the Book of Genesis. The point here is that this fable did not come via any divine transmission or communication from God or the gods. Also, we are not dealing with any historical occurrences involving a global deluge. These fictionalized tales are cultural products of parochial people with little knowledge of the world beyond the sphere of their own cultures and involved human-to-human transmission, with the stories told and retold, altered and elaborated, and inscribed in variant forms. The unimaginative authors of the Bible merely copied the flood story from the mythology of the Sumerians or the Babylonians, added a few embellishments, and made it the basis of their fable. The sponsors of the Ark exhibition are peddling this yarn to the American public as historical and scientific truth. The skeptic Michael Shermer (2002: 130) has rightly put it in this regard that, "To try to turn a myth into science [...] is an insult to myths, and an insult to religion, and an insult to science."

The Kentucky Ark and the associated narrative improves upon the original tale in various details and is complete with cages containing models of small dinosaurs alongside farm animals. Dinosaurs are used to convey the message that the earth was created during the Bronze Age and that at one time (before the "fall") humans and dinosaurs were all vegetarians and lived side by side in harmony. Dinosaurs and humans appear in other exhibits in the museum as well. It seems that this is a point the sponsors of this project want to emphasize in an attempt to refute the fossil record categorically. Creationists have been engaged in such an enterprise ever since the publication of Charles Lyell's *Principles of Geology* (1830–33), which presented evidence that the earth was older than 6,000 years (see Chapter 2).

The farcical nature of this bizarre spectacle has not escaped critics who have pointed out that the creationist architects of the museum and theme park seem to have taken as literal the portrayal of human–dinosaur coexistence in the 1960s Hanna-Barbera cartoon *The Flintstones*. A May 24, 2007 piece in *The Los Angeles Times* after the opening of the Creation Museum acerbically described this enterprise as "Yabba-Dabba Science: The Bedrock Truth is that the Creation Museum may be a Gay Old Time, But it's Not a Page Out of History," borrowing a few lines from the popular cartoon. The Ark was an addition to the Kentucky biblical funfair in 2016. The cost of the giant model boat alone is estimated to be over a hundred million dollars. One wonders how many homeless people, sick children, and others in need the donors exercising Christian charity who financed this bizarre supernaturalist amusement park could have helped had their dollars been utilized differently.

Not surprisingly, the Ark looks remarkably like the model boat conceived by Hollywood special effects people for use in the 1966 John Huston movie *The Bible in the Beginning* rather than anything gleaned from the vague Genesis text. This is not unexpected because purveyors of paranormal and supernatural nonsense often get their inspiration from Hollywood movies (cf., Sidky 2015: 114). The museum and model boat are perfect examples of what the philosopher David Hume (1902 [1748]: 125) described as "pious frauds."

These deceitful exhibitions of superstition and baloney are more ambitious versions of an earlier kind of religious fraud widely perpetrated by American evangelical Christians during the nineteenth and twentieth centuries (Noll 1994: 187). One of these involved an entirely fictitious tale complete with references to the "scientific literature" about a British sailor who was swallowed by a whale near the Falkland Islands and survived and was rescued after three days. The message was that this extraordinary event proves that the Bible story of Jonah and the giant fish is true and Christianity is vindicated (see Davis 1991, and Chapter 11). There are, of course, numerous other such cons and impostures to be found in the works of these virtuous religionists. The creation museum and the Ark are merely the latest renditions of this sort of chicanery.

Children whom parents bring to the Ark wonderland learn that science, rationality, and critical thinking are bogus and that evolutionary theory and climate change are scientific deceptions. More importantly, they are encouraged to "believe" and embrace the absurdities contained in a text written thousands of years ago by unknown, ignorant, violent, and deeply superstitious Middle Eastern people who knew next to nothing about the world and universe. This entire charade forms an important element of the creationist propaganda campaign to undermine independent thinking and science because these are the nemeses of religious dogma and superstition. As Hume (1987 [1758]: 66) caustically put it, "Liberty of thinking [...] is always fatal to priestly power, and to those pious frauds, on which it is commonly founded."

One anthropologist (Bielo 2018) has studied the Ark theme park and the efforts of Kenneth Ham, the mastermind of this project, and the organization behind this religionist enterprise. Ham, a failed Australian schoolteacher, is a boorish mountebank and self-styled "ambassador from heaven," as Hume would have put it. His public debates reveal that he is adept at clever talk but knows nothing about science, scientific reasoning, world religions, the existence of elaborate creation myths in other cultures, the ethnographic record, and even less about the history of the Bible and Christian theology. Yet, he uses his Bible wonderland in Kentucky to pontificate about the errors of science and evolutionary theory. The anthropologist studying "the Ark experience," who certainly had plenty of material to deliver a useful and much-needed critique, opted to do what others in the field have done. That is, to offer a nuisance and respectful anthropological narrative instead of assessing this shameful exhibition for what it actually is, a religious deception that has wasted the vast sums of money provided by religious donors that could very well have been put to good use elsewhere to make a real difference in the lives of needy fellow human beings. After all, is not that the purpose of Christian charity?

By not describing this charade for what it is the anthropologist in question has done nothing more than dignify and legitimize a scam perpetrated upon a credulous and scientifically ignorant American public. This entire enterprise is a disservice to the young minds polluted by the nonsense Ham and his unscrupulous evangelical creationist colleagues are disseminating that will leave them unable to compete in the global economic market with their counterparts in other countries such as China, Russia, and India, where children learn science and mathematics. The education of young people and their futures, of course, are of no concern because to religious fundamentalists their superstitious dogmas take precedence over all other matters. The anthropologist studying the Ark is also not concerned with the matter. This kind of anthropology is unfortunate. It is as reprehensible as the efforts of those who have taken up promotion of indigenous paranormal beliefs and superstitions in the name groundbreaking of inquiry (see Chapter 5).

Overall, such scholarship is abhorrent because it has prevented the honest assessment of the nature and consequences of supernatural and paranormal beliefs, attitudes, and behaviors across space and time. Scholars in disciplines such as critical philosophy of religion, evolutionary biology, and cognitive science have not shied away from weighing the evidence in this manner (cf., Philipse 2014: 330). In this study, therefore, I side with the scientists and philosophers rather than humanistic anthropologist colleagues.

Refusal to engage the content of religious beliefs is tantamount to endorsement and advocacy. Here the scholar comes dangerously close to committing the fallacy of "moral relativism," that is, that any beliefs, customs, practices, or traditions are worthy of tolerance and respect as long as the people in a given culture themselves consider those beliefs and practices as acceptable. When it comes to peoples' religious beliefs, this is particularly the case. However, this entails the fallacious extension of the general philosophical precept in anthropology known as "cultural relativism," that is, that cultures must be understood in their own terms and contexts rather than in terms of the standards of the outside observer's cultural traditions and beliefs. The fallacy of extending this idea to moral relativism becomes immediately apparent when we consider some of the grotesqueries of our time committed in the name of God or religion. These include abortion clinic bombings, beheadings, the Taliban treatment of women, putting women who have had abortions in jail for life in many places in Latin America because of Church injunctions, and the twenty-first-century form of child abuse of placing suicide vests on children so that they can kill themselves and others in the name of God. How about throwing acid on girls going to school, honor killings, racial and gender apartheid, infanticide, ethnic cleansing, and denying medical help for seriously sick children in favor of intercessory prayer? Regrettably, this list can go on ad infinitum.

Critical thinkers would argue that in our globally connected world there are certain beliefs and practices (select one from those mentioned or add others) that do not deserve respect or tolerance according to the standards and values of any culture. To do otherwise in these cases, to acquiesce to the hands-off approach, transforms the anthropologist into a willing or tacit apologist for unequivocally false and objectionable fantasies called religious beliefs. In this regard, researchers and scholars who otherwise pride themselves on their courageous battle against racism and exploitation, and who are advocates of human rights and social justice, have abrogated their intellectual responsibilities. The ever-insightful Thomas Paine (1880 [1807]: 152) made a similar point about scholars in his time. Perhaps it is time for anthropologists and scholars in all relevant fields to be more courageous. We cannot dignify patently false and irrational ideas and archaic absurdities just because they are labeled "religious."

Having said all this, I wish to move past the picture painted by the New Atheists who have stressed the futility, irrationality, falsehood, and dangers of religion. The questions I *also* want to address are: Why do humans have the proclivity for religion, the supernatural, and the paranormal in the first place? Why have people remained fettered to sets of ideas from a violent and barbarous past, or the delusions of a prescientific cosmology, that have no basis in reality and which bequeath nothing but illusionary succor that has come at a terrible cost? Why are such tenets deemed to be more sacrosanct among many than the sanctity of human life, secularism, democracy, human rights, gender equality, tolerance, and peace on earth? Why have ancient and patently false ideas and absurdities been maintained as sacrosanct truths while other parts of the archaic belief systems to which they belonged have long been abandoned? Why have not humans outgrown religion?

The objective of this study is to examine religion and all its associated supernatural and paranormal precepts critically and as comprehensively as possible without the usual obsequiousness. Deferential treatment and epistemological comprise are no longer feasible because the purveyors of supernaturalism, paranormalists, home-grown ayatollahs, and religious fundamentalists are now touting their beliefs as equally if not more valid and legitimate than scientific knowledge. Oxymoronic scientific creationists are actively engaged in political campaigns to make their superstitious beliefs part of school curricula by winning votes. However, by crossing over into the domain of science, these religious polemicists, who are purveyors of supernaturalism, superstition, and pseudoscience, have rendered their own premises legitimate subjects for critical scientific scrutiny.

The topics examined in the following chapters include psi phenomena, extraterrestrial visitations and abductions, divine miracles, religious experiences, paranormal monsters, magical healings, supernatural visions, life after death, corpse reanimations, the divine authorship, inerrancy, and the miracles of the Bible and Qur'an, creationism, arguments from supernatural design, cosmic fine-tuning, and more.

# Chapter Two

# THE UNREAL REAL: THE SUPERNATURAL, RELIGION, AND THE PARANORMAL

*Terms such as supernatural, metaphysical, and nonempirical reality are, in fact, oxymorons. It would make as much sense to talk about the "unreal real."*

—James Lett, Science, Religion, and Anthropology (1997)

*The unexplained is not supernatural.*

—Michael Scriven, Science, *Primary Philosophy* (1966)

Words such as religion, supernatural, and paranormal refer to transcendental realities, beings, and forces. These terms are very imprecise, and the boundaries of the purported phenomena which they denote are fuzzy. The first question to ask is, What makes something religious rather than supernatural or paranormal? Consider the following: Why is a late-night visitation by an androgynous being with wings, that is, an angel, deemed to belong to the realm of religion, while a similar nocturnal appearance by another androgynous but wingless creature, the occupant of an extraterrestrial spacecraft, considered to belong to the domain of the paranormal? Are beliefs in the existence of ghosts or souls part of religion or the supernatural? Alternatively, are they paranormal? Some conceptual clarification is necessary before we can proceed further.

## What Is the Supernatural?

The term "supernatural" comes from the Latin *supernaturalis* that was in use during the Middle Ages to describe the miracles of God mentioned in the Bible and the prodigies associated with the Christian cult of saints (Bartlett 2008: 9–17, 2013: 3–26). This concept was brought into theological discourse by the great Christian theologian Thomas Aquinas during the thirteenth century. It was juxtaposed with the ideas of *natura* and *naturalis*, "nature" or "natural," and was an aspect of the theological discussions of the time about the world of people and the spirit world. As the theistic philosopher William Shea (1984: 308) has pointed out, understandings of supernatural are framed in relation to "nature" and "natural," so that the meaning of one term is "dialectically coupled" with the comprehension of the other term. However, medieval thinkers concerned with the supernatural and natural struggled with the distinctions between these concepts. As the historian Robert Bartlett (2008: 26) has put it, "the categories and definitions used for discussing the natural and the supernatural were fluid, potentially contradictory, and often indeed unexamined." For reasons I shall discuss, these concepts have remained problematic to this day.

The philosopher of science Martin Mahner (2012: 1437) defines the supernatural as follows:

> the view that our lawful spatiotemporal world is not all that exists because there is another non-spatiotemporal world transcending the natural one, whose inhabitants—usually considered to be intentional beings—are not subject to natural laws.

The neuroscientist Yonatan Fishman and philosopher Maarten Boudry (2013: 924–25) provide a tentative but more detailed definition of the supernatural as referring to entities/phenomena characterized as follows:

> (1) They operate in ways that fundamentally violate our current understanding of how the world works, (2) they exist outside the spatiotemporal realm of our universe (though they may still causally interact with our universe), and (3) they suggest that reality is at bottom purposeful and mind-like, particularly in a sense that implies a central role for humanity and human affairs in the cosmic scheme.

Both of these definitions refer to a transcendental realm. Anything outside the spatiotemporal realm of the world is part of a purported nonempirical reality. It follows, therefore, that supernatural phenomena are inexplicable according to the current scientific understanding that addresses only empirical reality. These definitions approximate how the shamans and other supernatural practitioners with whom I have worked conceive of the world and universe (Sidky 2017b: 139–53). It is also more or less what most religionists and paranormalists think of when they talk about extraordinary beings and forces, such as ghosts, spirits, gods, God, and psi phenomena.

Making precise distinctions between supernatural and natural is extraordinarily problematic, and rigorous definitions are lacking. The word "supernatural" is what anthropologists consider to be an insiders' or *emic* term, denoting that it is comprehensible according to the consensual conceptual understandings meaningful and appropriate to members of particular human societies (Lett 1997: 109; Sidky 2015: 141). Thus, the sorts of things members of any culture construe as belonging to the transcendental realm vary across space and time. Even in the West, demarcating between what is natural and supernatural has shifted over time. For example, phenomena such as disease, bat sonar, meteorites, lightning, and comets were once considered to be supernatural/paranormal phenomena until naturalistic explanations consistent with other empirically grounded theories were provided (Fishman 2009: 824).

The case of lighting is a good example. It was once thought that lightning was God's instrument for punishing the wicked, illustrating the idea that nature and the cosmos are mind like and human focused and have a moral dimension, as stated in the definitions of supernatural given above. For this reason, religionists found Benjamin Franklin's lightning rod particularly vexing as an invention they saw to be thwarting the Lord's will, although how a small piece of metal could foil the all-powerful Creator of the universe was never discussed. However, statistical data of the kind collected by insurance agencies made it clear that lighting strikes the sinful and the righteous without due consideration of their religious affiliations or moral statuses (Fishman 2009: 822).

A further difficulty is that the delineations between natural and supernatural collapse under different scenarios (Fishman and Boudry 2013: 929). For instance, if there are supernatural beings beyond the spatiotemporal realm of our universe that can still intervene in our physical world, are those physical effects part of nature or beyond it? As this shows, the supernatural is epistemologically problematic. As Fishman and Boudry (2013: 930) observe, "At most, the concept of supernatural is a convenient term to capture a rough-and-ready distinction between mundane stuff and extraordinary, transcendent, mind-like stuff." Such difficulties justify not attributing any epistemic significance to the concept of supernatural (Fishman and Boudry 2013: 924).

In a diatribe concerning the problems of naturalism in science, the theistic philosopher Michael Rea (2004: 54) asserts that, as in the case of the supernatural, the concept of "nature" is also culturally constructed, arbitrary, and controversial, rather than being an observational statement. As Rea (2004: 54–55) puts it,

> There are common paradigms: men, beasts, plants, atoms, and electrons are natural; God, angels, ghosts, and immaterial souls are supernatural. But even these paradigms are controversial; and, in any case, it is not clear what the items on each list have in common with their other list-mates that makes them examples of natural and supernatural.

Rea is in the company of other religionists who believe that naturalism is science's Achilles heel. By attacking science in this way, these ideologues or religious polemicists think that they have opened the way for their version of "science," in which supernatural forces and Christian background beliefs play a significant role, an issue to be discussed in the next chapter. For now, it suffices to make two points. First, Rea exaggerates the problem of demarcating the natural from the supernatural or why these things are classified in this way. As the philosopher Graham Oppy (2018: 94) points out, these two domains are clearly distinguishable because humans, animals, plants, and atoms are scientifically established phenomena, while there is no such evidence for the existence of ghosts, deities, souls, and the like.

Second, it is necessary to note that we as humans are empirical beings operating within the parameters of an empirical world (nature) in which we survive because our senses do not interminably lead us to misapprehend that reality; otherwise we would bump into walls, walk off cliffs, step into traffic, and make other such disastrous blunders. Our perceptions of the natural world, therefore, do in some degree cohere with empirical reality outside our heads rather than being entirely the outcome of interpretive processes and arbitrary classifications disconnected from nature. Science is merely a more systematic way of trying to apprehend nature through methods that address our in-built subjective biases. Construals of the supernatural, therefore, do not have epistemic parity with scientific understandings of nature or the natural world based on systematic empirical testing and evaluations. Moreover, as discussed below, the fuzziness of the boundaries between natural and supernatural is not a science stopper. Therefore, the worn-out cultural construction of reality argument Rea attempts to harness here does not help the religionist case against science.

The point to keep in mind is that people in nearly all cultures differentiate between a realm in which humans dwell and a transcendental realm or realms wherein supernatural beings reside, regardless of which emic terms they may employ. In the cosmology of the shamans with whom I have worked, there are multiple supernatural worlds juxtaposed on the world of people. Moreover, the boundaries between these domains are permeable, and shamans do not recognize an explicit dichotomy between what we call "natural" and "supernatural." It is the same in many other cultural contexts (Saler 1977). The shamans, oracles, and god-men I studied for many years, who routinely traffic with the realm of the spirits and gods, are undoubtedly able to differentiate between what we would call the natural and supernatural. Thus, even in cases when members of particular cultures do not have a word that translates into "supernatural," or they do not make explicit distinctions between the natural and supernatural realms, they still recognize the existence of a transcendental world or worlds. It is an error to think that there are people who cannot differentiate between the domain of transcendent beings, such as spirits and gods, and the world of people, or distinguish mystical and ordinary realities (cf., Winzeler 2008: 7).

To solve these difficulties, Oppy (2018: 32–33) has opted to employ an umbrella term, the "non-natural," under which he includes the paranormal, preternatural, and the supernatural. In his view paranormal phenomena, which include such things as ESP, cryptids, and UFOs, are nonreligious, the preternatural is concerned with "religious marvels," and supernatural pertains to ghosts, spirits, and similar entities but "not essentially tied to religion."

Such a characterization is problematic, however, because supernatural beings and forces are an essential part of religions across cultures and through time. This is the only point where I disagree with Oppy's cogent ideas. What he refers to as the "preternatural" associated with demons, witches, and wizards is also questionable because magic, demons, and demonic forces are part and parcel of many religious cosmologies. In Christianity, at least since the late fifteenth century and probably much earlier, witchcraft was associated with "devils" and other supernatural entities, such as *incubi* and *succubi* acting under the direction of Satan, which are all supernatural beings of Christian theology (Sidky 1997: 31–47, 101–14). Moreover, the definition of paranormal as nonreligious phenomena is based on media portrayals and overlooks the considerable overlap between paranormal and religious phenomena. As parapsychologist Caroline Watt and psychologist Richard Wiseman (2009: xvii) point out, the paranormal encompasses not only beliefs in psychic abilities but also "beliefs in all-powerful deities and the power of prayer," survival of the soul after death, communication with the dead, psychic healing and harm, as well as visitations by intelligent alien life forms. Chapter 4 provides a discussion of the religious aspects of the paranormal. For these reasons the term "supernatural" remains highly problematic.

The concept of supernatural poses other epistemological difficulties as well. Anything outside the spatiotemporal realm of the world and universe is part of a purported nonempirical reality. Yet this putative reality that transcends the physical universe is thought to exert a direct and causal effect upon empirical reality somehow. The scientific anthropologist James Lett (1997: 109) points out the intrinsic problems involved in this line of reasoning by asking, If such a nonempirical reality exists, how can humans as empirical beings know or describe it? Moreover, what is the mechanism connecting this nonempirical reality with physical reality? Finally, if such a connecting mechanism exists, then why is there no scientific evidence for it? The philosopher Kai Nielsen (2001: 34) raises a similar question: How can we apprehend a reality that transcends the empirical world? Efforts to answer this question, he adds, have yielded propositions about an incoherent "something we know not what" (Nielsen 2001: 34). In other words, the replies verge on being and often are incoherent and meaningless.

The French philosopher René Descartes thought he had an answer to this problem. For him, the link between the supernatural or the spiritual (i.e., the mind/spirit) and the material or natural (i.e., the brain) was the pineal gland, what he called the "seat of the soul." However, he was wrong (see Chapter 6). Others have sought an answer in quantum physics. Assertions that quantum mechanics holds an answer (e.g., Hunter 2012: 25; Keener 2011: 124, 135) are merely a form of mystification due to a poor understanding of physics. The physicist Tanner Edis (2008: 49–52) calls this "quantum mysticism." Also, the psychologist James Alcock (1981: 114–15) points out the facetious nature of references by those with superficial understanding of physics to the principles of quantum mechanics and Heisenberg's uncertainty principle to imply that determinacy disintegrates at the subatomic level, that consciousness has an exalted role in reality, and that objectivity is an impossibility (cf., Edis 2008: 49, 51). All of this is sheer nonsense. As Edis (2008: 49, 51) points out, there is nothing in the quantum world that indicates "mysticism or any special role for consciousness." Philosopher Peter Slezak (1996: 211) holds a similar view and considers the assertion that quantum physics provides support for the supernatural to be nothing more than "sophistry." Even though the new physics is different from the mechanistic theories of the nineteenth century, he adds, "the new physics provides no more support for [supernatural] or mystical claims than the earlier physics."

Substituting alternative terms for the supernatural, such as metaphysical or transcendental, does not solve the problems. Such words, as Lett (1997: 110) observes, are oxymorons and make as much sense as talking about the "unreal real." In other words, these terms are unintelligible, self-contradictory, and hence meaningless. The "unreal real" stands for that for which there is no empirical evidence and cannot be comprehended. It belongs to the realm of imagination and fantasy. No naturalistic explanations are possible because the unreal real does not exist. The phrase "unreal real," therefore, highlights the fundamental problems one encounters when discussing transcendent realities, regardless of whether one calls them religious, paranormal, supernatural, or something else.

How does one talk about the unreal real? Take the idea of God construed as a putative supernatural nonphysical, bodiless being that theologians describe as radically transcendent (Swinburne 2004: 7). How can we discuss such an entity through the medium of language developed for designating physical reality? As the philosopher Herman Philipse (2014: 96) points out in his book, *God in the Age of Science*, the best that we can do is to use analogy or metaphor. The outcome is invariably a lapse into anthropomorphism whereby God becomes a human-like but fantastically powerful invisible man. In other words, God is nothing more than a glorified superhuman without a mortal body (Elbert 2003: 254). In his treatise *Dialogues Concerning Natural Religion* (1779), David Hume disparagingly described this as "the grossest and most narrow partiality" whereby we "make ourselves the model of the whole universe" (Hume 1779: 27). Such conceptions are problematic and patently false.

The absurdity of this line of thinking is also evident when theologians in the Judeo-Christian tradition refer to God as "him" or "he." How does one assign gender to an entity that by definition is nonphysical and bodiless and hence cannot possess reproductive organs? Theologians who provide descriptions of God also employ other human attributes such as purposeful, "perfectly free, omnipotent, omniscient, perfectly good" (Plantinga 2011: ix; Swinburne 2004: 7), which are psychological expressions that apply to human beings. Ascribing such human mental qualities or emotions to a radically transcendent and incorporeal being is incoherent. So, what is being discussed?

Anthropomorphic theisms, which entail Zeus-like gods, are unequivocally false. Theisms extricated from animistic principles by sophisticated theologians who offer spiritual conceptions of God as "unlimited," "pure spirit," self-caused, utterly independent being, or "God as the mysterious ground of the universe," to address the challenge from science, verge upon incoherency. To what does the notion of an ultimate self-caused, utterly independent being who transcends the universe refer? A transcendent being is, by definition, incomprehensible. Treating the idea in metaphorical terms, as Nielsen (2001: 33) says, raises the question: what is the referent of the metaphor?

Perhaps this difficulty explains why the philosopher Daniel Dennett (2006: 220) says that in reality theologians do not know what they are talking about and hence their insistence on the fundamental incomprehensibility of God and the elusiveness and mysterious nature of religious precepts as the central tenets of faith. Along similar lines, the ever-insightful Thomas Paine (1880 [1795]: 148) observed that theology is the study of nothing, is baseless, and cannot demonstrate anything. Take, for example, how certain theistic theologians construe the fragmentary, inconclusive, and contradictory evidence for the resurrection of Jesus, the central supernatural/paranormal event literalists claim is at the core of Christianity. These narratives are not merely elusive; they disagree on nearly all the key points. Indeed, the evidence for this purported miracle is the worst sort anyone could expect (see Chapters 14 and 15). However, instead of this impeding belief or raising questions and doubts, such problematic evidence is treated as a "divine mystery" to be embraced. The biblical scholar John Barclay (1996: 28) expresses this point of view as follows:

> One may interpret the fact that none of the gospels describe the actual moment of resurrection as marking this "event" in a special way as of ultimate and unique significance. The elusiveness of the narratives at this point signals the mystery of faith, the enigma of divine action which human reason cannot comprehend.

However, assertions that this or that is an incomprehensible ultimate mystery, as Nielsen (2001: 34) points out, is a dishonest way of saying we do not know what we are discussing.

The philosopher Herbert Spiegelberg describes two understandings of the supernatural in the context of religious discourse similar to that under discussion here. According to one conception, supernatural entities have natural attributes conceived according to familiar natural properties but to a greater degree, such as a deity that has superpowers and is omniscient in comparison with humans. Such supernatural beings tend to be anthropomorphic and can operate in earthly time and space. Another conception is of supernatural entities that categorically differ from natural ones to the extent that they are ineffable, mysterious, incomprehensible, and "Wholly Other," with no points of reference to anything natural (Mahner 2012: 1446). Spiegelberg (1951: 343) adds that supernatural entities that are comprehensible because they have quasi-natural properties and are therefore amenable to scientific appraisal may be termed *overnatural*. Entities that are categorically distinct from anything natural and are therefore incomprehensible and scientifically inaccessible can be called *transnatural* (Mahner 2012: 1448).

While theistic philosophers usually vacillate between these two characterizations of supernatural beings contingent upon the contexts in which they are operating (Mahner 2012: 1447), the extraordinary entities associated with religious beliefs across space and time have been overnatural anthropomorphic beings with naturalistic properties. There is a good reason for this. Overnatural beings combine human psychological characteristics with attributes that contradict intuitive expectations about humans, such as being invisible, omnipotent, omnipresent, and omniscient. As such, they violate ontological categories and to use the current jargon are "counterintuitive agents." Cognitive science and evolutionary psychology indicate that such counterintuitive ideas are attention-grabbing, memorable, and more likely to be retained and passed on (Boyer 2001: 65–69; Czachesz 2017: 8183, 133–38; Czachesz 2012: 141–89; Noenzayan and Atran 2004). The prevalence of anthropomorphic supernatural beings across cultures and time may be explicable in these terms. This line of research is covered in detail in Chapter 6.

The philosopher Kelly Smith (2001: 707) refers to transnatural and overnatural entities, respectively, as the utterly unknowable "mysterious God" premise and the "reasonable God" premise that grants the possibility that humans can to a degree comprehend His ways and purposes. Smith also points out that there would be very little to say about a "mysterious God" and his role in the creation of the universe because it is impossible to discern His divine purposes and creative mechanisms. Any statement about such a deity will be wholly arbitrary and groundless. Hence, endorsing this conception of God makes theology impossible. Advocating the "reasonable God" premise enables general claims about His actions and the empirical consequences of those actions. But this puts the burden of proof on the religionists who have to demonstrate how their claims are consistent with empirical evidence (Smith 2001: 710). In other words, the burden of proof that comes with this stance renders theistic claims vulnerable to empirical disconfirmation, such as the decisive disconfirmation of the Young Earth creationist postulate that a supernaturally caused global deluge explains the fossil record.

If the posited supernatural beings and forces can interact with the physical world in a way that we can detect their activities, that is, if they are overnatural entities, then they may be evaluated according to empirical evidence. What would such evidence include? One way to indirectly validate supernatural claims of this kind is to specify empirical happenings for which there are no plausible naturalistic explanations. Fishman and Boudry (2013: 930) provide a list of empirical observations that, if validated, could constitute tentative evidence for supernatural entities or phenomena in the world:

1. Intercessory prayer re-grows amputated limbs.
2. Only Catholic intercessory prayers are effective.
3. Anyone who speaks the Prophet Muhammad's name in vain is immediately struck down by lightning, and those who pray to Allah five times a day are free from disease and misfortune.
4. Gross inconsistencies in the fossil record, and independent dating techniques suggesting that the earth is less than 10,000 years old—thereby confirming the biblical account and casting doubt upon Darwinian evolution and contemporary scientific accounts of geology and cosmology.
5. Specific information or prophecies acquired during near-death experiences or via divine revelation that are later confirmed—assuming that conventional means of obtaining this information have been conclusively ruled out.
6. Scientific demonstration that proves extra-sensory perception or other paranormal phenomena (e.g., psychics routinely winning the lottery).
7. Mental faculties persist despite the destruction of the physical brain, thus supporting the existence of a soul that can survive bodily death.
8. Star alignments in the heavens that spell the phrase: "I Exist—God."

Evidence for any of these items would constitute provisional support for the supernatural. They would be tentative, because as in the case of lighting, disease, and meteorites natural explanations may eventually be provided. Similarly, the repeated failure to find evidence for these things would amount to provisional evidence against the supernatural (Fishman and Boudry 2013: 931).

Discussions of what is natural and supernatural will no doubt continue as they have for centuries. It is easy to get caught up in semantics and overlook the critical point that calling something supernatural versus natural is not the critical issue. What counts is evidentiary justification (Fishman 2009: 824; Fishman and Boudry 2013: 930). As Fishman (2009: 830) has cogently stated, the central question is not whether something is natural or supernatural, but instead whether there are any good reasons to believe that a claim is true? This is because the fundamental aim of science, he adds, is to reveal the nature of reality and in this pursuit science must venture wherever the evidence leads. In other words, in science, the ultimate arbiter of whether or not a claim is warranted is the evidence.

## What Is Religion?

As in the case of the supernatural, the concept of religion also poses various epistemological problems. Phenomena referred to as "religion" comprise different things across space and time and even between different classes within the same society (Nielsen 2001: 45). The problematic nature of the word is evident in the different ways scholars since the second half of the nineteenth century have defined religion, most of which fit the Abrahamic religions, but not all classes of "religions" (Oppy 2018: 30). Hence, there are no widely accepted designations of religion, although various viewpoints are on offer (Horton 1960; Nye 2008: 17–19; Smart 1989: 12–21; 1996: 10–11; Spiro 1966). Here I shall only discuss a few of these definitions before presenting the perspective adopted in this study.

In his book *The Elementary Forms of Religious Life* (1912) the noted French sociologist Émile Durkheim defined religion as:

> a unified system of beliefs and practices relative to sacred things, that is to say, things set aside as forbidden—beliefs and practices which unite into one single moral community, called a Church [disregard the Christian connotation], all those who adhere to them. (Durkheim 1961: 62)

Durkheim considered religion to be sui generis (self-generated) and irreducible to individual psychological states or defined with reference to the ideas of gods or spirits (Durkheim 1961: 50). To make the point that belief in spiritual beings is not the defining criterion of religion, he pointed out the existence of non-deistic faiths, such as Buddhism and Jainism. The problem, of course, is that in practice, gods, spirits, and divine beings play a prominent role in both Buddhism and Jainism.

In Durkheim's view, religion is a collective sociological phenomenon, comprising sets of shared beliefs and attitudes toward the sacred. These beliefs bring individuals together into a single moral community. Central to this understanding of religion are the ideas of the *sacred* and the *profane*. The sacred manifests itself when group members gather together to engage in collective rituals. Such rituals create and maintain group cohesion. It is when people come together that the power of group thought as a whole, or its collective consciousness, presents itself to and impinges upon individuals as an awesome and external force and has a determinative influence on thought and behavior. From the collectivity of the group emanates collective power, which seems to transcend the individual and, because it is a manifestation of the collective, endures beyond the earthly existence of any single person. It, therefore, appears as something external and eternal. It is this that becomes the focus of worship and ritual. Thus, the object of reverence and worship is the collective, or society itself (Sidky 2004: 27). Although Durkheim wanted to provide a naturalistic or scientific explanation, his idea of religion as an irreducible self-generating phenomenon immunized it from critical scientific ontological examinations and analysis according to psychological or other meaningful scientific categories.

In contrast to the Durkheimian social functionalist approach, the anthropologist Bronislaw Malinowski propounded an emotionalist-psychological functionalist perspective. For him, religion is comprehensible in relation to the human psychological needs it addresses under conditions of uncertainty. As he put it,

> Both magic and religion arise and function in situations of emotional stress: crises of life, lacunae in important pursuits, death and initiation into tribal mysteries, unhappy love and unsatisfied hate [...] religion [opens] up escapes from such situations and such impasses as

> offer no empirical way out except by ritual and belief in the domain of the supernatural. (Malinowski 1955: 87)

For Malinowski, religion enables humans to cope with the psychological stresses and the vicissitudes of existence. However, what he overlooked was that religion could also be an equally powerful source of fear, guilt, and anxiety: fear regarding wrathful deities, demons, devils, multiple hells, witchcraft, sorcery, eternal damnation, and of being punished for ritual infractions.

The anthropologist Clifford Geertz (1973: 4) offered a cultural definition of religion as

> (1) a system of symbols which acts to (2) establish powerful, pervasive, and long-lasting moods and motivations in men by (3) formulating conceptions of a general order of existence and (4) clothing these conceptions with such an aura of factuality that (5) the moods and motivations seem uniquely realistic.

Anthropologists, as well as researchers in the field of religious studies, generally accept this vision of religion. However, the Geertzian perspective is highly problematic. The first problem is that a definition of religion that excludes paranormal beings and the supernatural world is not only contrary to what anthropological findings reveal about religion but also indistinguishable from nonreligious ideologies, such as existentialism, communism, or Nazism. These are ideological perspectives that most anthropologists who are familiar with the ethnographic record of cultures around the world would refrain from calling religion.

Second, in this view, religion becomes the explain-all phenomenon, a worldview, the thing that provides the meaning of life. It is beyond truth or falsity but serves as a framework that allows people to comprehend various truths and falsehoods (Frankenberry and Penner 1999: 634). As such, Geertz placed religion outside the scope of rational scientific appraisal. Here Geertz's ideas to an extent harmonize with the views of the Christian existentialist philosopher Paul Tillich (1957: 82), who also sought to shield religion from scientific scrutiny, asserting that "scientific truth and the truth of faith do not belong to the same *dimension of meaning*." This smokescreen does not hold up because any religion involving overnatural beings and forces is open to scientific scrutiny.

The third problem with Geertz's definition of religion as meaning, moods, motivations, and feelings is that it valorizes the subjective, personal, and private. It verges on Mircea Eliade's notion of the irreducibility of religion, discussed in Chapter 1, as something that can only be interpreted sympathetically from the emic perspective, rather than as a phenomenon amenable to scientific scrutiny. Here critical ontological examinations and analysis of religious are precluded, and the scholar often slips into the role of advocate, guardian, and in some cases even endorser of the supernatural (Segal 1983: 111; Wiebe 1984a: 158).

In his book *Primitive Religion* (1871), anthropologist Edward Tylor presented what he called the minimal definition of religion as the belief in "spiritual beings." By this, he meant that wherever we find beliefs in extraordinary, noncorporeal entities such as souls, ghosts, fairies, angels, demons, devils, and gods that is where religion exists (Harris 1989: 399–400).

Tylor maintained that the belief in spirits developed out of efforts by early humans to explain the difference between living and dead people and images seen in dreams and visions. Early humans observing the difference between a living and deceased person tried to understand the difference and concluded that people must have a spiritual as well as a material body. Ancient people, according to Tylor, also believed the spiritual body roams around at night when people are dreaming and returns when they wake up. However, when someone dies, his or her spirit leaves permanently to become a soul. The body dies: the soul continues to exist. Tylor (1929: 24) thought that this is how early humans explained death, and he treated it as the principle underlying all religions.

Tylor was interested only in the cognitive dimensions of religion and did not incorporate the institutional aspects or sociological context of religious beliefs and actions into his analysis. While Tyler's cognitive perspective fell out of favor during most of the twentieth century, in recent decades, cognitive theories of religion similar to his have reemerged. Cognitive researchers have adopted a perspective like that of Tylor, which holds that religion centers upon beliefs in humanlike spirits and deities and is an effort to interpret physical reality (Guthrie 2007: 51–52).

This construal encompasses what may be called "the supernatural" defined as beliefs and practices linked to extraordinary beings, such as God, gods, angelic beings, souls, spirits, ghosts, and demons, which are culturally universal and are typically subsumed under the label of religion (cf., Coyne 2015: 114; Pandian 2003: 163). Here, religion and the supernatural refer to the same phenomena. However, such a conception of religion is too constricting because it does not incorporate beliefs and behaviors that are virtually identical in form and function to religious beliefs and practices but would not commonly be called religious (Lett 1997: 110).

For this reason, the anthropologists Arthur Lehmann and James Myers (2001: 3) advocate augmenting our conception of religion to incorporate extraordinary and mysterious powers and forces for a more comprehensive view that includes magic, sorcery, witchcraft, and related practices. This is the understanding of religion used in the context of the present study. It is also the reason why the analysis provided in this book includes all things referred to as religious, transcendental, mystical, supernatural, and paranormal.

## What Is the Paranormal?

Paranormal claims are in many ways similar to supernatural and religious ones. Moreover, like the supernatural and religious, the paranormal also entails putative phenomena and causal mechanisms that transcend the empirical world and are inexplicable according to the current scientific understanding of physical reality. However, the concept of the paranormal is conventionally used to refer to phenomena such as telekinesis, clairvoyance, telepathy, precognition, astrology, and so forth that appear unrelated to religion or the supernatural.

Like beliefs in the supernatural, paranormal precepts are widely held in modern Western societies, as well as being prevalent across space and time (French and Stone 2014: 7). There are no known societies where such beliefs are absent. During my fieldwork with Nepalese shamans and Tibetan oracles and mediums, the paranormal was everywhere. I also found such beliefs elsewhere I have conducted research, such as Central Asia, Australia, and the Pacific Islands. We do not see many explicit references to paranormal concepts in the anthropological literature on religion because most anthropologists employ emic or indigenous conceptual categories rather than using terms found in the vast parapsychological literature on the paranormal. Yet, the paranormal is present everywhere in the ethnographic record. As the parapsychologists Harvey Irwin and Caroline Watt (2007: 11) point out, paranormal and parapsychological phenomena are to be found in all cultures and across time, and the church's hagiographic record supplies many examples.

The universality of such ideas says a great deal about how beliefs and wishful thinking impact human perceptions and memory, and factor in on how people think and make decisions about the natural world (French and Stone 2014: 17). For these reasons, beliefs about the paranormal and the supernatural are of anthropological interest not merely as aspects of particular human societies but also because of what they can generally tell us about human experience and cognition.

The term "paranormal" ("beyond normal") denotes the existence of mysterious and occult forces in the universe. Psychologist James Alcock (1981: 3) defines the paranormal as putative phenomena inexplicable in terms of current scientific understanding of the world. In this respect, paranormal, like the supernatural, also refers to phenomena outside of the spatiotemporal realm, or a nonempirical reality, and similarly qualifies as the unreal real. For this reason, contradictions have beset the scientific study of the paranormal from the start, the main one being how to provide scientific evidence for something that, by definition, is inexplicable in scientific terms. A more precise definition beyond this does not exist, and the word "paranormal" is sometimes used synonymously with "supernatural, transcendental, or miraculous" (Kurtz 1985a: 503). Coyne (2015: 113), for example, includes the paranormal under the category of supernatural because such phenomena are contrary to the laws of physics.

To complicate matters further, construals of what constitutes the paranormal vary depending on whom one asks. The media incorporates an extensive and almost baffling array of items in this category. The list includes such things as crop circles, the now unfashionable Bermuda Triangle, Bigfoot, the Loch Ness monster, crystal power, dowsing, "the hundredth monkey" phenomenon, hypnosis, Kirlian photography, "the force," the Shroud of Turin, flying saucers (UFOs), astrology, astral projections, talking to the spirits of the dead, ghosts, and much more. The list of items anomalous psychologists provide is even more all-encompassing. These researchers, who seek explanations for paranormal phenomena according to known psychological and physical facts, consider as part of the paranormal "everything weird and wonderful" (French 2001a, 2001b; French and Stone 2014: 9).

## The Paranormal and Pseudoscience

Some of the items listed as paranormal, such as beliefs in UFOs or Bigfoot, are strictly speaking pseudoscientific claims. Here again, some clarification is necessary. Pseudoscience means fake or pretended science. The distinguishing features of pseudoscience include indifference to facts, use of subjective methods, dependence on arbitrary cultural conventions and mythology, and reliance on explanations based on "scenarios" or stories (Coker 2001; Lilienfeld 2005). It entails forwarding extraordinary claims in the absence of the necessary extraordinary evidence.

Other attributes of pseudoscience include heavy reliance on anecdotal and testimonial evidence, persuasion through rhetoric, the deliberate omission of crucial data, misrepresentation, emphasis on confirmation rather than refutation, failure to build upon existing knowledge, and the attempt to place the burden of proof on the nonbeliever (Coker 2001; Gardner 1957: 12–14; Lilienfeld 2005; Sidky 2004: 25, 397). Pseudoscience possesses its own large, scientific-sounding, pretentious but imprecise jargon that is used to generate an aura of authority. Proponents of pseudoscientific claims have an aversion to critical scrutiny and peer review and generally avoid submitting their premises to any meaningful tests.

Another characteristic of pseudoscience is the dependence on ad hoc hypotheses that serve as loopholes to render its assertions unfalsifiable. For example, oxymoronic scientific creationists argue that God created the earth a few thousand years ago (during the Bronze Age!), a claim that is contradicted by masses of scientific evidence that the earth is billions of years old. The creationist ad hoc rejoinder is that all the evidence indicating that this planet is ancient, including the fossil record, was put into place by God when He created the earth to test our faith. An alternative version is that it was the Devil who made this evidence to deceive us. This assertion is referred to as the "Omphalos hypothesis" after the title of the book by the religionist Philip Gosse, *Creation (Omphalos): An Attempt to Untie the Geological Knot* (1857). Gosse tried to harmonize the creation myth in the Bible with scientific geological findings of his time, especially Charles Lyell's work *Principles of Geology* (1830–32) that presented evidence that the earth was much older than 6,000 years.

Scientific creationism is part of the same genre of pseudoscientific paranormalism that the media and entertainment industry have been pushing on the American public for years. However, creationist and pseudoscientific ideas are not innocuous. They tend to support one another while taking advantage of and magnifying the gullibility and scientific illiteracy of the public. The skeptic, humanist, and author Arthur C. Clarke (2003: 185) described this turn of events as a descent into "cultural barbarism" characterized by mind-rotting rubbish such as UFOs, ESP, and creationism touted by home-grown ayatollahs of the airwaves and in bookstores and newsstands. The barrage of pseudoscientific and supernatural bunkum has intensified in the current post-truth era. Such beliefs are a testament to the predilection of human cognitive systems to be hijacked by supernatural ideation. These circumstances are very troubling. As the psychologist Thomas Gilovich (1991: 6) has cogently stated, tolerating flawed thinking and superstitions has a heavy cost because occasional acceptance of erroneous beliefs endangers our ability to see the world clearly the rest of the time and renders us "susceptible to the arguments and exhortations of those with other than benign intentions."

Clarke (2003: 185) was particularly angered by the nonsensical pseudoscientific ideas espoused by creationists. However, it is incorrect to label creationism merely a pseudoscience (contra Scott 2001). It is something more insidious. Those making pseudoscientific claims aspire to achieve the respectability of science by adopting scientific sounding nomenclature, but creationists while impudently using the trappings of science want to demolish science and replace it with the archaic superstitions of the Bible, or what the Christian apologist Alvin Plantinga calls an "Augustinian science" (see Chapter 3). In other words, the call is for the reestablishment of discarded medieval and archaic credulities associated with a bygone and defunct worldview. Creationists strive to accomplish their objective using political pressure and amassing votes rather than by offering for appraisal alternative methodologies and data superior to those of science (Bridgestock 2009: 45; Forrest and Gross 2004; Pennock 1999). These ideologues call their strategy to sway public opinion in favor of their superstitious beliefs, "the wedge" (Forrest and Gross 2004). For this reason, creationism is one of the biggest confidence games played on the American public. But more on this later.

Pseudoscience is different from "erroneous science" because its hypotheses are framed to be proof-exempt. For this reason, pseudoscientific knowledge does not grow, it does not yield new information, and nothing concrete is ever learned (Coker 2001). Pseudoscience appeals to emotion and sentiment and encourages distrust of established scholarly traditions. Advocates of pseudoscience attribute the skeptical scrutiny and criticism of their views by scientists to the vested interests of the scientific establishment in the subject matter and a grand conspiracy on their part to suppress the truth (Sagan 1995: 21). Hence, proponents of pseudoscientific claims frequently appeal to "the Galileo Argument," which entails drawing parallels between the rejection of their claims and the rejection of Galileo's ideas by an "establishment" terrified of being proven wrong. However, this is a spurious argument because it was the ecclesiastical establishment that persecuted Galileo—the scientists of the time accepted his findings. A distinction must be made here between legitimate skepticism and dogmatic close-mindedness—Galileo's persecutors refused to look at the evidence (Gilovich 1991: 51). Scientists look at the evidence before rendering any judgments (see Chapter 3).

Finally, pseudoscience eschews rational standards and argues from logical fallacies, such as the argument from ignorance, reduction to absurdity, appeal to authority, special pleading, and the least plausible hypothesis, among others. Here pseudoscience and religious apologetics have much in common. Pseudoscience and religion both are based on archaic irrational modes of thought that predate science by millennia and have been the source of all sorts of deceptive, fanciful, and patently false beliefs about humans and the nature of the world and universe (Sagan 2001: 385). As physicist Rory Coker (2001) has put it, "Pseudoscience encourages people to believe anything they want. It supplies specious arguments for fooling yourself into thinking that any and all beliefs are equally valid."

An excellent example of a pseudoscientific idea is the belief in the existence of a giant bipedal cryptid called Bigfoot (Sasquatch) that is of interest to cryptozoology (Card

2018: 45–46; Regal 2011). The claim that such a creature exists is controversial, and the evidence is highly problematic (contra Meldrum 2006). The evidence for this giant ape consists of bogus plaster casts of footprints, faked film footage and photographs, a stack of other hoaxes, and overall questionable anecdotal and paltry eyewitness testimonial reports about strange noises in the woods, fleeting figures in the dark, and rocks being flung from the bushes (see Daegling 2005). However, the claim is not paranormal, at least in the original versions. The discovery of such a creature would add to our basic knowledge of life forms on earth, but such a find would not require that we revise biology or physics as fields of study or necessitate any paradigm shifts (Dawkins 2001: 412; Goode 2012: 20). It would be different, however, if one could demonstrate that Bigfoot exists and that it is a pan-dimensional being who can live anywhere without a resource base and who can be summoned psychically (as more recent versions of the claim hold). Then, Bigfoot would be classified as a paranormal phenomenon because the discovery of such an entity would require that we rethink our fundamental understandings of biology, physics, and the nature of the universe.

Similarly, declarations regarding the existence of flying saucers as interplanetary vehicles fall into the category of pseudoscience. However, making assertions, as some have, that flying saucers are multidimensional machines whose occupants can psychically transport humans, objects, and entire cities from place to place renders such claims paranormal ones (Smith 2010: 6–7).

It is easy to ascribe paranormal explanations for odd events or anomalous experiences that one cannot easily explain (Alcock 1990: 10). However, to paraphrase the philosopher Michael Scriven (1966: 155), the unexplained is not supernatural or paranormal! Inexplicability may be due to the observer's unfamiliarity with what science knows or errors in human perception and information processing, none of which has anything to do with transcendental powers or forces (Alcock 1985: 539). In such instances, the paranormal merely is "a substitute for our ignorance of the causes at work" (Kurtz 1985a: 505). A mistake made by proponents of the paranormal is that our inability to provide a "naturalistic" explanation at the moment for an anomalous phenomenon by default validates a paranormal explanation. It does not! Nor does it shift the burden of proof from the person who is making the claim on to the skeptic (Dawkins 2001: 56; Gilovich 1991: 181; Humphrey 1999: 145). Religionists make the same mistaken assumption when they assert that since no natural scientific explanation exists for a purported religious event or miracle, see none forthcoming, they conclude that a supernatural force is involved, that is, God did it. This is called the god-of-the-gaps argument and involves the logical fallacy of argument from ignorance (Philipse 2014: 164). Time and time again, god-of-the-gaps explanations have failed to support the religionists' case.

To take another example from pseudoscience, let us once again consider UFOs (i.e., flying saucers or extraterrestrial spacecraft). When enough information does not exist to resolve a particular sighting, by default, believers forward a paranormal explanation (French and Stone 2014: 177). The majority of UFO sightings are due to perceptual errors, hoaxes, delusions, or misidentifications of natural objects, such as the planet Venus, the northern lights, weather balloons, missiles, flares, and so forth. However, a few cases are unresolved because there is simply insufficient information to determine whether we are dealing with a human-made object, a natural phenomenon, or a hoax. UFO believers take these instances as significant anomalies, or *an irreducible minimum*, that they claim cannot be explained away and must, therefore, be the genuine article (Hines 2003: 256). They conclude, therefore, that UFOs do exist. The scientific rejection of this claim provides ammunition for conspiracy theories about government cover-ups and so on. The 1997 comedy film *Men in Black* pokes fun at the "official explanations" when Kay, one of the leading characters, states:

> All right, Beatrice, there was no alien. The flash of light you saw in the sky was not a UFO. Swamp gas from a weather balloon was trapped in a thermal pocket and reflected the light from Venus.

However, the simplest answer is that these unresolved cases are also due to natural effects, perceptual errors, hoaxes, or delusions as in the cases for which sufficient evidence is available to decide (Stenger 1990: 104). As we shall see in Chapter 7, it is a universal human cognitive tendency to ascribe wrong explanations based on insufficient data.

There are many instances in which erroneous paranormal explanations were supplied for phenomena for which the science of the day had no answers. For example, bat navigation was once believed by some to involve an extrasensory mechanism until the 1940s when zoologist Donald Griffin and neuroscientist Robert Galambos identified the existence of an echo-sounding apparatus and bat navigation was incorporated as a verifiable and significant phenomenon into the domain of science (Alcock 1990: 17: Dawkins 2001: 50).

Another example of this involves scientific views of meteorites during the seventeenth and eighteenth centuries. At that time, the idea of "stones falling from the sky" was thought of as an impossibility and contrary to the known laws of physics (Gardner 1957: 9). Subsequently, with the expansion of knowledge (i.e., more data became available), not only was the existence of meteorites confirmed scientifically, but with an increased understanding of the physics of planetary development, it became apparent that Newton's laws actually predicted their existence (Schick and Vaughn 2014: 23).

It is important to note, however, that meteorites and bat sonar are real phenomena and given sufficient data and time naturalistic explanations for such things are eventually discovered (Stenger 1990: 23). These instances rather than indicating flaws in the scientific enterprise show that science can solve puzzles that entail empirical things, like rocks falling from the sky or bats successfully navigating in total darkness, although it may take some time. They also show how scientific knowledge changes over time as new evidence comes to light. Paranormal and religious beliefs, on the other hand, remain unchanged, although many ad hoc hypotheses and rationalizations may be attached to them to address contradictory evidence. For these reasons, as the scientific anthropologist Russell Bernard (1995: 25) has observed, "every phenomenon, including human thought and behavior, to which the scientific method has been systematically applied over a sustained period of time, by a large number of researchers, has yielded its secrets." Only things belonging to the category of the unreal real, such as supernatural happenings, the case of Bigfoot, psi phenomena, and extraterrestrial spacecraft and traces of their occupants, continue to remain obdurate over time despite extensive investigations because they are cultural constructs or the products of human imagination.

Ultimately, however, as in the case of the supernatural, there is no reason to get caught up in semantics as to whether a proposition is scientific or pseudoscientific. There may be cases where researchers have diligently attended to the requisites of scientific methodology in testing a paranormal proposition, such as near-death experience, or some psi phenomena, such as telekinesis or clairvoyance. Should such research be automatically dismissed as pseudoscientific because of the object of analysis? The answer is no. Playing the semantics game is not helpful. The reason for this is because science aims to explore the nature of reality and the ultimate arbitrator is whether or not there is evidentiary justification for believing a claim about some aspect of existence to be true regardless of where that conclusion takes us (Fishman 2009: 830).

One suggestion is that instead of getting entangled in the demarcation problem, the easiest solution may be to abandon the idea of pseudoscience altogether and directly discuss "bad, poor, or even stupid theories" (Truzzi 1996: 574). However, the fact that there is no widely accepted set of criteria for distinctly separating science from pseudoscience does not mean that such a distinction is imaginary or capricious (Holt et al. 2012: 84). By analogy, the boundary between night and day is blurry, but this does not mean that one cannot distinguish night from day (Leahey and Leahey 1983). Many of the characteristics of pseudoscience provided above can serve as "warning signs." The greater the number of such indicators associated with an investigatory enterprise, the more likely that the line between science and pseudoscience has been traversed (Holt et al. 2012: 84).

This chapter has highlighted the various conceptual and epistemological difficulties that arise when we talk about phenomena categorized as supernatural, religious, and paranormal. Such problems persist and will probably never be resolved because the terms in question take us into the realm of the unreal real and incoherency. One way to bypass these quandaries is to categorize all things religious, supernatural, and paranormal under what the philosopher Stephen Law (2016) refers to as "X-claims." These refer to false beliefs about incorporeal agents, miraculous powers and forces, extraordinary events, magical healings, and holy relics. These beliefs and perceptions stem from particular human perceptual and cognitive biases and proclivities. People everywhere rely on X-claims to explain phenomena that they cannot otherwise explain, and they also comprise the foundational tenets in many religions, including mainstream ones (Law 2016: 16, 23).

X-claims are almost always based on *testimony* and *subjective experience* and are systematically unreliable. The human cognitive and perceptual apparatus is particularly vulnerable to cyberattacks by X-claims that create false impressions and conclusions that render eyewitness accounts of such phenomena highly and consistently suspect. The cognitive underpinnings of X-claims, which will be explored in depth in later chapters, have far-reaching implication because they potentially demystify or debunk religious and paranormal ideas that have otherwise perplexed and enthralled humans across time and space (cf., Law 2016: 32).

# Chapter Three

# CAN SCIENCE SAY ANYTHING ABOUT RELIGION AND THE SUPERNATURAL?

*The God hypothesis is a myth [and] a myth is not a good explanation, and widespread encouragement of this particular myth undercuts a correct understanding of the Universe's and [humankind's] origin, nature, and destiny.*

—Michael Scriven, *Primary Philosophy* (1966)

*The best explanation for why there has been so far no convincing, independently verifiable evidence for supernatural phenomena, despite honest and methodologically sound attempts to verify them, is that these phenomena probably do not exist. Indeed, the absence of evidence, where such evidence is expected to be found after extensive searching, is evidence of absence.*

*To declare the study of supernatural phenomena out of bounds to scientific investigation imposes artificial constraints on scientific inquiry [and] denies science the noble task of purging false beliefs from the public sphere [and] the opportunity to discover aspects of reality that may have significant worldview implications.*

—Yonata Fishman, Can Science Test Supernatural Worldviews? (2009)

*It is not controversial that science does not recognise ancestor spirits, astral intelligences, demons [...] ghosts, gods [...] and the like. There is no reason to doubt that the listed entities and powers will not be recognised by any future science [...] we have enough securely established science to rule out that future science will [...] recognize the listed entities and powers.*

—Graham Oppy, *Naturalism and Religion* (2018)

*Reality stubbornly refuses to be bent to our desires or ideologies. Reality does not yield to wishful thinking.*

—Douglas Futuyma, *Science on Trial* (1982)

The "thou shalt not speak ill of religion" stance, discussed in Chapter 1, is associated with another problematic conviction on the part of many scholars, namely that religious and supernatural phenomena are not amenable to scientific analysis. The widely held opinion is that science and religion have different aims and realms of inquiry. Science is relegated exclusively to the investigation of physical phenomena and the search for naturalistic mechanisms based on an a priori commitment to methodological naturalism. Religion, in contrast, is consigned to addressing questions relating to ultimate meaning and ethical values that presumably only religion can address.

## Science and Religion: Non-Overlapping Magisteria?

The idea that religion and science have separate domains is not new. However, the most explicit contemporary formulation of this idea appears in the work of the late evolutionary paleontologist Stephen Jay Gould. He discussed this view in his book *Rock of Ages: Science and Religion in the Fullness of Life* (1999). In Gould's (1999: 119) words,

> Science simply cannot (by its legitimate methods) adjudicate the issue of God's possible superintendence of nature. We neither affirm nor deny it; we simply can't comment on it as scientists.

For Gould (1999: 6),

> The net, or magisterium, of science covers the empirical realm: what is the universe made of (fact) and why does it work this way (theory). The magisterium of religion extends over questions of meaning and moral value. The two magisteria do not overlap, nor do they encompass all inquiry (consider, for example, the magisterium of art and the meaning of beauty). To cite the old cliches, science gets the age of rocks, and religion the rock of ages; science studies how the heavens go, religion how to go to heaven.

Gould fails to specify in what ways purveyors of supernaturalism are more qualified than others to attend to profound cosmological questions of "ultimate meaning" and moral and ethical conduct. Religious specialists, be they priests, rabbis, or mullahs, are people who professionally tout archaic credulities and obscurantist myths initially propounded by cruel, ignorant, and superstitious tribesmen in the Middle East who died 2,000 years ago. How does this qualify them to say anything about morality and ethics? For some, religion co-opting morality has been a dreadful turn of events for humanity. The skeptic and humanist Arthur C. Clarke (2003: 183) lamented that one of the greatest tragedies in human history was the "hijacking of morality by religion." Such an arrangement, he adds, may have enforced good behavior among ancient primitive people, but it is now counterproductive. Yet, remarkably, he added, at the very time when archaic religious credulities and morality should be detached, "sanctimonious nitwits are calling for a return to morals based on superstition" (Clarke 2003: 183). It is difficult to imagine any way Gould could have specified how religious specialists are best qualified to adjudicate matters of morality given their ghastly and appalling track record as child molesters, abusers of women, fomenters of dissent, inciters of intolerance, architects of othering and scapegoating, and advocates of violence, whose primary skills have been bluster, hubris, and deception.

Gould (1999: 5) referred to his territorial demarcation as the "non-overlapping magisteria," or NOMA. As far as he was concerned, science has nothing to do with people's faith, and therefore, science and religion are not in conflict and can peacefully coexist in "respectful noninterference." Major scientific institutions, such as the American Association for the Advancement of Science (AAAS) and the National Academy of Sciences (NAS), have adopted Gould's unfortunate ideas as their official stance. In a publication called *Teaching about Evolution and the Nature of Science* (1998) the NAS states categorically that "science is limited to explaining the natural world by means of natural processes" and that explanations that entail supernatural or nonnaturalistic phenomena "are outside the realm of science and not part of a valid science curriculum" (NAS 1998: 126, 127). Along the same lines, Eugenie Scott (1999: 29), former director of the National Center for Science Education (NCSE), says, "Science is a way of knowing that attempts to explain the natural world using natural causes. It is agnostic toward the supernatural—it neither confirms nor rejects it."

To what extend Gould or the officers of the organizations mentioned here have taken this stance as a political strategy to avoid alienating religious people is hard to say. If their objective was to gain more supporters through this strategy of "respectful noninterference," it is clear that their efforts have been a dismal failure (Coyne 2015: 113). Science and religion have never been and cannot ever be complementary enterprises because, as the anthropologist Jacob Pandian (2003: 168) has observed, religion has commandeered and continues to try to commandeer and harness "scientific discourse in support of supernaturalism." Today, this is the central objective of the evangelical Christian proponents of "scientific (sic) creationism" or "creation science."

Gould's proposed construal of science and religion is patently false. Consider his understanding of religion:

> Religion just can't be equated with Genesis literalism, the miracle of the liquefying blood of Saint Januarius [...] or the Bible codes of Kabbalah and modern media hype. [...] [If] colleagues wish to fight superstition, irrationalism, philistinism, ignorance, dogma, and a host of other insults to the human intellect (often politically converted into dangerous tools of murder and oppression as well), then God bless them—but don't call this enemy "religion." (Gould 1999: 208)

It is as if Gould, sequestered in his ivory tower, had no grasp of the contemporary world and human history. His conceptualization of religion as a utopian, almost agnostic, humanistic philosophy altogether devoid of supernatural assertions about the material world, paranormal beings, and magical happenings is contrary to anthropological findings and the historical record. Gould excludes from religion such features as creationism, miraculous events, literalism, irrationalism, philistinism, ignorance, dogmatism, and all those things that are an "insult to the human intellect," whereas, in fact, these are the defining features of the majority, if not all, of the religions that exist today (Coyne 2015: 109–10). As physicist Taner Edis (2008: 31) has put it, such "a bloodless ultraliberal metaphysics" as the core of religion proposed is implausible.

Also, as various scientists and philosophers have pointed out, religion continuously makes claims about how the world and the universe operate, penetrating deep into the heart of the magisteria Gould treats as the exclusive preserve of his agnostic scientists (Dawkins 1997, 2006; Edis 2008; Fishman and Boudry 2013; Stenger 2007). Moreover, theistic philosophers such as Michael Ruse (2011: 5, 183) take issue with NOMA because it excludes crucial questions about the universe from the domain of religion for which they are ready to supply their faith-based, non-scientific answers. In other words, just adjudicating over ethics and values, as Gould would have them do, is insufficient for religious believers. Gould and those who have adopted his NOMA stance overlook the plain fact that many religionists want to replace science with their supernaturalism rather than coexist with it. They do not just want schools to teach Jesus alongside Darwin, they do not demand "respectful noninterference," they wish to replace empirical science with an "alternative" fundamentalist science based on the Bible (cf., Noll 1994: 186).

By restricting the scope of science to the empirical world, Gould infers that science has limitations and can say nothing about what is outside its specific domain. NOMA thus provides space for and legitimizes "other ways of knowing" as worthy of belief, such as Christian metaphysics and an endless array of other egregious paranormal and supernatural beliefs. Ruse uses this very argument in his book *Science and Spirituality: Making Room for Faith in the Age of Science* (2011). He contends that it is possible to overcome the limitations of science because we have a choice between "alternative metaphysics" (Ruse 2011: 183). The only choice for Ruse and true believers like him, of course, is Christian metaphysics. As the philosopher Peter Slezak (2012: 406) points out, while these religionists talk about "alternatives," it is unlikely they would ever grant equal consideration to metaphysics based on the theology of Quetzalcoatl or the precepts of Zarathustra.

Moreover, what such religionists fail to understand is that the limitations of science do not by default elevate positions that have nothing more to recommend them besides "Scriptural faith."

The tactic religionists employ here is to assert that scientific theories are provisional or even raise the bogus idea that scientific knowledge is fiction (a concept for which religionists must thank postmodernism, see Kakutani 2018: 18; McIntyre 2018: 141–48; Otto 2016: 199; Sidky 2018), and therefore their superstitious precepts have equal validity (Sidky 2018). Sadly, this is not the case; the validity of egregious theories and propositions is not enhanced merely because scientific knowledge is provisional (Slezak 2012: 408).

Claims that there are other equally valid metaphysical options, such as the God hypothesis, are what the philosopher David Hume (1902 [1748]: 165) called "sophistry and illusion." What we have, the totality of our theories in physics, chemistry, biology, genetics, neuroscience, archaeology, scientific anthropology, and geology, is the best there is (Pinker 2018: 393–95). As Slezak (2012: 406) puts it, science is the only game in town: "There is no alternative to our best theories other than the worse ones." Christian metaphysics or the metaphysics of the myriad other supernatural perspectives cannot offer better understandings of cosmology, quantum physics, molecular biology, the structure of DNA, epidemiology, or the evolution of life on earth. Moreover, as the philosopher of science Michael Scriven (1966: 157) pointed out years ago, the God hypothesis is "a myth" and hence is not a useful explanation. Encouraging this myth, he added, undermines an accurate comprehension of the Universe and humankind's origin, nature, and destiny.

Gould failed to anticipate how NOMA provides a convenient out for the purveyors of obscurantist and paranormal ideas who can claim that all supernatural phenomena belong to their exclusive domain and empowers them to make any outrageous claims they wish with impunity. As Ruse's work exemplifies, NOMA legitimizes superstitious beliefs by casting them as truth claims beyond or outside the scope of scientific appraisal (cf., Dawkins 2006: 59). In other words, in the case of supernaturalism, evidentiary justification is unnecessary.

This fact is evident in the Christian apologist Alvin Plantinga's claims about science and evolutionary theory:

> It is extremely hard to see how an empirical science, such as biology, could address such a theological question as [to] whether a process like evolution is or isn't directed by God [...] How could an empirical inquiry possibly show that God was not guiding and directing evolution? (in Scott 2008)

Here, Plantinga is implying four things: (1) that his supernaturalism is immune to any evidentiary challenges from science; (2) theological questions are outside the legitimate domain of science; (3) that he is privy to God's special truths and insights about nature and evolution inaccessible to all others; (4) that these unique insights qualify him to pontificate about the theological implications of biological evolution. Ruse also tries to make this point in his discussion of alternative metaphysics.

Contrary to such religious polemicist claims, as discussed below, science has a great deal to say not only about whether or not God is directing evolution or any other processes or forces in the universe but also about the God hypothesis itself. Moreover, what credentials do true believing theologians have that qualify them to say anything relevant about evolutionary theory or, for that matter, God that is of relevance to today's world when their imagination is weighed down by the tiresome and arcane superstitions they advocate?

Gould's construal of science is similarly faulty, which is surprising because he had an adequate grasp of scientific methodology, and the history of science was one of his specialties. Science has, can, and must address the evidentiary basis of religious pronouncements and their factual claims about the world and universe, a point the anthropologist James Lett (1997a) made years ago. Thus, because religion makes all kinds of factual assertions, as the philosopher Herman Philipse (2014: 85) observes, religion cannot be exempted from critical assessment by scientific methods.

## Methodological Naturalism and Its Religionist Critics

A common assumption is that science has an a priori commitment to methodological naturalism (e.g., Scott 2001: 246). The assertion is that the methods of science are integrally naturalistic and in principle and by definition, science is unable to examine supernatural phenomena. We can refer to this position as *intrinsic methodological naturalism* as opposed to *provisional methodological naturalism* to be discussed below. Thus, in this view science in principle can say nothing regarding the existence of entities and forces such as spirits, gods, ghosts, miracles, revelations, and psi, all of which are by definition outside its investigatory scope.

This construal of science developed in the context of the legal controversy over Intelligent Design in response to religionist imputations that science is a priori yoked to naturalism/materialism at the metaphysical level. The legal case that generated this controversy is called *Kitzmiller v. Dover Area School District* (2005). *Metaphysical naturalism* means that scientists adhere to the view that nature and material forces and processes constitute the whole of reality and dismiss the possibility of supernatural forces beforehand without justification. To counter the charge of metaphysical naturalism/materialism, scientists involved in the debate with creationists forwarded the principle of *methodological naturalism*, which specifies that science is naturalistic at the level of methodology alone and is neutral at the ontological or metaphysical level (Boudry et al. 2010: 228). Hence the assertion that science is "agnostic" regarding such matters, as noted, and that it neither confirms nor denies supernatural and paranormal phenomena (Scott 1999: 29). In other words, supernatural claims are off-limits to science (Fishman and Boudry 2013: 923). This entails the mistake of taking the fact that science does not appeal to supernatural beings or forces in its explanations to mean that assessing the reality of the supernatural is outside the scope of scientific assessment because such entities and forces are beyond or outside nature (e.g., Mahner 2012; Ruse 2001).

Epistemological confusion over this issue is widespread and many, including well-meaning science writers, have subscribed to the idea that methodological naturalism is the defining feature of science and all that it implies. For example, in their book, *Unscientific America: How Scientific Illiteracy Threatens Our Future* (2009), the journalist Chris Mooney and science writer Sheril Kirshenbaum (2009: 103) take this idea for granted. They differentiate methodological naturalism from "philosophical [metaphysical] naturalism," which they say holds that all of existence is explicable solely in empirical terms, processes, and forces. Mooney and Kirshenbaum (2009: 104) add that, in contrast, methodological naturalism "is not a claim about the fundamental reality of the world," does not rule out the possible existence of supernatural and paranormal entities and forces, and is not inherently atheistic. In other words, science and religion are not incompatible because they are concerned with wholly distinct phenomena. Hence, in their view, science and religion are broadly compatible, and a rapprochement is possible (Mooney and Kirshenbaum 2009: 106). Here, we are back to Gould's foolhardy notion of NOMA.

Several prominent scientists and philosophers of science have correctly asserted that the idea of intrinsic methodological naturalism stems from an ill-advised effort to demonstrate that there are no conflicts between science and religion. The motive behind this claim is the desire to neutralize opposition to evolutionary theory and ensure that religious taxpayers continue their support for science (Fishman 2009: 830; Fishman and Boudry 2013: 923). However, intentionally or not, this stance serves to shield and safeguards religion from critical scientific analysis.

The position that science has a hands-off policy in matters dealing with supernaturalism is an imprudent strategy for several reasons. As critics of this view have observed, intrinsic methodological naturalism is not an accurate characterization of science, it is conceptually flawed, and it needlessly imposes restrictions on the scope of scientific research. One significant implication of this view is that if scientists make any assertions regarding the supernatural, they are overstepping the legitimate boundaries of their intellectual enterprise.

Consider the following example, which reveals how outsiders have received the idea of methodological naturalism. Based upon such a misunderstanding of science, Mooney and Kirshenbaum accuse the New Atheists—their list includes Sam Harris, Richard Dawkins, Christopher Hitchens, and Daniel Dennett—of illegitimately collapsing the distinction between methodological and philosophical naturalism by making assertions regarding the existence of God. For Mooney and Kirshenbaum, it is one thing to exclude supernatural causal forces from scientific explanations and another to assert that science can resolve the debate over the existence of God. The latter question, they contend, is entirely outside the legitimate scope of scientific inquiry. These writers, of course, are adopting the exact position that theistic philosophers and religious polemicists take, namely that science cannot say anything about the supernatural. The religionist Craig Keener (2011: 121–25), for example, uses this very argument to make a case for the veracity of the miracles in the New Testament by arguing that supernatural forces are beyond the purview of science (see Chapter 8).

Moreover, Mooney and Kirshenbaum (2009: 101) add that the very suggestion that it is unjustified in believing in something for which there is no evidence is problematic because the term "evidence" presumes naturalism. As they see it, given that God is a supernatural entity, and not subject to physical laws, therefore science and methodological naturalism can say nothing about such a being (Mooney and Kirshenbaum 2009: 100). They approvingly quote the evolutionary scientist Matt Cartmill (1998: 78–79), who says that the disbelief in the existence of supernatural beings is "not a research finding" but merely a matter of personal belief. As noted, this is also a long-standing claim made by religionists and evangelical ideologues. For example, in his book *The Scandal of the Evangelical Mind* (1994), the evangelical professor of Christian thought Mark Noll (1994: 186) says that the grand cosmological claims of science about the nature of the universe are not scientific but merely faith-based assertions analogous to religious beliefs. The reasons why such statements are nonsensical are detailed later in this chapter.

What Mooney and Kirshenbaum overlook is that religionists are not content with such a characterization of the relationship between science and religion and have actually made methodological naturalism the primary focus of their efforts to delegitimize science. The extent of their confusion over the place of naturalism in science is evident when they equate methodological naturalism with the scientific method (Mooney and Kirshenbaum 2009: 182). Hence their assertion that legitimately science can say nothing about the supernatural phenomena. They take issue with and consider as highly dubious Richard Dawkins's contention that the existence of God is "a scientific question." Furthermore, these writers assert that scientists who do make any statements about the supernatural are reaching beyond the limitations of science that "end at the natural world" and are seeking to turn science into an antireligious doctrine. Religionists espouse the same belief, namely that science can only address empirical phenomena, and the moment scientists extend their discussion beyond the natural world they are no longer speaking "as scientists" (Keener 2011: 125).

What Mooney and Kirshenbaum fail to realize is that subscribing to the notion of methodological naturalism presents a barrier to the primary goal of science, which is "to pursue the truth about the nature of reality on the basis of evidence, wherever it may lead" (Fishman and Boudry 2013: 923). More importantly, this stance prevents science from its central task of purging false beliefs from the public sphere (Fishman 2009: 814).

Christian apologists, as noted, have capitalized on these conceptual flaws and have made the principle of methodological naturalism itself a significant point of contention by accusing scientists of an unjustifiable a priori philosophical prejudice and dogmatism toward supernaturalism or religion (Boudry et al. 2010: 228). Alvin Plantinga (2009), one of the paragons of Christian apologetics, uses the concept of methodological naturalism in a deliberate effort to subvert the legitimacy of science in favor of the superstitions and credulities he touts. He expresses his staunch supernaturalist bias with an avowal that for him no naturalistic process, including such things as the operation of the heart, liver, or brain, is comprehensible "absent a designer and outside the context of theism" (Plantinga 2009: 145). Such a position amounts to stating that "God does everything" and that without considering God's paranormal effects, it is impossible to understand anything about the world and universe. Plantinga's supernaturalism is also evident in his tedious ruminations about the goodness of faith, references to "the great things of the Gospel," and copious quotations from the Scriptures. His critique of science is based on this supernaturalist stance as developed in several publications (Plantinga 1993, 2000, 2001, 2009, 2011).

What theistic philosophers like Plantinga and others to be mentioned offer is a mixture of superstition and heavy doses of philosophical sophistry that lends their ideas an aura of erudition. These sanctimonious spokesmen of Christian fundamentalism have shrewdly emulated many of the techniques of contemporary philosophy and harnessed them to defend supernaturalism and the pious nonsense they espouse (cf., Nielsen 2001: 16). Such an enterprise has seldom yielded anything other than mystification and obscurantism. In his book *The Natural History of Religion* (1757), the eminent Scottish philosopher David Hume long ago pointed out the consequences of philosophy harnessed in support of irrational systems of theology:

> philosophy will soon find herself very unequally yoked with her new associate; and instead of regulating each principle, as they advance together, she is at every turn perverted to serve the purposes of superstition. For besides the unavoidable incoherencies which must be reconciled and adjusted, one may safely affirm that all popular theology, especially the scholastic, has a kind of appetite for absurdity and contradiction. If that theology went not beyond reason and common sense, her doctrines would appear too easy and familiar. Amazement must of necessity be raised; mystery affected; darkness and obscurity sought after; and a foundation of merit afforded the devout votaries, who desire an opportunity of subduing their rebellious reason, by the belief of the most unintelligible sophisms. (Hume 1889 [1757]: 46)

Not surprisingly, obscurantism and mystification are precisely what present-day theistic philosophers offer.

Plantinga alleges that methodological naturalism undermines the credibility of science because it excludes "by definition" all of those things near and dear to his heart. These include the existence of the Christian God, the reality of Christianity's other supernatural agents, the validity of knowledge obtained by way of revelation, the possibility of demonic possession, and the array of value and moral judgments that constitute the Christian "evidence base" or background knowledge (Plantinga 2009: 149; 2011: 167). He, therefore, calls foul and claims that in the "game" of science the dice is unjustifiably loaded against supernatural explanations. Exponents of Intelligent Design creationism, such as William Dembski (2003: 91, 96), have similarly claimed that the scientific community has unfairly stacked the cards against creationism by "artificially defining science as limited to material mechanisms" that has "conveniently eliminated design from scientific discussions." In other words, there is an atheistic materialist conspiracy to hide evidence of God's actions in the world.

Plantinga (2009: 151) adds that science is flawed because it excludes any theory that does not conform to methodological naturalism, "whatever its virtue." He neglects to provide or suggest any procedures as to how one assesses the "virtue" of such alternative theories. On faith? Revelation? What the gospels state? Ouija boards? Here, religionists provide nothing but value judgments. This is a critical omission, given that "value judgments" and "moral judgments" based on theistic supernaturalism have been the fuel for superstition, dogmatism, prejudice, bigotry, persecution, *jihads*, crusades, and other atrocities. The history of religion, especially the track record of theistic religions, speaks for itself regarding these virtuous and charitable deeds by "moral" religious believers. Moreover, Plantinga's theistic commitments and supernaturalism prevent him from realizing that the reason science has been so massively successful in every field where it has been systematically applied in a sustained fashion is precisely because it jettisoned the ancient religious superstitions and medieval delusions, what he calls the Christian "evidence base" and is trying to justify and promote.

At this point, one should remember that by touting this purported "evidence base" in the context of his invective against science, Plantinga makes it a legitimate topic for scrutiny following the scientific tradition of systematic skepticism. This evidence base includes beliefs in the existence of God, proof of supernatural design in the world, cosmic fine-tuning, the divine authorship and inerrancy of the Bible, the veridicality of religious experiences, the reality of miracles, and the occurrence or non-occurrence of paranormal events, such as the resurrection of Jesus. The veracity of the central premises of this "evidence base" is open to skeptical scrutiny by means of textual analysis, examination of historical records, anthropological findings, the principles of evolutionary and cognitive psychology, prior probabilities, the presence or absence of disconfirming evidence, and the availability of non-supernatural explanations that accord with empirical evidence (see Chapters 13 and 15).

Plantinga's assertion, to restate it concisely, is that science unjustifiably refuses to entertain the possibility of supernatural explanations due to a dogmatic naturalistic bias (Fishman and Boudry 2013: 932). Even some professional scientists have made such proclamations. For example, the evolutionary biologist Richard Lewontin (1997: 3) wrote the following in his review of Carl Sagan's book *The Demon-Haunted World*:

> It is not that the methods and institutions of science that compel us to accept a material explanation of the phenomenal world, but, on the contrary, that we are forced to by our a priori

> adherence to material causes to create an apparatus of investigation and set concepts that produce material explanations.

A similar idea has been forwarded by Cartmill (1998: 78–79), as already mentioned. The validity of such assertions will be discussed shortly. For now, it suffices to note that writers such as Lewontin forget the consequences of a priori commitments to supernaturalism that religionists wish to reinstate: absolutism, anti-intellectualism, dogmatism, sectarianism, prejudice, bigotry, xenophobia, and all the other associated pleasantries. Indeed, one can make a solid case that of all the brands of supernatural credulities to which humans are shackled, the theistic variety is the most pernicious because of its grisly historical track record and massive body count. Also, one wonders if Lewontin is willing to discard his "prior adherence to material causes" in the context of his own scientific investigations.

For religious apologists, it follows that it is this unwarranted prejudice and dogmatism that leaves no other options for scientists but to solely pursue materialist explanations that, in their view, are tantamount to atheism (e.g., Keener 2011: 138). Plantinga (2009: 153) sarcastically questions how one can "settle a disputed claim by declaring that one of the disputants is wrong just by definition," adding that this amounts to settling a dispute "just by looking up the term 'science' in the dictionary." He adds that the reasons evolutionary psychologists come up with explanations that religious beliefs are not produced by "truth-aimed cognitive processes" is because their intransigent naturalism "necessarily" compels them to a futile, atheistic, and defective materialistic vision of reality.

Believing that he has revealed science's Achilles heel, Plantinga (2009: 151) offers to solve the horrible predicament that scientists have gotten themselves into by asserting that methodological naturalism is not the only path to a genuine science. Here, this theistic philosopher is assuming that he has the necessary qualifications to pontificate about what science is and to disclose the true nature of "the game" scientists play. Yet, he questions the qualifications of scientists with impeccable credentials, such as theoretical physicist and Nobel laureate Steven Weinberg, philosophers and cognitive scientists Jerry Fodor and Daniel Dennett, and the noted evolutionary biologist Richard Dawkins, for suggesting that evolutionary theory disconfirms the argument from design that is central to the theistic perspective.

Plantinga goes on to maintain that methodological naturalism "is a proposed condition or constraint on science" and "not a statement about the nature of the universe." In other words, empirical phenomena, which are the focus of methodological naturalism, are not the defining condition of knowledge and stating that they are so is an arbitrary choice by scientists. Plantinga believes that he has thus established epistemic parity between his faith-based premises and scientific empirical propositions. If it is indeed true that methodological naturalism is based merely on a priori and unjustifiable metaphysical prejudice, then it follows that we should reject this kind of science. However, as I shall discuss below, faith-based premises and scientific premises based on empirical evidence do not have epistemic parity. Moreover, I shall show that Plantinga and the other religionists have misrepresented the role of naturalism in science.

In his book *Naturalism and Religion* (2018), the philosopher Graham Oppy has unambiguously demonstrated that such religionist critiques characterize naturalism in ways that naturalists themselves do not accept—most of them are strawman arguments (Oppy 2018: 12–14, 95). As he adds, it is inaccurate to say that naturalists consider current science as absolutely authoritative. The history of science suggests that significant parts of current science will turn out to be incorrect and that much of our current scientific knowledge is incomplete. Such is the nature of science—meaning that it does not traffic in the kinds of absolute inviolate truths found in religion. However, it is important to stress that scientists do indeed consider that current established naturalistic science has yielded the most reliable information that we have to date in the areas investigated by science. But this does not mean that current established science will be accorded special place in the future (Oppy 2018: 95). The history of science has demonstrated this to be the case.

## A Theistic Science Instead of an Empirical Science?

Having brought methodological naturalism into question to his satisfaction, Plantinga proposes a different set of background assumptions that admit supernatural causation, which is one of the primary objectives of Christian apologetics. In his mind, this opens up the possibility for a brand of science in which supernatural and paranormal forces can take center stage. Charles Taliaferro (2009: 213), another theistic philosopher, Christian apologist, and Plantinga admirer, explains that once we accept the "naturalism is profoundly problematic" in reference to human beliefs we no longer need to accept its claims regarding religion.

Plantinga's term for such a non-naturalistic enterprise is "Augustinian science." Such a purported "scientific approach" is superior, he adds, because it is not committed to methodological naturalism and can include Christian background knowledge, that is, the laundry list of Christian supernatural and paranormal claims and superstitions. In his words,

> a theory according to which God periodically adjusts the orbits of the planets, or has created life specially, or has intelligently designed certain features of the natural world [all of which would] fall under a general concept of science, but not under any of the cluster of scientific activities or enterprises characterized by methodological naturalism. (Plantinga 2009: 159)

Thus, superstition is once again respectable through the sophistry of this theistic philosopher. Or so it seems.

By proposing an "Augustinian science," Plantinga is really saying that we can substitute our personal faith-based beliefs for knowledge. Of course, in his case, these beliefs can only be Christian beliefs. However, what this pious philosopher is advocating is beyond imprudent because what he is really saying is that we can choose whatever suits us. The outcome of similar proposals has invariably been horrific. Indeed, disaster has followed whenever and wherever people because of religious reasons, political fiat, or expedience have come to believe that all truths are consensual, that one interpretation is as good as another, and when ideologues and politicians have promoted alternative facts, alternative knowledge, and "other ways of knowing." At this point, subjectivism, literalism, dogmatism, mysticism, and irrationalism supplant rational analysis and careful evaluation of evidence as justifications for propositions (Sidky 2004: 110). Consider the following two anti-science and antireason passages that capture this exact stance:

> From the fact that all ideologies are of equal value, that all ideologies are mere fictions, [we] deduce that everybody is free to create for himself his own ideology and attempt to carry it out with all possible energy (in Ross 1980: xxvii).

> We stand at the end of the Age of Reason. A new era of the magical explanation of the world is rising. There is no truth, in the scientific sense. That which is called the crisis of science is nothing more than that the gentlemen are beginning to see on their own how they have gotten onto the wrong track with their objectivity. (in Slakey 1993)

Sounds familiar? These seem to be what our religionists are proposing. However, these are not their words but those of two of our endearing historical figures and shining examples of humanity, Mr. Benito Mussolini (the first passage) and Adolf Hitler (the second passage) in defense of Fascism and Nazism.

Once such viewpoints are admitted, they create the circumstances that allow fanatical purveyors of supernaturalism and followers of esoteric absurdities, counter-culturalists, and cultural Luddites to find champions among self-serving and vote-hungry politicians. History is replete with cases of what happens when societies go down this cheery path. Here is when we get such sublime contributions as the "Aryan science" of the Nazis and their research institute the *Ahnenerbe*. The latter was the branch of the *Schutzstaffel* (SS) that fostered Aryan pseudoscience and Aryan anthropological and archaeological theories in support the Third Reich's racial program of the mass extermination of Jews and other undesirables, including gays, the mentally disabled, communists, and Roma (gypsies). In four years, eight to ten million helpless human beings were murdered because of the psychopathological Nazi program of racial hygiene based on paranormal and "alternative ways of knowing."

As the historian Jacob Bronowski (1973: 186) remarked about Nazi horrors, it was not science that dehumanized and converted people into numbers and consigned them to concentration camps and crematoriums; it was dogma, arrogance, and ignorance. He added, "when people believe that they have absolute knowledge with no tests in reality, this is how they behave" (Bronowski 1973: 186). This was knowledge based upon political fiat and expedience and claims to ownership of immunized truths. Whenever the espousers of irrational counter-science perspectives have gained political power, catastrophic consequences have often followed (Holton 1992: 125).

Similar circumstances also led to Lysenkoism, a glowing achievement of Stalinism, when ideology and authority became substitutes for scientific knowledge, with devastating consequences (Sidky 2004: 80). At the forefront of this program was Trofim Lysenko, a shrewd political functionary who convinced Joseph Stalin that scientific evolutionary genetics was merely false Western capitalist class-centered propaganda and offered his personal genetic theories that were compatible with his understanding of Marxist philosophy (Medvedev 1969; Soifer 1994). What he provided was only a crude rendition of Jean-Baptiste Lamarck's idea of the inheritance of acquired characteristics. Lysenko had his rivals, some of the finest scientific minds and leading geneticists in the Soviet Union among them, executed, imprisoned, or threatened into silence. He then applied his Marxists genetics to transform Soviet agriculture.

In his book *Science on Trial* (1982), the evolutionary biologist Douglas Futuyma (1982: 162) describes the outcome of Mr. Lysenko's science. After gaining control over biological research and agriculture in the Soviet Union beginning in the 1930s, Lysenko destroyed them, and agricultural production slid further and further into disaster. Yet, Lysenko's political clout left him unassailable. It was only in 1965, after Khrushchev resigned, that Lysenko fell from grace. However, Soviet biological sciences had been set back many decades compared to the West. This is a grim example of what happens when political fiat is substituted for scientific research and should be a warning to contemporary politician in the United States who are striving to undermine science and wish to extricate the input of scientific research from policy decisions.

The grim lesson of Lysenko's fiasco, as Futuyma (1982: 162) observed, is that reality "stubbornly refuses to be bent to our desires or ideologies" and nature cannot be altered and made subject to our wishes and desires no matter how much "faith" we have, how diligently we try, how many votes we take, how much we flex our political muscles, and how many other people we convert to our views (Sidky 2004: 380). Those who try to substitute religiously or politically expedient opinions for science lead us into folly and take us down the same road to perdition traversed by the architects of Nazi genocide and Stalinist science. Moreover, those who make bogus claims block us from the principal human goal of understanding the operation of the world and the universe. Hence, "playing fast and loose with the truth is a serious matter" (Sagan 1993: 55). Yet, this is what advocating for an "Augustinian science" and other "alternative sciences" means.

Plantinga does not see it this way. For him, science is a "game," and scientists play different games, and methodological naturalism only applies to some of these but not others. Some of these games are about "true theories," he maintains, and others about something more nefarious, "empirically adequate" theories. Here Plantinga clearly demonstrates his scientific illiteracy because he is attempting to cast one of the central virtues and epistemological strengths of the scientific approach, which is that all conclusions are tentative and provisional and are subject to revision, into its principal weakness because it can only produce "empirically adequate" theories (Plantinga 2009: 154). What this entails is the crude strawman argument that a valid or genuine science seeks absolute truths.

Contrary to such deceptive assertions, science is not and has never been about finding "true theories." All scientific conclusions are provisional and subject to revision (Sidky 2018). Hence, scientific knowledge changes and grows over time as researchers uncover new data, develop new methodologies and instrumentation, and correct errors (see Kuznar 2008: 17–49; Lett 1997b: 41–87; Sidky 2004: 25–32; 2007b). These features differentiate science from religion with its inviolable supernatural declarations and superstitions that have not changed for thousands of years.

### What Are the Unassailable Foundations of a Theist Science?

Having declared methodological naturalism as a groundless dogmatic stance, religionists forward the same old worn-out arguments for theism that philosophers refuted long ago. Consider how Taliaferro takes issue with Daniel Dennett's naturalistic approach to religion. Dennett (2006: 24–25) has said that religion is a "human phenomenon" rather than a supernatural one, comprising events, organisms, objects, structures, and patterns that are subject to the laws of physics and biology, not miraculous happenings.

Many scientists would have no problems with such a characterization of religion.

My ethnographic field research during the last 30 years has led me to the exact conclusion. I continuously hear about God, the gods, wrathful deities, spirits, ghosts, transcendental realities, and magical happenings, but it is always humans who say these things, acting as ambassadors of heaven, mouthpieces of the gods, the implementers and enforcers of divine legislation, channelers of spirits, and so forth. It is humans who devise and use the magical objects of religion and perform human-invented rituals. It is humans, not gods or God, who have written the purported sacred texts. It is humans who build the houses and shrines wherein gods and spirits ostensibly reside. The ubiquitous holy relics that enthrall religionists consist of parts of someone's body or something that came into contact with it. The holy water and wine are liquids a person collected or produced. The voices of the spirits, gods, and demons always come from the mouth of humans. And spirits and ghosts are ideas thought up by some person or persons. There is nothing supernatural, paranormal, or transcendental about any of this.

By attacking Dennett's naturalistic perspective, Taliaferro (2009: 204, 208) believes he has undermined "the hegemony of naturalism" by bringing to bear "positive theistic arguments," meaning the standard list: the cosmological argument, argument from design, argument from miracles, argument from religious experience, the ontological argument, and so forth, all of which were laid to rest long ago (see Chapters 8 to 12). As the philosopher Kai Nielsen (2001: 20) has pointed out, these metaphysical accounts for the existence of God have been abysmal failures. The arguments from miracles, design/fine-tuning, religious experience, and the argument from scripture are treated elsewhere in this book; here I shall focus on the one explicitly discussed by Taliaferro, that is, the cosmological argument.

As Taliaferro sees it, the various arguments for God have been extensively defended and form the unassailable foundation of the theist perspective that God is the best explanation for the cosmos, life on earth, and so forth. But of course, saying this does not make it so. He asserts that theism has greater explanatory unity in accounting for both the existence of the cosmos and its goodness (Taliaferro 2009: 208). I wonder if this philosopher considers as part of that "goodness" the endless evils of human existence, the brutality of nature, the suboptimal design of biological life forms, and the vast array of natural evils. More on these later in this chapter.

Religionists unvaryingly spout forth such aphorisms, along with accompanying phrases such as "our Lord Jesus Christ" did this or that, or the Creator is wise, loving, glorious, God sustains a good world, and, of course, humanity's "sinfulness" and "fall" are rarely forgotten (e.g., Barrett 2009: 96–98; Plantinga 2009: 144; Taliaferro 2009: 208). It is as if reciting these phrases, like magical incantations, will bestow cosmic significance to superstitious premises. In this context, Taliaferro refers to the works of various theistic philosophers, the most notable being the esteemed Oxford theologian Richard Swinburne (2004), whose sweeping defense of theism is based on taking all the arguments for the existence of God together to form a cumulative case. His project, however, has been soundly refuted (e.g., Everitt 2004; Martin 1990; Philipse 2014). The religionist premise on which Swinburne constructs his case—that is, that the different arguments for the existence of God entail or refer to the same entity and therefore support each other—is unsubstantiated, and years ago Schriven (1966: 109) rightly called such strategies a massive "confidence game" (see Chapter 9).

Taliaferro (2009: 214) chastises Dennett for spending only "five pages" on these independent theistic arguments. About the cosmological argument, he claims that Dennett is merely going "through the motions" by asking "What caused God?" Such a stance is surprising. The cosmological argument holds that every known thing came from or was caused by something else, and therefore the Universe came from something else and that something else is an "uncaused" God. A variant and equally problematic version of this is the so-called Kalam cosmological argument based on the work of the eleventh-/twelfth-century Islamic scholar Al-Ghazālī.

A brief digression from our present discussion about the possibility of a theistic science is necessary to explain why Al-Ghazālī's work has been revived by Christian apologists who have tried to harness it to their own cause. Al-Ghazālī's ideas have been a topic of much debate in recent years. The astrophysicist Neil deGrasse Tyson (2012), in several online video appearances, has attributed the end of the "golden age" of Islamic scientific advancements to the influence of Al-Ghazālī, who is said to have judged mathematics to be the work of the devil, hence terminating the possibility of further scientific explorations. Muslim scholars, however, consider Al-Ghazālī to be one of the great theologians of Islam who was known by his peers as the "renewer" or "reviver" of the faith and "proof of Islam" (Janin 2005: 83; Watt 1963). For this reason, Tyson's assertion has been challenged on various grounds. Indeed, true believers have spent considerable energies to vindicate Al-Ghazālī from such a dubious role in intellectual developments in the Islamic world. Their efforts, however, are entirely unconvincing.

Whether or not Al-Ghazālī said or did not say that mathematics is useless is not the point. Nor is it relevant whether this is an "orientalist" argument, the late Edward Said's term of opprobrium often used by Middle Eastern writers and Islamic scholars to label their opponents. What is relevant is that Al-Ghazālī's theological epistemology that elevated revealed knowledge above all else, like its Christian counterpart, in principle undermines all non-scriptural or non-revelation-based investigations of the natural world and the development of any scientific research program.

Not all Muslim philosophers, however, advocated elevating mystical or revealed knowledge over reason and empirical evidence. The twelfth-century rationalist philosopher

Averroes (Ibn Rushd), who was born and lived in Muslim Spain, provided a refutation of Al-Ghazālī's Islamic epistemology and advocated an approach to knowledge based on rationality, naturalism, and evidence as opposed to strictly revealed authority (Ibn Rushd 2005: 55–180). Averroes had an essential role in the history of science. It was the Latin translation of his commentaries on the works of Aristotle that were instrumental in renewing interest in Greek philosophy among Western European scholars. However, the relevant point here is that in the Islamic world, Averroes's ideas did not make headway, and it was Al-Ghazālī's Islamic epistemology that prevailed with dismal lasting impact.

As propounded in his book *Incoherence of the Philosophers*, Al-Ghazālī espoused a form of *occasionalism* (see below), rejecting the existence of any causal connections among created phenomena and positing that all physical events are due to the direct will and intervention of God and that the laws of cause and effect are illusory (Al-Ghazālī 2000: 116–17; Griffel 2016). I have yet to encounter a Muslim theologian who would dispute this claim, and I have come across many purveyors of that brand of supernaturalism, ranging from highly educated and sophisticated *uluma* to ignorant and uneducated village mullahs. Such a stance is a science stopper. To the degree and where and when the perspective advocated by Al-Ghazālī is adopted, all pursuits of objective forms of knowledge have come to a halt. In plain English, this is choosing the "God did it" hypothesis, which can be stated something like "all things are made and sustained by Allah," or "Allah is the cause of all causality." Al-Ghazālī went on to propose a Muslim science in a book called *The Revival of Religious Sciences*, which involves an amalgamation of Islamic superstitions, mystical knowledge, and philosophy and has become an essential text of Sufism.

Theistic philosophers are enamored with this kind of perspective because in their minds such an omni-explanation renders all theistic propositions invulnerable. I address the flaws of occasionalism and omni-explanations below and in Chapter 7. What is important to note here is that Al-Ghazālī's idea of a faith-based science (sic) is, in fact, a perspective similar to that being advanced by Plantinga, as already discussed. Al-Ghazālī's supernaturalism is highly compatible with the Christian variety. It is not surprising, therefore, that his epistemological perspective has found receptive ears among Christian apologists, like William Craig (1979), who has revived Al-Ghazālī's so-called Kalam cosmological argument to argue for the existence of the Christian God.

Now let us return to our discussion of the cosmological argument, of which the Kalam idea is a variant. The foundation of both cases is an a priori and unwarranted premise that everything but God needs a cause or a creator (Mackie 1982: 92–95; Oppy 2002). Dennett has merely stated one of the common objections to such an assertion by asking: "Where did God come from, or what caused God? Contra Taliaferro, this is not going through the motions. There have been extensive philosophical discussions postulating that an intelligent designer with complex attributes itself raises the question of who designed the intelligent designer, thereby creating an infinite regression (Fishman 2009: 819). The philosopher Ernest Nagel (1997: 7) calls attention to the problematic nature of postulating a first cause as a way of evading the convolutions of "an infinite series." This is because if all things must have a cause, then why is it that God does not require one for His existence? The standard reply that God is self-caused leaves open the question of why the universe cannot be self-caused as well (Nagel 1997: 7).

The question itself is improper because it is only solvable with reference to "something" else. However, the origin of this "something" else is itself part of what requires an explanation. Hence philosophers have asked: Where did God come from, or what caused God? Perhaps the universe is the sort of phenomenon that was not caused by anything. It could have come from itself, or it did not have a cause. Bringing God into the picture has a cost. In Scriven's (1966: 120) words, introducing a being whose own origin is exactly unexplained merely introduces additional unfathomables.

The introduction of a supernatural creative act, or an "intentional, purposive explanation" for everything, as Taliaferro (2009: 213) proposes, is nonexplanation for two reasons. First, the creative process is itself incomprehensible and has no observable effects to set its outcomes apart from a non-paranormal spontaneously originated universe. Second, it entails an entity whose own origin brings back the mystery it is meant to solve. The theist readily accepts a mysterious origin for a mysterious paranormal creator but not for ordinary material things. Such a stance, of course, entails unconvincing special pleading. The answer to the question about the origins of the universe, as Nagel puts it, could simply be that it came from nowhere, it just exists! How is the theist paranormal assertion that God was not caused, "He just exists!" any better than the non-paranormal thesis that "the universe just exists?" I submit that it is not.

It should be clear from this brief discussion that the purported theistic science on offer rests on very flimsy rather than unassailable foundations. Taliaferro and Plantinga make two assumptions about science: (1) that naturalism is problematic; (2) that scientific hypotheses are established on philosophical grounds rather than from evidence. They are wrong on both counts, and this illustrates the extent to which these pious philosophers misunderstand science, intentionally misrepresent it, or perhaps both.

## The Actual Meaning of Naturalism in Science

We can examine NOMA another way by asking, Is science entirely about empiricism and knowledge obtained via the five senses and religion about a transcendental reality beyond the empirical world only accessible by "other means of knowing?" The answer is no. As the scientific anthropologist Jame Lett (1997a: 111) observes,

> Religion and science are not at odds because religion wants to be "supernatural" [i.e., non-empirical], while science wants to be "empirical;" instead religion and science are at odds because religion wants to be irrational (relying ultimately upon beliefs that are either unfalsifiable or falsified), while science wants to be rational (relying exclusively upon beliefs that are both falsifiable and unfalsified).

Various scientists now concur with what Lett (1997b: 54) stated years ago, that the issue here is a clash between rationalism and irrationalism, or between rationality and superstition (Coyne 2015: xii).

The rules of scientific inquiry, such as testability, observer independence, parsimony, explanatory power, and replicability, are guidelines for evaluating a proposition, or a statement that is either true or false, according to the evidence. However, these do not commit science to the search for empirical knowledge. Instead, they commit science to the acquisition of *propositional knowledge*. Science does not reject any proposition that is not self-contradictory in an a priori fashion because any factual statement could be true. Also, the requirement is not just that evidence offered for a statement must be empirical but that the evidence must be objective (Lett 1997a: 105; 1997b: 44–59). What this means is that for an account to meet the scientific criterion of objectivity, it must be publicly verifiable and testable, that is, tested in relation to publicly ascertainable evidence. In other words, a proposition is scientific if it is publicly verifiable and testable.

Science is restricted to empirical data collection because this is the only approach available *for now* for the acquisition of propositional knowledge that has met the requirement of public verifiability and testability (Lett 1997a: 106). Thus, it is because science is objective that makes it empirical, not the other way around. Public verifiability provisionally requires empiricism and a naturalistic approach. If a nonempirical approach that fulfills the criterion of public verifiability is ever developed, it would readily be incorporated into science (Lett 1997a: 105).

The criterion of testability of propositional assertions also requires that they be falsifiable, that is, the specification of evidence to demonstrate that a claim is false. Moreover, actual attempts to falsify claims to knowledge are required (Coyne 2015: 30). An example of an unfalsifiable claim is the "Omphalos hypothesis," that all the evidence indicating that the earth is very old, including the fossils found in the rocks, was placed there by God to test our faith. This "God did it" hypothesis explains all evidence, and nothing can be presented that would not be attributable to divine action. Plantinga (2011: 303) also uses such a "God did it" hypothesis to account for everything, including the patterns and regularities in nature, why physical reality is mathematically describable, and even the human cognitive capacities that make science possible. This postulate is discussed further in Chapter 7; for now, it suffices to say that it represents an omni-explanatory hypothesis that purportedly accounts for all things. It is defective because it is overly complicated. The reason is that such a supernatural creator is by definition an intentional agent, who sees, comprehends, makes plans, has knowledge of everything, down to the subatomic level, and has a complex mind that can design things as complex as His own mind. God thus infinitely complicates the picture. This hypothesis, therefore, has a lower probability than alternative naturalistic explanations for the universe that correspond to observable data, and because "an explanation that explains everything explains nothing" (Fishman and Boudry 2013: 940–41; Mahner 2012: 1450–52).

Another example of an unfalsifiable claim is one used by believers in psychic powers who assert that psi phenomena disappear in the presence of skeptical scientific observers, known as the "psi experimenter effect" (see Chapter 4). Hence, no objective scientific tests can apply to phenomena defined in these terms. Yet another example would be claiming that there is a ghost in my house that vanishes whenever someone else is present or whenever video cameras and other recording devices are in operation. In science, the accumulation of contradictory evidence leads either to the alteration or abandonment of a hypothesis. Religious and paranormal claims, in contrast, are immune from appraisal because they are unfalsifiable. For this reason, such propositions are never modified or discarded in light of contradictory evidence. Hence, theistic philosophers are still touting archaic and medieval superstitious nonsense about worldwide floods, boats on mountaintops, talking snakes, corpses coming back to life, apparitions magically walking through locked doors, and so forth.

## Unfalsifiable Claims and the Scientific Criterion of Replicability: The Story of N-Rays

Science demands that findings must be replicable by neutral researchers who have the knowledge and means to attempt a replication but who are not believers and enthusiasts (Alcock 2003: 35). Examples from the history of science illustrate how easily our senses and cognitive biases can mislead us into accepting false propositions (see Chapter 7). Here a brief digression is necessary because of the relevance of this issue for the discussions of religious and paranormal claims in the following chapters.

A classic cautionary tale in the history of science is the case of N-rays. The story involves a French physicist named Prosper-René Blondlot (1849–1930), a highly respected member of the French Academy of Science, who held a post at the University of Nancy, in France. In 1903, Blondlot announced the discovery of a new type of radiation that he named N-rays, after his university (Hines 2003: 22; Lagemann 1977; Nye 1980). Blondlot reported that certain metals emitted N-rays and that the human eye could detect their presence (Schick and Vaughn 2014: 105). News about N-rays came at the heels of the discovery of X-rays in 1895 and subsequently of alpha, beta, and gamma rays. Hence, the field of physics was ready for another such breakthrough (Klotz 1980).

One of the reported properties of N-rays was that it could enhance the brightness of electric sparks and make objects coated with luminous paint brighter. Also, Blondlot claimed that sheets of lead could block such rays. It is here that the French physicist started getting into trouble because if one observer reported the presence of N-rays while another did not, Blondlot attributed this to different degrees of sensitivity to the rays by different observers, rather than to conclude that the rays were not present. The N-rays hypothesis was thus rendered unfalsifiable in the same way that the premise of the psi experimenter effect makes psychic phenomenon immune from appraisal.

Soon after Blondlot's announcement, French physicists in other laboratories following the same procedures began studying the new phenomenon, confirming his findings, as well as reporting the discovery of additional properties of N-rays (Lagemann 1977). There is a valuable lesson here relating to the fallibility of human perception and cognitive biases that we shall examine in later chapters. It also illustrates why scientific research is so difficult given the biases and presuppositions that impinge upon those engaged in this enterprise. In the case of N-rays, the mistake made by otherwise highly qualified and respectable physicists was that they relied upon the subjective judgments of observers regarding luminosity as a means of measuring the presence of the rays rather than using instrumentation that could establish an objective gauge of brightness (Hines 2003: 22).

Blondlot and his supporters were inattentive to how powerfully expectations and the confirmation bias can influence subjective perceptions leading to the emphasis of data that support a priori assumptions and wishful thinking, and the disregard or omission of disconfirming data that humans generally seem to abhor (see Chapter 7). Indications that something was amiss arose when scientists in Britain and Germany who relied upon objective measures of brightness in their laboratories could not replicate Blondlot's findings (Carroll 2003: 63). The decisive blow to the N-ray hypothesis came when the American physicist and skeptic Robert Wood, from Johns Hopkins University, visited Blondlot's laboratory to assess the validity of the experiments personally and to investigate whether N-rays were real or a figment of imagination and belief.

One experiment Wood took part in was designed to show that inserting a lead sheet between the source and a card coated with luminous paint could block N-rays. Wood's task was to put the lead plate in place, and Blondlot acted as the observer. During the testing, however, Wood surreptitiously made a few changes. In one test he told Blondlot that the lead sheet was in place when it was not, and in another, that it was not in place, when it was. Wood discovered that Blondlot's ability to detect the increased brightness of the luminous paint depended upon whether or not he believed that the lead sheet was in place (Hines 2003: 24). Wood used a similar procedure with other observers in various additional experiments, with the same results. If the observer believed that N-rays were present, they claimed they could detect them. If the test subjects thought that the rays were blocked, they reported that they could not identify them.

Wood (1904) published his findings in the journal *Nature* in 1904, effectively ending the debate over the existence of N-rays. However, Blondlot, like all true believers, doubled down on his convictions (backfire effect) and remained convinced that the phenomenon was real until his death in 1930 (Gardner 1957: 345; Lagemann 1977). The case of N-rays is a useful illustration of the human tendency to maintain a firmly held belief despite overwhelming contradictory evidence that we shall encounter as we further examine believers in the supernatural and the paranormal. Blondlot had become a true believer, which made disconfirming evidence irrelevant (Randi 1982a: 198).

These events demonstrate how the French scientists, most of whom honestly believed that they were working on a real phenomenon, were fooled by their own perceptual constructs and biases (Schick and Vaughn 2014: 107). The N-ray incident also shows the process of assessment of hypotheses in the context of scientific research, why the requirements of independent falsification and replication are so crucial, as well as to demonstrate the self-correcting nature of science (Hines 2003: 21). Without such safeguards, we are prone to be fooled by methodological errors, expectations, self-deception, our confirmation bias, and a host of other perceptual flaws and biases (see Chapter 7).

In the context of paranormal research, some investigators have tried to argue that it is inappropriate to apply the scientific criteria of falsifiability and replicability to psi phenomena because they are radically different from the sort of things ordinarily investigated by science. Purveyors of religious credulities and superstitions similarly claim that their assertions are exempt from the criteria of scientific evaluation; Plantinga's comment on evolution cited earlier is a case in point. Many scientists maintain, however, that such exemptions should not be afforded. As the professor of psychology James Alcock (2003: 35) states, this entails special pleading, and it is unwise because it calls for relinquishing the very conventions of scientific investigation that are needed to eliminate mistakes, self-deception, and fraud just to make room for assertions that violate the basic precepts of science. Science seeks to counteract our confirmation bias by requiring the replication and falsification of propositions. Religionists and paranormalists persistently yield to this bias. To reiterate an earlier point, science asks, "What is the evidence?" Paranormalists and religionists say, "I wish to believe this."

Science is about the accumulation of knowledge through public verification of falsifiable claims, relying on logic and experience, reason, and observation. In other words, science is committed to rational beliefs, that is, beliefs that are falsifiable and have not been falsified. However, because it is logically possible that new evidence could lead to the falsification of a hitherto unfalsified assertion, scientific knowledge is always provisional. Science, to put it differently, only makes probabilistic conclusions, not absolute ones. However, this does not undermine the scientific approach, contra writers such as Plantinga. What it means is that scientific knowledge is *self-correcting* because it gets revised as new data come to light or our instrumentations for studying the world improve. Such an effort is not merely adding more and more ad hoc hypotheses, such as when conspiracy theorists or paranormalists add such secondary justifications to prevent disconfirmations of their claims. In science, disconfirmation leads to the discarding of hypotheses. Here lies the strength of science as opposed to perspectives that are immune to such self-correction.

## Provisional Methodological Naturalism: How Science Really Works

The correct characterization of the methodology of science is *provisional methodological naturalism*, which is an empirically grounded guideline based on the historical pattern of the uniform successes of naturalistic explanations and the consistent failure of supernatural postulates (Boudry et al. 2010: 230). In other words, this stance is not based on an a priori presupposition, as religionists maintain, for example, Keener (2011: 138) but is a conclusion of science based upon an inference to the best explanation given all the available scientific data (Fishman 2009: 830; Fishman and Boudry 2013: 924; see Carrier 2005a; Edis 1998, 2008: 28–32; Fishman and Boudry 2013; Gauch 2009; Isaak 2002). Hence, "the rejection of the supernatural is not *a priori*; it is not declared before examining the facts" (Carrier 2005: 211). On the contrary, it is in relation to empirically grounded a posteriori conclusion from scientific evidence that scientists make the crucial assumptions that nature is lawful, that things do not come into existence from nothingness, and that supernatural and psi phenomena are unsubstantiated (Fishman and Boudry 2013: 926–27).

Declaring that supernatural and paranormal claims are beyond the scope of scientific assessment, as proponents of intrinsic methodological naturalism have done, is therefore erroneous and unjustified. More importantly, as Fishman (2009: 814) says, declaring supernatural phenomena as being out of bounds prevents science from doing what it is designed to do, that is, *the elimination of false beliefs*. Contra the assertions by theistic biologist Jeffrey Schloss (2009: 8) and Mooney and Kirshenbaum (2009: 182), using science to refute religious beliefs is not distorting science, it is doing what science is meant for—the eradication of erroneous beliefs about the world and universe!

Supernatural beliefs at the core of religion belong to the category of unreal real. They are, in other words, X-claims. Such premises are in the same group as the following postulates: the earth is flat, our planet is at the center of universe, nature is designed by an invisible Superman, the earth was created during the Bronze Age, disease is caused by evil spirits, lightning is God's instrument for punishing the wicked, ghosts and goblins exist, the universe is fine-tuned for human life, UFOs are extraterrestrial spacecraft, cryptids exist, vaccines thwart the Lord's will, global climate change is a fraud perpetrated by a conspiracy of scientists, cadavers can come back to life, the Holocaust is a hoax, ancient extraterrestrials created human civilizations, nicotine is not addictive, Elvis lives, and so forth.

The very fact that supernatural and paranormal claims are not compatible with scientific findings means that science provides evidence against such claims. Moreover, if there is evidence for or against a claim, it is scientifically testable (Fishman 2009: 815). Consider proof for the existence of God. Unless God is engaged in a cosmic plot to completely hide the evidence of His existence making himself undetectable to humans, there should be no difficulty finding godly traces in the world (Boudry et al. 2010: 241). Such is particularly the case with the God of theism who by definition has quasi-natural anthropomorphic characteristics and manifestations, as discussed in Chapter 2. As the philosopher of science Martin Mahner (2012: 1447) points out, a God that is "wholly other" is incomprehensible, unknowable, and unintelligible. This concept has no content, is incoherent, and can be rejected (Fishman and Boudry 2013: 931). Also, this is not the kind of God with which theists are concerned. Their God is a meddling paranormal being, one that causally interacts with the physical world. For this reason, there are no inherent obstacles to stop science from investigating claims associated with such a supernatural being.

So what sorts of things would the handiwork of a meddling God entail? Consider the following: evidence of fossilized monkey bones in Precambrian geological formations; a fossil species lacking any indications of evolutionary descent or relationship with other species; finding the letters of the book of Genesis encoded in human DNA; dating methods that indicate that the earth and the universe are 6,000 years old; intercessory prayers regrowing amputated legs; consciousness surviving the destruction of the physical brain; the spirit of dead relatives providing prophecies that are confirmed by independent investigators (Boudry et al. 2010: 241; Fishman 2009: 831). However, no such evidence has ever come to light anywhere at any time.

The principle of intrinsic methodological naturalism, as discussed earlier, goes against the fact that science has, does, and can assess supernatural hypotheses. As Fishman and Boudry (2013: 924) observe, "Science can (and has already evaluated) supernatural claims according to the same explanatory criteria used to assess any other 'non-supernatural' claim." Unfortunately for theists and paranormalists, the results of such systematic evaluations have unvaryingly been negative. Thus, "supernatural claims do not fall beyond the reach of science; they have simply failed" (Boudry et al. 2010: 227). As Coyne (2015: 113) says, "over its history, science has repeatedly investigated supernatural claims and, in principle, could find strong evidence for them. But that evidence has not appeared."

Supernaturalists continuously allege that scientists reject their claims just because they refer to nonempirical phenomena (e.g., Tart 2009: 65). For instance, the paranormalist and religious apologist J. Harold Ellens (2008a: 2), in a chapter in his edited three-volume anthology *Miracles, God, Science, and Psychology in the Paranormal*, asserts that scientists have been remiss in the investigation of the spirit world. He gives this as the reason for the lack of "hard data" for "the action of the divine spirit and in the areas of psyche and spirit." However, science has been doing this all along. The hard data are simply not there. Thus, this religionist is misleading and disingenuous in making such an egregious claim.

As our discussion shows, science does not reject supernatural explanations because it has an intrinsic problem dealing with supernatural phenomena or by philosophical fiat based on a priori metaphysical position but on purely evidential grounds. The continued failure of supernatural hypotheses justifies seeking naturalistic explanations when encountering peculiar phenomena rather than hastily jumping to supernatural or paranormal conclusions (Boudry et al. 2010: 241). A significant question to ask at this point is, Why has science been unable to find evidence for the supernatural? As Fishman (2009: 831) notes, the reason why no convincing and independently verifiable evidence for the supernatural has been forthcoming, despite honest and methodologically rigorous efforts, is that such phenomena probably do not exist. He adds that "the absence of evidence, where such evidence is expected to be found after extensive searching, is evidence of absence" (Fishman 2009: 831).

Many scientists will agree, however, that it is possible that evidence yet to be discovered may provide support for supernatural or theistic accounts as opposed to naturalistic explanations (Fishman 2009: 831). Religionists and paranormalists are placing their bets on this being the case. However, contrary to this view, as the philosopher Oppy (2018: 14–15) has cogently argued, there is enough firmly corroborated science for the nonexistence of such things as ancestral spirits, astral intelligences, demon, fairies, ghosts, gods, vampires, witches, werewolves, yeti, zombies, karma, ch'i, or psi to rule out the possibility that a future science will recognize these things.

Moreover, if such evidence were ever to appear—if someone can conclusively prove that the paranormal and supernatural exist—it would make anthropology and history very uninteresting enterprises because the fascinating aspect of religion and the paranormal is the persistence of such beliefs for which there is no evidence. However, this is very unlikely. The totality of evidence for theism amassed for well over two thousand years is not very convincing. As Scriven (1966: 155) cogently pointed out, "the evidence of theism is either good now, or else it never will be good." The reason for this, he adds, is because if all of a sudden incontrovertible miracles and resurrections and all the rest began to happen all over the world and mystics and psychics began providing incontestably verifiable prophecies and predictions, this would not constitute proof of the Judeo-Christian God. All it would show is that a "Johnny-come-lately" God has appeared on the scene (Scriven 1966: 155). There would be no reason to connect this late-arriving deity to the being to whom theists pray today because there is no evidence for the latter deity's miracles, prophecies, or actions in the world now or anytime in the past.

The real issue is not the inability of science to evaluate supernatural and paranormal claims but accepting such declarations without compelling evidence. If science accepted phenomena such as the miracles in the Bible on the insubstantial and contradictory evidence on offer, then it would also have to accept the miracles in other sacred texts, and indeed all kinds of supernatural claims. Such a verdict is not the same as rejecting a supernatural hypothesis because of an a priori bias; it is rejection using rigorous scientific investigation and weighting of the evidence (Fishman and Boudry 2013: 993). Tirades by religionists such as Plantinga about the defects of methodological naturalism are part of an old strategy that if one cannot refute a perspective on evidentiary grounds, then one should discredit it. Effort by such religious polemicists and vendors of superstition is an example of what the inimitable Thomas Paine (1776) called "Jesuitical cunning which always endeavors to disgrace what it cannot disprove."

## How Science Assesses Non-Falsifiable Claims

To reiterate, science has, does, and must evaluate supernatural and paranormal claims. The reason is that such claims do not pertain to a paranormal realm or some supernatural space but are statements made by humans (as empirical beings) about aspects of the natural world and universe in which they live. Although many such supernatural declarations are deemed to be non-falsifiable, they are nevertheless open to critical scientific appraisal. Science evaluates non-falsifiable claims according to the following three criteria: (1) prior probabilities, (2) the existence of disconfirming evidence, and (3) the availability of alternative non-paranormal explanations (Fishman 2009: 825). These considerations fall within what is called the "Bayesian confirmation theory" that many consider being an accurate depiction of the way scientists assign or revise degrees of confidence in a hypothesis based on new evidence and a given prior probability. In other words, this approach entails inferences according to prior probabilities that allow the placement of an explanation between the two extremes of "certainly right" and "certainly wrong" (Howson and Urbach 2006: 6–9, 91–130). The Bayesian perspective is an alternative to the classical approach in science that prevailed during most of the twentieth century under the influence of the philosopher Karl Popper and the statistician Ronald Fisher (Howson and Urbach 2006: xi).

## Assessing Claims to Knowledge: Zeus, Circe, Santa Claus, God, Unicorns, and the Problem of Evil

Criterion 1: Let us begin with Carl Sagan's (1980) reiteration of David Hume's (1902 [1748]: 112) stipulation regarding the occurrence of miracles, which is that "extraordinary claims require extraordinary evidence" (cf., Truzzi 1978: 11). As Fishman (2009: 817) explains, the more extraordinary a claim, meaning the lower its prior probability based on our background knowledge of the world, the heavier the burden of proof upon the person making the claim to provide evidence of such force and quality as to overcome the low probability of proposition on offer. In other words, the initial low probability of a fantastic or extraordinary claim based on what we already know about how the world operates—and we now know a lot—is grounds for skepticism.

A skeptical stance is justified even if there is no direct evidence against the claim. Take, for example, Santa Claus, a being with many magical powers that violate what we know about the operation of the world and the laws of nature, who is therefore no different from the paranormal beings in many religions, including the God of theism. Children at an early age learn about Santa from their parents. They hear stories about Santa's red costume, his flying reindeer, his workshop in the North Pole, his little helpers, and the wonderful presents he brings good little boys and girls every Christmas. In a single night, Santa simultaneously appears in person in peoples' homes over vast geographic regions, eats cookies and drinks milk, deposits presents, and returns to his abode in the icy North Pole.

By adulthood, however, most people know that Santa is not real. Many things just do not add up that provide clues (Brain 2014: 133–36). Why this apostasy? Because like the effects of the gods, God, or other supernatural beings, Santa's actions as culturally described have implications for the empirical world that we can evaluate. As children grow up, this is precisely how they realize that this being is not real. Consider the following observations. Strangely, parents always seem to be buying gifts at shopping malls around Christmas time. These gifts somehow vanish, until the time comes for presents to appear under the Christmas tree. Santa's notes are in mom's or dad's handwriting. Reindeer do not fly, and there are no levitating beasts anywhere on earth. Google Earth does not reveal any workshops in the North Pole. No scientific texts describe a toy factory run by elves in the icy fields to the north. Given what every adult knows about the population of the United States, it becomes evident that the transportation of all the toys for the children in this country alone would require a sleigh the size of many aircraft carriers, and its considerable weight would demolish any house on which it landed. A simple calculation tells us that if Santa visits 100 million houses in one night to make deliveries and it takes one second per home, that amounts to 100 million seconds, or three years to complete the task (Brain 2014: 133–36). Something is obviously amiss here.

Thus, based on their knowledge of the world, most rational adults do not believe that a paranormal being such as Santa Claus exists instead of being agnostic about it, that is, holding the belief that the probability of Santa's existence or nonexistence is 50-50 (Fishman 2009: 817). However, we cannot entirely prove that a flying fat man with levitating reindeer does not exist. Additional and surprising data might come to light that could conflict with our accepted models of how the world works. All scientific hypotheses, as already stated, are provisional and subject to revision. Again, our certainty in relying on what we know about the world involves probabilities extending from complete skepticism to a 50-50 agnosticism, to a near certainty. However, the crucial point is that because we cannot definitively disprove the existence of a supernatural being such as Santa Claus it does not justify opting for the 50-50 agnostic stance. What it does is to render Santa's existence extremely improbable.

It is the same with other paranormal beings. As Scriven (1966: 156) put it, "Ancient myths chiefly concern creatures of whose existence no *disproof* could be given, but that lack scarcely affects our view that there is not now, nor was there ever, a centaur, a unicorn, a Zeus, a Circe." The complete lack of evidence for a phenomenon provides justification to doubt its existence.

As the philosopher of science Norwood Hanson (1971: 323) pointed out, if seeking and not finding evidence for the existence of God is not grounds for denying the existence of such an entity, then seeking and not finding evidence does not give us grounds to deny the existence of goblins, witches, devils, five-headed Welshmen, Unicorns, mermaids, Loch Ness monsters, flying saucers, Hobbits, and Santa Claus. However, he added, there are solid reasons for denying that such things exist, not simply because we have failed to find such creatures but because there are no good reasons at all for supposing that such creatures do exist (Hanson 1971: 323). Our background knowledge, based on prior probabilities, and the absence of any corroborative evidence for the existence of entities such as Santa Claus or Circe make their reality highly improbable (Fishman 2009: 818). The belief in God is identical to the belief in Santa Claus, centaurs, unicorns, mermaids, the Loch Ness monster, goblins, witches, devils, Zeus, Circe, and flying saucers. What is involved here is not a formal, deductive demonstration, such as a mathematical proof for the existence of a highest prime number, which entails calculation, but proof based on the inductive description of gathered evidence, which requires looking for actual evidence and relying on what we know about the world (Norwood 1971: 310–11).

As an aside, one might ask, if Santa Claus is like the paranormal beings of the various religions, why don't people believe in him in the same way they believe in the gods? Do the gods of these religions have something Santa Claus lacks? No. The answer is simple: Santa's epistemic status is alterable with the inclusion of a few buttressing elements and social reinforcement as with all religions, that is, providing the belief in institutional support. First of all, apply continuous peer pressure and impose threats of ostracism to maintain childhood beliefs. Then add Claus temples and churches, a devoted priesthood, seminaries, and a holy book of mysteries and miracles written in an arcane language and impenetrable prose that requires specialists to interpret and explain.

A Clause creation myth would be invaluable. We might also extend Santa's sphere of influence to include all things. Require the faithful to pray to "the holy one" nine times a day facing north and always wear red clothing as a sign of their devotion. Add Claus Sunday school classes or Santa *madrassas*. Don't forget some handy immunizations against doctrinal disconfirmations, such as the assertion that Santa's miracles are beyond human comprehension and it is sinful and prohibited to ask questions about such sublime and mysterious matters. Throw in some terrorism in the form of punishments for sin and blasphemy. Brand critics and nonbelievers misguided fools and servants of a satanic being bent on misleading the faithful. Finally, include an icy hell of perpetual suffering and we have the religion of the God Claus. Blessed be his name and Peace be Upon Him! Anthropological and historical evidence shows that any absurdities encapsulated in such institutionalized structures that preserve, support, and expand them will appear plausible.

Criterion 2: Another way to evaluate a supernatural or paranormal hypothesis is to expect to find evidence for it if it is true and to find none if it is false. Either way, we have degrees of probabilities for or against supernatural declarations, such as the existence of Circe, Zeus, or Santa Claus. Take, for example, the God of Judaism, Christianity, and Islam. This being is described as an all-knowing, all-benevolent, all-present, and all-powerful being who answers prayers, bestows afterlife, and performs wonders and miracles. He, therefore, has observable effects on the material world (see Chapter 2). If this is the case, then this being is the sort of entity whose existence is ascertainable through empirical data. To reiterate, a God that does not have such tangible effects and is undetectable would only have fools as believers and is not of concern here (Scriven 1966: 159). Also, theologians who assert that God is unknowable and leaves no fingerprints upon the world not only talk themselves out of a job, but their stance also goes against nearly all existing religious creeds that state otherwise.

Therefore, it is possible to evaluate any supernatural claims that postulate some condition in the world by seeing if such conditions are present or absent. For example, the pronouncement that there is an intelligent, loving supernatural designer is unsupportable by the observable cruelty and wastefulness of life on earth and the suboptimal structural designs of life forms that competent human engineers would never undertake. Similarly, the claim for the existence of a moral, benevolent super-intelligent all-knowing being interested in peoples' lives is irreconcilable with the observation of the random distribution of natural disasters in association with the degree of religiosity, religious affiliation, or moral status (Fishman 2009: 823).

The existence of evil in the world is especially strong evidence against the existence of the theistic God and is known as *the argument from evil*. As Scriven (1966: 158) points out, "Unless there are really impregnable proofs that God exists, the existence of inexplicable evil *virtually* precludes the existence [of God]." Some elaboration is necessary here. There are instances when we can know that something is evil and not just "apparently evil," such as the sadistic murder of an innocent infant. We also know that such an evil thing could have been prevented if someone had been present with even a modicum of physical power and understanding of the situation. It follows that if a benevolent and all-powerful God existed, he would not allow such evils to take place. As Scriven (1966: 160) observed, by definition, God knows, is able to, and has reasons to prevent much of the pain and suffering experienced by those who do not deserve it. Therefore, He would prevent such events if He existed. Because such evils occur, He does not exist. In other words, Scriven adds, "the existence of this kind of evil is evidence which disproves the existence of God."

This argument has generated perverse and pernicious theistic rationalizations to vindicate the Deity and to explain the existence of human suffering. The objective of such ad hoc apologetics is to show that what we consider as evil is not *really* evil, or that its presence does not detract from God's goodness and power, a perspective known as *theodicy*. None of these contentions are compelling. Nor do such arguments provide any support for the God hypothesis. Even if humans are ignorant of all the facts and hence erroneously believe that evil is being tolerated, there are no theological explanations for those instances of suffering and grisly deaths that we do know to serve no useful ends, such as the murder of an innocent newborn for sadistic amusement or an infant born with terminal cancer.

Stating that the pain and evil suffered by an innocent victim will be made up in the hereafter does not expunge the wickedness of allowing them to occur in the first place. If a benevolent God existed, he would prevent such evil that is well within his powers to stop. Not to do so is a gross sin of omission. Alternatively, there is the argument that God is good in a nonhuman sense, which means he is not good in our sense, and hence he is not the God as conceived by believers (Scriven 1966: 159–61). To say that evil has already been reduced to a minimum by God's hard work and that otherwise things would be much worse, that is, that this is the best God can do, renders it futile and foolish for people to pray to or ask help from such an ineffectual entity (Scriven 1966: 162).

An appalling contention by theistic Christian philosophers is that God has given humans free will and all evil actions are the responsibility of humans. Here, the moral error is that God as a bystander completely capable of preventing such human evils is exempt for inaction by saying that "he did not do the evil" (Scriven 1966: 160). Another theological claim that preventable evil occurs as merited punishment does not justify the murder of a blameless child, a baby born with a terminal illness, or the torment and death of other innocents.

Then there is the theological defense of God that evil is necessary to help us understand our choices between what is bad and good and builds moral character. If evil did not happen, we would not recognize it, the argument goes, and hence, it is in our best interest for there to be evil in the world. Consequently, any improvements in earthly conditions would spoil the world as a moral testing ground. However, considering the many wars, famines, epidemics, pogroms, *jihads*, crusades, genocides, holocausts, ethnic cleansings, exploitation, abject poverty, and other horrors and inequities, we surely do not need all the evil in the world to recognize what evil is.

Alternatively, there is the argument that evils in the world are a form of divine punishment. But it makes no sense for God to test his puny creations in this way to find out what they will or will not do, since he knows beforehand what lurks in the human heart or could find out without such horrendous tests (Scriven 1966: 164). Also, why is this deity so vindictive and bellicose to punish humans by allowing tragedies such as the Holocaust to happen? The specious answers offered by theologians are merely efforts to justify and rationalize sets of beliefs in which such ideologues have a vested interest to preserve and promote. It is puzzling why anyone would defend such a malicious and unpleasant entity and why others would worship Him.

The fact that purported "godless" malefactors, such as Hitler, Stalin, Mao, and Pol Pot, enthusiastically committed mass murder does not exonerate God and justify religion, as believers often claim. Why would an all-powerful, all-loving, all-compassionate and benevolent God allow the horrors by such vile nonbelievers when by definition He can stop such catastrophes? Also, using these examples to justify religion amounts to saying, "their evil was greater than religious evils, and, therefore, religion is good." Finally, there are natural evils. A benevolent God would not allow the pain and suffering caused by earthquakes, floods, and tsunamis if he can prevent them. There are such events that even a human in the right place and time could have stopped had he or she been present, such as warning of an impending avalanche or a tsunami. If God does not prevent such events, as Scriven (1966: 161) pointed out, and there is no evidence of even one instance of supernatural mitigation of evil acts and disasters, it follows, therefore, that he is not God.

Another way to evaluate the God hypothesis is related to the claim made by religious people that various paranormal forces have a direct impact on their lives, such as the positive effects of intercessory prayers. The tangible effects predicted by this paranormal postulate are amenable to scientific evaluation. In fact, researchers have conducted several studies on the effects of prayer. The most ambitious one was called "The Study of the Therapeutic Effects of Intercessory Prayer" or STEP (Benson et al. 2006). It involved a three-year double-blind controlled study comprising 1,802 coronary bypass surgery patients in six hospitals. The pro-religion John Templeton Foundation sponsored the project with a 2.4 million dollar grant. Unfortunately, the findings of the study failed to support the assertion regarding the power of prayer. Other such studies have also failed to support the effectiveness of prayer on health (Krucoff et al. 2005; Galton 1872; see Master and Spielmans 2007 for an overview).

How religionists have responded to such disconfirmations falls into a familiar pattern that recurs in connection with other supernatural and paranormal claims, as we shall see in the following chapters. True believers embrace the slightest bit of evidence that tangentially supports their views. However, if their claim is disconfirmed they call foul, offer ad hoc excuses, deem the results irrelevant, and ultimately adopt a NOMA stance, that is, that their beliefs are outside the scope of scientific appraisal after all (Fishman 2009: 828; Kelly 1998: 527–28). The reaction of Chibnall and his colleagues (2001) to the findings of STEP exemplifies this stance. Their rejoinder is that the epistemology governing prayer and all other matters of faith is distinct from the epistemological principles governing nature. It is doubtful that these believers would have raised this kind of objection had the STEP yielded the slightest significant positive results (Dawkins 2006: 65). Such equivocations and special pleading are disingenuous.

As the physician Philip Smith (2002: 1420) observes, when a claim is made that prayer and faith have physiological effects, then that claim should be scientifically assessed. However, one cannot make such a claim, on the one hand, and demand exemption from scientific scrutiny, on the other hand. Surely, he asks, the infinite creator of the universe would not feel in jeopardy from such scientific evaluation. Smith (2002: 1420) notes, however, that while God may not take issue with such a test, his self-appointed earthly spokesmen certainly are threatened by this prospect. Chibnall and his colleagues offer another excuse, stating the STEP findings are irrelevant because the Bible forbids "testing God." However, as medical researcher William Harris and physician William Isley (2002) have pointed out, there are passages in the Bible that demonstrate that "testing God" is entirely appropriate.

Criterion 3: Science evaluates supernatural and paranormal claims in relation to the availability of plausible alternative hypotheses that are more consistent with other empirical explanations and observations. Such alternatives justify skepticism regarding any paranormal explanation. Science has provided alternative empirical explanations for many phenomena once considered to be supernatural, such as comets, meteorites, bat sonar, paranormal causes of disease, the idea that nature is the handiwork of a supernatural designer, and much more (Fishman 2009: 824). The existence of more plausible and parsimonious alternate and empirically grounded explanations is always an ample reason to justify skepticism toward any paranormal claim on offer. In the following chapters, several such alternative explanations to central supernatural and paranormal postulates are explored.

## Why the Absence of Evidence Is Evidence of Absence

Given that continuous efforts to look for proof for the existence of God (and other supernatural and paranormal beings and phenomena) have not yielded any sort of explicitly and publicly verifiable evidence, the skeptic would concur with the conclusion that the theistic God does not exist. As the philosopher Keith Parsons (1989: 9) observes, religious apologists and theologians have tried for thousands of years to conceive of a plausible argument or evidence for God's existence and have failed. Moreover, none of the sciences presuppose God and yet have been enormously successful on entirely naturalistic assumptions. Also, Parsons (1989: 9) adds, no "Spielbergian, Zeus-like figures" have manifested in the heavens, and there have been no Second Comings, no raptures, or any other signs to indicate that such an entity exists. Thus, as in the case of such paranormal phenomena as Bigfoot or the Loch Ness monster, persistent efforts to uncover "objective, unambiguous publicly available evidence" that God exists have failed. Hence, it can be concluded that such an entity is nonexistent. Along the same lines, Coyne (2015: 204) observes that the absence of evidence for any god is too conspicuous and religionist special pleading too unpersuasive to render the existence of such a being anything more than "a logical possibility." Hence, a reasonable conclusion is "that the absence of evidence is indeed evidence of absence" (Coyne 2015: 204).

Logical possibility, it must be noted, does not mean that a proposition is true. All sorts of outlandish things are logically possible, including the premise that chemical bonding is the result of sexual attraction between the integral atoms or the idea presented in Douglas Adams's story *The Hitchhiker's Guide to the Galaxy* (1979) that the earth was created by white lab rats to conduct psychological and behavioral experiments on humans (Smith 2001: 719). To this one could add that it is logically possible that you are merely a brain in a vat plugged into a device that generates the illusion that you have a physical body that is active in a material world out there. Logical possibility is a *necessary* but not a *sufficient* requirement for any hypothesis, but this does not mean in any way that such a hypothesis is a good one (Smith 2001: 719).

## Some Further Religionist Anti-Science Assertions

Religious polemicists and proponents of paranormal tenets are preoccupied with the effort to safeguard their supernatural worldviews, which they claim are rooted in something beyond the ordinary and vulgar material world and hence are sublime and worthwhile. They accuse their scientific critics of various sins and evils. These include: (1) the accusation of *scientism*; (2) science and Enlightenment values caused the Holocaust; (3) Adolf Hitler was a proponent of Darwinian evolutionism that was the basis of the Nazi genocide; (4) science is merely a worldview and a religion. These allegations are nothing more than religionist efforts to disgrace what they cannot disprove. Indeed, once we look past the theological veneer of sanctity, the erudite purveyors of such ideas are merely striving to elevate absurd credulities and archaic nonsense from a benighted time of ignorance and barbarism. A brief examination follows.

### *Scientism: What Does It Really Mean?*

This is a pejorative term that implies a dogmatic commitment to a materialistic (naturalistic/empirical) worldview that hinders new ways of thinking and whose proponents are fixated upon finding "absolute truths," with the sole preoccupation to debunk spirituality rather than study it in an honest and open-minded manner (Tart 2009: 12, 53, 192; Williams and Robinson 2015). The indictment is actually a mixture of various exaggerated and inaccurate charges that mean anything about science disliked by the person making the allegation (Coyne 2015: 201).

Such assertions are false because the objective of science is not to debunk spirituality but, as the scientific anthropologist Lawrence Kuznar (2008: 31) points out, to discover the workings of the world and the universe. In science all claims to knowledge, whether natural, supernatural, paranormal, or pseudoscientific, are evaluated according to the evidence and whether such claims meet basic criteria such as parsimony, testability, falsifiability, and explanatory power (Fishman and Boudry 2013). Moreover, all scientific conclusions are accepted provisionally, and science is never about absolute truths (Kuznar 2008: 33–34). Absolute truths, as already stated, are the domain of religion. Those who raise the charge of scientism are uninformed about how science works, or they are being dishonest.

### *Science Caused the Holocaust*

Another line of argument religious polemicists use to malign science is to attribute such evils as the Holocaust to scientific arrogance. Here religious apologists and propagandists have plenty to draw upon from the anti-science postmodernist discourse that flowed from the halls of higher learning in the United States during the 1980s and 1990s. Religionists, paranormalists, white supremacists, and snake-oil merchants touting an array of "alternative ways of knowing" and magical remedies have capitalized on the discursive space opened up by mendacious postmodern intellectuals to express their voices and claim to be heard with vehemence and hubris (Kakutani 2018: 18; McIntyre 2018: 141–48; Otto 2016: 199; Sidky 2018).

Postmodernist philosophers, following the semi-Marxist social theories of the Frankfurt School and the ideas of the German philosopher Friedrich Nietzsche (one of Adolf Hitler's favorite philosophers), undertook a systematic campaign to demonize and discredit science, rationality, modernity, and the entire philosophical foundations of the Enlightenment. Of interest here are the views of the highly adulated French postmodern guru Michel Foucault, whose vision of history was as skewed as his understanding of science, although he endlessly pontificated on both topics. Foucault blamed the horrors of the Nazi Holocaust on modernity and arrogant Enlightenment efforts to reconfigure society scientifically. Many have since echoed this specious assertion. Remarkably, it escapes these science-bashers that this bizarre construal of history in a way exonerates the Nazis whose monstrous atrocities are blamed upon and explained away as the consequences of "modernity" (Pinker 2018: 397), rather than condemning them as heinous acts by loathsome human beings.

Religious propagandists intent on forwarding their version of science, an "alternative" ethical and true science based on biblical precepts, or Plantinga's Christian evidence base, thus have a powerful argument for the evil and immoral nature of science and its philosophical underpinnings. In this context, an Augustinian science sounds enticing. However, is this assertion a legitimate one? No! The foundation of Hitler's ghastly enterprise was not science but paranormalism, pseudoscientific fantasies, and "alternative ways of knowing."

The Nazis were not putting into practice Enlightenment ideals; they vehemently opposed such ideals along with conventional science and rationality. The foundations of their perspective were the writings of various anti-science, anti-Enlightenment ideologues and the irrationalism touted by the *völkisch* or "people's" groups active during World War I and the following decades. These groups were devoted to German nationalism, spiritualism, astrology, and other occult practices. One of their influential ideologues was the philosopher Julius Langbehn, whose ideas centered upon a fanatical hatred of science, positivism, rationalism, empiricism, materialism, technology, secularism, democracy, and skepticism. He also endorsed pan-Germanism (*Pangermanismus*) and the superiority of the white German race. The other sources of inspiration for the *völkisch* groups and the Nazis were the ideas of the paranormalists Guido von List, Jörg Lanz von Liebenfels, and Karl Maria Wiligut.

Especially significant were the works of von List and von Liebenfels, who adopted the schema of "root races" in Helena Blavatsky's bogus paranormal theology called Theosophy. They transformed the idea of root races into the doctrine of Ariosophy, in which they presented race mixing as the cause of all the ills of the world. This dogma, furthermore, provided guidelines for the purification of the German Aryan blood through the elimination of the *untermenschen* or inferior races (Goodrick-Clarke 2005; Kurlander 2017: 3–61; Newman 2005: 73; Regal 2009: 28–29). Thus, the intellectual climate that propelled Hitler and his goons into power was one of paranormalism, irrationalism, and zealous anti-science viewpoints (Holton 1992: 124).

Even before the Nazis seized power, they were calling for a replacement of science with a German-made Aryan "alternative" in a manner analogous to what Plantinga recommends. When National Socialism came to power in 1933, massive efforts went into developing officially sanctioned counter-sciences. These Nazi "alternative" sciences included forms of astrology, a mystical physics, and Aryan archaeology and anthropology, all in the service of the Third Reich's racist program of genocide (Holton 1992: 124; Regal 2009: 28–29). Nazi racism was a pseudoscientific perspective, legitimized by scientific-sounding jargon but grounded in mythologized history involving the lost continent of Atlantis and the fictional northland of Thule as the mystical homeland of the superior white Aryan race. An important fact here is that this ideology tapped into racist and paranormal beliefs that have been around for millennia before modern science was developed and have often been justified religiously as part of God's grand design (Fagan and Hale 2001: 85; Pinker 2018: 397).

### *Hitler Was a Darwinian*

Creationists have attempted to besmirch the scientific theory of evolution by asserting that Hitler was a Darwinian and offer this as the explanation for the mass murders that ensued under the Nazis. As the historian of science Robert Richards demonstrates in his book *Was Hitler a Darwinian?* (2013), this is a patently false allegation (Richards 2013: 192–243). Darwinian evolutionism, which posits that all humans belong to a single species that evolved from a common ancestor, is irreconcilable with the Nazi beliefs. The latter posited that races comprised separate and innately distinct species hierarchically organized according to the superiority or inferiority of their cognitive traits and physiological attributes, with white-skinned, blond hair, and blue-eyed Germans at the pinnacle of this biosocial order (Pinker 2018: 398; Richards 2013: 192–243). Moreover, the officially sanctioned Nazi anthropology and archaeology relegated the Neanderthals to a subhuman lineage and forwarded the bogus theory that paranormally endowed superior Aryan progenitors faring from Atlantis and Thule outcompeted and replaced these early primitive subhuman creatures and are destined to rule the world. There is nothing Darwinian about any of this.

### *Science Is a Worldview or a Religion*

Anti-science ideologues assert that science is not an investigative method but a particular "worldview," in this case a materialist, anti-spiritual, and atheistic one. This is patently false, as philosophers Theodore Schick and Lewis Vaughn (2014: 160) point out, because science is "a method of discovering the truth, not a particular body of truths" and a way of solving problems, not specific solutions for them. It is erroneous, they add, to link science to any particular worldview, equate science with its applications, or link it with its results.

Related to the science as a worldview claim is the avowal that science is itself a faith-based belief system, that is, a religion (e.g., Roy 2005; Smith 2015). Joan Roughgarden (2006a: 3–12), a Christian biologist, is among those who assert that science is merely a religious belief and therefore its postulates are no more authoritative than the precepts of the Bible. This assertion is untrue for several reasons. First, science is not a system of inviolate or sacrosanct beliefs like religion but *a method* of discovering how the world and universe operate. Second, of all the ways of knowing, science alone turns critical judgment and skepticism upon itself. No religious belief systems have ever allowed or can afford to permit this option. Religious premises lack evidential foundations, and such belief systems provide no non-arbitrary means of differentiating between various and often conflicting religious assumptions. For this reason, because an appeal to objective evidence is impossible, disputes over matters of faith, as discussed in Chapter 1, invariably deteriorate into charges of heresy, apostasy, and atheism, along with intimidation, physical force, and, of course, religious violence.

Third, in contrast to religious premises whose validity is based on appeals to higher powers and postulated paranormal or supernatural beings outside the spatiotemporal confines of the universe, the evidentiary foundations of science are of *this world*, are open for assessment by others, and scientific claims are subject to falsification by independent and impartial parties. Think about the case of N-rays as one example. Unlike religion, it is a requirement that all scientific propositions be publicly verifiable and testable, that is, tested in relation to publicly ascertainable evidence. As Carl Sagan (1993: 20–21) put it so eloquently long ago,

> Science thrives on errors, cutting them away one by one. False conclusions are drawn all the time, but they are drawn tentatively. Hypotheses are framed so they are capable of being disproved. A succession of alternative hypotheses is confronted by experiment and observation. Science gropes and staggers toward improved understanding. Proprietary feelings are of course offended when a scientific hypothesis is disproved, but such disproofs are recognized as central to the scientific enterprise.

Hence, science consistently appeals to self-correcting epistemological foundations (Lett 1987: 21). Stated in other words, science is a systematic, self-correcting mode of generating knowledge (Kuznar 2008: 6). This explains the astonishing growth of knowledge and scientific successes (Bernard 1995: 17; Harris 1994: 73). The "faith" that scientists place upon rational analysis and empirical evidence is not due to some a priori ideological or religious-like commitment but, as discussed, is a conclusion of science based upon an inference to the best explanation given all the available scientific empirical data. In science, to say it again, the final arbiters are the data (Kuznar 2008: 25).

Also, religion appeals to purported absolute truths set forth in so-called sacred books that are laden with plagiarisms, contradictions, and gross factual errors, written long ago by ignorant, superstitious, and violent tribal people (see Chapter 10). These texts ultimately rest upon the authority of self-styled ambassadors from heaven and their true-believing acolytes who claim that they and they alone have a direct channel to God's mind and His divine truths, a mysterious kind of knowledge that is unavailable to anyone else but the divinely elect. Hence, we always have to take someone's word regarding the truth of their statements and assertion that their words have cosmic origins and sacred significance.

Scientific propositions, in contrast, are subject to independent appraisal instead of being based on someone's paranormal authority (Kuznar 2008: 23–26). As the anthropologist Marvin Harris (1979: 27) eloquently put it,

> In the entire course of prehistory and history only [science as] a way of knowing has encouraged its own practitioners to doubt their own premises and to systematically expose their own conclusions to the hostile scrutiny of nonbelievers.

Finally, to reiterate, there is no religion or any other available metaphysical and supernatural perspectives, now or in the past, that has offered better explanations of cosmology, quantum physics, the evolution of life on earth, molecular biology and genetics, the origin of hominids, the emergence of language and culture, the evolution of cultural similarities and differences, the nature of human psychology and cognition, epidemiology, chemistry, neurology, rock formations, continental drift, thunderstorms, earthquakes, tsunamis, volcanic eruptions, climate change (yes it is real!), depletion of the ozone layer (scientists discovered that not shamans!), and any other physical facts (Harris 1994: 62;

Schick and Vaughn 2014: 160; Slezak 2012: 406). Only the scientifically illiterate would claim that science is just another religion.

A final observation regarding these anti-science allegations is that they stem from the fallacious assumption that depreciating science by default elevates or automatically validates the paranormal or supernatural views that anti-science critics offer. For instance, Roughgarden (2006b) makes the preposterous claim that the limitations of science raise the credibility of the Bible. Furthermore, she asserts that the Bible—a text that may correctly be described as a catalog of superstitions and primitive credulities—has greater believability because it has been around for several thousand years. Thus, once again, a believer misconstrues the self-correcting nature of the scientific approach as a limitation to support superstition and supernaturalism. The validity of a claim or proposition is an epistemological question, not a matter of how long it has been around. Sadly, arguments such as these make their exponents look stupid.

## Subjecting the Entire Range of Religionist and Creationist Assumptions to Critical Scrutiny

Based on our discussion in this and the previous chapters, it is abundantly clear that paranormal and religious claims are amenable to scientific investigation. The "thou shalt not say ill of religion" and the reticence of many to critique such beliefs on scientific and philosophical grounds is untenable. Such a stance, to reiterate, is an ill-advised and an unjustifiable deterrent to the primary purpose of science—*the elimination of false beliefs* (Fishman 2009: 814).

Even under circumstances in which belligerent evangelical ideologues and oxymoronic creation scientists have directly and systematically assaulted the theory of evolution, scientific anthropology, and science in general, anthropologists have been embarrassingly equivocal in their response. They have either proposed NOMA or responded to only a narrow set of creationist assertions, such as their preposterous claim that the earth came into existence during the Bronze Age, their fatuous contention regarding a global deluge, or their premise that people were spontaneously created in the middle of the Holocene. Yet, they have been willing to tolerate other equally preposterous ideas touted by religionists and paranormalists (Lett 1997a: 112; 1997b: 54). These include the God hypothesis, claims about the inerrancy of the Bible, virgin births, zombie saints pouring forth from graves, the divine origins of Christianity, the resuscitation of cadavers, the existence of souls, the reality of miracles, and the idea of life after death. There are, of course, numerous other irrational and superstitious beliefs to add to this list with which religionists and paranormalists daily assault the intelligence and sensibilities of rational people.

The significant question is, Why is the single religionist idea of supernatural intervention in the evolution of life on earth unacceptable to anthropologists, while the many other equally fallacious and nonsensical claims that science-bashing evangelical ideologues tout are thought to be worthy of toleration and respect? I cannot admonish my anthropologist colleagues enough for their equivocation, double standards, and injudicious cultural sensitivities in this regard. Perhaps many have not yet realized or realized too late the true nature of the religionist assault on science and rationality. The issue is not merely about a supernatural mechanism for the development of life on this planet. What is taking place is an uncompromising assault on the scientific enterprise as a whole along with the entire body of scientific knowledge amassed over the last 400 years about the world, universe, human origins, prehistory and history, the operation of cultural systems, scientific medicine, human cognition, psychology, and reproduction. For religionists, it is not just about purging Darwin from the classroom but about demolishing secular society and establishing the Caliphate of Christ or the Emirate of Jesus. These descriptors are appropriate because there is an alarming similarity between the political and ideological agendas of evangelical Christians and those of the members of grotesque entities such as ISIS and the Taliban.

Lett's (1997a: 112) observation years ago, which is more pressing today than ever, is that anthropologists can no longer pick and choose which truths they reveal publicly and which ones they do not. It is imperative and indeed an ethical obligation that we follow where the evidence leads. The arbitrariness and inconsistency in choosing which paranormal claims to tolerate and which ones to oppose are a sign of indecisiveness and weakness. "Respectful noninterference" has never been the case for the vendors of supernaturalism in the past, and it is indeed not the case at present. We cannot afford equivocation at this time when institutions of higher learning have become beleaguered citadels in an ocean of irrationalism, supernaturalism, post-truths, alternative facts, conspiracy theories, and other bunkum espoused with bluster and hubris by the adversaries of rationality and science, secularism, human rights, peace on earth, and democratic principles (Sidky 2018).

# Chapter Four

# GHOSTLY RAPPINGS, THE SCIENCE OF THE SOUL, AND THE RELIGIOUS NATURE OF THE PARANORMAL

*But the work in parapsychology does more than refute materialism. It is more, too, than a new method of solving problems. There are, at least, still other definite implications and possibilities. Since this new science has penetrated the physical barrier that has hidden man's true nature from the scientists of the past, it has literally become the science of the spiritual aspect of nature.*

—Joseph Banks Rhine, *New World of the Mind* (1953)

*Parapsychological investigations tend to undermine [the] "physicalist" view of the world and, thus, to remove one of the obstacles to religious belief [...]. Parapsychological research seems to reveal a world in which it is more reasonable to suppose that God and the supernatural play a part.*

—Robert Thouless, "Implications for Religious Studies" (1977)

*Often our brains can mislead us, and can lead us to believe that we have had a paranormal experience even when no such thing has happened. Indeed, even if there is no such thing as a paranormal phenomenon, human information processing works in such a way that we are all likely from time to time to have experiences that seem for all the world to be paranormal.*

—James Alcock, Parapsychology as a "Spiritual Science" (1985)

*Not only have [parapsychologists] failed to discover significant new facts, but by nagging away at the few facts they thought were already in the bag, they have slowly but surely taken away the credibility even from those.*

—Nicholas Humphrey, *Leaps of Faith* (1999)

The term "paranormal" was adopted by researchers during the first half of the twentieth century to define the subject matter of the emergent field of parapsychology (Thouless 1942). Parapsychology[1] represents the continuation of the scientific search for ghosts, spirits, and the soul that started in 1882 with the formation of the Society for Psychical Research (SPR) in Britain. The counterpart of this organization was the American Society for Psychical Research (ASPR), established in the United States in 1884 (Beloff

---

1. I would like to thank Dr. Jeb Card, Department of Anthropology, Miami University, Oxford, Ohio, for reading an earlier draft of this chapter and for his many insightful comments and suggestions. His thoughts on Theosophy and the influence of Helena Blavatsky have been especially useful. I alone assume responsibility for any errors and the views expressed here.

1977: 4–16; Kurtz 1985b: 192–209). The search for ghosts and the soul as a coherent field of study began with the spiritualist movement in the United States during the middle of the nineteenth century that later spread to Britain and Europe and lasted well into the first two decades of the twentieth century (Beloff 1977: 5–7; Irwin and Watt 2007: 13; Kurtz 2003b: 220–21). Some historical background is useful at this stage.

## Spiritualism and the Quest for the Soul

Spiritualism developed around a hoax perpetrated by three mischievous girls, the Fox sisters, beginning in Hydesville, New York, during December 1847. The girls claimed that they could communicate with the spirits of deceased people who transmitted their messages through rapping sounds (Weisberg 2005: 72–77, 89–103). The ghostly signals were generated by the girl's themselves cracking their toes (Brandon 1983: 3; Hyman 1985: 8). To the witnesses, these miraculous messages were from the beyond. The unreal real had arrived in New York!

There is nothing remarkable about what the girls did; mischievous children, frauds, and charlatans are never in short supply across space and time. What is astonishing is the rapid and widespread public reception of the outlandish paranormal claim that ghosts could communicate with the living by making knocking sounds (Brandon 1983: 1–41; Weisberg 2005: 11–29, 59–72). Before the rise of spiritualism, the most widely known paranormal phenomena in the United States were hauntings and poltergeists (Beloff 1977: 6). What the Fox sisters claimed was something new and different. They were offering a novel X-claim. Soon a large following of enthusiastic supporters and true believers congregated around the girls. These included not only the uneducated and gullible but also many purported sophisticated and intelligent people, comprising prominent philosophers, scientists, newspaper editors, judges, and public officials. Here is a perfect illustration of how the desire for the paranormal to be real is so strong that many are willing to set aside the critical faculties operational in other aspects of their lives to accept the legitimacy of the most outrageous claims. This enthusiastic reception of the ghostly phenomenon announced by the Fox sisters launched the widespread spiritualist movement. This is yet another example of how easily X-claims can hijack the human cognitive apparatus.

The Fox girls quickly became national and later international celebrities. They soon embarked on a cash-generation tour around the country, improving their act over time, including hiring accomplices to assist them in their shenanigans. Everywhere they went, they left behind multitudes of true believers. At the same time, hundreds of new mediums cropped up around the country to provide similar services, and spiritualism became a national phenomenon (Brandon 1983: 42–76). These spirit conjurers worked in darkened séance rooms, where they offered proof of contact with the beyond by tipping tables, levitating objects, producing ectoplasmic emissions, engaging in teleportations, materializations, automatic writing, and so on (Kurtz 2003b: 220). Yet, no one wondered why his or her dead relatives needed such bizarre procedures to reveal themselves. By 1855 around 30,000 mediums were holding daily séances in the United States with millions of committed followers (Kurtz 2013: 325).

Among the dubious characters who benefited from this cultural climate was a Russian quack named Helena Blavatsky, a self-proclaimed clairvoyant and telepath who came to New York in 1873 at the height of spiritualism. Blavatsky espoused a form of mystical knowledge that she purportedly acquired from masters of the occult arts while traveling in India and Tibet that came to be known as Theosophy (divine wisdom). In the United States Blavatsky found a very receptive audience. She astounded people with bogus séances during which she magically produced letters allegedly written by ancient "ascended masters" who were said to reside in a paranormal dimension and possess lost arcane spiritual knowledge. In 1875 she founded the Theosophical Society. As a result, Blavatsky gained international fame and is considered one of the key figures in the New Age movement in the West during the 1970s (Hutton 1999: 18). By the time of her death in 1891, there were as many as 100,000 Theosophists around the world (Kurtz 1985b: 196).

Theosophy was not bestowed upon Blavatsky by any hidden Indian or Tibetan spiritual masters but was her own fabrication based on odds and ends plagiarized from various religious traditions. Her mediumistic feats and occult and psychic abilities were fraudulent as well. Richard Hodges, a member of the SPR, who investigated Blavatsky's marvels and miracles demonstrated that like all the other fakes and charlatans, she also used props and gimmicks. He also discovered that the letters from the "masters" were written in her own handwriting (Brandon 1983: 23).

These developments cannot be treated as a passing and harmless fad because there was a dark side to Theosophy. Blavatsky's work contributed to the racialist program developed by the Nazis in Germany. As noted in the previous chapter, her book *The Secret Doctrine* (1888), a German translation of which appeared in 1901, provided a human spiritual evolutionary typology that was adopted by the Austrian occultists Guido von List and Jörg Lanz von Liebenfels. They developed it into the doctrine of Ariosophy in the period after World War I that inspired the program of genocide devised by Adolf Hitler and Heinrich Himmler (Goodrick-Clarke 2005: 33–55, 90–105; Kurlander 2017: 18; Newman 2005: 73; Regal 2009: 28).

Not everyone fell for spiritualism. Indeed, from the start, some staunch critics and detractors saw through the hoax and even demonstrated how the sisters made the ghostly noises (Kurtz 1985b: 180). The true believers, however, were unconvinced and undeterred. Instead, such disconfirmations only magnified their faith in the genuine nature of spiritualism. Even a confession of fraud by one of the sisters (Kane 1985: 225–34) some years later, who detailed the various tricks she and her sisters used along with toe cracking to fool spectators, failed to dissuade the faithful. Believers denied that the confession had ever happened or attributed it to alcoholism and the influence of unscrupulous men who misled the poor lady, or enticed her with money, into making false statements (Brandon 1983: 228–54: Kurtz 1985b: 181–83). Devotees to this day discount the admission of fraud and affirm that spiritualism is a genuine "scientifically proven" phenomenon (e.g., Tart 2009: 258).

There are many lessons here that shed light on human desire and the nature of belief. The pervasive reception of spiritualism and the refusal of believers to give up their faith even when confronted with evidence of fraud and deception indicates how much humans yearn for the extraordinary and the marvelous. What this shows is that X-claims are highly alluring and can establish a powerful hold on believers' minds. The philosopher David Hume (1902 [1748]: 119) long ago pointed out this human predisposition in his book *Enquiries Concerning the Human Understanding* (1748):

> All proceeds from the usual propensity of mankind towards the marvelous, and that, though this inclination may at intervals receive a check from sense and learning, it can never be thoroughly extirpated from human nature. (Hume 1902 [1748]: 119)

In the case of spiritualism, the miraculous and the marvelous were the premises that there is life after death, that souls are real, and by extension that there is a God in Heaven. All of this, of course, is the stuff of religion. The will to believe has rendered humans throughout history and around the world susceptible to the frauds and the sleight-of-hand trickery of magicians, charlatans, and religious demagogues claiming miraculous powers and passing themselves as gods on earth or the divinely appointed impresarios of such beings. The Greek philosopher Celsus (1830: 30), writing two thousand years ago, described the multitude of charlatans in his time who "in temples and out of temples" go around claiming to be God or the son of God, promising salvation and deliverance to those who worshipped them and eternal fire for those who did not, hoodwinking the gullible with their stories. Hume (1902 [1748]: 125) called such pretenders "ambassadors from heaven."

The will to believe is a potent force. No one is immune to it, not even those trained in science. Indeed, expertise in a scientific field does not overcome this desire to believe. It also does not supply the necessary credentials to spot conjurers' tricks, and sleight-of-hand deceptions mediums and other paranormalists use to fool their clients. Only a highly skilled stage magician like Harry Houdini (1924) could competently investigate the spiritualists (Brandon 1983: 165–89; Randi 1976). Houdini had a great desire for spiritualism to be real because he wanted to communicate with the spirit of his beloved deceased mother and sought extensively, but was unable to discover a single genuine medium. His findings eventually contributed to the demise of spiritualism during the twentieth century. However, the practice of contacting the dead or "channeling" the spirits of the departed later returned and remains a popular and lucrative enterprise. Today, the skeptical conjurer James Randi has assumed Houdini's role as a debunker of paranormal fraud (Randi 1982a, 1982b, 1985, 1987). More recently, Penn Jillette and Raymond Teller of the Penn and Teller magic team have taken up this task as well (see Jillette 2014a, 2014b).

The human craving to believe in the unreal real is how members of our species mystify the world around. Special-pleading and multiple outs serve to insulate the true believers' faith from disconfirmation. Ad hoc hypotheses to achieve this are plentiful. In the case of spiritualism, for example, if a medium's fraud were detected, the retort would be "Oh she cheats some of the time, but not always" or "some mediums cheat, but there are others who have genuine powers."

The conclusions reached by members of the SPR (1883: 3) concerning the reality of the paranormal illustrates the depths of the desire for the paranormal to be real. After extensive but failed investigations, having established nothing conclusive, and being fully aware of the many fraudulent cases, their conclusion was as follows:

> From the recorded testimony of many competent witnesses, past and present, including observations made by scientific men of eminence in various countries, there appears to be, amidst such delusion and deception, an important body of remarkable phenomena, which are *prima facie* inexplicable on any generally recognized hypothesis, and which, if incontestably established, would be of the highest possible value.

Sadly, the important body of remarkable phenomena has failed to be established despite immense efforts by diligent researchers. It seems, however, that no amount of delusion, deception, and negative findings could deter the faithful from holding on to their beliefs and hopes for the miraculous and the extraordinary. These are anthropological and human psychological phenomena that beg for an explanation, something that I shall attempt in the following chapters.

Spiritualism was not a religion in the sense that its key players did not during that historical moment claim to be messiahs or prophets with a desire to establish churches or temples. Nevertheless, spiritualist claims were religious ones influenced or bolstered by society's central theological assumptions (Kurtz 2013: 321). Indeed, the implicit desire on the part of the researchers involved in the investigation of spiritualism was that by establishing the veracity of psychic phenomena they could offer a scientific basis for religious faith (Kurtz 2013: 339, 1985: 171). The fact that organized religion targeted spiritualism does not undermine the theological implications of the movement (contra Hines 2003: 45).

The religious premises of spiritualism included the belief in the existence of individual souls, life after death, the idea that certain individuals can conjure up and converse with the spirits of the dead, move objects at a distance with their thoughts, and perform other miracles. A glance at the Bible confirms the parallels between these phenomena and their religious counterparts (Larue 1990: 17). For spiritualists, psychic phenomena represented proof for the existence of a transcendental reality, and in this sense, as the philosopher Paul Kurtz (2013: 321) put it, spiritualism was a religious phenomenon "in motive and function."

The ultimate objective of the scientific research of psychic phenomena was to demonstrate that human thought and personality were not epiphenomena of material bodies or brains (Alcock 1985: 548, 553). Unlike science, the aim of this enterprise was not merely to understand some aspect of the natural world and universe, but to demonstrate that there was more to human existence than what was offered by the materialistic model proposed by science. Thus, in contrast to the founders of modern science, who carried out their efforts despite religious needs, psychic researchers undertook their task because of religious requirements and wishful thinking (Alcock 1985: 555).

## Parapsychology and the Religious Nature of Psi Phenomena

Those conducting psychic research today go under the label of parapsychologists. These individuals have taken up the mantle left behind by the nineteenth-century psychic researchers. Parapsychologists are concerned with a more limited range of phenomena than their predecessor. They are engrossed specifically with extrasensory perception, psychokinesis, and the idea of life after death collectively referred to as psi (Alcock 1990: 16; French and Stone 2014: 7; Thouless 1942).

The field of parapsychology owes its development to a researcher named Joseph Banks Rhine (1895–1980), who sought to provide a reliable empirical basis for psi phenomena through investigations conducted in a laboratory setting using scientific methods (Rhine 1977). Before Rhine's work, evidence for psychic phenomena consisted mainly of anecdotal accounts and information gathered by observations of psychic and mediums in uncontrolled settings that were conducive to fraud.

The psi phenomena of interest to parapsychologists fall into two groups: (1) extrasensory perceptions and (2) psychokinesis. Extrasensory perception includes precognition (knowledge about future events), retrocognition (seeing the past), telepathy (thought transference without the involvement of biological sensory apparatus), and clairvoyance (obtaining information from external sources, but not other minds) (Smith 2010: 245). Psychokinesis involves the direct effects of thoughts on material objects without the mediation of any recognized physical energy.

Underlying psi phenomena is the idea that consciousness is related to the physical world in a way that is "radically different from that held to be possible by contemporary science" (Alcock 1990: 19). In other words, psi phenomena stem from a very ancient premise basic to many religions that human consciousness, or some aspect of it, interacts with a more authentic transcendental spirit world (Stenger 1990: 8). As John Beloff (1977: 21), a leading paranormalist theoretician of his day, put it, the paranormal refers to the "domain of mind liberated from its dependence on the brain" and parapsychology provides evidence of the "essentially spiritual nature of man."

The notion of the mind as something separate from the physical brain leads to the presupposition that the mind, or spirit, can somehow survive after the physical brain and body have ceased to function, or the idea of life after death, which is a core belief in many of the world religions. Parapsychologists believe that the forces and powers with which they are concerned represent not yet understood aspects of the universe and that the existence of these forces will come to light with advances in scientific knowledge. However, the confirmation of the paranormal would not merely entail the incorporation of such phenomena into the domain of science, as in the case of the once misunderstood bat sonar or meteorites, but will result in an unprecedented paradigmatic shift that will usher a new millennium for humankind (Alcock 1990: 16–17). The paranormal thus promises miraculous and extraordinary possibilities, all familiar territories of religion.

Although not all contemporary researchers will admit it, the entire thrust of paranormal research is to overturn the empirical scientific view of the universe and replace it with one in which there is room for a spiritual or religious worldview (Kurtz 1985a: 503). Identical to this is the agenda of theistic philosophers and Christian apologists, such as

Alvin Plantinga, whose ideas are discussed in Chapter 3. Hence, directly or indirectly, parapsychology provides validation for a spiritual or supernatural outlook and the reality of souls, spirits, God, or the gods. It is a way of counteracting what the German sociologist Max Weber referred to as "*die Entzauberung der Welt*," or science taking "the magic out of the world."

Humans seem to desire and crave the marvelous and the mysterious. As noted, David Hume (1902 [1748]: 118) long ago pointed out humankind's inextricable and irrepressible propensity for the extraordinary and the marvelous. The philosopher Robert Pennock (1999: 277–78) has made a pertinent observation about this human proclivity stating that humans have a sincere desire to understand how the world operates. Yet paradoxically at the same time they are fascinated with the supernatural and want to believe that there are other planes of existence and that there is more to reality than meets the eye. Thus, they are constantly tempted by "cover-ups" and conspiracy theories that do not lend themselves to verification. During my fieldwork, I never ceased to be amazed by the fixation that members of our species have for the transcendental, paranormal, and supernatural. The question that seldom left my mind was: Why are we so compelled to seek the ethereal and the miraculous? The religious true believers pursue it, and this is the quest that drives all those researchers who have dedicated their lives and careers in search of otherworldly powers and energies.

There is no doubt that Rhine was on such a quest. His objective from the very start of parapsychology was to demonstrate the limitations of the physicalist view of the universe by showing that psi phenomena operate outside the boundaries of ordinary reality. In his view, parapsychology addresses "the experiences and behavior of living organisms that fail to show regular relationships with time, space, mass, and other criteria of physicality" (Rhine 1954: 801). The overly optimistic Rhine had no doubts about the reality of what he was investigating. Thus, in his book, *New World of the Mind* (1953), he made the following pronouncement: "the work in parapsychology does more than refute materialism [...] it has literally become the science of the spiritual aspect of nature" (Rhine 1953: 277).

By adopting the term "paranormal" to describe the subject of study, Rhine attempted to disassociate his efforts from overt supernaturalism. Nevertheless, he was well aware of the similarities between what he was studying and the supernatural events reported in the Bible. Indeed, he specifically pointed out the close parallels between parapsychological findings and the contents of the religious scriptures (Rhine 1972: 117).

For Rhine psi phenomena were at the foundation of religious beliefs, and he asserted that these systems were constructed upon an understanding of the powers and forces that were the subjects of his parapsychological research (Kurtz 2013: 364). If Rhine's assertions were correct, religion would be vindicated and given renewed validity. Some parapsychologists went beyond seeing psi and religion merely as kindred phenomena and maintained that psi, in fact, bolsters all the supernatural beliefs delegitimized by science. Such a perspective was a twentieth-century cloaked religious response to the threat that scientific knowledge posed to faith-based beliefs. The British parapsychologist Robert Thouless (1977: 175–76) clearly expressed this point of view observing that the findings of parapsychology eliminate the obstacles imposed upon religious beliefs by science and make it reasonable to believe once again that "God and the supernatural play a part in the world."

Thus, parapsychologists were and remain covert religionists. For the American parapsychologist, the late Douglas Rogo, religious miracles from levitation and the stigmata to Marian apparitions are genuine paranormal events. As Rogo (1982: 9) put it with a play on David Hume's words, "The evidence authenticating the existence of miracles is [...] so strong that its collective falsehood would be quiet literally miraculous." The possibility of miracles is discussed in Chapter 8. For now, we need merely to acknowledge the enthusiastic way paranormalists embrace such phenomena. Similarly, Robert McConnell (1982: 140), another American parapsychologist, sees psi phenomena at the foundations of religion itself, pointing out that "religion is nothing more than the cultural expression of psi phenomena."

At present, some people tend to demarcate religion and the paranormal. Beliefs and behaviors associated with God, the gods, the devil, angels, souls, ghosts, heaven and hell, and the resurrection of Jesus (in Christianity) are classified as religious. Beliefs in ESP, telepathy, clairvoyance, spirit communication, channeling, UFOs, the Loch Ness monster, Bigfoot, alien abductions, and so forth are subsumed under the classification of paranormal. The paranormal has thus become a general repository for all things unknown and unexplained, primarily due to the media and the efforts of some popular writers. Such designations obscure the fundamental religious or quasi-religious nature of the paranormal. Things such as Bigfoot and other cryptids, and the no-longer-fashionable Bermuda Triangle, really belong to a distinct category to be called "the mysterious and inexplicable."

The paranormal beliefs I have investigated in the context of shamanic performances, spirit possession events, exorcisms, mediumistic and oracular sessions, psychic healing, and while observing the magical feats and miracles of god-men and mystics are all firmly embedded in foundational religious and broader supernatural assumptions in every culture. In his investigation of the relationship between the religion and the paranormal, scientific researcher Alan Orenstein (2002: 309) has also found that "paranormal beliefs are profoundly religious in nature" and that "some amount of religious belief is a necessary condition for paranormal belief."

Religious and paranormal beliefs, to state it differently, are not distinct phenomena. The main reason people perceive them as such is that supernatural concepts are part of organized religions, have more adherents, have long historical traditions, have institutional support, and are deemed to be mainstream. Phenomena classified as paranormal do not have these attributes or institutional backing. As sociologist Christopher Bader and his colleagues (2017: 158) point out, "religious phenomena and paranormal phenomena appear to be one and the same." Both sets of beliefs share a spiritual orientation, hold that there is more to reality than what science can reveal, and require "a measure of faith and a willingness to accept the ephemeral" (Bader et al. 2017: 85–86).

Sociologist Erich Goode has also pointed out parallels between paranormalism and religion. This is not to say that various organized religions do not show adversity to some alternative forms of belief in the paranormal. The Catholic Church, for example, opposes the use of the toy called Ouija board based on the following statement against divination in the *Catechism of the Catholic Church* (no. 2116):

> All forms of divination are to be rejected: recourse to Satan or demons, conjuring up the dead or other practices falsely supposed to "unveil" the future. Consulting horoscopes, astrology, palm reading, interpretation of omens and lots, the phenomena of clairvoyance, and recourse to mediums all conceal a desire for power over time, history, and, in the last analysis, other human beings, as well as a wish to conciliate hidden powers. They contradict the honor, respect, and loving fear that we owe to God alone. (Conference of Catholic Bishops 2016: 513)

However, every item of traditional religious dogma that is refuted by science, such as angels, the devil, demons, miracles, holy visions, divine creation, magical healing, virgin births, and resurrections of the dead, are instances of paranormalism (Goode 2012: 220). As I shall discuss in detail in Chapters 13 and 14, the central themes of paranormalism in the West derive from the miracles of Jesus described in the gospels (Humphrey 1999: 93–94). Moreover, various paranormal claims, such as the belief in life after death, spirits, and the soul, directly support religious beliefs (Bridgstock 2009: 53). As the biblical scholar Gerald Larue (1990: 9) observes, paranormalism "draws energy from the pervasiveness of religious supernaturalism and evokes pseudoscience to promote its teachings."

Goode (2012: 221) points out other similarities between paranormal beliefs and religious supernaturalism, noting that religion and paranormalism both reject materialism, espouse a mind–body dualistic perspective, and their central premises are non-falsifiable. Furthermore, in both cases, propositions are accepted on faith rather than because of evidence. And Orenstein (2002: 309) points out that the driving factor in both religion and the paranormal is faith rather than rationality. The convictions of believers of both sorts are unshakable by evidence or compelling scientific counterarguments.

The claim here is not that paranormalism and religion coincide, at least in the West. In certain respects, they constitute mutually exclusive domains. In Larue's (1990: 12) words, the supernaturalism of the Bible and paranormal and occult beliefs are two sides of the same coin. Paranormalism and religion both are about the unreal real, that is, they comprise X-claims. Also, in some cases, paranormalism can become a functional alternative to religious beliefs (Goode 2012: 236). Hence, seeking an exact correspondence between religious beliefs and paranormal ones is bound to be unsuccessful (e.g., Rice 2003; Sparks 2001). As Goode (2012: 227) sums it up, "the folk epistemology for paranormalism and traditional religious thinking are similar." While certain paranormal beliefs may run counter to traditional Christian beliefs, he adds, the general thinking process of both beliefs systems are the same.

Paranormal and religious beliefs emanate from the same cognitive and psychological wellsprings and desires to affirm the spiritual nature of humankind. They let us know that we are more than merely biological machines. These beliefs also serve as a shield against the widely abhorred, bewildering, and unsatisfying scientific worldview

(Humphrey 1999: 7; Kurtz 2013: 339). Paranormal and supernatural beliefs, to reiterate, are responses to what science has taken away, that is, they are reactions to the disenchantment of the world by science and rationality. The psychologist Nicholas Humphrey (1996: 8) has eloquently described the perceived impact of science on the spiritual sensibilities of humankind:

> Science, with its chain-saws and bulldozers of reason, has felled the tropical rainforest of spirituality. It has wreaked ecological destruction on fairyland. Is has extinguished the leprechauns, the elves and goblins. It has caused a global change in the weather of imagination. It has made a dustbowl of our Eden, and created an inner drought. And all this, not to bring greater peace or happiness, but to satisfy people's hunger for the Big Macs of technology.

People throughout history and across cultures have time and again demonstrated that they would grasp the flimsiest and most ephemeral proofs to satisfy their desire and yearning for there to be a spiritual or transcendental dimension to existence. This is a clear indication that human cognitive systems are highly vulnerable to and are easily hijacked by such ideas. The unreal real thus becomes a possibility. When the desire for something to be true is so strong, and the evidence for it so weak and imperceptible, people are willing to fool themselves and to bamboozle others, as revealed by the history of psi research and religious miracles. Hence the paranormal, the supernatural, fraud, and gullibility always seem to go together. Why humans have this deep desire for the transcendental requires explanation and is a topic that I shall discuss in detail in the following chapters.

## On the Persistence and Weirdness of Ghost Beliefs and Otherworldly Powers

My investigations of religion and the paranormal have taken me to different places and cultures around the world. Everywhere, I have found believers in spirits, ghosts, the gods, or God. The ubiquity of paranormal and supernatural ideas across cultures is astonishing. Also, my research on the origins of religiosity and shamanism has revealed the pervasiveness of such beliefs through time (Sidky 2008, 2017b).

The questions to ask at this point is, Why do so many people in so many places and times believe in such things? The most straightforward explanation for the prevalence of such beliefs across space and time could be that the paranormal and the supernatural actually exist. This stuff is real! In other words, ghost, spirits, and ESP actual exist, reality is purposeful and mindlike, and humans have a central role in the cosmic scheme (cf., Fishman and Boudry 2013: 924). It would make sense, therefore, that people around the world and throughout history have constructed complex belief systems and entire theologies around such phenomena. Such a proposition is fascinating. However, it is not true. Scientific investigations of the paranormal conducted for over two centuries have failed to substantiate such a supposition. Two rather intriguing questions now arise. First, if paranormal and supernatural beliefs are not based on actual phenomena, what prompts humans to believe that such things are real? Second, why do such beliefs persist over time? Here, I shall focus on the second question, the persistence of such beliefs. What prompts humans to entertain such ideas will be discussed in later chapters.

## Why Believers Won't Quit: The Legacy of the Nineteenth-Century Search for Ghosts and the Soul

As discussed above, beginning in the late nineteenth century, bright and talented individuals, such as the philosopher and psychologist William James, the philosopher Henry Sidgwick, and the physicist Oliver Lodge invested their time, intellectual resources, and reputations in the search for ghosts and spirits, convinced that they were on to "something" mysterious, real, and worthwhile. We can call these men seekers of the soul and explorers of the unreal real. These intrepid pioneers searched long and hard to uncover the mystery.

In the end, however, after decades of painstaking effort, souls, spirits, and other transcendental energies and forces remained intractable and as elusive as ever. The unreal real turned out to be especially uncooperative and recalcitrant. As James (1909: 580) explained,

> [Sidgwick and his associates] hoped that if the material were treated rigorously and, as far as possible, experimentally, the objective truth would be elicited, and the subject rescued from sentimentalism on the one side and dogmatized ignorance on the other. Like all founders, Sidgwick hoped for a certain promptitude of result; and I heard him say, the year before his death, that if anyone had told him at the outset that after twenty years he would be in the same identical state of doubt and balance that he started with, he would have deemed that prophecy incredible. It appeared impossible that the amount of handling evidence should bring so little finality of decision.

It was the same for James (1987: 1250) himself who described his efforts in psychical research as follows:

> My own experience has been similar to Sidgwick's. For twenty-five years I have been in touch with the literature of psychical research and have had acquaintance with numerous "researchers." I have also spent a good many hours (though far fewer than I ought spent) in witnessing (or trying to witness) phenomena. Yet I am theoretically no "further" than I was at the beginning; and I confess at times I have been tempted to believe that the Creator has eternally intended this department of nature to remain *baffling*, to prompt our curiosities and hopes and suspicions all in equal measure, so that, although ghosts and clairvoyances, and raps and messages from the spirits, are always seeming to exist and can never be fully explained away, they also can never be susceptible of full corroboration. [...] The peculiarity of the case is just that there are so many sources of possible deception in most of the observations that the whole lot of them *may* be worthless, and yet that in comparatively few cases can aught more fatal than this vague general possibility of error be pleaded against the record. Science, meanwhile, needs something more than bare possibilities to build upon so your genuinely scientific inquirer—I don't mean your ignoramus "scientist"—has to remain unsatisfied.

Yet, despite the admission of failure and acknowledgment of the prevalence of fraud, James did not reject the existence of psi but merely stated that such phenomena are unexpectedly obstinate. These statements reveal the powerful role of the confirmation bias and the backfire effect on psi beliefs (see Chapter 7).

## How Paranormal Beliefs Are Immunized: Explaining Away Disconfirmations

This refusal to relinquish beliefs in the unreal real is a significant attribute of all believers and seekers of otherworldly things. The unwillingness to abandon such ideas is one reason why the paranormal persists. Many others who subsequently picked up where the nineteenth-century soul seekers left off have ended up in the same position, in a pattern that has been repeated over and over (Bridgstock 2009: 107). The deep yearning for the miraculous and the transcendental is astonishing, and it has led seekers of souls to make innumerable compromises on standards of evidence and methodology to obtain the answers they desire. For these reasons, the history of psychic research has been peculiar if not downright weird. The unreal real doesn't just refuse to cooperate; it often acts most bizarrely.

Paranormalists have devised various tactics in response to their critics to address the problems of proof and replicability rather than abandon their central premise regarding the existence of psi itself. Thus, the ability of some researchers but not others to detect psi does not raise the issue that psi may not be real, or that there are methodological problems, but is ascribed to an inherent property of psi to act weirdly—a phenomenon called the *psi experimenter effect*. Simply put, some researchers obtain positive results because of their own psi capabilities or psi friendliness and sensitivities, but others who lack this capacity fail to do so. In other words, only those who are believers in psi can obtain positive psi effects in the laboratory, something that should set off alarms about confirmation bias, the distorting effects of expectation, and perceptual errors and illusions to which all humans are susceptible (see Chapter 7). The psychologist James Alcock (2003: 38–39) refers to this as "the ultimate Catch-22" wherein both finding and not finding evidence for psi are used to support the case for the paranormal. Other failures are similarly explained away. When a subject fails so entirely that the data statistically fall in an unpredicted direction, that is, fewer hits than expected by chance, it is referred to as the *psi-missing effect* and is actually taken as positive evidence for the psi hypothesis, thus transforming failure into success (Gilovich 1991: 181–82).

Finally, when an exceptional subject's high scores on a psi test drop down to chance level after initial success, as they invariably do as demonstrated by the history of psychic research, this is taken as revealing another weird characteristic of psi, referred to as *the decline effect*. However, rather than being an attribute of psi phenomena, the more plausible explanation is that as experimental controls are increased, false positives decline until the effect no longer occurs (Stenger 2003: 342). Alternatively, the initial findings may be due to a statistical effect that disappears with the inclusions of more data (Stenger 2003: 342). Again, failure becomes success and psi persists.

In actuality, these ostensible "effects" are merely arbitrary post hoc labels for failed outcomes. They render psi phenomena unfalsifiable and are touted because proponents refuse to accept any disconfirmation, despite the strength of the counterevidence (Smith 2010: 104). The continual piling on of ad hoc hypotheses is why psi phenomena have become weird and difficult to understand.

## The Cumulative Weirdness of Psi Phenomena

The more extensively psi phenomena have been investigated, the weirder and fishier they have become. We find that such energies and power can manifest only under highly conditional circumstances. Psi phenomena never appear on demand on the spot. Much preparation is required before the paranormalist, whether a medium, spirit channeler, shaman, prophet, messiah, or some other miracle worker, can perform. Rooms have to be darkened. Objects and props have to be arranged. Instructions to those present have to be given. Restrictions must be put in place. I often had to wait several days while the shamans with whom I worked completed their preparatory tasks before conducting their rituals and displaying their paranormal powers.

As Humphrey (1999: 74) observes, the weirdness of psi is evident when the transcendental powers of the universe work on metal spoons, but never on solid blocks of iron or wooden cutlery. Spoons bend if they are touched but not from a distance. Objects nearby move or levitate, but nothing happens long distance. Some props display paranormal powers, such as staffs turning into serpents, but not others, such as swords transforming into dragons. Psi powers manifest themselves in laboratories, but remarkably rarely during everyday circumstances. Also, such effects happen in the presence of believers, but for some odd reason not when skeptics are around. The dead can send messages from the beyond, but only in cryptic form. The deity possessing a medium speaks, but in a language only the medium or an appointed specialist can translate. Psi appears in dark rooms, but never when the lights are on. Paranormal beings reveal themselves and communicate with just a few individuals often in a covert fashion, rather than before gathered masses of skeptics. Ghostly manifestations and spirit encounters are never predictable. Statues of saints and the Virgin Mary move at night under special conditions, but never during the daylight. Psi can manifest itself as vague images of faces on burnt toast or water stains on a wall, but never clearly and explicitly evident to all observers, such as in Times Square. Psi powers can tip or levitate tables but never buildings or cars. Finally, tapping into the power of the soul and other mysterious forces and energies from the beyond can accomplish what any ordinary conjurer can, but never anything more significant. Why this weirdness?

There is also the lack of significance and relevance of the paranormal powers on display. Paranormalists can dazzle and amaze people with their ectoplasmic emissions, levitations, teleportation, materializations, automatic writing, table-tipping, making musical instruments play by themselves, mind-reading, producing ghostly rapping noises in the dark, bending spoons, and making stopped watches operate again. Yet, none of these extraordinary powers have any relevance for human life (Humphrey 1999: 121–22).

Moreover, while paranormalists display their abilities before audiences, usually for a fee, they seem to make no use of them offstage in their own daily lives. Nor are such powers harnessed to cure cancer, eradicate HIV, or help people in other ways. Finally, why do those who possess such transcendental skills work as entertainers rather than getting rich by divining winning lottery numbers or predicting the stock market? Why aren't these gifted individuals in positions of power and authority rather than trying to make money selling books, engaging in circus-like sideshows, or scamming the gullible and the desperate?

These characteristics have become standard attributes of paranormal phenomena, which are declared to be things that are uncontrollable, unpredictable, and unrepeatable. For this reason, even the faintest hints or signs of such energies and wonders are admissible as proof that such extraordinary powers are real and in operation. Thus, the worthy efforts to demonstrate the transcendental and spiritual nature of humans have devolved into settling for almost anything at all that could bolster the transcendental and count against scientific materialism, which is considered "the soul's enemy" (Humphrey 1999: 72).

There is an extensive literature that is claimed to provide "scientific evidence" for psi phenomena. For believers and parapsychologists, this is sufficient if not definitive proof of psi (Radin 1997, 2006; Tart 2009). However, these purported "scientific studies" suffer from numerous methodological defects. We cannot find even a single convincing case of a robust and replicable psi manifestation that would be considered adequate by the broader scientific community (French and Stone 2014: 271). Hence, quantity does not compensate for the absence of quality (Gilovich 1991: 157).

Controlled experiments have been conducted, but they do not meet the stringent standards that exist in mainstream sciences. As philosopher and physicist, the late Victor Stenger (2012: 242) pointed out, assertions about the discovery of positive effects of something miraculous are made based on findings involving such minimal statistical significance that a simple numerical fluctuation would yield the same result once every 20 times the experiment is repeated. What this suggests is that we are dealing with nothing more than a statistical artifact or quirk. In physics, a novel effect is not taken seriously unless it can be demonstrated that it would not be reproduced as a statistical artifact once in 10,000 cases (Stenger 2012: 242). As Stenger (2012: 242) put it, the fact that no psi claim has withstood scientific scrutiny compels us to conclude that such phenomena do not exist.

The rejoinder by proponents of paranormal beliefs is that the scientific community has imposed unreasonable standards of proof upon them and hence demand special dispensations. As an aside, the religionist Craig Keener (2011: 146) who has attempted to demonstrate that miracles are genuine supernatural events asserts the same thing (see Chapter 8). However, psi phenomena must be held to the highest standards because a single incontrovertible case of the unreal real would require the revision of the entire scientific worldview (French and Stone 2014: 270). Paranormal claims are extraordinary claims, and for this reason, they require extraordinary evidence. This is not an unreasonable stipulation.

The seekers of the transcendental do not see it this way. They are willing to accept evidence that under any other circumstances would set off alarm bells for fraud, perceptual illusion, or chance. It is for this reason that believers fall prey to charlatans and hoaxers all the time. As Humphrey (1999: 74) points out, there is a lot of evidence from many areas of life suggesting that humans are adept at fooling others and themselves. Yet, there is no evidence that the paranormal behaves this way. Or putting it another way, evidence for miraculous and ethereal powers is nonexistent, but proof that people cheat, lie, falsify results, delude themselves, and misperceive is overwhelming (French and Stone 2014: 154). David Hume (1902[1748]: 128) pointed this out long ago:

> the knavery and folly of men are such commonplace phenomena, that I should rather believe the most extraordinary events arise from their concurrence, than admit a single violation of the laws of nature.

For these reasons, the quest to reveal the spiritual and transcendental nature of humankind, the search for the soul and spirits, has not brought to light anything extraordinary, but instead it has uncovered an embarrassing, unremarkable, and perhaps unwanted fact, "human untrustworthiness," or the tendency of members of our species to lie and commit fraud (Humphrey 1999: 148).

What is also remarkable is that such negative findings have spectacularly failed to diminish the enthusiastic reception of paranormal and supernatural beliefs as numerous polls and surveys have shown. The tenacious way that proponents of the paranormal maintain their beliefs, despite disconfirmations and evidence of fraud, is nearly identical to how religious true believers uphold their views in the face of contradictory evidence and rational critique. As Alcock (2003: 48) observes, no evidence would convince psi believers that paranormal phenomena do not exist. Careful studies that have failed to replicate the psi hypothesis do not seem to accomplish this. Such findings are attributed to the experimenter effect, ignored, or more often taken as failure only in one particular instance where psi has not been found, rather than as disconfirmation of the hypothesis itself. Humphrey (1999: 153) sees this as a type of religious reaction or a kind of paranormal fundamentalism.

Of course, rather than arguing about the relevance of infinitesimal statistical values or methodological criteria, there is a straightforward real-life way believers can convince the skeptics of the reality of psi phenomena. For example, to reiterate, providing unequivocal evidence that psychics routinely win the lottery. Alternatively, presenting a solid case that telepaths hold positions of power and authority in society because of their psi abilities. Or evidence could be offered that psychics have changed the outcome of political elections. A single case of a faith healer regrowing an amputated limb would do the trick. Then again, believers could show that clairvoyants continually and correctly predict the stock market. Or they could provide examples of prophecies from the beyond that include new knowledge of the world that researchers can check against empirical data (Fishman and Boudry 2013: 929; Stenger 2008: 171). Paranormalists have had thousands of years to provide such proofs. To date, no such evidence has appeared. Yet, this is precisely the type of evidence one would expect if paranormal and supernatural forces and powers were actually operative in the world.

## Why Don't Paranormalists Accomplish Great Things?

Instead of accomplishing great things, we find psychics and paranormalists who presumably have tapped into the mysterious powers and energies of the transcendental world acting just like run-of-the-mill conjurers and stage magicians (Dennett 1999: xi). They can do what ordinary conjurers can do, but no more. Why? The answer is simple; they really do not possess any genuine powers (Dawkins 2001: 127–28).

All of this does not bode well for the psi researchers and true believers in the supernatural and the paranormal. As anomalous psychologists Christopher French and Anna Stone (2014: 268) sum it up, the history of parapsychology has been one of false starts. Despite enormous efforts, parapsychologists have failed to offer a single replicable demonstration of psi powers. Humphrey's (1999: 114) verdict is even more damning, observing that quest for the paranormal has been one big mistake. Centuries of effort has not yielded a single authenticated case of such powers. This, he adds, has been a disaster for parapsychology and indeed for the entire antimaterialist campaign and the quest to establish the spiritual nature of humankind (Humphrey 1999: 142).

Things look dismal indeed. However, none of this seems to matter. The faith of believers in the reality of psi powers remains steadfast as ever, and they are sure that there is "something" to all of this that close-minded scientists simply don't get. Thus, psi persists. So, what is that "something" that has lured so many to invest their intellectual resources, emotions, and, in some cases, their reputations and entire careers to find? There is no doubt that "something" is going on. The near universality of paranormal and supernatural beliefs attests to this fact. I cannot remember how many times I asked myself "again?" as I have encountered paranormal beliefs and practices among different groups of people in the course of my field research. But is this something otherworldly and transcendental as the faithful seem to think? Well, the evidence for that is almost nonexistent. So where does that leave us? The question to be asked is, If paranormal and supernatural phenomena are not manifestations of purposeful, mind-like forces and energies outside the spatiotemporal realm of the universe, as over two hundred years of negative scientific findings indicate, what are they and from where do they emanate?

For nearly thirty years, I have worked with shamans, mediums, mystics, various types of faith healers, and god-men. I have observed their magical feats and recorded episodes of spirit possession, exorcisms, the summoning of the spirits of the dead, and oracular witch-finding sessions. For most of this time, I was entirely open to considering all possibilities as explanations for such phenomena, meaning that I was operating on the assumption that there might be something extraordinary to all of this, or something more than people engaging in what is, in fact, *a kind of human behavior*. In many instances, while paranormal happenings were occurring, such as objects moving on an altar, or persons displaying paroxysms as spirits or gods entered their bodies, the magico-religious specialists with whom I was working were convinced and assured me that the spirits were all around and that mysterious powers were in full operation. Many times, I should have and expected to experience or at least detect a glimpse of something remarkable and extraordinary. However, I did not. I encountered nothing that could not be explained in non-paranormal terms, such as deceptive sleight of hand, perceptual illusions in dark rooms, hallucinations, expectations, suggestion, the effects of group dynamics on beliefs, and the confirmation bias.

Of course, such findings pose a problem for the anthropological fieldworker who has entered a research site to describe and document rather than debunk. I have avoided the latter as much as possible. However, it is also intellectually dishonest not to follow the evidence wherever it leads. The problematic epistemic status of paranormal and supernatural beliefs does not change, and such ideas do not become exempt from critical scrutiny and skepticism just because people in a particular culture dignify them. It is easy to overlook that paranormal experiences are a human phenomenon because people everywhere attach cosmic and mystical significance to them. The explanation for the paranormal is not in the unreal real—that track has led nowhere—but in humans themselves and their biopsychological and cognitive dispositions that make occasional paranormal experiences inevitable for some people across space and time (cf., Bridgstock 2009: 50).

This perspective finds support from research in clinical psychology and human behavior. Such findings suggest that the human perceptual apparatus while reliable most of the time has limitations and operates in a way that guarantees that we will have "ostensibly paranormal experiences" even if the paranormal did not exist (Alcock 1985: 538–39; French 2001b: 4). Such experiences are the cost of possessing the type of cognitive and information processing capacities conferred upon us by evolution that is capable of rapidly processing large amounts of data and yielding conclusions for action (Gilovich 1991: 2). These information processing capacities that involve perception, thinking, and memory are the basis of our evolutionary success as a species. Yet, these same capacities sometimes lead us to weird conclusions and delusional beliefs. Put differently, our evolved cognitive attributes can generate the impression that we have experienced events of a paranormal or supernatural nature that have not actually occurred or not occurred in the way we have perceived them (French and Stone 2014: 115; Schick and Vaughn 2014: 98).

If correct, these findings have tremendous implications in clarifying the true nature of supernatural and paranormal belief systems and the purported cosmic and metaphysical significance people attach to such beliefs that are at the core of all religions. Moreover, they help explain the weirdness and persistence of paranormal and supernatural experiences and ideas. Beliefs in the unreal real are of interest not because they point the way to some hidden miraculous spiritual truths but are significant from an anthropological perspective because of what they say about human cognition, experience, psychological needs, credulousness, and wishful thinking.

# Chapter Five

# GHOSTLY ENCOUNTERS IN THE FIELD: ANTHROPOLOGY OF THE PARANORMAL OR PARANORMAL ANTHROPOLOGY?

*Anthropology has taught us that the world is differently defined in different places. [...] the worlds of different people have different shapes. [...] space does not conform to Euclidean geometry, time does not form a continuous unidirectional flow, causation does not conform to Aristotelian logic, man is not differentiated from non-man or life from death, as in our world.*

—Walter Goldschmidt, foreword to Castaneda's *The Teachings of Don Juan* (1968)

*When [anecdotes] are the only source of data they cannot be used to reach extraordinary (or even ordinary) conclusions. The plural of anecdote is not "data."*

—Victor Stenger, *God and the Folly of Faith* (2012)

In contrast to anthropologists who subscribe to the hands-off approach to religious truths and paranormal beliefs, there are those who embrace the spiritual and paranormal suppositions of the people they study. This kind of anthropology developed around the personal anomalistic or weird experiences of several researchers while they were engaged in field research in cultures away from home. These types of events are nothing new or unique. What is new is how some researchers have interpreted such occurrences.

During my fieldwork in Nepal, the paranormal was always around. Nepalese shamans with whom I worked are practitioners who claim to have access to recondite, otherworldly knowledge and to possess the capacity to interact with and embody spirits, foretell the future, and divine the sources and causes of misfortune and illness. Paranormalists, psychics, clairvoyants, evangelical faith-healers, and other such practitioners in the West more or less say the same thing. Nepalese shamans can also purportedly communicate with ghosts, raise the souls of the dead in cremation grounds during late-night ceremonies, exorcise evil spirits, and summon demons at crossroads to harm enemies. There is also a remarkable parallel between the "alien abduction" narratives commonly reported in the United States and the supernatural kidnapping stories associated with the shamanic calling in Nepal (see Sidky 2008: 147–62).

In the Tibetan community in Northern India, I encountered individuals who claim to be the reincarnations of known deceased personages and say they can recall their past lives. Some Tibetan monks avow that they can levitate during meditative states and invited me to observe their remarkable abilities. Others say they can channel or physically incarnate specific Tibetan deities and engage them as oracles. The government of Tibet before the Chinese invasion in 1950 used such oracular knowledge as the basis of policy decisions. I call this "governance by soothsaying." The Tibetan government in exile in India, whose figurehead the Dalai Lama has attracted the admiration, adoration, and donations of Western celebrities, scholars, and political leaders, still relies on such oracular performances. While incarnated, the Tibetan gods communicate with government officials using a mystical language and reveal various truths and provide answers to specific questions (see Sidky 2011). This credulous arcane occultic practice may seem anachronistic but is reminiscent of Ronald and Nancy Reagan's reliance on psychic fortune-telling, daily horoscope readings, and astrology to guide their decision-making. Nancy Reagan also retained a full-time fortune-teller whose advice she used when making out her husband's day-to-day schedule. It seems that cultural boundaries or other considerations do not restrict supernaturalism and superstition.

The Sufi mystics I encountered in various parts of Central and South Asia possess auras of sanctity through which they can confer blessing and good fortune upon supplicants. They can also purportedly read peoples' thoughts and physically appear in two places at the same time. Sufi saints are revered in many countries, and their graves serve as pilgrimage sites.

I had a personal share of paranormal experiences as well, such as "the sensed presence," nocturnal entity experiences, seeing apparitions at graveyards and cremation grounds, and a close encounter with the primordial god of the shamans in the forest (Sidky 2017b: 43). The similarities between these experiences and claims by supernaturalists and paranormalists in the West are quite remarkable. The question one must ask is: Don't these cross-cultural parallels signify that there must be "something" to the paranormal and the supernatural? Before answering this question, it is necessary to discuss the perspective of other anthropologists on this matter.

## Anthropology and Paranormal Phenomena

In a chapter called "Parapsychology and Anthropology" in Benjamin Wolman's massive *Handbook of Parapsychology*, published in 1977, Robert Van de Castle, a professor of clinical psychology and ardent paranormal believer, urged anthropologists to be "humble" and embrace as genuine the paranormal phenomenon they encounter during fieldwork. Van de Castle cited anthropologist Walter Goldschmidt's foreword to Carlos Castaneda's book *The Teachings of Don Juan: A Yaqui Way of Knowledge* (1968) as an exemplar of the "kind of tolerance one might hope from anthropologists."

Castaneda was a Peruvian-born writer who earned his PhD in anthropology from the University of Californian, Los Angeles, in 1973. During the late 1960s and 1970s, he attained considerable fame and fortune from his books on shamanism, and some consider him to be one of the key figures in the New Age movement. In *The Teachings of Don Juan*, Castaneda weaves a tale of psychotropic adventures in alternate realities and magical worlds while apprenticing for an enigmatic Yaqui "sorcerer" or shaman named Don Juan. Castaneda vividly recounted visionary experiences and insights gained while he was under the influence of powerful hallucinogenic drugs, such as peyote and datura.

He described an alternate spaciotemporal reality infused with magic and miracles, where people can fly and operate free of the physical constraints and limitations of the ordinary world, and a place of endless possibilities and fantastic happenings (Sidky 2015: 36–37). Here is how he described one of his magic flights:

> My legs were rubbery and long, extremely long. I took another step. My knee joints felt springy, like a vaulting pole; they shook and vibrated and contracted elastically. I moved forward. The motion of my body was slow and shaky; it was more like a tremor forward and up. I looked down and saw Don Juan sitting below me, way below me. The momentum carried me forward one more step, which was even more elastic and longer than the preceding one. And from there I soared. I remember coming down once; then I pushed up with both feet, sprang backward, and glided on my back. I saw the dark sky above me, and the clouds going by me. I jerked my body so I could look down. I saw the dark mass of the mountains. My speed was extraordinary. My arms were fixed, folded against my sides. My head was the directional unit. If I kept it bent backward, I made vertical circles. I changed directions by turning my head to the side. I enjoyed such freedom and swiftness as I had never known before. The marvelous darkness gave me a feeling of sadness, of longing, perhaps. It was as if I had found the place where I belonged—the darkness of the night. I tried to look around, but all I sensed was that the night was serene, and yet it held so much power. (Castaneda 1968: 91)

Goldschmidt's (1968: xxi) foreword to Castaneda's book included the following remarks:

> Anthropology has taught us that the world is differently defined in different places. It is not only that people have different customs; it is not only that people believe in different gods and expect different post-mortem fates. It is rather that the worlds of different people have different shapes. The very metaphysical presuppositions differ: space does not conform to Euclidean geometry, time does not form a continuous unidirectional flow, causation does not conform to Aristotelian logic, man is not differentiated from non-man or life from death, as in our world.

Goldschmidt is offering nothing less than a full endorsement of the reality of the paranormal world, at least in "different places." His comments imply ontological relativism and are very puzzling because at that time anthropologists were still paying lip service to the epistemology of science and the principles of scientific research.

The depressing part of this affair is that Castaneda's work was a deliberate and systematic fraud. A few anthropologists had doubts, but they never took Castaneda to task on this matter. Instead, it was the journalist Richard de Mille (1976, 1990) who exposed Castaneda's imposture and plagiarism. It turns out that there never was a Don Juan, no apprenticeship, no magic flights, or any of the rest. Here is yet another example of how the desire for the paranormal to be genuine is so powerful that many, including professional anthropologists, are willing to accept the legitimacy of almost any claim, setting aside the critical faculties operational in other aspects of their lives. Such credulous reception of all things paranormal is the reason why there is an almost irresistible temptation on the part of unscrupulous mountebanks to take advantage of true believers by committing fraud. Hence, as noted in Chapter 4, the paranormal, dishonesty, and gullibility seem always to go together. Such was the case with the spiritualist movement that it was spawned by a hoax perpetrated by the mischievous Fox sisters during the nineteenth century as well as the entire history of the ensuing scientific study of ghosts, souls, and spirits leading to the development of parapsychology. Castaneda, who made a considerable amount of money from his books, is one such example of a charlatan peddling the paranormal to gullible audiences.

Van de Castle (1977: 667–68) went on to chastize other anthropologists for their "condescending" attitude toward the paranormal beliefs of local people and bemoaned the fact that more of these researchers have not embraced and incorporated the truths of parapsychology into their fieldwork. However, his concerns were entirely misplaced. A few anthropologists indeed reject the idea that paranormal beings have an ontological reality independent of the observer in a particular culture. In other words, they construe spirits and ghosts as being part of a given culture's consensual reality rather than being a part of a universal reality of all cultures (e.g., Murdock 1980: 54; Spiro 1982: 52). However, in American anthropology, beliefs in the paranormal are not the exception but the rule. Indeed, the same year Van de Castle's chapter was published, an ethnographer named Joseph K. Long published *Extrasensory Ecology: Parapsychology and Anthropology* (1977). Long (1977: vii, 248, 375, 384–85) vouched for the reality of "ghosts, astral projection, and poltergeists," the probability of levitation and the genuine nature of psychic surgery. Long also endorsed the authenticity of the fake psychokinetic tricks of Uri Geller, one of the biggest frauds and con artists of the time (Kurtz 1985: 209–17; Randi 1982b). As the scientific anthropologist James Lett (1997a: 117) has put it, this book is "perhaps one of the most regrettable examples of the irrational approach to the paranormal within cultural anthropology."

Margaret Mead, one of the icons of American anthropology, almost a revered mother goddess among the older generation, was another ardent advocate of paranormal beliefs (Lett 1997b: 67; Mead 1977: 48). She publicized her views on the subject in her talks and writings. She was also instrumental in gaining membership for the pseudoscientific Parapsychological Association into the American Association for the Advancement of Science (Lett 1997a: 113). Such a move on Mead's part was appalling. As the noted physicist John Wheeler (1979) remarked, giving parapsychology a place on the same platform as science only serves to dignify a "pathological" pseudoscientific enterprise (Gardner 1989: 185–92).

The regrettable credulities of Long and Mead are shared by many others who have since entered the field with a priori paranormal cultural beliefs of their own, including the late Bruce Grindal (1983), Edith Turner (1998), and Paul Stoller (1989), to name but a few. Their perspective entails "subjective-cognitive engagement" to attain knowledge impossible to acquire "through normal means of objective observation" (Hunter 2012: 37).

What paranormal anthropologists are espousing is "alternative ways of knowing" and "subjective truths," which is a coy way of justifying positions that lack rational and evidentiary warrant and to express beliefs presented as being exempt from all scientific challenges. The same impetus in the culture to which these anthropologists belong is behind the efforts of evangelical con artists, paranormal gurus, faith-healers, and various purveyors of other mystical bunkum. The stance has also empowered boorish politicians seeking exemption from accountability to audaciously espouse obscurantist nonsense that "facts and opinions are indistinguishable," that for every fact there is an equally valid "alternative fact," that truth is in the eye of the beholder and, best of all, that "truth is not truth." In other words, the anthropologists in question are relying on these very justifications for the nonsense they are peddling that has been a dominant theme associated with promoters of pseudoscientific beliefs in their culture (Sidky 2018).

## Paranormal Anthropology: Ghostly Encounters in the Field

To provide one example of anthropology in the service of supernaturalism and paranormalism, consider Stoller's work among Songhay people in Africa in his *In Sorcery's Shadow: A Memoir of Apprenticeship among the Songhay of Niger* (1989). This anthropologist proudly claims that he essentially adopted the entire range of Songhay superstitious beliefs. Among the various paranormal experiences he had, Stoller (1989: 148) recounts a frightening panic attack, which he describes as an entity encounter, and how the magical incantations he learned from the locals saved him from this supernatural assault. Stoller (1989: 229) describes what he took away from his field research experience as follows:

> As anthropologists, we must respect the people among whom we work. [...] For me, respect means accepting fully beliefs and phenomena which our system of knowledge often holds preposterous. I took my teachers seriously. They *knew* that I used divination in my personal life. They *knew* that I had eaten powders to protect myself. They *knew* that I wore objects to demonstrate my respect for the spirits. They *knew* I had an altar in my house over which I recited incantations.

Here, respecting, appreciating, and taking religion "seriously"—an aphorism that these anthropologists endlessly recite—as religious studies scholar Robert Segal (1983: 110) pointed out long ago, amounts to taking the stance of the devotee over that of the skeptic on metaphysical issues and entails an understanding of religion with endorsement, in short, something close to religious "conversion" (Wiebe 1984a: 158). This sort of cross-cultural gullibility and paranormalism among anthropologists is most regrettable.

Also, as discussed in Chapter 1, this sort of cultural conversion may sacrifice one's objectivity, but that does not mean that one has grasped the essence of a new cultural identity (Klausner 1994: 18). In the case of the new convert, these are not impressed upon a blank slate as in the experience of a child in that culture through the process of enculturation. Indeed, no one is so well-placed as to grasp the actual insider's perspective (Oppy 2018: 33), although he or she may claim that they have attained such a view.

The trend toward treating one's own paranormal experiences as ethnographic evidence continues (e.g., Glass-Coffin 2010; Koss-Chioino 2010). One example is the work of Henry Wesselman, who like Castaneda, also capitalizes on his credentials as a PhD in anthropology to gain the confidence of his audience. Here is yet another self-styled messiah-shaman aspirant. His claim to this lofty status is that he is the recipient of earth-shattering revelations through personal spiritual contact with a purported paranormal shamanic personage from the future. In his book, *Spiritwalker: Messages from the Future* (1996), and sequels with clichéd titles reminiscent of Castaneda's popular paperbacks, Wesselman reveals his mission to deliver humankind from its current terrible and hopeless predicaments.

Like other religious pretenders before him, Wesselman makes the same wearisome apocalyptic predictions about an imminent collapse of Western society that such messiahs have been articulating for over two thousand years, none of which has ever come true across space and time. As to be expected, this messiah also predicts the subsequent restoration of a better and more spiritually awakened society. It seems that there is hope for us after all. Such ideologues thrive by taking advantage of the human psychological and cognitive dispositions that under the right circumstances compel people to believe in all kinds of absurdities and fatuous fairy-tales. These same cognitive vulnerabilities have enabled bogus cults like Mormonism, Scientology, Peoples Temple, Branch Davidians, Order of the Solar Temple, Heaven's Gate and Aum Shinrikyô and movements such as spiritualism to attract followers.

## Extraordinary Anthropology and Paranthropology: Epistemological Quandaries

Several anthropologists who study the paranormal as described refer to their perspective as "extraordinary" or "experiential" anthropology or, more recently, "paranthropology" (Goulet and Miller 2007; Goulet and Young 1994; Hunter 2012). They use these labels to avoid "the negative connotation of paranormal [...] as irrational thinking and charlatanism" (Hunter 2012: 23). I prefer the label "paranormal anthropology" (see Sidky 2017b: 193–204).

The investigative agenda these researchers adopt is the study of paranormal phenomena in other cultures. The reason they focus on these so-called ancient, traditional, non-Western societies is the assumption that authentic psychic or "psi" phenomena only exist in such faraway places "outside of the Western conceptual bubble," where such phenomena are considered to be "normal." This is the same perspective espoused in 1957 by Joseph Bank Rhine, the chief architect of parapsychology, that "psi manifestations appear more prominent in 'primitive' non-scientific, pre-literate cultures" (Rhine and Pratt 1957: 109). In psi research some things, it appears, do not change. As the paranormalist Paul Devereux explains in a blurb on the cover of Jack Hunter's book *Par anthropology: Anthropological Approaches to the Paranormal* (2012), studying these faraway societies allows us to put "our repressed experiences of the paranormal into context" against the "whole testimony of humanity." It is as if finding more believers in the paranormal will somehow legitimize the beliefs in such things back home. But the notion that genuine paranormal phenomena only exist in non-Western cultures is sheer nonsense. What these researchers also overlook is that the epistemic status of egregious propositions and patently false assertions do not change just because this, that or many cultures dignify or attach cosmic significance to them.

The claim that "authentic" paranormal beliefs only exist in a few remaining strongholds in faraway non-Western societies is sheer nonsense. Various polls indicate that more than 50 percent of the people around the world, including the citizens of the United States, believe in the paranormal (Chapman University Survey of American Fears 2018; Irwin 2009: 1–2; Watt and Wiseman 2009: viii). Thus, the actual anthropological question should be, Why do lots of people in so many places hold such patently false beliefs?, not How do our distorted or suppressed paranormal beliefs compare to the genuine ones elsewhere?

Paranormal anthropologists describe their approach as "non-judgmental engagement" of other people's paranormal experiences (Hunter 2012: 38). They include their own psi experiences during field research as part of their data sets. Whatever "mystical truths" or "transpersonal insights" gained through these procedures are then used to bolster and validate the paranormal claims and convictions of fellow-believers back home. What this actually means is that we have professional scholars in American universities espousing superstitions (e.g., Hunter 2018).

Paranormal anthropology has the following features:

1. The anthropologist's own subjective experiences of ghosts and goblins are treated as data and incorporated into the ethnographic narrative along with a higher degree of gullibility than is usual among academics. Such subjective impressions are then offered as valid anthropological revelations regarding the reality of spirits and the spirit world.
2. The ghost beliefs of ghost-believing local people are used to establish the legitimacy, authenticity and veracity of the paranormal experiences. Paranormal anthropologists consider such ideas as authoritative because they are part of a "spiritual worldview" of non-Western cultures, something allegedly lost in the disenchanted West. The anthropologist thus becomes the true believing advocate for indigenous spirituality or, more accurately, the purveyor of the credulities of non-Western people.
3. This perspective entails the adoption of subjective and mystical approaches to knowledge because spiritual wisdom is thought to be beyond conventional empirical analysis.

Here the anthropologist is not merely suspending judgment, which is a corollary of the principle of cultural relativism (i.e., looking at beliefs and practices in their specific contexts), but rather suspending disbelief. The suspension of disbelief is a corollary of ontological relativism (i.e., accepting as real the construal of reality by members of the cultures under investigation). These writers reject cultural relativism because framing beliefs in spirits and other paranormal phenomena in this way, they claim, removes such precepts from "serious consideration" (Glass-Coffin and Kiiskeentum 2010: 113). Instead, they advocate taking such precepts "seriously"—whatever that means—and consider the role of the anthropologist to be the "first-person witness to the reality of the unseen world," that is, that spirits and the spirit world exist universally as mind-independent phenomena and are not just a part of the consensual reality of any given culture (Glass-Coffin and Kiiskeentum 2012: 125).

The volume edited by the aspiring anthropologist Jack Hunter called *Paranthropology* (2012), which is as scientifically lamentable as Long's *Extrasensory Ecology*, requires brief discussion (see also Hunter 2018). The book is dedicated to none other than Joseph Long. The foreword is by Van de Castle (2012: 15–19), who is still a psi true believer, convinced of the reality of out-of-body travel, and remains a faithful devotee and champion of Uri Geller, the despicable Israeli flimflam artist. In the introduction to this book, Hunter makes the same grandiose claims regarding the reality of psi phenomena and predictions about soon to come significant theoretical breakthroughs and paradigm shifts that parapsychologists have been making since at least the days of Joseph B. Rhine and his Zener cards. As Hunter puts it,

> If psi phenomena are real, as the evidence from parapsychological research and ethnographic accounts would appear to indicate, traditional anthropological theories of magico-religious beliefs and practices will, by necessity, require some very significant revisions.

These are egregious misrepresentations. Neither ethnographic findings nor over two hundred years of parapsychological research have produced anything close to support the existence of psi phenomena. Moreover, as discussed in Chapter 3, science has systematically and repeatedly investigated paranormal and supernatural claims and has not found any supporting evidence (Coyne 2015: 113; Fishman 2009: 831; Fishman and Boudry 2013: 924; Boudry et al. 2010: 227).

Hunter also heaps praises on Castaneda for his contributions to the field of paranormal anthropology, only casually acknowledging the "debate" concerning the authenticity of his work. Sadly, there is no debate; that research was a shameful fabrication. Hunter (2012: 35) goes on to revel in the "tantalizing glimpses of the underlying nature of reality, a world occupied by spiritual beings, non-physical intelligences and paranormal powers" made possible by paranormal anthropological research.

The premise that other people (i.e., non-Western folk) are enmeshed in a different reality based on separate "metaphysical presuppositions," where spirit and matter are not distinct, as Goldschmidt put it, entails the fallacious stereotype of the so-called magical or mystical other. The notion that "other" people do not or cannot distinguish between the real and unreal is not only grossly ethnocentric, naïve and racist but also factually incorrect. Nepalese shamans, for example, wholeheartedly believe in the reality of the spirit world, just as we believe in the reality of the physical or material world. However, I have never encountered anyone who could not tell the ordinary world apart from the spirit world. Nor was there a shortage of skeptics regarding shamanic powers and the existence of ghosts, goblins, witches and demons in the communities to which the shamans belong (Sidky et al. 2002: 158). The same is the case for all of the other societies where I have conducted fieldwork, from Rapa Nui (Easter Island) to Aboriginal communities in the Australian outback.

The unfortunate fact is that paranormalism and supernaturalism everywhere and in all cultures across space and time entail irrational thinking, gross superstitions, fraud and charlatanism. As Lett (1997a: 111) put it bluntly, every paranormal belief in every culture, regardless of whether their sponsors are shamans, priests, rabbis, mullahs or psychics, is demonstrably untrue.

Employing alternative ways of knowing and treating private subjective psychic experiences as data, as paranormal anthropologists advocate, opens us to accepting as veridical all sorts of imaginary things, such as "sensed entities," ghosts and fairies. These "alternative" procedures do not provide any means of differentiating between hallucinations, illusions or dreams. To dispense with objective methods for assessing such beliefs lands us in what the philosopher Herman Philipse (2014: 329–30) calls "the swamp of gullibilism."

As replicable empirical evidence has not been produced for any paranormal or supernatural phenomena anywhere and at any time, all that paranormal anthropologists have is an endless array of anecdotal accounts and subjective impressions of their psychic experiences. Such reports are X-claims and are hardly sufficient to support extraordinary claims regardless of how many such cases one brings to bear. As the philosopher and physicist Victor Stenger (2012: 235) put it, the plural of anecdote is not "data." In his essay on miracles, the philosopher David Hume (1902 [1748]: 128) also warned that accumulating lots of anecdotes does not amount to evidence for paranormal claims.

## From Paranormal Anthropology to Theistic Anthropology

Paranormal anthropology, as encompassed in the works of Edith Turner, Jean-Guy Goulet and Paul Stoller, has not only emboldened miracle mongers to dignify superstitions (e.g., Keener 2011: 220–27) but also served as the inspiration for the growth of "theistic anthropology" (Bielo 2015: 40–41). Its foundational premise is that "the anthropologist can affirm the ontological reality of religious worlds through their research" (Bielo 2015: 39). These writers set themselves apart from the others in the field whom they dismiss as positivists, agnostics and atheists merely engaged in "role-play."

The efforts of theistic anthropologists are as much at odds with the core epistemological principles of the discipline as are the efforts of their paranormalist counterparts. Like the latter, these writers also insist that they are exempt from scientific evidentiary standards and assessment because of the nature of the sublime truths and ontological realities with which they are concerned. As Bielo (2015: 39) states it explicitly, theistic anthropology "directly challenges some core social science tenets: to rely strictly on empirical data, to maintain a critical distance from what you are studying, to be skeptical of your one subjective experience." By eschewing these tenets, these writers feel that they have glorified and legitimized supernaturalism and superstition.

Theistic anthropologists are evangelical Christian academics. While their stated objective is the scholarly anthropological study of Christianity, these religionists are, in fact, trying to create a Christian anthropology, an enterprise for giving witness to the risen Lord. What else could affirming the ontological reality of religious worlds denote? As is the case with theistic Christian philosophers and polemicists, these so-called anthropologists are merely dignifying credulity as a method. This is an embarrassing development within the discipline of anthropology. The books and articles produced under the auspices of theistic anthropology, therefore, belong to the general genre of Christian apologetic literature and suffer from the same flaws as detailed in the upcoming chapters.

Paranormal and theistic anthropologists are comparable in that they both rely on alternative ways of knowing and private subjective insights—which is what they call "ethnography"—to prove the existence of imaginary worlds and unseen realities, phenomena for which there is no evidence anywhere across space and through time. They differ in that the first group is concerned with establishing the veracity of ghosts, spirits, goblins and mystical worlds, while the second group seeks to prove the truth of the gospels of Jesus Christ.

## What Do Paranormal Experiences in the Field Signify?

Now we may return to the question raised at the beginning of this chapter regarding the reality of the paranormal,which was, Does the cross-cultural recurrence of paranormal events signify that there is something to all this? The answer is yes; there is "something" here. However, as scrutinized in the following chapters, that something has nothing to do with nonphysical intelligences, mysterious spirit worlds, paranormal powers, soul energies or mind-independent supernatural realms.

Finally, what about my paranormal encounters in the field? These have entirely naturalistic explanations in terms of hypnagogic hallucinations, certain human cognitive predispositions and the effects of psychotropic drugs on the human mind. Also, Nepalese shamans do not actually venture into the land of the spirits or talk to ghosts. Such locales and entities are cultural assumptions, not mind-independent phenomena. Tibetan monks cannot levitate, although some can bounce pretty high off the ground while seated. This is what they call levitation! Tibetan mediums do not incarnate gods, and the deity messages are not veridical. Sufi mystics are not telepathic and do not simultaneously appear in different locations. Finally, the fact that some anthropologists have had psychic or paranormal experiences is not a novel or earth-shattering discovery of some ultimate and previously unknown mystical truth. Nor are ghostly encounters during fieldwork a sufficient basis for proclaiming significant theoretical breakthroughs or predicting paradigmatic shifts. At best, such experiences may contribute to a better understanding of why humans everywhere come to hold beliefs of this kind—anthropologists included—not that there is some significant underlying ontological validity for any of these views.

# Chapter Six

# WHY WE THINK THE WORLD IS HAUNTED

*All proceeds from the usual propensity of mankind towards the marvelous, and that, though this inclination may at intervals receive a check from sense and learning, it can never be thoroughly extirpated from human nature.*

—David Hume, *Enquiries Concerning the Human Understanding* (1748)

*It is as if there were in the human consciousness a sense of reality, a feeling of objective presence, a perception of what we may call "something there," more deep and more general than any of the special and particular "senses" by which the current psychology supposes existent in realities to be originally revealed.*

—William James, *The Varieties of Religious Experience* (1902)

*We impose order [on the world] even when there is no motive to do so. We do not "want" to see a man on the moon. We do not profit from the illusion. We just see it. [...] The predisposition to impose order can be so automatic and so unchecked that we often end up believing in the existence of phenomena that just aren't there.*

—Thomas Gilovich, *How We Know What Isn't so* (1991)

*The human information-processing system is such that we should expect ostensibly paranormal experiences to be frequently reported even if paranormal forces do not exist.*

—Christopher French, *Paranormal Perception* (2001)

*The ease with which we see faces, in particular, has led to the idea that we are inclined to see supernatural characters at the drop of a hat. Each year some bagel, muffin, burnt toast, potato chip, or even ultrasound of a fetus showing the face of some deity is paraded as evidence for divine miracles.*

—Bruce Hood *Supersense* (2009)

In this chapter, I begin my examination of the cognitive and psychological foundations of religious and paranormal beliefs. The main question addressed is, How and why do people think of such things? My anthropological investigations of religious specialists over many years that brought me into contact with a variety of paranormal and supernatural practitioners have led me to the conclusion that humans seem to have particular cognitive biases that naturally result in paranormal ideation. It is as if the misunderstood and mysterious workings of their own minds have mystified humans across space and time. If this conclusion is correct, then all beliefs about goblins, ghosts, gods, and spirits and all the assumptions and musings of philosophers and theologians contemplating the nature of God are actually attempts at making sense of particular fundamental features of how human minds operate and process information. Thus, understanding the paranormal and supernatural requires moving beyond the observation of rituals and recording what people say and do (the standard strategy anthropologists employ in fieldwork) and to focus upon the types of minds that generate such ideation. I am talking about the human mind.

## How Our Cognitive Biases Predispose Us to Paranormal Ideation

Research in evolutionary and experimental psychology during the last several decades shows that human cognitive and perceptual systems evolved to enhance survival rather than as mechanisms to accurately evaluate the actual condition of the world in an absolute sense (French and Stone 2014: 188). The human mind is actually a kind of "bag of tricks" cobbled together through the process of natural selection that made it heavily biased toward noticing things of greatest importance to our ancestors' reproductive success (Dennett 2006: 107, 120). For this reason, certain kinds of thoughts and ideas are remembered more easily than others through a process of mental rehearsals during which pertinent ideas are fixated upon and what is trivial is rejected after a single tryout. The cognitive psychologist Bruce Hood (2009: 9) calls these features "mind design," hinting at the way our brains have been evolutionarily configured to comprehend and interpret the world in a manner that makes some ideas evident and easy to grasp and others more difficult to apprehend and remember.

Our minds are always engaged in an automatic ongoing process of figuring out how the world operates. We do this by perpetually seeking patterns and causes and making inferences about them convinced that we draw our conclusions from objective evidence (Gilovich 1991: 30). This cognitive tendency to see order, pattern, and meaning in the world is so powerful that we cannot help ourselves from imposing regularity on randomness and seeing configurations where we have no compelling reasons to do so. Hence we see faces in the clouds, the man on the moon, and Jesus on toast (Smith 2010: 145). As the professor of psychology Thomas Gilovich (1991: 10) has put it, "we impose order even when there is no motive to do so. We do not "want" to see a man on the moon. We do not profit from the illusion. We just see it."

Thus, in part, the inherent pattern-seeking mechanisms of our brains that order or organize data powerfully impact how we perceive (Hood 2009: 65). Another factor impinging upon our perception is that when there are ambiguities in the data or where sensory stimuli are weak, our minds fill in the missing information using what we already know. A remarkable example of such a perceptual illusion or mental construction in the history of science was the claim by the Italian astronomer Giovanni Schiaparelli in 1877 that there was a vast network of furrows on the surface of the planet Mars. In 1908, the American astronomer Percival Lowell popularized this idea. Lowell translated Schiaparelli's word *canali*, which in Italian means grooves or channels, into the English word canals, a term that implies agency and design (Sagan 2006: 105). Lowell claimed that a network of waterways crisscrossed the surface of Mars. Ideas about the existence of a civilization on Mars were prevalent aspects of the popular culture and imagination of the day, as reflected in H. G. Wells's *The War of the Worlds* that was first serialized beginning in 1897, as well as many other stories about Martians and a civilization on the red planet.

Remarkably, Lowell was not alone in seeing the Martian canals. Others reported spotting these structures and named and mapped them. Lowell was even able to show similarities between his canal maps and those drawn independently by other observers. Of course, there are no canals or any surface features on the red planet that could be mistaken for such structures as shown by photos of the Martian surface taken by the spacecraft Mariner 9 and the many subsequent images obtained during other Mars missions. As the astronomer and astrophysicist Carl Sagan (2006: 106–7) observed, this illusion was due to a failure of the human hand–eye–brain combination under unclear observation scenarios.

What this case reveals is that when confronted with ambiguity or weak data streams, our brains adjust for and make sense of the inputs by falling back on what we already know and believe by filling in the gaps in the information (Gilovich 1991: 2; Hines 2003: 238–39). This is known as *top-down processing*. This makes us prone to render conclusions and posit causal connections on the basis of incomplete or unrepresentative information, such as deducing that the lights in the sky are alien spacecraft, or seeing a ghost or spirit in the shadows, or believing that we have had a prophetic dream (cf., Gilovich 1991: 30).

Thus, our evolved abilities to detect meaningful patterns, order, connectedness, and cause-and-effect relationships, which conferred enormous evolutionary advantages to our species to navigate the world effectively, come with a high price because at times it leads us to see patterns and meaningfulness when there are none (Gilovich 1991: 10). These cognitive biases have a direct bearing on paranormal and supernatural thinking. Hood (2009: 11) explains:

> The ease with which we see faces, in particular, has led to the idea that we are inclined to see supernatural characters at the drop of a hat. Each year some bagel, muffin, burnt toast, potato chip, or even ultrasound of a fetus showing the face of some deity is paraded as evidence for divine miracles.

The general tendency to make meaningful connections in random data or meaningless noise is called *apophenia*. Examples of this included perceiving patterns in randomly drawn lottery tickets, detecting hidden codes in holy books, positing conspiracy theories, and more (French and Stone 2014: 196). A wide range of ostensibly paranormal and pseudoscientific phenomena are attributable to these factors, including electronic voice phenomena (EVPs) involving ghost communication via tape recordings, backward masking (reverse-speech embedded with Satanic messages in rock music), and seeing Jesus's face on a corn tortilla.

A specific type of apophenia is called *pareidolia* that leads to the perception of shapes, like faces, in random stimuli. An enthralling example of this phenomenon is "the Face on Mars," in the Cydonia region of the planet photographed in 1976, where once again ambiguous data influenced by our prior knowledge and expectations have created a remarkable illusion of a human-like face on that distant planet. Here the prior knowledge was the idea that Mars once had a civilization that built canals as well as influences from science fiction novels and movies. These probably include Edgar Rice Burroughs's numerous popular books about Mars and John Carter published between 1912 and the

1940s, Orson Welles's infamous 1938 radio adaptation of H. G. Wells's novel, and, of course, a host of other films and publications. Since the identification of the Cydonia face, diligent enthusiasts peering over NASA photographs have discovered other such images on the Martian landscape, such as the "crowned face" and the "Nefertiti face" detected by the late astronomer Tom van Flandern (2002).

## Why We Think about Ghosts and Other Uncanny Entities: Intentional Agents and the Theory of Mind

In the randomness around us, we not only regularly discern human-like figures, but our peculiar cognitive biases also make us perceive agency behind events. Some evolutionary psychologists have argued that humans possess an "agency-detection" cognitive module. We are thus continually scanning the environment for possible signs of agency and agents. Such a mental capacity had considerable evolutionary significance. As anthropologist Scott Atran (2002: 60–61) has put it,

> Identifying animate beings as agents, with internal motivations, would allow our ancestors to anticipate goal-directed actions of predators, prey, friend, foe, and to profit from this in ways that enhance hominid survival and reproductive success.

Moreover, it is posited that this agency-detection module is hyperactive and hair-triggered and is prone to overdetection under ambiguous, uncertain, or scary conditions (Atran 2002: 78), that is, it generates false positives. Again, the advantage of this bias is that when we encounter ambiguous data, such as hearing sounds in the bushes, we are instantly able to infer an intelligent agent, such as an enemy or predator. If our inference is correct, we benefit immensely by being able to flee in time or take some other appropriate action and survive, while a mistake would cost us relatively little aside from an adrenaline rush and some sweat. The advantage of this "better safe than sorry" approach mostly outweighs its disadvantages (Schick and Vaughn 2014: 136). The trade-off here, however, is lots of false positives, or our susceptibility to detect agents where there are none, and is conducive to supernatural and paranormal interpretations of puzzling or scary events.

In the ancestral environment, possessing this hyperactive and easily tripped agency detector made evolutionary sense because the greatest threat of all was probably other humans and carnivorous beasts. Thus, being able to detect these threats and respond to them rapidly based on very slight information had immense survival value, enabling those who had this capacity to survive long enough to pass on their genes to the next generation. For this reason, the agency-detection mechanism became widespread among our kind (Schick and Vaughn 2014: 136). This capacity is not only extensive but also exists in children, leading some researchers to conclude that it is hard-wired into our brains (Schick and Vaughn 2014: 136).

This discussion is highly relevant for our inquiry because of the part played in paranormal ideation by our tendency to infer agents under puzzling, uncertain, or scary conditions. Such inferences contribute to beliefs in ghosts, spirits, gods, demons, angels, and the like. As discussed in my book *The Origins of Shamanism, Spirits Beliefs and Religiosity* (2017), our agency-detection system makes us prone to perceive agents in the most unlikely locations and is especially active in spooky or dangerous circumstances. On several occasions, while accompanying my Nepalese shaman friends to graveyards and forests late at night to observe them summon up souls of the dead or nature spirits, I began inferring agency at the faintest sounds and the slightest movement of leaves, all of which acquired sinister and threatening significance (Sidky 2017b: 101). Such experiences can be quite alarming and convincing as well.

It is not surprising that people are especially vigilant and scan for menacing agents under circumstances when they are under the threat of predators or pestilence (Whitehouse 2008: 34). This priming of the agency-detection system contributes to high levels of perceived encounters with sinister paranormal beings (Whitehouse 2008: 34–35). To put it in other words, our constant scanning for agents is the basis of our "proclivity for finding disembodied agents everywhere" (Barrett 2004: 31; Guthrie 2008: 243).

Since such inferred paranormal beings are incorporeal, their presence or absence may not be readily determined because, unlike people, they do not leave behind physical evidence of their existence. Ghosts, for example, do not leave behind footprints. Some researchers think that one reason the idea of supernatural beings has endured over space and time is that the existence of such entities cannot easily be disproven (Schick and Vaughn 2014: 137). Our constant preoccupation with paranormal beings, such as ghosts, gods, demons, extraterrestrial abductors, and so on, is due not only to the cognitive biases that predispose us to infer agency continually but also to find intentional agents everywhere.

Evolution, to put it another way, has provided us with a ghost and paranormal agent-generating minds and that is why we think we live in a world inhabited not just by humans and animals but also by incorporeal intentional beings (Sidky 2017b: 203–4). The species-wide delusion that the world is haunted by ghosts, demons, spirits, gods, or God is an evolutionary by-product of the human cognitive and perceptual apparatus. The proclivity toward such delusions is thus built-in or intrinsic to human brains. Sigmund Freud, in his book *The Future of an Illusion* (1927), described religious beliefs are unprovable "illusions" and "obsessional neurosis," but saw them as useful for some in addressing existential anxieties (Freud 1961: 21). However, the term "delusion" is more appropriate because supernatural/paranormal ideation has no evidentiary justification and has historically and across cultures come at enormous psychological and physical costs to humankind. The philosopher Stephen Law (2016) refers to these beliefs that stem from false positives generated by the human cognitive propensity to overdetect agents and related biases as "X-claims," to be discussed below.

## Why Spirits, Ghosts, and Gods Have Human-Like Minds

Humans relate to perceived paranormal agents in the same way they socially relate to other people using what is known as "the theory of mind" (Pinker 2006: 7). This concept refers to the human capacity to think about minds, or the ability to reason about what others are thinking, seeing, feeling, believing, and intending (Bering 2013: 22). MRI studies have shown that the location of the neural system committed to the theory of mind is the prefrontal cortex. According to the evolutionary psychologist Michael Tomasello (1999: 202), this capacity to understand the minds of others as intentional agents was a relatively recent evolutionary development among *Homo sapiens* that radically altered the nature of human social interactions.

The evolutionary psychologist Jesse Bering (2013: 33) points out that theory of mind is a part of our cognitive blueprint and a hallmark of the human species in the same way as language and bipedal locomotion. Theory of mind was an indispensable adaptation and was "foundational to social cognition and human life" (Guthrie 2007: 49). Evolutionarily speaking, individuals who could determine the "strategic interests of allies and enemies and to manipulate social relations accordingly," using theory of mind would have had a reproductive advantage (Whitehouse 2007: 220). This aptitude appeared with our capacity for language and, according to Bering (2013: 173) whose findings I shall discuss in detail below, was an evolutionary "game changer" (cf. Cosmides and Tooby 2000: 74).

Inferring intentionality, or taking "the intentional stance," is how our minds comprehend things moving around us in the world and guessing their motives and desires. The intentional stance flows from our theory of mind. Humans can, therefore, have thoughts about thoughts and even thoughts about thoughts about thoughts, or representations of representations (Barrett 2011: 75). Another term for this is meta-consciousness. This ability initially evolved to handle the problems of modeling other minds under increasingly more complex social settings during our evolutionary past (Cosmides and Tooby 2000: 105; Sperber 2000).

Moreover, the intentional stance also became the foundation for the development of religious thinking. As the religious specialist and cognitive scientist Todd Tremlin (2006: 103) has put it,

> This level of reflection takes place when you wonder what someone else is thinking or feeling, when you assess the source of your own thoughts or feelings, or when you attempt to evaluate the consequences of an action. The water-shed comes with third-order intentionality, which is what it takes to represent the contents of the mind of someone who does not actually exist. At increasing orders of intentionality, this ability deepens and the range of cognitive skills broadens. The uniquely human capacity for detached, creative thought, which includes the ability to conceive of imaginary beings and alternative worlds, stands behind literature, art, science, and, of course, religion.

Minds possessing this kind of higher-order intentionality belonged exclusively to modern humans (Stringer 2012: 116). Modern human minds can operate up to a fifth or even sixth level of intentionality; after that, test subjects in experimental settings seem to falter (Dunbar 2004: 45). In the words of evolutionary psychologist Robin Dunbar (2003: 117–18), everyday interpersonal interactions require three levels of intentionality and religious conceptualizations are possible beyond the fourth level. The evolution of this extraordinary cognitive attribute for inferring intentionality is linked to the development of the theory of mind (Tattersall 2012: 214).

We cannot help but automatically experience the world as containing not only animate human bodies but also rememberers, forgetters, thinkers, dupes, promise breakers, allies, and foes (Dennett 2006: 111–14). Adopting the intentional stance is so inherent that it is challenging to shut it down even when it is no longer appropriate. For example, when someone close to us dies, we continue taking the intentional stance toward them, although they are no longer physically present. In the same way that we cannot see thoughts radiating from brains, we cannot observe agentive properties terminate when someone dies (Pyysiäinen 2007: 57). Therefore, it is difficult for us to think that these processes stop when someone's bodily functions cease. Thus, instead of deleting the file containing their memory we transform them into virtual persons because of our intentional stance, and we continue to experience their presence as a ghost or spirit, conjured up by our troubled mind-sets as survivors (Dennett 2006: 112–13). Overactivation of the intentional stance thus yields perceptions of nonexistent bodiless or *virtual agent* ideas, which along with ghosts and spirits also include angels, demons, gods and goddesses, Osiris, Jupiter, Yahweh, Allah, Quetzalcoatl, and so forth.

Theory of mind and our ability to take the intentional stance coevolved with our linguistic capacity, and these abilities reinforced each other (Dunbar 2003: 117–18). In the process of using language, humans thought up and talked about otherwise elusive topics in the virtual world of the imagination populated by intentional virtual agents (Dennett 2006: 111–14). Thus, the imaginative by-product of our hyperactive tendency to infer agency, minds, and intentions was a proliferation of billions of agent ideas in the mental theaters of our ancestors. Some of these had qualities that made them memorable enough to be copied and passed on. They were "copy-me" memes, or non-genetic replicating coded pieces of information (see Chapter 1) that ultimately yielded the weird and fantastic entities that populate the mythologies of cultures around the planet (Dennett 2006: 123).

Dennett (2006: 123) postulates how some agent concepts were selected from the vast array of possibilities, elaborated upon, and incorporated into religious belief systems. Many imagined agent concepts would have been too obtuse, nonsensical, and not attention-grabbing enough to remain in our minds for very long. However, a few beat others in the gauntlet of mental rehearsals, vying for our attention, or rehearsal time in our brains, to remain, change, improve, and become more attention-grabbing over time and get passed on. These were the successful coded pieces of information with copy-me programs.

Hood (2009: 54–55) points out that ideas that caught on were the ones that fit our mind design. Heath and Heath (2007: 3–51) describe these as ideas the "stick" or are sticky. Agent ideas with supernatural or paranormal attributes that violate physical laws are central to all religions around the world (see Boyer 2001). The ideas that were passed on via oral transmission all seem to have such features. Their supernatural aspects make an impact when embedded in an ordinary storyline, thereby creating a "contrast effect." They make an impression on the recipients because they depart from expectations, that is, they contradict our intuitive ontological expectations about basic categories and seem miraculous. Another way of saying this is that they were weird and extraordinary.

Agent concepts that lack a substantial contrast effect are less appealing. However, such concepts are also less alluring if they have too many fantastic attributes. Paranormal agents that have only a single or limited number of violations of our intuitive ontological expectations seem more memorable than ones that are overly preposterous. Hence a statue that cries is more apt to make an impression and be treated as a believable paranormal phenomenon, or miracle, is remembered, and stories about it are transmitted to others, compared to one that simultaneously cries, bleeds, converses, flies, disappears and reappears, and plays poker.

Religious beliefs, therefore, emerged as part and parcel of our cognitive attributes that conferred an evolutionary advantage upon our ancestors by affecting how they acted in the world. According to the anthropologist Pascal Boyer (2001: 123), aspects of the theory of mind seem to have evolved "as a way of catching prey and avoiding predators more efficiently:" In the ancestral environment, individuals possessing these mental attributes could better deal with predators as well as the developing social complexity, larger group sizes, and the need to establish social alliances.

The extension of beliefs, desires, motives, and other mental states to the environment using our minds as models enabled humans to predict, control, and explain the unknown aspects of the social and natural worlds (Boyer 2001: 123; Hubbard 2002: 32). Our theory of mind thus not only became indispensable but completely flooded our evolved social brains so that we constantly overattribute mental states even to things that are mindless (Bering 2013: 37). As experimental psychologist Steven Pinker (2006: 7) points out concerning religious thinking, from our proclivity to attribute an invisible "mind to other bodies, it is a small step to imagine minds that can exist without bodies."

Here arises the notion of unanchored agency. Theory of mind thus renders the possibility of the existence of all sorts of other nonmaterial paranormal beings, such as ghosts of dead people, primordial ancestors, and deities (Whitehouse 2007: 220). A variant of the theory of mind is called the "existential theory of mind," which appears in association with the detection of signs of supernatural beings (Gray and Wegnewe 2010: 10). Our agency-detection capacity, the theory of mind, and existential theory of mind all seem to underpin our cognitive capacity for supernatural ideation (Tremlin 2006).

Nearly all supernatural and paranormal belief systems that exist include whole taxonomies of spirit beings of various shapes, varieties, and functions, covering an entire range from lowly nature spirits, to elves, fairies, unicorns, *jinn*, demons, devils, Lilith, Circe, Zeus, Jupiter, Tlaloc, Gaia, Artemis, Yahweh, and so forth. A perfect example of this from the context of my fieldwork is the cosmology associated with Nepalese shamanism, which is elaborate, highly complex, and profuse with various classes of supernatural entities (Sidky 2008: 115–34, 2017b: 135–52).

The perceptions of minds behind events in the world, or intuitions about spirits, souls, and deities, seem to have explanatory values connected to basic human psychological needs. These cognitive mechanisms underlie the intuitive feeling we tend to have that there is a consciousness higher than ours, somewhere out there, watching, listening, and acting. William James made a note of this sensation, although he did not have an explanation for it. In his words,

> But the whole array of our instances leads us to a conclusion something like this: It is as if there were in the human consciousness a sense of reality, a feeling of objective presence, a perception of what we may call "something there," more deep and more general than any of the special and particular "senses" by which the current psychology supposes existent in realities to be originally revealed. (James 1902: 58)

At times, we all seem to have this sensation of something out there, watching, lurking, and waiting. If this view is correct, then God who is an autonomous paranormal agent "out there," or a supermind, if you will, with thoughts and intentions, an entity believed to exist outside the human brain, may be merely a cognitive illusion generated by the overextension of our theory of mind. As Bering (2013: 38) points out, once we push aside theological embellishments attached to the notion of God found across cultures, we are left simply with just another mind. Supernaturalism and paranormalism arise from the attribution of mental states and psychological properties to various postulated entities: ghosts, souls, demons, devils, gods, and God. If these ideas are correct, then a point to consider here is that it is not God who has made humans in his own image, as some of the sacred texts claim, but it is humans who have made God in their image.

## Why the World Is Mind-Like, Souls Persist after Death, Animism, and Anthropomorphism

Another relevant aspect of the theory of mind is its linkage to animism (from the Latin *anima* or soul), which involves the attribution of sentience and goal-directedness (qualities of living things) to animals, plants, rocks, mountains, rivers, natural events, and even manufactured objects, such as computers, or automobiles (Guthrie 1993: 39–40). It flows from our tendency to "spontaneously and intuitively" extend or overattribute our theory of mind and the intentional stance to living objects and entities that have mental lives as well as nonliving entities or objects that do not have mental lives (Guthrie 2007: 49; Hood 2009: 120).

The nineteenth-century British anthropologist Edward Tylor used the concept of animism as a first principle that generates beliefs in paranormal beings. Tylor focused on logical inferential steps early humans might have taken to formulate the ideas of spirits and souls. He observed that early humans rationally inferred spirits (non-empirical agents) and souls (aspects of humans that survive after death) from an attempt to solve two categories of "biological problems:" (1) the difference between a living and a dead person; (2) why images appear in dreams and visions. For Tylor (1929: 110), the theory of souls served as the model for the development of "ideas of other souls of lower grade" and spirit beings in general from the tiniest elf to the idea of an "all-powerful Creator." In other words, once formulated, the concept of spirit beings was extended through extrapolation to cover a wide range of phenomena as a principle of causation or explanation for the experience. As he put it,

> It was no spontaneous fancy, but the reasonable inference that effects are due to causes, which led [early *Homo sapiens* to populate] with such ethereal phantoms their own homes and haunts, and the vast earth and sky and beyond. *Spirits are simply personified causes.* As men's ordinary life and actions were held to be caused by souls, so the happy or disastrous events which affect mankind, as well as the manifold physical operations of the outer-world, were accounted for as caused by soul-like beings, spirits whose essential similarity of origin is evident through all their wondrous variety of power and function. (Tylor 1929: 108–9)

Tylor thus proposed a kind of cognitive theory of religion, although at the time the findings of neuroscience and evolutionary and cognitive psychology were not available to lend substance to his ideas (Guthrie 2007: 51–52).

Animism is a way of comprehending or modeling the world by inferring unseen agency, purposeful forces and energies, and mysterious mechanisms at work behind events in the surrounding environment (see Guthrie 1997a, 1997b). In other words, animism is a nonscientific way of trying to figure out the complex underlying powers involved in earthly phenomena by using the human mind as a model (Hood 2009: 61). Such inferences used to make sense of the world also contributed to the rise of ideas about supernatural agents and forces (Guthrie 1997b). As Hood (2009: 24) has put it, "a mind designed for generating natural explanations also generated supernatural ones."

A particular case of animism is anthropomorphism, projecting not just sentience and goal-directedness, but using models of the self (as a symbol and language using entities with thoughts, motives, desires, and feelings) to nonhuman entities and events in the environment (Guthrie 1993: 39–40, 1997a). We, therefore, construe our surroundings as living and humanlike. The payoff of seeing the phenomena in question as living intentional agents is enormous if we are correct and the costs of being wrong relatively minor (Guthrie 2001: 99, 107).

In his book *The Natural History of Religion* (1757), the philosopher David Hume wrote about the pervasiveness of anthropomorphic thinking and linked it with conceptions of God or the gods. In many ways, Hume anticipated some of the ideas now being forwarded by cognitive and evolutionary psychologists regarding the workings of the human mind:

> There is a universal tendency amongst mankind to conceive all beings like themselves, and to transfer to every object those qualities with which they are familiarly acquainted, and of which they are intimately conscious. We find human faces in the moon, armies in the clouds; and by a natural propensity, if not corrected by experience and reflection, ascribe malice and good will to everything that hurts or pleases us. Hence [...] trees, mountains, and streams are personified, and the inanimate parts of nature acquire sentiment and passion. [...] [and] each grove or field is represented as possessed of a particular genius or invisible power, which inhabits or protects it. Nay, philosophers, cannot entirely exempt themselves from this natural frailty; but have oft ascribed to inanimate matter the horror of a vacuum, sympathies, antipathies, and other affections of human nature. The absurdity is not less, while we cast our eyes upwards; and transferring, as is too usual, human passions and infirmities to the deity, represent him as jealous and revengeful, capricious and partial, and, in short, a wicked and foolish man, in every respect but his superior power and authority. No wonder, then, that mankind,

> being placed in such an absolute ignorance of causes, and being at the same time so anxious concerning their future fortunes, should immediately acknowledge a dependence on invisible powers possessed of sentiment and intelligence. The *unknown causes*, which continually employ their thought, appearing always in the same aspect, are all apprehended to be of the same kind or species. Nor is it long before we ascribe to them thought, and reason, and passion, and sometimes even the limbs and figures of men, in order to bring them nearer to a resemblance with ourselves. (Hume 1889 [1757]: 11–12)

The anthropologist Stewart Guthrie in his book *Faces in the Clouds: A New Theory of Religion* (1993: 3) has offered a systematic cognitive and evolutionary theory of religion based on anthropomorphism. Guthrie's theory of anthropomorphism, first propounded in his article "A Cognitive Theory of Religion" (1980) and developed in subsequent publications (Guthrie 1997a, 1997b, 2001, 2007, 2008), offers a novel way of thinking about animism and anthropomorphism and was instrumental in inaugurating the cognitive approach to religion in anthropology.

## Why Humans Believe in the Soul and an Afterlife

Another aspect of the theory of mind that underlies paranormal and supernatural ideation is that it leads us to perceive ourselves and other people as entities with more than just flesh and blood bodies. The awareness of our own minds, or consciousness, as well as those of others strongly inclines us to think that the mind, which seems to exist inside us, is somehow distinct from our physical bodies which are "outside" us (Humphrey 1999: 192). This mind/body distinction arises from the fact that we, as individuals, experience our mental lives as operating independently of our bodies. Hence, we feel as if we are piloting a complex biomechanical chassis that is our physical body (Hood 2009: 121, 124, 128). A person has a thought about moving his or her hand, for example, and their hand moves. The psychologist Leonard Zusne (1985: 690) describes this phenomenon as follows:

> We are aware that the subjective self is quite different from our physical bodies or anything else in the visible, tangible world. There is the I, the mind, the soul even, and then there is the body and all the rest of the physical world, and they are different. [...] The illusion that the self-aware I is an entity separate and distinct from the physical body is an overwhelming and inescapable one. The ego and all its functions—perceptions, thoughts, dreams, images, memories, wishes, emotions—achieve such a degree of apparent autonomy that it may seem quite plausible to think that a wish or a thought should be able to lead an independent existence outside the brain.

In other words, we infer that we have both a material body and an immaterial essence or "soul" (Weisman 2015: 84). This is a pervasive X-claim. Here we have hit upon one of the foundational premises of religion and paranormalism. Such thinking led the French philosopher René Descartes to accept the postulate of dualism that the mind and body are qualitatively distinct from one another and that consciousness stems from nonmaterial spiritual forces, energies, and powers. Specifically, Descartes conceived human bodies as elaborate physiological/material machines fundamentally different from their minds, which he construed as intangible and immaterial in makeup. It was this line of reasoning that led him to generate the famous phrase *Cogito ergo sum*, "I think therefore I am." Descartes was in error, but his mental exercise reveals how powerfully intuitive it is for humans to perceive themselves not just as a body but as a thinking entity that occupies a material chassis of the body, like a pilot operating an airplane (Bloom 2004: 202).

In this view, the mind (consciousness) does not arise from the physical brain, but emanates from paranormal sources and is not explicable in material scientific terms. Today, philosophers refer to this as "substance dualism," the mind–body problem, or the problem of consciousness (Humphrey 1999: 195). The people that I have encountered in cultures as different as the Australian aborigines, the inhabitants of Rapa Nui, Tibetans, Nepalese, Afghans, and Indians are all dualists, as are most of the people around the world because of our shared cognitive biases. This belief, as Stewart-Williams (2015) observes, is a powerful meme across cultures.

In contrast to the dualistic perspective, the scientific view of this problem is that there is no mind–body split and that our brain generates our mind, or that consciousness emerges from the physical brain (Hood 2009: 133). We are, in other words, material beings, rather than supernatural ones, we do not "possess" or inhabit our bodies, we are our bodies (Bloom 2004: 202). Moreover, no one has found any scientific evidence that there is a soul that is linked to the body (Papineau 2015). Our mental life is entirely dependent on the brain without which mental life cannot exist (Augustine and Fishman 2015: 203–4, 227). The subjective impression that our minds can survive death is a "psychological illusion" among the living (Bering 2013: 130; Augustine 2015). A powerful indicator that our mental life is a product of our physical brain is the fact that consciousness is alterable if the brain is damaged, probed, stimulated, or drugged (Bloom 2004: 225; Hood 2009: 125). As Gennaro and Fishman (2015: 112–22) point out, the argument from brain damage, which demonstrates the dependence of consciousness on the brain, or what is termed "the dependency thesis," disconfirms the life after death hypothesis.

However, despite what science reveals, people everywhere are natural dualists or natural Cartesians, and dualism dominates their thinking. Thus, when we are in the sad situation of watching someone die, it seems as if something has just left our presence. This impression of the departure of an essence, life force, or "something" makes intuitive sense because of our dualistic bias (Hood 2009: 152).

Parapsychologists and other proponents of paranormalism stake everything on the supposition that the mind and body are distinct. As the paranormalist Charles Tart (2009: 195–96) maintains,

> there's the data from a hundred years of scientific parapsychological research, using the best kind of scientific methodology, that shows us we can't simply dismiss the idea that the mind is something more than just material body.

Unfortunately, like nearly every other claims made by such writers, Tart's assertions are a gross exaggeration. The research he mentions consists mostly of a collection of lots of anecdotal accounts, and to quote Stenger (2012: 235) once again, "the plural of anecdote is not 'data.'" Moreover, the scientific methodology employed by parapsychologists he describes is, in fact, the worst kind there is and not the best, as discussed in Chapter 4.

The proclivity for dualism also exists in children, and some researchers argue that the idea that the mind (consciousness, spirit, soul) is separable from the physical body is an innate cognitive design feature (Bloom 2004: 149). Our dualism is at the basis of the near-universal idea found in nearly every religion that there is life after death and the belief that we can transcend the demise of our physical chassis and continue to live on in some other place or realm and even come back in a new body.

Indeed, humans have constructed elaborate theologies around this meme, each culture providing its particular details as to how disembodied spirits behave, whether or not they interact with the living, and their final destination (Zusne 1985: 690). One of the main foundations of Christianity is the survival-after-death meme, which was the most effective proselytizing tool exploited by the Apostle Paul while he spread his supernaturalism among non-Jewish communities beyond Palestine. Many other religions have also capitalized on the promise of life following death as a powerful recruitment tool. The idea of the spirit separate from the body is also the fundamental premise in shamanistic traditions and has probably been around for millennia, or for as long as the existence of the modern human mind that appeared 200,000 years ago or even earlier (Sidky 2017b).

Dualism explains why the idea of a soul distinct from the body, and the possibility of its persistence beyond death, has such a grip upon the human imagination. It makes intuitive sense and provides psychological assurance that our inner selves or minds are associated with an immaterial soul that can survive the demise of our physical bodies (Bloom 2004: 226; Zusne 1985: 690). It is the power of the afterlife meme and the associated promise of heavenly rewards that compel some young Muslim men and women, with encouragement from pious enablers working on behalf of their merciful and compassionate God, to happily and willingly take their own lives and those of others in grotesque acts such as suicide bombings and other forms of deliberate martyrdom.

The problem that all humans face, of course, is that it is impossible to know what it is like on "the other side," or what it is like to be dead. There have been no genuine communications from the beyond to offer any clues, not from mediums, spirit channeler, oracles, mother-goddesses, mystics, prophets, messiahs, shamans, or any other paranormal practitioners. Present-day pretended spirit communicators who offer bogus messages from the beyond are capitalizing on the psychological vulnerabilities, existential anxieties, and wishful thinking of their desperate clients. The same is true of hallucinatory phenomena referred to as near-death experiences (NDEs), to be discussed in Chapter 9.

We postulate that there is life after death because we have never experienced being dead or being without any sensations and consciousness. We, therefore, cannot conceptualize our psychological nonexistence. All we have to work with to solve the puzzle or mystery of what happens after our demise is what we already know when we are alive, which leads to the illusion that our mind continues as it is in life even after our passing and is hence immortal (Bering 2013: 114–17). Beliefs about life after death entail "psychological-continuity reasoning" and also involve the operation of the theory of mind. Our illusion-generating theory of mind not only allows us to conceptualize the minds of the dead or dearly departed who no longer have bodies but also our minds without bodies (Bering 2013: 123).

Afterlife beliefs, as noted, are found across cultures and throughout time. The discovery of ancient burials with associated grave goods, taken as indicators of afterlife beliefs, dates back to at least the Upper Paleolithic (Pettitt 2011; Sidky 2017b: 109–11). All cultures have developed distinct mortuary practices guided by and reflecting dualistic reasoning aimed not only at the disposal of the corpse but also to ensure the spirit or soul of the deceased reaches its posited intended destination. Among the Jirels of eastern Nepal, where I conducted fieldwork, funeral rites begin with the disposition of the body through cremation. However, the spirit of the deceased is believed to linger afterward for 40 days. At the end of that period, the spirit is ritually summoned by the surviving family members to enter the body of a living relative and relate whether the funeral arrangments were satisfactory and for the departed to relay his or her final wishes and thoughts. The spirit speaks through the possessed person and conveys its feelings and last desires. If pleased, it will then depart to the realm of the dead. Ensuring that the spirit of the deceased is happy and will, therefore, leave in peace is very important to the Jirels because an unsatisfied soul may continue to linger on and become a hungry ghost feeding off the energy of the living and cause sickness and all sorts of mischief. If the spirit expresses unhappiness, other rituals are necessary to rectify the situation and placate the ghost (Sidky 2008: 118–34; Sidky et al. 2002: 114–29).

Construing the mind as separate from the body seems to be the "intuitive default" of our theory of mind. From it flows an entire range of related concepts and presuppositions, such as an everlasting incorporeal mind not limited by physical laws, gravity, time, and space (Hood 2009: 133; Zusne 1985: 690). Humphrey (1999: 196) concurs with a point made at the start of this chapter that paranormal beliefs arise from our puzzlement about our own mental life and its association with our physical being. Without an obvious mechanism linking the mind to the brain (Descartes erroneously identified this linking mechanism as the pineal gland), the influence of the mind to make the body move and engage in complex actions seems magical and paranormal. Thus, we have a ready-made exemplar of the concept of "mind over matter" that is the model for other types of paranormal events (Humphrey 1999: 196, 216). Thus telepathy, clairvoyance, telekinesis, the idea of life after death, communication with the dead, and just about everything else paranormal all become possibilities (Humphrey 1999: 191).

To summarize our discussion so far, a complex set of interrelated cognitive biases give rise to and bolster supernatural and paranormal ideation, including beliefs in the existence of transcendental realities, and the illusion of God. These cognitive design features include the agency-detection mechanism, theory of mind, dualistic thinking, teleo-functional reasoning, our sense of paranormally ordained destiny, conviction about the immortality of the soul, the perception of meaning and intentional design in natural events and processes, and the proclivity to link misfortunes to moral breaches or the action of supernatural intentional agents.

## Responses to Naturalistic Cognitive Explanations of Religion by Theistic Philosophers

Scientific explanations for religious beliefs based on the findings of cognitive, experimental, and evolutionary psychology strongly suggest that religion is a natural phenomenon, the outcome of evolutionary processes and mental attributes (Guthrie 2008, 2001). Evolved human cognitive proclivities explain why people have supernatural beliefs and why such ideas are nearly ubiquitous across space and time. Whatever version of the various theories of religion on offer is considered, that is, cooperative adaptationist, non-adaptationist spandrel, or memetic pathogen (see Chapter 1), the implications are that humans have supernatural beliefs irrespective of whether there is a God, gods, or transcendental realms, as mind-independent realities (Guthrie 1997b). A further implication of such findings is that they challenge the rationality of those who hold supernatural beliefs (cf., Bloom 2009: 124) because such ideas do not have an accurate relationship to the object of belief.

Confronted with the possibility that evolutionary theory has explained God away, religious polemicists and theistic philosophers, as to be expected, have attempted to harmonize theism, specifically Christian beliefs, with these findings and provide rejoinders by asserting that religious beliefs are justified regardless of what the scientific evidence indicates. Once we weed out the strawman and *ad hominem* arguments, religionist responses to the challenge by cognitive evolutionary research are nearly identical.

The cognitive psychologist and believing Christian, Justin Barrett (2009: 96–97) maintains that explaining how a belief came about says nothing about whether that belief is justified in the same way that the scientific understanding of the workings of the human visual system does not raise doubts about the existence of a visible world out there. Barrett is a person of faith, and his theistic orientation skews his perspective on this matter. The problem with his assertions is, of course, that vision entails empirical phenomena that may be checked to determine if our eyes are deceiving us (see Chapter 9), while beliefs about spirits, ghosts, gods, or God refer to the unreal real, they are X-claims, meaning non-empirical realities with no possibilities of validation in the same way as tangible, visible objects in our surroundings. Similarly, the theistic philosopher Peter van Inwagen (2009: 133) asserts that the fact that there are psychological mechanisms that "cause" supernatural beliefs does not mean that those beliefs are irrational. Theistic philosopher Michael Murray (2009: 169) also avers that the origins of supernatural beliefs in mental tools or cognitive modules have no bearing on the justification of those beliefs.

From this point in their religionist diatribe onward, Barrett and like-minded theists descend further and further into supernaturalism and Christian superstitions. Such a plunge occurs when they aver that since Christian theology teaches that God created humans so that they may "enjoy a relationship with Him," therefore, the cognitive proclivities that generate beliefs in God are part of the divine design. In other words, God "instantiated" this world to bring about people capable of a loving relationship with Him and he supernaturally guided natural selection to bring about humans with the kind of minds that can apprehend God (Barrett 2009: 96). Religionists like Barrett and his associates think that they have thus addressed the dilemma posed by science. Their argument, however, is grossly defective.

Their answer, to state it in different words, is, "God did it!" Along the same lines, Van Inwagen (2009: 137) argues that a naturalistic explanation is not "all the explanation" and that the findings of cognitive and evolutionary psychology are subsumable into a "comprehensive supernaturalistic explanation of the phenomena." What is this comprehensive explanation? His answer is, "Our omniscient Creator chose the evolutionary accidents," and they were "part of the Creator's plan." Taliaferro (2009: 208) also asserts that everything in the cosmos is ultimately caused by God, who intentionally sustains a "good world."

In other words, we are back again to an omni-explanation. Plantinga (2009: 148), who is considered by some theists to be "the greatest Christian philosopher alive," does no better (see Chapter 3). He forwards the same tired argument that the evolved cognitive modules suggested by evolutionary psychologists as the basis for religious beliefs were, in fact, designed by God "with the objective of enabling us to see the truth and the great things of the Gospel" [gospels?]. The theistic philosopher Michael Murray (2009: 178) says pretty much the same thing: "God configured evolutionary history to make belief in the supernatural reality easy or natural for us." So, again, the answer is something like, "It was the Lord's doing!"

Barrett realizes that the evolved human cognitive proclivities account only for belief in supernatural agents but not a conception of the Christian God. To deal with this problem, he predictably appeals to the archaic myths and superstitions contained in the Bible. These beliefs include the idea of the fall of "mankind," sin (something that is *never* absent from Christian discourse), paradise lost, the truth of the Scriptures, the veridicality of divine revelations, the reality of miracles, and, of course, Jesus as God incarnate and the actuality of the resurrection. I will address the flaws in these ideas in more detail later in this chapter when discussing Plantinga's idea of a god-sensor, or *sensus divinitatus*. For now, I shall explore Barrett's assertions more closely. In his words,

> A perfectly adequate concept of God does come as part of our biological heritage but […] living in a sinful, fallen world this concept grows corrupt as we grow. […] the diversity of god concepts we see is a consequence of human error and not divine design. The biblical story of Adam and Eve suggests a similar account. (Barrett 2009: 97–98)

These statements require some comments. The idea that polytheistic beliefs, that is, "a diversity of god concepts," are degenerate forms of an earlier belief in the one true God is refuted by overwhelming anthropological, historical, and archaeological evidence. Religionists have been trying to push this bogus claim as a legitimate historical fact since at least the nineteenth century. For example, in his twelve-volume study *Der Ursprung der Gottesidee* (*The Origin of the Idea of God*) published 1926–55, father Wilhelm Schmidt of the failed German diffusionist (*kulturkreise*) school of ethnology argued that the humans initially believed in a single Supreme God, but that this idea subsequently degenerated into pantheons of deities (Sidky 2004: 102).

Based on the premise that other religious beliefs degenerated from a postulated true monotheistic one, Barrett (2009: 98–99) adds,

> God has equipped people with the prerequisite cognitive equipment to have an opportunity to have an appropriate relationship with God. Clearly, this relationship has been disrupted [...] But God has not given up on the relationship. Rather, God has revealed Himself in a variety of ways to trigger these cognitive capacities to suspect superhuman agency. [...] Further, he used scriptural and other forms of revelation to clarify this confusion [...] Then, ultimately, He became human in the person of Jesus of Nazareth [...] Perhaps one of the motivations for God to reveal Himself in the form of a human is that an anthropomorphic form is one that our fallen cognition could conceive.

In his book, *Why Would Anyone Believe in God* (2004), Barrett adds the sin of *scientism* to the list of evils that have contributed to the assault on the belief in a perfect God concept, ending on the note that since belief in God comes naturally, atheists are human aberrations in a world full of good believers (Barrett 2004: 118). This is sheer bunkum because if the world were full of good people, we would not have the kind of conditions we have today where poverty, violence, suffering, oppression, inequality, and injustice are rampant.

As for the scientism canard, we might recall from Chapter 3 that this refers to the disingenuous view that nature and material forces and processes constituted the whole of reality and science has all the truths in an absolute sense of the term. This assertion is a variant of how religionists construe methodological naturalism. It is understandable when true believing religionists such as Plantinga appeal to Christian supernaturalism to support claims about Jesus and God. For a purported scientist such as Barrett to do so is very unfortunate indeed. In later chapters, I shall discuss the problematic nature of revelatory knowledge, the implausibility of sacred texts as messages from the supernatural, and the questionable nature of the stories about Jesus and his purported return from the grave. All of these superstitious beliefs collapse under the skeptical scrutiny of science.

While most of the rejoinders to naturalistic explanations of religion discussed thus far are merely instances of special pleading, Murray raises some specific objections to the findings of evolutionary psychology that require comments. As noted, in his mind, cognitive explanations only indicate that humans possess particular mental proclivities that under certain conditions produce supernatural agent beliefs. Such explanations say nothing as to whether those beliefs are justified (Murray 2009: 169). However, he overlooks the fact that whether or not supernatural beliefs are or are not justified is an empirical question that is ascertainable by evaluating the evidence. Theistic special pleading and sophistry will not do.

Murray begins his diatribe by questioning the role of the hyperactive agent-detection mechanism in generating supernatural agent beliefs. When this mechanism is triggered, such as when one hears footsteps in the upstairs bedroom, the sounds may produce an agent belief, but other cognitive tools are activated to assess the reliability of that conclusion, such as one going upstairs, looking, and finding that it was a family member who had returned home earlier than expected. Murray points out that the agent-detecting mechanism is often reliable in helping us identify the presence of a human, animal, or moving object. So how does this mechanism generate false positives, he asks, as suggested in the case of supernatural beliefs? In other words, what leads to the generation of a false positive that one has detected a nonexistent supernatural agent? Murray (2009: 171) is doubtful about the context under which the agent-detecting mechanism results in supernatural ideation.

The point Murray misses is that supernatural agent concepts arise in instances of false positives that the activation of other cognitive tools *cannot* resolve. In the example given here, someone hears footsteps upstairs; the perception generates an agent concept in his/her mind, the person goes and looks, but finds no one. The situation now becomes puzzling and somewhat frightening because it suggests that some intentional agent is present in their house, but they cannot be observed. It is under such circumstances that supernatural interpretations arise, especially under stressful or scary situations and when factors such as low lighting or other conditions impede clear sensory perceptions, as in the example of my nocturnal experience with Nepalese shamans in the forests and graveyards.

Murray then raises the issue of justification to address the assertion that religious beliefs are unjustified because they do not have an accurate relationship to the object of belief, that is, that they are false positives. Here Murray talks about two types of justification that philosophers refer to as *truth by correspondence* and *truth by coherence* (he calls these internalist and externalist perspectives). Truth by correspondence depends on whether a proposition relates to the "way the world is," that is, whether it corresponds to empirical data, or is "true of the world" (Williams 2001: 32, 139). The premise here is that humans live in a world and universe that exists independently of the thoughts and beliefs they have about them and that *these external circumstances comprise the condition of knowledge* (Sidky 2004: 18, 27, 398). The scientific enterprise is based upon the premise of truth by correspondence.

Truth by coherence refers to self-contained sets of beliefs that are mutually consistent and support and reinforce one another. All religious ideologies fall into this category (Sidky 2004: 18). This type of truth, as the anthropologist Frederick Bailey (1991: xviii) puts it, "is a matter of convention," something that people decide is true, a premise that is unconstrained by empirical reality.

Murray enters into very precarious epistemological territory by asserting that beliefs based upon truth by coherence are warranted if there is a *source* that generates those beliefs. From this, he concludes that Christian beliefs, which have God as their source, are entirely justified, regardless of what cognitive science suggests because such beliefs could not arise if there were no God (the source generating the beliefs). This, of course, is a paranormal assertion that entails the a priori acceptance of God's existence. The argument amounts to the claim that if there is a God, then religious beliefs are justified. Religious polemicists use this tiresome argument repeatedly. For example, the religionist Craig Keener (2011) uses it in an effort to demonstrate the authenticity of New Testament miracles (see Chapter 8).

Murray attempts to establish God's existence by appealing to the standard religionist arguments for the existence of such an entity, all of which philosophers have resoundingly defeated (see Everitt 2004; Martin 1990; Nielsen 2001: 20; Philipse 2014; Schriven 1966: 109; also see Chapters 3 and 11). For Murray, there simply would be no world, people, believers, cognitive scientists, or universe without God (Murray 2009: 175). Murray thus offers an omni-explanation that God is the cause of all things, including why humans have supernatural beliefs. He then tries to shift the burden of proof on to the scientist to prove him wrong. In other words, prove that God does not exist!

There are several difficulties here. First, contrary to what Murray thinks, the burden of proof always rests on those who make extraordinary claims (see Chapters 3 and 8). Second, it is correct that science cannot disprove the existence of God or even beings such as Circe, Zeus, and Santa Claus. In science, no hypothesis can be definitively disproven because new evidence may come to light that will conflict with current explanations (Fishman 2009: 818). Hence religionists often raise this challenge. However, whether God's existence cannot be proven or disproven does not confer existence or nonexistence equal epistemic status. Just because something is logically possible, such as the existence of an invisible superhuman supernatural entity like the theistic God or Santa Claus, does not mean that their existence is probable. Thus, the issue is not whether the existence of God is disprovable, but whether it is probable (Dawkins 2006: 54). This subject is examined at length in Chapter 3, and only a brief discussion will be offered here. We can determine if a paranormal being such as God exists by looking at the observational earthly consequences of the claim according to the following criteria: (1) prior probabilities for it; (2) the presence or absence of evidence for the claim; (3) the existence of plausible alternative explanations that accord with empirical data (Fishman 2007: 816). We can thus assign a hypothesis a place on a range of probabilities going from uncertain, to a 50-50 agnosticism, to complete skepticism (Fishman 2007: 818). The argument from evil, the argument from nonbelief, and the argument from improbability all suggest that the theistic deity is highly improbable (Dawkins 2006; Drange 1998; Everitt 2004; Martin 1990). Thus, Murray's challenge for science to disprove the existence of God does not help his case.

Convinced that his argument is sound, however, Murray goes on to address the question of parsimony, that is, the scientific assertion that a naturalistic explanation is superior to the supernatural one proposed due to its simplicity. This is true, he notes, if all other things are equal. However, in the case at hand, Murray maintains, all other things are not equal. He argues that the criterion for selecting a hypothesis is how well it coheres with our background knowledge. For him, God coheres exceptionally well with his background knowledge, which makes the God hypothesis a superior choice. What Murray has in mind specifically is Christian background knowledge discussed in Chapter 3 (Plantinga 2009: 149, 159). Therefore, he argues, because God exists, religious beliefs are justified. But this argument is possible only if one has accepted the existence of God beforehand based on special pleading rather than any evidence. His flagrant epistemological blunder is placing Christian background beliefs, which are agreed-upon beliefs (truth by coherence) with no empirical evidentiary support, on equal footing with the background knowledge used in science that is anchored upon empirically grounded a posteriori conclusions that are true of the world (truth by correspondence) (Fishman and Boudry 2013: 926–27). These two types of beliefs do not have epistemic parity.

To summarize, apologist objections to the naturalistic scientific explanations of religion are that without God there would be no universe, humans, cognitions, theists, or religions, and so forth (Murray 2009: 175). Plantinga (2011: 303) takes this argument one step further and affirms that God created the universe with regularities and predictable patterns to be mathematically describable and to obey laws in a manner that humans can grasp them (Plantinga 2011: 277, 286). In other words, God has designed the universe in such a way for inductive reasoning to be successful and for empirical science to be a possibility. Furthermore, he says, it is only feasible for scientists to detect patterns and regularities in the natural world because God programmed human cognitive abilities to be able to do so in the first place (Plantinga 2011: 296, 301). Religionists thus assume that they have covered the necessary grounds in favor of supernaturalism.

The problem is that if God designed physical reality with these properties, as Plantinga says, then why is there so much ambiguity as to compel creationists to look for signs of supernatural design in the most recondite places, such as the structure of molecules? Also, if reality is devised in this way, why do creationists resort to clever-talk in the form of meaningless and incomprehensible mathematical proofs to make a case? Such design features, if Plantinga is correct, should be so self-evident as to leave the most entrenched and recalcitrant disbeliever mute in astonishment—but they are not (see Chapter 11). The obscurity of supernatural design explains why religionists resort to barrages of special pleading and why there is a massive body of philosophical refutations of the design argument and all the rest for the existence of God.

Moreover, if what these apologists say is the case, then why is doing science so arduous? Why are humans so powerfully prone to the confirmation bias and other perceptual distortions if God created the world to be unambiguously comprehensible to humans? Think about the example of N-rays covered in Chapter 3. Also, if science is part of God's design, then why are theists like Plantinga and evangelical Christians in general so perturbed by scientific findings that refute theism? Perhaps, if we adhere to Plantinga's line of reasoning, it is part of God's plans for scientists to conceive of the theory of evolution to explain life on earth as well as develop naturalistic explanations for religious thought that disconfirm what appears in the Bible and other books of supernaturalism and to silence theologians.

As to the fit between human cognitive capacities and the world that makes science possible, this is not a matter of magical endowment conferred by an invisible Sumerian superman in the sky (or wherever theists now posit His residence to be); these capacities were not always there in the form found among modern humans. They are the outcome of millions of years of evolutionary development—early hominids did not possess our cognitive abilities (Sidky 2017b: 105–16). Along with our genes, social and cultural adaptive forces over a very long time had much to do with shaping our cognitive capacities, which explains the differences in the cognitive abilities between *Homo sapiens* and earlier *hominins*. There is no supernatural mystery that there is a fit between our cognitive capacities and the world and universe in which we live—they are the consequences of our evolutionary development (cf., Oppy 2018: 71).

Nor is "God explains everything" or "the Lord did it" a novel premise. Religionists have often forwarded claims of this kind, such as the panentheistic stance that God is an intricate part of every aspect of physical reality. There is also the doctrine of *occasional causation*, a version of which holds that God is the cause of every feature of the world and universe down to the most inconsequential events (Fishman and Boudry 2013: 941). Occasional causation is a flawed and antiquated proposition that David Hume put to rest in his book *Enquiries Concerning the Human Understanding* (1748):

> They pretend that those objects which are commonly denominated as *causes*, are nothing but *occasions*; and that the true and direct principle of every effect is not any power or force in nature, but a volition of the Supreme Being, who wills that such particular objects should forever be conjoined with each other. [...] Thus, according to these philosophies, everything is full of God. [...] nothing exists but by his will, that nothing possesses any power but by his concession. (Hume 1902 [1748]: 70)

One of Hume's objections was

> this theory of the universal energy and operation of the Supreme Being is too bold ever to carry conviction with it to a man sufficiently apprised of the weakness of human reason, and the narrow limits to which it is confined in all its operations. [...] there must arise strong suspicion, if not absolute assurance, that it has carried us quite beyond the reach of our faculties, when it leads to conclusions so extraordinary, and so remote from common life and experience. We are got into fairy land. (Hume 1902 [1748]: 72)

Hume is saying that such knowledge of God's actions is beyond the capacity of human reason because: (1) we know nothing about the mechanisms used by this supernatural entity; (2) it is inconsistent with what is evident from nature; (3) this line of reasoning leads us to a mental fantasyland. Theistic philosophers, however, have no problems revealing the mysterious workings, thoughts, and intentions of the Supreme Being, something that they alone seem able to fathom but which is beyond the reasoning power and common sense of the majority of ordinary humans. Most of what they say, of course, is speculation, nonsense, incoherent, and meaningless.

Reiterating ideas discussed in Chapter 3, there are multiple epistemological flaws in an all-encompassing "God did it" hypothesis offered to account for everything. First, as the philosopher of science Martin Mahner (2012: 1450) points out, such a statement "explains nothing because it explains too much." If any proposed mechanisms for the workings of the world, including the existence of cognitive proclivities for supernatural ideation, and even science, can be accounted for by saying God willed it so, all further inquiry comes to a halt, leaving us in the dark. Thus, such "an explanation that explains everything explains nothing" (Mahner 2012: 1451). Indeed, it could be said that this is one of the most specious arguments religionist have devised. Of course, the termination of knowledge-building may not present a problem for religionists because, as the philosopher Kelly Smith (2001: 723) has pointed out in the context of his discussion of design-creationism, these ideologues are unconcerned about furthering human knowledge. However, this matters a great deal for those who are interested in how physical reality works and the importance of human understanding and the advancement of knowledge.

Second, using God as a causal explanation overly complicates things, as previously noted, because such an entity is an intentional agent, who sees, comprehends, makes plans, has knowledge of everything down to the subatomic level, and has a complex mind capable of designing things as complex as His own mind. Instead of being a simple entity, as theistic philosophers erroneously claim, God is the most complex type of entity conceivable and hence is highly improbable (Fishman and Boudry 2013: 941).

Third, omni-explanatory propositions are unsatisfactory because the principles and mechanisms of the supernatural are unknown. Explaining one unknown phenomenon by appealing to something that is even more unknown, in this case, the theistic God's operations, entails the logical fallacy of *ignotum per ignotius* (explaining an unknown by an even greater unknown). In other words, such an explanation substitutes one mystery with another mystery (Fishman and Boudry 2013: 941). Looking at arcane, self-contradictory and factually flawed religious texts rife with superstitious credulities and grotesque absurdities for clues about the Lord's mechanisms does not solve this epistemological conundrum. Appealing to supernatural revelations or religious experiences as a source of such information is equally problematic because these events are thoroughly unreliable and lack independent confirmation (see Chapter 9). Thus, an omni-explanation is not even a pseudo-explanation because, as Mahner (2012: 1452) puts it, "it is tantamount to saying that we do not know how a certain fact works or has come about."

Finally, theists contend that postulating supernatural entities is comparable to the postulation of unobservable theoretical entities in science (e.g., Roughgarden 2006a, 2006b). In other words, science itself is a faith-based religious ideology, an idea already addressed in Chapter 3. Such a proposition is fallacious because theoretical entities in science are assigned definitive properties. In contrast, as Mahner (2012: 1452) points out, while the term "God" may be meaningful in a local sense and to specific groups of believers, the properties of this supernatural being are variable and arbitrary among theologians, between religious traditions, and even from one believer to the next. Indeed, variance over the exact meaning of God is the reason why votaries belonging to one religion, sect, and cult and the other have for millennia been gleefully killing votaries of other religions under the labels of apostates, heretics, and atheists.

God is not a legitimate theoretical entity because even if we settle on a definition that does not vary indiscriminately, the "God did it" explanation is still arbitrary because other supernatural beings, such as aliens, demons, angels, a confederation of subpar divinities, a time-traveling scientist, or the Devil can fulfill the same explanatory task. There are no objective empirical procedures for deciding among these rival supernatural possibilities. Moreover, we are in the dark about the powers, capabilities, and intentions of such beings (Mahner 2012: 1453). In other words, the mechanisms of the supernatural are unknown to us. All that one can propose is that supernatural being X did Y for *some unknown reason*. Such a proposition, however, is no better than stating that we have no clue about the cause of X (Mahner 2012: 1453).

In contrast, science posits the existence of non-observable or theoretical entities in accordance with other firmly corroborated scientific postulates, not merely because they are logical possibilities or simply through pure guesswork or out of thin air. Hence, the supernatural beings postulated in religion are not analogous of the theoretical entities postulated in science. For these reasons, supernatural propositions are scientifically useless. From this discussion, it is clear that the religionist rebuttals to the cognitive scientific explanation that demystifies religious beliefs fail decisively.

## Is There a *Sensus Divinitatus* or God-Module in the Human Brain?

One last question needs to be asked regarding the implications of the cognitive perspective discussed in this chapter: Can we conclude from our discussion that there is a religion- or god-module in the human brain? Can this god-module be the reason why humans across space and time have sets of beliefs and behaviors that could be labeled religious? The answer is no. Religion is the outcome of cognitive attributes working together but evolutionarily selected for other reasons. This is not the same thing as a "God-module" or "God spot" that some experimental neuroscientists claim to have discovered in the temporal lobe regions of the human brain. They link these locations to subjective paranormal experiences, such as seeing apparitions, sense of entity presence, and mystical experiences (see Alper 2008; Cook and Persinger 1997; Fenwick 2001; Persinger 1993). While it is possible to generate mystical experiences through the manipulation of the brain, the idea of a "God-module" is controversial (Holt et al. 2012: 132–33). Religious polemicists and apologists have nevertheless seized upon this idea as a way of justifying their supernaturalism and superstitions.

In his book *Warranted Christian Beliefs* (2000), Plantinga suggests that there is a god-sensor, or *sensus divinitatus*, implanted into the human brain to enable people to know that God exists and requires worship without needing evidentiary justification for such beliefs (Plantinga 2000: 214, 259). A brief digression into theistic discourse is necessary to address this assertion. As we shall see, not only is this claim baseless but it also illustrates the mental contortions believing theologians engage in to make their superstitious claims appear plausible.

First, as Philipse (2014: 38) points out, if such a radar or antenna for detecting God did exist, then everyone who lives or has ever lived would believe in the Christian God. Adam and Eve would, therefore, be monotheists and Christians. The problem is, of course, that the earliest known religions were polytheistic and monotheism did not appear until late in human history, during the time of the Pharaoh Akhenaten, circa 1350 bce (see Hoffmeier 2015: 211–65). To address this discrepancy, Plantinga resorts to the doctrine of original sin. That transgression, the burden of which Christians say all of humankind must bear, occurred when a talking conspiratorial snake that the all-powerful God created, but could not control, deceived the child-like Eve, the first woman, into fooling the naïve Adam into eating an apple. In other words, in this theological fantasy, it is women who are culpable for the sins of "mankind." This act, the so-called original sin, Plantinga says, caused the god-sensor to malfunction, and hence humanity lapsed into polytheism and disbelief (Plantinga 2000: 205).

Positing a malfunctioning god-sensor, however, raises another problem. If the sensor is inoperative, then how are we to explain the presence of 2.1 billion Christians in the world? To address this quandary, Plantinga is forced to rely on the Jesus myth, arguing that some people were "saved" because God appeared on earth in the flesh, sacrificed himself to atone for the sins of humanity, died, and came back to life. In other words, the incarnation, crucifixion, and resurrection of Jesus was God's solution to the problem of a malfunctioning god radar (Plantinga 2000: 241, 246). Moreover, to inform humans about this solution and the path to salvation, God inspired the men who wrote the gospels, so God is the ultimate author of the New Testament (Philipse 2014: 40).

Several points require comment here. First, why does God need books? Second, if the omniscient Creator of the universe directly inspired these texts, then why do they contain a profusion of factual errors, contradictions, and sheer absurdities? What a book written by the omniscient and omnipotent Architect of the universe might look like is described in Chapter 10. The Bible or any of the other sacred tomes on offer do not fit the provided criteria. Also, does not the fact that there are multiple versions of these purported "inerrant" sacred texts and the history of the haphazard way they were selected, edited, and compiled in the forms available today through committee votes based on political fiat suggest that they were the handiwork of humans rather than God? Is this a minor theological point?

Also, why did God need to go through all this trouble of having himself nailed to a cross, wait three days, rise from the grave with no eyewitnesses, briefly appear to a handful of dubious characters in ghostly manifestations, and is then never seen again? Why didn't the omnipotent Creator repair the malfunctioning god-sensor remotely by magic? Aren't God's miracles boundless and his powers limitless? Such a deific fix would undoubtedly have saved all parties needless grief and avoided the many ugly religious wars between votaries of different faiths that have marred the pages of human history and continue unabated.

All of this aside, Plantinga's explanation for why there are Christians in the world today is that God sacrificed himself to save a select few from his own wrath, repairing the god-sensor in their brains. It follows that the god-sensors of all the unredeemed non-Christians (and the majority of scientists), who still bear the blame for a purported sin committed by fictional characters plagiarized from Sumerian mythology, remain inoperative. Hence the reason why there are believers in other gods (i.e., false ones from the Christian perspective) and non-believers (atheists) is that these unfortunates are suffering from a mental defect. What an astonishing claim! Instead, could it be that it is Mr. Plantinga's cognitive powers that are incapacitated by the brain virus of theism discussed in Chapter 1? How else can one explain why a cognitively normal person would forward the kind of fanciful argument described here that verges on the absurd?

The implausibilities that underlie Plantinga's proposition are numerous. First, consider the likelihood of the claim that an immortal paranormal being, the Creator of all that exists, visited an insignificant remote corner of an inconsequential planet to show solidarity with a small group of dubious humans for their suffering due to conditions that he himself created. Second, this omnipotent being could only do this by going through a paranormal charade during which, temporarily disguised as a man, he suffered, died, was magically resurrected, and retired to heaven from where he comfortably rules while human suffering continues unabated (Philipse 2014: 177). In other words, God went through a fake death to save an "elect" few from "his own unseemingly vengeance" (Bradley 2015: 25). Finally, if this is how God conveyed the message that death and suffering are defeated, as the Christian apologist Swinburne (2003: 1) adds to this line of reasoning, then why are we surrounded with human torment, misery, and death? For such arguments to have any credence religionists must first prove that the theistic God exists, that Jesus was that being in the flesh, and that a resurrection did, in fact, take place. As discussed in Chapters 12, 14, and 15, efforts by theistic philosophers and theologians to do this have been abysmal failures. Hence, we can only conclude that a god-sensor is a fallacious idea. Arguments offered in support of this notion are perhaps among the best pieces of evidence that sterile medieval scholastic thinking is still alive and well today and is being peddled by the paragons of religious apologetics.

## Implications: Supernaturalism Debunked

Cognitive, evolutionary psychology and the neurosciences have now demonstrated that the cognitive dispositions discussed in this chapter make people highly prone to accepting intuitively appealing false positives due to our innate pattern-finding pareidolia, meaning-detecting apophenia, hyperactive agent sensor, teleological reasoning, and inclination toward anthropomorphism (cf., Ambasciano 2018: xvi). Indeed, historical and anthropological evidence shows that such concepts easily hijack the human cognitive apparatus. To state it differently, humans are psychologically highly vulnerable to false beliefs about extraordinary human-like invisible intentional agents and paranormal forces. Long ago, David Hume (1902 [1748]: 119) perceptively called attention to this, pointing out "the strong propensity" of humankind to "the extraordinary and the marvelous." As already noted, the philosopher Stephen Law (2016) refers to such beliefs about counterintuitive superhuman agents, miraculous and paranormal actions, extraordinary events, magical healings, and holy relics as "X-claims." Humans evoke such ideas to explain what they cannot otherwise explain, and such notions form the core of many religions, including mainstream ones (Law 2016: 16, 23).

Hume (1902 [1748]: 119) made the further observation that these beliefs themselves "ought reasonably to beget a suspicion against all relations of this kind." Along the same lines, Law adds that X-claims are always justified by appeal to *testimony* and *subjective experience* and are systematically unreliable. He adds that "we are highly prone to false positive X-claims when they are grounded just in [testimony and subjective experience], and this provides us with a rationality defeater for such beliefs" (Law 2016: 32). The implications of this observation are momentous concerning religion. Put simply, the cognitive and neurosciences and evolutionary psychology have essentially demystified or debunked the extraordinary and miraculous underpinnings of the perception, diffusion, and receptions of all such ideas (Ambasciano 2018: xi).

# Chapter Seven

# COGNITIVE BIASES AND WHY PEOPLE THINK EERIE THOUGHTS

*It is the peculiar and perpetual error of the human intellect to be more moved and excited by affirmatives than by negatives; whereas it ought properly to hold itself indifferently disposed toward both alike.*

—Francis Bacon, *Novum Organum* (1620)

*When men wish to construct or support a theory, how they torture facts into their service!*

—Charles Mackay, *Memoirs of Extraordinary Popular Delusions and the Madness of Crowds* (1842)

*The influence of belief, on hypothesis, on perception is so striking that one might almost say, not seeing is believing, but that believing is seeing.*

—Reuben Abel, *Man Is the Measure* (1976)

*Anecdotes are unreliable for various reasons. Stories are prone to contamination by beliefs, later experiences, feedback, selective attention to details, and so on. Most stories get distorted in the telling and retelling. Events get exaggerated. Time sequences get confused. Details get muddled.*

—Robert Caroll, *Skepdic* (2007)

*Our memory of an event can be drastically changed if we later encounter new information about the event—even if the information is brief, subtle, and dead wrong.*

—Theodore Schick and Lewis Vaughn, *How to Think about Weird Things* (2014)

There is a close linkage between memory, thought patterns, human perception, and why we believe we have had supernatural and paranormal experiences and encounters. Some scholars have suggested that cognitive biases that distort perception and memory are at the foundation of many paranormal beliefs (Goode 2012: 296).

## Memory, Cognition, and Supernatural and Paranormal Ideation

One such set of cognitive biases are "quick and dirty rules of thumb" called heuristics (see Kahneman 2011: 97–195). These allow us to rapidly sift through messy, random, and ambiguous data and arrive at workable solutions. There are several such rules. The "representative heuristics" permit us to recognize patterns and categorize data by assessing the similarities between objects and events according to some common striking attribute. Thus, when trying to determine cause-and-effect relationships, we use such guidelines as "like goes with like" or "big events must have big causes." Another set of rules is known as the "availability heuristics" and entail the tendency to use past examples or events that come to mind immediately to render judgments in a current situation, such as using a recently viewed paranormal television show to explain an anomalous event one has encountered (French and Stone 2014: 126).

Heuristics usually work because categories that go together often do share a resemblance, effects typically resemble causes, and past experiences can solve problems in the present (Gilovich 1991: 18). Heuristics do not produce the best solutions but ones that are fast and adequate and hence this ability conferred an adaptive advantage to our ancestors by enabling rapid decision-making in the face of ambiguous information or data streams (Kahneman 2011: 98; Schick and Vaughn 2014: 132).

We encounter problems and slide into erroneous thinking using these rules when dealing with inaccurate, incomplete, or irrelevant information. For example, many Americans consider the Kennedy assassination as a "big event," and hence it seems implausible that an unimportant and obscure gunman could have been its cause. Instead, a grand political conspiracy is posited because of the bias that big events must have big causes (Goode 2012: 298). Similarly, the destruction of the Twin Towers on 9/11 was too big an event to have been caused by a small group of crazy Arab terrorists who got lucky, so higher forces, such as the US government and the Israeli Secret Service, must have been involved.

The representative heuristic can lead us astray when we make incorrect associations—for example, associating star signs with particular personality traits that are the basis of astrology. It is the same with beliefs about homeopathic or contagious magic, which operates on the premise that two things that have been in contact with one another are paranormally linked when apart. Thus, the view is that an article of clothing worn by a person can be used to cause him or her harm by subjecting the cloth to magical procedures. The availability heuristic, that is, using past experiences to solve problems in the present, can also lead to erroneous thinking because it can result in hasty conclusions and overgeneralizations (Smith 2010: 122).

Another relevant phenomenon is the way our minds and prior beliefs influence how we perceive. As the philosopher Reuben Abel (1976: 39) put it years ago, "the influence of belief, on hypothesis, on perception is so striking that one might almost say, not seeing is believing, but that believing is seeing." Research in human psychology and cognition during the last several decades has shown that human perception is constructive in nature (Smith 2010: 142). This factor has a significant bearing on supernatural and paranormal claims and experiences. As the professor of neurology Terence Hines (2003: 238) points out, perception entails not only sensory stimuli "but also what we know and believe about the world, even if that knowledge and beliefs are wrong." These factor in heavily when sensory inputs are weak or ambiguous.

Research has also revealed that memory, not just perception, is created inside our heads, being influenced by sensory data inputs as well as our prior knowledge and expectations (Schick and Vaughn 2014: 99). When recalling an event, we merely remember bits and pieces of information, never a total picture, and our minds fill in the gaps and missing details, embellishes, connects the dots, and even hallucinates nonexistent filler information (Smith 2010: 145, 170). The result is a constructed recollection that is partly based on facts and partly upon inconsequential data and imaginary details. The idea that our memory is like a video recorder accurately registering everything out there is, therefore, a significant misconception (Beyerstein 2007: 321).

In other words, memory is influenced not just by actual sensory input data (called *bottom-up processing*) but also by what we already know and expect (called *top-down processing*) (French and Stone 2014: 138). In circumstances when sensory inputs are weak, our prior knowledge and beliefs fill in what is missing, resulting in the perception of things that are not there or events that never happened. This aspect of the human cognitive and perceptual apparatus becomes particularly relevant when we evaluate eyewitness accounts and anecdotal reports of unusual or paranormal events and happenings in which misidentification, the constructive nature of memory and perception, and our susceptibility to X-claims factor in heavily. These include such things as seeing the Loch Ness monster, Bigfoot sightings that are now a national phenomenon, UFO reports, the Roswell incident, seeing ghosts and apparitions, encountering poltergeists, alien abductions, and the descriptions of various religious miracles, such as Marian apparitions, and the post-resurrection appearances of Jesus (cf., Hines 2003: 238, 412).

## What the Roswell UFO Crash Tells Us about Paranormal Ideation

The Roswell incident is of particular interest here. The episode centered upon a report on June 14, 1947 by a ranch foreman named "Mac" Brazel that he had discovered debris from a strange flying vehicle. The material was found 80 miles from the town of Roswell, New Mexico. What Brazel stumbled upon were parts of a crashed secret Project Mogul spy balloon employed by the US military to monitor atomic explosions inside the Soviet Union in those days of Cold War paranoia (Thomas 1997a). There is nothing extraordinary or weird about the recovered fragments contra claims by UFO enthusiasts. Descriptions of the retrieved material (pieces of a six-sided balloon-hoisted radar reflector) are an exact match to what we now know about the materials used in constructing the Mogul balloons (Emery 1997: 95; Goode 2012: 196; Ziegler 1997: 8–9).

Brazel did not bring the debris to anyone's attention until early July, probably on the seventh of the month. By that time one of the pivotal events that launched the modern myth of UFOs in the United States had taken place—the report on June 24, 1947 by a pilot named Kenneth Arnold about witnessing crescent-shaped objects that looked like "saucers" skipping across the surface of water in the skies over Mount Rainier, in Washington State (Thompson 1991: 1–10). News agencies quickly transformed this into a major story about the sighting of "flying saucers" from outer space (Sidky 2015: 111).

Brazel likely brought his find to the attention of the local sheriff after hearing about Arnold's flying saucers. For help, the puzzled sheriff contacted the intelligence officer of the Roswell Army Airfield, one Major Jesse Marcel. Marcel who thought an alien spacecraft might be involved (probably also because of the Mt. Rainier flying saucer story), went to the alleged crash sight, along with another officer, collected some of the material, and returned to the base. On July 8, the airfield provided a press release that the military had recovered fragments of a "flying disk." The headline of the local newspaper the *Roswell Daily Record* that carried this announcement stated that the US military had captured a "Flying Saucer." The sensational report quickly spread across the nation (Sidky 2015: 112–13).

Some of the debris was then flown to the Fort Worth Army Airfield in Texas. At this time the seven now-famous Roswell photographs were taken showing Brigadier General Ramey and Colonel Thomas Dubose examining the debris, including two images of Marcel and the balloon parts. The remainder of the evidence was shipped for evaluation to Wright Patterson Air Force Base, in Dayton, Ohio, which makes perfect sense because no one at the Roswell Army Airfield was familiar with the Mogul project and the debris would have seemed puzzling. At that time, there were several conjectures about the nature of the debris, including a possible secret US or even a Soviet military aircraft. The idea that the wreckage was from an extraterrestrial spacecraft was not in the forefront.

At a news conference held that evening at the Fort Worth Army Airfield, the officials dismissed the UFO story and described the debris found at Roswell a part of an ordinary high-altitude "weather balloon." Interest in the story quickly faded it, and the entire incident was more or less forgotten for several decades, but the two conflicting military communications sowed the seeds of a vast conspiracy theory.

In the late 1970s, two paranormal researchers, Charles Berlitz and William Moore, resuscitated the Roswell incident. One of the key informants they interviewed was the then aging Marcel, who was now convinced that the wreckage he obtained came from an extraterrestrial spacecraft. The two writers presented this material in their book *The Roswell Incident* (1980). The role of memory and recall is highly significant here. What these writers offered was a story pieced together from the recollections of an elderly gentleman about events more than 30 years earlier. To do this, they ignored a range of problems. For example, they accepted the accuracy of Marcel's account of the extraterrestrial materials even though he was unable to recount the exact year of the event, the fact that he had personally appeared in two rather than a single photograph, and that all the photos show the same debris (Goode 2012: 194). Berlitz and Moore embellished their tale further by appending anecdotal accounts of the retrieval of multiple alien bodies at another purported crash site located 150 miles away from where the Roswell debris had been recovered in 1947. The source of this information was a second- or third-hand account of a claim by a man who had died in 1969 (Goode 2012: 195). This tale was no doubt highly contaminated by the well-developed folk tradition of extraterrestrial humanoid visitations that had developed since the Kenneth Arnold event hit the news media, along with the appearance of various UFO religions with messages from wise angel-like beings remarkably reminiscent of themes portrayed in the 1951 movie *The Day the Earth Stood Still* (Sidky 2015: 114).

It is quite clear that the alleged "eyewitness" reports used by the UFO researchers, in this case, stemmed from "a single oral milieu" involving an uncorroborated folk tradition that had developed about extraterrestrial visitors and their flying vehicles (on the problematic nature of such narratives, see Vansina 1985: 159). This tradition crystallized after Arnold's flying saucer story, the original 1947 Roswell flying saucer crash report itself, along with the impact of Hollywood movies, and other cultural factors. One of these movies was the iconic 1956 film *Earth vs. the Flying Saucers* released by Columbia Pictures.

The inspiration for the story was the nonfiction book *Flying Saucers from Outer Space* (1953) by Donald Edward Keyhoe, a Marine Corps naval aviator turned UFO investigator. Thus, not only is the Roswell story based on information collected years after the events, and hence subject to a whole range of distorting effects upon memory and perception to be discussed below, but it also relies on secondhand anecdotal information and the flaws associated with this type of evidence.

Years later, the Roswell legend acquired its fullest form in a book written by science fiction writers Kevin Randle and Don Schmitt, with the title *The Truth about the UFO Crash at Roswell* (1994). They placed particular emphasis on Berlitz and Moore's saga about the alien corpses. We are now offered new anecdotal information from previously unknown witnesses who came forward years later with remarkable details about the secret goings-on and nefarious activities by American military personnel involving "aliens." Randle and Schmitt completed the Roswell myth with forensic details describing US government investigators recovering tiny alien bodies, removing them in secret, testimony from a mortician about receiving an official request for "child-sized coffins," and, of course, alien autopsies. This account is in part based on the eyewitness testimony of a nurse, who claimed to have seen the alien autopsy being performed in 1947, although she was not posted to the Roswell facility until 1956 (Gildenberg and Thomas 1998: 31–36; Goode 2012: 195).

Similarly, the mortician's testimony is implausible because it is unlikely that the medical examiners would choose to transport such highly valued and perishable specimens in coffins. Instead, these astonishing bodies would have been bagged, refrigerated, or packed in ice and transported to a major medical facility for analysis rather than autopsied in an inadequately equipped room at the base (Emery 1997: 95).

These ideas also inspired the faked 17-minute "alien autopsy" film produced by a British filmmaker and scam artist named Ray Santilli that surfaced in 1995. Experts almost immediately pointed out that the film was a hoax, but enthusiasts embraced it as the genuine article and irrefutable proof of alien visitations and, of course, a massive government cover-up (Bauer 1997; Emery 1995; Musella 2006; Nickel 1995; Stokes 1996). In 2006, the filmmaker admitted that the film was, in fact, a reconstruction ("restoration") based on "a single frame or two" from purported original footage that had completed deteriorated, which was tantamount to saying that he faked the entire production.

All of this material on the Roswell crash makes for a delightful science fiction story. The episode also attests to the ingenuity of paranormal hoaxers such as Santilli. However, today, nearly 75 million people in the United States believe that the Roswell UFO crash was a real event and that the US government has covered it up (Goode 2012: 198). The Roswell story is identical to many revered religious miracle myths that also have millions of believers. It illustrates how human cognitive and perceptual errors and the constructive nature of memory involving anecdotal and eyewitness reports contribute to the formation of entirely fictional narratives or X-claims about things that never happened and in some cases could not have happened. For these reasons, I shall refer to the Roswell incident again in the chapter on the resurrection of Jesus, which entailed similar circumstances.

## Memory Distortions and Beliefs in Paranormal

There are various memory-distorting effects that are relevant to paranormal ideation and claims, such as the Roswell UFO crash and similar stories. One effect is the *hindsight bias*, which enables a particular outcome to tightly fit a prediction, such as a prophetic dream, through a process of retrofitting. For example, taking a supposed prescient dream that happened after the foretold event as having taken place before the incident occurred (Schick and Vaughn 2014: 117).

Another distortion is known as *selective memory*, which refers to our tendency to recall events that stand out and forget those that are uninteresting. A typical example of this is when we receive a phone call from someone about whom we were thinking at the moment. This event may seem like a solid case of telepathy rather than a coincidence because we tend not to recall the thousands of other instances when we have thought about someone but did not receive a call from them at that moment. Another example is when a psychic provides an array of predictions, as they invariably do, often in succession. However, people only remember the statements that seem to fit their particular case or come true by coincidence, while forgetting as nonevents the many other predictions that did not come true or included details that did not match their circumstances.

A phenomenon identified as *cryptomnesia* (also known as "source-monitoring error") also biases perception. These are hidden memories that seem like original ideas and are based on things forgotten. These are recollected in modified form from the original memory and are erroneously considered to be a new and original conception. Thus, an idea from a book someone read years ago may be recalled as a memory of a past life or alien abduction. This phenomenon could also include a mixture of actual events, dreams, other people's claims, and imagination (Smith 2010: 171).

Our recollection of an event can also radically change after the fact if we get new information regardless of the veracity or extent of that information because as noted memory is constructive in nature (Schick and Vaughn 2014: 116; Hines 2003: 243). Presenting test subjects with new information about an event, experimental psychologists have shown, can alter their memory after the fact. Such a distortion can result in a recollection very different from what really took place (Hines 2003: 243). The subject, however, is usually sure about the reliability of such altered memories. Leading questions and exposure to new information, for example, has led some people to report having had near-death experiences (NDEs) years after the event took place, even though they made no such claims at the time of the supposed occurrence (French and Stone 2014: 140). The same process is involved in stories about UFOs, such as the Roswell incident, and religious miracles based on eyewitness memories and anecdotal accounts.

Related to this is the phenomenon of *false memories*. Research in this area started in the late 1980s and early 1990s, mostly in response to situations involving "recovered memories" and the idea of "repressed memories" associated with cases involving satanic ritual abuse and alien abductions (Wilson and French 2006: 1494). The key but unproven premise was that traumatic memories, such as ritual torture by Devil-worshippers or horrific medical procedures extraterrestrial abductors are claimed to perform on humans, are automatically repressed or hidden from consciousness but can be retrieved using visualization and hypnosis (Smith 2010: 181). It turned out that these techniques employed by therapists are conducive to creating memories of events that never happened (Baker 1997a, 1997b). The memories were implants by the therapists, and the phenomenon is known as "false memory syndrome." For this reason, the therapists involved acquired the reputation as "memory hackers."

The misunderstanding of the phenomenon of false memories had tragic consequences. Some patients who underwent repressed memory treatment were led to believe that they had been sexually abused in satanic rituals and even ate babies during diabolical rites, allegations that disrupted families and destroyed peoples' lives. Many of those who underwent such therapy later realized that their recollections were false, and some even sued their former therapists (Loftus 1993; Smith 2010: 182).

Experimental psychologists have demonstrated the ease with which it is possible to implant false memories (Loftus 1993). Several studies indicate, for example, how a significant number of people have been led to report seeing film footage of dramatic events that do not exist (French and Wilson 2006: 167). These include the crash of the Boeing 747 in Amsterdam in 1992 (55 percent of respondents); the actual car accident that killed Princess Diana in 1997 (44 percent of respondents); and CCTV footage of the 2002 Bali nightclub bombing that caused the death of many tourists (39 percent of respondents). The test subjects not only recalled seeing these nonexisting videos but also provided details, such as where they were at the time they saw the footage.

The finding that extensive memory effects can be created by implanting pseudomemories has considerable relevance to retrospective reports of supposed paranormal and supernatural experiences and events, which are invariably anecdotal accounts dependent on the memory of the claimants long after the supposed events are said to have happened (French and Wilson 2006: 167; Holt et al. 2012: 28). Reports of the paranormal resurrection of Jesus, if it indeed happened, for example, are based on second- and third-hand anecdotal accounts of a few people that were told and retold, circulated among and between communities and recorded 50–70 years after the fact. That is even longer than the amount of elapsed time between the alleged UFO crash at Roswell and the stories of alien bodies and the rest that appeared in the United States three decades later. How are we to evaluate such statements in light of the problems and unreliability of anecdotal information and testimonials? Consider what the late philosopher Robert Carroll (2007) said about such evidence:

> Anecdotes are unreliable for various reasons. Stories are prone to contamination by beliefs, later experiences, feedback, selective attention to details, and so on. Most stories get distorted in the telling and retelling. Events get exaggerated. Time sequences get confused. Details get muddled. Memories are imperfect and selective; they are often filled in after the fact. People misinterpret their experiences. Experiences are conditioned by biases, memories, and beliefs, so people's perception might not be accurate. Most people aren't expecting to be deceived, so they may not be aware of deceptions that others might engage in. Some people make up stories. Some stories are delusions. Sometimes events are inappropriately deemed psychic simply because they seem improbable when they might not be that improbable after all. In short, anecdotes are inherently problematic and are usually impossible to test for accuracy.

Psychologists Leonard Zusne and Warran Jones (1989: 220) add about psychic anecdotes that "retrospective falsification, the mixing of imagination and memory, is the rule in these stories rather than the exception." Imagination and memory enter in as well, they add, with "significant but inconvenient details being omitted and other details added."

That absence of objective informants is an ongoing concern for those engaged in ethnographic fieldwork. During field investigations of shamanic ritual healings and exorcisms, I frequently found that accounts reported by spectators of such rituals interviewed days later were at odds with each other and with what was on the videotape recordings. People exaggerate, distort, or fail to provide crucial facts and figures all the time. We, therefore, face serious questions about the reliability and accuracy of such information. Such data are especially problematic in cases where external corroboration of statements is not possible. Such fallibility is the reason why the philosopher David Hume was so adamant that testimonies regarding miraculous events are entirely unacceptable (see Chapter 8).

Many other factors that diminish accuracy seem to impinge upon perception and memory and can lead to paranormal ideation. One is poor viewing conditions, such as darkness or semi-darkness, when our minds fill in the blanks using existing beliefs. Below, I describe my own experiences with such perceptual distortions during field research. What people perceive and recount is also impacted by altered states of consciousness. These are brought on by tiredness or the use of psychotropic drugs, physiological trauma, intense engagement in ritual activities, emotional arousal, bereavement, expectations, religious attitudes and zeal, and the will to believe (French and Wilson 2006: 167–68; Martin 1991: 75).

## Witnessing the Resurrection of the Dead during Anthropological Fieldwork: What Does It Mean?

How quickly such circumstances can lead to paranormal ideation is evident from the case of anthropologist Bruce Grindal (1983) who reported "witnessing" a Ghanian man rise from the dead during a Sisal funeral "death divination" ritual involving singing, dancing, and drumming. The event is said to have occurred on October 23, 1967, in the town of Tumu in Ghana. Grindal's (1983: 67–69) narrative is as follows:

> I was [...] alone among strangers in the outer yard of the burial place. Near midnight I heard the goka singing in the inner yard, and I proceeded alone through the passageway to the dead man's compound. [...] The body of [...] the drummer was propped against the west wall of the compound, near the door to his rooms. Above his head, on the roof, were the talking drums. The corpse was seated upright and cross-legged on a cowhide, covered from the head by a cloth. The goka, "praise singers," were bent over the corpse, beating upon their hoes of iron and singing bayila ("man songs"). [...] As I watched them, I became intensely aware of their back-and-forth motion. [...] Then I saw the corpse jolt and occasionally pulsate, in a counterpoint to the motions of the goka. At first, I thought that my mind was playing tricks with my eyes, so I cannot say when the experience first occurred; but it began with moments of anticipation and terror, as though I knew something unthinkable was about to happen.

> [...] What I saw in those moments was outside the realm of normal perception. [...] The corpse, shaken by spasms, then rose to its feet, spinning and dancing in a frenzy. [...] [Then the] talking drums on the roof of the dead man's house began to glow with a light so strong that it drew the dancers to the rooftop. The corpse picked up the drumsticks and began to play. I cannot say whether what transpired took a matter of minutes or even an hour. Nor can I be sure about the sequence of events which I witnessed. But after a while, the power which had filled the compound began to cool, and the body of [...] the drummer was once again sitting propped against the west wall of the compound.

Grindal had an anomalous experience. He did acknowledge that this experience took place in an "altered state of consciousness" due to physical and psychological stress, but he did not construe it in psychological terms as a hallucination or delusion (Grindal 1983: 60). Instead, he inferred that he had witnessed an *actual* paranormal event—a dead man coming back to life, an experience beyond the limits of empirical understanding (Hellweg et al. 2015: 205–16). He is asking his readers to accept the resurrection event as a real event but a kind of reality not accessible through empirical procedures. Such an experience, in Grindal's (1983: 76) words,

> does not lend itself to empirical verification or replication under experimentally controlled conditions. Had I chosen [...] to set up some objective recording device, such as a camera or tape recorder, the event simply would not have happened. Truly to witness such an event precludes one's being a detached observer. [...] The canons of empirical research limit reality to that which is verifiable through consensual validation of rational observers. Understanding of death divination must depart from these canons and assume that reality is relative to one's consciousness of it.

In other words, this is a phenomenon that is only comprehensible in terms of the anthropologist's subjective-intuitive grasp of the experience. The conclusion is, therefore, that the canons of empirical research must be set aside if we are to achieve an accurate understanding of what is real in such cases (Hellweg et al. 2015: 207). The claim here is that reality is contingent upon the observer's subjective perceptions, or reality is whatever a person wants it to be. Grindal's Ghanian resurrection story is an excellent example of how Western observers, enamored with the exoticism of far-away cultures, lose all critical faculties, and treat mundane anomalous experiences as genuine paranormal events. It also demonstrates that claims about seeing the resurrection of the dead are not a phenomenon restricted to ancient historical settings. Finally, it illustrates how powerfully humans are susceptible to X-claims based on subjective experience and testimony.

I also had comparable "paranormal" experiences while accompanying my Nepalese shaman friends to graveyards and forests late at night to summon spirits of the dead. As a result of long hours of waiting in total darkness, sleep deprivation, fatigue, and expectations of paranormal happenings, the faintest sounds and the slightest motion of leaves and grass acquired sinister significance. Staring into the darkness, I could discern sinister human-like shapes manifesting all around us, including figures raising from ancient graves. Remarkably, some of these forms closely resembled the beings prominent in the cosmology of Nepalese shamans with which I had become familiar. The shamans reported seeing the same or similar entities and provided explanations for them. Such experiences can easily attain paranormal significance. Unlike Grindal, however, this event did not lead me to the paranormal conclusion that I saw mind-independent paranormal entities or the dead rising from their tombs.

## Additional Distorting Effects on Memory and Perception

Another feature of human perception that under certain circumstances can contribute to paranormal ideation is the phenomenon of *group-think* (French and Stone 2014: 119–20). Group-think becomes operational when enthusiastic people with similar beliefs and attitudes congregate. In such settings, individuals may express an even stronger version of the ideas that brought them together to obtain in-group approval, popularity, and dominance. In such circumstances, contrary views are not sought out and, if expressed, are ignored or ostracized. Group-think was powerfully operative among members of the Heaven's Gate UFO cult, who upon seeing the Hale–Bopp comet agreed that "the mothership" had come to take them away and committed suicide. Comparable to this is the case of the members of the Peoples Temple, who convinced themselves that US soldiers were coming to kill them and also committed mass suicide. This phenomenon was also probably at work among the 500 brethren who, according to the Apostle Paul (if he was not engaging in a pious fraud), saw the risen Jesus (see Chapter 15).

Another factor that influences accounts by multiple eyewitnesses—testimony usually considered to be more reliable than reports by an individual observer—is the phenomenon of *memory conformity*. It occurs when multiple spectators of an unusual or anomalous event, such as a crime, sightings of UFOs, apparitions of the Virgin Mary, ghosts, or monsters, discuss the incident among themselves before offering a formal statement. Under such circumstances, the testimony of one observer can alter the testimony of the other witnesses (French and Wilson 2006: 171). The growth of the Roswell myth is a perfect illustration of memory conformity at work among the so-called witnesses who came forward decades later to affirm that they saw aliens and even autopsies performed on extraterrestrial cadavers that never happened.

In addition to the distorting effects described so far, some reports have been shown to contain entirely false memories not based on *any* actual event seen by *any* eyewitnesses. This phenomenon is particularly relevant in cases involving claims of alien abductions and past life memories. Some psychologists maintain that believers in the paranormal are more susceptible to such memory distortions. Such believers also tend to display fantasy-proneness and possess overactive imaginations (Nickell 1997). The reports they provide are manifestations of personal fantasies rather than the experience of a genuine mind-independent event. Such fantasy-proneness creates ostensible experiences of a paranormal event that, in turn, results in the conviction that such phenomena are authentic (French and Wilson 2006: 176). It is difficult to convince those who have experienced the fantasy firsthand that the event has a natural explanation (French and Wilson 2003: 154).

Another biasing factor is the "backfire effect." This refers to circumstances when believers confronted with evidence that their deeply held beliefs are wrong, reject the evidence, and double down on their erroneous beliefs. In his book *Post-Truth* (2018), the philosopher and historian of science Lee McIntyre (2018: 36–58) shows how the confirmation bias and the backfire effect are at the center of the present era of post-truths, alternative facts, counter-knowledge, and anti-intellectualism.

Then there is the *confirmation bias*, a potent phenomenon that distorts how we process information. It refers to the proclivity to seek out any confirmatory evidence for one's beliefs while systematically ignoring information that disputes them (Goode 2012: 296). The confirmation bias poses a challenge in scientific research, and scientists are careful to pay attention to it. However, this bias is a predominant feature of the work of believing theologists, religious apologists, psi researchers, and proponents of other types of paranormal ideas.

In his book *Novum Organum* (1620), the philosopher and scientist Francis Bacon described the confirmation bias in great detail and its role in bolstering paranormal and supernatural ideation:

> The human understanding when it has once adopted an opinion (either as being the received opinion or as being agreeable to itself) draws all things else to support and agree with it. And though there be a greater number and weight of instances to be found on the other side, yet these it either neglects and despises, or else by some distinction sets aside and rejects, in order that by this great and pernicious predetermination the authority of its former conclusions may remain inviolate. And therefore it was a good answer that was made by one who, when they showed him hanging in a temple a picture of those who had paid their vows as having escaped a shipwreck, and would have him say whether he did not now acknowledge the power of the gods—"Aye," asked he again, "but where are they painted that were drowned after their vows?" And such is the way of all superstition, whether in astrology, dreams, omens, divine judgments, or the like; wherein men, having a delight in such vanities, mark the events where they are fulfilled, but where they fail, though this happen much oftener, neglect and pass them by. (Bacon *Aphorisms*, Book I, chapter 46, 1902: 23–24)

Bacon also pointed out another significant human cognitive predisposition:

> Besides, independently of that delight and vanity which I have described, it is the peculiar and perpetual error of the human intellect to be more moved and excited by affirmatives than by negatives; whereas it ought properly to hold itself indifferently disposed toward both alike. Indeed, in the establishment of any true axiom, the negative instance is the more forcible of the two. (Bacon *Aphorisms*, Book I, chapter 46, 1902: 23–24)

Along the same lines as Bacon, Gilovich (1991: 31) observes that confirmatory or supporting information seems to be more comfortable to handle cognitively than negative data. Thus, believers easily find confirmation for their beliefs even in the presence of masses of contrary evidence. The confirmation bias is exceptionally deep-seated among those heavily committed to a particular set of supernatural or paranormal beliefs. Consider the following example. The Christian apologist Gary Habermas (2003: 15–32) argues that the Shroud of Turin is evidence for the resurrection of Jesus. In the context of this discussion, he confidently cites all of the evidence that seems to support his argument, even quoting sources out of context, while refusing to acknowledge any evidence that refutes his case. This strategy is never convincing. As the philosopher Michael Martin (1991: 96) observes regarding this case, Habermas's "failure to acknowledge negative evidence hardly adds to the credibility of his other arguments for the truth of the Resurrection." The Shroud of Turn is discussed later in this chapter.

The confirmation bias, as psychologist Richard Wiseman (2010: 169) points out, has characterized psi research since the inception of the field. He describes this as "the heads I win, tales you lose" approach, which entails treating perceived positive results as confirmation but never considering negative outcomes as disconfirmation of a psi hypothesis. Thus, as Wiseman explains, starting at the turn of the twentieth century, systematic scientific research on psi involving mediums and psychics only revealed the prevalence of fraud and self-delusion. Rather than this embarrassing fact leading to the conclusion that psi does not exist, researchers doubled down on their convictions and simply shifted their focus to a different set of subjects and their psychic abilities. Thus, psi research under J. B. Rhine targeted exceptional individuals, who unlike mediums did not profess to have psychic powers but could purportedly obtain better than chance scores on ESP tests.

As discussed in Chapter 4, Rhine felt sure that he had scientifically established the existence of psi, although no one has been able to replicate his results. However, once again, rather than paranormal fundamentalists abandoning the psi hypothesis, they simply changed their approach, forwarding the view that psi abilities are far more subtle than hitherto suspected, are inconsistent, and seem to be present in a diffuse pattern among the general population. This inconsistency is what the neuropsychologist Nicholas Humphrey (1999: 74) calls the "fishy" characteristics of psi phenomena that have been adding up so that over the years psi manifestations have become more and more conditional, unpredictable, and unreliable and are said to operate under a limited set of conditions (see Chapter 4). Hence, as sociologist Christopher Bader et al. (2017: 158) observe, the paranormal is "messy" and elusive. Bigfoot is always behind the bushes, ghosts never materialize before qualified observers, and UFOs seem to forever vanish before the arrival of expert photographers. This vexatious attribute of psi is so prevalent that researchers will often grasp even the flimsiest tidbit of evidence as a confirmation for their hypotheses.

Wiseman (2010: 171–76) shows how at each stage in the history of psi research, proponents have refused to treat nonsignificant results as evidence against the existence of psi abilities. Either they have done this by not publishing such findings in their journals, thereby creating a publications bias, or they have attributed the negative outcome to other factors, such as the effects of non-psi conducive laboratory settings or researchers. Alternatively, as noted, they have merely abandoned one line of research and adopted a new set of procedures rather than consider the actual implications of disconfirmations (Alcock 2003: 37). Another strategy has been to resort to meta-analysis or the post hoc data mining of a group of studies. Again any statistical result deemed significant is presented as confirmation, while contrary outcomes are explained away according to the operation of non-psi conducive variations (Wiseman 2010: 173–74). The cases used in these meta-studies, none of which may have yielded any positive findings individually, are thus manipulated to generate an overall positive result (Smith 2010: 260).

Confirmation bias enables people who have invested a great deal in a particular array of beliefs to avoid the psychological effects of cognitive dissonance, which arises when one holds two sets of conflicting views (Smith 2010: 144). The understanding of this bias is valuable in shedding light upon why purveyors of supernatural ideas, such as members of religious cults, like the followers of Jesus, Sabbatai Şevi, and Menaḥem Schneerson, discussed in Chapter 16, have resisted and explained away all disconfirmations of their failed prophetic claims.

Another perceptual phenomenon that can play a part in paranormal claims is the *autokinetic effect*, which refers to the fact that when people are observing a small light source in a dark room or against a dark background, it will appear to move. This effect is thought to be due to minute eye movements that cause the image to shift across the retina. The brain interprets these as a movement at the source. Moreover, this effect is subject to social influence. Thus, if one person states that the light is moving in a particular direction, others will report seeing the same thing (Hines 2003: 242).

Other types of perceptions can also be affected by social influence. The expectation of perceiving a stimulus often leads to its perception even when such a stimulus is absent. For example, during a fake psychic spoon bending demonstration, participants who were told that the spoon would continue bending after the psychic placed it on the table were more likely to report seeing the object continue to warp (Wiseman and Greening 2005).

Another effect is the illusion of *apparent motion*. If one places two small lights at locations A and B in a dark room and first turn the light at A on and off and then turn on the light at B, the observer will report seeing a single light moving across space between the first and second points. The autokinetic effect and the apparent motion illusion are often the basis of reports of flying saucers moving in the night sky. These moving objects may appear real, but they are constructs of the human brain (Hines 2003: 242).

## Misunderstanding Probabilistic Events and Paranormal Beliefs

An entirely different factor that plays a role in paranormal ideation is the misunderstanding of probabilistic events (Gilovich 1991: 20). Probabilities are counterintuitive, and random dispersion of events usually looks nonrandom. Take, for example, a case of flipping a coin. The law of large numbers (i.e., the law of averages) states that there will be close to a 50-50 split between the number of heads and tails after a large number of tosses. However, after only a few tosses unbalanced splits are likely, creating a seemingly inexplicable clustering effect. The mistake is that people expect to obtain the appropriate numbers of heads and tails not just in a large number of tosses but also in short sequences. Consider a study investigating the power of the mind to influence the outcome of dice throws. If the researcher stops the procedure once a perceived result is obtained, called the "arbitrary endpoint," the clustering effect will give the false impression that something unusual or paranormal is in operation (Smith 2010: 258).

As discussed in Chapter 6, humans are highly predisposed to seeing patterns (Holt et al. 2012: 18) and have great difficulty recognizing randomness or random events.

We regularly detect order and patterns in what is chaotic and random, even when such patterns are absent (Gilovich 1991: 21). We then proceed to offer post hoc explanations for these seemingly astonishing impressions and coincidences that are only the effects of our misidentification of a random pattern due to a poor grasp of the nature of probabilities (Hines 2003: 148). As the eminent statistician Ronald Fisher (1937: 16) observed long ago, "for the 'one chance in a million' will undoubtedly occur, with no less and no more than its appropriate frequency, however, surprised we may be that it should occur to us." In other words, certain odd or unusual things do happen on occasion. This, however, does not mean that such singular events are paranormal or supernatural.

Some scholars conjecture that the very notion of randomness or chance is a recent cultural innovation and that before this people may not have even had the means of suspecting the existence of random events (Dennett 2006: 133–34). This development would explain why humans across cultures and through times have devised and relied upon many divination techniques (see Curry 2010). As I have pointed out elsewhere, people abhor uncertainty or randomness and rely on divination in efforts to reduce it. Divination is a type of supernatural communication used to obtain information about the future and things unknown through the detection of patterns and associations (Sidky 2015: 96).

Paranormalists and religionists treat misidentified patterns perceived in randomness as remarkable mysteries, using Carl Jung's idea of "synchronicity," or "meaningful coincidence," for which there is no actual evidence (Carroll 2003: 186; Smith 2010: 125). As statistical mathematicians Persi Diaconis and Frederick Mosteller (1989: 860) point out, "In a culture like ours based heavily on determinism and causation, we tend to look for causes, and we ask: What is the synchronous force creating all of these coincidences?" Indeed, they add, humans are "swimming in an ocean of coincidences" and "tend to find coincidences everywhere if they try hard enough" (Diaconis and Mosteller 1989: 860).

## Synchronicity and the Bible Code

One example of bizarre coincidences is the so-called Bible Code. If we circle every tenth letter in the Bible, some of the selected letters will form words that appear to be messages. This approach is taken by paranormalist Michael Drosnin in his best-selling book *The Bible Code* (1997). Drosnin claims to have discovered purported prophecies hidden in the Bible "for three thousand years." He treats these codes as evidence that some divine intelligence was involved in the creation of the Bible. This example is yet another of those hackneyed sham arguments made respectively by Jews, Christians, and Muslims that their holy books contain miraculous and profound predictions and prophecies.

The Bible Code is a spurious supernatural claim (see Thomas 1997b, 2001). As Goode (2012: 297) points out, with enough words, similar messages are discoverable as well in stacks of comic books or even pornographic novels. Drosnin, confident that he had come up with a divine mystery, issued a challenge to anyone to detect similar prophecies in other books. The challenge appeared in a piece in *Newsweek Magazine* (Begley 1997). As he put it, "When my critics find a message about the assassination of a prime minister encrypted in Moby Dick, I'll believe them." Mathematician Brendan McKay (1997), who took up this challenge, found assassination predictions in Moby Dick for Indira Gandhi, Leon Trotsky, Martin Luther King Jr., and Robert Kennedy. McKay has also refuted the work of a group of scholars who have forwarded a similar claim that the Book of Genesis encodes events that happened millennia after the writing of the text (Brendan et al. 1999). Similarly, the physicist and mathematician Dave Thomas (1998) put the code hypothesis to the test and found a prediction that the Chicago Bulls would win a sixth National Basketball Association Championship in Leo Tolstoy's novel *War and Peace*. Thomas wittily concluded that either the Bible Code idea is nonsense or "Leo Tolstoy is the Supreme Being who created the world."

None of these findings showing the spurious nature of the Bible Code hypothesis have made Drosnin change his mind or prevented publishers from picking up his equally deceptive sequels, *Bible Code II: The Countdown* (2002) and *Bible Code III: Saving the World* (2010). This fact is not surprising. The media is always ready to push any sort of phony paranormal claims upon a preconditioned gullible public hungry for wonders and mysteries. The paranormal sells books and increases ratings.

It is clear how paranormal ideation can arise when people do not understand the chance occurrence of an event or the probability of separate events coinciding (French and Stone 2014: 120). As Diaconis and Mosteller (1989: 860) have put it, "co-incidences occur in the minds of observers."

Moreover, once a paranormal explanation based on such misunderstandings arises, it is retained and becomes the basis for the interpretation of other such events in the future (Gilovich (1991: 23).

As discussed in this section, there are a range of commonly misunderstood memory and perceptual factors that explain why we think eerie thoughts. Many, if perhaps not all, paranormal reports and ideation may be attributed to these biasing factors that make us believe we have seen ghosts, spirits, angels, demons, and alien visitors when such entities are absent.

## What the Shroud of Turin Tells Us about Paranormal Believers

In the previous section, I discussed the role of the confirmation bias and the backfire effect in sustaining paranormal beliefs. A related influential cognitive biasing factor is called *evidence distortion*. This factor safeguards preexisting supernatural conclusions from disconfirmation. This strategy entails looking for errors in hostile evidence, offering ad hoc explanations or relying on multiple outs for one's own views, misrepresenting the claims of opponents, and even committing fraud (cf., French and Stone (2014: 132).

The case of the Shroud of Turin is a perfect example of the lengths to which believers are willing to go to distort contrary evidence to confirm their biases, double down on disproven beliefs, and even perpetrate pious fraud (for an overview, see Nickell 2003). This case is also relevant because Christian apologists consider the Shroud as tangible proof that the resurrection of Jesus was an actual paranormal event, which is the topic of discussion in Chapters 14 and 15.

### *The Shroud as a Paranormal Object*

The Shroud of Turin is claimed to be an uncanny object of considerable religious significance (Mueller 1986). It consists of a piece of cloth measuring roughly 14 feet long by 3.5 feet wide that bears a full body front and back imprint of a bearded man with long hair depicted with wounds to the scalp, side, feet, and hands suggesting crucifixion on the basis of someone's conjecture that this is what a crucified person would look like. Moreover, the locations of the injuries appear red and resemble the color of blood. To create such an image, one section of the cloth would have had to be placed under the body, and the other half then folded over the head and draped over to cover the front of the corpse.

Today, this holy object is housed in the reliquary of the Cathedral of St. John the Baptist in Turin, Italy. Many believers consider the Shroud of Turin to be the actual burial cloth of Jesus, which, if true, would make it the holiest relic in Christendom (Nickell 1998a: 7). Indeed, Christian apologists such as Kenneth Stevenson and Gary Habermas have argued in their book *Verdict on the Shroud: Evidence for the Death and Resurrection of Jesus* (1981) that the Shroud is tangible evidence that Jesus physically rose from the dead and visited his associates in person. Since then numerous other books have appeared making similar claims. Habermas (2003: 27–28) himself remains committed to this position.

### *Holy Things, the Christian Cult of Saints, and Relics of the Christ*

The existence of such an object is not unusual and is part of the Christian cult of saints that appeared in the centuries after the death of Jesus, probably as early as the second century CE (see Bartlett 2013: 3–26; Freeman 2011). People cherished these objects as enduring sources of supernatural power because of their association with holy personages (Bartlett 2013: 3). The belief in the magical powers of the relics and bones of saints was so strong as to make St. Augustine ask the following question: "Why can the dead do such great things?" The fixation upon or craze for holy Christian relics was at its height during the early medieval period and created a massive demand for such items big and small (Tattersall and Névraumont 2018: 29).

Christian entrepreneurs realized quickly that there was money to be made and thus began the enterprise of relic forgeries. In medieval Europe, where counterfeiting and selling "holy relics" had become big business, there were many "relics of the Christ." These included vials of his mother's breast milk, hay from the manger where he was born, nails from the cross, numerous pieces of the cross itself, his foreskin (a total of 18 were known), and as many as 43 "authentic" burial shrouds of Jesus (Humber 1978; Tattersall and Névraumont 2018: 38). As the historian Charles Freeman (2012: 24) has pointed out, the shroud must be understood against the background of "the wider world of medieval relics, in which the Shroud [of Turin] is one of the thousands associated with the Crucifixion and tomb alone."

In his remarkable book, *Memoirs of Extraordinary Popular Delusions and the Madness of Crowds* (1842), the Scottish author Charles Mackay provided a delightful survey of the holy relic industry and the significance of relics to medieval European supplicants and worshippers:

> The first pilgrims to the Holy Land brought back to Europe thousands of apocryphal relics. In the purchase of which they had expended all their store. The greatest favorite was the wood of the true cross, which like the oil of the widow, never diminished. It is generally asserted, in the tradition of the [Catholic] Church, that Empress Helen, the mother of Constantine the Great, first discovered the veritable "*true cross*" in her pilgrimage to Jerusalem. The Emporer Theodosius made a present of the greater part of it to St. Ambrose, Bishop of Milan by whom it was studded with precious stones, and deposited in the principal church of the city. It was carried away by the Huns, by whom it was burnt, after they had extracted the valuable jewels it contained. Fragments, purported to have been cut from it, were, in the eleventh and twelfth centuries, to be found in almost every church in Europe, and would, if collected together in one place, would have been almost sufficient to have built a cathedral. Happy was the sinner who could get a sight of one of them; happier he who possessed one! To obtain them the greatest dangers were cheerfully braved. They were thought to preserve from all evils, and to cure the most inveterate diseases. Annual pilgrimages were made to the shrines that contained them, and considerable revenues collected from devotees. [...] Next in renown were those precious tears of the Savior. By whom and in what manner they were preserved, the pilgrims did not inquire. Their genuineness was vouched by the Christians in the Holy Land, and that was sufficient. Tears of the Virgin Mary, and tears of St. Peter, were also to be had, carefully enclosed in little caskets, which the pious might wear in their bosoms. After the tears, the next most precious relics were the drops of blood of Jesus and the martyrs, and the milk of the Virgin Mary. Hair and toe-nails were also in great repute, and were sold at extravagant prices. Thousands of pilgrims annually visited Palestine in the eleventh and twelfth centuries, to purchase pretended relics for the home market. The majority of them had no other means of subsistence than the profits thus obtained. Many a nail, cut from the filthy foot of some unscrupulous ecclesiastic, was sold at a diamond's price, within six months after its severance from its parent's toe, upon the supposition that it had once belonged to a saint or apostle. Peter's toes were uncommonly prolific, for there were nails enough in Europe, at the time of the Council of Clermont, to have filled a sack, all of which were devoutly believed to have grown on the sacred feet of that great apostle. Some of them are still shown in the cathedral of Aix-la-Chapelle. The pious come from a distance of a hundred German miles to feast their eyes upon them. [...] At Port Royal, in Paris, is kept with great care a thorn, which the priests of that seminary assert is the identical thorns that bound the holy head of the Son of God. How it came there, and by whom it was preserved, has never been explained. [...] Europe still swarms with these religious relics. There is hardly a Roman Catholic church in Spain, Portugal, Italy, France or Belgium, without one or more of them. Even the poorly endowed churches of the villages boast the possession of miraculous thighbones of innumerable saints of the [Catholic] calendar. Aix-la-Chapelle is proud of the veritable *châsse*, or thigh-bone of Charlemagne, which cures lameness. Halle has a thigh-bone of the Virgin Mary; Spain has seven or eight all said to be undoubted relics. Brussels at one time preserved, and perhaps does now, the teeth of St. Gudule. The faithful, who suffer from toothaches, had only to pray, look at them, and be cured. Some of these holy bones have now been buried in different parts of the Continent. After a certain lapse of time, water is said to ooze from them, which soon forms a spring, and cures all the diseases of the faithful. [...] It is curious to remark the avidity manifested in all ages, and in all countries, to obtain possession

> of some relic of any persons who have been much spoken of, even for their crimes. (Mackay 1842: 696–98)

The existence of this relic manufacturing industry in medieval Europe alone provides plenty of reasons to be suspicious about all of the alleged holy relics of the Christ or that of anybody else. Mackay was astounded by the absurdity of the enthralled crowds who venerated such things. This tendency, it seems, has not dissipated in our time as is evidenced by the frantic efforts of devotees to cast a glimpse upon the Shroud of Turin and for others to go to any lengths to somehow prove that it is indeed an actual miraculous object.

### *How the Shroud Became a Magical Object of Veneration*

The Turin relic acquired its current paranormal fame after a photograph was taken for the first time in 1898. The glass plate negative revealed what looks like a photographic "negative image" that was sensationalized as "a miracle." Before this optical illusion, the shroud was one dubious relic among thousands of others, and no one considered it as extraordinary. A medieval cult of the shroud did not exist, and the modern-day adoration the Turin Shroud began in 1898 after the miracle photo appeared (Freeman 2012).

### *How Shroud Believers Have Misrepresented the Evidence*

Miracle-mongering believers clamored about the impossibility of a medieval forger creating "a photographic negative" before the invention of photography. The assertion is that they had in hand a genuine miraculous object. However, the allegation about a photographic negative is false (Nickell 2013: 122). As Steven Schafersman (1998), one of the scientists who has evaluated the evidence on the Shroud points out, the image is only an apparent photographic negative. In contrast to a true photographic negative, the dark features on the shroud, such as the beard, mustache, hair, and blood, are dark on it and light on the positive. In other words, it suggests that Jesus was white-haired, and his blood was white as well.

To assert that this optical illusion of a quasi-negative image proves the shroud is a miraculous or supernatural object is as absurd as maintaining that the Jesus optical illusion found online is supernatural. This illusion consists of several black and white patches. There are four dots placed vertically at the center. Looking at the dots for 30 seconds and then gazing at a white surface leads to the perception of a positive image of a bearded man with long hair, that is, a Jesus-like face. This effect is even more remarkable than the so-called negative image of the Turin relic. A miracle? Not really. Calling the image on the Turin cloth a miracle is akin to calling this optical illusion on the internet a miracle of God.

The same is the case for another phony claim that there is a paranormally produced three-dimensional image embedded in the shroud (Habermas 2003: 28). There is a crude three-dimensional property about the picture because it was created using a rubbing technique on a bas-relief model. Several three-dimensional reproductions of the figure depicted on the shroud and touted as the actual representations of Jesus appear all over the internet. Remarkably, the various renditions of Jesus look like completely different individuals. Another miracle? No. The paranormal investigator Joe Nickell (1998a: 27–28) has been able to create a negative-like image with three-dimensional properties identical to the Turin Shroud using the non-miraculous method of wet-molding cloth to a bas-relief, which is allowed to dry and then rubbed with powdered pigment in the same way as making a rubbing from a tombstone.

Religionists dismiss, ignore, and misrepresent disconfirming evidence. More troubling is that they make patently false claims to give the impression that the authenticity of the Shroud is a scientifically and historically proven fact. Their scientifically illiterate audiences conditioned to believe have easily fallen for this sham. The strategy seems to be to pile falsehoods upon lies until the reader is no longer able to tell fact from fiction. William Meacham's (1983) paper that surprisingly appeared in an issue of *Current Anthropology* on the authentication of the Shroud is an excellent example of such a strategy. This paper, as Schafersman (1983: 301) aptly describes it, is "a blatant example of human credulity [that] rarely finds its way into the professional scholarly literature."

Contrary to Meacham's claims, the image is not anatomically perfect (Cole 1983: 296). The left-hand fingers are shorter than the right-hand ones, and the right forearm is abnormally elongated. The body itself is elongated, which is a characteristic of Gothic art but not of the human anatomy. One rejoinder by believers is that this discrepancy is caused by joint dislocation due to the ordeal of crucifixion. This is purely conjecture and unconvincing. But even if this is the case, the leap from hints of a crucified victim to the resurrection of a dead individual is unwarranted.

In addition to these issues, contrary to Meacham's assertion, there are no impressions of coins placed over the eyes as part of a burial rite. In fact, the gospels state that with sunset approaching, there was not enough time to carry out the burial rites. There was barely enough time to place the body in a tomb. So, there were no coins placed anywhere. This contention involves a case of *pareidolia*, seeing patterns in randomness, a trick of the observer's mind that also leads people to see Jesus on toast, faces in the clouds, and pyramids and sphinxes on Mars. Meacham falsely says that forensic pathologists agree that the image is the result of contact with a corpse in rigor mortis. To the contrary, forensic pathologists assert that bodies never create such image transfers (Mueller 1983: 299). Also, the wounds are not accurately portrayed, contra to what Meacham says, because real blood from actual wounds does not flow in the way depicted in the picture. Similarly, the image-forming process is not unknown and has been replicated, as noted above.

Meacham also misrepresents the data regarding other points. The history of the relic, for example, does not include any verifiable facts. It is not well-established that the shroud is an archaeological document of Jesus's crucifixion. Available archaeological evidence does not support the antiquity of the Shroud. The history of this object before the fourteenth century is unknown. Efforts to reconstruct such history by apologists and believers (e.g., De Wesselow 2012; see Wilson 2011) have been a dismal failure amounting to fiction writing rather than historical research (Freeman 2012). Pollen samples taken from the cloth do not indicate that the object was once in Palestine. Finally, it is patently false that the amount of data obtainable from this object about the death and resurrection of Jesus is so considerable that we could consider the shroud to be "fifth gospel," as Meacham overconfidently claimed. These constitute a series of pious lies and wishful thinking.

As far-fetched as claims about the Shroud's authenticity seem to be, the various supernatural explanations for the creation of the image are even more unbelievable. So once again, we are in the realm of the unreal real or the territory of X-claims. One assertion is that the image is a "vapor picture" caused by the fumes emitted by the blood, sweat, and mortuary oils and spices applied to the body. However, even if we are to accept the fictional accounts provided in the gospels about the burial of Jesus, there is significant disagreement in these texts as to whether or not anyone anointed the corpse. The other even more far-fetched and stolid explanation provided is that "the images were created by a burst of paranormal light, such as Christ might have produced at the moment of resurrection" (in Mueller 1986: 325). We are asked to believe that Christ was radioactive and emitted radiation! How does anyone know this? We have now ventured into the land of science fiction and Hollywood special effects.

Shroud cultists and sindonologists (those engaged in the pseudoscientific study of the shroud) who are attempting to prove the authenticity of the relic can debate as much as they want about particles, fibers, pigments, patches, blood drops, pollen, cryptic signs and symbols, and so forth. What are they really trying to establish? That the resurrection happened? Believers do not understand that even if it could be proven that this fabric was wrapped around a crucified human body that left its impression and real blood stains on the material, this does not show that the resurrection indeed occurred. All it would indicate is that the cloth was in contact with a dead body. None of the properties of this object suggest that the person whose image is on the fabric rose up from the dead, which is the basis of declaring the shroud a miracle of God. Nor is there any evidence that this cloth came from Palestine and specifically from the nonexistent tomb of Jesus (see Chapter 14).

Moreover, before claiming that the Turin relic is the burial cloth of Jesus, it must be proven that Jesus's body was retrieved from the cross, ritually prepared, wrapped, and then placed in a tomb. There is considerable evidence that none of these things happened. The fate of Jesus's body is unknown (see Chapter 14). The best guess is that the body either decomposed on the cross or was dishonorably buried in the ground by the same people responsible for his crucifixion. The evidence provided in the Synoptic Gospels and the Gospel of John for the burial of Jesus is the worst kind one could have. Thus, efforts to establish the Shroud of Turin as a paranormal object is wishful thinking and nothing more on the part of believers desperate to substantiate their supernatural fantasies and superstitions.

However, even if we go along with the argument that this relic could contain a genuine image, there is another major problem. Whose image does it depict? There are no contemporary portraits or images of Jesus. Indeed, St. Augustine, writing during the early fifth century, lamented the fact that no one knew what the Savior or his mother looked like (Nickell 1998a: 22). From an iconographic perspective, the image on the shroud appears precisely like the stylized depictions of Jesus with Semitic features, long hair, bear, accentuated eyes, and a prominent nose, that replaced the earlier Jesus images as the Greek god Apollo. The Semitic-looking depiction based on someone's imagination of what a Palestinian Jew might have looked like gained currency between the third and the fourth centuries, that is, hundreds of years after Jesus's death (Nickell 1998b: 24, 2007: 68). Thus, just as portrayals of gray extraterrestrial beings today resemble popular images of aliens in comic books and movies, the image on the Shroud resembles the popular conceptions of what Jesus was believed to have looked like during medieval times. These facts alone suffice to cast complete doubt on the authenticity of the relic. However, true believers are undeterred by any such evidence.

### *What Historical Records and Iconography Reveal*

An analysis of the historical records by Canon Ulysse Chevalier unmistakably reveals that the shroud is not authentic (Chevalier 1903: 5–24). First, there is the surprising fact that there is no mention of this supposed holiest relic of Christianity until 1353, when a soldier named Geoffroy de Charney presented it to the Lirey Abbey, in the dioceses of Troyes, in north-central France. Geoffroy proclaimed that the cloth was the authentic burial shroud of Christ. However, he provided no information about how, where, and when he acquired the holy article. So the provenance of this relic is entirely unknown. Second, how the body was enveloped in the cloth to produce a front and back image is inconsistent with Jewish burial practices. The gospels only mention pieces of fabric, not a one-piece shroud being used to prepare the body for burial. In other words, the New Testament texts fail to support the claim that the Turin fabric was Jesus's burial cloth. Had such an astonishing object been present, the disciples would have certainly retrieved and exhibited it as proof of the claim that Jesus was alive to silence their many cynics. So why didn't this happen? Simple, there was no such burial cloth.

Third, none of the gospels, where the story of Jesus's burial and resurrection is found, mention the existence of a burial shroud with a miraculous image impressed upon it. Given the gospel writers' desperate need for apologetic propaganda against the assertions in their time that there was no bodily resurrection, they would surely have mentioned this tangible piece of evidence for the miracle they were defending had it existed.

Fourth, during the fourth century, when the Christian emperor Constantine's men are said to have discovered the Holy Sepulcher—the alleged tomb of Jesus in Jerusalem—they proclaimed that they recovered the actual crown of thorns the Romans placed on Jesus's head, the lance that pierced his side, and pieces of the real cross (cf., Guignebert 1958: 493; Onfray 2011: 115; Tobin 2009: 544). However, there is no mention of a burial shroud, with or without an image impressed on it (see Chapter 14). Why not? If such a remarkable object existed, this is where it would have shown up. In other words, had those zealous religious propagandists behind the unearthing of the purported tomb of Christ known about the existence of the shroud they would have included such a magical object along with the other counterfeit artifacts they claimed to have discovered. We find, therefore, that even Christian propaganda does not support the authenticity of the Shroud of Turin.

Fifth, if this cloth had been deemed to be authentic at the time it first surfaced in 1353, it is impossible to explain why Church officials or the Pope did not jump at the opportunity to acquire it and capitalize on its propaganda value. It is clear that none of the religious authorities of the time considered this relic to be the genuine article. We might recall that there were numerous burial shrouds of Jesus in existence.

By 1357, the Shroud went on display as an authentic relic of the Christ, and, as to be expected, it was proclaimed to possess miraculous healing powers. This exhibit drew multitudes of venerators who could cast eyes on the fabulous object for a fee. The relic thus became a lucrative cash generator for those who put it on exhibition. Given its uncertain provenance and the fact that none of the gospels mention a shroud bearing the imprint of the Christ, skeptics at the time raised objections as soon as it was placed on public display. Thus, Henri de Poitiers, the Bishop of Troyes, at the recommendation of the learned men and theologians of the day, launched an official investigation into the matter. As a result, the Shroud was taken off public display and hidden away. However, the relic resurfaced in 1389. We know this from a letter written by Pierre d' Arcis, the person who succeeded Henri, sent to Pope Clement VII, dated 1389. The letter reads as follows:

> The case, Holy Father, stands thus. Some time since in this diocese of Troyes the dean of a certain collegiate church, to wit, that of Lirey, falsely and deceitfully, being consumed with the passion of avarice, and not from any motive of devotion but only of gain, procured for his church a certain cloth cunningly painted, upon which by a clever slight of hand was depicted the twofold image of one man, that is to say, the back and the front, he falsely declaring and pretending this was the actual shroud in which our Savior Jesus Christ was enfolded in the tomb, and upon which the whole likeness of the Savior had remained thus impressed together with the wounds He bore. This story was put about not only in the kingdom of France but, so to speak, throughout the world, so that from all parts people come together to view it. And further to attract the multitude so that money might cunningly be wrung from them, pretended miracles were worked, certain men being hired to represent themselves as healed at the moment of the exhibition of the shroud. (Thurston 1903)

D'Arcis also referred to the inquest undertaken by his predecessor Henri de Poitiers and the conclusions of that investigation:

> Eventually, after diligent inquiry and examination, he discovered the fraud and how the said cloth had been cunningly painted, the truth being attested to by the artist who had painted it, to wit, that it was a work of human skill not miraculously wrought or bestowed. (Thurston 1903)

According to this letter, not only is the Shroud a fake, but extensive chicanery was involved in fooling the public about its magical powers, including the hiring of stooges and shills to stage miraculous healings (Nickell 1998a: 25–26). It appears that this was another loathsome run-of-the-mill paranormal hoaxes that continue to be perpetrated by evangelical preachers and other charlatans in our own time, with the sole purpose of preying on the desperately ill and the gullible and defrauding them of their savings with bogus claims of miraculous cures.

Eventually, Pope Clement declared that the shroud was a painted fabric or "a representation" of the actual burial cloth. He issued a Bull (public decree) pronouncing that the actual nature of the shroud as a copy had to be stated whenever it was placed on public exhibition. However, the papal injunction was eventually forgotten, and the Shroud was once again declared to be the genuine article and Christianity's most significant holy relic (Mueller 1986: 327).

Subsequently, Geoffroy de Charney's granddaughter, a woman named Margaret, acquired the cloth and took it on a roadshow to make money. This display again raised questions about its authenticity. Eventually, Margaret sold (not donated, as apologists claim) the Shroud to Duke Louis I of Savoy, who proclaimed it to be genuine and housed it in his castle at Cambéry (Nickell 2013: 120). A fire in 1532 nearly destroyed the relic at this location, a fact that later surfaces during the modern debate about the authenticity of the cloth. Eventually, a later duke took the cloth to Turin, where it remains and where a cameraman took the 1898 photograph.

This historical evidence proves beyond any reasonable doubt that the Shroud of Turin is a case of pious fraud, although even a pious fraud is questionable in this case because the relic was used most impiously to fleece the public of their cash. Predictably, however, none of the evidence reviewed here has raised doubts in the minds of believers about the authenticity of their Savior's burial fabric. Nickell (1998a: 29) describes the all too familiar pattern in such cases when an array of post hoc apologetics are piled atop one another by religionists to explain away evidence refuting their beliefs.

True believers have exerted monumental efforts to prove the authenticity of this sordid piece of religious imposture, including additional acts of fraud. At the behest of shroud-believers, there were two scientific studies of the Shroud, one in 1969 and the other in 1973. The motive of the sponsors was authentication, not actual unbiased historical or scientific assessment. Expert serologists were employed to establish the presence of blood on the cloth using microscopal, chemical, and biological tests. An art specialist was asked to analyze the image itself. The serologist failed to find any traces of blood, and the art expert determined that the image was the result of an artistic printing technique (Nickell 2007: 132, 137). For believers, this was terrible news.

### *Scientific Evidence, Pseudoscience, Pious Frauds, and the Shroud*

The religionists' response to these negative findings is a typical one used when dealing with contrary scientific evidence. Coyne (2015: 72) describes this pattern as follows: if the evidence supports the believers' paranormal claim it is vigorously broadcast, but if the evidence disconfirms their hypothesis, it is explained away, ignored, or suppressed. This is also a good example of the backfire effect, which refers to the fact that when believers are confronted with evidence their deeply held beliefs are wrong, they reject the evidence, and double down and even intensify their erroneous beliefs.

In the case of the negative findings regarding the Shroud not only were the results squelched, but an alternative account was immediately publicly circulated attesting that the authenticity of Jesus's burial cloth was not in doubt (Nickell 2007: 137). All subsequent "scientific investigations" of the relic underwritten by believers have followed the same pattern: distinguished experts are called in to render their verdict, their findings are negative, and the experts are attacked (Nickell 2007: 133). These efforts represent cases of pretended science harnessed to religious motives and gross supernaturalism (Mueller 1986: 324).

In 1978, another research team was formed with the scientific-sounding title "The Shroud of Turin Research Project" to authenticate the relic. Most of the team members were believers, and several belonged to an organization dedicated to proving the authenticity of the artifact. Once again, science was applied for crass supernaturalism (Nickell 2013: 124). Again the believers were provided with a contrary verdict. The finding came from Walter McCrone, the team's sole forensic chemist (McCrone 1986). He concluded that the alleged blood on the cloth was composed of red ochre and vermillion pigments, substances commonly used by medieval artists to depict blood. Thus, once again, the scientific evidence revealed that there is no blood on the cloth and that the image was the result of artistic techniques (McCrone 1999; Schafersman 1998: 35–36).

Predictably, the religionists suppressed McCrone's findings, and later he was expelled from the research team. Moreover, two team members, neither one an expert in blood analysis or the study of pigments, went public declaring the discovery of blood on the shroud. In 1983 forensic specialists refuted this shameful deception. A subsequent claim was the detection of human DNA on the fabric. Jesus's DNA? Not really. Anyone handling the cloth or crying over it, as many religionists do when they see holy relics, could have deposited the DNA.

At this stage, a different tactic appeared. A Swiss criminologist named Max Frei-Sulzer announced that he had discovered and identified 33 different pollen grains in the tape-lifted samples collected during the 1978 investigation that could only have originated in Palestine during the time of Jesus. Remarkably, there was no evidence of pollen from the region of France where the Shroud first came to light and where it was located for centuries. However, the other tape-lifted samples gathered at the same time as the one used by Frei contain very few pollen, a discrepancy that Steven Shafersman attributed to sample tampering. In other words, this was an act of pious fraud or hunger for publicity on the part of the Swiss criminologist. The deception also brought attention to Frei's questionable reputation as an investigator who had been censured earlier for tampering with evidence at the police crime laboratory in Basel, Switzerland, where he was employed (Nickell 2013: 268–69). In another incident, Frei, passing himself off as a handwriting expert, had erroneously declared the fake diaries of Adolf Hitler as the genuine article. Frei was a shady character all around.

## Radiocarbon Dates: Disgracing What Cannot Be Disproved

The final and decisive blow for the pro-authenticity crowd was the radiocarbon dates of the shroud obtained in 1988 in separate laboratories in Oxford, Zurich, and the University of Arizona (Damon et al. 1989). The tests provided dates between 1260 and 1390 CE, which confirm Pierre d'Arcis's assertion that the Shroud was a forgery dating to the fourteenth century. The scientific evidence thus matches the historical records. A complete account of the investigation appears in physicist Harry Grove's book *Relic, Icon or Hoax? Carbon Dating the Turin Shroud* (1996).

Again, rather than accept the evidence indicating that the relic is a forgery, believers launched a campaign to discredit the carbon dates. The effort by such purveyors of supernaturalism is an example of what Thomas Paine (1776) perceptively referred to as "Jesuitical cunning which always endeavors to disgrace what it cannot disprove." Into the fray entered a Russian researcher named Dimitri Kuznetsov, with his ad hoc hypothesis to explain why the carbon tests yielded dates during the medieval period. He asserted that according to his tests, fire can affect carbon-14 dating and that the 1532 fire had altered the radiocarbon signature of the cloth resulting in false dates. Experts were unable to replicate his results. Moreover, it turned out that Kuznetsov had plagiarized his data, even duplicating an error in the original materials. Another pious or not so pious fraud.

A further effort to discredit the carbon dates was the assertion that false dates were due to microbial contamination of the samples. However, physicist Thomas Pickett demonstrated that to get such a discrepancy in the dates, the amount of microbial contamination would have to be twice the weight of the cloth sample used in the tests. Another baseless allegation to refute the carbon dates was that the samples came from repair patches made after the 1532 fire, rather than the original materials. Finally, the most ludicrous of all explanations forwarded is that the paranormal radiation emitted from Jesus's body at the moment of resurrection altered the carbon-14 ratio in the shroud (Nickell 2013: 126; 1998b: 151), that is, the radioactive Jesus hypothesis. It is important to note that none of these denunciations have survived critical scrutiny (Schafersman 1998; Tattersall and Névraumont 2018: 49). A concise summary of these and other major mistaken assumptions regarding the Shroud are to be found in Colin Berry's (2019) site "Sindonology's 10 Biggest Mistakes."

This bizarre psychodrama continued with others accusing the scientists of deliberate fraud and for being part of a grand conspiracy to discredit this holy relic, a plot that included the Archbishop of Turin and even the Vatican. Why individuals and organizations whose own status and authority depend on the authenticity of the resurrection would conspire to suppress such confirmatory evidence is not explained.

The reaction of the religious enthusiasts, who have been dealt a decisive blow based on the historical, iconographic, and radiocarbon evidence, is a classic example of efforts to avoid cognitive dissonance that arises when someone confronts with two sets of conflicting beliefs, as already discussed in the context of the treatment of the confirmation bias. Rather than change or abandon a disconfirmed premise, shroud believers, like other paranormalists and religionists in comparable circumstances, have doubled down on their beliefs and embarked on an energetic propaganda campaign to convince themselves and recruit others to the truth of their beliefs (Bromley 1996: x). The words of Canon Ulysse Chevalier (1903: 5–24), the Catholic scholar who uncovered the documentary evidence proving that the shroud is a medieval artifact, are relevant here: "The history of the shroud constitutes a protracted violation of the two virtues so often commended by our holy books: justice and truth" (in Nickell 2013: 128).

The media and popular presses continue to treat this appalling religious imposture as a true paranormal object of great significance (Schafersman 1998: 29). Since 2001, there were more than 400 books published proclaiming the authenticity of this forgery, with only ten books presenting a skeptical perspective (Nickell 2013: 119). The stream of books and videos proclaiming authenticity continues today. Treatment of the Shroud of Turin illustrates a point made in an earlier chapter that science seeks to counteract the ever-present confirmation bias by demanding evidence and requiring the replication and falsification of propositions. Moreover, science demands that one follow the evidence to whatever conclusion it may lead. Religionists and paranormalists, such as those discussed here, yield to the confirmation bias. Science asks, "What is the evidence?" Paranormalists and religionists say, "I wish to believe this."

Ultimately religionists are not interested in where the evidence leads or the spirit of inquiry but the truth of their superstitious beliefs that always take precedence over something so inconvenient as the facts (e.g., Craig 1994: 36). What is unfortunate is how religionists and paranormalists seek to disguise their superstitious premises by adopting the trappings and terminology of modern scholarship and science. Sadly, the outcome of all this effort and mental contortions used to try and prove paranormal premises is that seemingly intelligent people look stupid. As stated before, this travesty makes it extremely difficult to take seriously anything these purveyors of supernaturalism say. Finally, to reiterate a point already made, believers fail to realize that even if there is proof beyond a shadow of a doubt that the cloth had been wrapped around a human body, this does not prove that a dead man came back to life, an event on which the entire case pivots.

Believers persist in their effort to validate somehow the authenticity of the Shroud relying on questionable methodologies and conclusions that do not meet minimum scientific standard. This is to be expected because they are dealing with the unreal. A case in point is the paper by religionists Carlino et al. (2017) published in the scientific journal *PLoS ONE* that claimed authenticity. The editors (2018) of the journal were compelled to retract the article due to its methodological shortcomings, insufficient controls, problematic conclusions, and because the sample used was provided by the religionist organization Shroud of Turin Education and Research Association Incorporated (STERA) that the authors failed to mention in their paper.

Meanwhile, the evidence against the authenticity of this relic keeps piling up. A more recent blood pattern analysis (BPA) of the Turin cloth has revealed that the flow patterns of the alleged blood from the different parts of the body are inconsistent with one another and are unrealistic even if one infers non-documented episodes of bleeding due to movement of the cadaver or postmortem bleeding (see Borrini and Garlaschelli 2018: 7). These findings further indicate that the Shroud of Turin is a fourteenth-century artistic representation and is consistent with the historical records, the radiocarbon dates, and the extensive chemical analyses of the cloth.

# Chapter Eight

# MIRACLES AS EVIDENCE OF GOD'S ACTIONS IN THE WORLD

*The knavery and folly of men are such common phenomena, that I should rather believe the most extraordinary events to arise from their concurrence, than admit of so signal a violation of the laws of nature.*

*No testimony is sufficient to establish a miracle, unless the testimony be of such a kind, that its falsehood would be more miraculous, than the fact, which it endeavors to establish.*

—David Hume, *Enquiries Concerning the Human Understanding* (1748)

*[A miracle is] the most equivocal sort of evidence that can be set up; for the belief is not to depend upon the thing called a miracle, but upon the credit of the reporter who says he saw it; and, therefore, the thing, were it true, would have no better chance of being believed than if it was a lie.*

—Thomas Paine, *Age of Reason* (1794)

*All the pretended miracles near enough to be examined are referable to illusion or imposture [...] miracles only exist when people believe in them. The supernatural is but another word for faith.*

*If a single miracle had ever been proved, we could not reject in a mass all those of ancient history; for, admitting that very many of these were false, we might still believe that some of them were true. But it is not so.*

—Ernest Renan, *The Apostles* (1866)

*Extraordinary claims require extraordinary evidence.*

—Carl Sagan, *Cosmos* (1980)

Miracles are thought to be direct instances of supernatural or paranormal interventions in the natural order of the world and the course of human history. In these events, the normal and the supernatural converge. It is for this reason that objects such as the Shroud of Turin described in the previous chapter acquire so much significance in the minds of the faithful. The "argument from miracles" for the existence of God is a standard part of the arsenal of theist philosophers and religious polemicists. However, are miracles what they are claimed to be?

## The Role of Miracles in Religion

Nearly every religion possesses accounts of strange and extraordinary happenings and deeds associated with the authors or originators of those beliefs systems, such as Moses, Jesus, Buddha, and Muhammad, not to mention the founding holy personages or leaders of "indigenous religions" and new religious movements, which number in the thousands. Religious miracles persist today in the form of Marian apparitions, weeping and bleeding statues, figurines that drink milk, faith-healings, marvelous cures at holy shrines, and images of holy figures appearing on the sides of buildings, window panes, and pieces of toast. Alongside these are reports of similarly weird and extraordinary happenings that are not (necessarily) religious, such as sightings of cryptids, monsters, alien beings, rapacious abducting extraterrestrials, crop circles, psychic surgery, and other unexplainable and mind-boggling things.

Records of ancient religious miracles appear in the sacred texts of different cultures. These writings are profuse with narratives of mysterious happenings that are used to substantiate each religion's truth claims. As the philosopher David Hume (1902 [1748]: 121) noted in his essay "Of Miracles" (1748), all religions "abound in miracles," and they use these miracles as evidence for the truth of their supernatural beliefs. Believers make such assertions, Hume (1902 [1748]: 131) observed, because mere reason is insufficient to convince us of the veracity of their implausible postulates.

The gospels contain stories about the miracles of Jesus, who was born of a virgin, performed magical healings, walked on water, changed water into wine, fed masses with a few pieces of bread, expelled demons, healed the sick, and returned from the grave. The paramount miracle in Christianity is Jesus's resurrection. As the historian of the New Testament and early Christianity Gerd Lüdemann (1995: 1) observes, "The resurrection of Jesus is the central point of the Christian religion." Similarly, the theologian Ernest Barnes (1948: 84) noted the centrality of miracles for the Christian faith. For these reasons, a detailed evaluation of the miracles in the gospels is provided in Chapters 13 and 14.

The great Christian theologian St. Augustine defined a miracle as an event that happens "in defiance of the natural laws known to us." Philosophers refer to these as "violation miracles" in contrast to "coincidence miracles," which are cases of unexpected good fortune. More specifically, Thomas Aquinas, during the thirteenth century viewed miracles as phenomena distinct from natural causes, beyond nature, and caused directly by God (Bartlett 2008: 19). False miracles, or marvelous feats, Aquinas added, although similarly astonishing, are due to misunderstood natural causes or achieved through the action of demons or magic. During the Middle Ages, miracles were thus understood as "that which is done contrary to the usual course of nature and amazes us [...] [and that] the author of miracles is God," a point that theologians continuously try to emphasize (Bartlett 2013: 335).

A miraculous phenomenon contradicts our intuitive ontological expectations about basic categories, such as solid objects, living things, and personal agents (Pyysiäinen 2004: 82, 2008: 18). Hence, these sorts of things are attention-grabbing and highly memorable and can evoke powerful emotional reactions. The nature of such stories is significant. Those that are memorable and are adopted and transmitted are the ones that violate intuitive ontological categories or have certain fundamental counterintuitive aspects, such as a statue that bleeds, talking snakes, humans turning into pillars of salt, dead persons coming back to life, and so forth. To give a prosaic example, reading a newspaper article about a dog biting a human is not attention-grabbing or memorable, we hear of this frequently. But think of a news report that says "girl bites dog." That one does the trick. The extreme improbability of miraculous events and their counterintuitive attributes leads to the conclusion that a supernatural agent or otherworldly power must be involved (Shapiro 2016: 55). Such a supposition, however, does not mean that miracles are real. These are all X-claims and suspect for that reason.

For believers, miracles always have religious significance (Overall 2003a: 156). While miracle stories serve to establish the religious credentials of particular saintly figures, they ultimately presume more general religious doctrines, such as the reality of God (Martin 1990: 189). As already noted, the "argument from miracles" has been one of the mainstays of support for theism (Mackie 2013: 13). For religionists, miracles provide evidence that behind what is perceptible there is at work an all-knowing, all-powerful cosmic intelligence, or God, making His presence known by intervening in earthly affairs through extraordinary intrusions, therefore proof that a miracle is genuine proof of the existence of God. Some theologians continue to rely on this argument to support their claims about theism (e.g., Swinburne 2004). The problem here, as the philosopher Michael Scriven (1966: 139) put it, is that the evidence for the occurrence of miracles as supernatural interventions into the natural order of events "is in an unhappy state."

Miracles are such extremely improbable events, so contrary to all that is known, that they are explicable only through recourse to a supernatural force operating outside the natural order of the universe (Shapiro 2016: 2). Moreover, it is the infrequency and uniqueness of such events that allow us to recognize them as miracles. If a preternatural intelligence were to intervene in the world all the time, it would be impossible to differentiate a natural from a supernatural occurrence. Miracles may, therefore, be described as "one-off events," as Coyne (2015: 120) has put it, which are extraordinary in kind.

The theistic philosopher Charles Taliaferro (2009: 206) takes a different stance, arguing that miracles are simply acts of God and for him, the cosmos itself is a continuous miracle, and that "the cosmos could not exist for an instant were it not for the creative, conserving act of God." The problem here is, How do we know this? Because of statements in arcane and absurd texts written thousands of years ago by people who knew next to nothing about the world and universe? Also, if everything is a miracle as suggested here, how could we possibly distinguish a miracle from an ordinary event? To say that everything is a miracle and that this proves the existence of God tells us absolutely nothing.

Another way to think about this is that something is deemed to be miraculous because the percipients cannot imagine a possible explanation for it either due to a lack of knowledge or unfamiliarity with an already existing naturalistic explanation for the phenomenon in question. As philosopher Paul Kurtz (2003b: 218) pointed out, the word miracle, like paranormal, is interjected when we do not understand the causes of phenomena. This entails the logical fallacy of arguing from ignorance, that is, that since we do not know of a naturalistic explanation for some event or occurrence, it must, therefore, be paranormal, or "God did it." I have already discussed the flaws in this kind of omni-explanation that purportedly explains everything in Chapters 3 and 6.

## David Hume on the Nature of Testimonial Evidence and the Psychology of Miracle Claims

In his book *Enquiries Concerning the Human Understanding* (1748), David Hume presented a decisive refutation of claims regarding the occurrence of miracles. Ever since its publication, this work has exasperated all religionists and theistic philosophers who depend on miracles to further their superstitious claims (e.g., Keener 2011). As the philosopher Robert Fogelin (2003: 39) points out, Hume's opponents are invariably miracle mongers. Let us follow Hume's line of thought. As he put it,

> Nothing is esteemed a miracle, if it ever happen in the common course of nature. It is no miracle that a man, seemingly in good health, should die on a sudden; because such kind of death, though more unusual than any other, has yet been frequently observed to happen. But it is a miracle that a dead man should come to life; because that has never been observed, in any age or country. (Hume 1902 [1748]: 115)

Here, Hume is using background evidence and prior probabilities of extraordinary claims being true or false based on our knowledge of how the world operates.

Miraculous occurrences depend upon eyewitness testimonies to the effect that an extraordinary event has indeed taken place, was seen by those witnesses, and that those rendering the report are truthful (Philipse 2014: 170). Thus, assertions about miraculous events always come to us in the form of anecdotes. Anecdotes, as discussed in Chapter 7, are entirely unreliable. As New Testament scholar Bart Ehrman (2009: 175) points out, reports about the miracles of Jesus, especially the resurrection stories, come from second- or third-hand accounts written down 35 to 65 years or more after the fact. Moreover, he adds, the narratives are rife with incongruities.

Thomas Paine (1880 [1794]: 49, 51) perspicuously pointed out a significant attribute of miraculous events, observing that a miracle is "the most equivocal sort of evidence [because it depends] upon the credit of the reporter who says he saw it; and, therefore, the thing, were it true, would have no better chance of being believed than if it was a lie. [...] it requires a transfer of faith from God to man to believe a miracle upon man's report." Compounding the problem is the fact that miracles always take place under questionable circumstances, occur covertly, and often before a handful of dubious characters. The French philosopher Ernest Renan (1866: 12) noted the tendency for miracles never to take place before qualified skeptical witnesses who are the ones to convince. He adds that all miracles require credulity of the witnesses.

In such reports, claimants are asserting that we should trust the veracity of their account that a violation of a law of nature has occurred in favor of their argument. The central issue, therefore, is the reliability of testimonial evidence itself. As the philosopher Nicholas Everitt (2004: 117, 308) has pointed out, Hume was concerned with the epistemology of miracle reports and not strictly with the reality of miraculous happenings.

The aspect of Hume's ideas on this subject that is of interest to this discussion is how he underscored the psychological and cognitive foundations for why people are so receptive to accepting tales about miraculous occurrences (Fogelin 2003: 21). The two key factors he pointed out are (1) the predisposition to believe and (2) the "knavery and folly of men" who readily commit pious frauds and impostures. Regarding the first point, he wrote,

> The passion of *surprise* and *wonder,* arising from miracles, being an agreeable emotion, gives a sensible tendency towards the belief of those events, from which it is derived. And this goes so

> far, that even those who cannot enjoy this pleasure immediately, nor can believe those miraculous events, of which they are informed, yet love to partake of the satisfaction at second-hand or by rebound, and place a pride and delight in exciting the admiration of others. (Hume 1902 [1748]: 117)

We know from history that in various cases miracle tales have become entrenched in particular populations, spread widely, become the subjects of further elaboration and theoretical embellishments, and even acquire institutional sponsorship (Oppy 2018: 172). Miracle stories are, therefore, copy-me bits of information or memes. These are the kind of circumstances associated with the claim that a dead person came back to life, which is the basis of Christianity. Even where such stories do not have official institutional acceptance, such beliefs can become embedded and persist over time. Consider how many people in the United States believe on the basis of flimsiest evidence in such things as Bigfoot, the Loch Ness monster, UFOs, alien abductions, ESP, satanic ritual abuse, and other marvelous, weird, bizarre, and paranormal tales. Like miracles, these things are attention-grabbing because they violate intuitive expectations, which makes them memorable. Being attention-grabbing, however, does not make them real. True or not, such beliefs can be resilient indeed. In some cases, such ideas have endured for thousands of years, as exemplified by the religious miracle stories associated with the "world religions."

Hume's statement about the "knavery and folly of men" stresses human psychological and cognitive dispositions that under the right circumstances compels people to believe in all kinds of absurdities and fatuous narratives. These are the proclivities identified by cognitive and evolutionary psychologists that include our hyperactive agency detection mechanisms, the tendency to trust what authority figures tell us, and the propensity to soak up particular types of fantasies. Indeed, these researchers have substantiated Hume's ideas by showing that the human cognitive apparatus is highly vulnerable to and is frequently hijacked by such false counterintuitive beliefs or X-claims based on subjective impressions and anecdotal evidence (Law 2016).

For Hume (1902 [1748]: 119) miracles flow from the human propensity toward "the marvelous." He adds that although this proclivity may be suppressed based on sense experience, it can never be "extirpated from human nature." But as Hume further observed, "the strong propensity of mankind to the extraordinary and the marvelous [...] ought reasonably to beget a suspicion against all relations of this kind." The philosopher Stephen Law (2016) forwards a similar idea regarding the persistence and unreliability of such beliefs (see below).

Regarding the first point, the will to believe and the intense desire for wanting those beliefs to be true are so compelling that they tempt some to perpetrate fraud and others to accept such impostures uncritically. For these reasons, in contrast to all other aspects of human experience "violations of truth" are widespread in testimony regarding matters of religion and the paranormal (Hume (1902 [1748]: 128–29). Religious polemicists vigorously object when skeptics call attention to the fact that true believers are prone to committing pious frauds to prove what is in their minds a meritorious cause, as Hume put it (e.g., Keener 2011: 193). Yet, the many misrepresentations and outright falsehoods in their own works as discussed throughout this book alone support this contention.

Moreover, history is replete with cases of false miracles that provide solid reasons for rejecting the veracity of all such paranormal and supernatural claims. For example, the propensity for fraud and deception is now well-known with respect to nineteenth-century spiritualism. An appropriate description of its history is a catalog of hoaxes and scams. There is also considerable evidence that present-day faith healers, neo-shamans, and televangelist preachers use trickery to convince their gullible and often despairing clients that they have miraculous powers. The same is true of the various mediums, psychics, and fortune tellers who make a living by defrauding the public using numerous impostures.

Moreover, the great talents members of our species have for deceptiveness has in several cases duped trained scientists in parapsychology laboratory settings. For this reason, exceptional control protocols have become necessary to prevent cheating in laboratory studies of paranormal phenomena. Psi researchers themselves have on various occasions resorted to deception to fool others that they have found long-awaited proof for some psi phenomenon. In my work, I regularly encountered sleight-of-hand trickery in the repertoire of shamans and faith healers in several cultures. In other words, none of these practitioners possess genuine paranormal capacities. Their success depends entirely upon how well they hoodwink the gullibility, insecurities, and psychological vulnerabilities of their customers. Hence, the religionists' case is not bolstered in any way when a believer such as Keener (2011: 229) seek to dignify and validate the authenticity of the miraculous antics of a conman such as Oral Roberts due to their purported similarities with shamanistic practices around the world.

The ease with which paranormal scam artists can bamboozle people today suggests that the credulous and superstitious people in biblical times were probably more susceptible to trickery and deceit. As Martin (1990: 197) observes, if special precautions are needed to prevent fraud in modern scientific laboratories, what sort of credence should we attach to miracle reports by "less educated and less sophisticated people without systematic controls against fraud?" His answer is "very little." Along the same lines, Renan (1866: 12) observed that miracles are never proven and, upon close inspection, turn out to be due to "illusion and imposture." He adds that miracles "only exist when people believe in them. The supernatural is but another word for faith." By illusion, Renan is referring to the various factors that lead to perceptual errors and self-delusion. The great deal we now know about the different perceptual and cognitive errors to which eyewitnesses are prone, as discussed in Chapter 7, supports this assertion. These include hallucinations, collective delusions, misunderstanding of probability, memory errors, hindsight bias, top-down processing, the role of expectation, and the psychological phenomenon of group-think and memory conformity. Such factors suggest that assertions regarding any miracles rest on extremely flimsy grounds.

It is for these reasons that Hume adopted an uncompromising skepticism regarding the reality of miracles attested to by testimony. Thus, as some say, while the possibility that miracles can happen should not be ruled out, that is, "improbable events are not impossible events" (Shapiro 2016: 78), one can never relinquish the demand for extraordinary evidence. However, conceding that miracles are logically possible does not mean acknowledgment that they are probable according to how physical reality operates (Everitt 2004: 118).

## Pious Frauds, Miracles, and Why Extraordinary Claims Always Require Extraordinary Evidence

Hume (1902 [1748]: 117) elaborated on the role of religious orientation upon the nature of testimonies regarding miracles, pointing out that when religion is combined with the propensity toward the marvelous, reason vanishes and human testimony loses all credibility. Anyone who has spent time with believers, whether evangelical Christians, Taliban ideologues, Jehovah's Witnesses, Mormon missionaries, shamans, or New Age mystics and healers to provide a few examples with which I am familiar, will quickly discern this fact. Also, as Hume noted, religious people are highly motivated to spread lies if they think it is for a higher purpose. In his words,

> A religionist may be an enthusiast, and imagine he sees what has no reality: he may know his narrative to be false, and yet persevere in it, with the best intentions in the world, for the sake of promoting so holy a cause. (Hume 1902 [1748]: 117–18)

Such purveyors of false tales or pious lies, Hume (1902 [1748]: 118) argued, are also more motivated in their efforts than other scam artists. Hume (1902 [1748]: 118) also emphasized how the miracle-monger relies on his or her oratory skills to take advantage of the ignorance of his or her listeners and their propensity to react in an emotionally receptive way to extraordinary religious claims and miraculous happenings. It is remarkable how closely these words apply to the present with the proliferation of impudent religious fundamentalists, evangelical preachers, New Age gurus, televangelists, exorcists, and conspiracy theorists and their beguiled and entranced audiences.

Hume also stressed that the true believer also has other powerful personal motives to pursue their deception and demagoguery:

> But what greater temptation than to appear a missionary, a prophet, an ambassador from heaven? Who would not encounter many dangers and difficulties, in order to attain so sublime a character? Or if, by the help of vanity and a heated imagination, a man has first made a convert of himself, and entered seriously into the delusion; whoever scruples to make use of pious frauds, in support of so holy and meritorious a cause? (Hume 1902 [1748]: 125–26)

Such "ambassadors from heaven" flourish in our day in the form of evangelical preachers such as Billy Graham and his imitators, so-called neoshamans, New Age gurus, and magicians. Included in this group are pretenders like David Koresh, Jim Jones, Marshall Applewhite, Shoko Asahara, Bin Laden, and Ashin Wirathu, to name just a few.

Thus, as Hume said it, given the prevalence of fraud, the human propensity to want to believe in the wondrous, the claim itself is "proof against a miracle" (Hume 1902 [1748]: 114). Hume (1902 [1748]: 116) provided the resurrection of a cadaver as an example, asserting that if someone reports that a dead man has come back to life, one must weigh whether the reporter is lying or deceived against the claim that a corpse came back to life, which never happens. To accept a resurrection, Hume adds, the testimony should be so strong that its "falsehood would be more miraculous" than the event being reported. Otherwise, we are entitled to be skeptical.

The philosophical niceties of whether or not improbable events are impossible in a case such as the resurrection of the dead should not even be part of the debate. There is no evidence now or at any time in the history of humankind that a cadaver has come back to life and walked among people, although religionists want us to think that the dead do sometimes rise from the grave even today (e.g., Keener 2011, see below). The deaths of many billions of humans, none of whom have returned from the dead, substantiate this point. As Loftus (2011: 80) puts it concerning the resurrection of Jesus, "such prodigious events never happen in our days, then they did not happen in first-century Palestine either." Similarly, Thomas Paine (1880 [1794]: 50) asked what is more probable that the laws of nature have ceased to operate, or that the reporter is telling a lie? He adds that there is no evidence that the laws of nature deviate, whereas there is ample evidence "that millions of lies have been told in the same time" and hence the odds are "at least a million to one, that the reporter of a miracle tells a lie." Therefore, instead of considering a report of a miracle as evidence for the truth of a claim, it should be treated as evidence of the falsity of that assertion (Paine 1880 [1794]: 50).

The type of testimonies Hume rejected, therefore, are those provided in support of religious miracles (Fogelin 2003: 26). Hume's rejection of such declarations, as Fogelin (2003: 29, 31) points out, stems from an examination of the historical record which reveals a "consistent pattern of ignorance, deceit, and credulity." In other words, Hume made his case based upon the empirical facts, sufficiently attested to by history, that testimonies regarding religious miracles are exceptionally untrustworthy (Fogelin 2003: 29). Religionist efforts to refute this argument are discussed below.

However, Hume did not deny that miracles are a priori impossible, *contra* his religionist critics (e.g., Johnson 1999: 18). As Fogelin (2003: 26, 28) points out, Hume does provide a specific scenario, one that does not include religious motivations, where the appropriate type of testimony could overrule background knowledge of how the world operates. Hume (1902 [1748]: 127–28) put it as follows:

> suppose, all authors, in all languages, agree, that, from the first of January, 1600, there was a total darkness over the whole earth for eight days: suppose that the tradition of this extraordinary event is still strong and lively among the people: that all travelers, who return from foreign countries, bring us accounts of the same tradition, without the least variation or contradiction: it is evident, that our present philosophers, instead of doubting the fact, ought to receive it as certain, and ought to search for the causes whence it might be derived. The decay, corruption, and dissolution of nature, is an event rendered probable by so many analogies, that any phenomenon, which seems to have a tendency towards that catastrophe, comes within the reach of human testimony, if that testimony be very extensive and uniform.

Thus, while the required standards for testimony in support of miracles are very high, they can in principle be met (Fogelin 2003: 31). However, religionists past and present who cite testimony to support miracles fail to attend to any standards. Hence the Christian apologist William Warburton (1841: 313), a contemporary detractor, sought to refute Hume by arguing that a miraculous scenario such as the absence of the sunlight for eight days is on par with Jesus's resurrection from the dead, both being contrary to the laws of nature. Hume is therefore arbitrarily biased, Warburton declared, for accepting one case and not the other. Warburton was mistaken. For his assertion to hold up, he has to provide the same type of testimonies for the resurrection that Hume requires for the eight-day eclipse. The point is not that both of these events—an eight-day eclipse and a cadaver rising—are violations of natural laws, but rather the nature of the testimonies in each case. The evidence religionists are required to provide must, as Hume (1902 [1748]: 116–17) said,

> be attested by a sufficient number of men, of such unquestioned good sense, education, and learning, as to secure us against all delusion in themselves; of such undoubted integrity, as to place them beyond all suspicion of any design to deceive others; of such credit and reputation in the eyes of mankind, as to have a great deal to lose in case of their being detected in any falsehood; and at the same time, attesting facts performed in such a public manner and in so celebrated a part of the world, as to render the detection unavoidable: all which circumstances are requisite to give us a full assurance in the testimony of men.

In other words, the witnesses have to be numerous, exceptionally trustworthy, and of unimpeachable character. Moreover, they must be unbiased and have no stakes in the matter, concur and not contradict each other, have relevant expertise, not be gullible, and must not be visually impaired (Fogelin 2003: 8; Hume 1902 [1748]: 112–13). However, there are no cases in human history of any miracle attested by testimony that meets these criteria. True believers, of course, cry foul and declare that these standards are too rigid and demand that they should be relieved of the burden of proof (see below).

What Hume underscored is the cognitive disposition for people to believe the unreal real or their susceptibility to X-claims. This was not a mere supposition, and the findings of the neurosciences and cognitive and evolutionary psychology have confirmed this to be the case. The desire for the supernatural and paranormal to be genuine is so powerful, as already discussed, that many are willing to accept the legitimacy of almost any claim, setting aside the critical faculties operational in other aspects of life. Such willingness renders all such claims susceptible to fraud, deception, and self-delusion. Religious indoctrination reinforces this by encouraging followers to accept on faith, which means "believe" without asking for evidence. As Mackie (2013: 15) points out, in the context of religion, this kind of credulity is considered meritorious. Or to put it another way, in religion, doubt and skepticism are construed as vices and sins (Martin 1990: 198).

Such uncritical reception of all things paranormal and supernatural among true believers offers an almost irresistible temptation on the part of the not so pious to take advantage of them by committing fraud. In our own time, we have evangelical preachers, the likes of Peter Poppof and other religious conmen with their onstage theatrics and mail and online scams, and Uri Geller, the Israeli spoon-bending swindler, and sadly innumerable others. This also brings to mind the exploits of Peregrinus, the pretender and con artist, to be discussed in Chapter 12, who joined the church to exploit the credulity of the early Christians, "who took him for a God, accepted his laws, and declared him their president," as Lucian of Samosata describes in his satirical tract *The Death of Peregrinus*.

The same desire for the supernatural to be real is also the reason that reduces to the ranks of liars and cheats all of our present-day self-styled "ambassadors from heaven" wishing to forward what they deem is a meritorious cause. A case in point is the ludicrous Creation Museum in Kentucky and its giant boat, the so-called Ark of Noah, discussed in Chapter 1. Religionists themselves acknowledge that when it comes to a choice between evidence of facts and faith, they will always choose the latter. Consider Ken Ham's response during his February 4, 2014 debate with Bill Nye at the Creation Museum when he was asked by the moderator "What, if anything, would ever change your mind?" Ham's response was "God has shown me very clearly through his word [...] the Bible is the word of God [...] as far as the word of God is concerned, no, no one is going to convince me that the word of God is not true" (Nye and Ham 2014). Christian apologists, such as William Craig, hold the same position. He has openly stated that

> Should a conflict arise between the witness of the Holy Spirit to the fundamental truth of the Christian faith and beliefs based on argument and evidence, then it is the former which must take precedence over the latter, not vice versa. (Craig 1994: 36)

Given the problematic nature of religionist testimonies in support of miracles, Hume (1902 [1748]: 115–16) formulated his famous maxim:

> No testimony is sufficient to establish a miracle, unless the testimony be of such a kind, that its falsehood would be more miraculous, than the fact, which it endeavors to establish.

Hume's maxim is, of course, applicable to all paranormal claims. He extended his idea to such phenomena as prophecies, divinations, and prodigies. Carl Sagan (1980) reformulated this adage as "extraordinary claims require extraordinary evidence." An earlier formulation of this statement was by the Eastern Michigan University sociologist and skeptic Marcello Truzzi (1978: 11) who said: "Extraordinary claims require extraordinary proof." What this means is that in the case of miracles and similar weird and extraordinary happenings the nature and quality of the eyewitness testimonies have to be of a standard that outweighs the extreme improbability of the miraculous event (Philipse 2014: 176). Such a stringent demand for evidence is necessary because miracles on offer in the context of religious claims—such as angelic beings carrying messages, cadavers rising from graves, the moon splitting into two, virgins giving birth, oceans parting, women turning into pillars of salt, burning bushes talking, non-corporeal beings having intercourse with maidens, and hordes of zombie saints invading towns—are such improbable events that the proof of such singularly unlikely happenings must be very, very strong (Shapiro 2016: 89).

For this reason, Hume (1902 [1748]: 116) rejected testimonial evidence regarding miracles. Along the same lines, Renan (1866: 12) observed that if there were conclusive evidence for a single miracle, then we would be unjustified to reject all such claims in totality. Since then, we could argue that some accounts are false, but others may yet be true. However, no such evidence has been provided in any place or time.

However, what about the miracles that have been officially certified by an organization such as the Catholic Church? It is the case that the Vatican has ruled various occurrences as genuine miracles, such as the Marian apparition at Fátima, Portugal. Given the nature of that event, to be described in Chapter 9, little confidence can be placed in the procedures used to make such a determination. Indeed, ecclesiastical standards are hardly scientific ones, regardless of the purported stringent guidelines and investigative methods. The Vatican relies on interviews and amassing anecdotal accounts. In other words, this is theological validation, not a scientific confirmation.

Consider the miracles that qualified Mother Theresa for beatification, which means that she is blissfully dwelling in heaven, can be revered, and can intercede on behalf of those who pray in her name. The purported miracle was the claim by an Indian woman named Monica Besra that her cancerous tumor disappeared when she looked at the nun's image (Brown 2016). However, it turns out that Besra only had a cyst caused by tuberculosis, not a cancerous tumor, and she had undergone conventional medical treatment in a hospital under the care of a physician who took credit for her recovery (Coyne 2015: 117; Orr 2003). Besra's case is rather embarrassing, but it is probably not unlike hundreds of other such certified miracles of God provided for us by the astute investigators at the Vatican.

Hume (1902 [1748]: 122) extended his argument to all miracle-based religions, pointing out that irrespective of who provides the testimony, a few "barbarous Arabians" for Islam, or gullible and ignorant people for Judaism and Christianity, "all the authors and witnesses […] who have related any miracle in their particular religion […] we are to regard their testimony in the same light."

Hume pointed out further that when the miracle-believers of one religion refute the tenets of another miracle-based faith, they undermine their own position in the same process. For example, one Christian apologist asserts that simply because some miracles are fake, that does not mean that all of them are fraudulent (McDowell 1973: 125). In other words, the assertion is that the miracle stories of the Bible are genuine and conclusive evidence for the existence of the Christian God, but identical fables and fantasies in other holy books are false (Narveson 2003: 99). Proponents of spiritualism and psi phenomena use the same sort of sham special pleading, namely that some cases may have been fakes, but this does not mean that all claims are fraudulent. Such a spurious stance does not hold up. As Hume (1902 [1748]: 121) observed,

> Every miracle, therefore, pretended to have been wrought in any of these religions (and all of them abound in miracles), as its direct scope is to establish the particular system to which it is attributed; so has it the same force, though more indirectly, to overthrow every other system. In destroying a rival system, it likewise destroys the credit of those miracles, on which that system was established; so that all the prodigies of different religions are to be regarded as

contrary facts, and the evidence of these prodigies, whether weak or strong, as opposite to each other.

Even if one disagrees with Hume's argument on this point, it is the case that since the evidence of purported miracles in one religion is exceptionally weak, then it is the same in the case of the ostensible miracles in other religions (Martin 1990: 202).

To state it differently, to establish the veracity of such extraordinary happenings the proponents of any one religion must be able to demonstrate that *their* story is more believable than similar claims forwarded by members of other religions and, as Oppy (2018: 173) stresses, more credible than all the reports of extraordinary events and entities not connected to any religion. Thus, if one cannot find firmer historical corroboration for the miracles ascribed to Jesus than is possible for the ones credited to other similar characters, then there is insufficient justification to accept either set of claims (cf., Oppy 2018: 173). These include the miracles attributed to Apollonius of Tyana, Asclepius, Attis, and Empedocles, who were also considered to be the sons of God and mortal women, raised the dead, were deemed "saviors" from heaven, appeared after death, and ascended to heaven (see Chapter 13).

As for the assertion that the falsehood of some miracles does not mean all of them are false, Renan (1866: 12) acknowledged this possibility but pointed out that all miracle claims have proven to be false upon close examination. In other words, under scrutiny, all miracle stories collapse. Moreover, the sheer number of so-called miracles on record does not help the believer's position in any way, although religionists often try to make this claim as will be discussed below. Hundreds of unsubstantiated cases do not amount to a substantiated one. As Nickell (1998a: 11) has observed, for example, "an accumulation of Elvis Presley sightings" does not prove that Elvis is still with us (see Reece 2006: 161–65). It is the same with claims regarding paranormal and supernatural happenings.

As to the contention that it is impossible to prove that a miracle has not happened, here again, the believers falter. Is it true that "the positive savant who denies the supernatural argues as gratuitously as the credulous one who admits it," Renan (1866: 12) asked? Not so, he added, because the burden of proof rests with those who assert paranormal claims. As he put it, "It is the duty of him who affirms a proposition to prove it, while he to whom the affirmation is made has only to listen to the proof and decide whether it is satisfactory." The burden of proof never shifts, no matter how sincere, enthusiastic, or crafty the special pleading.

## Evaluating Extraordinary Claims

The philosopher Larry Shapiro (2016: 71, 73), following Hume, suggests the following steps for the evaluation of miracle claims, a process already covered in Chapter 3. First, we should weigh the probability of the truth of the testimony relative to the probability of the event. Second, consider the probability of whether something other than the occurrence of the event generated the testimony based on our background evidence and knowledge. And, of course, we must look at the availability of alternative non-paranormal explanations. These are relatively reasonable criteria given our current state of knowledge and background evidence, which provides reliable clues about what types of events are likely and which ones are not.

Unlike the ancients, today we do not ascribe things we cannot explain to mysterious supernatural interventions. However, religionists still find it expedient to ensure that the faithful continue believing in miracles "as unexpected and extraordinary evidence of God's power" (Carveri 1967: 118). Hume is reviled in religionist circles for this reason. Most rational people, however, no longer think that seeds sprout in the fields through magic, that evil spirits cause disease, or that thunder, lightning, hurricanes, tsunamis, and volcanic eruptions are God's actions because Americans tolerate homosexuality. Nor do they think that a mere touch can heal spleens, that the application of saliva and mud can restore sight to the blind, or that prayers can return life to a cadaver. Only an utterly enthralled person of faith (e.g., Keener 2011: 537, see below) can claim that evangelical preachers across the globe today can bring the dead back to life. Thus to argue for the possibility of miracles as events outside of nature, as Craveri (1967: 118) put it, hoodwinks people's ignorance and encourages their superstitions.

Our background knowledge and evidence are significant factors in this case. As Shapiro (2016: 81) puts it, our current knowledge of the world is vast. We now know what eclipses are and how tsunamis occur. We also know that the dead do not come back to life, people cannot tread water, and stone statues do not bleed or cry. Religionists and paranormalists would object and point out that the available background knowledge we have does not mean that everything about reality is known. Another way this is stated is that you have not looked at every single case and, therefore, divine miracles may be happening (Keener 2011: 143–45, 148). By taking this position, believers hope that the universe may yet operate in the way they wish it to do so, that is, that behind what is apparent there is a cosmic intelligence, an omnipotent, all-knowing God who is personally concerned with the details of the lives of every single person. Such a tactic is not very useful because the evidence for the paranormal and supernatural is not going to get any better.

As Scriven (1966: 155) forcefully pointed out, "the evidence for theism is either good now, or else it never will be good." He points out further that even if all of a sudden there is a proliferation of indisputable miracles all over the planet and if religious mystics were able to offer confirmable wonders, this would be evidence not of the God of theism but that of the arrival of a "Johnny-come-lately" supernatural being. There would be absolutely no reason to think that this is the theistic God. In other words, the best explanation of the evidence we have just described would be that "a god has *arrived*; there would be absolutely no reason to think that he had access to all the times and places that are part of the nature of the God to whom theists pray now."

The inference that a cosmic intelligence outside the spatiotemporal realm of our universe is the best explanation for an improbable event stems from several far-fetched unverifiable assumptions, at least unverified during the more than 200,000 years *Homo sapiens* have been around. These include the premise that a cosmic super-intelligence exists, has human-like desires, expectations, intentions, emotions, and is personally involved in the daily affairs of people, is worried that we might steal or covet a neighbor's spouse, and uses miracles to reveal His presence. No explanation is ever on offer for why an omnipotent, omniscient God should choose such a recondite way to disclose his existence, rather than through an unambiguous and direct method.

As the philosopher Jan Narveson (2003: 99) asks, "Why on Earth (or in heaven) would the Deity engage in such shenanigans anyway?" He creates an orderly universe but then tries to induce people to believe in his existence by talking out of burning bushes, walking on water, sacrificing himself to himself to allay his own anger and to absolve people of purported sins committed long ago by somebody else, dying and coming back from the dead, and so forth (cf., Narveson 2003: 100). Such behavior is very odd, indeed. How are his rational-minded worshippers to make sense of this? Narveson (2003: 100) adds that God's capricious activities, producing a miracle here but not there, before this group rather than the other undermines such narratives. The one rational conclusion is that these tales were the inventions of beguiled true believers, and in particular, ones "not inclined to ask too many embarrassing questions." Miraculous events resonate in human minds—we invent them to mystify ourselves, this is also why we love Houdini, James Randi, David Copperfield, Penn and Teller, and other stage magicians or illusionists, but they have nothing to do with a God or any other paranormal beings or forces.

There is another major problem. As Shapiro (2016: 87) rightly asks, how do we know that an alleged miracle is the handiwork of the God of our particular religion? Why is the Christian God a better choice than Shiva, the destroyer and creator? What about Kukulkan, Zeus, Teshub, or Baʿal? They were pretty good creator deities as well! There are many other equally plausible alternative possibilities, such as a scientifically advanced extraterrestrial being masquerading as God to toy with our minds, a group of lesser gods, a near-god entity, or even a super magician. These possibilities are as good or as bad as the God hypothesis to account for an observed paranormal phenomenon. In other words, why is the Christian God, Allah, or Jehova the more reasonable explanation over aliens masquerading as God, multiple gods, an assemblage of lesser deities, or even a super magician? Can we say that we just know that aliens, lesser gods, and super magicians are imaginary, but the Christian God, Allah, or Jehova do exist? How can this stance be justified? Opting for the God hypothesis, from among other equally plausible explanations leaves the miracle-believer begging the question (Shapiro 2016: 83).

To make a credible case, miracle-believers must present evidence for a miraculous event that is so extraordinary as to render all alternate explanations entirely improbable. Thus, to reiterate, the burden of proof is entirely and always upon the proponent of the miracles. As Fishman (2009: 817) observes, the more extraordinary a claim is given our background knowledge, the higher is the burden of proof on those making the claim. Consider the following: declaring that clothes are hanging in one's closet is not extraordinary because many people have closets full of clothes based on our background knowledge. Such a statement carries a low burden of proof. But professing that one has an "invisibility cloak" in one's closet "carries a high burden of proof, given the unprecedented nature of such entities" (Fishman 2009: 817). In such a case, there is a rational basis for skepticism based on the low probability of the claim even where direct evidence is not available against the assertion.

## What Do Miracles Actually Signify?

One crucial question believers fail to address is, How does a miracle prove the veracity of a theological claim? The theologian and philosopher Hermann Reimarus (1879: 69, 74–75) observed that simply because some purported prophet is alleged to have performed miracles establishes nothing because there are multitudes of bogus prophets, magicians, and "false Christs" who have performed miracles to the astonishment of the masses. Moreover, he added, that effort to establish any article of faith based on miracle claims is nothing more than a sign of the doctrine's inauthenticity.

Similarly, one could ask: In what ways do miracles offer proof that God exists? Some philosophers suggest that if a miracle were actually to occur, it would be evidence *against* the existence of God (Overall 2003a). How? Miracles are puzzling, capricious, biased, makeshift, and arbitrary solutions (Overall 2003b: 161). Some are healed, but many others are not, one prayer is answered, another is not (Martin 1990: 192). Some are fed, others go hungry. Consider the reports of "miracle cures" in recent times. These consist mostly of instances of "faith healing," which is a commonplace phenomenon and is attributable to the placebo effect or suggestibility. Most people overlook the sad fact that the little old lady that the evangelical preacher magically compels to stand and walk away from her wheelchair before the enthusiastic throng collapses in pain shortly after the cameras are turned off.

Moreover, there is the fact that of the over half-million or more people who every year visit paranormally charged locations such as Lourdes only a handful experience a miraculous cure of the placebo kind (Scriven 1966: 139). Here, the supernatural is again being fishy and quirky. Why not heal all the miserable, desperate, and suffering supplicants? Why only miraculous cures that fall in the category of short-lived psychosomatic illnesses? Why no restorations of amputated limbs? Why not eyesight to those without eyeballs?

All of this is at odds with the nature of a benevolent God. Religionists might say that God responds to emergent needs, which is saying that God has His own mysterious and unfathomable reasons. It expresses nothing, other than "don't ask, just believe." Alternatively, the assertion may be that God only helps the deserving (Overall 2003b: 161–63). But then why exclude from miraculous cures the innocent children born with terminal cancer or other deadly ailments? Why are they not worthy of miraculous curative effects? Such circumstances comprise cases of injustice and the creation of undue suffering. Why would a benevolent God be the cause of these things? Such conditions are inconsistent with the existence of the theistic God.

Another puzzling feature of miraculous happenings is that most of them are trivial. They fall into the category of what Scriven calls carnival sideshow exhibitions that appear in the news from time to time, such as bleeding statues or apparitions of virgin ladies in the sky, for which there is simply a lack of evidence based on a careful examination by those familiar with naturalistic explanations for such phenomena. It seems that the Almighty participates in medical marginalia (Scriven 1966: 140). The trivial nature of these so-called miracles rules them out as evidence of divine suspension of physical laws. Efforts to use such unsubstantiated and insignificant events in the present as proof that such wonders occurred in the past, as Keener (2011) does, are wholly unconvincing (see below).

Given the amount of suffering and misfortune in the world that require miraculous fixes, what is the cosmological significance of such trivial things as changing water into wine, statues weeping, pictures bleeding, Jesus's face appearing on toast, or the manifestation of purported stigmata? Also, how do parlor magic tricks, which is what miraculous deeds reported in religious texts resemble, validate the divinity of any religious figure? They do not! These things, to cite Craveri (1967: 118) once again, merely hoodwink the gullibility of the percipients. Miracles only appeal to human weaknesses, such as fear, anguish, suggestibility, and awe of the unknown (Overall 2003a: 154). They make God look like a circus performer out to dazzle us with his latest but trivial conjuring act. These are not the sorts of tactics worthy of a perfect, benevolent, all-knowing, all-powerful Deity (Martin 1990: 192; Overall 2003a: 154).

Finally, miracles demonstrate a flaw in the order and regularity of the universe (Overall 2003a: 154). Why did God create such a problematic world and universe in the first place that requires miraculous interventions to fix? Such violations are inconsistent with the existence of a perfect and benevolent God. Also, why does not God produce a continuous flow of beneficial effects via miracles? (Overall 2003a: 152). None of this makes sense.

## Are Miracles Logically Possible?

Are violation miracles even logically possible? Some philosophers maintain that they are not. If we accept a proposition as a law of nature, then, if it is a genuine law of nature, it cannot be violated. Thus, to say that an event has occurred that has violated such a law means that the statement of the law is not factual. Therefore, no laws of nature have been violated, and the event is not a miracle (Everitt 2004: 119). But if we hold that a law of nature cannot be violated unless God intervenes, what the Christian apologist Swinburne (2004: 279) calls a "non-repeatable exception," you have an exemption built into the proposition. Now we are saying something like "all male northern cardinals are red except for the rainbow-colored ones in the North Pole." In this case, finding a rainbow-colored cardinal, that is, the exception, does not violate the generalization that says all cardinals are red except for a rainbow-colored one. The problem here is that we cannot admit a proposition as a law and also believe in a fact that contradicts it, as Swinburne does. Either the contradicting fact is wrong, or we are in error in supposing that the proposition is a true law. Thus, as Everitt (2004: 122) observes, "since violation miracles by definition involve the violation of a non-violatable type of law, the very concept is an incoherent one."

Another perspective would be to think of miracles not as a violation of the laws of nature but as events that are "inexplicable" (Basinger 1984: 6). Such a view, however, raises another problem. As theologian John Hull (1974: 56) observes, there can never be "a theory of miracles" because the indispensable feature of miracles is their very "inexplicability." Why, if this is the case, should we believe theologians who attempt to explain these inexplicable events by inferring the action or motives of some supernatural being?

Let us for the sake of argument pursue this line of reasoning a bit further. Here we have to be clear about what we mean by "inexplicable." Is the event inexplicable to us with our present level of scientific knowledge? If so, then what may seem like a miracle today, as in the case of the belief among the ancients that the sprouting of seed in the fields was a miracle, will not be one according to future scientific knowledge. We could address this problem by tightening our definition to state that a miracle is "inexplicable in principle," and neither present nor future science can explain it (Everitt 2004: 124), in other words, asserting that there are no scientific explanations to be discovered at any time or place. How can we establish that an inexplicable event today cannot be explained by future science? Here we enter dangerous territory given the epistemic progress of science, how it has been able to explain one mysterious event after another, and the "accumulated force of centuries of practical accomplishments" that characterizes the history of science (Overall 2003a: 159). It would be possible if we could show that God produced the inexplicable event in question. Here, however, we are not using a miracle to prove theism, we are inferring the miracle from God. The theologian's purpose is to use miracles to prove theism or determine if God is inferrable from the miracle (Everitt 2004: 124). We cannot infer the existence of God from the occurrence of a naturalistically inexplicable event without providing further evidence that God exists.

If miracles are logically impossible, then what generates the reports that such events have happened? As already noted, something is a miracle when people believe it is one. Hence miracles are no different from any other paranormal phenomenon, such as encountering a ghost, receiving a telepathic message, or seeing a UFO. These events are explicable according to such factors as a misunderstanding of probabilities and other cognitive, perceptual, and memory errors that result in beliefs in paranormal phenomenon. We do not need to enter into deep theological debates or venture into epistemological and ontological discussions about the nature of reality to explain them.

Many miracles are due to misidentifications or erroneous interpretations of mundane events as supernatural one. Here we may think of the miracle of water flowing from the crucifix at Our Lady of Velankanni Church in Mumbai, India, when people mistook a plumbing problem as a wonder from the Lord. We might consider the miracle of the inscribed eggs in Leeds, England, in 1806, when a prank fooled the local people that the Day of Judgment was upon them. A description of these incidents is provided in Chapter 9. There is also the miracle that resulted in the beatification of Mother Theresa by the Vatican discussed in this chapter. History is replete with such spurious "miracles."

In other cases, miracles are nothing more than lucky coincidences. These are known as "coincidence miracles" (Everitt 2004: 125). For example, an alarm clock does not ring, and someone misses a plane that crashes. Such an event has a naturalistic explanation. The person forgot to set the alarm the night before, or there was a power outage, and the alarm failed to ring. Inadequate maintenance, metal fatigue, or mechanical failure is responsible for the plane crash. Such persons may thank their lucky stars, or God, for this bit of good fortune, even though the event has a naturalistic explanation. Coincidence miracles happen all the time, but their occurrence provides nothing to establish the existence of God or any other supernatural being (Everitt 2004: 126). One wonders just how many of the events touted as genuine miracles of God in the religious literature of different cultures are "coincidence miracles" mistaken for violation miracles. Thus, there are alternative explanations for purported miracles that are consistent with our background knowledge and supported by considerable empirical evidence that obviates the need to resort to paranormal causality. The only reason miracles abound is because humans have an unlimited desire and innate cognitive proclivities for the wonderous and the extraordinary to be true.

## The Theist Case for Miracles and Efforts to Refute David Hume

Some of the standard religionist objections to scientific skepticism regarding miracles have already been pointed out. Here a brief examination is offered of the massive two-volume study *Miracles: The Credibility of the New Testament Accounts* (2011) by biblical studies professor Craig Keener. This writer is a devout religionist who personally believes in "supernatural causation" for healing and the raising of the dead, and this study is his effort to validate the miracles described in the gospels and Acts of the Apostles (Keener 2011: 766–67). This work is perhaps the best and most authoritative exemplar of the religionists' stance on miracles and their ostensible refutation of Hume's ideas. The critical assessment provided here should, therefore, also apply to other religionist tracts on miracles.

To proceed, Keener first attempts to establish that his paranormal perspective is exempt from scientific appraisal using postmodern anti-science ruminations (Keener 2011: 189, 192, 222–23). A brief explanation is necessary to clarify the epistemological underpinnings of Keener's study. As I have pointed out elsewhere (Sidky 2018; 2007a: 68, 2004: 399), the systematic efforts of postmodern academics to delegitimize science during the 1980s and 1990s have provided religionists and paranormalists considerable ammunition to advance the validity of their bogus and irrational ideas (Kakutani 2018: 18; McIntyre 2018: 141–48; Otto 2016: 199; Sidky 2018). While postmodernism is now mostly defunct, its spurious anti-science legacy has spread far and wide.

In publications and classrooms, postmodernist gurus expressed their disdain for the rationalist tradition of the Enlightenment and their total disregard for empirical data and logic. They especially stressed the idea of "the cultural construction of knowledge" and extolled subjective and intuitive approaches to knowledge. The postmodern assault on science centered on the idea of epistemological relativism. This entails the premise that conditions of knowledge are such that the truth and falsity of assertions are entirely context dependent, situated, and always relative to cultural and social backgrounds, political position, class, gender, ethnicity, race, and religion. According to this view, non-scientific and irrational perspectives all have validity.

For postmodernists, it followed, therefore, that no representations of reality or story can be privileged because there are multiple and equally valid realities and truths. Moreover, because all truths are relative, these academic virtuosos asserted, whose truth prevails is a coefficient of power and coercion. The West is dominant and hegemonic, and hence its "truths" (i.e., science) are privileged. In such a presentation, science became merely a "worldview," one of many around the world, and the idea that scientific knowledge depends upon objective empirical evidence was declared to be false. Of course, such statements are sheer distortions. By strategically excluding the empirical dimension of the scientific enterprise, postmodernists grossly misrepresented science as merely a "story" or narrative like any other that relies on rhetorical ornamentation and language games to persuade people of its legitimacy and authority (Sidky 2018).

The science-bashing postmodern academics are mostly responsible for the current dismal post-truth intellectual and cultural conditions by creating the space in which "fake news," "other ways of knowing," alternate truths, pseudoscience, conspiracy theories, climate change denial, "ancient alien theory," misinformation, religious fanaticism, supernatural bunkum, and many other bizarre and outlandish notions are flourishing. Paraphrasing Ambasciano (2018: 176), post-truth is the digital version of postmodernist skepticism about knowledge. Under these circumstances, those touting paranormal and supernatural hypotheses can assert that scientific appraisal and validation of claims to knowledge are now defunct and brazenly demand that their voices be heard. Religionists such as Keener (2011: 140–41, 160) have appropriated the postmodernist supposition that if science is merely a worldview, a faith-based cultural prejudice, or just one culture's story, it can no longer be privileged and religious claims are not only exempt from scientific appraisal but have equal or even greater epistemic validity. This is another way of saying scientific evidentiary criteria do not apply to our beliefs. These are disingenuous assertions. As discussed in Chapter 3, science is *a method* of discovering how the world and universe operate, not a worldview or a faith-based set of beliefs. Theological beliefs and scientific postulates do not have epistemic parity.

Keener (2019: 100–1, 107), however, avers that science is a worldview and stresses that "a worldview is not an argument" against miracles and religion. He adds that "In the wake of postmodernity in the West, the collapse of traditional Western paradigms has led to the reevaluation of a number of long-held interpretations of reality" (Keener 2011: 99). For him, it follows that because the scientific perspective has been discredited (it has not!), therefore supernaturalism has automatically been validated. Even if it were the case and science has collapsed, the validity of any perspective is an epistemological question and depends upon how well it holds up in relation to empirical evidence, not because of the failure of a rival perspective (cf., Ayala 2016: 326).

In support of his supernaturalist stance on miracles, Keener (2011: 178) employs epistemological relativism to declare that science is simply a historically contingent, a priori culturally biased philosophical construct that has blinded scientific skeptics to the truth of the miracles of Jesus Christ and miraculous events in general. Like other paranormalists, Keener goes one step further by advocating ontological relativism, meaning that reality itself is culturally determined (see Chapter 5). As he puts it, "assumptions about reality are often culturally formed, and events that function as 'reality' by the criteria of one culture can shape its history even if these assumptions are foreign to other cultures" (Keener 2011: 96–97). He adds that the ancients who subscribed to "different plausibility paradigms may well have experienced genuine [miraculous] events that many modern Western interpreters would attribute to different causes." The overall point of these contentions is that the miracles of Jesus were genuine supernatural events.

Keener strives to demonstrate that miracles are real in an ontological sense. Scientific skepticism regarding such events, he reiterates, is merely an a priori opinion due entirely to a Western ethnocentric bias (Keener 2011: 121, 124, 138, 154, 166, 219). Elsewhere, he says that scientific skepticism regarding eyewitness reports of miraculous events arose entirely from the bias of particular philosophers, specifically David Hume (Keener 2011: 107, 166, 178). These are gross misrepresentations as well because science does not dismiss eyewitness testimony because of some prior bias but on epistemological grounds and in terms of overwhelming evidence that has persistently shown the unreliability of such reports (see Chapters 6 and 7).

The focus of Keener's critique is Hume's essay on miracles, discussed above, which he identifies as the principal source of scientific "anti-supernaturalism" (Keener 2011: 83, 107–208). He adds that Hume's case is flawed, and his views hold sway because he stated his case very eloquently (Keener 2011: 121, 169), that is, acceptance of his ideas is based on persuasive argument rather than reason and evidence. Keener and the post-modern writers whose work he draws upon are under the mistaken assumption that scientific knowledge is generated through arbitrary group consensus (what philosophers call "truth by coherence") rather than what it is actually based upon, namely correspondence with empirical evidence that is true of the world (or "truth by correspondence"). The religionist Alvin Plantinga (2009: 151) raises a similar point about methodological naturalism, as discussed in Chapter 3. This, of course, is another misrepresentation. In science, the final arbiter is the data. Also, in science, no hypothesis is rejected a priori without first examining all the evidence. This is why scientific knowledge changes and grows over time as new discoveries are validated and incorporated into the scientific knowledge base. If new discoveries are rejected in the manner Keener suggests, this should not happen. Also, the scientific view on the impossibility of the supernatural and paranormal is not an a priori agreed upon assumption asserted before examining the evidence. As discussed in Chapter 3, scientists have arrived at this position based on an empirically grounded a posteriori conclusion from scientific evidence that constitutes our background knowledge.

Keener's (2011: 108) main criticism of Hume's view on miracles is that it entails circular reasoning. As he puts it, Hume stated that miracles are counter to the unwavering laws of nature (i.e., he was discussing *violation miracles*) and do not happen and then proceeded to rule out eyewitness testimony for miracles (i.e., others' experience) on the assumption that miracles do not happen. Hume's fundamental error, Keener adds, was that he based his stance concerning the unreliability of eyewitness accounts of miracles on the "uniformity of human experience." Keener (2011: 108) construes this statement to mean Hume's own limited personal experience and perhaps the experience of his social circle. Hume, however, was referring to scientific background knowledge. For Keener (2011: 114), Hume's stance is merely a presupposition because he did not seek to marshal all the evidence in support of his assertion, that is, he did not consider all the cases everywhere. Remarkably, this religionist thinks that science operates purely on narrow inductionism (Keener 2011: 198) of the sort advocated by Francis Bacon in the early days of science. Bacon's premise was that only after looking at all the facts are we justified in making conclusions, which was a corrective measure in the early days, but it is not how the scientific enterprise operates today (see Chapter 3). Keener (2011: 143–45) goes on to counter Hume by stating that in today's world, testimonials for miracles are overwhelming compared to what was available in Hume's day, and this fact refutes this stance. Keener refers to this body of material as the "majority world perspective," which is another way of saying uniform human experience as he interprets Hume's remarks.

Keener also criticizes Hume for emphasizing the gullibility of religionists and labeling miracle reports and holy books as the handiwork of "ignorant and barbarous nations." He insists that this is merely a derogatory Western prejudice toward religion (Keener 2011: 193, 222). Such postmodern sensitivities collapse, however, in light of the terrible things recounted in the books provided by these ancient tribal people. The contents of these purported holy volumes are ample evidence that their authors were ignorant, superstitious, violent, and delusional people (see Chapter 10). Skeptics agree that Hume was fully justified in pointing out "the futility of religion for morality and its penchant for bringing out and justifying the worst violent behaviors" (Ambasciano 2018: xiv).

In opposition to Hume, Keener (2011: 194) insists that miracle reports are reliable and that blind faith may distort accounts, but that does not mean that testimony offered by believers is false. For this reason, he accepts the complete veracity of the anecdotal materials in the Bible, which he treats as a book containing reliable historical and biographical accounts (Keener 2011: 35, 55), rather than what it is, namely Christian recruitment literature (see Chapter 12). He states, for example, that it is ethnocentric and prejudicial to suggest that the member of the Jesus cult (among Hume's ignorant and barbarous people) "could not distinguish between a corpse and a dinner guest," referring to the postmortem appearances of Jesus to his followers (Keener 2011: 223). Their testimony about paranormal events, he adds, is therefore entirely reliable and Jesus appeared to them in the flesh. This is untrue. The disciples did confuse an apparition for an actual physical encounter, as discussed in Chapter 15. Only an ardent religionist would make the assumptions that biblical reports recount the occurrence of genuine supernatural events. As discussed in Chapters 12, 14, and 15, accounts of Jesus's miracles and his resurrection, which are of central concern to Keener, were provided by the worst sort of witnesses one could encounter and recorded in second- and third-hand versions many decades after the fact by unknown writers in a different language who lived far from the location of the events in question.

Finally, Keener (2011: 150–51) adds that Hume's standard of proof (i.e., that extraordinary claims require extraordinary evidence) is too high and if applied outside of the realm of the supernatural or paranormal would be a science stopper and prevent scientists from believing others who announce a new discovery. This is a misrepresentation as well. Science does not work this way. Whether such a discovery is accepted or not depends on independent verification and replication not when someone claims a novel finding, as the case of the N-Rays shows. Where evidentiary confirmation fails, it is reasonable to be skeptical.

Another tactic Keener employs is to allude to Gould's fatuous concept of NOMA. Supernatural and paranormal events, he maintains, are beyond or outside the scope of scientific research. In his view, science can only legitimately address "normal happenings of nature" and repeatable events, hence it cannot pronounce judgments on unique anomalous occurrences such as miracles (Keener 2011: 125–26). Therefore, once scientists speak of things outside "the normal," they are no longer speaking "as scientists," and their statements carry no weight (Keener 2011: 125–26). This is the same specious argument made by Mooney and Kirshenbaum (2009: 100–1), namely that supernatural phenomena are outside the legitimate scope of scientific inquiry. I have detailed the flaws of this perspective in Chapter 3. Science assesses all phenomena, whether normal, anomalous, paranormal, or pseudoscientific, entirely based on evidence.

However, as Keener sees it, if the legitimate domain of scientific inquiry is only "normal happenings," that is, empirical phenomena, and science is incapable of addressing supernatural events or unique "singular anomalies," such as miracles, resurrections, and so forth, then empiricism has to be "neutral" regarding God's existence and activities that underlie miracles (Keener 2011: 121). This means that when scientists express skepticism toward miracles, Keener (2011: 2, 107, 123, 166) reiterates, they do so entirely due to philosophical fiat and ethnocentrism.

Keener bolsters his NOMA case further by pointing out that science is not qualified to address theological truths. In other words, paranormal and supernatural events are the exclusive preserve of religionists. Following Plantinga and Swinburne, Keener avows that Christian miracles involve divine causation, and hence, they are theological rather than scientific issues (Keener 2011: 126). In his words, such miracle claims "are best explained by supernatural causation" (Keener 2011: 2, 107).

What does Keener offer in place of the scientific perspective? Nothing new. He maintains that we must take "the special religious context of miracles" into account (Keener 2011: 160). This requires that we start with a theistic assumption that allows the possibility of a deity who acts purposefully in nature. Once this is granted, then it becomes unreasonable not to accept miracle testimonies (Keener 2011: 140). In other words, he is postulating a universe that includes "an order-maintaining yet occasional miracle-working God" before he undertakes the task of showing that miracles are real events caused by God (Keener 2011: 141). To clarify his perspective on miracles, Keener (2011: 159) provides the following example. He says that the claim that an elephant flew over London would be incredible in ordinary terms but not incredible under the conditions he sets for his work, meaning if you don't a priori exclude the possibility of a deity known to make elephants fly in other cases then flying pachyderms are possibilities. He extends this view to biblical miracles, asserting that if God exists and produces miraculous happenings in the present era, then the many miracle reports found in the Bible must be genuine events (Keener 2011: 160). Stated differently, Keener is inferring that a miracle-working deity exists; therefore, miracles are real. He does not see the circular reasoning in this premise. What he is asking his readers is to accept the existence of God as an a priori postulate, whereas the validity of his argument depends upon first demonstrating that such an entity exists, acts intentionally, and periodically interferes in physical reality and human affairs. Theists have consistently failed in this task (see Chapters 3, 9, 10, and 11).

The problematic nature of Keener's supernaturalist position can be demonstrated by way of analogy. If we allow the possibility that there are technologically advanced humanoid extraterrestrials with the capacity to travel faster than the speed of light and who have an interest in our planet and human affairs, then it would be unreasonable not to accept a whole range of claims. These include the notion that UFOs are alien spacecraft, that beings from outer space regularly abduct people and sexually abuse them, that space people draw pictures of farm fields and mutilate livestock, and that earthly civilizations were the handiwork of ancient alien visitors from other galaxies. However, before one can accept any of these propositions, the person who is making these claims is required to provide irrefutable and corroborated evidence that extraterrestrials of this sort exist. It is the same with Keener's assertion that genuine miracles occur in the present.

Keener is trying to convince the reader that the scientific requisite propounded early on by Hume, which is that *extraordinary claims require extraordinary evidence* (see Chapter 3), does not apply to his supernaturalist approach. He elaborates by saying that "how much evidential value one attaches to a given claim depends on the nature of the burden of proof one demands, reflecting one's presuppositions about divine activity in the world" (Keener 2011: 250). Purveyors of all sorts of paranormal, pseudoscientific, supernatural, and other irrational and bogus assertions perpetually make the demand that they should be relieved of the burden of proof and exempted from evidentiary criteria of science. In contrast, science demands the highest burden of proof for extraordinary claims. This is not an a priori metaphysical position arrived at by philosophical fiat, contra Keener, but is based on evidential grounds. It is the persistent failure of supernatural hypotheses that serve as justification for seeking natural explanations when encountering extraordinary claims rather than jumping to supernatural or paranormal conclusions.

Having leveled the playing field where supernatural causation is admissible to his satisfaction, Keener brings to bear a range of subjective accounts and eyewitness testimonies or anecdotes by Christians around the world about miraculous happenings and supernatural occurrences. These claims, he asserts, must be treated as almost entirely truthful and admissible, with accounts by multiple witnesses all the more so (Keener 2011: 146). His uncritical treatment of these tales is remarkable but not unexpected of a zealous believer. In support of the contention that miracle claims by eyewitness should be admitted, Keener (2011: 156, 209, 213) points out that "hundreds of millions of people" around the globe (or "the majority world perspectives") have offered miracle claims comparable to the early Christian accounts. For him, it follows, therefore, that the eyewitness information to be found in "the miracle accounts in the Gospels or Acts" should be accepted as genuine. Supernatural claims, he writes, "belong to the widespread experience of much of humanity [and these reports] reinforce the plausibility of miracles in principle" (Keener 2011: 189). Or he says, "divinely driven supernatural phenomena" exist "on the premises of many faiths" (Keener 2011: 195). However, these are X-claims generated by human cognitive biases. For such assertions to be credible as mind-independent phenomena, one must first produce incontrovertible evidence of genuine paranormal events. Keener has not done this. Also, he gives no evidence anywhere that he has appraised every possible instance himself, although he generalizes about the whole of humanity. This is something for which he faults Hume. Moreover, he erroneously believes that piling up masses of multiple eyewitness anecdotal accounts constitutes data. It does not, as discussed in Chapter 7.

Even if Hume did rely solely on cases familiar to him and his associates (he did not!) and broader evidence was not available in his day, this is irrelevant because the problematic nature of eyewitness testimonies and anecdotal evidence is now well-established.

Indeed, the entire history of spiritualism, parapsychology, the efforts of believers' in the Shroud of Turin, Marian apparitions, the many witnesses who testified that witches in early modern Europe could fly and alter nature, the innumerable reports of cryptids and paranormal monsters, UFO sightings by millions around the planet, the many witnesses who think Elvis lives, and reports about the Roswell incident and eyewitness testimonies about alien autopsies that never happened all supports this conclusion. In other words, multiple independent witnesses do not increase the probability of testimony in extraordinary claims, contra Keener (2011: 152).

More importantly, cognitive science, the neurosciences, and evolutionary psychology have provided convincing evidence that the human cognitive apparatus is particularly vulnerable to and is easily hijacked by X-claims. As discussed in Chapter 6, these are false beliefs about counterintuitive agents and miraculous happenings due to our innate pattern-finding pareidolia, meaning-detecting apophenia, hyperactive agent sensor, and inclination toward anthropomorphism (Law 2016: 16, 23).

As Law observes, X-claims are always justified by appeal to *testimony* and *subjective experience* and stem from cognitive attributes that are prone to false positives. Law (2016: 32) adds that the X-claim argument provides a rationality defeater by underscoring the systematic unreliability of humans in the case of religious and other X-claims that are grounded on testimony and subjective experience (Law 2016: 32). Thus, as Ambasciano (2018: xi) observes, the neurosciences and cognitive science have demystified the "very perception, diffusion, and reception of miracles." Science, to put it bluntly, has debunked religious miracles. Perhaps, the greatest problem for works such as Keener's study is the reliance upon "X-claims" for establishing the reality of miracles.

Keener's work suffers from additional shortcomings. Throughout the narrative, Keener (2011: 69) repeatedly conflates the assertion that large numbers of people have witnessed "miracles" or that the early "Christians truly believed that these events were genuinely occurring in their time"—which is a non-problem—with the supposition that the existence of a large number of witnesses ("tens of millions" and "hundreds of millions of people" in the present, e.g., Keener 2011: 69, 156, 209, 21) who truly believed means that something paranormal indeed occurred (Keener 2011: 143, 145, 213, 240, 241, 249–50). There are also thousands and millions of eyewitness testimonials about UFOs, extraterrestrial visitations, Bigfoot, crop circles, mind-over-matter, and so forth. Or consider the purported eyewitness reports by 70,000 people gathered in Fátima, Portugal, on October 13, 1917, stating that the sun descended upon and almost crashed on earth (see Chapter 9). Adopting Keener's stance requires that we must grant that such an event did happen rather than being an illusion or hallucination. We have now landed in the swamp of sheer gullibility.

Keener (2011: 145) also conflates empirical experiences and paranormal ones as if they have epistemic parity. For instance, he states that "if experience is reliable in knowing that water is normally not turned to wine, why would it not be reliable in recognizing when water is turned to wine?" The problem, of course, is that the first premise is an empirical one that is true of the world, whereas the second one is a paranormal assertion that never happens without sleight of hand illusion and trickery. Other religionists make a similar argument, as discussed in Chapter 12, by equating the epistemic status of a run-of-the-mill claim that a Roman general marched his troops across a river and the paranormal claim about a corpse coming back to life.

Given all these suppositions, a wide range of extraordinary phenomena become genuine occurrences for Keener (2011: 227, 244). These include the practices of bogus Filipino psychic surgeons, the magical powers of the self-styled mystic Grigori Rasputin because of his influence over the Tsar of Russia and his credulous wife, magical healings of all sorts, and the raising of the dead by evangelical Christian ministers, such as the early twentieth-century Congolese preacher and conman Simon Kimbangu. He also recounts other cases of the raising of the dead reported more recently (Keener 2011: 537). Such miraculous happenings today, Keener (2011: 214) says, resemble those of the gospels, again implying that the latter were true paranormal events. Here, Keener (2011: 537) leaps from the assertion that "a number of such claims reflect genuine eyewitness experience" to the insinuation that dead people have, in fact, come back to life. Such an inference is a *non sequitur*; it does not follow. There are genuine eyewitness experiences of innumerable bogus phenomena that does not bestow ontological validity to such things. Moreover, Keener downplays the fact that religious conmen and self-styled miracle workers have been bringing purportedly dead people back to life for millennia for cash and self-aggrandizement. A contemporary and notorious example of one such charlatan who raised more dead people than Jesus is discussed in Chapter 13.

Keener (2011: 197) acknowledges that some miracle reports are false due to fraud or deception but insists that this does not mean all of them are false. This is a standard religionist contention (e.g., McDowell 1973: 125). A case could be made if there were an iota of evidence anywhere in space and time that a genuine miraculous event has taken place. If Keener's theistic magic premise were true, such evidence should be there in abundance but is not. As Ambasciano (2018: xi) puts it, millions of smartphones with cameras around the planet have failed to record a single incontrovertible instance of a divine or miraculous sign. He adds,

> no goddess, god, spirit, ghost or superhuman being has ever walked among us mere mortals [...] No divine intervention of some sort has ever interrupted our daily existence. No miracle has ever been ascertained beyond a reasonable doubt. Apparently, the era of miracles is closed, and rivers of theological ink have been shed to justify this absence.

Paradoxically, however, in this post-truth age, there is a deluge of "tearful" but unsubstantiated stories of whole varieties of bogus miraculous happenings on social media (Ambasciano 2018: xii).

Keener (2011: 220–21) also draws on the findings of various anthropologists, who he says have shown that people across many cultures experience visions or other altered states of consciousness and that the religious "vision reports in Acts or Revelation would, therefore, appear plausible to much of the world's population." The insinuation again is that these were genuine transmissions from otherworldly sources. Indeed, he adds that these events are difficult to explain without recourse to "superhuman entities" (Keener 2011: 221). This also does not follow. Of course, humans across space and time have such experiences, and these appear plausible to those around them. I have recorded numerous such instances during fieldwork. This is another non-problem. The real question is not whether such events appear plausible but rather if they constitute mind-independent phenomena and indeed entail otherworldly beings and forces. Unfortunately, they do not. Moreover, such visionary experiences can indeed be explained in naturalistic terms that accord with empirical evidence (see Chapter 9).

Keener also refers to the work of paranormal anthropologists, such as Edith Turner, Paul Stoller, Jean-Guy Goulet, and David Young, among others, who adopt an "experiential approach," the highly problematic nature of which I have discussed in Chapter 5. He also discusses Bruce Grindal's story about "witnessing" a Ghanian man rise from the dead (see Chapter 7), inferring genuine supernatural events in such cases (Keener 2011: 247–49). Keener asserts that such postmodernist perspectives that focus upon experiential phenomena challenge Western Enlightenment skepticism. Here, the gullibility and subjective impressions of a handful of overzealous and scientifically illiterate ethnographers become supporting evidence for biblical miracles.

Keener (2011: 541) goes on to make the astonishing claim that at present there is "abundant eyewitness testimony in which a number of people apparently dead are revived without brain damage, after a sustained period." The reader is asked to believe that the subjects of these magic shows were indeed deceased rather than "apparently dead." Again, Keener is inferring that abundant testimonies about dead people being revived—once more, a non-problem—denotes that in some cases the dead have come back to life. This simply does not follow. Yet, Keener insinuates the following: "To argue that ancient eyewitnesses could have believed that Jesus raised the dead, it is sufficient to demonstrate that eyewitnesses offer comparable claims today; one need not venture into an explanation" (Keener 2011: 541). However, venturing into explanations is indeed a requisite. Simply attributing such events to the mysterious machinations of some a priori postulated miracle-working paranormal being will not do. Contemporary and ancient corpse reanimators, including the instances when Jesus brought dead people back to life, as well as his own resurrection, are discussed in Chapter 13. These cases are not based on a shred of credible evidence for paranormal happenings. These are all X-claims and implausible for that reason. Moreover, there are perfectly plausible naturalistic explanations for such events that accord with overwhelming and well-established scientific evidence (see Chapter 16).

Keener's book, to reiterate, is a work by a true believer in desperate need to validate Christian superstitions (Keener 2011: 767). While other religionists may applaud this book, it is a highly problematic and wholly unconvincing study. The style of presentation hoodwinks the gullibility of readers who may not be familiar with anthropology, academic standards, the rules of rational inquiry, the nature of scientific research, and who are conditioned from childhood to believe without evidence. Without assuming a priori the existence of a miracle-working deity that purposefully acts in nature, as Keener (2011: 140–41) demands of his readers, his argument for the ontological reality of miracles fails. Asserting that a miracle-producing deity exists, therefore, genuine miracles happen, which is Keener's foundational premise, is tautological, and explains nothing. To put it bluntly, Keener dignifies credulity as a method in the same way other religionists tend to do (cf., Price 2010a: 274).

For skeptics to take what Keener offers seriously requires extraordinary evidentiary justification. Amassing a large number of anecdotal accounts, subjective impressions, and reports of someone telling someone else that a miracle took place here or there, along with a heavy dose of special pleading that these are trustworthy, as Keener has, simply will not do. Indeed, efforts by theists over the last several millennia have failed to make a case for the existence of a miracle-working God. Many have looked for such evidence long and hard, including scientists but without success. The evidence is not there.

# Chapter Nine

# WHEN GOD TALKS TO PEOPLE: ARE RELIGIOUS EXPERIENCE EVIDENCE OF GOD?

*He who is involved in ecstasies and visions, who takes dreams for reality, and his own imagination for prophecy, is a fanatical novice of great hope and promise, and will soon advance to the higher stage and kill men for the love of God.*

—Voltaire, *The Philosophical Dictionary* (1764)

*Something [...] revealed to a certain person, and not revealed to any other person [...] is a revelation to the first person only, and hearsay to every other, and consequently they are not obliged to believe it.*

—Thomas Paine, *The Age of Reason* (1794)

*If you talk to God, you are praying, if God talks to you, you have schizophrenia.*

—Thomas Szasz, *The Meaning of Mind* (1996)

One frequent claim for the existence of God is the "argument from religious experience." The philosopher Michael Martin (1990: 154) provides a concise definition of religious experience as an event "in which one senses the immediate presence of some supernatural entity." It is a claim to "direct, rather than inferential, knowledge of the existence of God" (Scriven 1966: 136). Many people in cultures across space and time have reported powerful, private, revelatory, visual, and auditory experiences involving contact with purported super-intelligent entities, or "Divine Others" who are believed to exist outside the spatiotemporal realm of the universe but can have observed effects upon the world. In this chapter, I shall examine the case for the existence of God and transcendental realms based on the argument from religious experience.

"Religious experiences" refer to different types of perceptions and feelings, and some demarcations are necessary before we can proceed. The philosopher Graham Oppy (2018: 173–77), for instance, considers several distinct phenomena to belong in this category. He includes thoughts generated during religious practice undertaken under the auspices of organized religious institutions, such as meditation sessions, religious dances, festivals, initiations, sermons, and so on. He also extends the term to circumstances when people witness "miraculous" events or when they have dreams construed as messages from supernatural beings or "the beyond." The most important category for our purposes is called *visionary experiences*. While various types of feelings and perceptions could be labeled visionary events, such as hallucinations due to brain disease and psychiatric disorders, or illusions resulting from drug addiction or alcoholism, some of which may have religious content, here the concern is with what is commonly referred to as "mystical," "spiritual," or "revelatory" visionary experiences. These are characterized by *ecstatic states*, sensations of the *numinous* (feeling the presence of "the Holy" or "Divine), *unitive states* involving the sense of oneness with the universe, and *salvific states* that entail feelings of deliverance and redemption.

Ecstatic states occur during altered states of consciousness (ASC) that could entail embodiment of supernatural beings brought on by ritual means, such as chanting, drumming, uttering mantras, or ingesting entheogenic substances (Sidky 2017b: 21–36, 37–52). Examples from my research include the visionary experiences of Tibetan mediums and oracles and Nepalese shamans (Sidky 2008: 89–114; 2017b: 21–36). The accounts of Sufi mystics I encountered in various parts of Central Asia exemplify experiences of the numinous. Numerous examples also occur in the context of the other Abrahamic religions. The German theologian Rudolf Otto used the term "numinous" (1923: 16–18, 19–37) to refer to sensations of the presence of the Divine that are self-generating, powerful, ineffable, indescribable, and at once overwhelming, mysterious, terrifying, and fascinating (*mysterium tremendum et fascinans*). Such experiences are often interpreted as theological encounters (Oppy 2018: 176). An example of unitive experience, or the sense of oneness with God, the Deity, or "ultimate reality" is exemplified by the concept of *fana*, described by the Sufi mystics I have encountered. It entails the dissolution of one's ego and a sensation of unity with the whole of creation or reality. Finally, an excellent example of a salvific state is the supernatural encounter of Saul of Tarsus (who became the Apostle Paul), on the road to Damascus, discussed in Chapter15.

## Visionary Experiences and the Rise of Religious Movements

Divine messages received by self-styled messiahs, prophets, or ambassadors of heaven have mobilized masses and launched religious movements, some of which have later transformed into full-fledged religions. Religious movements inspired by divine revelations have numerous cross-cultural similarities and are a well-known anthropological phenomenon explicable according to non-supernatural sociopolitical, economic, and ecological variables. As I have pointed out elsewhere (Sidky 2015: 199), all such movements begin with the ecstatic religious experience of a new prophet, messiah, or savior, carrying a message of redemption or salvation from God, the gods, spirits, or the ancestors. The messiah reveals the reasons why people are suffering and lays out plans for a remedy to the situation. The visions and dreams usually foretell the end of the world, the eradication of the oppressors and foreigners, and the establishment of a new order when the ancestors or gods will return, justice will prevail, and the righteous will rule the world. The new vision is often synthetic, or *syncretic*, and may incorporate aspects of traditional and impinging alien beliefs and practices. Some anthropological examples include the late nineteenth-century Native American Ghost Dance and the cargo cults in Melanesia that appeared during the nineteenth century and still exist today (Sidky 2015: 199–211). The same pattern is also true of major world religions, such as Judaism, Christianity, and Islam.

There is nothing particularly miraculous or supernatural about how some of these religious movements have risen rapidly and spread across space and, in some cases, have become established faiths, although their respective believers are taught to attach cosmic significance to the origins and proliferation of whatever creeds they profess. Believers, for example, see a miracle in the growth and spread of Christianity from a minor and marginal cult to the dominant religion in the Western world in just a few centuries. However, this rate of growth, estimated to have been about 40 percent per decade, is identical to the rate at which Mormonism spread during the nineteenth and twentieth centuries (Stark 1984, 1996: 5). Given that the details of the rise of Mormonism are reasonably clear, few others apart from its indoctrinated adherents would consider it to be a miraculous religious movement.

Religious experiences that have launched such movements form the core beliefs of Judaism, Christianity, and Islam and other religions, are recorded in sacred texts, and have had a significant impact on the course of human history. These include Moses receiving commandments from Yahweh, the Apostle Paul hearing Jesus's voice on the road to Damascus, and Muhammad's encounter with the archangel Gabriel in a cave. Innumerable humans have lived by, killed, and died for the ostensible revealed words of God received and disseminated by self-styled prophets, vatics, and messiahs. What are we to make of these extraordinary events?

Such visionary or ecstatic events, involving communication and interaction with the sacred or paranormal realm, was almost a daily part of my fieldwork with shamans, mediums, mother-goddesses, god-men, and oracles. Their behaviors and claims are highly reminiscent of the prophets of old. In many instances, I was able to observe such specialists before, during, and after their encounters with supernatural beings and paranormal realities. Aside from recording such occurrences and attempting to explore their sociocultural consequences as aspects of human behavior, I frequently wondered about their ontological significance. Such thoughts gave rise to several questions: What do such interactions between specific people and the gods really signify? Is there something more to these circumstances than humans acting out cultural roles? Have the shamans and miracle workers stumbled upon a gateway to the realm of spirits and gods?

Various scholars through the years have maintained that religious experiences are the driving force of all faiths (Whitehead 1974; Johnson 1963). Theistic philosophers suppose that religious experiences provide evidential justification for the existence of God (Taliaferro 2009: 214). Indeed, many believers consider religious or mystical experiences to be one of the most convincing arguments for the reality of the supernatural world and extraordinary beings (Stenger 1990: 104). As we shall see here, the argument from religious experience constitutes a central component of the case made for the existence of the theistic God by Christian theologian and apologist Richard Swinburne (2004: 293–327). Is there any substance to such a claim?

The major problem with revelatory experiences, or revelations, as I found out early in my field research, is that they are private. By this, I mean that during such encounters with the extraordinary only a particular individual is the recipient of the paranormal communiqué. While it was possible for me to observe the behaviors and listen to pronouncements of such miracle workers, I had no access to the subjective perceptions and sensations of what the percipients claimed had transpired between them and the supernatural and the paranormal realms. Long ago, the ever-insightful Thomas Paine (1880 [1794]: 3) noted the problem with such God-to-human communications in the context of his critique of Christianity:

> admitting, for the sake of a case, that something has been revealed to a certain person, and not revealed to any other person, it is a revelation to that person only. When he tells it to a second person, a second to a third, a third to a fourth, and so on, it ceases to be a revelation to all those other persons. It is a revelation to the first person only, and hearsay to every other, and consequently they are not obliged to believe it.

What this means is that religious adherents must take their visionary's word—that is, the words of another human being—that the revelation was genuine and was related to them accurately. Thus, the God-to-human communicative exchange is, in reality, a human-to-human message transmission. Believers, however, ascribe mystical and cosmic significance to such revelatory messages of their messiahs, prophets, and vatics, forgetting that ultimately the source of these magical memoranda is other human beings.

There is no doubt that in some cases the percipients are genuinely convinced of the veridicality of their extra-worldly encounters. It must be stressed, however, that this only means that a person comes to sincerely believe that he or she sees or senses the presence of something extraordinary, not that such an extraordinary something necessarily exists outside their minds. In other words, contrary to the assertion by the sociologist Rodney Stark (1999), the ubiquity of purported experiences of God, or whatever label one wishes to use, and how powerfully the percipient believes that the experience is genuine do not justify that such a supernatural being exists as an objective, mind-independent entity. The reason for this is that large numbers of people have experienced seeing and are true believers in comparably unwarranted things, such as UFOs (over 1 million cases since 1947), alien abductions, angels, ghosts, vampires, night demons, cryptids, and fairies, but this does not mean that such things exist anywhere, in any form, at any time (cf., Sagan 2006: 162).

## Do Religious Experiences Support the Existence of the God of Theism?

Another point to address here is that lots of people have religious experiences. Much is made of the ubiquity and similarities between these events as tangible evidence of the extraordinary and the supernatural. But do they, in fact, denote the marvelous or miraculous? No. In actuality, as the neuroscientist Peter Brugger (2001: 210) has pointed out in connection with paranormal experiences, such as seeing ghosts or apparitions, these events signify something rather trivial, namely that "the central nervous system of all human beings exhibit some common functional properties."

For such experiences to qualify as genuine paranormal or supernatural encounters, independent evidence of their veracity is necessary. It is not sufficient to claim, contra to what the theistic philosopher Charles Taliaferro (2009: 201) says, that people have religious experiences because of "the reality and activity of an omnipresent God." It is a question-begging assertion to claim that God revealed himself to me—therefore, God exists. In the words of the philosopher Michael Scriven (1966: 140), "No account of their experience by itself can contribute to the argument in any way." Similarly, the philosopher Kai Nielsen (2001: 32, 34) observes that there is an abundance of revelations from the beyond, or from above, they are often at odds with one another, and there is no basis for differentiating between the genuine and putative claims. Criteria independent of the supposed revelations are needed to judge whether what confronts us is an actual or false religious experience. He adds further that the argument for the existence of God from religious experience has been refuted so decisively that few try to defend it anymore, and those who still take on this task do so in mitigated forms (Nielsen 2001: 32). However, this is not so in the case of some of the theistic writers as discussed below.

Claims about any direct interaction or communication between humans as empirical beings and a non-empirical cosmic paranormal super-agent outside the spatiotemporal realm of the universe classify as extraordinary or miraculous because, if true, they would violate the physical laws that govern the transmission of energy and information (cf., Everitt 2004: 156). As we know, extraordinary claims require extraordinarily strong proof (Truzzi 1978: 11). As with all miracles, the proof of genuine religious experiences, defined as contact with actual paranormal beings independent of the mind, is utterly absent. However, there is an overwhelming amount of evidence that human perceptions and memory are prone to all sorts of distortions and biases due to the effects of expectations, top-down processing, misidentifications, delusions, mental illness, and hallucinations, as discussed in Chapter 7. People also often fabricate stories and tell lies. Before we can justify that a cosmologically significant religious experience has indeed occurred, we must first rule out all of these factors.

Religious polemicists and theologians, ever in search of justification for their cherished fantasies and superstitions, nevertheless claim that religious experiences of God justify that such a supernatural being exists as an objective, mind-independent entity (Swinburne 2004: 293). However, they rarely consider the above-mentioned cognitive and psychological factors associated with such perceptions and feelings. It is difficult to conceive how such theologians can justify their lengthy discourses on the significance of religious experiences without attending to these considerations.

## Do Religious Experiences and Public Perceptions Have Epistemic Parity?: Swinburne's Theological Proof

Richard Swinburne (2004: 293–327) uses the argument from religious experience as one of the key elements of his overall project of bringing to bear the total evidence for the existence of God. That evidence includes the teleological and cosmological arguments, and the arguments from miracles and design, among others (see Chapters 3, 8, and 11,

12), in a cumulative strategy in support of theism. The adoption of this tactic derives from the presupposition that God's existence is the best explanation for all the facts when *taken together*.

Before we turn to Swinburne's views on religious experience, a brief discussion of his cumulative strategy is necessary. This amalgamation ploy is not original and is highly dubious as well. As the philosopher Michael Scriven (1966: 109) observed years ago, "the greatest confidence trick in the history of philosophy is the attempt to make the various arguments for the existence of God support each other by using the same term for the entity whose existence each is supposed to establish." Whereas how these supernatural beings are conceptualized varies considerably. Therefore, first, proof has to be presented that these entities are the same if any cumulative strategy or "combination trick" is to work. As we shall see, Swinburne has not managed to provide such proofs.

Swinburne begins his argument by differentiating between *publicly perceivable* objects associated with ordinary circumstances and *privately perceivable* objects related to religious experiences that come "from God." He then claims that perceptions of both types of objects are veridical. A veridical perception refers to "the accurate perception of what is real" (Aleman and Larøi 2009: 15). Swinburne resorts to this shrewd strategy to claim that religious experiences have epistemic parity with ordinary public perceptions. He then goes on to reason that proving the veridicality of religious experiences in effect proves the existence of God as the source of those experiences.

However, the two types of perceptions Swinburne wants to treat as being epistemically on par are, in fact, very different. As the philosopher Nicholas Everitt (2004: 161–62) points out, in the case of a publicly perceivable object anyone positioned correctly in space and time, who does not suffer from any sensory impairments, and is attentive will see it as real. Privately perceivable objects are things Swinburne associates with religious experiences. He describes these as occurrences that have the extraordinary power to make themselves selectively visible to one person, or a small group of people but remain invisible to others (Everitt 2004: 161–62). Moreover, in this line of reasoning since a privately perceivable object can control its perceptibility the failure to see it does not mean that it is not there but only that it has chosen not to reveal itself in that particular instance to that particular observer.

Here is a superb example of a non-falsifiable assertion because such a perceptual event can fail all the disconfirmation tests used to assess ordinary perceptions and still be construed veridical because it entails a selectively visible object. Skeptics would rightly disagree with such a view, pointing out that an object that can selectively make itself visible and invisible in its interactions with its surroundings is scientifically impossible. Swinburne does not see it this way and argues that religious experiences are paranormal or supernatural events and therefore do not conform to physical laws as skeptics demand. Here he uses the familiar strategy frequently employed by other religionists and paranormalists of asking for an exemption from all scientific evidentiary criteria by asserting that religious phenomena are outside the boundaries of legitimate scientific inquiry. As we shall see, Swinburne's entire case depends on such exemptions. Few skeptics, however, would acquiesce to such special pleading.

One essential element of the argument from religious experience is what Swinburne calls the "Principle of Credulity." As he puts it,

> I suggest that it is a principle of rationality that (in the absence of special considerations) if it seems (epistemically) to a subject that x is present; what one seems to perceive is probably so. (Swinburne 2004: 254)

A corollary to this is what Swinburne (2004: 322) calls the "Principle of Testimony." It holds that in the absence of exceptional considerations, the purported testimonies of others are perfectly reliable accounts of what is the case. Through this kind of sophistry, Swinburne is saying that a person's subjective perceptions are believable and are always what they appear to be unless there are some very, very good reasons to think otherwise. However, as we have seen in Chapters 6 and 7, there is overwhelming cognitive, neuroscientific, and psychological evidence demonstrating that perceptions are seldom what they seem to be. Given the enormous range of defects in human perception and memory, it is surprising that anyone finds Swinburne's argument to be credible.

To follow this theologian's line of reasoning further, he is saying that if people have a minimal experience of God talking to them, it is reasonable for them to believe that God is indeed talking to them, and that God exists. Someone is justified in doubting this only if there is proof that very, very probably God does not exist and his or her experience is an illusion. If such proof is not forthcoming, then this person is entitled to assume that God exists and is having a conversation with him or her (Everitt 2004: 161). The faulty reasoning should be clear. Swinburne employes the hypothesis of theism to support the veridicality of religious experiences that are in turn used to support the claim that the theistic God exists. In other words, he is assuming the veracity of the premise he is seeking to establish, which is a terrible case of circular reasoning. Moreover, this is a clever ploy on his part to shift the burden of proof on the skeptic.

Swinburne assumes that his cumulative case strategy has demonstrated the probable existence of the monotheistic God—meaning the Christian deity, not Shiva, Kukulkan, Jupiter, Teshub, or Baʿal—and uses that assumption to support his arguments for the veridicality of religious experience. For this reason, he dismisses David Hume's view on the improbability of miracles because Hume did not consider the fact that God exists and "can set aside the laws of nature he normally sustains" (Swinburne 2003: 25, 30, 2004: 284). In other words, like other apologists, he is asking us to accept the existence of God a priori to establish the veridicality of religious experiences. Skeptics are unconvinced by Swinburne's special pleading or that his cumulative strategy for the justification that theism has succeeded, at least to the satisfaction of those who are not devout votaries or indoctrinated (Everitt 2004; Martin 1990: Philipse 2014).

Swinburne's argument for religious experience hinges on the validity of his Principle of Credulity, or whether or not there is epistemic parity between publicly and privately perceivable objects as he describes them (Philipse 2014: 321–22). To find out, we can outline the argument provided by the philosopher Everitt (2004: 157–58, 172). Let us say we are in Scotland walking along the shores of Loch Ness. A few minutes into the walk, a beast raises its head out of the water. We, therefore, believe that we have seen the legendary Loch Ness monster and now think that the cryptid is real. The reasoning is as follows:

(1) It seems that I had an experience of the monster. So:
(2) I probably did have an experience of the monster. So:
(3) The monster exists.

Here we have gone from a perceptual experience to a claim about a mind-independent entity. Swinburne uses the same type of argument to make a case for experiencing God. Is this move justified? The answer depends upon the existence of epistemic parity between religious experiences and ordinary perceptual experiences. The epistemic circumstances of ordinary perception hinge on whether the experience coheres with one's other experiences. Minimally, one can employ three types of confirming and disconfirming procedures (Everitt 2004: 157–58). Let us say there is an orange before us and we want to know if it is actually there, that is, it is veridical, or if it is an illusion or hallucination. First, one can use further visual procedures that would provide the needed evidence to make such a determination, such as changing one's position relative to the object. One could do this by walking around it, drawing nearer, or changing the intensity or angle of the light in the room. If the object experienced is real, then the experiences of it will change in predictable ways as a result of such tests.

Second, if these procedures do not suffice to resolve the question, we could use other sensory modalities, such as touching or smelling the object. If our fingers pass through the orange, or we cannot smell it, then it is reasonable for us to conclude that the orange is probably not there. Another approach would be to test the causal interactions between the perceived orange and other objects in the surrounding environment. Will it cast a shadow when we shine a light on it? Will it be displaced when hit by another orange rolled toward it? If there are no such interactions, then the orange is probably not real.

Third, we could seek corroboration from other people who are in a position to perceive the orange. If the object is real, then others will probably be able to see it as well, although here we must be wary of group hallucinations that happen under certain circumstances (see below). If under normal conditions others cannot see the orange, then it is justifiable to conclude that the orange is probably a perceptual illusion. It is not justifiable to conclude from this, however, that we have extra-sensitive paranormal abilities to detect such objects and others who have fewer sensitivities are unable to do so (Everitt 2004: 158). The French physicists studying the presence of N-rays, discussed in Chapter 3, made this mistake by attributing the varying ability of test subjects to detect the rays to differences in degrees of sensitivity to the rays by various observers, rather than to conclude that the rays were not present.

Similar tests outlined above concerning objects such as an orange do not apply to religious experiences (Martin 1990: 167). What this suggests is that the Principle of Credulity is not the ultimate "principle of rationality," but must be justified on inductive grounds. In other words, in the case of ordinary perception for any object we see, there are confirming and disconfirming experiences we can use by applying different modalities of sense experience as described. However, what confirmation or corroboration procedure can we use in the perception of God, who by definition is invisible and nonmaterial, and is able to choose who may or may not perceive Him? There are none! Corroborating a purported experience of God is not feasible through the kind of exploration and testing that is possible in the case of the perception of an orange. If the Principle of Credulity were valid, these procedures should, in principle, be possible. However, they are not because the two types of perceptual experiences do not have epistemic parity.

Let us now return to our example of the Loch Ness monster. This entity is a cryptid creature of pseudoscience, but God is a paranormal being. One may catch a glimpse of Nessie but not of God. The monster, if it is real (it is not), would be a physical object, with a particular chemical composition, odor, a definite size, shape, and color, with limbs, a body, head, and eyes. It could be detectable with motion sensors and photography (the Plesiosaur-like creature in the so-called surgeon's photograph from 1934 is a fake and does not count). God, however, is by definition a nonphysical entity without any discernible features, such as size, shape, color, odor, body, limbs, head, eyes, or chemical composition. None of His attributes are perceivable. We cannot detect God with motion sensors, cameras, or other instrumentations. Such a being is an impossible object of sensory experience. As Everitt (2004: 172–73) sums it up, in religious experience the alleged object, that is, God, does not have any perceivable properties and therefore the experience cannot have the phenomenal constituent religionists claim it does. Thus, given that Swinburne argues that "in the absence of special considerations, if it seems (epistemically) to a subject that x is present" then it is present, all the purported perceptions of God fall under the "special considerations" clause because it is impossible to experience God.

## What Do the Experiences of God Really Signify?

The philosopher Herman Philipse (2014: 328) argues that a purported experience of God by a subject is not an "of-God experience," but of something else that is not identical with God. When we look at the five categories of religious experience Swinburne describes as part of his case, this becomes evident.

(1) Perceiving a supernatural object as a public, ordinary non-supernatural object, for example, seeing God's handiwork in the starry night sky. This is not an of-God experience, however, because the product, in this case, the starry night sky, is not the same as its maker. For it to qualify as such, God and the night sky have to be identical, but they are not. The theistic God, as Philipse (2014: 325) points out, is by definition not identical with any publicly visible objects.

(2) The experience of an extraordinary public supernatural object in its own guise. An obvious and uncontroversial case of this would represent compelling evidence for a religious experience (Martin 1990: 162). For example, Muhammad seeing the archangel Gabriel as a mind-independent event, but no such evidence exists. Alternatively, if there had been an actual resurrection of Jesus, then that could count. However, as discussed in Chapters 12, 14, and 15, the resurrection of Jesus

is very controversial. The Christian sources, such as the Synoptic Gospels and the Gospel of John, or the Apostle Paul's letters, contradict one another, and there are no Roman or Jewish documentations for the event (see Chapter 12). Also, even if some people actually saw a resurrected Jesus, those individuals would have perceived an extraordinary public object, the risen body of a man. This is not an of-God experience because in that situation God was in the earthly form of a human being, and God is bodiless. The appearances of Jesus are consistent with several alternative supernatural explanations, such as a finite god, a deity among deities, a group of lesser gods, or even the Devil (Martin 1990: 162).

(3) A nonpublic subjective experience of a supernatural being that is describable in ordinary vocabulary. For example, God's voice that only the percipient can hear (something commonly associated with various psychological maladies, see below). An example of this was the Apostle Paul's experience on the road to Damascus when he claimed he heard Jesus's voice. But here, to identify the voice as that of God's necessitates that the voice is heard by others who could then tell us that it was the voice of such an entity. However, this is impossible because God is immaterial, has no vocal cords, and hence no audible voice. Thus, this is not an of-God experience but a purported experience of something allegedly produced by God. The Principle of Credulity can justify the idea that the product exists, but not that God produced it (Philipse 2014: 328). Similarly, we may add that the "experience of God's goodness, glory, love, greatness," which is how Taliaferro (2009: 208) characterizes religious experiences, is not of-God experiences but sensations purportedly produced by God.

(4) Experience of specific sensations that are ineffable and indescribable in words. This has no phenomenal content, and such occurrences do not provide epistemic support for the existence of God because there is no way to determine that such an indescribable experience is of-God. Thus, the principle of credulity does not apply to this case.

(5) A religious experience without any sensations. This also lacks phenomenal content because it is, by definition, unknowable.

Neither of the experiences (1) or (2) is sufficiently similar to ordinary perceptions to justify the application of the Principle of Credulity. If an of-God experience exists, as Philipse (2014: 326) points out, it would belong to categories 4 and 5 on Swinburne's list because they fit the definition of God as a bodiless entity. However, the Principle of Credulity is even less justifiable when applied to these because they are phenomenologically different from ordinary sense perceptions. Thus, by definition, experiences that would qualify as of-God experiences are the ones to which the Principle of Credulity applies the least (Philipse 2014: 326–27).

Given the phenomenological characteristics of these five kinds of religious experiences, how can one know that the object is the experience of God, given God's attributes as an entity that is bodiless, absolute, unique, transcendent, and totally free? In fact, what is perceived in these cases is not God but specific perceptible effects that He allegedly produces, like hearing a voice we think is His, having a feeling of unity with the universe, getting a realization of profound significance, or feelings of salvation purportedly caused by Him. To construe these events to be of-God is to offer a more robust interpretation than is justifiable by the phenomenology of such experiences themselves (Philips 2014: 333). In other words, such a claim transcends what one can reasonably expect to know by what is experienced (Martin 1990: 185). Hence, there are convincing defeaters both for one's own religious experiences and those of others as related to us through second-hand testimony.

Religious experiences, which are reports of having perceived things that cannot by their very nature be perceived, undermine the credibility of all assertions regarding of-God experiences. Swinburne, however, is optimistic that despite such difficulties, the percipient will be able to identify the source of the experiences because of the sheer awesomeness and magnitude of the attributes of God. Thus, even if inductive procedures are needed to detect lesser degrees of these attributes in other circumstances, he adds, we can know this in the case of God (Philipse 2014: 327). Alternatively, Swinburne (2004: 318–19) makes the following suggestion:

> The description of God as the one and only omnipotent, omniscient, and perfectly free person may indeed suffice for someone to recognize him—by hearing his voice, or feeling his presence, or seeing his handiwork, or by some sixth sense.

However, how does one determine that a voice one is hearing or a feeling is that of an awesome infinite being and not that of an awesome finite being? There is no background information available to help us make such a determination (Martin 1990: 181). Also, the difficulty with the suggestion that the percipient can know something through some sixth sense is that ESP and all psi phenomena are unreliable and unproven (Martin 1990: 183). From the issues raised here, Philipse (2014: 328–29) concludes that "there are no good reasons to suppose that any real perceptual of-God experiences have occurred among the multitude of religious experiences."

For the sake of argument, however, let us assume that a genuine of-God experience is possible. Here the question that arises is, What would one need to determine that the voice one is hearing is that of an invisible, utterly unique, omnipotent, omniscient, transcendent, and perfectly free being? How about if it offered the solution to a mathematical problem no one has ever been able to solve? Alternatively, what if it provided hitherto unknown knowledge that is testable and verifiable by independent investigators, such as how to build a spacecraft capable of traveling faster than the speed of light? These might suffice. The problem is that there are no documented cases of an of-God experience in the vast corpus of reported religious experiences recorded over the millennia across cultures in which God has revealed anything that the members of the community to which the percipient belonged could not have known or discovered by themselves (Philipse 2014: 328). Also, if religious experiences were indeed the sources of extraordinary revealed knowledge of the profound significance claimed for them by true believers, they should be so overwhelmingly impressive as to convince even the most recalcitrant atheists immediately. No such experience has occurred. Otherwise, there would be no atheists or even agnostics anywhere on this planet.

Another problem religionists must address is the availability of non-paranormal explanations for religious experiences that attribute such events to internal mental processes and not to a hypothetical and by definition unknowable mind-independent paranormal entity. Swinburne's (2004: 320) response is that demonstrating that an apparent experience of God has a natural cause does not invalidate its veridicality as a supernatural event. The reason for this is that God, as the creator and sustainer of the universe, is omnipresent and cannot be absent from any location and is a part of all causal processes. We have already encountered this sort of special pleading. Swinburne is thus resorting to the fallacious "God did it" or "God is in everything" omni-explanatory hypothesis, already dispelled in Chapters 3 and 6. It is false because, among other defects, "an explanation that explains everything explains nothing" (Fishman and Boudry 2013: 940–41; Mahner 2012: 1450–52).

The other problem is that if all purported experiences of God are veridical then so would the of-God experience of Peter Sutcliffe, the Yorkshire Ripper, who murdered 13 women and tried to kill 7 others, claiming that God told him to do so (Philipse 2014: 335). The same would be true of the experience of the self-styled Messiah of the Heaven's Gate cult who committed suicide along with 38 of his followers based on a message from "his Father" from "the Kingdom of Heaven" (Sidky 2015: 119). Therefore, the contention that all of-God experiences are veridical because God is part of their causes fails.

Our discussion thus far has focused on religious experiences associated with the monotheistic God. However, all sorts of people from various religious and cultural backgrounds have reported such experiences. Are all of these experiences veridical? A significant epistemic problem arises here. If the Principle of Credulity applies to all religious experiences, then we must accept as veridical the experiences not only of the monotheistic God but also of Baʿal, Amun Ra, Jupiter, Ahura Mazda, Shiva, Dorji Drakden, along with experiences of aliens, demons, goblins, and so forth. Philipse (2014: 329) refers to this as falling into "the swamp of gullibility." However, if the monotheistic God is real, as theists claim, then assertions about the other deities must be false. If this is correct, it means that religious experience itself is an altogether untrustworthy epistemic source, so that the argument from religious experience for the monotheistic God is also vanquished.

## Are Religious Experiences Cosmically Significant Supernatural Events?

In contrast to the religionist perspective discussed in the previous section, there are non-paranormal explanations for religious and mystical experiences that are supported by considerable amounts of independent empirical evidence (Everitt 2004: 171). These explanations do not depend upon unproven processes and mechanisms, such as divine interventions in the evolution of the human brain or the existence of a hypothetical supernatural being that is by definition unknowable and for whose presence there is no scientific evidence. Instead, they draw from the fields of neuroscience and evolutionary, cognitive, anomalistic, and experimental psychology and scientific anthropology.

As already discussed, religious experiences involve anomalous events, such as seeing apparitions, hearing voices, the "sensed presence effect," reception of supernatural messages and mandates, and the feeling of oneness and connectedness with the universe (French and Stone 2014: 65–67). Science, however, does not consider these phenomena to be unknowable, ethereal, supernatural, or otherworldly. In the words of the psychologist Barry Beyerstein (2007: 314), neuroscientific and psychological research has demonstrated that mystical or religious experiences are nothing more than by-products of how our brains work. Thus assertions by votaries that "religious experience involves more than just fantasy-driven altered states of consciousness" (e.g., Fontana 2003: 109) are highly problematic.

Religious and mystical experiences involving loss of personal and spatial boundaries are relatively common. Surveys in the United States and the United Kingdom indicate that between 20 and 44 percent of these populations have reported having such experiences (Fenwick 2010: 12). While there is no reason to doubt such occurrences, which can be powerful and at times life-changing for the experient, what is in question is whether these events entail contact or communication with some Cosmic Being as claimed (Stenger 1990: 104). Moreover, the possibility of fraud is also ever-present. In some cases, claiming to have had such an experience can yield many rewards, such as attention, admiration, and social status. Thomas Paine (1880 [1795]: 142) astutely pointed out the central problem posed by such experiences:

> [The thing revealed] is a revelation to the person *only to whom it was made*. His account to another person is not revelation; and whoever puts faith in that account, puts it in the man from whom the account comes and that man may have been deceived, or may have dreamed it, or he may be an imposter and may lie. There is no possible criterion whereby to judge the truth of what he tells, for even the morality of it would be no proof of revelation. In all such cases the proper answer would be, "When it is revealed to me, I will believe it to be a revelation; but it is not, and cannot be incumbent upon me to believe it to be revelation before; neither is it proper that I should take the word of a man as the word of God, and put man in place of God.

The inability to verify claims to visions and auditions leaves open the opportunities for fraud. As the New Testament scholar Luke Johnson says in his book *Religious Experience in Earliest Christianity* (1998: 53),

> For a variety of reasons, humans have found it profitable to fake religious experiences, not unlike the way some people fake the experience of pain for the sake of gain or attention. And when in principle such experiences lack the possibility of verification, the possibilities for widespread fraud and deception are obvious.

Religious experiences are sometimes classified under the labels of "ASC" and "anomalous experiences." These two terms are somewhat confusing because they refer to overlapping phenomena. ASC relate to changes to aspects of consciousness from our ordinary wakeful state. It can involve visual, auditory, and tactile hallucinations, encounters with paranormal beings and spirit helpers, as well as experiences of oneness with the cosmos. Many of the shamans with whom I have worked, for example, claimed to see, hear, and have contact with an array of paranormal entities. The Sufi mystics I have encountered, however, describe their experience in terms of the idea of oneness or unity with ultimate reality, or God, something they call *fana-fil-haq* and *fana-fil-tawheed*.

The idea that humans have multiple states of consciousness was discussed over a century ago by the noted American psychologist William James in his book *The Varieties of Religious Experience* (1902): In his words,

> Our normal waking consciousness, rational consciousness as we call it, is but one special type of consciousness, whilst all about it, parted from it by the filmiest of screens, there lie potential forms of consciousness entirely different. We may go through life without suspecting their existence; but apply the requisite stimulus, and at a touch, they are there in all completeness, definite types of mentality which probably somewhere have their field of application and adaptation. No account of the universe in its totality can be final which leaves these other forms of consciousness quite disregarded. How to regard them is the question—for they are so discontinuous with ordinary consciousness. (James 1902: 298)

Subsequent researchers have elaborated upon this concept (see Ludwig 1990: 18).

## What Do Altered States of Consciousness and Anomalous Experiences Really Signify?

Theists and various researchers enthralled by mysticism, spirituality, and shamanism attach a great deal of mystery and significance to ASC, as I once did, and consider them as the mind's doorway to alternate realities and the means for the acquisition of transcendental truths and paranormal powers. This claim is, in fact, the bread and butter of the purveyors of New Age and eastern mysticisms. Religionist professor of Scripture John Pilch (1998: 57–58) maintains, for instance, that ASC provide access to an actual mind-independent "alternate reality," or access to a real supernatural domain.

I have investigated this idea for a long time in the context of fieldwork attempting to be as accommodating as possible. However, after years of research with religious practitioners who routinely employ ASC in their ritual activities, it became clear that the transcendental truths received always amount to restatements of ideas that are already part of the extant worldviews and knowledge base of the communities to which such practitioners belong. I have never encountered examples of any radical epistemological or ontological breakthroughs by anyone undergoing ASC, whether shamans, mediums, mystics, god-men, rinpoches, and so forth. None of these specialists were ever able to reveal anything startlingly novel. They could not even provide simple mundane information, such as the location of my house in the United States, the weather conditions in my hometown, and similar information, although I often asked them to provide such reports. These observations made me rethink the notion of religious experiences as a kind of human behavior, rather than a manifestation of the miraculous, or an intervention of a supernatural force or intelligence outside of space and time into empirical reality. Reports of such experiences, therefore, are X-claims.

As noted, religious experiences are sometimes called "anomalous experiences," which also refer to subjective perceptions that deviate from ordinary awareness and normative or conventional perceptions of reality (Cardeña et al. 2000: 4; Holt et al. 2012: 2). Researchers with definite leanings toward paranormal beliefs use the term "anomalistic," as in "anomalistic experiences" or "anomalistic psychology," in place of "abnormal psychology" or "abnormal behavior" to avoid the negative connotations of psychopathology that is attached to those words. Anomalous experiences include auditory and visual hallucinations, states involving the impression of contact with non-ordinary reality, the sensed presence effect, ESP, prophetic dreams, and seeing ghost, angels, fairies, and so forth (Holt et al. 2012: 2; Wulff 2000: 397). Henceforth, I shall avoid using the terms ASC and anomalous experiences as much as possible because they encompass overlapping phenomena and can be a source of confusion.

The phenomenological attributes of religious or mystical experiences to which believers attach considerable cosmic significant as evidence of God's actions in the world are achievable through the physical manipulation of the brain (Beyerestein 2007: 318–19). Thus, neuroscience is perfectly capable of explaining such subjective experiences in naturalistic terms. Similar effects are achievable through the use of a variety of hallucinogenic and psychotropic drugs, such as psilocybin, DMT, and ketamine, among others (Sidky 2017b: 37–52). As I have discussed in *The Origins of Shamanism, Spirit Beliefs, and Religiosity* (2017), archeological data indicate that the ritual use of drugs dates back to ancient times. Swinburne (2004: 314) dismisses the role and significance of hallucinogens in religious experience, which is a further indication of how oblivious believing theologians are to the relevance of the anthropological and scientific evidence to their central debates and arguments.

Other religionists argue that such scientific findings do not detract from the cosmological significance of religious experiences because it was God who created the brain mechanisms involved in facilitating the reception of His transcendental truths (Fingelkurts and Fingelkurtz 2009). Once again, these believers are resorting to the problematic "God did it" or "it is all part of God's plan" omni-explanation. Moreover, the same objections raised regarding Swinburne's argument from religious experience apply here as well. In other words, such an assertion would be credible if any of the revelations purported to be direct divine transmissions from God during "a drug trip" contained any novel, previously unheard of truths unknown to or beyond the capacity of members of the group to which the visionary belongs to discover by themselves.

Humans have had religion for at least 150,000 to 200,000 years or more (Sidky 2017b). In all that time, no visionaries, shamans, prophets, vatics, or messiahs have revealed anything genuinely extraordinary to their culture, time, and place. Considering the vast periods involved, one would expect at least one or a few such revelations. There are none! Why? Of relevance here is Victor Stenger's (1990: 107) observation that the visions and hallucination have never involved new knowledge about the universe or "neutrinos or airplanes or computers before the twentieth century."

## Are Religious Experiences Veridical or Paranormal Fantasies?

In an article on religious experience, the sociologist Rodney Stark (1999) correctly emphasizes the importance of the cultural and social contexts of supernatural experiences by pointing out that individuals who receive revelations come from cultures that accept the reality of such experiences. However, he moves into the realm of the paranormal and pseudoscience by stating that we cannot rule out the possibility that "revelations actually occur." By this, he means the transmission of genuine messages from the supernatural world. As Stark puts it (1999: 287–88), "We do not know that revelations are impossible; it is entirely beyond the capacity of science to demonstrate that the divine does not communicate directly with certain individuals."

However, as already discussed, such demonstrations are well within the parameters of science. Science can indeed demonstrate that supernatural revelations are impossible. To reiterate, one reason is that these messages never contain new knowledge unattainable by members of the society to which the percipient belongs. It is also clear that Divine memoranda are almost always wrong. The Jewish Messiah never appeared, Christ did not come back, the Kingdom of God on earth never materialized, white people were not swept away by the Ghost Dance ritual, the ancestors never brought the promised cargo in Melanesia, and so forth. Also, there are the many gross errors of fact contained in the divine communications that suggest human rather than supernatural or divine sources.

Stark (1999: 288) also suggests that divine communications are veridical because "normal" people can "sincerely believe" that they have communicated with God. He admits that delusion and deception exist in religion but adds that it is more reasonable to attribute truly profound revelations to authentic divine sources (Stark 1999: 305). On what grounds is this stance more reasonable? Just because someone sincerely believes that Yahweh, Jesus, Allah, Sananda, or even the Devil have spoken to him or her and acts accordingly despite hostility and persecution does not prove the supernatural origins of the message. All sorts of fanatics sincerely believe in outlandish absurdities purportedly transmitted from the beyond and act upon them often at enormous costs to themselves and others. Delusional extremists who believed that they were exercising God's mandates are a recurrent theme in human history. Nor does the fact that someone sincerely believes that a paranormal being has spoken to them rule out the psychopathological model of revelation, contra Stark.

Similarly, the sincerity of belief does not refute the fraud hypothesis as Stark thinks it does. David Hume astutely (1902 [1748]: 113) pointed this out long ago, which I shall cite once again:

> A religionist may be an enthusiast, and imagine he sees what has no reality: he may know his narrative to be false, and yet persevere in it, with the best intentions in the world, for the sake of promoting so holy a cause.

Given that Stark is open to the possibility of genuine supernatural revelations in human affairs he takes as veridical (i.e., actual communications with God) the disclosures to that effect made by individuals such as Moses, Jesus, Muhammad, Joseph Smith (the prophet of Mormonism), Bernadette Soubirous (the girl who saw apparitions of Mary in Lourdes, France), and Sun Myung Moon (the founder of the Unification Church). Yet, there are plenty of reasons to doubt the veracious nature of the claims made by such individuals because ultimately, we only have the word of these self-styled vatics and ambassadors from heaven regarding the veracity of their claims. That lots and lots of gullible or desperate people believed or still believe their declarations and venerate them as holy personages do not alter the epistemic status of their claims.

Stark (1999: 290) also makes the erroneous assertion that archaeology has confirmed the historicity of the New Testament. Such statements are religionist nonsense. He also accepts as genuine the revelation by the Holy Spirit to Mary, related in Luke 1:26–56, about her conception of the "Son of God." However, the idea of Jesus's divine parentage was conceived long after the time of Jesus, and hence, his mother could not have known it. The determinations of Jesus's divinity as the son of God as well as the doctrine of the Trinity were not based on an announcement by some supernatural agency or through a divine transmission and were unknown at the time Jesus was alive. These ideas were decided upon through committee vote by the First Council of Nicaea (now İznik, Turkey) convened in 325 CE by Emperor Constantine. The potentate who saw the effectiveness of Christian beliefs as a means of social control in the eastern provinces sought to create an authoritative and standardized version so he could use it to extend and consolidate his political power. Stark's assertions are incorrect.

Finally, Stark (1999: 292) adds that "some revelations seem genuine" because they are "so culturally impressive as to be worthy of divine sources." The examples he gives, such as the poetic language of the Qur'an and the words in the Book of Mormon, are actually very unimpressive and well within the capacity of humans. The Qur'an, for example, was assembled from dispersed verses written on various types of materials by different people with varying literary skills. These bits of anecdotal data were compiled possibly as long as 20 years or more after the death of the Prophet Muhammad, the alleged recipient of the revelations (Donner 2008: 29–37; see Warraq 1998: 150, 2000). This either happened during the reign of Abu Bakr (632–634 CE), the first Caliph of Islam, who succeeded Muhammad, during the time of Uthman (644–656 CE), the third Caliph, or even later (see Warraq 1998: 11–13).

The final version of the Qur'an thus created was heavily impacted by the vagaries of orally transmitted information, which is open to alterations and embellishment. Also, there are errors of judgment and selection, loss of data due to the death of many who had initially memorized the verses because of the Arab wars of expansion, the limitations and unreliability of human memory, and the vicissitudes of the human hands. Therefore, like other ostensibly inerrant sacred tomes, this one is also a human artifact, notwithstanding the alleged cosmic significance attached to it by believers and the infantile rage they display toward anyone who disagrees.

Although some scholars have stated that Islam, in comparison to other religions, emerged "under the clear light of history" (Andræ 1960: 11), we know as little about Muhammad as we do about Moses or Jesus. Apocryphal tales abound, but the historical evidence is almost entirely absent. While all of this evokes a sense of sacrilege among true believers, the fact of the matter is that we do not know who initially wrote down these verses. All of these factors would have impacted the language in that holy book. Also, the original text was in the old unstandardized Arabic script lacking diacritical marks that made it conducive to variant readings. Standardize Arabic did not appear until the end of the ninth century. Addressing this problem would have required numerous emendations and redactions. Hence the language contained in the final standardized version of the holy book was very different from the first recitations or revelations (see Warraq 1998: 11–13). There is nothing impressive enough to warrant the conclusion that the source of this tome was an otherworldly power or supernatural being.

There are more significant problems with claims about the miraculous nature of the Book of Mormon. It is full of gross factual errors, racism, and sheer nonsense contrary to anthropological findings and historical evidence. These include assertions that Jesus visited North America in person and that the Native Americans are the descendants of Middle Eastern people fleeing the Tower of Babel around 2500 BCE. This holy book is also full of racist avowals, such as the claim that the lost white-skinned tribe of Israel that settled the Americas millennia ago were the actual builders of the sophisticated civilizations in the New World rather than these being the accomplishments of the indigenous peoples, thereby denying and depriving them of their cultural and historic heritage. Also, there is the declaration that Native Americans are the descendants of the Lamanites, one of the purported Middle Eastern tribes that allegedly came to the Northern Hemisphere. These are a cursed and degraded lot, the text says, because they exterminated the Nephites, their righteous kinsmen, a sin that caused their skins to turn dark (see Bushman 2008). None of these and the many other absurdities in this text would be there if its source were indeed a Divine all-knowing supernatural being, as believers profess. Also, the history of how Joseph Smith, the self-styled ambassador from heaven, and the founder of Mormonism, forged this so-called holy book is well known (Shapiro 2016: 97–107). It did not originate from the supernatural realm. These facts make it difficult to comprehend Stark's statements.

Even avowed new syntheses of cultural elements into new models for social action and moral behavior that sometimes follows religious revelations do not constitute miraculous or paranormal events that are inexplicable according to conventional or prosaic ecological, sociocultural, political, and economic forces. These include Yahweh's messages to Moses, Jesus's post-resurrection appearances to Peter and the disciples, Jesus's communiqué to Paul, Allah's directives to Muhammad, Joan of Arc's fantasies, Martin Luther's delusional visions, Handsome Lake's reception of messages from the Creator, Wovoka's Ghost Dance dream, and the lurid visions of the Melanesian cargo prophets.

## Religious Experience and Brain-Based Hallucinations

Religious experiences, as neuroscientists Jeffrey Saver and John Rabin (1997: 498) have put it, are "brain-based." Those in search of the unreal real desperately wish to avoid such a conclusion (e.g., Fingelkurts and Fingelkurts 2009; Hay 1990; Stark 1999). However, evidence that these experiences are brain-related hallucinatory phenomena is overwhelming. Indeed, the use of such terms as "vision," "revelations," "sense of presence," and "mystical oneness" to describe such events are merely dignified descriptors of well-known hallucinatory experiences in various sense modalities (Zusne and Jones 1989: 114). The word "hallucination" comes from the Latin *hallucinere*, meaning "to wander in mind." Cognitive neuropsychiatrists André Aleman and Frank Larøi (2009: 23) define hallucination as "a conscious sensory experience" that does not have corresponding external stimulation of the relevant sensory organ but seem sufficiently real to resemble "a veridical perception."

The word "vision" is derived from magico-religious lore and means the same thing as "hallucination," but with the added theological ornamentation of sacredness and cosmic significance (Beyerstein 2007: 300). Visions are thought to come from supernatural beings intending to send the "chosen" recipients dispatches containing prophetic mandates and missions. If we focus exclusively on the visions of the revered religious figures already mentioned, we could easily overlook others who also believed that they were "chosen" for special missions through paranormal visions (cf., Beyerstein 2007: 320). These paragons of virtue included Atilla the Hun, Adolf Hitler, Idi Amin, Charles Manson, Jim Jones, Marshall Applewhite, Peter Sutcliffe, Soko Asahara, and David Koresh, to name a few. Here, Voltaire's cynical observation is highly relevant:

> He who is involved in ecstasies and visions, who takes dreams for reality, and his own imagination for prophecy, is a fanatical novice of great hope and promise, and will soon advance to the higher stage and kill men for the love of God. (Voltaire 1901 [1764], 5: 16)

If we set aside the theological trappings, our topic merely becomes hallucinations. Reports of these occur throughout history, often in connection with religious phenomena (Aleman and Larøi 2009: 9–10; Leudar and Thomas 2000: 1–13; McCarthy-Jones 2012). Many supernatural and paranormal experiences, past and present, are hallucinations misinterpreted and ascribed celestial meaning by the percipients. As Beyerstein (2007: 320) sums this up, the sense of presence, out-of-body experiences (OBEs), and visions of ghost and other supernatural beings have for millennia produced new religions. While these have been accepted as proof of afterlife, higher planes of existence, and cosmic consciousness, he adds, they have prosaic explanations. In the present, these take the form of sightings of alien spacecraft piloted by rapacious crews of incubi and succubi who abduct people for sexual abuse and bizarre medical experimentation.

Hallucinations may involve different sensory modalities: auditory (nonverbal sounds), verbal (voices), visual (seeing), olfactory (smelling), kinesthetic (body movement and sensations), tactile (touch), and gustatory (taste). Also, there are hypnagogic (onset of sleep), or hypnopompic (waking up from sleep) hallucinations (Reed 1988: 49–58). Multimodal hallucinations involving several simultaneous perceptual experiences also take place (Aleman and Larøi 2009: 32). Neuroimaging studies indicate that a hallucination in a particular modality involves brain locations that ordinarily process information in that modality. For example, the activation of brain locations associated with the perception of speech causes auditory hallucinations, indicating that inner speech occurs at the same time as auditory hallucinations. Activation of the right inferotemporal cortex related to the perception of faces causes the hallucination of faces. Also, the stimulation of the area of the brain associated with reading produces hallucination of letters or pseudo-words (Sacks 2012: xi).

Although commonalities exist across different societies, the metaphysical attitudes of time and place influence the contents of hallucinations. Religious phenomena, we might recall, are part and parcel of cultural traditions. They cannot be otherwise. Moreover, the culturally determined content of hallucinations can change over time. For example, Aleman and Larøi (2009: 30) point out that unlike the present-day pattern in Europe, during the Middle Ages hallucinations were universally religious in nature, involving messages from God, saints, and interactions with angels or demons. Moreover, the recorded cases from the Middle Ages were almost entirely visual hallucinations (Kroll and Bachrach 1982). Such occurrences are rare at present.

There are also cross-cultural variations in the predominance of particular kinds of hallucinations. For example, visual hallucinations associated with schizophrenia predominate in Africa and the Middle East, while these hallucinatory phenomena are the least frequently reported symptoms among European and American patients (Aleman and Larøi 2009: 30; Bentall 2000: 96–97). One would not expect such variations if these experiences were actually tapping into some singular universal cosmic source or ultimate reality beyond the material universe, rather than being the effects of the human brain and nervous system with input from culture. The significant cultural component of such experiences is a rationality defeater for such claims.

Since the latter part of the nineteenth century, hallucinatory experiences have been viewed by psychiatrists and psychologists as pathological. For example, as the eminent psychiatrist Thomas Szasz (1996: 13) put it regarding auditory hallucinations, "If you talk to God you are praying, if God talks to you, you have schizophrenia." Acoustic, visual, and other types of hallucinations associated with religious experiences frequently occur in cases of schizophrenia, affective disorders, post-traumatic stress disorder, and borderline personality disorder. Such hallucinations also arise among non-psychiatric patients suffering from neurological conditions, such as cerebrovascular disorders, brain tumors, brain injuries, epilepsy, narcolepsy, and migraines (Aleman and Larøi 2009: 48; Bentall 2000: 93).

Mystical or religious experiences are found in association with high levels of activity in the temporal lobes of the brain that may be caused by temporal lobe epilepsy (Landsborough 1987; Saver and Rubin 1997). Zusne and Jones (1989: 69) point to the close resemblance between mystical experiences and what happens to epileptic patients, making it difficult to differentiate between them. Such brain activity produces a range of perceptions and sensations (Saver and Rabin 1997: 498–500). These include déjà vu, jamais vu (perceiving what is known as if it is unknown), detachment, ineffable unity with the cosmos, autoscopy (seeing one's double and OBE), double consciousness (sensing a quasi-consciousness of the self with a different perception of reality). Visual and auditory hallucinations involving perceptions of apparitions occur as well.

Patients with temporal lobe epilepsy tend to develop morose personalities, are humorless, display an extreme obsessive preoccupation with religious, mystical, and cosmological problems, have a desire to preach about the moral failures of those around them, along with many other psychopathological traits. Such individuals also have a powerful conviction that God has chosen them for some special mission (Clarke 2010: 101; Zusne and Jones 1989: 69). As Beyerstein (2007: 330) points out, the symptomology of temporal lobe epilepsy and the experiences of the prophets of old indicated that they suffered temporal lobe anomalies that convinced the experiencer that he or she has been chosen for a special mission in life.

William James (1902: 29) was familiar with the psychopathological behavioral displays of many of the major religious figures:

> Even more perhaps than other kinds of genius, religious leaders have been subject to abnormal psychical visitations. Invariably they have been creatures of exalted emotional sensibility. Often they have led a discordant inner life, and had melancholy during a part of their career. They have known no measure, been liable to obsessions and fixed ideas; and frequently they have fallen into trances, heard voices, seen visions, and presented all sorts of peculiarities which are ordinarily classed as pathological. Often, moreover, these pathological features in their career have helped to give them their religious authority and influence.

James's (1902: 45) explanation for this phenomenon was not that these personages were psychiatric patients but that perhaps such psychopathologies provided the "requisite receptivity" for divine inspiration from "a higher realm." However, inferring cosmic significance for such purported paranormal communications is problematic given the banal nature of the messages. Thus, to justify the attribution of celestial weight to them external corroboration of the content of the alleged revelation is a requisite (Stenger 1990: 104).

Subclinical hyperactivity in the temporal lobes with non-convulsive symptoms, the occurrence of which is distributed widely in the general population, is known to produce mystical-like spontaneous anomalous experiences (French and Stone 2014: 98; Persinger and Makarec 1987; Zusne and Jones 1989: 69). Electrical stimulation of the temporal lobes during neurosurgery also produces similar experiences. Such findings further support the conclusion that paranormal and religious experiences are indeed brain-based (Stenger 1990: 106).

Temporal lobe activity is also affected by neurochemical changes in the brain associated with bereavement, hypoglycemia, hypoxia, anoxia (no oxygen), fatigue, and the use of psychotropic drugs that cause the same types of perceptions commonly associated with religious experiences (French and Stone 2014: 99). There is, therefore, considerable empirical data demonstrating the involvement of the temporal lobes in the generation of mystical and religious experiences. Stenger (1990: 106) observes that the ease with which epileptic visions have been taken as having paranormal significance suggests that humans have allowed themselves to be massively influenced by "people with brain disease."

One conclusion someone could reach regarding the phenomenological similarities between religious experiences and a psychotic worldview is that religions "are a form of madness and the religious merely insane." Alternatively, we could take the cultural relativist perspective that clinically diagnosed psychotics in this culture are merely prophets and visionaries falsely labeled as mad by those who lack their "sensitivities and insights" (Clarke 2010: 75). Most researchers do not make such determinations. The type of hallucinatory phenomena associated with psychosis is now known to also occur among a significant proportion of the nonclinical population (David 2004: 111; Johns and van Os 2001). These include individuals ranging from the psychologically well-adjusted to those who display some symptoms of psychopathology but do not fit the category of clinically psychotic (Aleman and Larøi 2009: 83; Peters 2010: 127).

Christian apologists who try to portray the post-resurrection appearances of Jesus to his grieving followers as something more than hallucinations often claim that hallucinations only affect those with mental illness (see Chapter 15). Since the disciples were not mentally ill, they conclude, the appearances were not hallucinations but actual visits by a dead man who came back to life. However, this is a misrepresentation because such group experiences are frequent and well-documented among nonclinical populations.

In connection to this, scientific researchers have forwarded what is known as the "continuum hypothesis," which holds that the primary difference in hallucinatory experiences between pathological and normal populations is quantitative rather than qualitative (Aleman and Larøi 2009: 86). The significant difference between these two groups may be due to how individuals react to their experiences rather than being related to the nature of the hallucinatory experience itself (French and Stone 2014: 67). Another possibility is that the same set of symptoms are deemed to be religious experiences if the subject is mentally stable and considered psychotic if he or she is unstable (Tobert 2010: 45).

Yet another factor is the attitude of those around the experient, whose acceptance of the psychological condition allows the person to be socially assimilated rather than the symptoms deemed pathological (French and Stone 2014: 67). I encountered situations like this in connection with the terrifying subjective experiences that launch particular individuals along the path to a shamanic vocation in Nepal. In cases where the resulting ontological crisis that occurs due to the encounter with the paranormal world is socially accepted and culturally mediated, the result is a practicing shaman and a functioning member of the community. Where such experiences are not socially recognized and culturally negotiated and mediated, the outcome is a psychiatric patient (Sidky 2008: 57–78).

Another example of this comes from the history of Islam. Muhammad was deeply frightened and puzzled about his supernatural encounter with the paranormal being he saw in the cave (identified as the archangel Gabriel) that began his career as the Prophet of Allah (Watt 1961: 21). At first, he even doubted his own sanity. It was only because of the support and encouragement of his wife, cousin, and close associates that he was able to overcome his doubts and was convinced that he was the recipient of a divine mission. Thus, sociocultural factors and historical contingencies impact whether an experience obtains designation as mystical, spiritual, psychotic, or pathological in different circumstance (cf., Claridge 2010: 76).

It is correct to say that experiences that Western psychiatry may label as pathological, such as hearing voices or seeing visions, are valued and sought after in some cultures (Fenwick 2010: 9). However, relativistic perspectives that place too much emphasis on the cultural dimensions of psychopathology are problematic. As the cognitive neuropsychiatrist Anthony David (2004: 111) has pointed out, it is a mistake to conclude that there is nothing inherently pathological about "hearing voices" except in those cases when the voices compel the patient to cause harm to themselves or others. Thus, contrary to Stark's (1999: 294, 305) assertion, it is not more plausible to treat such hallucinatory experiences as genuine paranormal events rather than ascribing them to psychopathology. It is even possible to make a case that religious experiences and magical thinking are a form of psychosis.

## Does God Speak to People? Julian Jaynes's Eccentric Theory of the Bicameral Mind

Maybe God or the gods did speak to people once upon a time. Here I want to discuss a particular theory linking religious experiences and hallucinations. It is a remarkable and rather peculiar perspective, and I include it here for the sake of comprehensiveness and because of its unconventional nature. The Yale University psychologist Julian Jaynes proposed this theory in a fascinating and controversial study of human consciousness called *The Origin of Consciousness in the Breakdown of the Bicameral Mind* (1976). The book provides a psycho-historical analysis of human civilization drawing on neuroscience, psychology, archaeology, history, and the examination of ancient texts (Persinger 2008: vii–x; Sher 2000: 239).

Jaynes argued that in the past, between 10,000 and 1000 BCE, the human mind was two-chambered or bicameral. People with bicameral minds did not have consciousness as we understand and experience it. They did not have thoughts about thoughts, or awareness about awareness described in connection with the theory of mind and the intentional stance in Chapter 6. In the bicameral mind, according to Jaynes, cognitive functions were divided between the two halves of the brains. Those possessing such minds understood or took their internal thought processes, or their internal dialogue, as communication between the self and an external entity, such as a god, or some other supernatural being. In Jaynes's (1976: 75, 93) view, the transmission of the messages was associated with "the visual aura of an authority figure or god, or sometimes as a voice alone." A person obeyed these hallucinated voices because he could not " 'see' what to do by himself." Jaynes compared the guiding hallucinations of the gods in antiquity to the delusions of schizophrenic patients in the present.

According to this theory, a massive alteration in human mentality occurred toward the end of the second millennium, that is, after 1000 BCE. The factors that led to the weakening of the auditory hallucinations or the breakdown of the bicameral mind included the advent of writing, various historical upheavals, environmental changes, and the emergence of meta-consciousness (Jaynes 1976: 216–21). At this time, people began to apprehend that the external voices they thought they were hearing that originated inside their own heads were actually the kind of internal dialogue we have and understand today. With this shift came the rise of the contemporary subjective, introspective conscious mind. After this time, the gods stopped speaking, and this is why they are "no longer heard and seen" (Jaynes 1976: 320).

According to Jaynes, however, vestiges of the bicameral mind as a carryover from the previous mentality still exist today in association with schizophrenia, hypnotic states, and appear in connection with a variety of religious phenomena, such as states of possession and prophecy. As Jaynes (1976: 320) put it,

> Thus, as the slow withdrawing tide of divine voices and presences strands more and more of each population on the sands of subjective uncertainties, the variety of technique by which man attempts to make contact with his lost ocean of authority becomes extended. Prophets, poets, oracles, diviners, statue cults, mediums, astrologers, inspired saints, demon possession, tarot cards, Ouija boards, popes, and peyote all are the residue of bicamerality that was progressively narrowed down as uncertainties piled upon uncertainties.

Cognitive and evolutionary psychological findings discussed in Chapter 6 do not concur with Jaynes's ideas. The theory of the bicameral mind remains controversial because of its multidisciplinary scope and a general misunderstanding of Jaynes's construal of consciousness and the role of hallucinations (see the volume by Kuijsten 2008). For this reason, Richard Dawkins (2006: 350) has aptly described Jaynes's work as a book that is "either rubbish, or a work of consummate genius, nothing in between."

### Out-of-Body and Near-Death Experiences

One hallucinatory phenomenon that has various religious implications entails perceptions of the self and body, referred to as the OBE. Such events have a close association with near-death experiences (NDEs). The neural system underlying this type of anomalous incident involves aspects of the cerebral cortex and subcortical limbic structures with linkages to memory, mental imagery, motivation, emotion, and "the spatiotemporal mapping of the self and surrounding environment" (Beyerstein 2007: 327).

Stimulation of the exposed surface of the cortex during surgical procedures using a weak electrical charge has evoked vivid and realistic memories, meaningful and cosmically significant visions, déjà vu, ecstasy, as well as OBEs when subjects have reported floating above and seeing their bodies. There is nothing paranormal about such experiences. They involve momentary disruptions of the brain's capacity to integrate the positional information sent to the neural system by the muscles, tendons, and joints; gravitational and motion data from the balance mechanism in the inner ear; and spatial information from the audiovisual systems (Beyerstein 2007: 328).

OBEs are sometimes part of the initial stage of NDEs that are taken as evidence that the soul or spirit survives after death (see Stenger 2012: 230–38). Surveys have shown that more than 70 percent of Americans believe in life after death (Harris Poll 2009; Pew Forum on Religion in Public Life 2008). The works of psychologists Raymond Moody (1975) and Kenneth Ring (1989) made the phenomenon of NDE famous. *The Handbook of Near-Death Experiences: Thirty Years of Investigation* (2009), edited by Janice Holden and associates, provides a compilation of the findings of NDE investigations over the past several decades.

Up to 20 percent of people whose hearts and breathing have temporarily stopped report such experiences (French and Stone 2014: 95). French and Stone (2014: 277–78) define NDE as a transcendental state among people who are near death or believe themselves to be so. The sensations include feelings of bliss, OBE, movement through a tunnel with a light at the end, encounters with angels and other supernatural beings and dead relatives, receiving prophetic messages, obtaining paranormal healing powers, and a life review culminating with a decision to return (cf., Jansen 1997: 8).

The implication here is that the mind is separable from the brain and body and that our consciousness can survive the physical demise of our bodies, an idea discussed in Chapter 6 in connection with mind–body dualism and paranormal beliefs. As noted before, the notion that the mind survives the body is very ancient and is central to the dogma of a number of the major world religions and is probably held to be true by the majority of people around the world (French and Stone 2014: 258). This belief, as Stewart-Williams (2015) observes, is a powerful meme found across cultures. Another descriptor for this phenomenon is the "survivalist hypothesis" (Braithwaite 2008).

NDEs have a variety of components, with different experients providing very dissimilar accounts, although researchers have tended to treat all of these reports as if they represent the same phenomenon (French and Stone 2014: 109; Osis and Haraldsson 1977). In other words, there is far more variability in the accounts, and many narratives lack central features, such as the tunnel effect and the heavenly ambiance, which is puzzling if all these narratives relate a visit to the same afterlife (Hines 2003: 101). Moreover, not all of these experiences are euphoric or pleasant. Some subjects have reported horrifying visits to hellish locations where they have encountered terrifying demonic beings. Also, none of the prophetic messages have ever come true, and the purported healing powers that percipients sometime claim to have acquired are unimpressive and bogus.

Finally, NDEs do not occur in all societies around the world, which suggests the underlying role of culture rather than the percipients encountering the same universal transcendental reality (Augustine 2015: 542–50; Stenger 2012: 236). The cultural dimension of this phenomenon means that the NDE postulate fails the anthropological dictum that any valid claims about some aspect of human experience (which these are) must apply to many places and many times, and if it does not, then we are justified to be skeptical. The fact that NDEs do not occur in all cultures suggests that these experiences are merely a type of "culture-bound syndrome" or a culturally specific psychological aberration of the sort reported in the ethnographic literature about far-away places, for example, conditions such as *amok*, *pibloktoq*, *susto*, and the old hag (see Simons and Hughes 1985: 469–506). This is a powerful rationality defeater for the life after death hypothesis.

Another point to consider is that the drug ketamine can produce psychological states similar to NDEs, and experiences commonly reported during mystical states, including movement through a dark tunnel, the vision of a bright light at the tunnel's end, the belief that one is dead, sensations of a presence, and an OBE (Jansen 1997: 8). Damage to the temporal lobes or cortical stimulation can also produce experiences comparable to NDEs, including OBE, and memory recall, or "life review." Analogous experiences ensue in connection with g-force acceleration during aerial combat maneuvers in jet planes and centrifuge training of pilots. These activities affect the flow of blood and oxygen to the retina, the visual cortex, and other parts of the brain, along with an increased release of endorphin, serotonin, and dopamine and loss of consciousness. This phenomenon, referred to as *g-force-induced loss of consciousness*, causes "dreamlets," tunnel vision sometimes involving a bright light at the end of the tunnel, floating sensations, euphoria, and a sense of serenity as the subjects regain consciousness, which are reminiscent of NDEs (Comings 2008; Shermer 2011: 152–53; Whinnery 1979, 1997, Whinnery and Whinnery 1990). These factors suggest that NDEs have underlying physiological and neural correlates. OBE and NDE phenomena, which are often on offer as evidence of life after death, are actually the result of complex internally generated fantasies or hallucinations caused by transient anomalies of the brain (Beyerstein 2007: 329; Augustine 2015: 542).

NEDs have been explained in terms of the hallucinatory experiences caused by cerebral anoxia (see Blackmore 1993; Woerlee 2003). When the heart ceases beating even for a short interval, the oxygen supply to the brain is cut off, which impairs the function of neurons. The effect of this is a feeling of well-being and power, followed by a sensation of being detached from reality, passing through a tunnel, and finally perceptions of paranormal beings, and so forth (French and Stone 2014: 111; Hines 2003: 101).

Religious enthusiasts acknowledge that anoxia does produce the types of hallucinations on which they base their hypothesis but argue that this is true of most, but not all cases of NDEs because we cannot definitively prove that every single patient reporting an NDE suffered from anoxia. These are instances for which there are insufficient data about the patient to indicate whether or not anoxia occurred and are considered proof of the NDE hypothesis. These contentions are analogous to the "irreducible minimum" number argument used by proponents of UFOs after the majority of their cases have been disconfirmed by critical analysis, as reviewed in Chapter 2.

NDE studies have numerous and very significant flaws, many of which are detailed in the book *The Myth of an Afterlife: The Case against Life after Death* (2015), edited by Michael Martin and Keith Augustine. The earliest investigations by Ring and Moody employ masses of anecdotal information obtained from second-hand sources, such as reports by doctors and nurses, rather than the percipients themselves, or the accounts were collected months or even years later. Such retrospective reports are subject to a wide variety of memory distortions that impact recall after the event, as examined in Chapter 7 (Alcock 1981: 76; Hines 2003: 101). In many cases, NDE reports are provided by individuals who made no such claims at the time the experience allegedly happened but did so upon questioning, later on, sometimes many years later. As David Lester (2015: 633) points out in his review of the overall evidence for NDEs, nearly all of the reports are based on memories of events long ago. The likelihood of false memories is, therefore, very high in such cases.

One study in support of the survivalist hypothesis, which appears in the high-impact journal *The Lancet*, addresses some of the methodological issues raised by skeptics and challenges the anoxia hypothesis (Van Lommel et al. 2001). This investigation involved 344 resuscitated cardiac patients, 18 percent of whom reported NDEs. The study claims that if cerebral anoxia caused the reported NDEs, then all of the clinically dead patients should have had NDEs, instead of just 18 percent of the patients. However, this assertion also undermines the survivalist hypothesis because if the afterlife is real, then all of the subjects should have glimpsed the other realm, rather than a percentage of the individuals involved (Braithwaite 2008). Indeed, not everyone who has had a close call reports NDEs, and such experiences are also reported in non-life-threatening circumstances (Lester 2015: 638).

The biggest problem with the study by Van Lommel and colleagues, and others like it, as psychologist and neurocognitive researcher Jason Braithwaite (2008) has pointed out, is that if the brain is dead, as believers claim, then how is it possible for memory to be operational and the event remembered, even if the experience was in a paranormal realm? The physician Mark Crislip (2008) raises another point by asking whether the subjects involved "were dead or nearly dead." As he points out, the EEG cannot distinguish between the flat line that happens when the brain is oxygen deprived and when it is dead. These circumstances support Lester's (2015: 647) overall conclusion that to date, there are no methodologically sound studies of NDEs.

Braithwaite's (2008) conclusion is that given the fact that NDEs are similar to experiences associated with various pathologies and neurological conditions and direct brain stimulation, there are substantial indications that these experiences have an underlying neural correlate located inside peoples' heads rather than in a purported paranormal or supernatural reality somewhere "out there." In other words, like many other supernatural experiences, these are brain-based phenomena. Also, the argument from brain damage, which demonstrates the dependence of consciousness on the brain (i.e., that without a brain there is no consciousness), or what is termed "the dependency thesis," rules out the possibility that consciousness survives after bodily death (Augustine and Fishman 2015: 203–4, 227; Gennaro and Fishman. 2015: 112–22).

Claims made that subjects who have had NDEs have upon resuscitation recalled information they could only have obtained during out-of-body events are untrue (Beyerstein 2007: 329–30). Hospitals in several countries took part in a study which involved placing a target photograph in coronary care units visible only from above near the ceiling. Any patient having an NDE could report the target image after resuscitation and hence provide indisputable proof that human consciousness can exist apart from the brain and body. There are no such reports despite the occurrence of several NDEs at these sites (French and Stone 2014: 258). Indeed, despite over a century of anecdotes, no convincing evidence has been produced by anyone that supports the survivalist hypothesis.

## Cognitive Mechanisms of Hallucinatory Phenomena

Further clarification of hallucinatory phenomena is possible through the examination of the cognitive mechanisms involved. All hallucinations are explicable according to how the human brain processes sensory data in combination with information from memory to create a virtual model of reality. This virtual mental model includes not only the sensory stream of external stimuli but also a mixture of information we already have, such as prior beliefs, dreams, mental imagery from long-term memory, and even illusions and fantasies that shape our conscious awareness. It is an established scientific fact that top-down processing and related cognitive factors can produce perceptions without a source in the external world (Aleman and Larøi 2009: 91; Beyerstein 2007: 321). The operation of such mechanisms indicates the constructive nature of perception, as discussed in

Chapter 7. The balance between input from the external world and information stored in our memories is fluid but ordinarily stable and predictable. Any interference in this balance, however, can lead to the domination of our conscious awareness by dreams, memories, and fantasies that are often indistinguishable from real mind-independent events (Beyerstein 2007: 321, 327).

Factors that bias the brain's representational system toward internal sources and memory images over external sensory information inputs will trigger hallucinations by weakening the mechanism that suppresses vivid imagination during ordinary waking states. Such hallucinations can involve seeing supernatural beings or the apparitions of deceased loved ones. These precipitating factors include isolation, a decrease in external stimuli, extreme stress, use of psychoactive drugs, sensory overload, bereavement, and the strong desire for reassurance that our deceased loved ones continue to exist happily in another realm (Beyerstein 2007: 321, 327). Also, similar effects are achievable by prolonged fasting, dehydration, hypoxia, hyperventilating, hypoglycemia, high fever, and extreme pain. Malfunctions of the sleep-waking system, such as extended sleep deprivation, hypnogogic and hypnopompic states (hallucinations at the boundary between falling asleep or waking up) may also trigger visionary experiences.

When the prevailing reality model is disrupted, producing a deluge of internal memory-based imagery, the processes that construct the virtual model of reality inside our brains will harness these available but disorganized bits of information, like pattern-seeking pareidolia, to make sense of and produce a coherent picture. Excellent examples of this are the hallucinations experienced during NDEs when the mind compensates for the disruption of the sensory data stream by filling the gaps with stored memories and information (Braithwaite 2008). Such hallucinatory scenarios are tied to and express the experient's needs, problems, preoccupations, and cultural background.

Sometimes such alternative virtual models of reality constructed inside our heads using internal memory-based imagery and fantasies may also disrupt the mental model of the body as existing inside a physical chassis in three-dimensional space. Accompanying this state are sensations of unity and oneness with the cosmos commonly reported during religious experiences. Such events can be scary if they happen spontaneously. Mystics deliberately seek them out. Religionists and cult members call this phenomenon transcendence or "Nirvana," while psychologists and psychiatrists refer to it as "depersonalization" and "derealization." These ASC can be powerful, hyper-emotional, and cathartic. Religious demagogues and charismatic political leaders have chanced upon sets of rituals and activities involving rhythmic movement, music, sensory overload, and physical and emotional exhaustion to produce such effects among their followers. These techniques come into play during mass rallies and revival meetings to encourage people to become converts and to persuade them that the dogma on offer has celestial and supernatural significance (Beyerstain 2007: 327; Ray 2009: 143). In the church settings, such experiences are easily misconstrued as spiritual states, and astute evangelical ministers have capitalized upon such procedures to generate mass emotional appeal among their congregations (Ray 2009: 143).

Another cognitive dimension of hallucinations is the involvement of information below the level of consciousness. A great deal of mental activity involving perception, recognition, reasoning, decision-making, and memory occur below our conscious awareness. However, we are only aware of the output of these processes (Velmans 2000: 200). In some circumstances, subconscious data cross over into our conscious awareness. The crossing over of a threshold of the content of preconscious or unconscious regions of the mind into conscious awareness is referred to as transliminality (French and Stone 2014: 101–2). Transliminality occurs in association with mystical experiences and paranormal ideation (Thalbourne and Delin 1994: 31).

Transliminality is related to temporal lobe activity caused by hyperconnectivity between the temporal lobes and the sensory areas of the brain that can result in oversensitivity to internally generated information (French and Stone 2014: 102). These below-consciousness processes that sometimes initiate behaviors that seem to be outside our control, evoke feelings the sources of which we are unable to identify, or throw up images and information we cannot remember experiencing before. These strike us as paranormal, supernatural, or something cosmically meaningful (Beyerstein 2007: 316). These are, however, the ordinary but counterintuitive ways our brains operate. This phenomenon underlies trance states, transcendental states of consciousness, mystical revelations, and the so-called born-again experiences of evangelical Christians. These states occur when unconscious materials, dreams, fantasies, and emotions from one part of the brain leak into systems underlying subjective conscious experiences (Stone and French 2014: 146).

Another perspective indicates that hallucinations are related to impairments in our capacity for reality monitoring that ordinarily enables us to distinguish between real and imagined events (Aleman and Larøi 2009: 118). When such a monitoring failure happens, it leads to the attribution of subjective thoughts to an external source and is called "externalizing bias." This perceptual malfunction interferes with our source monitoring ability that ordinarily allows the identification of and discrimination between external sources (perceptions of mind-independent events) and internal sources (mind-dependent thoughts and beliefs). An example of this is auditory hallucinations involving the misattribution of inner speech (the internal dialogue we use to monitor our behavior) to an external source (Aleman and Larøi 2009: 110). Such voices may speak the subject's thoughts out loud, comment on his or her actions and behavior, or issue commands and instructions. The voice may seem to be located inside the subject's head or appear to come from the outside, from trees, behind walls, animals, or rocks. In some cases, the voice comes from the sky or some remote region of the universe (Watkins 2008). For Moses, the alleged voice emanated from a burning bush, for the Apostle Peter it came from the sky, and for Muhammad, the voice sometimes also came from the heavens.

Expectations impact hallucinatory experiences as already noted. Thus, expecting that spirits exist or that a particular location is haunted will result in perceptions of such anticipated entities. This entails top-down influences on experience (Holt et al. 2012: 136). The role of expectation in such hallucinatory phenomena suggests that apparitions will appear when they are psychologically needed and relates to the perception of control over life events (Houran and Thalbourne 2001). Such a process explains why the shocked, terrified, and grieving followers of Jesus thought they saw his apparition after he was executed (if the reports of these sightings were not later fabrications, which is a definite possibility, see Chapter 15).

Most of the time, we can tell reality apart from internal imagery and daydreams. This capacity, however, can break down, creating hallucinations and generating paranormal experiences. Hallucinations may be the cost we have to bear for our remarkable ability to think and remember using virtual scenarios or "mental dry runs" in our mind's eyes or models of the world created by the complex neural systems inside our heads (Beyerstein 2007: 321–22). Hallucinations are the side effects of this sophisticated representation systems. As Brugger (2001: 195) has put it, "paranormal experiences are the outcome of distributed neural systems inside our heads that produce beliefs the origins of which we project into the outside world." What is remarkable is the sort of significance humans have attached to these manifestations, building entire belief systems and theologies around them.

The research findings reviewed in this section provide ample grounds for dismissing paranormal and supernatural explanations for religious and mystical experiences. These are brain-based phenomena with physiological explanations. In other words, such experiences, no matter how powerful and life-altering they may be for those who have them, are ordinary rather than miraculous or extraordinary events. The unreal real is merely an attribute of our particular neural and cognitive architecture. Therefore, it can be stated with great confidence regarding religious experiences, as Stenger (1990: 107) has put it, that "we have a suitable explanation for these reports that do not require invoking any hypotheses other than those relevant to the science of neurophysiology."

## Apparitions: Perceiving Figures

A different type of hallucination that recurs in the context of religious experiences and in association with paranormal themes is the subjective perception of figures called *apparitions* (Irwin and Watt 2007: 192). Apparitions are a near-universal phenomenon across space and time (Zusne and Jones 1989: 225). Until the nineteenth-century hallucinations were known as apparitions and were generally considered mystical or spiritual experiences (Aleman and Larøi 2009: 10).

An apparition is a perceptual-like experience of a known person (alive or dead), entity, or animal that is not physically present. The figure is superimposed on the environment, but the surroundings of the percipient are unchanged. A single person can perceive apparitions, or a group of people may experience them at the same time (Evans 1984: 76; Green and McCreery 1975: 1; Holt et al. 2012: 125–26; Irwin and Watt 2007: 192–93). Religious polemicists and apologists who frequently state that apparitions are only seen by single individuals and never by groups of people are being deceptive or have failed to consult the relevant scientific literature (see Chapter 15).

Like other types of hallucinations, apparitions appear real to the percipient, although, as noted, the entity observed is never physically present. Such an experience is a more complex form of the "sense of presence" often reported during religious experiences (Holt et al. 2012: 131–32). They can occur when the percipient is either asleep or awake. Apparitions can appear and disappear and pass through walls and locked doors (Evans

1984: 85–86). Apparitional hallucinations tend to be visual and auditory, with a small proportion of cases being exclusively auditory (Irwin and Watt 2007: 195). Apparitions of deceased loved ones, who may be visible and are heard and felt, are relatively common during bereavement (Aleman and Larøi 2009: 67; French and Stone 2014: 99). However, there are also reports of apparitions of living people in their "etheric" bodies, which casts doubts on the usefulness of this phenomenon as evidence for life after death (Zusne and Jones 1989: 226).

People often experience apparitions at locations where they are expected, such as places of religious significance, gravesites, and buildings reputed to be haunted. All of this has a bearing on specific examples of apparitions to be discussed in Chapter 15, namely the postmortem appearances of Jesus to the disciples, to the Apostle Paul, and the 500 brethren that Paul mentions in his first letter to the Corinthians.

Apparitions also occur during a condition known as sleep paralysis, which is a relatively common but highly misunderstood phenomenon that mainly affects adults and occurs across cultures and through time (French and Santomauro 2007: 382). People with sleep disorders frequently report this experience, but between 25 and 40 percent of the general population has had or will have at least one such experience (French and Stone 2014: 219). Sleep paralysis happens when someone is lying in bed during the stage before falling asleep or just before waking up. One characteristic of this phenomenon is a temporary but total inability to move. The paralysis can last up to a few minutes and usually terminates abruptly. It is accompanied by breathing problems, sensing the presence of a numinous intruder in the room, feeling pushed or pinned down, the sensation of an entity sitting on one's chest, harrowing dread, and scary vivid audio and visual hallucinations (Alder 2011: 8–36).

Perceptual experiences that happen during the onset of sleep are referred to as hypnagogic hallucinations, while those that occur during the waking stage are known as hypnopompic hallucinations (Aleman and Larøi 2009: 40). The subject may perceive apparitions of demonic beings, monsters, or animals and hear voices, footsteps, and other sounds. Sometimes sleep paralysis may result in the sensation of floating and may even produce an OBE. Autoscopy or seeing one's own body from above may accompany such an event.

What sets these experiences apart from bad dreams is that the subjects are awake, can open their eyes, and are aware of their immediate surroundings but cannot speak, scream, or move. Hence the experience fits the original meaning of "nightmare" as a nocturnal assault by a demon or evil spirit, known as the fiend or incubus (in Latin, "one who presses or crushes") (Adler 2011: 3; French and Santomauro 2007: 390).

The apparition of demons and the sense of presence ("the intruder experience") can both trigger the hyperactive vigilant agent detection system and heighten expectations of threat and danger (Holt et al. 2012: 134–35), as assessed in Chapter 6. The activation of these mechanisms accounts for the frightening nature of such hallucinations. Thus, sleep paralysis is predominantly terrifying and unpleasant (Aleman and Larøi 2009: 40–41). Across cultures, people interpret this phenomenon in paranormal terms as a spiritual or supernatural assault. Sleep paralysis is thought to account for a wide range of ostensibly paranormal happenings, such as encounters with ghosts, angels, demons, and in Western societies with rapacious extraterrestrial alien abductors (Alder 2011: 37–58; Blackmore 1998; Clancy 2005; Proud 2009; Spanos et al. 1995). These variations in the contents of hypnagogic and hypnopompic hallucinations are explicable according to top-down processing that always shapes the nature of hallucinatory phenomena. It is through this mechanism that elements of belief and appropriate imagery from the experient's memory and cultural background are interjected into the experience (French and Santomauro 2007: 392).

Although sleep paralysis involves perceptions of demonic beings and other rapacious supernatural entities and is considered to be supernatural by most people, it is explicable according to the workings of the human sleep cycle. When we fall asleep, we go through a progression of stages of sleep. The sequence associated with dreaming is called the rapid eye movement (REM) phase. When in REM sleep, our muscles are paralyzed to prevent us from acting out our dreams (Hinton et al. 2005). Ordinarily, we are not aware of the paralysis because we are only cognizant of the contents of our dreams. However, sometimes, there is a disruption of this process, and we awaken while still in the REM stage (French and Stone 2014: 220). We are now conscious while bursts of dream imagery invade and become mingled with our waking consciousness. The result is that the percipient is awake in bed able to see the room clearly but is unable to move and has vivid hallucinations. As this occurs while our vigilant agency detection system is activated, we perceive threatening presences such as demons, witches, ghosts, and goblins (Holt et al. 2012: 135).

## Collective Hallucinations and Group Delusions

Collective hallucinations are another phenomenon relevant to our overall discussion. Many instances of collective visionary events are on record throughout history. Some familiar examples include the visions of the Virgin Mary in locations such as Lourdes in France, Fatima in Portugal, and Guadalupe in Mexico. Sociologists Robert Bartholomew and Erich Goode (2000: 302) describe such collective delusions as being characterized by the rapid spread of false beliefs in a population that can affect a region and even an entire nation.

Believers, however, do not consider such occurrences to be instances of delusion. Indeed, Christian apologists altogether deny the reality of mass hallucinations and perceptual contagion (e.g., Habermas 2003: 25–26). Alternatively, some paranormalists claim that such shared visions prove their mind-independent nature. However, these occurrences are indeed cases of shared or collective delusions involving perceptual contagion, examples of which are plentiful in the psychiatric literature (Brugger 2001: 201).

History is full of episodes of highly emotionally charged group delusions (Bartholomew 2001). These bizarre incidents reveal the remarkable power of cognitive predispositions, human psychological insecurities, wishful thinking, and gullibility and the extent to which they are susceptible to perceptual errors. Some of these events express exaggerated feelings of threat within the community, such as the plague-spreader panics that began in France in 1348 and spread across Europe, resulting in the murder of thousands of falsely accused individuals. A plague-spreader panic also gripped Milan, Italy, in 1630 (Sidky 1997: 87–94).

Another form of group delusion involves flight panics, such as the one in London in 1761, initiated by an earthquake prophecy. Mackay (1842: 260) describes a particularly curious mass panic during the nineteenth century:

> A panic terror of the end of the world seized the good people of Leeds and its neighborhood in the year 1806. It arose from the following circumstances. A hen, in a village close by, laid eggs, on which were inscribed the words, "*Christ is coming.*" Great numbers visited the spot, and examined the wondrous eggs, convinced that the Day of Judgment was near at hands. Like sailors in a storm, expecting every instance to go to the bottom, believers suddenly became religious, prayed violently, and flattered themselves that they repented them of their evil courses. But a plain tale soon put them down and quenched their religion entirely. Some gentlemen, hearing of the matter, went one fine morning, and caught the poor hen in the act of laying one of her miraculous eggs. They soon ascertained beyond doubt that the eggs had been inscribed with some corrosive ink, and cruelly forced up again into the bird's body. At this explanation, those who had prayed, now laughed, and the world wagged as merrily as of yore.

A different kind of group delusion involves episodes of wishful thinking that seem to address psychological and emotional needs (Bartholomew 2001: 21). One example of this is perceptions of statues that move, weep, bleed, or exude holy liquids. A somewhat seamy incident of this kind occurred in 2012 in Mumbai, among a group of Indian Christians. In this incident, believers noticed "holy water" miraculously flowing from the feet of a statue of Jesus at Our Lady of Velankanni Church. The event was declared a miracle. The news drew large numbers of the faithful who came, drank some of the holy liquid, and began devoutly worshipping the sacred image. An Indian skeptic Sanal Edamruku solved the mystery when he discovered that the so-called miracle was due to a nearby blocked toilet leaking fecally contaminated water that poured out of the base of the Jesus statue. Rather than accepting the reality of the situation, the enthralled votaries reacted with outrage over the debunking of their "miracle." They had Edamruku legally charged under Indian law for damaging religious sentiment (Shaffer 2013). The poor fellow had to flee the country to avoid imprisonment as a refuge from religious fatuity and superstition (Coyne 2015: 122). One wonders how many other such fallacious miracles have passed undetected and have been taken as the genuine article in the long history of such occurrences.

## Marian Apparitions: What Do They Signify?

Another type of mass hallucination is the apparitions of the Virgin Mary, of which church historians have recorded many instances over the centuries (Horfall 2000). The biblical historian and archaeologist Gerald Larue (1990: 175) refers to these collectively as a modern-day "cult of the Mother Goddess." These sightings almost always occur in association with Christianity, and especially Roman Catholicism. Indeed, as paranormal researcher Hilary Evans (1984: 104–5) has put it, the Catholic Church seems to have "a virtual monopoly over the phenomenon." Comparable apparitions in other religions are rare or have been underreported (Evans 1984: 104). Moreover, since the middle of the 1800s, Mary has appeared only to young, illiterate children in cultural backwaters (Dash 2000: 52).

Such collective visionary events are nearly always religious in nature and occur under particular conditions. According to Bartholomew and Goode (2000: 303), these include the role of mass media, rumors, extraordinary anxiety or excitement, and cultural beliefs and stereotypes. Zusne and Jones (1989: 117) add that emotional arousal is a prerequisite of collective hallucinations:

> The most common causes of emotional excitement in groups are religious, and indeed, phenomena related to religion are most often the subject of collective hallucinations. Second, the categories are limited by the fact that all participants in the hallucination must be informed beforehand, at least concerning the broad outlines of the phenomenon that will constitute the mass hallucination. This may take the form of a publicly announced prophecy, for example, or someone suddenly looking up and saying, "Lo, in the sky!" or words to that effect. Things in the sky, or at least overhead, are the most commonly seen collective hallucinations: radiant crosses, saints, religious symbols, flying objects, and sometimes all of these in combination. Once the general type of hallucination is identified, it is easy to harmonize individual differences in the accounts. This may take place during the hallucination or in subsequence discussions.

Many of those involved may have a visual experience, but they do not really see the purposed miraculous apparitions or even see the same things (Evans 1984: 111). Such was unmistakably the case with the Virgin Mary miracle that occurred on May 25, 1953, in Sábana Grande, Puerto Rico, where a crowd of 150,000 people had gathered to witness a predicated manifestation. Fortunately, several sociologists led by Melvin Tumin and Arnold Feldman (1955) were present and recorded the event. The researchers noted that some people reported seeing such things as the silhouette of Mary in the clouds, other said they saw colored rings around the sun, some experienced healing, while others stated that they did not see or experience anything extraordinary. I strongly suspect that the same pattern occurs in other such events across space and time. Zusne and Jones (1989: 117) elaborate that there are always individuals who have no visionary experiences. However, they rarely admit this since it raises doubts about their worthiness. Subsequently, the phenomena of groupthink and memory conformity come into play (see Chapter 7) when the beliefs of the group as a whole impinge upon and shape those of individuals who will go along with the shared consensus out of a desire for acceptance, worthiness, or enhanced status. They may even be convinced that they had visions as well. Zusne and Jones (1989: 117) add that it is often the case that the alleged "eyewitness" on closer inspection did not see anything.

I recorded an example of this in the context of a shamanic healing ritual during fieldwork in Nepal. It was late in the evening, and a group of five shamans, the patient, several members of the patient's family, and approximately 30 villagers tightly packed in a large empty room of the village schoolhouse. The patient was an elderly village woman who had become the target of a supernatural assault by the primordial god of the shamans, a supernatural being known as Ban-Jhãkri. At one stage of the ritual, the shamans who were furiously pounding their drums and chanting compelled the spirt to relent and cease its attack. They and others present whispered that they saw the spirit detach itself from the woman and stand in the middle of the room. Onlookers who were seated on the floor quickly repositioned themselves, creating an open space as a path leading to the doorway. The spirit ostensibly strolled past them and out of the room. I was unable to see the paranormal entity, but those present agreed unanimously that they had witnessed the supernatural entity appear and depart from the place. Unmistakably, this was a case of a collective visionary experience. In the days that followed, I spoke individually to several villagers who were present during the exorcism and asked them to describe in detail what they had witnessed. None of these individuals had actually seen the spirit and admitted that they went along with the opinion of the group because of a conviction that others in the room had seen the paranormal being.

One event during which the factors described were operative was the apparition of Mary in Fátima, Portugal, on October 13, 1917 (Bennett 2012; De Marchi 1952, 1956). More than 70,000 people allegedly saw the vision, and the occurrence is among those officially recognized by the Vatican as a genuine miracle (Laurentin 1990: 47; Nickell 1998: 176–81; Rogo 1982: 222–47). A Roman Catholic website describes this event as follows:

> On October 13, 1917, there were more than 70,000 people gathered in the Cova da Iria in Fatima, Portugal. They had come to observe a miracle which had been foretold by the Blessed Virgin to three young visionaries: Lucia dos Santos, and her two cousins, Jacinta, and Francisco Marto [...] Shortly after noon, our Lady appeared to the three visionaries. As the Lady was about to leave, she pointed to the sun. Lucy excitedly repeated the gesture, and the people looked into the sun [...] Then a gasp of terror rose from the crowd, for the sun seemed to tear itself from the heavens and come crashing down upon the horrified multitude [...] Just when it seemed that the ball of fire would fall upon and destroy them, the miracle ceased, and the sun resumed its normal place in the sky, shining forth as peacefully as ever. (in Dawkins 2000: 134)

If this counts for a genuine miracle, meaning that it is considered to have better documentation than other such happenings, the evidence is remarkably deficient. First, the evidence is purely anecdotal, which is never reliable under any circumstances. It is merely an uncorroborated story about impossible things. Second, none of the thousands at the scene truly saw Mary. All we have is the word of a few youngsters who claimed they saw the apparition. It is even unlikely that all of the children saw the figure and it is very possible that the event involved the phenomenon of folie à deux, which entails the transmission of delusional beliefs and hallucinations from one individual to another. It is also highly probable that the youngsters were lying as in the case of the Fox girls. Third, this description fails to specify just how many people "gasped" or how many genuinely saw the alleged misbehavior of the sun. Was it one person, one hundred, ten thousand? Estimates indicate that nearly 50 percent of those present at Fátima said they saw nothing, those who claimed they did perceive something have provided contradictory reports (Nickell 1998: 177; Tobin 2009: 382). Others who were caught up in the momentary frenzy and not wanting an exclusion from God's grace kept silent and were later convinced of the reality of the event by the testimony of others and sensational reporting by miracle mongering journalists. The event at Fátima is an excellent example of how information received after the fact can create false memories, a process discussed in Chapter 7.

Given what we know about the role of expectation, the problematic nature of memory and eyewitness reports, groupthink, memory conformity, emotional contagion, the constructive nature of perception, hindsight bias, the phenomenon of folie à deux, and top-down processing, there is nothing miraculous about this or similar events (see Chapter 7). It is a sad testament to human desperation, wishful thinking, gullibility, proneness to fantasy, perceptual and memory errors, and vulnerability to X-claims. The event at Fátima also clearly demonstrates, as Tobin (2009: 384) has observed, that "the presence of many witnesses does not guarantee the actual occurrence of the event reported."

Marian apparitions, in general, are highly problematic. The phenomenon entails appearance of a female figure said to be the mother of Jesus. However, the entities described, as the historian Mike Dash (2000: 52) observes, never resemble a middle-aged Palestinian woman from the first century CE. Even in alleged cases where that apparition has identified herself as Mary, there is no guarantee that it is who it claimed to be (Evans 1984: 109). Let us also not forget that the portrait of Mary is unknown. Indeed, as noted before, St. Augustin, writing during the fifth century, bemoaned this very fact (Nickell 1998: 22). Thus, the descriptions of Mary vary widely. To some, she appears as "a little girl," to others "a young girl," or "a woman between sixteen and eighteen years of age." Descriptions of the entity involve different types of clothing, such as "a white dress," "clothed in the sun," or wearing "a crown of stars." Thus it is unclear that the visions in various places are even of the same entity, which is strong evidence that the appearances are idiosyncratic hallucinatory phenomena. Religionists, however, are unperturbed by these discrepancies and attribute these variations to "the property of glorified bodies," which can appear at any desired age or outfit (Laurentin 1990: 33). In other words, the assertion is that the paranormal acts in mysterious ways. What this means is that people can interpret nearly any vision according to what they desire. Hence, the paranormal is once again acting fishy.

There are two possibilities to consider regarding the 1917 miracle at Fátima. The first is the ostensible believers' perspective, that the virgin mother of God, actually a Palestinian lady and mother of several children, who died 2,000 years ago, appeared to a few obscure little girls and that the solar system stopped operations. The second is the scientific position that the girls were caught up in a pious fraud or delusion, and the thrill of all the attention, like the Fox sisters, and a few in the crowd led by expectations and desperation hallucinated and others went along with their assertions. Is it not odd that a celestial being wanting to make some significant theological point with an eager audience of tens of thousands present and waiting chose to reveal herself only to some children? Evans (1984: 119–20) points out how improbable it is for the mother of a first-century Middle Eastern messiah to appear to some young peasant child in a faraway place 2,000 years later. Theologians, however, attribute this to the transcendental secrets of religion, which really means they are making up stories.

In other words, theologians are telling the faithful that they are confronted with a supernatural mystery and to believe without evidence, which is not very convincing. It also does not answer the following question: Why deprive the throngs of the poor, desperate, and miserable faithful of the grace and glory? Would a loving and compassionate lady, the mother of the benevolent God no less, do that? If she had appeared to the purported 70,000 supplicants all at once and if anyone in the region, the rest of the country, Europe, or around the world had noticed that on that particular and fateful day the sun misbehaved, then we would have a real miracle. However, we do not have such evidence. The sad fact is that while the evidence of genuine miracles is entirely absent, evidence that people lie, commit pious fraud, misperceive, hallucinate, and delude themselves is overwhelming. Fátima is a case in point.

To reiterate, in the case of Marian apparitions, we again have the paranormal acting fishy. Mary leaves us guessing. Also, it is bizarre that the mother of God often asks for certain ludicrous conditions to be met, such as a desire that the local villagers build a chapel in her honor. Really? The mother of the Creator of the universe will not be happy until some villagers construct her a shabby building?

The divine communications associated with these apparitions are also incongruous. Like the communiqués from the occupant of UFOs, these often entail edifying lectures, such as "pray more," and vague threats, such as behave or "my son [i.e., God] will become angry!" The heavenly messages never contain anything not already know to the recipients. There are significant parallels between the messages conveyed by such apparitions to the faithful and those revealed by extraterrestrial UFO pilots to contactees. Carl Sagan (1995: 101) wondered why the alien visitors never seem to provide information that can help us solve crucial problems. He was also puzzled by the fact that these outer space emissaries always seem to reveal their messages to questionable characters and never take over television stations or appear before the United Nations Security Council. Finally, he wondered why these visitors who have mastered interstellar space travel at faster than light speed never know more than the people to whom they relay messages.

The lady at Fátima emphasized that she had a significant message for the Pope. Yet, she chose to convey this critical communiqué via some children instead of transmitting it directly to the Vatican or even through the local bishop, priest, or village officials (Dash 2000: 55). Moreover, if there were truly some earth-shattering supernatural revelation, the Vatican would indeed have revealed it. The propaganda value alone would make this an astute move. No such announcements have been forthcoming. However, none of this makes any sense. Believers say that Mary's appearances are meant to bring faith and solace to local communities. This task would undoubtedly be better accomplished by appearances to people with the resources to make a difference in the lives of the locals, such as before government leaders, the General Assembly of the United Nations, or the president of the United States in the White House.

Another line of proof presented by devotees is the purported miraculous healings that accompany Marian apparitions. If any such events occur, they fall into the category of commonplace placebo-based recoveries, such as the cases I have encountered in the context of shamanic healings (see Sidky 2010). There is nothing miraculous about these. Also, the evidence is paltry at best that any genuine cures have taken place at Fátima or other Marian sites. Moreover, even if documentation of such a cure could be provided, there is no substantiation that its provenance is the visionary entity or that the healing validates the identity of the paranormal being (Evans 1984: 109). A genuine unequivocal miracle may be declared if an amputated arm or leg grows back or if sight is restored to a person without eyeballs. However, this has never happened at Fátima or at any of the other locations where Mary is known to have appeared. Why is the mother of God unable to do such things?

Finally, of the over half-million or more suffering and desperate pilgrims seeking healing who flock to supernaturally charged locations such as Lourdes and similar locales every year only a handful receive the benefits of the experience (Scriven 1966: 139). Here, once again, the unreal real is being fishy. Why doesn't Mary heal all the miserable, despairing, and suffering supplicants? Why only miraculous cures that fall into the category of psychosomatic illnesses? Why no restorations of amputated limbs? It is clear from this discussion that the Marian apparitions do not signify what miracle enthusiasts and church officials claim.

# Chapter Ten

# BOOKS AUTHORED BY GOD? SACRED TEXTS AS EVIDENCE OF THE SUPERNATURAL

*Here then we are first to consider a book, presented to us by a barbarous and ignorant people, written in an age when they were still more barbarous, and in all probability long after the facts which it relates, corroborated by no concurring testimony, and resembling those fabulous accounts, which every nation gives of its origin.*

—David Hume, *Enquiries Concerning the Human Understanding* (1748)

*A book that really came from the all-powerful, all-knowing, perfect creator of the universe would be unimaginably brilliant. […] Each point made each idea expressed would be inarguable and stunning. […] It would blow us away. It would be impossible to put down. It would touch each of us personally, regardless of our ages, our education, or our experiences.*

—Marshall Brain, *How "God" Works* (2014)

*All that is necessary, as it seems to me, to convince any reasonable person that the Bible is simply and purely of human invention—of barbarian invention—is to read it.*

—Robert Ingersoll, *Lectures of Col. R. G.* Ingersoll (1907)

The three major world religions, Judaism, Christianity, and Islam, possess revealed texts, the Old Testament, The New Testament, and the Qur'an. These are the purported written records of God's communication to humans by way of a selected emissary, messiah, prophet, vatic, and so forth. While humans are involved in the transmission process, the ultimate author of these books is claimed to be none other than God himself.

These mighty tomes are the basis of the theological "argument from Scripture" for the existence of God. Given that this is part of the arsenal theists and religious apologists employ in their invectives against naturalism and science, claims about the miraculous nature, inerrancy, and supernatural origins of these books are legitimate issues for scrutiny according to the tradition of systematic skepticism in science.

## Proposed Evidence of the Divine Origins of Sacred Texts

How do we know that these books are of divine origins? First, the very fact that such texts exist becomes proof for the reality of their supernatural author. In other words, if God does not exist, then how can the existence of the holy book be explained? What this involves, of course, is the question-begging assertion that God wrote the book; therefore, the book is evidence that God exists. If we were to accept this claim, then logically we must also accept the divinely ordained nature of *The Book of Mormon* (1829), the scripture of the Church of Jesus Christ of Latter-day Saints, and *Dianetics* (1950), the foundational text of Scientology (Dennett 2006: 240). No one outside of these two religions would do so, however, because we know for a fact that these books are the handiwork of a couple of dubious self-aggrandizing con artists, respectively Joseph Smith and L. Ron Hubbard.

Other proofs offered by religionists for the authenticity of their holy tomes include such things as their literary merits, the purported accuracy of the predictions they contain, the superiority of their moral messages, and the ostensible "scientific knowledge" they hold (Oppy 2018: 180). Such arguments are flimsy because they depend upon the texts themselves to validate those texts. What is needed is evidence outside the documents in question (cf., Scriven 1966: 134–35, 140). But no such evidence seems to exist for any of these magnificent works. Moreover, while it is obvious why believers would attribute vast cosmic importance to these volumes, there is no consensus among scientifically minded experts regarding any of these grandiose pronouncements. There is also the fact that these texts contain numerous historical, scientific, philosophical, and theological errors that categorically rule out anything extraordinary, divine, or sacred about them.

There are lots of other puzzling facts. The messages contained in the sacred texts purportedly stem from the same paranormal source, the revelations of the Abrahamic God. Oddly, rather than divulging a single unmitigated and unambiguous set of instructions to steer desultory and aimless wayfaring humans along the path to righteousness, this God has provided different and contradictory iterations of His message to sundry earthly representatives at various times and places. The ever-perceptive Celsus (1830: 30) drew attention to this long ago, asking,

> does Moses or Jesus lie? Or, was the Father who sent Jesus forgetful of what he had formerly said to Moses? Or, condemning his own laws, did he alter his opinion, and send a messenger to mankind with mandates of a contrary nature?

All of this is surprising. Why could not the omniscient and omnipotent Creator of the universe get it right the first time? Why so many prophets with different messages, revelations, and miracles at various times?

This pattern of God-to-human transmission has led the respective recipients of God's revelations to maintain that they have got it right, that they are the sole possessors of the truth, and accuse others of atheism or heresy. The faithful in each of these religions assume that their particular holy books contain the literal, perfect, inerrant, and final words and truths put forth by their omnipotent, infallible, and veracious God. For the believers, it is sufficient that their holy tomes say that they contain God's actual words. No further evidence is necessary. What believers fail to understand, however, is that their sacred books represent the claims about and not the proof of their religions.

What is also puzzling is why God in every case transmitted His divine message intended for the whole of humanity to a handful of obscure, uneducated, often dubious and ignorant individuals, in a local language, in the remote cultural hinterlands of a place like the Middle East? Why not make blazing and glorious revelations to notable figures of humanity in the centers of major civilizations?

A detailed discussion of the problematic nature of revelations as a basis of religious truths has been provided in detail in the previous chapter. It was shown that revelations and visionary experiences are not what the believers claim them to be. Here, let us suppose that such divine transmissions did indeed take place and they are recorded in humankind's sacred literature. However, before we proceed further, we need to ask some additional questions. First, why does God need books? There are many far more effective ways of transmitting and storing information, including direct implantation into human neural circuitry. Second, to create His Scriptures, why did God depend on people whose literary skills are limited and who are subject to making mistakes? These are puzzling questions that need answers. Attributing these issues to the mysteries of religion and repeating the aphorism "have faith, just believe" is unconvincing to anyone but the fully conditioned and indoctrinated true believer.

## What Would Books Written by God Really Look Like?

Let us say, for the moment, that God had good reasons to write a book or even several books. What would any reasonable person expect about the nature of a text written by the omniscient, omnipotent, and veracious Creator of all that exists? The skeptic Marshall Brain (2014: 183) provides some useful diagnostic markers for such a production. Such a text authored by the all-knowing and all-powerful creator of the universe should be "unimaginably brilliant" and perfect, with such wisdom and beauty as to astound the more recalcitrant non-believers. It should contain passages of such power and persuasion that any skeptic who reads it will immediately become a devotee. Also, God's book would be entirely devoid of nonsensical tales of barbarism, incest, misogyny, slavery, or genital mutilation. Yet, these sacred books contain passages not fit to be read to anyone. As the skeptic Robert Ingersoll (1907: 787) pointed out regarding the Bible,

> It contains pages that no minister in the United States would read to his congregation for any reward whatever. There are chapters that no gentleman would read in the presence of a lady. There are chapters that no father would read to his child. There are narrative utterly unfit to be told.

In addition, God's book would be free of factual errors, half-truths, and nothing contrary to established scientific facts (Brain 2014: 183). The impact of reading such an awesome and excellent book would be so overwhelming that its veracity and divine authorship would be instantaneously self-evident to every person who lays eyes on it. If such a book existed, then there would no longer be a diversity of religions, sects, or denominations. Atheists would vanish overnight, and all theologians would be out of a job.

Moreover, such a miraculous text would be accessible to the speakers of all languages on earth, as well as the illiterate and the blind (Brain 2014: 183–84). Such a universal divine message would also be comprehensible without the need for translators or specialists such as the multitude of tendentious theologians to explain the true meanings of the words. That God's Scriptures are not simultaneously available in every known language and universally comprehended is alone sufficient evidence that these were the handiworks of fallible humans, not that of a super paranormal being possessing unlimited knowledge, power, and wisdom wishing to transmit His divine will to the whole of humanity (Brain 2014: 185).

Also, such mighty works would be an endless source of utterly new knowledge not already possessed or accessible to people on their own, explained so clearly that every reader could easily comprehend it. We would also expect useful information, such as warnings about the dangers of bacteria, viruses, as well as cures for cancers. Yet, what is blatantly missing is information beyond the state-of-knowledge of the time when these texts appear.

Then there are the purported true predictions said to exist in these books. Here again, what is on offer is disappointing. As astrophysicist and skeptic Neil Degrasse Tyson (2003: 75) observes in regard to this question, "I have yet to see a successful prediction about the physical world that was inferred from the content of any religious document." The effort to find accurate predictions has always been abject failure. We are not talking about "postdictions," that is, making predictions fit the facts after the stipulated events have already taken place, which is feasible to do with lots of ancient and modern texts, but ones demonstrably recorded before the events have occurred.

None of the sacred books contain unambiguous details on such things as the structure of the DNA, the nature of atoms, what viruses are, or anything else remarkable. Nor do they carry sentences like "the sun is a star" or "Mars has volcanoes." There is never a statement to the effect that "thou shalt not travel faster than light," or any other bit of information not known to the humans of that time that would attest to the extraordinary paranormal source for the data (Sagan 2006: 166). The philosopher and physicist Victor Stenger (2008: 176) suggested a passage that would have clinched the case:

> Before two millennia shall pass since the birth of our Lord, a man will stand on another world within the firmament, and he will smite a tiny orb with his staff such that it will fly from sight.

The reference here is to astronaut Alan Shepard's famous golf shot, February 6, 1971, during the Apollo 14 mission to the moon. No such passages exist in any of these marvelous books. We do not even get minor bits of useful information, such as how babies are made, how contraception works, or even something as rudimentary as instructions that boiling water prevents waterborne diseases (Barker 2016: 299). Why not?

Not only are all these things missing, but the volumes currently on offer as sacred works of Almighty God are full of all of the things they should not contain: absurdities, contradictions, gibberish, bigoted and barbaric precepts, misogyny, mythology, and gross errors of fact (see Mcafee 2011: 65–82). The factual errors are particularly glaring. A massive flood never inundated the earth. This is a fable plagiarized from the Sumerians. The dead do not come back to life—zombies are Hollywood fiction. Virgin women do not give birth, but desperate unmarried victimized or sexually assaulted pregnant teenage girls do lie. Evil spirits or devils do not cause diseases; there are things called viruses and bacteria that cause sickness. And there is no evidence that the world came into existence during the Bronze Age. The earth is 4.5 billion years old.

Adroit religionist argumentation, casuistry, and apologetics cannot satisfactorily resolve such gross errors of scientific fact, although erudite theologians have been at this task for millennia. One of their common feeble explanations is that the sacred books have two components, one holding immutable, eternal truths, and the other outdated messages in the vocabulary of the recipients of the revelation at the time of transmission. These messages, it is argued further, were relative to the time and the fact that they are scientifically false does not invalidate the eternal truths of God's message contained therein (Swinburne 1992: 77). If this is true, then the omniscient God tricked his audience in a patronizing way by giving them false but comforting fables, such as "you are at the center of creation," instead of revealing the true nature of the universe and all it contains (Philipse 2014: 10). This raises a serious concern. As the philosopher Herman Philipse (2014: 10) asks, if one part of the message provided by a deceiving and patronizing Deity is false, why should we believe the other parts?

If we treat these texts as "revealed theology" and the handiwork of an all-knowing and unerring God, the errors and contradictions they contain confound us. However, these contradictions vanish instantly if we take them for what they actually are, texts written by error-prone humans who were the products of their respective times and cultures, living in different locations and possessing different motives, prejudices, and objectives (Philipse 2014: 6–7). As Ingersoll (1907: 790) put it,

> If there are mistakes in the bible, certainly they were made by man. If there is anything contrary to nature, it was written by man. If there is anything immoral, cruel, heartless or infamous, it certainly was never written by a being worthy of the adoration of mankind.

In sum, God's books should contain the "extraordinary," but the extraordinary is conspicuously absent from humankind's sacred literature. What we find instead is indeed what one would expect if these texts were written by ignorant, superstitious, delusional, and deeply disturbed tribesmen who lived thousands of years ago and knew next to nothing about the world. This point was even apparent to the Greek philosopher Celsus nearly two thousand years ago, whose devastating critique of Christianity is discussed in Chapter 13. Celsus (1987: 101) wrote that "Moses and the prophets who put together this record had absolutely no inkling how the world came to be, and their books are absolute garbage." Or as Ingersoll (1907: 787) put it, "Few books have been published containing more filth than this inspired word of God."

There is also the problematic character or nature of the purported author of humankind's sacred literature. We do not find a benevolent, omnipotent, all-knowing Creator but a being displaying all the loathsome human passions of vindictiveness, wrath, insecurity, gynophobia, homophobia, racism, and genocidal delusions. But of course these attributes are explicable if these messages were not revelations from a divine Creator but ideas from the minds of unidentified superstitious people.

Then there is the problem of the vagueness of the sacred narratives and why believers receive so little upon which to justify their faith in their Author. Religious apologists will take issue and point out that God does not reveal too much because doing so would inhibit the ability of humans to choose between good and evil freely. This argument from hiddenness, or *Deus absconditus*, is an exasperating and recurrent theme in Christian theology. It states that God conceals himself even from those who need him or desire to see him (Philipse 2014: 302; Schellenberg 2006: 2). However, if there is a God that loves and has a unique purpose for humans, why has he taken exceptional measures to hide from them? The argument from hiddenness also raises the problem of religious experience. If God is hiding, then who or what is generating the spiritual experiences of the prophets and mystics? The real puzzle is that God provides so little evidence of his presence that many are led to doubt that he even exists (Philipse 2014: 307).

To put it differently, as Carl Sagan (2006: 167) asked, why is God so conspicuously present in the holy books but so absent in the world? The evidence for theism is very feeble, and "this weakness of evidence is evidence against it" (Philipse 2014: 118). And as Coyne (2015: 118) observes, given the fact that scriptural predictions have never come to pass, science has failed to validate any religious postulate, and evidence for the existence of God is nonexistent, one can conclude that such an entity does not exist. The absence of evidence where such evidence should be overwhelming supports this conclusion.

Aside from these difficulties, there are also moral and ethical problems. There is no mention anywhere in the holy tomes about the value of intellectual curiosity, the importance of religious tolerance, equality among men and women, the evils of racism and slavery, benevolence to nonhuman lifeforms, or care for the planet (Philipse 2014: 12). Instead, these texts extol the opposite of these values and ethical precepts. How is this fact compatible with the attributes of the theistic God who is, by definition, loving, wise, and just?

Although in this chapter I shall look on at the Bible, there is no need to try and understand the perspicacity of every holy book in circulation. The reason for this is as Hitchens (2007: 126) pointed out, "if one comprehends the fallacies of one 'revealed religion' one comprehends all of them." Or to put it another way, what can be said about the absurdities of one set of scriptures applies equally to the others.

## The Old Testament: God's Message to Humankind 1.0

We may begin with the Old Testament, a book that David Hume (1902 [1748]: 124) aptly described as the handiwork of "barbarous and ignorant human beings" from a time of ignorance and superstition, minus any corroboration by concurring testimony and similar to the lore every culture offers about its origins. Historical analysis during the last two centuries has revealed that significant portions of the Old Testament come from earlier non-divine cultural sources, such as the view of the universe held by the ancient civilizations of Sumeria, Babylonia, Assyria, and Egypt. All of this denotes human-to-human rather than God-to-human transmission of information (Philipse 2014: 11).

Take the absurdity of the origin story in the Book of Genesis, which today's creationists consider the inerrant words of God. The opening line is, "In the beginning, God created the heavens and the earth." This is nonsense because the earth and universe were not created at the same time or through the same processes. As Brain (2014: 145) observes, this is a critical factual error by the author who is purportedly an omniscient and perfect being who was the cause of the creative process and should surely have had the same data upon which scientists have based their determination of the age of the earth and the universe.

That this grossly anthropomorphic creation story is a fable invented by nescient and unimaginative humans is also clear from other embarrassing assertions in the text. Celsus (1987: 101–2) pointed out these errors long ago:

> All that business about "Let there be light"—Are we to think that the creator of the world used light from above like a man who borrows a torch from his neighbor? [...] They allot certain days to creation, before days existed. For when heaven had not been made, or the earth fixed or the sun in the heavens, how could days exist? Isn't it absurd to think that the greatest God pieced out his work as a bricklayer, saying "Today I shall do this, tomorrow that," and so on, so that he did this on the third, and that on the fourth, and something else on the fifth and sixth days! We are thus not surprised to find that, like a common workman, this God wears himself down and so needs a holiday after six days, and gives orders like a foreman [and] is not acting very much like a god?

Oddly, a Greek author who lived nearly two thousand years ago could discern the nonsensical nature of this text. Yet, present-day creationists and evangelical Christians who have the benefit of modern education and masses of scientific information at their disposal actually believe that the Bible contains the inerrant words of God and that the Book of Genesis is an accurate description of the creation of the world and universe.

In this text, we also find the fable of the creation of "man." The creation of Adam from a lump of clay is, relatively speaking, a more or less elegant affair. But why the omnipotent creator of the universe had to use mud is puzzling. Why not create humans from a puff of smoke or a flash of light or some magical substances? Why mud? The historian Robert Gillooly (1990: 101) observes that the use of clay made sense to ancient people because that was the material they used to create things. What is puzzling is why Christians take this yarn as literal truth and have done so for two millennia.

The creation of Eve, the first woman, is a somewhat different affair and reveals that the God of the Old Testament was a gynophobe and an unabashed misogynist. As the noted nineteenth-century anthropologist James Frazer observed in his book *Folklore in the Old Testament* (1918), God's contempt for women is blatantly obvious. She is created after man, out of a piece of her master. And God's misogyny is further evident because all of the misfortunes of the human race are ascribed to "the credulous folly" of the first woman (Frazer 1988: 101).

The Book of Genesis also relates the abysmal tale of the fall of "mankind" or "Paradise Lost." As Gillooly (1990: 102) points out, the fable of a talking snake in a magic garden comes from a more ancient Sumerian story, so there is nothing original or supernatural about this tiresome and terrible narrative. The story's purpose is to explain the reasons for the existence of evil and suffering in the world under the watchful eye of a supposedly benevolent, omnipotent, and all-knowing Deity. Put simply, it renders humans, especially women, accountable for the sins and evils of the world, leaving the image of a capable and loving God untarnished.

The narrative also reveals God's temperament with his infantile tantrums and paroxysms, rancor, and vindictiveness toward his puny creations and the obnoxious recalcitrant and transgressing serpent. Frazer (1988: 101) provided some interesting insights regarding this archaic story, pointing out the farcical nature of God losing his temper over the disobedience, cursing the snake to forever crawl on its belly, eat dust, and become the enemy of humankind. He condemns the woman to bear children in pain and be the slave of her husband. He curses man to perpetual toil and a terrible death in old age to return to the dust from whence he came. Then after venting his anger with "these copious maledictions," God shows kindness by making clothes out of skins for the "shameful pair" who retreat into the wilderness—thus Paradise is Lost. One is forced to pause in disbelief when hearing that religionists propose this ludicrous text as an alternative to scientific biology and evolutionary theory to be taught to children in schools.

As an aside, creationists espousing these archaic credulities are to be found as well outside the United States. During the 1950s and 1960s, as part of their anti-science campaign, American evangelicals attempted to popularize their creationist superstitions by having their literature translated into other languages, including Turkish, for use in Islamic education (Noll 1994: 191). These materials no doubt shaped Islamic creationist thought as exemplified by the inane works of the Muslim religious cult leader Adnan Oktar, who under the pen name of Harun Yahya wrote *The Atlas of Creation*. Like other works in this genre, the *Atlas* is full of nonsense, deceptions, and plagiarisms. One also wonders whether Mr. Oktar is aware of or is willing to acknowledge his intellectual debt to American Christian evangelism. In 2007, this Turkish creationist kindly sent thousands of free copies of the English translation of his absurd book to American scientists and politicians, no doubt, to enlighten them about Allah's handiwork in the world and the truth of Islam. This book is an embarrassment to all concerned.

Dan Barker, a former evangelical minister, has compiled biblical stories from the 39 books of the Old Testament that reveal the repugnant characteristics of Yahweh, the God of Abraham, who is the main protagonist in this bizarre tome. Of these, the first five books are known as the Pentateuch of Moses, although Moses, if he even existed, had no hand in writing them. Here, in addition to the story of the wretched Adam and Eve, we also find the fable of the burning bush from whence God spoke to Moses. Also, there is the account of the infantile conjuring one-upmanship between Aaron and the Pharaoh's magicians to see whose serpent is the biggest, and the genocidal plagues the merciful Yahweh unleashed upon innocent people of Egypt, including killing their children, to demonstrate his might. What is described here is deliberate, systematic, and ruthless infanticide: "at midnight that the Lord struck all the firstborn in the land [...] and there was a great cry in Egypt, for there was not a house where there was not one dead" (Exodus 12:29–51).

Those who make this book the basis of their code of ethics rarely question why an all-powerful and all-knowing and supposedly compassionate and merciful supernatural being who could have easily vented His rage directly upon the Pharoah (a mere puny human and yet His mortal enemy) had to destroy innocent children who had no culpability whatsoever in the dispute. What sort of a supernatural moral being kills the innocent? Also, what sort of reader would not find this disturbing and repugnant? No amount of apologetics can render this ghastly passage more palatable.

The text portrays an angry, jealous, and insecure supernatural being, a cosmic tyrant, who in addition to being a callous infanticidal monster, deliberately and maliciously intimidates, bullies, and terrorizes his hapless human creations out of deep insecurity about his own awesomeness: "your God [...] is a jealous God [...] and he will destroy you from the face of the land" (Deuteronomy 6:15). Another passage reads: I [...] fill them with horror so they would know that I am the LORD" (Ezekiel 20:25–26). This God's tribal mentality and vindictiveness have no limits (see Mcafee 2011: 84–106). Absent from the legislative repertoire of this benevolent supernatural lawgiver is the principle that punishments have to be proportionate to the offense in intensity and extent. Instead, He says: "I the LORD your God, am a jealous God, punishing the children for the sin of the parents to the third and fourth generation of those who hate me" (Exodus 20:5). What sort of an all-powerful being is this that can only cajole worship and respect from his pathetic human creations by bullying and terrorism?

The degree of malice this being displays is dumbfounding. Yahweh also enthusiastically condones stoning to death and murder of parents, siblings, and children to ameliorate his deep insecurities and pathological fear that some other Deity, such as Ba'al, will usurp his position, and that His perfidious worshippers who are on a constant lookout for a better god would abandon him. Hence he directs Moses to kill all blasphemers: "Whether foreigner or native-born, when they blaspheme the Name, they are to be put to death" (Leviticus 24:13–16). Books containing such barbarity and absurd superstitions should be banned, not revered. Reflecting on such obscene passages, Thomas Paine (1880 [1795]: 58) rightly remarked: "to read the Bible without horror, we must undo everything that is tender, sympathizing, and benevolent in the heart of man." Paine (1880 [1807]: 159) added, "The idea that the writers of the Old Testament had of a God was boisterous, contemptible, and vulgar."

Yahweh's paranoia has no end, and he recommends that anyone contemplating the worship of other gods has to be put to death mandatorily: "Stone them to death, because they tried to turn you away from the LORD your God, who brought you out of Egypt, out of the land of slavery" (Deuteronomy 13:6–10). Or consider what is offered to ensure family values and harmony. God commands that rebellious children should be handed over to the elders and "all the men of his town are to stone him to death" to instill fear to all who hear about it (Deuteronomy 21:18–21). Only a beguiled and reverential religionist (e.g., Keener 2011: 222–23) could object to the use of terms such as "ignorant "and "barbaric" to refer to the loathsome individuals who thought up these ghastly things.

All of these terrible events make the world of the Old Testament a nightmarish one indeed. Putting it plainly, Yahweh is nothing less than a monstrous being who enjoys and even laughs about the horrors he indiscriminately unleashes upon both the deserving and undeserving of his pathetic and helpless creatures. He boasts about his ability to make people flee from his majesty and how he destroys "both the blameless and the wicked" and mocks at "the despair of the innocent" (Isaiah 2:19; Job 9:22–23). He also brags about the cruel and wholesale death and destruction he can unleash upon his woeful subjects "to make the land desolate and destroy the sinners within it" (Isaiah 13:9–10). Elsewhere he says, "I will dash them one against another without pity, or mercy, and destroy them all" (Jeremiah 13:14). For these reasons, Ingersoll (1907: 793) found the words in this book incongruous with a benevolent and wise Deity:

> No god ever upheld human slavery, polygamy or a war of extermination. No god ever ordered a soldier to sheathe his sword in the breast of a mother. No god ever ordered a warrior to butcher a smiling, prattling babe. No god every upheld tyranny. No god ever said, be subject to the powers that be. No god endeavored to make man a slave and woman a beast of burden.

None of these archaic tales of brutality, terror, and bloodshed can be rationalized, as Barker (2016: 4) notes, by arguing that if we look at the entire picture, these horrors actually denote a loving, merciful, just, and forgiving God, as religious apologists claim. Picking and choosing a verse or two from some other part of the text, written centuries apart, to demonstrate that "God is love" is an unconvincing and a feeble effort to justify the activities of a supernatural being who engages in infanticide, genocide, torture, and other acts that today would be labeled crimes against humanity.

Christian apologists want others to accept the large-scale atrocities of the monstrous Abrahamic God as part of a grander and more righteous program. However, as Barker correctly points out, you cannot make the gruesome dreadfulness of this holy book vanish by saying "context," and presto "evil becomes good." As he says, it is impossible to mitigate Yahweh's innumerable barbaric injunctions and thuggish behavior using a handful of ingratiating praise that "God is love" (Barker 2016: 5). It is horrifying to think that humans are made in the image of this ghastly Deity. As Christopher Hitchens (2007: 99) pointed out, the monarchical growlings about respect and fear along with constant boasting about unlimited powers and endless threats of revenge and retaliation in the form of "worship me or I will obliterate you" sound more like the petty and cruel Babylonian or Assyrian monarchs of the time, rather than an almighty divine and benevolent Creator.

Believers and apologists raise objections, averring that the Bible is not meant to be accepted literally but is to be viewed allegorically or metaphorically. This is an unconvincing and embarrassing bit of apologetics. What kind of sane individual uses rape and the slaughter of innocent women and children as objects for their allegories? Addressing this issue long ago, the ever-astute Celsus (1987: 80–81) wrote,

> Their books are full of stories about the treacheries [...] It is no wonder that the reasonable among the Christians, embarrassed as they ought to be by such stories, take refuge in allegory! as they are, all in all, very stupid fables. On the other hand, some of the allegories I have seen are even more ridiculous than the myths themselves, since they attempt to explain the fables by means of ideas that really do not fit into the context of the stories.

The assertion contemporary Christian theologians and polemicists make that no one really takes the Bible literally is spurious and mendacious. The existence of many millions of creationists in the United States alone suggests that lots of people accept the Bible literally. The entire inerrancy canard is about taking this text literally. The nonsense these people accept as the verbatim words of God include such absurdities as the world being a few thousand years old, that species are immutable, and that "man" was created in one stroke by magic in some ludicrous garden with talking snakes. In the same way, these believers accept Yahweh's endless misogyny, invectives against transgressors, and the incitement and extolling of genocide, homophobia, ethnic cleansing, and wholesale enslavement of people. Clearly, Dawkins (2016: ix) is on the mark when he says that the pretense that believers do not take the Bible literally is intellectually dishonest.

The bloodlust, cruelty, and atrocities of the biblical elders match those of their dreadful Deity. Consider Moses's order regarding a group of people known as the Midianites whom the Jews had vanquished in battle: "kill every male" [and] "every woman that hath known a man by lying with him," but save the young virgin girls "for yourselves" (Numbers 31:17–18). Reading this passage, an appalled Paine (1880 [1795]: 69) remarked about the villainous nature of Moses and added: "Here is an order to butcher the boys, the massacre the mothers, and debauch the daughters!" Paine (1880 [1807]: 142–43) rightly concluded that allowing "a thousand devils" to roam and preach their doctrine in public would be better than granting any credibility to such monstrous human beings as Moses and the Bible prophets.

Of course, the atrocities described in the Old Testament were acts in reality committed and valorized by very gruesome and deeply disturbed humans operating according to the credulities and superstitions of their time and place. Hitchens (2007: 99) contemplating these dreadful and offensive passages remarks, "It would be harder to find an easier proof that religion is man-made."

Or as Ingersoll (1907: 792) recommended,

> All that is necessary, as it seems to me, to convince any reasonable person that the bible is simply and purely of human invention—of barbarian invention—is to read it. Read it as you would any other book; think of it as you would any other; get the bandage of reverence from our eyes; drive from your heart the phantom of fear; push from the throne of your brain the cowled form of superstition—then read the holy bible, and you will be amazed that you ever, for a moment, supposed a being of infinite wisdom, goodness and purity, to be the author of such ignorance and such atrocity.

There is no evidence of any supernatural or extraordinary force here, merely human foibles, barbarousness, and an endless capacity for sadistic tortures and homicide. And there is Paine's (1797b) observation that "belief in a cruel God makes a cruel man," which is a statement that is fully substantiated by the long and repugnant history of religious violence across space and time. Paine (1880 [1794]: 12) added that reading the many passages filled with "voluptuous debaucheries, the cruel and torturous executions, the unrelenting vindictiveness," it is more appropriate to regard these as the words of a demon, not God. Along the same lines, Ingersoll (1907: 876) remarked,

> [had these words] been found in some temple erected to the worship of some snakes, or in the possession of some cannibal king, written in blood upon the dried skins of babes, there would have been a perfect harmony between its surroundings and its sentiments.

It is understandable why Voltaire cynically remarked that "The Bible [...] is what fools have written, what imbeciles commend, what rogues teach and young children are made to learn by heart" (Konner 2007: 66).

What is more remarkable is that none of the central episodes related in the Old Testament are actual historical events. Egyptian historians of the day who are known for the detailed records they kept about significant events and people say nothing about Moses, the genocidal plagues, or any other of the incidents reported in the Bible (Bradley 2015: 111). The apologist assertion that the Egyptians did not write about the exodus of the Jews because they were too embarrassed by their defeat at the hands of Yahweh is pure nonsense. This is using the absence of evidence as evidence. If an actual event was involved, then the Egyptian chroniclers would in their usual way have acted as spin doctors and declared that they intentionally expelled the Jews because of their vile nature, or something like that, in the same fashion that they spin doctored their failure against the Hittites during the Battle of Kadesh, in 1274 BCE as a major victory, rather than deny that it happened.

It is difficult not to conclude that the Old Testament accounts are sheer fabrications. Archaeological and historical research suggests that there was no captivity of 600,000 Jews in Egypt during the thirteenth century BCE, no mass exodus, no parting of any sea, and no wandering in the Sinai Desert for 40 years. Similarly, there were no battles in Canaan, no fortified cities to be destroyed, no walls around Jericho to be brought down, no empires ruled by David or Solomon, no historical records from neighboring states about these empires, no golden age in the Kingdom of Israel and Judea circa 1000 BCE. These are all fantasies of ignorant and petty desert tribesmen with illusions of grandeur.

Archaeologically, this part of the Middle East is one of the most extensively explored areas in the world, with research going back several centuries. Yet, while archaeologists have unearthed evidence of many other things, including the small encampments of prehistoric hunting-gathering people from the Paleolithic period, there is not a trace of any evidence for the events or activities described in the Old Testament (Dever 1990: 25, 80–81; Finkelstein and Silberman 2001: 57–63, 33–38, 128–31). The evidence should be there, but it is not.

It is astonishing that millions of people have anchored their worldview on this nightmarish fictional tome. All of this makes one wonder why the Gideons organization distributes millions of free copies of this ghastly book to make people aware of "God's love." Dawkins (2016: viii) speculates that perhaps the employees of this organization have never actually read this terrible book. Thomas Paine (1779: 15), however, knew the answer to this question: "The Bible is a book that has been read more and examined less than any book that has ever existed."

## The New Testament: God's Message to Humankind 2.0

From the same hinterlands and cultural backwaters of civilization that conferred upon us the Old Testament, we get the New Testament. This represents God's message 2.0. It is comprised of 27 books, including the canonical gospels, The Acts of the Apostles, the Epistles, and the Book of Revelation. These texts articulate the central dogma of

Christianity, including Jesus's divinity, the notion of the virgin birth, and the doctrine of the Trinity. Of interest to our discussion are the gospels which relate Jesus's life and career.

Remarkably, like the Old Testament, this book too is an accumulation of haphazardly cobbled together narratives that are full of contradictions, errors, inconsistencies, and nonsense. The principal sections, the canonical gospels, were not delivered by some supernatural agency or through a divine transmission but were selected by ordinary humans from over 50 texts in circulation through committee votes, such as the First Council of Nicaea in CE 325 and the Council of Rome in CE 382. The New Testament, therefore, is anything but an inerrant record of God's words that believers assume and apologists profess (see Chapter 14).

The endless absurdities of this book have been pointed out by various commentators, including the perceptive Celsus and Thomas Paine. That one was a pagan philosopher and the other a deist does not detract from the cogency of their commentary. Both of these essayists provided devastating critiques that anticipated many of the issues raised by present-day Bible de-mythologizers and critical historians. For this reason, I will present their arguments here in some detail. As is discussed in Chapter 13, Celsus presented his critique of the early Christians in his treatise *On the True Doctrine* (ca. 185), and Paine's ideas appeared in his book *The Age of Reason* (1794).

Employing his pagan frame of reference, the first discrepancy Celsus pointed out was the notion of God incarnating as a physical being, which he found to be inconsistent with the attributes of the God described in Christian theology, as an immutable spiritual being who is uncreated, eternal, invisible, incomprehensible, omnipotent, omniscient, omnipresent, and perfect. As the historian of early Christianity Robert Wilkin (1984: 103) explains, Celsus's (1830: 24) question was: How is it possible for a Deity who is by definition immutable to transform into a human or an imperfect being? Present-day philosophers have also pondered this question. Thus, Philipse (2014: 149) points out the incongruity of a "perfect being" creating something apart from himself that is imperfect.

Then there is also the problem of why an omniscient being chose that particular time in history to appear on earth and not earlier. Celsus (1987: 77) wondered why God stood by watching as evil escalated and only after a long interval decided to intervene as if he did not know or care about the fate of humanity before this. Related to this, Celsus asked why God had to appear in person. After all, as the omnipotent Creator of the universe, with dominion over all of existence he should know all about the affairs of people. Also, He undoubtedly has the power to defeat Satan and correct the evils of the world remotely by magic. So why, Celsus (1987: 76) asked, did God have to pay a visit to a domain over which he supposedly has total control?

Let us for the moment grant that perhaps a personal visit was necessary, why did the Deity choose such an odd method of achieving it? That is impregnating a Jewish village girl, going through gestation, birth, childhood, adolescence only to become an ineffective and failed itinerant preacher operating in the rural areas of Palestine (Tobin 2009: 359). Celsus (1830: 29) asked further:

> If God, like Jupiter in the comedy, being roused from a long sleep, wished to liberate the human race from evils, why did he send only into a corner of the earth this spirit of whom

you boast? Though he ought in a similar manner to have animated many other bodies, and to have sent them to every part of the habitable globe.

Here, Celsus is inquiring why an enterprise for the universal salvation of humankind unfolded in a remote spot in the world and was made known only to a handful of marginal and superstitious villagers in such a bizarre fashion.

Celsus (1830: 11) also pointed out Jesus's many un-Godlike characteristics, such as being disgracefully made a prisoner and betrayed by those whom he called his disciples. Then there is the issue of the virgin birth, which the gospel writers long after the fact copied directly from Isaiah 7:14: "Therefore the Lord himself shall give a sign; Behold, a virgin shall conceive, and bear a son, and shall call his name Immanuel" (Kurtz 2013: 120). Such plagiarism was part of a systematic reverse-engineering by the authors of the Gospel of Mathew and the Gospel of Luke to represent Jesus as God incarnate (see Chapter 12), which was an idea conceived around 85–90 CE.

The concept of the virgin birth and the incarnation of God created many logical problems. Celsus (1830: 5–6), for example, dismissed the grandiose claims about Jesus, pointing out that he was born in a poor Jewish village, rather than David's royal city of Bethlehem, to an impoverished woman who made a living by spinning. He added further that this woman was abandoned by her husband, a carpenter who found out that she had committed adultery and was impregnated by a Roman soldier named Panthera. As a consequence of being expelled by her husband, she became a disgraceful vagrant who delivered Jesus in secret and humiliation. Wilken (1984: 110) suggests that the idea that Jesus was fathered by a Roman soldier named Panthera (Pandera, or Pantera) was probably a story circulating in the empire and perhaps in the Jewish communities in Celsus's days (see Tabor 2007: 63–72, 344). Another story based on the apocryphal books of the New Testament says that Mary became pregnant by one of the high priests of the Temple, who then recruited Joseph to pose as her husband to cover up the scandal (Kurtz 2013: 125). Celsus (1987: 57–58) was also very perplexed by the particular method God used to come to earth. Why have his spirit enter the womb of a woman when he could have created a body through magic, something well within his power?

Not surprisingly, Thomas Paine (1880 [1795]: 115) found the virgin birth story "blasphemously obscene" in which a young girl about to be married is "debauched by a ghost" under the impious pretense that "the Lord shall come upon thee." And Paine (1880 [1795]: 118) asked how any rational human being could believe this terrible tale that is "naturally impossible, repugnant to every idea of decency, and related by persons already detected of falsehood?" Paine (1880 [1794]: 15) also pointed out many of the problems with the New Testament narratives that philosophers and critical historians are now talking about, namely that the book is rife with redactions, editorial mistakes, and outright forgeries, all of which is concrete evidence that this is the handiwork of people and not "the vehicle of the Word of God."

Of the many other paranormal happenings reported in this book, Paine (1835: 300) observed "all the tales of miracles, with which the Old and New Testament are filled, are fit only for impostures to preach and fools to believe." Christianity's truth claims would be believable, he added, had circumstances been different. In his words,

> Now, had the news of salvation by Jesus Christ been inscribed on the face of the Sun and the Moon, in characters that all nations would have understood, the whole earth had known it in twenty-four hours, and all nations would have believed it; whereas, though it is now almost two thousand years since, as they tell us, Christ came upon earth, not a twentieth part of the people of the earth know anything of it, and among those who do, the wiser part do not believe it. (Paine 1880 [1807]: 205)

There is also the puzzle of Jesus suffering and dying for the sins of humanity. As Paine (1880 [1794]: 18) observed, if suffering was the issue, then Jesus should have been allowed to live as a human, away from his cozy heavenly abode, to bear the inequities of life, and die in the same pathetic way as everyone else by succumbing to old age, disease, and infirmity. Such a fate would have made more sense rather than going through a fake death to be followed by a comfortable seat high in Heaven (cf., Bradley 2015: 25; Philipse 2014: 182). However, for Paine (1880 [1794]: 9) the entire story could have been less absurd had God compelled "Satan to exhibit himself on a cross, in the shape of a snake, as a punishment for his new transgression." Then, he added, the story would have made sense. Yet, it is the transgressor that appears triumphant, not God. In other words, the story entails the near deification of Satan, who in the shape of a snake was created by God but with such great god-like powers as to require that the Almighty intervene in the affairs of this world personally and exhibit "himself upon a cross in the shape of a man" (Paine 1880 [1794]: 9). Paine (1858: 338; 1892: 377) also called attention to the fact that the Bible contains so many contradictions as to make it impossible to separate fact from fiction. He rightly described the whole thing as "an outrage to common sense and an insult to human intelligence."

Aside from the issues noted thus far, the nature of the message contained in the New Testament raises many problems. As noted earlier, the New Testament was religion 2.0, purportedly a better and friendlier version of the previous obscene and scandalous communiqué. This, however, is not the case. As Barker (2016: 294) points out, here was the perfect opportunity to replace the old model with a genuine moral one. Yet, what we find is more of the same and more anger and jealousy instead of compassion and understanding. Jesus says, "Think not that I am come to destroy the law, or the prophets [...] but to fulfill" (Matthew 5:17–19). Also, there is more fire, burning, and crying, along with gnashing of teeth, and other unspeakable torments. Jesus says, "If a man abides not in me [...] he is cast forth into the fire" (John 15:6). The number of people burned alive as heretics, apostates, and witches because of these words is heartrending. Look at the history of the Inquisition, the Church's anti-heresy campaigns, or the witch hunts in Europe, just to mention a few examples (on the witch hunts, see Sidky 1997).

On top of this, the loving and compassionate Jesus offers us an entirely new form of terror, everlasting incineration in Hell for eternity (Mark 9:42–48; Matthew 13:41–42, 25:41). The philosopher Bertrand Russell (1957: 17–18) found Jesus's image as a compassionate savior utterly inconsistent with his remarks about wailing and gnashing of teeth and his vindictive fury against those who would not listen to him preaching. Even Celsus (1987: 70), a pagan living nearly two thousand years ago, was horrified by these cruel proscriptions.

Then there are the failed prophecies. One of the colossal fiascos in the New Testament is the disconfirmation of its most significant prophecy, the Second Coming, or the Parousia. The gospels relate that Jesus foretold that his second coming and the establishment of God's kingdom on earth would occur within the lifetime of his disciples. But this did not happen, and all the disciples went to their grave with the promise unfulfilled. Here, the gospel writers employ ingenuity and reverse-engineering to explain away this glaring predicament using a strategy that all failed messianic cultists employ, which is to reinterpret the prophecies (see Chapter 16). One after-the-fact excuse for the postponed Parousia is that for God "a day is like a thousand years, and a thousand years are like a day," while still boasting that the day will surely come. Such a proclamation, of course, is coupled with the promise of more hellfire and other pyrotechnics to baffle the believers. With no sign of Jesus after nearly two thousand years, Christian apologists have been changing their story as well as "moving the goal posts" ever since (Loftus 2010: 333). Also, there is another usually overlooked failure in Christian theology, namely the promise that the resurrection of Jesus signifies triumph over death (Romans 6:9) and the defeat of evil. However, the promise (or more aptly wishful thinking) was false. Death has yet to be overcome, there is no redemption for the faithful, and evil persists as robustly as ever.

Evangelical Christians and other literalists in the United States today consider the New Testament to contain the actual words of God. However, the voluminous inconsistencies, contradictions, the gross error of facts, barbaric injunctions, gynophobia, homophobia, and misinformation in these texts rule out the likelihood that an omniscient, omnibenevolent, omnipotent paranormal Being was the source of the words. Moreover, the failure of the biblical prophecies is substantial evidence against the involvement of some extraordinary magical being or supernatural power.

These errors place the hapless true believers in a terrible bind because if one part of their holy text is shown to be fallible then, as the Christian apologist Gleason Archer (1982: 22) points out, it follows that trust cannot be placed in matters of religion in other parts. The option chosen by Archer and other believers is the inerrancy canard or a radical fundamentalist stance that every word in the Bible is God's literal truth, which is an infantile and pathetic refusal to acknowledge the problematic nature of these texts. Sadly, pretending that these errors do not exist and emphatically insisting that it is all true does not make them magically vanish; it only makes those who espouse such nonsense look stupid. Here we see exactly how faith renders evidentiary challenges irrelevant and is a barrier to intellectual honesty and the spirit of inquiry, or search for truth.

Plantinga (1991: 8, 12), a paragon among the apologists, expresses this view, writing that the Scriptures contain the "inerrant words of God" and that "the Lord makes no mistakes." Really? Do these texts contain no mistakes? Plantinga (2000: 241, 357) tries to circumvent the evidentiary challenge altogether by averring that evidence is not necessary because the belief in God is a "basic belief," that is, is self-evidently true. But cutting through this smokescreen of theological jargon, clever talk, and sheer nonsense, we see that this amounts to saying, "I believe it is true because I wish it to be true."

Another apologist, Peter van Inwagen (1993: 97), says: "I fully accept the teachings of my denomination that the Holy Scriptures of the Old and New Testaments are the revealed word of God." What about the teachings of the other denominations? If they are divergent enough for Inwagen to make this stipulation, then what happened to the inerrancy of the texts? Or are the followers of other denominations wayward heretics and apostates? Alternatively, from the point of view of the other denominations, is it van Inwagen's congregation that is guilty of getting it wrong? Why are God's inerrant words so difficult to understand? Why do they lend themselves to divergent interpretations? Claiming the inerrancy of the Bible entails ignorance of history, mythology, archaeology, and anthropology as well as substantial doses of utter intellectual dishonesty. Belief without evidence, no matter how cleverly presented, is irrationalism.

Apologists who try to defend their will to believe resort to specious arguments, special pleading, and rhetorical subterfuge and try to capitalize on their audience's gullibility and ignorance and unfamiliarity with scholarly standards. Through such tactics, they create the false impression that history and reason are on their side. Having chosen this path, these writers besmirch their integrity when they make false claims about the inerrancy of their dubious holy book or when they assert that an event such as the resurrection of Jesus described in the gospels is among the most well-documented events in human history (see Chapter 12). The objective of these ideologues, of course, is not scholarship, historiography, or rational argumentation but to make converts. Sadly, this amounts to "dignifying credulity as a method" (Price 2010a: 274).

The unabashed mendacity of such dogmatists clearly illustrates the difference between science and religion. Science and religion, to reiterate, are at odds because the hallmark of science is the question, "What is the evidence," while the hallmark of religion is "I wish to believe." Religionists are therefore intellectually perfidious and will never follow the evidence where it leads. Instead, they will strive to dismiss or savagely suppress any evidence that disconfirms their beliefs and silence voices of opposition, by force and violence if necessary. For this reason, wherever and whenever religionists assume political power, they have happily incinerated and gleefully stoned to death and beheaded those who disagree.

According to the overview in this chapter, only one very distressing conclusion is possible. None of the revered sacred texts on offer look anything like a book authorized or written by the omnipotent, omniscient, omnibenevolent, veracious Deity. If the purpose of religion is to offer wisdom, comfort, guidance, and solace for the weak, needy, and the suffering, then the nonsense contained in these books does not fit that definition.

The God of theism described in these terrible tomes is not wise, benevolent, or all-loving. What we find is an infantile, insecure, obscene, vindictive, paranoid, and bellicose blackmailer. All that this narcissistic Deity does in page after page and verse after verse of these dreadful volumes is to brag about his own might and awesomeness and continuously threaten his puny and helpless creatures with bodily harm, incineration, fire and brimstone, scalding water, pain, wholesale slaughter, destruction, and eternal suffering. He is to be worshipped not because of his infinite love and benevolence, or by virtue of his awesomeness, greatness, goodness, or righteousness, but because the alternative he offers is incineration and interminable suffering in some hellish location, one more terrible than the next. The theistic God is the supreme narcissist and terrorist. This is why I have said that humankind's sacred literature reads like a catalog of psychopathology. Perhaps Thomas Paine was correct when he said that these are the attributes of a demonic being, not of God. Only a demon bullies, torments, and brutalizes helpless sentient beings. If this fiend is "the Creator," then it seems that he made sentient lifeforms solely for the pleasure of getting the full effects of the pain and suffering he inflicts on these helpless creatures.

Of course, we are not talking about God. These books are indeed an affront to God, any God. The contents of these dark tomes are human inventions and childish anthropomorphic projections of ignorant and barbaric people living in inhumane and brutal times. What these books say has nothing to do with the Creator of the world and the universe, if such an entity exists. Yet people around the planet have made the nightmarish fantasies of superstitious, ignorant, and delusional people who wrote these ghastly books the basis of their moral and ethical codes.

As a final point, to reiterate, the texts contain nothing extraordinary. There is no radically new information, no revolutionary medical cures, and nothing else to make life more tolerable on a planet where more than two billion humans are barely scratching a living. We find no universally applicable ethical precepts, such as the value of human life, equality for all, compassion for nonhuman life, or respect for the planet. There is nothing that extols intellectual inquiry and reason and naught that denounces bigotry, racism, slavery, misogyny, the abuse of women and children, or inhumanity to those who are different. In fact, we find the extolling of values that are the exact opposite of these and which bring out the worst in human behavior.

The ambiguity and contradictory nature of the revealed messages has often served as a license for unrestrained dogmatism bolstering fanaticism and inhumanity. Such ambiguities and inconsistencies make nearly any reading possible. Hence, rabid fundamentalists and the so-called moderate and peaceful votaries use the same books and recite the same passages and verses as the basis of their religious perspectives. For this reason, these delightful tomes have been the bane of humankind.

Following God's words contained in the holy books in a literal sense, as is required of the faithful—moderate and radical militants alike—means one thing, absolute belief without evidence. Conditioned in this way to believe on faith and not to question makes people commit unthinkable atrocities as well as rendering them susceptible to the manipulation of all sorts of dubious ideologues, whether evangelical preachers, mullahs, *jihadis*, crusaders, fundamentalist racists, and home-grown and overseas ayatollas. This is the hallmark of all religions. In Ingersoll's (1907: 792) words,

> According to the theologians, God, the Father of us all, wrote a letter [the holy tomes] to His children. The children have always differed somewhat as to the meaning of this letter. In consequence of these honest difficulties, these brothers began to cut out each other's heart. In every land, where this letter from God has been read, the children to whom and for whom it was written have been filled with hatred and malice. They have imprisoned and murdered each other, and the wives and children of each other. In the name of God every possible crime has been committed, every conceivable outrage perpetrated. Brave men, tender and

> loving women, beautiful girls and prattling babies have been exterminated in the name of Jesus Christ.

Thomas Paine (1880 [1795]: 195), as if peering into our time, said, "no falsehood is so fatal as that which is made an article of faith." The precepts contained in these horrific religious volumes provide an unrestricted license to act irrationally, irresponsibly, and inhumanely and feel virtuous about it.

## Chapter Eleven

# GOD'S FINGERPRINTS IN THE NATURAL WORLD: INTELLIGENT DESIGN, IRREDUCIBLE COMPLEXITY, AND COSMIC FINE-TUNING[1]

*At every turn, we seem to think there are subtle messages scratched into the woodwork of nature, subtle signs or cues that God, or some other supernatural agent, is trying to communicate a lesson or idea to us—often us alone. Usually, it's about how we should behave.*

—Jesse Bering, *The God Instinct* (2013)

*The 'appearance of design' tracks prior belief, and so cannot be taken to be any kind of vindication of that belief.*

—Graham Oppy, *Naturalism and Religion* (2018)

*Modern-day "creationism" [is] the effort to construct an alternative fundamentalist science based on the Bible. [...] Millions of evangelicals think they are defending the Bible by defending creation science, but in reality, they are giving ultimate authority to the merely temporal, situated, and contextualized interpretations of the Bible that arose [during] the early nineteenth century.*

—Mark Noll, *The Scandal of the Evangelical Mind* (1994)

A long-standing argument for the existence of God arises from a human cognitive tendency for teleo-functional thinking associated with our theory of mind (see Chapter 6). This is known as the "teleological argument" or "argument from design." Before discussing this line of reasoning, however, I wish to discuss the cognitive foundations of this type of thinking. Teleological or teleo-functional thinking refers to inferences that things exist for a purpose rather than merely being the result of physical or natural processes (Bering 2013: 46–47, 55). Attributing purpose to things implies a purposeful creator or designer. We think in this way as easily about a showerhead that pours water on our heads as with rain that falls from the sky. Teleo-functional thinking involves the attribution of reason and purpose to aspects of the natural world and the universe.

1. I would like to thank Dr. William C. McGrew, Department of Archaeology and Anthropology, University of Cambridge, UK, for reading an earlier draft of this chapter and for his many useful comments and suggestions. I alone assume responsibility for any errors and the views expressed here.

## The Cognitive Foundations of Arguments from Design

Developmental psychologists have shown that teleo-functional thinking also exists among children, which is why humans, in general, are innate creationists and why most individuals cannot easily grasp evolutionary theory. As the evolutionary biologist Richard Dawkins (1996: xviii) has lamented, "It is almost as if the human brain were specifically designed to misunderstand Darwinism and find it hard to believe." However, he emphasizes a different set of intuitive problems people have for accepting evolutionary theory, such as the erroneous popular perception that evolution by natural selection operates by chance and the immense timescales associated with the evolution of life on earth. These timescales are on the order of millions of decades. People just cannot get their minds around this because they think in minutes, hours, days, years, decades, and centuries.

However, creationist thinking and the idea that there is design in the world comes more easily for people than evolutionary thinking because it flows from "the propensities of the human mind." As Bering (2013: 59) points out, our theory of mind ensures that we will always favor a "purposeful-design framework." What is paradoxical is that this propensity that generates hostilities toward evolutionary theory is due to the way natural selection (i.e., evolution) has impacted how we think about our origins.

Along similar lines, cognitive psychologist Bruce Hood (2009: 57) observes that the reason creationism is so appealing to many is that it has greater cognitive resonance with our mind design, which compels us to see order, structure, and purpose in nature. It must be stressed, however, that because design beliefs are generated by "properly operating" cognitive processes, or are based on what one could call "common sense principles," they have a warrant or are justified (contra Plantinga 2011; Ratzsch 2003). These are X-claims or what science has shown to be easily produced false beliefs. People will form design beliefs, even if supernatural design forces are absent (Eyghen 2019: 81).

As Hood (2009: 61) puts it, our intuition leads us to think in terms of the following premises:

1. There are no random events or patterns in the world.
2. Things are caused by intention.
3. Complexity cannot happen spontaneously but must be a product of someone's plan to design things for a purpose
4. All living things are essentially different because of some innate but invisible property inside them.

The Darwinian theory of evolution through natural selection, while simple and elegant, is just too counterintuitive to fit our mind design that seeks order and causality, infers intentions, and abhors chance occurrences or randomness. Evolutionary theory also violates our hard-core essentialism that species have immutable essences and because of our proclivity to believe that design requires a designer (Hood 2009: 62). Developmental psychologists have found that even children from a very young age view living entities as intrinsically distinct, with fixed properties that are considered immutable (Kelemen

1999). In other words, children are innate creationists. This conceptual bias continues into adulthood (Kelemen and Rosset 2009). Hence Christian fundamentalism is only a partial explanation for the popularity of creationist thinking.

The reason why creation myths abound across groups and throughout time is that the human mind is innately compatible with a creationist perspective. For this reason, nearly all cultures, including the Incas, Aztecs, ancient Egyptians, and many others, had creation stories (Hood 2009: 61). The irony is that the hostile anti-evolution creationism in the United States is an expression of the way evolution structured human minds to operate. Here is yet another example of how the misunderstood mysterious workings of their own minds mystify people.

As discussed in Chapter 6, our theory of mind, which compels us to think about human origins and existence in intentional terms, also gives rise to teleo-functional fantasy about a super-intelligent mind and First Agent who deliberately designed the universe and put us on earth for a divine purpose. Theory of mind thus supplies all the stuff of religion and the ideas that have preoccupied theologians and philosophers for millennia. This type of reasoning is the basis of the various renditions of the design argument for the existence of God. It is also the foundation of "natural theology," an endeavor based on the premise that observations of the natural world can lead to clues about what is inside God's mind, or the attempt to show the probable existence of God using empirical evidence from the natural world (Philipse 2014: 3). Natural theology is, therefore, distinct from "revealed theology," which stipulates that religious truths originate in divine communiqués. The philosopher Peter Slezak (1996: 201) describes natural theology as "finding rational arguments and evidence for religious claims *a posteriori* instead of establishing these claims through revelation *a priori*."

Humans frequently think they detect signs, symbols, messages embedded into the framework of nature, and other cues that God or some other supernatural being is conveying messages that usually tells them how to behave (Bering 2013: 77). Hence natural events become messages from the other world. Even natural disasters are construed as acts of God or some other hidden intentional agent. Thus, earthquakes, forest fires, hurricanes, and tsunamis become more than what is apparent because the design of our minds compels us to ponder unknown paranormal causes behind events. An inane and perverse example of this is the assertion by staunch Christian evangelists and washed-up right-wing pundits looking for cheap publicity that Hurrican Harvey that hit Houston and Hurrican Katrina in New Orleans were signs of God's wrath toward Americans for tolerating homosexuality.

We are also cognitively uncomfortable with randomness, chance occurrences, and fortuitous life events because we think in intentional terms. Thus, when people, who are social beings, encounter misfortunes, they personify these events and immediately seek morally culpable intentional agents, which tragically usually means other people. The guilty parties are identified and subjected to punishments in God's name, imbuing the misfortune with meaning and providing a sense of control (Gray and Wegner 2010: 10). Innumerable cases of scapegoating and witchcraft persecutions have resulted from this human cognitive tendency. Some of these horrible religious atrocities and misogynistic crimes are discussed in my book *Witchcraft, Lycanthropy, Drugs, and Disease* (1997).

I have also encountered such cases of personifying misfortunes in the form of witchcraft accusations in the context of fieldwork in Nepal. Such incidents result in the humiliation, torture, and even murder of women for causing sickness, the death of a child through magic, or poisoning people's food, actions for which they could not have possibly been responsible (Sidky 2008: 135–46). Where the causes of misfortunes are indeterminate and accountable human malefactors are not available, as in the case of major disasters, such as avalanches or hurricanes, people may infer the actions of more powerful moral agents, such as the gods, or God, punishing them directly (Gray and Wegner 2010: 11).

## The Nature of Design Arguments

The German mathematician and astronomer Johannes Kepler believed that the face we perceive when we gaze at the moon is evidence of God's handiwork and proof of intelligent design (Sober 2006: 98). Kepler came to this conclusion because of the human cognitive tendency to see patterns in randomness, a near-universal phenomenon reported by people in many different cultures (Smith 2010: 145). Like many others, Kepler mistook this cognitive illusion for a mind-independent feature of the solar system (see Chapter 6). Inferring the presence of a purposeful paranormal designer from some perceived element in nature or the cosmos is the defining attribute of all design arguments.

Our theory of mind powerfully predisposes us toward purposeful design interpretive frameworks. Design jumps out at us almost everywhere and seems significant and profound. All sorts of phenomena from the wings of a butterfly to the structure of the human eye scream out design. Cognitively, design without a designer seems improbable. We thus intuitively postulate purposeful designers, and this renders all of us adept creationists. Also, we are prone to perceive design even where none exists. Design-based insights, however, tell us more about the workings of the human mind than about the operation and structure of the world around us. Creationism is, therefore, a human cognitive illusion around which people across cultures and through time have constructed myths, belief systems, and entire theologies.

As the evolutionary biologist Francisco Ayala (2016: 313) has pointed out, the design argument has two parts: (1) that design exists in nature and (2) only God could be responsible for the design. The postulated designer is always thought of in human terms as an awesome but human-like paranormal being, with motives, objectives, and intentions (Ratzsch and Koperski 2016). For theists evidence for the existence of this designer is His handiwork, the structure of the world.

The argument from design goes back at least to the ancient Greeks and is grounded in prescientific conjectures about the nature of the world and universe (Ratzsch and Koperski 2016; Ruse 2006: 13–14; Shanks 2006: 19–49). However, design arguments are not "tenacious weeds" lingering "in the minds of men" from ancient times, as the philosopher Niall Shanks (2006: 19) believes, but are the ongoing productions of such minds.

There are several versions of the argument from the apparent design of the world. The shared underlying reasoning of all these perspectives is that the perceived order and functionality in nature is the achievement of a super paranormal designer. David Hume provided an eloquent elucidation of this idea to critique it in his book *Dialogues Concerning*

*Natural Religion* (1779), a work the philosopher Nicholas Everitt (2004: 85) rightly describes as "one of the masterpieces of Western philosophy:"

> Look round the world: contemplate the whole and every part of it: You will find it to be nothing but one great machine, subdivided into an infinite number of lesser machines, which again admit of subdivisions to a degree beyond what human senses and faculties can trace and explain. All these various machines, and even their most minute parts, are adjusted to each other with an accuracy which ravishes into admiration all men who have ever contemplated them. The curious adapting of means to ends, throughout all nature, resembles exactly, though it much exceeds, the productions of human contrivance; of human designs, thought, wisdom, and intelligence. Since, therefore, the effects resemble each other, we are led to infer, by all the rules of analogy, that the causes also resemble; and that the Author of Nature is somewhat similar to the mind of man, though possessed of much larger faculties, proportioned to the grandeur of the work which he has executed. By this argument *a posteriori*, and by this argument alone, do we prove at once the existence of a Deity, and his similarity to human mind and intelligence. (Hume 1779: 47–48)

The philosopher John Stuart Mill (1874: 167) provided a similar formulation:

> Certain qualities, it is alleged, are found to be characteristic of such things as are made by an intelligent mind for a purpose. The order of Nature, or some considerable parts of it, exhibit these qualities to a remarkable degree. We are entitled, from this great similarity in the effects, to infer similarity in the cause, and to believe that things which it is beyond the power of man to make, but which resemble the works of man in all but power, must also have been made by Intelligence, armed with a power greater than human.

Religionists have been using the design argument to make theological points for millennia. For example, the Apostle Paul, in his letter to the Romans, used design in the world as unequivocal evidence for the existence of God to instill fear in the hearts of would-be nonbelievers:

> The wrath of God is being revealed from heaven against all the godlessness and wickedness of people, who suppress the truth by their wickedness, since what may be known about God is plain to them, because God has made it plain to them. For since the creation of the world God's invisible qualities—his eternal power and divine nature—have been clearly seen, being understood from what has been made, so that people are without excuse. (Romans 1:18–20)

The argument from design was highly popular during the eighteenth century, a time many believed that science was uncovering persuasive evidence of God's handiwork in the make-up of the natural world (Mackie 2013: 132). Indeed, before Darwin provided a naturalistic mechanism for the evolution of life in the next century, the idea of a paranormal designer was considered to be the best and most convincing explanation for the complexity of life on earth. However, Hume tore through and decisively demolished the argument in his *Dialogues Concerning Natural Religion*. Religionists, however, have refused to abandon the worn-out case. Among believers, Hume's arguments fell upon deaf ears.

Religionists disparagingly described Hume as "God's greatest gift to the infidel" (Ruse 2006: 17).

## William Paley, Natural Theology, and the Argument from Design

The best-known form of this argument was provided during the nineteenth century by the theologian and Christian apologist Archdeacon William Paley of Carlisle, in his influential book *Natural Theology, or Evidences of the Existence and Attributes of the Deity, Collected from the Appearance of Nature* (1802). Paley (1802: 5) stated his case as follows:

> In crossing a heath, suppose I pitched my foot against a *stone* and were asked how the stone came to be there, I might possibly answer that for anything I knew to the contrary it had lain there forever; nor would it, perhaps, be very easy to show the absurdity of this answer. But suppose I had found a *watch* upon the ground, and it should be inquired how the watch happened to be in that place, I should hardly think of the answer which I had before given, that for anything I knew the watch might have always been there. Yet why should not this answer serve for the watch as well as for the stone? Why is it not as admissible in the second case as in the first? For this reason, and for no other, namely, that when we come to inspect the watch, we perceive—what we could not discover in the stone—that its several parts are framed and put together for a purpose [...] This mechanism being observed—it requires indeed an examination of the instrument, and perhaps some previous knowledge of the subject, to perceive and understand it; but being once, as we have said, observed and understood—the inference we think is inevitable, that the watch must have had a maker—that there must have existed, at some time and at some place or other, an artificer or artificers who formed it for the purpose which we find it actually to answer, who comprehended its construction and designed its use.

For Paley, the analogy between a human artifact and nature was so powerfully compelling as to justify the conclusion that as in the case of the watch there is a purposeful, intelligent agent behind the apparent design we detected in nature. As he put it, "There can be no design without designer; [no] contrivance, without a contriver" (Paley 1802: 15–16). This design, Paley argued further, is noticeable in things ranging from the solar system and the human eye to the structure of the cardiovascular system (Bradley 2007). As Paley saw it, natural theology thus confirmed the Book of Genesis (Philipse 2014: 267). For this reason, I consider all works expressing versions of this argument to belong to the genre of paranormal literature.

Paley's argument entails analogical reasoning and is highly problematic. As Philipse (2014: 97–98) observes, we use an analogy to talk about something not well understood as if it is something else that is better known, for example, comparing the human brain to a computer. However, such comparisons are appropriate only to a certain degree because while the brain could be treated as a type of computer, it also has attributes that computers do not have. Analogies may make it easier to think about the brain, but they do not transform the brain into an artifact.

Paley's analogy between watches and organisms, therefore, is weak and too remote to justify inferring similar causality. In other words, there is a "dis-analogy" between the watchmaker and the putative maker of organisms and universes (Sober 2006: 110). As the philosopher Graham Oppy (2006: 177) points out, beyond the considerations of function, background knowledge is in use when we inspect a watch and conclude that it was human-made. The background knowledge used includes knowing that brass does not occur in nature, that clear glass is fabricated in a factory, and that the constituent metal parts, such as cogwheels, do not come from trees (Oppy 2018: 66). These are the considerations that justify our inference that the object in question is the result of human hands. However, the criteria used to support our judgment that a watch is the result of intelligent design do not transfer to the reasons used to suppose that an intelligent agent has designed the natural world (Oppy 2006: 177). This undermines the overall argument. As Oppy (2006: 177) explains, our background knowledge about the constituent materials and elements of manufactured items is not the equivalent of any data about the production of biological materials and components.

Inferring the existence of an invisible paranormal super creator from his purported effects in the world, such as the perceived symmetry of butterfly wings or the structural arrangement of the human eye, is highly problematic because there are no literal descriptions of God the designer that we can use. The theistic creator God, we may recall, is conceived as an anthropomorphic spirit entity who is bodiless, eternal in nature, unique, radically transcendent, incomparable with any other entity, unknowable, absolutely free, with moral attributes such as omnibenevolence, omnipotence, and omniscience (Swinburne 2004: 1). He is the maker, designer, and sustainer of all things aside from himself. How does one describe an entity that is radically transcendent and infinitely different from all finite entities? How does one know anything about the motives, methodology, creative intentions, and desires of such a being?

Determining such attributes about other humans is possible because we have background information (Philipse 2014: 147). For example, from their biological characteristics, we can infer that they need to eat, rest, and desire companionship. From their historical, cultural, and psychological background information, we can deduce such characteristics as disposition and personality traits. Thus, when we infer that somebody designed an object suitable for some purpose, we employ such independent background information that makes it possible to ascribe intention and make sense of their handiworks, such as a watch. Also, we have independent information about the existence of humans, and we can observe their behavior (Narveson 2003: 95). We have none of this for God—stories in sacred books are utterly useless because their authors knew less than we do (Narveson 2003: 96). Also, so-called divine revelations are notoriously unreliable and are of no help. We have no biological, psychological, cultural, or historical background information about God that would allow us to non-arbitrarily attribute intentions, such as the reasons why he created people in the form they appear and where they exist, or why butterfly wings look the way they do, and so forth (Philipse 2014: 147).

Theological savants who do assign motives and intentions to God do so arbitrarily. Thus, as Philipse (2014: 158) says, assertions that God created humans because of his need to share, love, and interact are anthropomorphic projections. Social animals, such as humans, interact and share to survive and procreate, as explained by evolutionary theory. God, however, is bodiless, eternal in nature, unique, incomparable with any other entity (Swinburne 2004: 1), and cannot have any such attributes (Philipse 2014: 158). Moreover, words such as free, knowledgeable (omniscient), and good (benevolent) are developed in reference to people; they cannot apply to God as defined by theism (Philipse 2014: 97–98). In other words, the God of theism is an anthropomorphic projection, that is, as noted in Chapter 6, humans conceive of God in their own image, rather than the other way around.

As Slezak (1996: 206) has put it, anthropomorphism is at the core of the design argument. However, he adds, the cognizance of design or the presence of order and regularity does not warrant the extrapolation of an intelligent designer. Such reasoning about the mental states of invisible intentional agents using the human mind as a model arises out of the overextension of the theory of mind and the human cognitive bias to overdetect agency, as discussed in Chapter 6. Or to state it differently, these are all X-claims, as discussed in Chapters 6 and 8, and are merely a testament to the fact that humans are prone to false paranormal and supernatural ideation.

Hume (1779: 81–82) dealt with this problem long ago, pointing out the audacity on the part of those who claimed to know God's attributes and noted how this line of thinking devolves into absurd anthropomorphic ideation:

> may it not render us presumptuous, by making us imagine we comprehend the Deity, and have some adequate idea of his nature and attributes? [...] His ways are not our ways. His attributes are perfect, but incomprehensible. And this volume of nature contains a great and inexplicable riddle, more than any intelligible discourse or reasoning. [...] [Thus] by representing the Deity as so intelligible and comprehensible, and so similar to a human mind, we are guilty of the grossest and most narrow partiality, and make ourselves the model of the whole universe.

Hume also noted that we could say that an unobservable exists if our statement is based on effects we can experience but only if such a causal regularity is inductively established. For example, from footprints in the sand, we could conclude that a person walked there because we know from recurring experience that humans walking on sand leave behind prints. However, we cannot justifiably take aspects of the universe and conclude that it was created by God in the same way as we can about footprints in the sand or even machines designed and built by engineers because we lack the experience of God (Philipse 2014: 23). The argument from analogy is feeble because the differences between humans and an incorporeal God are greater than the similarities between them.

Thus, Paley's assertion that because the eye is analogous to a telescope, we can conclude that an intelligent designer designed it involves an unwarranted inferential leap. This is the flaw in all design arguments. As Shanks (2006: 166–67) points out, to bridge the inferential gap requires that we provide evidence about who designed the object in question, how, and for what purpose. Here a mechanical metaphor, that is, telescopes as eyes, fails. The reason for this is because we know that telescopes are human artifacts and as such have human designers, even if the identities of those designers are unknown. However, in the case of the eye, we do not have such background information. Merely stating that the eye is like a designed artifact does not make it an artifact. To substantiate this claim requires unequivocal "evidential justification," which means we must provide information that answers by who, how, and why the object in question was made (Shanks 2006: 166–67). Creationists have never been able to provide such evidence. Natural theology fails because it lacks explanatory details about who (proof for the existence of God), how (mechanism of creation), and why (evidence of purpose) (Narveson 2003: 93–94).

So why do religionists think they perceive design? As Oppy points out, there is a universal tendency for humans to detect design in cases where there are parts that seem to fit together to accomplish some seeming function. However, only in cases involving an a priori belief that animals and plants are designed do people perceive design in such entities because parts fit together to perform a function (Oppy 2018: 66–67). In other words, prior beliefs, such as the idea that there is a God, impinge in those cases where people think they see design in plants and animals. As Oppy puts it, the "'appearance of design' tracks prior belief, and so cannot be taken to be any kind of vindication of that belief" (Oppy 2018: 67).

Hume elaborated other weaknesses of using the analogy between organisms (the objects purportedly made by God) and human artifacts, such as a watch. For instance, God is postulated as a single unitary designer, but we know from experience that very few artifacts are produced by a single designer (Everitt 2004: 99). Large complex objects usually have groups of cooperative designers and creators. So, if the analogy is to hold, it is more justifiable to infer a group of paranormal designers for the things in the world. Thus, Hume argued, the beings of polytheism, rather than a single super paranormal creator, such as Yahweh or Allah, are more appropriate candidates as the designers. Also, human designers work with prefabricated materials, such as brass, glass, cogwheels, but God creates ex nihilo ("out of nothing"). Thus, for the analogy to hold, the supernatural designer would have to be described as a fashioner or assembler of preexisting stuff (Everitt 2004: 99).

Experience also tells us that makers of artifacts are physical entities with a human form. The analogy breaks down if we say that things in the world are the creations of a bodiless, nonphysical entity (Everitt 2004: 100). Thus, if the apparent design of organisms is all there is to work with to analogically infer God's attributes, then religionists are presuming more than is possible to establish based on the design argument alone (Gaskins 1976: 335). Our judgment of the signs of design in a watch, to state this differently, derives from what we know humans do. But the further afield we move from human cases, from watches to butterfly wings, the more ephemeral the ground rules for inferring design become. In the words of the philosopher Elliott Sober (2006: 111) signs of intelligent design are contingent upon an empirical understanding of what designers do. This works in the case of human designers. However, the further we move from human designers, the less certain our inferences become about intelligent design.

Hume (1980 [1779]: 74) made a final point that the design argument, which posits a morally perfect designer, fails because what we perceive in the world does not indicate a benevolent designer. Here the reference is to the argument from evil discussed in Chapter 3. Religionists tend to downplay, dismiss, and try to explain away the evils and imperfections of the world. In his efforts to portray the Creator's perfect nature, Paley (1802: 46) simply ignored the flaws, defects, and cruelty that characterize nature as "of little or no weight." A crucial problem such as this, however, cannot be so easily dismissed. As Hume (1980 [1779]: 74) put it,

> Look around this universe. What an immense profusion of beings, animated and organized, conscious, and active! You admire this prodigious variety and fruitfulness. But look a little more closely at these living things (the only ones worth thinking about). How hostile and destructive they are to each other! How far they all are from being able to achieve their own happiness! How contemptible or odious they are to the spectator! The whole picture is one of a blind nature impregnated by some powerful life-giving force and pouring forth from her lap, without discernment or parental care, her maimed and abortive children!
>
> Here the Manichaean system—according to which the universe is governed by two fundamental forces, one good and the other bad—comes to mind as a good hypothesis to solve the difficulty. No doubt it is in some respects very attractive, and it's giving a plausible account of the strange mixture of good and ill that appears in life makes it more probable than the common hypothesis of a single benevolent God.

In other words, given such mixed phenomena in the world that embody benign and malevolent aspects, it is not possible to justifiably infer the morally perfect deity of theism. At best, it leads to an inference of an indifferent designer (Bradly 2007: 249). Here someone could object that the existence of the designer is distinct from the attributes of the designer (Sober 2006: 107). While this may be true, however, religionists often infer God's goodness from his creative actions. The theistic philosopher Richard Swinburne (2004: 130) states, for example, that God created the world and universe out of his desire to love and interact with human moral agents that he embodied and situated in a physical universe specially designed so that humans can develop morally.

Alternatively, Hume (1889 [1759]: 111) humorously surmised that the faulty and imperfect nature of the world is because

> [it] was only the first rude essay of some infant deity, who afterward abandoned it, ashamed of his lame performance: It is the work of some dependent, inferior deity; and is the object of derision to his superiors: It is the production of old age and dotage in some superannuated deity.

There is another difficulty with arguments from design, such as the one offered by Paley, because they entail the logical fallacy of argument from ignorance, also called the god-of-the-gaps fallacy. There are several steps in this line of reasoning. First, an empirical phenomenon which appears not to be due to random processes is identified. Second, it is shown that scientific explanations for this phenomenon are not available. Third, the absence of current scientific explanations is taken to mean that any such explanations are, in principle, impossible. Fourth, it is concluded that the phenomenon is designed by a super-intelligent purposeful paranormal agent (Philipse 2014: 164). Another way to put this is that everything about which we are ignorant is due to God's magic. However, to paraphrase the philosopher Michael Scriven (1966: 155), the unexplained is not supernatural or paranormal.

For instance, Paley's comparison of a telescope and the human eye led him to conclude that such a complex biological system is undeniable evidence of intelligent design for which there could be no scientific explanation. What impressed him is the intricate arrangement of the iris, lens, retina, and cornea that make up the "camera eye" found in vertebrates as well as in mollusks, such as the squid and the octopus (Coyne 2009: 141). Since Paley's time, other creationists have adopted this as their favorite example of God's handiwork. Evangelical Christian students have raised it more than once during my classes dealing with human evolution. Believers cannot fathom how science could explain such an intricate biological structure.

Paley's god-of-the-gaps dilemma became evident 57 years later when Charles Darwin demonstrated how the camera eye developed through a series of adaptive steps, each conferring better visual perception and aiding survival (Ayala 2016: 323). This process has been replicated through mathematical modeling, beginning with a patch of light-sensitive cells, or a simple eye precursor, that has resulted in a sophisticated camera eye similar to those of vertebrates through a series of 1,829 small adaptive changes (Coyne 2009: 142). The required evolutionary time frame calculated was less than 400,000 years. Animals with these type of eyes existed 550 million years ago, which is plenty of time for the camera eye to have evolved 1,500 times. In fact, the eye developed independently among at least 40 separate groups of organisms. Paley was wrong. As we shall see, the god-of-the-gaps dilemma recurs in the case of other variants of the argument from design on offer since the nineteenth century. Unfortunately, it has never been of much help to the theistic case.

Darwin's idea of evolution through natural selection presented in his book *On the Origin of Species* (1859) challenged the biblical fable that life appeared through special divine actions that produced separate, perfect, and immutable species, each containing its own defining essence (Everitt 2004: 101). That such an idea appears in the Bible is not surprising. It expresses the ancient human cognitive bias to believe that design requires a designer, which is the foundation of our hard-core essentialism that species have immutable essences (Hood 2009: 62). Coyne (2015: 2) refers to Darwin's book as "the greatest scripture-killer ever penned," which refutes all biblical postulates by explaining patterns of nature that earlier could only be accounted for by invoking a supernatural designer.

Similarly, the philosopher Sahotra Sarkar (2007: 39) states that Darwinian evolutionism "permanently removed divinity from nature, ensuring that the organic world should never again be regarded as the special handiwork of a divine 'Creator.'" It is for this reason that Dawkins (1996: 4) feels that it was Darwin, not Hume who delivered the ultimate death blow to the design argument. Darwin demonstrated how the evolution of species by descent through modification based on the mechanism of natural selection explains the design features that engrossed Paley. This obviated the need to resort to paranormal or supernatural forces to explain the diversity of life on earth. As Darwin (1887: 279) put it in his autobiography, "The old argument of design in nature, as given by Paley, which formerly seemed to me so conclusive, fails, now that the law of natural selection has been discovered."

Darwin's *Origin of Species* represents a sustained effort to scientifically resolve the problem of design addressed by Paley (Ayala 2016: 286). Darwin pointed out that organisms do display design and complexity, but this design is the outcome of natural selection that leads to the adaptation of organisms to their environments. Specifically, the mechanism involved is natural selection nonrandomly operating on random mutations in the contexts of specific environmental factors, or the interaction of chance and necessity (Ayala 2016: 314). The result is adaptation through differential reproduction.

The philosopher Daniel Dennett (2006: 243–44) provides a splendid description of precisely what Darwin's scientific explanation entails:

> a non-miraculous account: a massively parallel, and hence prodigiously wasteful, process of mindless, algorithmic design-trying, in which, however, the minimal increments of design have been thriftily husbanded, copied and re-used over billions of years.

Overwhelmed and flabbergasted by the astonishing advances in our scientific understanding of life on earth made possible by Darwin's approach, theists have ever since sought to demolish this rival of supernaturalism through more clever reformulations of the timeworn design arguments under such labels as irreducible complexity and cosmic fine-tuning (see below).

Religionists thus continue to cling to the design hypothesis praying for vindication. However, it must be stressed that science may eventually find a better alternative to the theory of evolution because science, unlike religious dogma, is continuously being updated with better understandings of the data or the discovery of new evidence. The alternative, therefore, is not between Darwinism and creationism but between Darwinian evolutionism and a better scientific theory. Thus, whatever an alternative to Darwinian evolutionism may be, it is unlikely that it will be anything that involves the supernatural beings described in the theists' specious antiquated holy books written thousands of years ago by ignorant and superstitious tribal people in the Middle East who knew next to nothing about the world and even less about the universe.

Religionists are operating under the deluded assumption that any legitimate rival to scientific evolutionism will, by default, validate their paranormal designer hypothesis (Schick and Vaughn 2014: 195; Stenger 2003: 94). As Ayala (2016: 326) observes, the failure of one explanation does not validate an alternative explanation. Each one stands or falls on its own evidentiary merits, not on the failure of an alternative. For instance, Darwinian evolution by natural selection was accepted because many tests sustained it. It was not adopted by default because Jean-Baptiste Lamarck's theory of evolution based on the inheritance of acquired characteristics was a failure. This religionist view stems from the logical fallacy of the false dilemma, which posits an erroneous either–or scenario, whereas, in fact, alternative explanations that depart from these two perspectives are always possible.

There is also no hope for the theists regarding theories about the origins of life, which is a phenomenon not addressed directly by evolutionism. Evolutionary theory is concerned only with the various developmental trajectories life took after it emerged rather than how it originated. However, several distinct scientific theories address the origins of life. While at the moment there is no scientific consensus regarding which one of these is the most plausible, what is clear is that none of these theories invoke ancestral spirits, ghosts, divinities, or a paranormal superman as creator (cf., Everitt 2004: 106).

## Paley Updated: Swinburne's Case

In his book *The Existence of God* (2004), Richard Swinburne has attempted to reformulate and update Paley's argument. He begins by looking at the temporal order of the universe. Natural events are not random, he points out, but specific kinds of phenomena always succeed other specific types of phenomena. This regularity is puzzling, he adds, because the universe should be chaotic, but it is not. For Swinburne (2004: 136) the orderliness of the universe requires explanation. Science can explain one type of order in terms of another kind of order, but it can never account for the existence of orderliness in the universe as a whole. Here, Swinburne interjects a "personal explanation" involving an intentional agency. He believes that a godless universe cannot be orderly and only a paranormal creator, that is, the Christian God (not Zeus, Shiva, Ahura Mazda, Ba'al, Ennead, Pacha Kamaq, or Plato's Demiurge), can account for the order we perceive around us. For Swinburne, the existence of order proves the existence of God because order is more probable than not if God is in the picture. So, we are back to the same story; there is something we cannot explain, so God did it! What is on offer is a clever restatement of Paley's position. However, what it demonstrates, as Ruse (2006: 27) has observed, is simply that the argument from design has not changed since the nineteenth century.

The first problem with Swinburne's argument is the assertion that the universe would be chaotic in the absence of God. Any posited universe that contains any objects and substances cannot be utterly chaotic because objects and substances are defined in terms of regularities, meaning that order is intrinsic to them (Everitt 2004: 90–93; Philipse 2014: 263). Thus, any universe that contains substances and objects will have some degree of order. An utterly chaotic universe is not possible. Or as Slezak (1996: 203) points out, "any world will look designed, however it came into being." If this is the case, then what is the justification of interjection the hypothesis about an order-creating supernatural agent? As Everitt (2004: 90–91) points out, even if we start with the premise that the universe could have been chaotic but instead displays order, we are left with the question of how the order we perceive appeared from chaos? If the answer is that God created it, God is defined by theists as a magical Super Being who is rational, good, and not whimsical or capricious, that is, orderly; then physical order is being explained in terms of divine order. The argument fails because order itself has not been explicated (Everitt 2004: 91). Thus, the theist is worse off than the scientist in accounting for the existence of orderliness in the universe.

Alternatively, if we say that the universe was emergent or self-creating, we are suggesting that a universe with a limited degree of order (a wholly chaotic universe is not possible, as noted) gave rise to more order. Hence, there is no need to opt for a "personal explanation" or posit or interject a theistic order-creator because the order we see in the universe arose from an earlier state of the universe. Personal explanations are grounded in superstition and paranormal ideation.

The theist is not satisfied with any eventuality that excludes a paranormal human-like agent or designer, meaning the Superman of superstitious ancient Middle Eastern tribesmen. Thus, Swinburne observes that we have two choices, either accept the existence of the universe as a brute fact or explain it by interjecting an intelligent agent. He prefers the latter (Swinburne 2004: 204). This choice is based on faith, and as Slezak (1996: 202) has put it, faith entails beliefs "without rational warrant." Hence, for the theist, the self-explaining, self-caused deity is the ultimate brute fact (Philipse 2014: 126). However, as theism lacks adequate justification, this choice is nothing more than a groundless opinion or wishful thinking.

Why God, and specifically the Christian one, seems the most plausible option for Swinburne is because theists assume the truth of the God hypothesis beforehand on faith and all the supporting theological ruminations and casuistry offered as a rationale for the existence of such an entity are mere pretenses and hyperbole. There is no effort to explain the paranormal agent Himself (Gaskin 1976: 342). In other words, theists accept the truth of the claim they are seeking to establish beforehand and hence are begging the question. As philosopher Jan Narveson (2003: 103) sums it up, natural theology is thus smoke and mirrors, it lacks content, and the evidence referred to is "beside the point."

The non-theist can easily counter Swinburne that the most plausible option is to choose the emergent self-causing universe as the ultimate brute fact, one that obviates the tribal fantasy of an invisible Super Being and the medieval credulities that have sustained that antiquated myth. The unavoidable conclusion is that there is no divine intelligent designer. In an earlier time, it may have been reasonable for people to think that there was widespread evidence for a divine designer because of their superstitious background knowledge (Cordry 2006: 278). Science has long since repudiated these credulities. Religious apologists, such as Swinburne, however, sadly continue to tout these ancient and medieval absurdities although they no longer carry any weight in most quarters.

## What Would a Designed Universe Really Look Like?

If God created humans as intelligent beings who seek ultimate spiritual meaning, as theistic philosophers claim, then he would have had good reasons to incorporate design features explicitly at all levels and scales in the universe to make sure that humans could readily and unmistakably perceive and appreciate the design in the structure of the universe. In other words, design should be a prominent feature of every aspect of the world and the universe. Yet, this is not the case at any level. As the philosopher Benjamin Cordry (2006: 277) points out, looking at the universe on a cosmic scale there are no signs of design. Globular and spiral galaxies are entirely the outcome of material forces and are no more designed than a hurricane or a clod of dirt. Furthermore, the distribution of the galaxies is random and chaotic. Indeed, as Cordry (2006: 277) adds, there is nothing in the arrangement of the universe that conveys meaning to us. There is no concrete symbol of God, nothing that says humans are at the center of the universe, and nothing to suggest a cosmic architecture.

It is no different at the smaller scale of the solar system, Cordry adds. There are no aesthetic reasons for the arrangement of the planets anywhere. Mars's red color or the craters of the moon have no reasons. There are no messages in any of these things. Similarly, the position of the earth, its tilt, its geography, the shape and arrangement of its continents, or the fact that it has one moon are meaningless (Cordry 2006: 278). In sum, contra religionists, we find no design principle underpinning such things as the number and distribution or structure of the galaxies, the number and arrangement of the planets, or the topographical features of the earth. Yet, these are what we would expect if some intelligent entity designed the universe with a human-focused purpose in mind.

Given this fact, once again, we must ask: Why are so many people convinced that design and purpose are all around? Why is there a proliferation of creating myths, theologies, and dogmas across cultures and through time attesting the existence of supernatural designer-creator(s)? As noted earlier, these are explicable in terms of human teleo-functional cognitive biases that compel us to believe that a purposeful, intelligent agent must have wound up the universe at the singularity, touched off the Big Bang, and fashioned the algorithms of evolution (Bering 2013: 59). It is not surprising that theologians and creationists have devoted considerable amounts of time and effort forwarding design arguments for the existence of this purported deity. The irony in all of this, as Bering (2013: 107–8) observes, is that creationists are using "their mindlessly evolved theory of mind to make meaning of the meaningless." In other words, to reiterate, creationists have misconstrued an evolutionary-based cognitive illusion for a mind-independent feature of the world and the universe.

## Taking Reverend Paley to the Microbiology Laboratory: God's Handiwork in Molecular Structures

Religionists refuse to terminate their efforts to salvage the fallacious design argument, which they think holds their best hopes for refuting the detested theory of evolution. Another reformulation of the argument is offered by the advocates of "Intelligent Design," the pseudo-scientific branch of the crusading evangelical Christian movement in the United States. The primary objective of these ardent supernaturalists is to make Jesus, evangelical Christianity, and the medieval bunkum that supports it the center of American society, culture, and education (Pandian 2002: 2373) and replace science with the Bible (cf., Forrest and Gross 2004). As anthropologist Jacob Pandian (2003: 164) has pointed out, this is an effort to reinstate what Church fathers managed to do during the early medieval period, which is to make religion, specifically the Christian religion, the only legitimate "true knowledge" about the natural world and the human condition. However, this effort to amalgamate ancient Middle Eastern creation myths and "science" is an oxymoron and is simply "using the vocabulary of science to foster biblical discourse as scientific" (Pandian 2003: 168).

This program, carried out under the deceptive and oxymoronic label of "creation science," lacks any overarching research agendas to produce new knowledge or to test innovative theories. Its only purpose is to demonize science, attack evolutionary theory, and forward a religious agenda founded upon archaic superstitions and nonsense (cf., Forrest 2002: 80). The efforts of these purveyors of supernaturalism and merchants of superstition, to quote Thomas Paine (1776) once more, is an example of "Jesuitical cunning which always endeavors to disgrace what it cannot disprove."

The fact that it is impossible to transform the design argument into a scientific research program unmasks the vacuous and intellectually barren nature of this perspective. One might consider taking creationist claims seriously if they were to provide any novel or innovative ideas instead of touting the same arcane nonsense under the smokescreen of scientific-sounding jargon. If this were not the case, creationists would have established such an enterprise long ago. These zealots have no positive theory of their own, and their purported scientific explanations entail the same antiquated assertion, "God did it" (Sober 2006: 105). There is a simple reason for this failure. As mathematician David Shotwell (2003: 49) puts it, by opting for a supernatural hypothesis "anything goes" because the supernatural "provides no direction for research, suggests no testable hypotheses, and gives no reason to expect one result rather than another from any observations or experiment."

The paragons among these purveyors of supernaturalism keep promising that the bright young scholars who have joined their ranks will soon usher in significant breakthroughs in this area (e.g., Dembski 2003: 95). But what does this mean? That these young geniuses will provide evidence that the beliefs of delusional, ignorant, and barbaric tribesman in the Middle East who lived and died thousands of years ago are actually true? No such breakthroughs have come forth, and it is doubtful that any will appear anytime soon.

Given that Intelligent Design is bereft of any scientific foundations, its proponents attempt to justify their stance by appealing to the unfortunate broad popular support for creationism in the United States. Thus, William Dembski (2003: 89), a mathematician and leading philosopher in the movement, asserts that lots and lots of people in the United States believe that there is some sort of design in the world. Therefore intelligent design must be valid. Dembski acknowledges the logical fallacy of argument by popular consensus but still goes on to assert that the validity of Intelligent Design is clear because it is on its way to becoming "mainstream" in the United States. Really? Is this the most persuasive case to be made? Masses of people believing in the most outlandish absurdities is a recurring theme in human history. I have already discussed the horrifying consequences that often ensue when science is perverted to our wishes and desires and when alternative forms of knowledge supplant evidence through expedience, political fiat, votes, or agreement of groups. This is the road to Lysenkoism, Fascism, and Nazism. Is this what is advocated? This question is all the more crucial in the current climate of post-truths, anti-science irrationalism, and paranormal bunkum.

Popular consensus does not compensate for the problematic epistemic status of spurious claims. Nor does the fact that the public wants creationism taught in schools but not witchcraft or flat-earth geology as topics of study add to the credibility of Intelligent Design or distinguish it from other paranormal nonsense, as Dembski (2003: 90) maintains it does. We must not forget the regrettable fact that this public that believes in creationism also thinks that God was an ancient astronaut, demons exist, evil spirits cause diseases, witchcraft is real, prayers can cure cancer, and vaccines cause autism. This public also believes that Reptilian overlords run the US government, satanic ritual abuse is widespread, and that the US government and the Israeli Secret Service were responsible for the 9/11 attacks. Let us not forget the convictions that high-ranking officials of the Democratic Party are involved in a child prostitution ring and human trafficking using a local pizza restaurant in Washington, DC, as a front, NASA faked the moon landing, UFOs are extraterrestrial spacecraft, Elvis lives, and that aliens frequently visit peoples' homes and give them anal probes. Intelligent Design and these other "mind-rotting rubbish" and paranormal bunkum, as the skeptic Arthur C. Clarke (2003: ) put it, are all aspects of the cultural backwardness into which we have descended.

Proponents to Intelligent Design and scientific creationism are present-day self-appointed "ambassadors from heaven" who, like their many historical counterparts described so well by David Hume, will forward any specious and duplicitous arguments and make use of all types of pious frauds in support of what they perceive to be a holy or meritorious cause. There are, of course, many other examples of evangelicals engaging in such acts of pious impostures. One notorious case is the story that has been going around evangelical circles since the end of the nineteenth century, and espoused by some of the founders of creation science, about a British sailor who lived in the belly of a whale for many days (Noll 1994: 187), as discussed in Chapter 1. This was pseudoscience harnessed in support of Christian supernaturalism. Edward Davis (1991: 234), a historian of science who demonstrated the fictitious nature of this tale, described the motives of those who perpetuated this fraud:

> [They] wanted more than anything else to give people reasons to believe, to strengthen their faith in the gospel by strengthening their faith in the literal words of the Bible, to debunk the claims of atheistic scientists and apostate theologians. What better way to do this than to use scientific evidence itself as a weapon against the scoffers? [...] I want to emphasize that there was nothing unique about [their} anxiety. The tendency to muster pseudoscientific "facts" to defend the reliability of scripture against biblical critics was absolutely characteristic of much evangelical and fundamentalist literature of the period. This represents a significant change from the general state of affairs in the 19th century, when a number of highly respected Christian scholars had produced a substantial body of literature harmonizing solid, respectable science with the faith of lay believers. [...] However, there is no comparable body of literature from the first half of the present century.

Creationism, which attempts to harness scientific evidence to debunk science, is a grand pious fraud. Thus, as Dennett (2006: 61) explains, the work of creation scientists is characterized by shoddy arguments, misrepresentations, and evasions presented under the facade of science. Another of Thomas Paine's (1835: 295) observations is relevant here:

> There is scarcely any part of science, or anything in nature, which those imposters and blasphemers of science [...] have not, at some time or other, perverted or sought to pervert to the purpose of superstition and falsehood.

It seems that not much has changed in the religionists' agenda since Paine's time. Among the many tactics creationists use is to call foul by claiming that the close-minded scientific community is concealing the flaws in evolutionary theory by denying critics of evolutionism a fair hearing. They thus forward their deceptive anti-science agenda by portraying themselves as akin to Galileo Galilei, the lonely seekers of truth victimized by a callous and dogmatic academic establishment (Sarkar 2007: 95). The strategy, we might recall, is also used by paranormalists and purveyors of all sorts of other bunkum. The flaws of this ploy have already been discussed.

### *What Is Irreducible Complexity and Does It Prove "God the Designer"*

The central claim of creation dogmatists is that intelligent design is perceptible in complex biological systems that they characterize as "irreducibly complex," which they present as a challenge to Darwinian evolutionary biology (Behe 1996, 2001). Here is yet another version of Paley's case, as the philosopher Graham Oppy (2006: 188) points out, although its principal proponent the biochemist Michael Behe makes scientific pretensions by declaring that his objective is not to prove the existence of the God of monotheism but merely to offer evidence of an intelligent designer of some sort. Yet, Behe's claim to fame is that he has discovered the undeniable evidence of God's handiwork, and hence proof of his existence, at the molecular level.

While Behe confidently takes the credit for formulating the concept of irreducible complexity, this idea, as the philosopher and evolutionary biologist Francisco Ayala (2016: 321) has pointed out, was already articulated by none other than Paley (1802: 175–76) himself:

> When several different parts contribute to one effect, or, which is the same thing, when an effect is produced by the joint action of different instruments, the fitness of such parts or instruments to one another for the purpose of producing, but their united action, the effect, is what I call relation; and wherever this is observed in the works of nature or of man, it appears to me to carry with it decisive evidence of understanding, intention, art [i.e., a designer].

Moreover, as Shanks (2006: 161) has brought to attention, in modern times the idea of irreducible complexity had been proposed ten years before Behe by the late biochemist Alexander Graham Cairns-Smith (1986). However, Cairns-Smith did not resort to the paranormal to explain such complex structures and avoided the god-of-the-gaps fallacy (see below). He noted the silliness of invoking supernatural forces to explain something for which at present lacks a natural explanation, especially given the fact that many similar puzzles have been solved by science (Cairns-Smith 1986: 6).

Behe denies that he is a creationist and affirms his belief in science (Behe 1996: 5). By deemphasizing his supernaturalism, he is thus claiming much less than Paley did. One fails to see any distinctions here, however, because the putative designer in question is an intentional paranormal being, the invisible Super Being of theism. Indeed, elsewhere, Behe acknowledges the theological implications of his assertions. It should be noted that while in secular forums, proponents of Irreducible Complexity are disinclined to identify the supernatural designer as God, even unashamedly suggesting that the designer could be an extraterrestrial or a time-traveling biologist. In other settings, they openly express their religious and superstitious fervor. This is highly disingenuous. These zealots avoid explicit references to God to present Intelligent Design as a scientific rather than religious alternative to evolutionary theory that should be taught in schools bypassing the US Constitution that prohibits the teaching of religious dogma in public educational institutions (Ayala 2016: 315, 322).

Before examining the details of Behe's argument, it is necessary to point out several issues that undermine the case before it starts. First, why is complexity a criterion for intelligent design? One would think that a truly intelligent all-powerful paranormal designer would make the most efficient streamlined products that have no redundancies, which require no cobbling together of components, and whose creation is not wasteful, necessitates no algorithmic design-testing, and does not need the many massive extinction of species. That is how evolution through natural selection works, not divine magical creation. Perceptions of complexity, as biologist and hierarchy theorist Daniel McShea (1991: 319) suggests, may in part involve some innate human cognitive bias that leads us to perceive a cat to be more complex than a clam, even though by comparing their components and arrangments such a determination is not a straightforward task. In other words, humans think in terms of complexity, patterns, and causes. As already discussed in Chapter 6, that is how evolution has structured human minds. Creationism, as stated before, is a cognitive illusion. Complexity may be a relevant criterion for humans and in the context of naturalistic evolutionary processes, but for the putative divine designer, who can do anything whatever, operates magically under no material constraints, and is outside the scope of any physical laws, complexity may not even be a design parameter.

Second, why is the evidence of the so-called designer's handiwork so recondite that we have to search for it at the molecular level? This contradicts the theistic philosopher Plantinga's (2011: 248) assertion that design is not inferred but rather is a belief that is formed in an immediate or basic fashion, meaning that it is self-evident. After all, the creator God of intelligent design has not only fashioned all that we see, but He is said to be actively involved in the world. But if all of this is true, then why is clear and irrefutable evidence of his handiwork so hard to find? As the philosopher Benjamin Cordry (2006: 277) asks: if there is divine design in the world, why is it not a predominant attribute of what is all around us?

Here theologians resort to the inane idea of "argument from hiddenness," as noted before, which holds that God loves humanity and wants to have a personal relationship with people but conceals himself for good reasons (Swinburne 2004: 212). By veiling himself, the reasoning goes, God can find out who will act morally or immorally on their own volition. But why would God want to entrap in this way his miserable subjects with whom he wants to have a freely chosen loving relationship? Besides, as an omnipotent and omniscient being, one would think that God already knows what is in peoples' hearts and minds. So why does the purported all-knowing, all-powerful, all-loving paranormal entity need to play such a malicious and childish game of hide-and-seek? The hiddenness argument, of course, is an ad hoc postulate intended to give the theist hypothesis intrinsic unfalsifiability, which is a common strategy used by proponents of all pseudoscientific, psi, and paranormal claims, of which this is an example (Boudry and Braeckman 2011; Boudry et al. 2010: 239).

Third, it appears that before investigating the possible direct and indirect evolutionary pathways that can account for purported irreducibly complex structures, Behe has jumped to the conclusion that scientific explanations for the phenomenon in question are in principle impossible and interjects a magical designer (i.e., the Christian God) into the equation. Behe is thus committing the common and gross fallacy of "argument from ignorance" (aka god-of-the-gaps fallacy).

### *Intelligent Design and the Argument from Ignorance*

Advocates of Intelligent Design have failed to heed the caveat voiced long ago about this problem by the Scottish evangelical lecturer and biologist Henry Drummond. In his "Lowell Lectures on the Ascent of Man," Drummond (1896: 426) excoriated "reverend minds" who incautiously argue for God's existence from phenomena science cannot as yet explain, or from "gaps which they fill with God." Their concern, he added, is not with what science can explain but with what it cannot and that their "quest is ignorance, not knowledge." This tactic is always a risky maneuver, given the spectacular growth of scientific knowledge, how science has solved one purported inexplicable problem after another, and the "accumulated force of centuries of practical accomplishments" that characterizes the history of science (Overall 2003a: 159).

The eminent evolutionary biologist Theodosius Dobzhansky (1967: 13) long ago made the following observation regarding the fallacy of arguing from ignorance:

> There are people [...] to whom the gaps in our understanding of nature are pleasing for a different reason. These people hope that the gaps will be permanent, and that what is unexplained will also remain inexplicable. By a curious twist of reasoning, what is unexplained is then assumed to be the realm of divine activity. The historical odds are all against the "God of the gaps" being able to retain these shelters in perpetuity. There is nothing, however, that can satisfy the type of mind which refuses to accept this testimony of historic experience.

### *The Case for Irreducible Complexity and Its Flaws*

Having outlined these preliminary quandaries, we are now in a position to evaluate the case of Irreducible Complexity. Behe does not deny that evolution through natural selection is operative, which is wise given that the scientific evidence for it is overwhelming. Instead, he asserts that the volition of a paranormal intelligence is at work *in addition* to natural selection. What is not explained is why this intelligent designer, who is purportedly all-knowing, wise, and competent, has chosen to inefficiently double the effort by dividing the workload of creating between one set of mechanisms that are mindless, wasteful, violent, bloody, and operate naturally and another that works under his direct omniscient magic. Behe's position thus grossly violates the principle of parsimony (Ockham's Razor) and clearly dispells his scientific pretensions. However, this critique would be applicable only if what is on offer is scientific. It is not! Behe is a paranormalist and the purveyor and advocate of supernaturalism disguised as science.

So what constitutes an irreducibly complex biological phenomenon? According to Behe's (1996: 39) definition, irreducible complexity refers to

> a single system that is composed of several well-matched, interacting parts that contribute to the basic function, and where the removal of any one of the parts causes the system to effectively cease functioning.

We might note that Behe does not provide a concrete definition of complexity other than as something that is juxtaposed in contrast to simplicity. Yet, such a definition is necessary if we are to compare purported irreducibly complex biological systems, such as the bacterial flagellum at the micro-level to the process of eye-building at the macro-level (Forrest and Gross 2004: 82).

To clarify what he means for his scientifically naïve readers, Behe uses the analogy of the common five-part spring-operated mechanical mousetrap. Here the mousetrap is the equivalent of Paley's pocket watch or telescope.

> A common mousetrap has several parts, including a wooden platform, a spring with extended ends, a hammer, holding bar, and a catch. Now, if the mousetrap is missing the spring, or hammer, or platform, it doesn't catch mice at all. Therefore, it is irreducibly complex. It turns out that irreducibly complex systems are headaches for Darwinian theory, because they resist being produced in the gradual, step-by-step manner that Darwin envisioned. (Behe 1996: 39)

The basic idea is that such a structure could not evolve by natural selection because it requires that all the beneficial mutations occur at the same time (Sarkar 2007: 99). This analogy is then extended to putative irreducibly complex biochemical systems that are said to operate as integrated wholes and which would cease to function with the removal of any of the interlocked constituent parts. In other words, the component of such systems by themselves have no selectable functions and as such are therefore useless. Since natural selection can only operate upon already functioning systems, irreducibly complex systems must have arisen as integrated wholes in "one fell swoop" (Behe 1996: 72). There can be only one explanation for this, design by a supernatural intelligent agent, and that agent can only be the Christian God.

The mousetrap, however, is a poor model for an irreducibly complex system and does not hold up because each of the five parts of the mousetrap can be shown to be useful on its own and hence selectable in different contexts. More importantly, it is not a good analogy because Behe has assumed that the mousetrap was created ex nihilo, all at once, in the manner that theists think God creates things. The mousetrap he describes is actually the outcome of numerous iterations of mouse-capturing device designs over an extended period, as indicated by the numerous patents on file. The mechanical mousetrap, to state it differently, was not designed and created out of nothing in one go but is based on various earlier mousetrap patterns. Behe's mousetrap is, as philosopher Niall Shanks (2006: 168) has demonstrated, a "technological hybrid, descended with modification from earlier traps in a complex, historical, evolutionary process." It is not a case of special creation as Behe treats it. Hence this device is inappropriate as a model for an irreducibly complex object.

Furthermore, it should be noted that in the same fashion as the purveyors of other paranormal claims, Behe is not above mendacity to capitalize on the scientific illiteracy and intellectual unsophistication of his readers. He reassures them that:

> There is no publication in the scientific literature—in prestigious journals, specialty journals, or books—that describes how molecular evolution of any real, complex, biochemical system either did occur or even might have occurred. (Behe 1996: 185)

This is an egregious misrepresentation (Ayala 2016: 329, 2007: 151). At the time, there were several papers published in peer-reviewed journals that addressed precisely this issue (see Catalano 2004). Darwin (1859: 189) himself had tackled the question of complexity.

> If it could be demonstrated that any complex organ existed, which could not possibly have been formed by numerous successive, slight modifications, my theory would absolutely break down. But I can find out no such case.

There is also the work of Cairns-Smith (1986) mentioned earlier. Behe believes that irreducibly complex systems are a demonstration that such arrangements could not have been produced through "numerous, successive, slight modification," reiterating Darwin's words, and concludes that the Darwinian theory of evolution has been refuted. Like the proponents of other paranormal mysteries, Behe attributes enormous significance to his own work and feels that it has earned him a place among the intellectual giants of science:

> The result of these cumulative efforts to investigate the cell—to investigate life at the molecular level—is a loud, clear, piercing cry of "design!" The result is so unambiguous and so significant that it must be ranked as one of the greatest achievements in the history of science. The discovery rivals those of Newton and Einstein, Lavoisier and Schrödinger, Pasteur, and Darwin. (Behe 1996: 232–33)

One could grant this intrepid scientific trailblazer such honors if only his case were sound. Sadly, it is not! Behe's work has received considerable thoughtful scientific evaluation and has been found to be wanting. Moreover, his ideas have not compelled evolutionary biologists and anthropologists, individually or en masse, to abandon the sinking ship of Darwinian evolution, as creationists would have it.

The case of Irreducible Complexity suffers from various problems. First, as in the case of Paley, Behe makes an unwarranted inferential leap from functional order to the designer. To bridge the inferential gap requires independent evidence about who designed the object in question, how, and for what purpose. The failure to offer such evidence, as already noted, is the flaw in all design arguments (Shanks 2006: 166–67). Second, as Oppy (2006: 188–96) has shown, there is nothing in principle to indicate that irreducibly complex biological systems cannot result from numerous successive, slight modification. Third, let us suppose that an actual irreducibly complex structure comes to light for which Darwinian evolutionary theory has no explanation. That fact alone is not sufficient to justify inferring that the cause is the God of theism, or for these ideologues the Christian God. Yet, apologists such as Plantinga (2011: 264) and like-minded religious polemicists wager heavily that Behe's irreducible complexity offers support for theism over naturalism. As already noted, the spurious creationist assumption is that any evidence that could count against evolutionary theory by default counts in favor of their God hypothesis. It does not. Claims to knowledge stand or fall on their own respective evidentiary merits.

While Behe includes in his portfolio of antievolution evidence such phenomena as the cascade of blood clotting proteins and antibody production in the immune system, the showcase of Irreducible Complexity is the bacterial flagellum, a structure that is really an ion-driven rotary engine used for swimming. The flagellum has gained iconic status among Intelligent Design creationists (Sarkar 2007: 111). The Intelligent Design ideologue William Dembski (2003: 94), for example, affirms that this case is definitive proof of God's direct intervention in the world and does not foresee any possibilities that a non-paranormal explanation is ever likely to be provided.

Behe presents the bacterial flagellum as a complex molecular machine, the non-selectable, non-functional constituent parts of which were produced at the same time to work as an integrated system. This is his showcase example that Darwinian evolutionism is false. However, scientific research on genes and proteins comprising such structures has demonstrated that several proteins of the flagellum are fully selectable and functional in different contexts. One such case is the secretory pump, or syringe, known as a type III secretory system, found in the *Yersinia pestis* bacteria that causes the bubonic plague. This syringe is used to inject toxins through the host cell membranes into the cytoplasm. Molecular investigations of the proteins in this secretory pump have shown that they are directly homologous with the proteins in the basal section of the bacterial flagellum. In fact, 80 to 88 percent of the proteins in the flagellum have homologs in other structures (Sarkar 2007: 113). Hence, the flagellum is itself a type III secretory system (Miller 2006: 85). Therefore, the required beneficial mutations of the parts of irreducibly complex structures do not have to co-occur. Complexity, in other words, can arise incrementally, and fragments of the flagellum can operate fully for a different function (Sarkar 2007: 113).

Moreover, the indication is that the bacterial flagellum is not an irreducibly complex structure as defined by Behe (Liu and Ochman 2007; Miller 2006: 85; Pallen and Matzke 2006). Indeed, the bacterial flagellum is an excellent example of the cobbling together or mix-and-match opportunism of the evolutionary processes that produce novel functions (Miller 2006: 87). The mistake Behe has made is to assume that the parts of complex systems have always had their present functions. He makes the same mistake in treating the mechanical mousetrap as a device created all at once in its current form and function. There are numerous examples of a component selected for one function that is subsequently adapted for another function. Hence, because the individual parts of Behe's molecular machine that is said to be only functional as a whole have demonstrable selectable functions, the irreducible complexity hypothesis is refuted. Scientists have convincingly demonstrated that biological structures such as the flagellum and other organs are not irreducibly complex, and never come about in one fell swoop (Ayala 2007; Brauer and Brumbaugh 2001; Miller 2006; Pennock 2002)

To state this differently, because the flagellum contains within it a smaller functional group of components, such as the type III secretory system, it does not qualify as an irreducibly complex system (Miller 2006: 85). Thus, the assertion that the flagellum could not have evolved because the total system had to be created first to produce a selectable function is false. Not only is Behe's example not irreducibly complex, but there are also questions about whether irreducible complexity even exists in nature, or whether very complex structures have been misrepresented as such by Intelligent Design polemicists (Darper 2002; Everitt 2004: 108; Pigliucci 2003: 104).

As an aside, it may be noted that the entire question of complexity is a problem in many fields. To address this issue, different operational definitions would be necessary. For instance, the basic pentadactyl appendage in extant vertebrates ranges widely from highly derived in the leg of the horse to a much reduced, simple flipper of the dolphin. So the real question would be, which one is more complex or more "evolved?"

The evolutionary steps leading to the development of bacterial flagellum is an example of a *structure co-option pathway* that operates at every organizational level, not just at the molecular one (Sarkar 2007: 101–2). Another example at a different organizational level is the feathers of birds. Feathers evolved from scales, and any intermediary form between scales and feathers would not produce flight. However, feathers provide excellent thermal insulation, and there is evidence that feathers were first selected for this purpose. Feathers initially developed for thermal regulation and later incorporated into a more complex system for flight (Sarkar 2007: 102). Thus, like the efforts of Paley and Swinburne, the endeavor to salvage the fallacious design argument by the oxymoronic creation scientists is an abject failure.

## Looking for God's Handiwork in the Cosmos: Taking Reverend Paley to Outer Space

From the effort to find evidence of God's handiwork in molecular structures and biochemical pathways, some creationists have shifted the search for such evidence to the features of the universe as a whole. This perspective is called the argument from fine-tuning or the *anthropic principle*, a term coined by the Australian theoretical physicist Brandon Carter (Barrow and Tipler 1988; Davis 1992; Rees 2001). The discussion provided here is because cosmic fine-tuning is a paranormal hypothesis that is part of the religionists' case against science.

The basic idea is that intelligent life depends upon the fundamental physical forces to be exactly as they are, and any deviation would have rendered such life impossible (Everitt 2004: 91). The fine-tuning thesis, in other words, holds that carbon-based life would not exist if the fundamental properties of the universe were slightly different from what they are. The *anthropic coincidences* refer to basic numbers in physical theory, the values of which make life possible. These include such things as the strength of electric forces holding atoms together, the strength with which atomic nuclei bind together, the number that determines the amount of matter in the universe, the number that allows galaxies to form, and so on (Shanks 2006: 205–7).

It is reasoned further that it is highly improbable that random factors are the cause of the existing properties of the universe. Random here indicates anything not due to the handiwork of a purported intelligent agent (Shotwell 2003: 48). Thus, given that there is an improbable life-permitting universe rather than the more probable life-prohibiting one, it is posited that some non-random supernatural intelligent power fine-tuned the universe to permit the emergence of sentient life. Without such critical adjustments, life would not have emerged. No natural force can account for these numbers, believers maintain, and science has no explanation. Therefore, the fine-tuner had to be the God of Abraham, although one would think that Quetzalcoatl, Shiva, or Zeus would be equally suitable candidates for this achievement. Also, as mathematician David Shotwell (2003: 48) points out, the argument that the order of the universe is the work of an intelligent agent because that order could not exist otherwise is question-begging.

### *The Fine-Tuning Argument as Natural Theology and Physics Mysticism*

Fine-tuning falls in the genre of natural theology based on the well-worn argument from design discussed above (Slezak 1996: 203). In other words, the argument from fine-tuning is a theological claim, not a scientific one. It is one way to interpret a puzzling aspect of the universe, in this instance, the anthropic coincidences. It is not surprising that a theistic philosopher and Christian apologist such as Plantinga includes fine-tuning in his array of arguments and apologetics. The contention is that a fine-tuned cosmos is improbable under the non-theist hypothesis (Plantinga 2011: 224, 226). Placing so much weight upon fine-tuning is a significant risk given that this argument is not as conclusive as theists want or wish to believe.

First, let us ask the following question: What is enigmatic about people living in a sector of the universe that is suited to sustain human life? If humans did not occupy a position in the life-permitting zone of the universe, they would not be here to ponder that question. Life forms occur in "life-scapes," where it is possible for them to exist. Being puzzled by this is akin to being mystified about the facts that there are whales in the oceans and wildebeests and zebras on the Serengeti plains.

Here again, what is operational are the cognitive biases that make us see patterns, faces, design, infer intentionality, and to think of phenomena in animistic and anthropomorphic terms as mind-independent features of the universe. It seems that the inherent human cognitive bias for teleo-functional reasoning simply will not allow some people to discard the wearisome design argument. The fine-tuning data itself, a set of values or the fundamental constants, do not warrant inferences of intelligent designer any more than saying "the sky is blue; therefore God exists." Such arguments are forwarded entirely because of the personal religious and supernatural motives of their advocates. It is anthropocentric presumptuousness to think that the fundamental physical principles have something to do with us, with humankind. Whereas the fact of the matter is, as the physicist Steven Weinberg (1993: 253) points out, that "as we have discovered more and more fundamental physical principle they seem to have less and less to do with us." Positing anthropocentric significance for the cosmic fine-tuning, that is, inferring a divine paranormal plan in the universe in which humans have a pivotal meaningful role, reflects an overextension of our theory of mind and an expression of our teleo-functional reasoning in hyper-drive, imputing human-centered meaning to the entire cosmos. Or, to put it another way, this is an X-claim.

Physicists who advocate the fine-tuning argument are playing the role of scientific mystics by proclaiming that somehow the phenomena they are studying have spiritual meaning or significance beyond what is justifiably inferrable from the data. To reiterate a point made earlier, belief without any evidentiary warrant, as is the case here, is irrationalism and mystical bunkum. The publishing industry realizes that there are big profits in books written by scientists that tie astrophysics to God (Tyson 2003: 74). These publishers are catering to the same type of need that parapsychologists and New Age mystics and our home-grown ayatollahs attempt to meet, which is to bring God back into the picture and affirm the true spiritual nature of humankind. What is on offer, however, is merely irrational anthropocentric wishful thinking that attributes cosmic significance to human life. Certain people have been trying to retrieve this position for humankind since the days of Copernicus, Galileo, Hume, and Darwin.

In the same way that psi researchers seek to elevate the credibility of their mendacious pronouncements, the sponsors of fine-tuning also attempt to lend an air of respectability and authority to their claims by using the language of biochemistry, information theory, thermodynamics, astrophysics, and cosmology. Thus, they present inchoate and meaningless assertions in the form of erudite and scholarly sounding arguments brimming with mathematical equations and symbolic logic to emulate mainstream scientific research. Hapless readers are baffled with the endless and pretentious jargon and baffling and meaningless mathematical equations. As Dennett (2006: 242) puts it, none of this is very compelling or comprehensible to anyone who does not have a proclivity for math, theoretical physics as well as the "niceties of scholastic logic."

The creationist intellectual enterprise under discussion, to reiterate, takes us from the Scottish moorlands out into the cosmos, again in desperate search for Jesus and God, to resuscitate Paley's case yet again, but by shifting the focus to the design of the universe and physical laws rather than the entities made possible by those laws (Dennett 1995: 166). In other words, its proponents are merely trying to dignify the archaic design argument by bringing cosmology, physics, and scientific jargon into the equation. However, as Slezak (1996: 204) observes, all the new evidence has failed to bolster the basic design argument in any way. Indeed, he adds, the evidence of a finely tuned universe after the Big Bang is, in principle, no better than that available to Paley. Finally, he says that the vast insights of physics and cosmology do not warrant conclusions concerning intelligent purpose behind it and are no better than the animistic beliefs of preindustrial cultures that attributed intelligence to trees and rocks. Whether we are talking about rocks or the entire universe, the analogy is the same and equally deficient (Slezak 1996: 206).

The fine-tuning argument is also dubious because we actually do not know how much some constants can vary to make life impossible (Coyne 2015: 161). Moreover, the argument is not even innovative. It is a reformulation, down to the last word, of the standard run-of-the-mill design argument that the philosopher Bertrand Russell addressed in 1927:

> Everything in the world is made just so that we can manage to live in the world, and if the world was ever so little different, we could not manage to live in it. (Russell 1957: 9)

In his novel *Candide* (1759), the philosopher Voltaire offered a parody of this line of reasoning:

> It is demonstrable [...] that things cannot be otherwise than as they are; for all being created for an end, all is necessarily for the best end. Observe, that the nose has been formed to bear spectacles—thus we have spectacles. Legs are visibly designed for stockings—and we have stockings. (Voltaire 1918: 1)

### *Inferring God's Handiwork from Cosmic Features: Isaac Newton and Laplace's Response*

Using features of the cosmos to infer God's handiwork is not an original idea. Isaac Newton provided a version of this in 1792. For him, the unwavering arrangement of the planets and their moons and why the celestial bodies do not shatter through gravitational forces and centrifugal motion could only be explained through miraculous fine-tuning by God. For an eminent scientist such as Newton, who was a significant actor in the Scientific Revolution, to lapse into this type of supernaturalism may surprise some. However, Newton was not the earliest of the scientific geniuses but the final paranormalists or sorcerers (see White 1998). As the British scholar John Maynard Keynes (1947) put it,

> Newton was not the first of the age of reason. He was the last of the magicians, the last of the Babylonians and Sumerians, the last great mind which looked out on the visible and intellectual world with the same eyes as those who began to build our intellectual inheritance less than 10,000 years ago.

Newton's explanation turned out to be a god-of-the-gaps argument because the French physicist and astronomer Pierre-Simon Laplace accounted for the problem by proposing his nebular hypothesis that explains the orbits of the planets and their movement as well as the formation and evolution of the solar system. Laplace demonstrated that the behavior of heavenly bodies could be adequately explained using his physical theory without the need to postulate a supernatural fine-tuner or Divine cosmic engineer (Philipse 2014: 163).

There is more to this story. On one occasion, when Laplace presented the French ruler Napoleon a copy of his book on astronomy, the monarch asked why he did not mention the Divine author of the heavens. To which Laplace famously replied, "Sire, I had no need of that hypothesis" (Ball 1895). Whether or not this incident is apocryphal, it reflects the mood of the time. By the end of the eighteenth century, scientists and astronomers had become convinced that explanations for astronomical phenomena should never invoke paranormal forces (Philipse 2014: 163). Philipse (2014: 163) maintains that this is why Paley concluded that biological phenomena rather than astronomical ones were the best place to seek evidence of God's handiwork (Paley 1802: 199). But, as we have seen, Paley also ventured into the god-of-the-gaps territory when Darwin convincingly demonstrated a naturalistic mechanism for the evolution of life on earth.

### *The Theological Underpinnings of the Fine-Tuning Argument and Its Inconsistencies*

The fine-tuning perspective is a personalized or intentional explanation for an event—in this case, the creation of a universe suitable to generate human life by an intentional supernatural being with motives and a particular and almost obsessive interest in human beings. However, the theological underpinnings of this line of reasoning are arbitrary, absurd, and meaningless. We are again presumptuously told that God created the universe to allow the genesis of humans because He loves people, consciousness, or souls. But a race of spirit beings would not suit His purpose because souls as moral agents need to be embodied physically, hence the reasons for the creation of the physical universe (Swinburne 2004: 130). No compelling explanations are put forward for why embodiment is necessary for this purpose. Theologians ruminate that thus embodied and emplaced human souls could on their own efforts and volition develop moral character through the physical hardships they encounter in the world (Bradley 2001: 463). Such suffering provides humans with an opportunity to freely choose to believe or not to believe and to be good or evil.

In other words, all the evils and hardships on earth are in place for a good reason by the benevolent Creator, which is the basis of a pernicious theistic rationalization for the existence of human suffering (theodicy), discussed in an earlier chapter. Thus, once again, we are supplied with the designer's motives and intentions. Theologians never tell us how they know such details. All of this, of course, raises the same problem encountered by proponents of other versions of the design argument. That is, how they can decipher the creator's motives and intentions in the absence of independent background information in a non-arbitrary fashion without resorting to anthropomorphic projections? The fine-tuning argument is, of course, arbitrary and nonsensical.

Cordry (2006: 279) correctly observes that the fine-tuning argument really amounts to "writing the significance of human life into the cosmos." It says that "the laws of nature are what they are so we can exist" (Weinberg 1999). The argument is a religionist effort to undo Copernicus and Galileo who knocked humans off the pedestal at the center of creation and cast them adrift in a callous, purposelessly, and impersonal universe. It is another way of counteracting what the German sociologist Weber referred to as "*die Entzauberung der Welt*," or science taking "the magic out of the world." However, the entire discussion is pointless to begin with because theists are striving to explain an unknown, that is, why there are anthropic coincidences, by postulating another unknown, the involvement of an all-powerful paranormal spirit Being for whose existence there is absolutely no scientific evidence.

Here we encounter the fallacy of the false dilemma once again. Efforts to determine the significance of anthropic coincidences are in the form of an either–or choice between intelligent fine-tuning and blind luck. There is no evidence to suggest that these are the only options (Shanks 2006: 211). Creative nonpersonal forces, Plato's Demiurge, Hume's unintelligent infant deity, or a senile and ludicrous superannuated deity are as plausible as the suggestion that a gigantic invisible anthropomorphic being, that is, the Christian God, put the universe together because He "loves us" (Martin 1990: 133). In other words, fine-tuning does not warrant the inference that the God of theism is responsible for the anthropic coincidences. To demonstrate that such a being is involved requires non-arbitrary independent evidence that tells us how and why these anthropic constants occur in the first place. Theological musings based on archaic superstitions are not sufficient. That ludicrous, contradictory, and gibberish-filled sacred texts written long ago by ignorant and superstitious tribesmen in the Middle East say that a designer was involved in the creation of the universe does not suffice (see Chapter 10). The stories in these tomes, which portray the creator as a Sumerian bricklayer who divides his task into days, and even takes a one-day holiday, are at best farcical. What is needed is proof that a non-corporeal paranormal being exists, is capable of designing a physical universe, had reasons for wanting to do so, and what those reasons were.

As the philosopher of physics John Earman (1987: 314) points out, the anthropic principle expresses nothing more than "a lack of robustness of explanation, of the standard hot Big Bang scenario" that potentially could be explained by further theoretical developments. Science does better and better all the time, but we can never know everything at any given time. The words of the British geneticist and evolutionary biologist John B. S. Haldane (1927: 298) are appropriate here: "Now my own suspicion is that the universe is not only queerer than we suppose, but queerer than we can suppose." Given that the universe is so odd and peculiar, there will always be a lacuna in our knowledge in which one can cram God. Physicist Richard Feynman's (1992: 208–9) remarks are relevant:

> God was always invented to explain mystery [...] to explain those things that you do not understand. Now when you finally discover how something works, you get some laws which you're taking away from God; you don't need Him anymore. But you need Him for the other mysteries. So, therefore, you leave Him to create the universe because we haven't figured that out yet; you need Him for understanding those things which you don't believe the laws will explain, such as consciousness, or why you only live to a certain length of time—life and death—stuff like that. God is always associated with those things that you do not understand.

Attributing causality to a super-agent said to possess knowledge beyond what we have is intuitive and comes naturally because we continuously over-attribute our theory of mind and agency detection. However, such a move is erroneous. These ideas constitute X-claims and tell us more about how human minds can be hijacked by paranormal ideation rather than shed light on the workings of the universe.

As for probabilities and coincidences, the extant universe may be a low-probability event, but low-probability events do happen (see Chapter 7). To quote Ronald Fisher (1937: 16) once again: "for the 'one chance in a million' will undoubtedly occur, with no less and no more than its appropriate frequency, however, surprised we may be that it should occur to us." Alternatively stated, unanticipated things happen from time to time without the need for us to suppose supernatural forces as their cause. The philosopher of science John Worrall's (1997: 11, 13) words on this issue are worth repeating:

> It is notoriously easy to play the coincidence game. Coincidences—"massively improbable" events can be created at will—especially if you are happy not to think too sharply about what you treat as the random variables underlying probabilities. Even in cases where probability talk is justified, it's just plain silly to say that some event has such a low probability of happening that it "cannot have happened by chance"—chance is what governs both high and low probability events: low probability events tend to occur less often. [...] by insisting that some feature of the universe cannot be accepted as "brute fact," we cover up our inability to achieve and deeper, testable descriptions in some sort of pseudo-explanation—appealing without any independent warrant to alleged a priori considerations or to designers, creators and the rest.

Along the same lines, evolutionary biologist Jerry Coyne (2015: 163) points out that if we are the inhabitants of the only universe, the simple explanation for the cosmic fine-tuning is that we got lucky and drew the perfect hand in the bridge game of the cosmos. In fact, the entire argument is incoherent and meaningless because it attests to the improbability of an event that has already taken place (Carroll 2015).

### *Does Fine-Tuning Imply the Existence of a Fine-Tuning Deity?*

Rather than delve further into the probabilities and coincidences of possible life-permitting or life-prohibiting universes, here I shall focus on further inconsistencies of the theological foundations of the fine-tuning argument. The reason is that no matter what words are in use and the number of adroit scientific-sounding jargon terms and flummoxing and extraneous mathematical equations harnessed to the task, this is a paranormal claim, not a scientific one. First, even if being puzzled by the fine-tuning of the physical constants of the universe is warranted, inferring the God of theism from this fact does not follow (Earman 1987: 314). As already noted, there are plenty of other equally plausible supernatural candidates for this job. Second, it makes no sense for a being who is by definition a supremely intelligent, non-capricious being who desires to produce human moral agents to have created a universe the natural evolution of which in the first instance was not life-permitting and then need to fine-tune the whole thing to make specific sectors of it life-permitting (Everitt 2004: 96). As an omnipotent being, God could just have easily fine-tuned life to any universe, rather than fine-tune the universe for life (Coyne 2015: 162). As the philosopher Jan Narveson (2003: 99) observes, the fine-tuning argument "implies that the Deity prefers vastly improbable ways of bringing about intended results (the existence of people) to the much more plausible ones He could have done at the drop of the divine hat." Moreover, the fact that the universe is conducive to human life under only a minuscule set of unlimited possible states suggests that there is no design, or that there is poor design (Licon 2015: 417). It is stupid rather than intelligent design.

If the theistic hypothesis is correct, then everything about the universe becomes baffling. If God had the objective of creating humans, as the philosopher Philipse (2014: 312) asks, why is the universe not constituted on a human-compatible scale, as a finite system with the earth at its center, as stated in the Book of Genesis? Instead, the universe is an estimated 2 million trillion miles across and contains 100 trillion galaxies, each with a billion star systems (Everitt 2004: 217). Also, if theism is on the mark, then the universe, galaxies, and planets should be teeming with sentient life. Yet life is exceedingly scarce, and most of this expanse is inhospitable to life (Philipse 2014: 145). Nearly 80 percent of all matter in the universe is dark matter that cannot be detected and is inert rubbish. As Everitt (2004: 217) asks, what explains this scale and the massive amounts of celestial stuff of which the majority of humans who have lived or will ever live will never become aware? All of this renders the theistic hypothesis very unlikely if God aimed to create the universe to foster human life.

Another question, as Coyne (2015: 165) asks, is why did God wait to create life so late in the evolutionary history of the earth, some 10 billion years after the universe came into existence? Why is it that for 99.99 percent of that time, humans, who are said to be "the jewels of creation," were missing (Everitt 2004: 218)? And as Cordry (2006: 284) points out, the scarcity of intelligent life, why there is life on earth and not on Mars or the other planets, and the "deafeningly barren cosmos" all refute the theistic proposition that God values intelligent life. The universe is not a cradle for life; living things are "not at home here." He adds that it is "stultifyingly perplexing that the things God finds to be 'good' and 'very good' are so exceptionally scarce" (Cordry 2006: 284–85). This should not be the case if God engineered the universe to contain intelligent, spiritually minded human life.

Circumstances on planet earth also fail to support the theistic hypothesis. Up to 70 percent of the planet is inhospitable for human life, and the world seems to be out to get us. Think of the number of our hominin ancestors who did not make it. Evolution has permitted us just barely to hang on (Coyne 2015: 165). Cordry (2006: 285) points out how scarce and thoroughly conditional life is on earth. Most life forms fail to develop to maturity, and life is constantly at the mercy of chance. Instead of this planet being a sanctuary or incubator for life, he adds, here life is under continual threat from external forces.

Moreover, for up to half of the total time life has existed on earth, bacteria have been the sole form of life. Regarding abundance, hardiness, temporal durability, adaptability to the most extensive range of habitats, genetic variability, and overall biomass, bacteria surpass all other life forms (Everitt 2004: 218). By all measures, these organisms seem to have been the dominant form of life on this planet. Thus, as Everitt (2004: 218) points out, if God loved life and activated his divine powers to enable such life to flourish, the recipient of such divine favor is bacteria, not people. There are other candidates as God's favored creatures, for example, insects. These are among the most successful life forms on earth. They are estimated to exist in the trillions, as opposed to a few billion humans, which would suggest that God fine-tuned the universe for bugs and creepy crawling things (Shotwell 2003: 48).

The theistic hypothesis also makes no sense from a biological standpoint. For an omnipotent being to choose to facilitate the emergence of human and animal life on earth via the process of evolution, which is a mindless, ruthless, and wasteful process, is incompatible with His purported omnibenevolence. As the philosopher of science Adolf Grünbaum (2001: 32) queries, how does theism explain the numerous mass extinctions and the horrible ways species have perished that characterize the planet's biological history? For theists to say that God had competing goals in mind when he created these things and set processes in motion only further undermine the purported power of the God hypothesis.

Swinburne (2004: 189) claims that God evolved humans rather than create them in one fell swoop because the process is beautiful. Moreover, God is said to have created animals in this way because of his desire for them to have pleasant sensations. Really? These are merely doleful theological rationalizations for what no theology can justify or explain away. Cordry (2006: 284) notes that considering evolution beautiful given the mass extinctions, wastefulness, and terrible violence it entails begs the question.

Furthermore, beauty is not a species-independent property of objects, and we cannot assume that the universe as a whole is beautiful to anyone. Theologians who claim that it is are spouting pure nonsense. Beauty and ugliness are attributes of local phenomena (Philipse 2014: 277). Some things are beautiful, and some are ugly. Asteroid impacts and lunar craters and mass extinctions are sinister, not beautiful. How are dark matter and dark energy, which are now thought to consist of the greater part of the universe, beautiful? Also, what proof is there that animals have more pleasant sensations than unpleasant ones?

As Philipse (2014: 277–78) sums it up, if God designed the universe to host humans and other life forms, then it would have been an entirely different place. Billions of years would not have passed before the appearance of life and life would not be so exceedingly rare given the spatial vastness of the universe. In a designed universe, the planets of the solar system should have been teeming with life, but they do not. The geology and geography of the earth should be based on aesthetic principles or convey meaningful messages, but they do not. He adds that the notion that the universe is fine-tuned for human life is as absurd as a fly in the palace of Versailles thinking that the palace was built especially for it (Philipse 2014: 277–78). But given the scale of the universe, this is an understatement.

Similarly, religionist efforts to explain the horrible circumstances confronting humans during their brief tenure as individuals on earth, and even the suffering of nonhuman life forms, as morality building (at least for people) and as "good disguised as evil" leads to a perverse justification of cruelty and suffering. We are back to theodicy and the argument from evil. One could reasonably argue that the anthropic principle is not an indication of God's love for humans but is intended to ensure the existence of humans so that they may suffer to the fullest extent all the hardships of life, sickness, become decrepit, and die miserable and pathetic deaths as most do.

As the philosopher Michael Martin (1990: 124) puts it, existential hardships humans confront are more than adequate to build character. The excessive suffering that exists, sometimes to the point of crushing individuals, cannot be explained away by the postulate that it is about moral character. Also, if this is God's method for bolstering moral souls, it is not working out very well. Finally, the theistic perspective fails to explain the massive pain and suffering before the advent of *Homo sapiens* experienced by nonhuman life forms that, according to theism, cannot develop a moral character. This is why Hume (1779: 186) was so puzzled about the Creator's motives for not preventing evil in the world and queried, quoting Epicurus:

> Is God willing to prevent evil, but not able? Then he is not omnipotent. Is he able, but not willing? Then he is malevolent. Is he both able and willing? Then whence cometh evil? Is he neither able nor willing? Then why call him God?

### *What the Anthropic Principle Says about a Purported Paranormal Fine-Tuner*

Even if we accept the theist argument and assume that the anthropic principle does, in fact, suggest a designer, we encounter a significant quandary. Given the problematic and miserable predicament of humans and animals on earth, we have to conclude that the creator of the universe is a malevolent rather than a benevolent being (Smith 1992: 348). Such an evil entity would want a universe with intelligent life, as much as a benevolent God, because actualizing moral evil necessitates the presence of intelligent life as much as achieving a moral good. An evil agent cannot unleash its malevolence on inanimate matter but can exercise the immense cruelty it desires and get the full effect of its malice if there are sentient beings with nerves and feelings, who are conscious of suffering, injury, and can experience painful and premature deaths. Bolstering the likelihood that the designer and fine-tuner is a malevolent spirit is the vast amount of seemingly random natural evils. While religionists have tried to argue that natural evils are, in fact, good, their argument collapses under its own weight.

One common tactic used by apologetic theologians attempting to address the existence of evil is to assert that it is all part of "God's plan" for a higher purpose. Really? How do these theologians know this? Did God reveal his plan to them directly? Do they have unique cognitive sensitivities and special mental acumen to comprehend the will of God that everyone else lacks? Or are they making up fairy tales? The justification that religious apologists such as Swinburne (2004: 207–8) offer to account for evil and suffering is that the positive benefits made possible by them obviate their negative values. These include expressing generosity, compassion for the victims of evil, which gives humans a chance to investigate and prevent its future occurrence (Philipse 2014: 296). As the philosopher Quentin Smith (1992: 350) correctly points out, however, this is a "self-evidently false moral principle."

The absurdity of this theist assertion is evident as soon as we apply it to the Nazi Holocaust, the Hiroshima and Nagasaki atomic bomb blasts, the Khmer Rouge killing fields in Cambodia, the millions of agonizing deaths caused by AIDS, and the Rwandan and Bosnian genocides, to name just a few of the pleasantries of recent human history. For rational human beings, no quantity of present or future good, be it compassion, knowledge, remorse, or opportunity to cure an incurable disease, outweighs the total evil and horrors of such dreadful events (Philipse 2014: 296). It requires little thought to realize the perverse nature of this so-called higher-order good defense offered by religious apologists. The philosopher John Stuart Mills (1874: 187) rightly described this effort not only as intellectually contradictory but also as one that "exhibits to excess the revolting Jesuitical defense of moral enormities."

Another strategy to exonerate God is to blame the evils of the world on humans. Granted humans cause wars, big and small. However, they do not make cancer, AIDS, polio, typhus, or the bubonic plague (Narveson 2003: 101–2). Humans do not generate earthquakes, landslides, hurricanes, and tsunamis (fracking causing earthquakes and deforestation causing landslides aside). Inane assertions that evil exists because God is punishing us for our sins or our souls are being tested to enable us to morally mature are unconvincing excuses and arbitrary bunkum and an attempt to address the cognitive dissonance of holding contradictory sets of beliefs. Another strategy is to bring up the so-called free will defense. However, genocidal maniacs murdering countless innocent people, sinless children included, are not excused because they are expressing their free will. Besides, why does God allow such behaviors to go on in the first place? How is cancer associated with free will? Does this exculpate the Creator?

"Gratuitous evil" abounds in the world. There are too many and too serious evils on earth, both natural and moral, which seem pointless and gratuitous despite the "higher order good defense" (Philipse 2014: 187). And as Smith (1992: 350) observes, in light of the pervasiveness of evil one cannot but conclude that natural evils are gratuitous. It follows that an all-powerful, all-knowing, and perfectly good God does not exist because such a being would not allow any gratuitous evil. However, such evils are precisely what one would expect if a malevolent supernatural being created the universe. Smith (1992: 350) concludes that "if any spirit created the universe, it is malevolent, not benevolent."

Alternatively, as a rival to the theistic thesis Shotwell (2003: 49) proposes the "gremlin hypothesis," which not only explains all aspects of the universe but also solves the problem of evil:

> Each subatomic particle is inhabited by a ghostly little gremlin. Each gremlin maintains the existence of its particle by a continuous creative act and is in instantaneous telepathic communication with all the others. By this means, they cooperate to produce the universe and its lawful behavior. This hypothesis "explains" everything that exists and every event that occurred. It accounts for those nasty features of the world that are so troublesome to believers in an omnipotent and perfectly benevolent creator; they exist because the gremlins are mischievous and, in some respects, malevolent.

Based on the discussion in this chapter we can conclude that the design argument, including its irreducible complexity and cosmic fine-tuning versions, is not only inadequate but that this idea, in fact, works against the theist contention regarding a benevolent creator God. Paley provided the most exhaustive case for the design argument. It was conceptually devastated by Hume and laid to rest by Darwin. Efforts to resurrect the design case by proponents of irreducible complexity and fine-tuning have not fared much better. These efforts involve wishful thinking by would-be science mystics and frantic religionists. These versions of the argument fail for the same reasons Paley's case collapsed.

# Chapter Twelve

# THE MIRACLES OF THE BIBLE: THE QUINTESSENTIAL FOUNDATIONS OF PARANORMAL BELIEFS IN WESTERN CULTURE

*The writers of the New Testament cannot be regarded as trustworthy witnesses to the resurrection—first because they were not eye-witnesses; second, because they were the slaves of a bewildering Old Testament exegesis and numberless current superstitions; and third, because they had little or no conception of any distinction between objective fact and subjective impression.*

—Charles Gorham, *The First Easter Dawn* (1908)

*We entertain a suspicion concerning any matter of fact, when the witnesses contradict each other; when they are but few, or of a doubtful character; when they have an interest in what they affirm. […] There are many other particulars of the same kind, which may diminish or destroy the force of any argument, derived from human testimony.*

—David Hume, *Enquiries Concerning the Human Understanding* (1748)

*What we remember about an incident can actually be changed after the fact. When this happens, the witness truthfully testifies to remembering something that never happened.*

Terence Hines, *Pseudoscience and the Paranormal* (2003)

The crux of the religionist assault on science and anthropology is the assertion that their supernatural and paranormal view of the world and universe based upon a Christian "evidence base" and "positive theistic arguments" provides a superior explanatory framework. In doing so, as noted before, religionists have made their theistic premises a legitimate subject for scientific and anthropological scrutiny in the tradition of systematic skepticism. In this chapter, therefore, I focus on the core premises of this "evidence base" and attempt to find out how well they hold up under such scrutiny and whether or not the religionist claim about the superiority of their supernatural framework, or what the theistic philosopher Plantinga calls an "Augustinian Science," has any evidentiary justification. The approach is the same one I use when evaluating similar types of evidence in the context of any other anthropological analyses of supernatural and paranormal claims. This entails an examination of historical records, textual analysis in relation to anthropological findings, use of the principles of evolutionary and cognitive psychology, prior probabilities, the presence or absence of disconfirming evidence, and the availability of non-supernatural explanations that accord with the empirical evidence.

The starting place for such an inquiry is, of course, to look at the supernatural and paranormal events described in the Bible. These constituted the foundational beliefs of the "evidence base" offered as a better alternative to the scientific worldview. In his book *The Supernatural, the Occult, and the Bible* (1990), biblical historian and archaeologist Gerald Larue has shown the powerful impact of the pervasive supernaturalism of the Bible on contemporary magical and paranormal thinking. It is here that we find the description of the archetypal paranormal events in Western culture, the miracles of Jesus, and the resurrection. One expects that if substantial and convincing evidence of the paranormal and supernatural exists anywhere, it should be in these texts that believers have for 2,000 years considered accurate historical descriptions of the miraculous origins of their faith. But given what we have discussed about paranormal and supernatural phenomena, human cognitive and psychological dispositions, eyewitness testimony, and the problematic nature of anecdotal evidence, we are justified in asking whether the events in question happened in the manner and scale described in this sacred and revered holy book.

## Who Narrated the New Testament Stories, Who Wrote Them Down?

Our investigation must begin with an assessment of the sources. Everything we know about the paranormal events in question comes from anecdotes and stories offered by members of the Jesus cult (the Jews who became the first Christians) after the death of their rabbi. Their stories were circulating by word of mouth among the early Christian communities for decades, passed on from person to person before they were written down. Bear in mind that what appears in the relevant information in these texts came from second-, third-, or even fourth-hand accounts, not from anyone present at the time of the purported events in question.

We may begin by asking several questions: What sort of people provided this information? Who were they? From where did they come? What were their backgrounds? How did they look at the world and their place in it? It is easy to forget that these individuals lived in a time and place entirely alien to us. It was a world governed by magic where many thought they were experiencing strange paranormal happenings all the time (Cotter 1999). This world also contained an abundance of prophets, oracles, miracle workers, and raisers of the dead who could foretell the future, restore sight to the blind with mud and spit, heal spleens with a touch, and routinely resurrect cadavers (Shapiro 2016: 123).

Based on historical evidence and the New Testament texts, the people in question were illiterate and deeply superstitious, fantasy-prone members of a fanatical eschatological cult (Acts 4:13; Carrier 2010: 305–8). Or, as the critical historian and philosopher Charles Gorham (1908: 132) put it, they were "ignorant and superstitious" folk "filled with Messianic expectations and proneness to the marvelous." The French philosopher and philologist Ernest Renan (1866: 22) similarly observed that Jesus's disciples were a simple uneducated lot who "believed in phantoms" and experienced miracles all around.

Consummate hallucinators and spirit-channelers, these persons fell into trances en masse, had group visions, spoke in tongues, believed that God communicated with them in dreams and visions, became spirit possessed, and were susceptible to psychosomatic maladies (Acts 2:1–13; Carrier 2014a: 124). As the philosopher Thomas Sheehan (2008: 110) points out, among these personages ecstatic visions and manifestations were frequent events. These paranormal experiences included theophanies, or seeing God (Acts 7:55), angelophanies, seeing angels (Luke 1:11), receiving revelations (Galatians 1:1–12), and having epiphanies of returning prophets (Mark 8:28). In many ways, the Jesus cultists are reminiscent of the members of the Melanesian cargo cults, to mention one anthropological example, who also fell into spontaneous, self-induced group trances, had visions, spoke to God and the ancestors, confirming the truth of the revelations of their prophets (Sidky 2015: 209).

The noted French Enlightenment writer Paul-Henri Thiry (Baron d'Holbach) (1813: 9, 259, 273) characterized the Jesus cultists as ignorant and rude individuals possessing an indefatigable credulity who were susceptible to accepting the most contradictory, unintelligible, and revolting doctrines and mysteries. The philosopher of religion John Hick says something similar in his book *The Metaphor of the God Incarnate* (1993: 16), noting that during the early "apocalyptic phase of the Christian movement the canons of plausibility were very different from those operating within today's mainline churches."

As simple and highly superstitious people lacking any critical thinking skills, the early Christians were easily swayed by any charismatic conman with a good story, ready to greedily accept without examination "whatever soothes superstition, and promotes wonder," as David Hume (1902 [1748]: 126) would have described it. The Greek rhetorician and humorist Lucian of Samosata captures the gullibility and superstitious nature of the early Christians in his satire *The Death of Peregrinus*, a story written as a denigration of superstition. Lucian describes the exploits of Peregrinus, a Greek Cynic philosopher and con artist who joined the church to take advantage of the credulous Christians:

> It was now that he came across the priests and scribes of the Christians, in Palestine, and picked up their queer creed. I can tell you, he pretty soon convinced them of his superiority; prophet, elder, ruler of the Synagogue—he was everything at once; expounded their books, commented on them, wrote books himself. They took him for a God, accepted his laws, and declared him their president. The Christians, you know, worship a *man* to this day,—the distinguished personage who introduced their novel rites, and was crucified on that account. Well, the end of it was that [Peregrinus] was arrested and thrown into prison. This was the very thing to lend an air to his favourite arts of clap-trap and wonder-working; he was now a made man. The Christians took it all very seriously: he was no sooner in prison, than they began trying every means to get him out again,—but without success. Everything else that could be done for him they most devoutly did. They thought of nothing else. […] Their officials bribed the gaolers to let them sleep inside with him. Elegant dinners were conveyed in; their sacred writings were read; and our old friend Peregrine (as he was still called in those days) became for them "the modern Socrates." In some of the Asiatic cities, too, the Christian communities put themselves to the expense of sending deputations, with offers of sympathy, assistance, and legal advice. The activity of these people, in dealing with any matter that affects their community, is something extraordinary; they spare no trouble, no expense. Peregrine, all this time, was making quite an income on the strength of his bondage; money came pouring in. You see, these misguided creatures start with the general conviction

> that they are immortal for all time, which explains the contempt of death and voluntary self-devotion which are so common among them; and then it was impressed on them by their original lawgiver that they are all brothers, from the moment that they are converted, and deny the gods of Greece, and worship the crucified sage, and live after his laws. All this they take quite on trust, with the result that they despise all worldly goods alike, regarding them merely as common property. Now an adroit, unscrupulous fellow, who has seen the world, has only to get among these simple souls, and his fortune is pretty soon made; he plays with them. (Lucian of Samosata 1905: 79)

Lucian's story may be satire, but his account of the credulity of besotted believers spellbound by supernaturalism is not off the mark.

All of this makes clear the absurdity of efforts by some present-day apologists to portray the early Christians as sound critical thinkers who would never have accepted the miracles associated with Jesus had they not possessed overwhelming evidence (e.g., Boyd and Eddy 2007: 64–66; Ellens 2008b: 1; Keener 2019; Wright 2003: 690). Moreover, such a suggestion also goes against what we know from history and anthropology regarding the beliefs of ancient peoples and present-day small-scale cultures. There is no good reason to dismiss characterizations of the early Christians as miracle mongering, hallucination-prone credulous people living in a world steeped in superstition (cf., Fox 1986: 117), contra Allison (2005: 201). As the skeptic Paul Tobin (2009: 360) points out, those who saw and heard Jesus were uneducated, ignorant, uncritical, and superstitious. This weighs heavily upon their credibility as witnesses to the historicity of biblical miracles. The people we are talking about, therefore, are the worst kinds of informants or witnesses to be found.

## The Nature of the Texts

But what about the written accounts in the New Testament, especially the canonical gospels? Did critical and meticulous scholars systematically and carefully assemble these texts? Who were the authors of these fabulous texts? Did the gospel writers check their facts? When were these texts written? These questions are crucial to this discussion.

We know that in the early stages of the Jesus movement, the transmission of the teachings of the cult was by word of mouth. Its members felt no need to write down their beliefs because as part of an eschatological cult they imagined that the end of the world was upon them (Hoffmann 1984: 27). At this stage, the Christian movement was sprawling and uncoordinated, characterized by a diversity of views and incompatible theologies (Doherty 2005: 126, 124; Goguel 1953: 6). However, as time passed, Jesus's apocalyptic prophesy was not realized, "the New Jerusalem" did not descend from heaven, and the original members of the cult began to die one after another (Spong 1995: 58). By this time, the oral traditions were starting to falter and diverge even more, and the concerns of the emerging church were taking priority. Thus the need arose to write the stories down (Loftus 2010: 318).

The four canonical gospels (the Synoptic Gospels and the Gospel of John), the principal texts that describe Jesus's miracles, were not written by his disciples but by evangelists many years later (Philipse 2014: 173). Moreover, as discussed below, these texts do not constitute four separate and independent accounts but are all based on a single and highly problematic source. These facts contradict the common belief among most Christians today—a belief that has been around for more than two millennia (Doherty 2005: 240)—that four individuals named Mark, Matthew, Luke, and John, who were close personal associates or students of Jesus, wrote the gospels. The conviction is that these men followed Jesus around during his brief one-year (Mark, Matthew, Luke) or three-year (John) ministry, watched him perform miracles, heard his sermons, and provided four independent transcripts of his life and accomplishments in Galilee and the events after his terrible death in Jerusalem. None of this is true (see Helms 1988, 1997, 2006).

Jesus's disciples were Aramaic-speaking Galilean peasants who, as noted, were illiterate and could not have written anything (Ehrman 2009: 105–6; Herzer 2001). If Jesus himself could read and write, he left no written accounts. Although Christian apologists claim that the gospels are eyewitness reports (Bauckham 2006: 6), it is now solidly established that this is not the case (see Redman 2010). These texts were written 40 to 70 years after the crucifixion by educated but completely anonymous authors. These individuals wrote in Greek and lived somewhere in the Greek-speaking areas of the Roman Empire far from the location of the events they describe (Ehrman 2009: 103–4, 2014: 73, 2016: 73, 100).

Moreover, the authors of the gospels were not historians but zealous evangelical propagandists, whose carefully crafted texts were intended to convince readers that Jesus is the risen Son of God (Parsons 2005: 440). Present-day apologists are merely preying on the trust and naïveté of their audiences when they affirm the historical accuracy of these narratives (Price 2011: 219).

The philosopher Porphyry of Tyre (died c. 305 CE), a fierce third-century opponent of the Church, called the evangelists who wrote the gospels "inventors, not narrators" (Wells 1996: 40). As an aside, the Christians destroyed Porphyry's books *Philosophy from Oracles* and *Against the Christians* of which only short quotes survive in the works of apologists who tried to provide refutations. It was the same with the works of many other critics of the Church, such as Celsus's book *On the True Doctrine* (see Cook 2000; Labriolle 1930, 1935; Wilkens 1984). Apologists such as Ellens (2008a: 1), who claim that had the stories about Jesus and his miraculous deeds been untrue "there would have been significant numbers of voices raised to counter the claims," are espousing nonsense. There were such voices, but they were silenced through book burning and other types of censorship by the Christians.

On the historical reliability of the gospel, Gorham (1908: 13, 16) wrote that their authors were not historians but unknown superstitious persons with imperfect knowledge of the facts living in an age of ignorance and credulity. The tales that have been passed down are of unknown origins and are "saturated with belief in miracles" and mythical elements. None of these persons, he adds, were eyewitnesses to any of the events they describe, including the resurrection of Jesus. From their writings, it is evident that they were unable to differentiate fact from subjective impressions and they labored under the influence of "bewildering Old Testament exegesis and numberless current superstitions" (Gorham 1908: 82).

Similarly, the noted historian of early Christianity Raymond Hoffmann (1984: 7) observes that the gospels, which were written around two generations after the events allegedly occurred, were not intended as biographies or historical tracts. They comprise the missionary propaganda of the cult of Jesus. Their authors had two objectives: (1) to express their belief that Jesus was the Messiah by picking select prophecies from the Old Testament; (2) to convert others to join them. These texts easily betray their propagandist nature. For example, the author of the Gospel of Mark (16:15–16) has Jesus actually preaching the gospel, which means "good tidings," or the Church's post-resurrection announcement that Jesus has died for the sins of the world and is the risen Son of God (Wells 1996: 146).

Concerning the New Testament in general, scholars now agree that it is "an arbitrary hodgepodge of dubious literature of uncertain reliability" (Carrier 2010: 297–99). Moreover, the inclusion of numerous forgeries in this text indicates a "pervasive dishonesty" among the early Christians who excelled at making up stories, forging documents, and even fabricating entire gospels (Carrier 2010: 307; Ehrman 2009: 121–33, 2011). As such, it is difficult to trust narratives provided by essayists known to routinely tell pious lies to promote their perceived meritorious cause (cf., Price 2005a: 425).

To further complicate matters, we must keep in mind that none of the texts have survived in their original form. They are known to us through handwritten copies of copies, produced later, in some cases centuries later (Wells 1996: 70–71; Ehrman 2009: 48, 133–84). Moreover, as the philosopher Larry Shapiro (2016: 124) points out, every line and passage of the gospels have been influenced by errant translations and tendentious redactions throughout two millennia. Their untrustworthiness should, therefore, not even be a debatable issue. New Testament scholars have known for a long time that the original authors of these texts would have difficulty recognizing the versions that are around today (Shapiro 2016: 124).

## Are the Gospels History?

Finally, the fantastic paranormal elements central to these stories exclude them from the genre of historical works as understood today (Doherty 2005: 1). These include uncanny happenings, angelic visitations from the skies, strange earthquakes, eerie supernatural eclipses of the sun lasting hours, hordes of the living dead humans invading cities, people appearing and vanishing instantaneously, apparitions walking through locked doors, and corpses coming back to life everywhere. Take, for example, the description of the eerie happenings that purportedly transpired at the moment of Jesus's death on the cross found in the Gospel of Matthew (27:51–53):

> Then, behold, the veil of the temple was torn in two from top to bottom; and the earth quaked, and the rocks were split, and the graves were opened; and many bodies of the saints who had fallen asleep were raised; and coming out of the graves after His resurrection, they went into the holy city and appeared to many.

This is like a scene from a bad Hollywood horror movie. Some contemporary theologians take this passage as creative imagery of apocalyptic eschatology and the holy city as referring to a "new, heavenly Jerusalem" (Brown 1994: 1118, 1131). However, the statement that they "appeared to many" clearly suggests that Matthew is talking about an earthly appearance. No matter how we look at it, the eminent Bible demythologizer David Friedrich Strauss (1902: 694) was being munificent when he said, "[rendering] this incident conceivable is a matter of unusual difficulty."

Thomas Paine (1880 [1795]: 120–21) was particularly annoyed with Matthew's supernaturalism and blatant prevarication about this legion of reanimated dead saints. Had this fable been true, he points out, it would have become the central topic of many treatises. But this is not the case. Paine (1880 [1795]: 121) queried further why the author of Matthew did not tell us what happened to the reanimated saints, who saw them, whether they emerged naked, men and women saints, or if they were fully clothed. He also does not say whether the risen saints went to their respective homes, to reunite with their spouses, and claim their property, and exactly how their relatives received them. In his words, "Strange, indeed that an army of saints should return to life, and nobody knows who they were, nor who it was that saw them, and that not a word more should be said upon the subject, nor these saints have anything to tell us!" In light of such passages, Gorham (1908: 18) made the following pertinent comment about such absurdities in these holy books: "the Gospels themselves furnish ample evidence that their compilers were ignorant and credulous men, whose statements of facts cannot be accepted without investigation."

Apologists go to extreme lengths to provide reasons why we should consider this genre of propaganda and paranormal fantasy as historical evidence. The results of such efforts, however, are never flattering, As the philosopher John Loftus (2011: 76) observes: "the contortionist ways Christian apologists defend their faith makes otherwise intelligent people look stupid." Some writers in a display of mind-boggling naïveté and absence of critical acumen advocate that accounts such as the living-dead saints invading Jerusalem described in Matthew are possibilities. One such ideologue is Bishop Nicholas Wright, who states in his massive book *The Resurrection of the Son of God* (2003: 636) that "Some stories are so odd that they may just have happened. This may be one of them, but in historical terms, there is no way of finding out." Gorham's (1908: 96) comment is appropriate here: "Before such an exhibition of critical fatuity sober reason stands aghast."

New Testament scholar and theologian Dale Allison (2005: 304–5) maintains that those who reject the veracity of the gospel tales have a bias toward the paranormal and argues that the inclusion of implausible claims does not mean these narratives are devoid of actual historical materials. This special plea for the historical substance of the kernel of these tales is an old apologetic tactic that, as the classical scholar Reginald Macan (1877: 34–35) observed long ago, is merely an excuse for passing off "unhistorical" narratives as reliable history. The fact that the gospel writers had no qualms about adding supernatural implausibilities to their narratives raises suspicions that they probably added non-paranormal fictional materials to their texts as well. They were inventors, not recorders of facts.

## Assessing Christian Apologist Claims Regarding the Historicity of the Gospel Accounts

Present-day Christian apologists such as Richard Swinburne (2003: 1, 70, 74), William Craig (1998: 256–57), Nicholas Wright (2003: 695, 710), and Gary Habermas (2003: 15–32) affirm that the canonical gospels are undoubtedly accurate historical documents that contain reliable information regarding the events described. How do they determine that this is the case? Oddly enough it entails asserting the veracity of these texts by quoting the same texts. This involves a crude form of circular reasoning or the logical fallacy of begging the question (Pyysiäinen 2004: 162; Watson 1987: 366). The philosopher Robert Price (2011: 220) has compared this form of reasoning to the argument that "the Emerald City of Oz must exist, since, otherwise, where would the Yellow Brick Road lead?"

Here apologists have already encountered an insurmountable obstacle because the texts on which they anchor their arguments represent *the claim*, not *the evidence* for their supernaturalism (Espinoza 2013: 60). As Paine (1880 [1795]: 57) stated emphatically, before admitting the Bible as proof of something, the book itself must be shown to be true. Apologists overlook all of these issues and proceed on the assumption that the gospels provide historical support that God exists, that Jesus was God incarnate, and therefore, his crucifixion and resurrection make rational theological sense. In fact, as we shall see, the stories in question do not make sense and entail some of the most problematic, poorly documented, and dubious events in the entire history of Christianity.

### *Is There Evidentiary Parity between the Resurrection and Julius Caesar's Crossing the Rubicon?*

Wright (2003: 717) describes the resurrection of Jesus, the central miracle of the Christian faith, as an event with "a historical probability so high as to be virtually certain, as the death of Augustus in AD 14 or the fall of Jerusalem in AD 70." Another apologist, Douglas Geivett (1997: 185–86), asserts that the proof for the resurrection meets "the highest standards of historical inquiry" and is as certain "as Caesar crossing the Rubicon in 49 BC." These are remarkably overconfident statements. But are they true?

Historian and philosopher Richard Carrier (2006a) has soundly refuted these assertions. Briefly, Carrier provides five reasons why historians believe that an event such as Caesar and his legions crossing the river Rubicon took place: (1) there is Caesar's own account in his book *The Civil War*, a Latin classic for 2,000 years; (2) there are accounts of the crossing by Caesar's enemies, such as the Roman philosopher and statesman Marcus Tullius Cicero; (3) there are inscriptions and coins produced after the civil war referring to the event; (4) nearly every historian, including prominent scholars of the period, wrote about the crossing; (5) there are implicating consequence of the Rubicon crossing, such as Caesar's troops meeting and defeating the opposing legions in battle and ultimately the advent of the imperial era.

Carrier points out that comparable evidence for the resurrection does not exist. First, there are no written accounts by Jesus or any of his close associates and followers. Indeed, the utter absence of information about Jesus during his lifetime is startling (Carrier 2014b: 281–358; Doherty 2005: 199–222; Wells 1996). As the New Testament scholar Bart Ehrman (2011: 256) puts it, there are no records of his birth, no mentions of his words and deeds, not trial transcripts, no descriptions of his death, indeed there are "no references to him whatsoever in any way, shape, or form." Moreover, he adds, one cannot even find the name of Jesus in first-century Roman sources.

This near-total paucity of information about Jesus has, in fact, led some scholars to question the historical existence of such a personage comparing him to legendary figures such as King Arthur or Ned Ludd, the mythical founder of the Luddite movement (Carrier 2014a, 2012: 11–15; Doherty 2005, 2009; Wells 1996). Another such comparable mythical figure is John Frum, the shadowy messiah of the cargo cult religion on the island of Vanuatu (formerly the New Hebrides). The problem with historical nonexistence hypothesis is that the ferocious first-century opponents of Christianity did not deny Jesus's existence (Kurtz 2013: 114). However, the issue of Jesus's historical nonexistence is not relevant to the present discussion, although there is the fact that the Christians burned or otherwise destroyed numerous critical texts, some of which could very well have included such doubts about the historicity of the man.

There are many other sources, besides the canonical gospels that potentially shed light on the resurrection. These include the gospels of Thomas, Peter, Philip, Mary, the Hebrews, Judas, the Egyptians, and many more. The non-canonical status of these texts does not diminish their value as historical sources. None of these provides an account of the resurrection itself. Moreover, some of these texts do not even mention Christ's return from the grave, which indicates that there were significant variations in beliefs within different early Christian communities regarding Jesus and the idea of his alleged return after death (Gorham 1908: 138; Philipse 2014: 173).

What is on offer in all of the available texts constitutes second- or third-hand descriptions of the discovery of an empty tomb, that is, "resurrection narratives" (Perrin 1977: ix; Philipse 2014: 172). These tales comprise rumors and imaginative constructions regarding the whereabouts of a missing corpse. Moreover, as discussed in Chapter 7, even if eyewitness reports were available, they would be of limited use given what psychological studies have revealed concerning the unreliability of such accounts (see Schacter 1995). Indeed, based on what we now know about the constructive nature of perception and the various factors that affect memory and recall of events, eyewitness information of this type is the worst kind of evidence imaginable. These include such variables as bottom-up and top-down processing, hindsight bias, and selective memory. Especially relevant is the phenomenon of false memories and the fact that memory can easily be altered after the fact when subjects receive new information about an event. There are also the phenomena of groupthink and memory conformity based on a consensus about how an event transpired that is due to social dynamics rather than conformity to objective data or actual occurrences. Finally, there are all the massive reliability problems associated with anecdotal information. All of these factors impact the nature of testimonies and information about any event. Moreover, a further magnification of such distortions occurs when information about an incident is gathered long after the fact, in this case, many decades after the alleged happenings took place. These are the same sociopsychological processes involved in the generation of the Roswell UFO myth, the bogus nature of which is solidly established.

Second, there are no contemporary accounts of the resurrection from hostile parties, such as members of the Sanhedrin, Caiaphas (the Jewish high priest who masterminded Jesus's doom), Pontius Pilate, the Roman prefect of Judea, Herod Antipas, the ruler of Galilee and Perea, the Jewish and pagan scholars writing at that time, or anyone else. This silence is particularly puzzling given that the gospels tell us that Jesus's fame went throughout Syria and that he traveled in these places performing amazing miracles accompanied by his disciples and followed by a vast multitude of people "from Galilee, the Decapolis [the 'ten Greek cities' in eastern Palestine], Jerusalem, Judea, and the region across the Jordan" (Matthew 4:24–25). The sources also relate how the miracle-worker from Nazareth delivered numerous sermons to large crowds all over Judea, astonishing the masses with his teachings and marvelous deeds (Fitzgerald 2010: 24). Yet there is not a word of this in any written accounts from that time. We have nothing until the gospels were written decades after the supposed time of the crucifixion.

Similarly, there is no mention by any contemporary writers of the astonishing and miraculous phenomena that supposedly occurred at the time of Jesus's death and rising, as described in the problematic passages in the Gospel of Matthew (27:51–54), such as the earthquake and the hordes of dead people coming back to life. If such dramatic events had occurred, they would surely have been noticed and recorded by independent sources, such as historians, philosophers, or anyone else. Once again, we have nothing.

Third, there is no physical evidence for the resurrection. There are no inscriptions, commemorative monuments, or coins that declare "year two of the era of Jesus Christ," or anything else (Carrier 2006a). If we accept the veracity of what the gospels say about Jesus's burial site, the vacant tomb contained nothing to be used as evidence for the resurrection. As the philosopher Larry Shapiro (2016: 115) puts it, "an empty tomb is an empty tomb," and it is "as much evidence of the work of body snatchers, tomb robbers, or extremely rapid decomposition" as it is of a resurrection. These suggested alternatives, including overnight disintegration and vanishing of the body, are just as plausible as the idea that a dead man came back to life after three days, which is something that has never happened anywhere on earth at any time. Moreover, as discussed in Chapter 15, there is considerable evidence that the story of the empty tomb was an expedient fictional embellishment suited to the needs of the evangelists writing long after the death of Jesus. In other words, there is a very high probability that there was no empty tomb!

Fourth, none of the known contemporary historians mention the resurrection. Jewish scholars living at the time, such as Justus of Tiberias or Philo of Alexandria, do not provide any such information. Philo, who was a contemporary of Jesus, wrote nearly fifty works that are still extant, covering topics ranging from history to religion. He talks about Pontius Pilate, yet he is silent about Jesus (Freke and Gandy 1999: 136). All of this is very puzzling.

Fifth, there are no implicating consequences of the events in question. The fact that the Christian religion spread after the death of Jesus as an implicating consequence has nothing to do with whether a dead man came back to life and strolled out of a tomb. The diffusion of this religion is explicable in terms of the same sociocultural, political, historical, and economic forces that account for the expansion and establishment of other faiths across time and space.

### *The Relevance of Josephus and Tacitus*

There is, however, a reference to Jesus who was "the Christ" who rose from death in the treatise *Jewish Antiquities* written sometime after 93 CE by the Jewish–Roman historian Flavius Josephus. Christian apologists incessantly cite this passage in support of their supernaturalism, and hence it requires some discussion. The significant text is as follows:

> Now there was about this time Jesus, a wise man, if it be lawful to call him a man; for he was a doer of wonderful works, a teacher of such men as receive the truth with pleasure. He drew over to him both many of the Jews and many of the Gentiles. He was the Christ [Messiah]. And when Pilate, at the suggestion of the principal men amongst us, had condemned him to the cross, those that loved him at the first did not forsake him; for he appeared to them alive again the third day; as the divine prophets had foretold these and ten thousand other wonderful things concerning him. And the tribe of Christians, so named from him, are not extinct at this day. (Josephus 2007, book 18, chapter 3.3: 964)

For centuries this passage has been a favorite bit of evidence among Christian apologists. It has been discussed so frequently that it has acquired the label *Testimonium Flavianum* (meaning the testimony of Flavius Josephus). Predictably, as the biblical scholar Robert Eisler (1931: 41) observed, "critics of the passage were chiefly philologists, and its defenders theologians." Eisler (1931: 36–37) adds that this passage would have been of immense value to Christian apologists because we have an unbelieving Jew and adversary of the faith reluctantly acknowledging Jesus as the true Christ foretold by the prophets endowed with the miraculous power of the Redeemer. The implications, he adds, are that "even the princes of the synagogue, who handed him over to death, acknowledged him to be God." This refutes those who doubt that a Christian interpolation in which a Jewish historian makes references to Jesus is pointless and of no use for apologetic purposes (e.g., Meier 1991: 64).

There are solid reasons to conclude that this passage is indeed a later Christian embellishment. First, it is very probable that if Josephus wrote about Jesus, he would have used terms like "false messiah," "blasphemer," and "charlatan." He had a great disdain for the many messianic figures of his day and considered them all to be brigands and impostors responsible for the destruction of Jerusalem. Second, as an orthodox Jew, Josephus would not have used this kind of flattering language or write sycophantic phrases such as "if it be lawful to call him a man" or "doer of wonderful works, a teacher," without providing explanations for his readers who were primarily Romans, as he does elsewhere in the book (Carrier 2014a: 334; Doherty 2005: 213). Nor would he have written that Jesus was "the Christ" who came back to life after three days and visited his followers, or that "the divine prophets had foretold these and ten thousand other wonderful things concerning him" without elaborating on the meaning of these points. Also, he would not have used the sentence alive on "the third day," which is a Christian creedal phrase, without explaining what it meant and discussing what happened to the man who came back to life (Carrier 2014a: 334). Josephus certainly would not have agreed that Jesus fulfilled biblical prophecy and "ten thousand other wonderful things" without explanation.

Throughout the book, Josephus talks about other individuals named Jesus, who he unambiguously identifies (e.g., Jesus, the brother of John; Jesus, the brother of Onias; Jesus, the son of Phabet; Jesus, the son of Sie; Jesus, the son of Damneus; and Jesus, the son of Gamaliel). However, he is silent about the identity of the Jesus mentioned in the *Testimonium Flavianum*, which strongly indicates the handiwork of a zealous Christian fabricator who presumed that everyone knew Jesus and did not bother to include the necessary descriptive information.

Moreover, Josephus does not explain why he suddenly alters the flow of his narrative to talk about this particular Jesus at that specific juncture in his text. The *Testimonium* appears amid his discussion of the misfortunes of the Jews, some of which transpired during the administration of Pontius Pilate. Skeptics have pointed out that the passage about a wise miracle-working teacher of the truth interrupts the logical structure and flow of the text, is inconsistent with the narrative about a series of national disasters, and must, therefore, be an interpolation (Eisler 1931: 43). The passage before it ends with an act of treason that leads to a massacre:

> there were a great number of them slain by this means, and others of them ran away wounded. And thus an end was put to this sedition.

The passage that follows says,

> About the same time also another sad calamity put the Jews into disorder, and certain shameful practices happened about the temple of Isis that was at Rome.

Following this second paragraph is a long, elaborate discussion of the religious controversy behind the event in question involving Judaism and the cult of Isis, which suggests that Josephus would have also elaborated upon the Christ passage if he had written it (Carrier 2014a: 336). Along similar lines, Wells (1996: 48) observes, if the flattering words used actually reflected what Josephus believed, he would not have limited his reference to such a short passage. It makes sense, however, that Christian interpolators would have inserted a reference to Jesus in between the two passages to correct Josephus's embarrassing silence on Jesus in the context of his discussion of Pilate (Carrier 2014a: 395; Wells 1996: 49).

Other clues also support the conclusion that this is a Christian fabrication. For example, Christian writers from the second, third, and early fourth centuries quote passages from Josephus but make no reference to the statements in the *Testimonium*. Yet, comments such as Jesus being the Messiah found in the *Testimonium* by a noted Jewish historian would have been of immense propaganda use in their efforts to defend Christianity against pagan antagonism (Doherty 2005: 208; Sandmel 1965: 18), which is indeed how present-day apologists use this passage. The ancient writers in question include Justin Martyr, Theophilus of Antioch, Melito, the bishop of Sardis, Marcus Minucius Felix,

Irenaeus, Titus Flavius Clemens (Clement of Alexandria), Julius Africanus, Tertullian, Hippolytus of Rome, Origen, Methodius of Olympus, and Lucius Lactantius. As the professor of classics and expert on Josephus Louis Feldman (1984: 659) observes, the text in the *Testimonium* should have been "the first passage that a Christian apologist would cite." However, these writers are silent.

There is yet another clue. The famous Christian apologist Origen quotes Josephus to establish the existence of John the Baptist but criticizes Josephus for not "believing in Jesus as the Christ," yet the *Testimonium* explicitly says that Jesus was the Christ. If the passage had been present in his edition of Josephus, or if the passage existed as it appears today, Origen would not have made such an odd comment. As Doherty (2005: 209) pointed out, Origen spent a quarter of a million words to refute Celsus's charges that Jesus was a charlatan and that the resurrection was a bogus Christian fable, drawing upon a vast range of sources, including a reference to Josephus, but recounts nothing mentioned in the *Testimonium*. Yet, affirmation by this eminent historian about Jesus being a "wise man" who did "wonderful works" and was a teacher of "the truth" who attracted to him "many of the Jews and many of the Gentiles" would have added considerable strength to his diatribe. But Origen is silent. Eisler (1931: 38) suggests that Josephus had written some text but not the one later Christian apologists quote because the original would have been hostile toward Jesus given that Josephus believed that the Emperor Vespasian was the Messiah of the Jews foretold in the Old Testament.

Others have interpreted Origen's silence as indicative that Josephus's original passage did exist and was neutral and hence the comment that he did not accept Jesus as the Messiah. But Origen's remark may well have been prompted by Josephus's statement in his book *Jewish Wars* that the Jewish messianic prophecies referred to Vespasian (Doherty 2005: 210; see also Doherty 2009: 533–96). An additional point to be made here is that if Josephus believed Vespasian to be the prophesied Jewish Messiah, as he says in *Jewish Wars*, he would not have referred to Jesus as the foretold redeemer.

The first quotation of the *Testimonium* as it is known today appears during the fourth century and was used by Eusebius, the Bishop of Caesarea, in his book *Historia ecclesiastica* [History of the Church]. Eusebius seems to have produced the text out of nowhere. The dubiousness of this character in itself raises lots of suspicions because he was not only a terrible and utterly unreliable scholar but also advocated pious fraud and was a notorious liar and falsifier of evidence (Carrier 2014a: 121). He has the distinction of being the foremost forger and plagiarizer in the entire history of Christianity. Unfortunately, nearly everything we know about the early history of Christianity comes from the pen of this unscrupulous plagiarist, teller of false tales, and propagator of disinformation. The noted culture historian Carl Jacob Christoph Burckhardt described Eusebius in his book *The Age of Constantine the Great* (1949) as "the first thoroughly dishonest and unfair historian of ancient times" (Burckhardt 1949: 283).

It is very likely that Eusebius himself forged the *Testimonium* along with his other fraudulent acts. These included forging letters exchanged between Jesus and the rulers of the city of Antiochia, falsifying dates, writing fake biographies of Christian martyrs using material plagiarized from Roman novels, and repeatedly changing and rewriting the history of the church as he deemed necessary for propaganda reasons (Fitzgerald 2010: 54;

Metzger 1987: 202). Eusebius's culpability has been pointed out by the religious studies scholar Ken Olson (1999). While some disagree (e.g., Whealey 2007), Olson (2013) demonstrates that the language and content of the passage closely parallel Eusebius's own work. Quotations of the *Testimonium* appear in three of Eusebius's extant works: *The Demonstration of the Gospel* (3.5.106), *The Ecclesiastical History* (1.11.8), and the *Theophany* (5.44). Olson (2013) argues that the most plausible hypothesis is that Eusebius either composed the entire text or rewrote it so thoroughly "that it is now impossible to recover a Josephan original." This suggestion is entirely plausible given that we have ventured into a time of political rivalries, power struggles, the blatant forging of documents and letters, redactions, and the systematic and wholesale destruction of anti-Christian books and historical evidence (Freke and Gandy 1999: 10).

There have been efforts to "rescue" the *Testimonium* by deleting certain things Josephus would not have said. For example, some have expunged such phrases as "if it be lawful to call him a man," "he was the Christ," "for he appeared to them alive again the third day," or "the divine prophets had foretold these and ten thousand other wonderful things concerning him" (cf., Meier 1991: 56–88). However, there are additional statements that could not have come from Josephus, as discussed above. As Carrier (2014a: 333, 335) has shown, deleting all of these, we would be left only with the phrase "there was about this time Jesus, a wise man" without any attached narrative, which is meaningless. Hence, the conclusion to be reached is that Josephus as well did not write this sentence (Doherty 2005: 206–13; Martin 1991: 85; Philipse 2014: 172).

Another reasonable place to look for evidence of the resurrection is, of course, the work of the Roman historians, such as Pliny the Younger, Tacitus, and Suetonius writing around 110–120 CE. They refer to the Christians as superstitious mischief-makers but say nothing about the resurrection (Philipse 2014: 172). However, there is a reference to the Christians in Tacitus's book *The Annals*, dated around 116 CE that apologists have interpreted as a reference to the resurrection. For this reason, a brief discussion is necessary. Tacitus talks about the Christians while writing about the burning of Rome during the reign of the emperor Nero:

> Nero fastened the guilt and inflicted the most exquisite tortures on a class hated for their abominations, called Christians by the populace. Christus, from whom the name had its origin, suffered the extreme penalty during the reign of Tiberius at the hands of one of our procurators, Pontius Pilatus, and a most mischievous superstition, thus checked for the moment, again broke out not only in Judaea, the first source of the evil, but even in Rome, where all things hideous and shameful from every part of the world find their center and become popular. Accordingly, an arrest was first made of all who pleaded guilty; then, upon their information, an immense multitude was convicted, not so much of the crime of firing the city, as of hatred against mankind. Mockery of every sort was added to their deaths. [...] Hence, even for criminals who deserved extreme and exemplary punishment, there arose a feeling of compassion; for it was not, as it seemed, for the public good, but to glut one man's cruelty, that they were being destroyed. (*The Annals of Tacitus*, book 15, chapter 44)

If this passage is authentic, then it is an essential historical reference to Jesus outside of the New Testament, although inferring the resurrection from it is highly debatable as we shall see. However, as Carrier (2014b) argues, the line beginning with Christus is a possible interpolation and that Tacitus was describing the followers of the Jewish instigator named Chrestus, prosecuted by Emperor Claudius. The insertion of the lines referring to the execution of Christus by Pilate probably happened after the middle of the fourth century.

However, even if the passage is not a forgery, the accuracy of its contents is questionable. It is unlikely that Tacitus, who is describing the crucifixion of an obscure Jewish rabbi nearly 90 years earlier, consulted original documents when the Christians in his day were themselves relating this fable from their books. Therefore, what the *Annals* provides is not independent evidence. However, even if we grant that this was not the case and actual archival materials were available, it is doubtful that records existed for each of the many thousands of individuals the Romans crucified in Judea. Moreover, if such individual records did exist, they would have referred to the condemned prisoner by his proper name Yeshua or Jesus, not Christ, which was the moniker Christians used to refer to their savior (Tobin 2009: 223). Finally, even if such records had been kept, they were probably destroyed when Rome's libraries burned at least two times in the interval between the crucifixion and when Tacitus wrote his book (Carrier 2014b: 344).

Another difficulty is that Tacitus incorrectly refers to Pilate as "procurator," a title in use in his day, whereas during the reign of Tiberius Roman governors were officially known as "prefects" (Wells 1979: 187). This reinforces the conclusion that Tacitus is reporting information that came from what the Christians in his day were saying (Doherty 2005: 202).

Finally, it more than grossly exceeds the warrant of this passage to suggest, as some apologists have, that the sentence "mischievous superstition, thus checked for the moment, broke out not only in Judaea, the first source of the evil but even in Rome" is an indirect testimony that Jesus was crucified and rose from the grave. Tacitus does not mention anyone returning from the dead. He did not even have the basic facts right and to suggest that somehow this passage contains a reference to the resurrection is pure apologist bunkum.

Thus, Tacitus is not a source helpful to the apologists' cause. To reiterate, overall historical evidence about Jesus is very scanty. The paucity of evidence is the reason why some of the scholars mentioned above have expressed doubts about the historicity of such a person (Carrier 2014a, 2012: 11–15; Doherty 2005, 2009; Wells 1996).

Returning the question of historical sources mentioning the resurrection, we find that it is not until the third and fourth centuries that writers first provide detailed descriptions of this event as the bedrock of the Christian faith. The authors in question include Clement of Alexandria, Origen, Sextus Julius Africanus, and the notorious forger Eusebius. These were Christian evangelists, ideologues, and apologists with religious motives whose purpose was to gain converts. Their works are late and hardly reliable objective accounts. They belong to the genre of Christian paranormal literature.

We are now in a position to ask the following question: How does the evidence for Jesus's resurrection fare in relation to the high standards of historical inquiry used in the analysis of run-of-the-mill historical events? The answer: Not very well. As Carrier (2006b) puts it, the only proofs of the resurrection are the New Testament sources that are perhaps the worst type of evidence one has for any event. Carrier adds, "Indeed, you really have to look hard to find another event that is in a worse condition than this as far as evidence goes." Carrier's rebuttal is so decisive that further discussion is unnecessary. A point worth making is that the fallacious claim that the evidence for the resurrection is as good as the evidence for any event in history is an old and often repeated apologetic assertion that Gorham (1908: 77) addressed over a century ago. It is as if saying that the evidence is good makes it so.

Another apologist assertion is that if "all" the evidence for the resurrection is "taken together," we have a solid case as good as any other well-supported historical event. Hence writers like Habermas (2003: 22) provide laundry lists of "evidences" to support the idea that a corpse decomposing for three days in a grave got up and walked away. Alas, multiplying many false accounts does not produce a true account. Bad evidence does become good evidence in this way. The early Bible critic David Friedrich Strauss (1873: 82–83) put it bluntly that the paranormal resurrection of Jesus is one of the worst documented events in history. Adding that, "comparing the immense effect of this belief with its absolute baselessness, the story of the resurrection of Jesus can only be called a world-wide deception."

However, there is more. We must keep in mind that the resurrection is not the same kind of event as Caesar crossing the Rubicon or the death of Augustus. The rising of the dead is a paranormal phenomenon and, as such, carries a weighty burden of proof (Tobin 2009: 554). What this means is that even if evidence of the highest standards of historical inquiry were to be produced for the resurrection (none exists as we have seen), it would still not be sufficient. The event was an extraordinary one, and it requires extraordinary evidence. As Shapiro (2016: 92) correctly puts it, the conventional standards of historical investigation are insufficient when applied to testimony regarding happenings that are "more improbable than the run-of-the-mill historical events." In his words, "If the 'highest standards' of historical inquiry demand that evidence for an event be *very* convincing, this still would not do when seeking to justify belief in miracles." Believing in such events requires *better* than convincing evidence or proof that is so strong as to render all other explanation for sightings of Jesus after his death implausible. Sadly, no such evidence is to be found anywhere.

Based on this discussion, we can conclude that the case for the resurrection rests on extremely flimsy foundations. The only evidence provided that a dead man came back to life through a singular miracle from God is secondary and tertiary after the fact anecdotes of the appearances of the risen Jesus to the disciples that I shall discuss in Chapter 15. Moreover, as we shall see, these reports are at variance with each other in every vital detail. As the biblical scholar John Barclay (1996: 26) admits, only a heavily committed religious believer, who has already accepted the truth of Christianity on faith, can honestly treat these texts as historical evidence.

### *An Assessment of Contemporary Christian Apologetic Scholarship*

Here it is necessary to highlight how Christian apologists approach the texts under discussion. Remarkably, their methodology is very much like that of the proponents of other types of paranormal beliefs. For this reason, the works of these ideologues may be classified as belonging to the broader genre of paranormal literature. Their works share the following attributes:

1. A "canon mentality" or an "it-is-written" perspective that assumes that the gospel narratives comprise "a faithful historical record," whereas, in fact, the historicity of these narratives is highly doubtful and cannot be assumed in an a priori fashion (Bater 1969: 51–52; Botha 1989: 46, 55; Watson 1987: 366). This is certainly something no legitimate historian would ever do (Craffert 1989: 334–35).
2. A will to believe. The writers in question may talk about "historical evidence" and "the sources," but ultimately they operate based on the will to believe. The question is never "What is the evidence?" Instead, the position taken is "I wish to believe." Thus, the theologian Hans Küng (1984: 348–49) says in the same sentence that there is no evidence for the resurrection in the entire New Testament and that there can be no doubt that this is a historical event.
3. An open admission that no evidence of any kind will sway them from their prior convictions regarding the divine truths to their holy book. For instance, as the Christian apologist William Craig (1994: 36) acknowledges:

    > Should a conflict arise between the witness of the Holy Spirit to the fundamental truth of the Christian faith and beliefs based on argument and evidence, then it is the former which must take precedence over the latter, not vice versa.

    In other words, this paragon among the contemporary Christian apologists is saying is that no facts or evidence of any kind will ever make him change his prior convictions regarding the divine truths of his holy book. Thus, these writers are offering religious propaganda and credulity as a substitute for scholarly analysis or historical methodology.

4. Apologists start with answers beforehand. Despite lip service to standards of scholarship and tenets of historical research, these religionists are not interested in understanding the emergence of Christianity in historical terms *as a historical phenomenon* but invariably pursue supernaturalism and paranormal hypotheses. They begin and end with the same propositions, namely that miracles are real, the resurrection was an actual physical and historical event, and Jesus was God incarnate.
5. These writers refuse to consider any non-paranormal and non-supernatural alternative possibilities. They find it impossible to imagine that the events in question did not take place as described in their sacred texts. William Craig's comments are a perfect illustration of this stance. This leads to massive confirmation bias because one will always find convincing any arguments that appear to confirm what one has already accepted as true (Watson 1987: 371–72).
6. The tendency by such authors for misrepresentations and deception. For instance, religionist Roy Varghese (2003: xiii) proclaims that "contemporary scholars who have done specialized work in this area now accept the historicity of the Resurrection." He does not provide any information about who these "scholars" are or whether they are true believers or critical historians, whereas, in fact, there is considerable

disagreement among contemporary scholars on nearly every aspect of the resurrection event. Long ago, David Hume (1902 [1748]: 125–26) drew attention to this tendency among believers to make "use of pious frauds" in support of what they think is "a holy and meritorious cause."

7. These writers mimic mainstream scholarship to provide "sophisticated, scholarly sounding arguments packed with footnotes, and symbolic logic, striving to look precisely like mainstream scholarship" (Loftus 2011: 378, n. 14). Thus the superstitious and supernatural foundations of their arguments are disguised by making them appear credible in the context of rational, scholarly discourse. This is analogous to the way advocates of pseudoscientific and paranormal bunkum adopt the trappings and terminology of legitimate science.
8. A refusal to consider the role of sociopsychological and anthropological factors in human affairs that prevents the realization that behind the texts there are "ordinary human beings with aspirations, ideals, prejudices, self-interests and quite a bit of irrationality" (Bater 1969: 55).
9. Such writers treat the resurrection as "a unique eschatological event" outside history and culture caused by God that is "beyond ordinary experience" (Watson 1987: 368). However, while apologists accept the historical veracity of extraordinary events or miracles in the biblical sources, they disqualify from such a designation similar phenomena in other literature or cultural contexts (Bater 1969: 55). Moreover, the assertion that the phenomenon in question represents "a unique eschatological event" is tantamount to saying that it is not amenable to scientific analysis or can be understood according to cross-cultural, systematic comparative approaches, which nullifies the legitimacy of any epistemological claims made by these ideologues. This stance is adopted because it opens space to offer personal subjective superstitions and paranormalism as a substitute for historical data. What is on offer in these works are assemblages of X-claims. Also, admitting that the phenomena under investigation are subject to arbitrary and ad hoc divine interventions that bring about unique sociocultural and historical consequences renders superfluous all historical and anthropological investigations, including what the apologists have to say (cf., Smith 1968: 12).

# Chapter Thirteen

# JESUS THE MIRACLE WORKER, MAGICIAN, AND SORCERER

*Those cures and resurrections, or feeding the crowds with but a few loaves [...] let us say for the sake of argument that such things were actually done by [Jesus]. Are they then so different from the sort of things done by sorcerers—who also claim to do wonderful miracles, having been taught their tricks by the Egyptians? As these men are able to do such wonderful things, ought we not regard them also as sons of God?*

—Celsus, *On the True Doctrine* (circa 185 CE)

*The miracles which Jesus performed [...] were in no way original; the healing of the lunatics, the expulsion of the devils, extraordinary cures, wonderful powers over nature, and even the resurrection of the dead, all were part of what the faith, both of Jews and pagans, expected of a genuine worker of miracles.*

—Charles Guignebert, *Jesus* (1958)

Paranormal beliefs everywhere draw upon and are linked to foundational religious or supernatural premises characteristic of the particular culture in which they occur. My research on shamanism in Nepal revealed that a broad set of Buddhist, Hindu, Bon (pre-Buddhist Tibetan), and various indigenous religious premises form the foundations of shamanic paranormal beliefs. This is also the case in many other cultural settings, including paranormal beliefs in Western society. Here the source that is drawn upon is the miracles described in the Bible, especially the wonders wrought by Jesus as described in the Synoptic Gospels and the Gospel of John (Humphrey 1999: 93). Miracles are central to Christianity and the divine status of Jesus. As the Italian biblical scholar Marcello Craveri (1967: 117) pointed out, the centrality of Christianity is Jesus's miracles because without these he would appear as an ordinary human.

## Jesus's Miracles as the Prototypical Examples of Paranormal Beliefs in the West

In his book *The Supernatural, the Occult, and the Bible* (1990), the biblical historian and archaeologist Gerald Larue discusses the powerful impact of the pervasive supernaturalism of the Bible on contemporary magical and paranormal thinking. The Bible is the book of miracles, the text of uncanny happenings, or the definitive handbook of the paranormal in Western culture. It has for millennia provided the central themes of paranormal beliefs and research. According to the neuropsychologist Nicholas Humphrey (1999: 93–94), Jesus's miracles are the prototype for what genuine paranormal phenomena would be like if they took place. Jesus can thus be considered the preeminent practitioner of the paranormal in Western society. As the religious texts say, he possessed superhuman abilities because he was the Son of God and his powers came from the absolute source of all paranormality, the architect of the universe himself in the transcendental world beyond the spatiotemporal realm of ordinary reality. As such, Jesus would have been able to alter physical laws and produce innumerable wonders. Moreover, because of who he was, Jesus would not be restricted by any physical or sociocultural parameters in the exercise of his magical abilities. The possibilities and range of his miracles would thus be limitless. In contrast to today's paranormalists, who seem to accomplish as much as any run-of-the-mill conjures and no more, Jesus as the foremost paranormalist would have surpassed all others. Or at least he should have.

## Assessing Jesus's Paranormal Feats

The question is, how does Jesus fare compared to present-day paranormalists, or better yet, to the sorcerers and magicians of his days? Jesus used his supernatural powers strategically to lend divine authority to his mission and convince people that he was the Messiah who would rule as King of the Jews with his disciples at his side (cf., Kurtz 2013: 126). Jesus's remarkable capabilities included precognition, clairvoyance, telepathy, the capacity to feed multitudes, heal the sick, walk on water, exorcize demons, and bring corpses back to life. Jesus's greatest paranormal feat—his resurrection from the dead—became the miracle Christians emphasize as the justification for and validation of their religion as a supernaturally ordained phenomenon. How well the resurrection holds up as a miraculous event is the topic of Chapters 14 and 15. Here I shall look at Jesus's other miraculous works.

As the all-powerful Son of God, Jesus's feats of magic should have been different in scope and nature from those performed by all other magicians. Such a demand is not unreasonable given the magnitude of his paranormal claims. In Jesus's day, wandering magicians, holy men, soothsayers, corpse reanimators, and prophets, who had been around for centuries throughout the Roman period, flourished and could be found all along the Eastern Mediterranian (Smith 2014: 96). Surprisingly, these individuals performed the same kind of feats Jesus is said to have accomplished. The Christian apologist and miracle-believer, J. Harold Ellens, in a chapter in his edited three-volume compilation *Miracles: God, Science, and Psychology in the Paranormal* (2008) suggests that Jesus's miracles were incomparable, awesome, and genuine or else there would have been refutations and rebuttals. As Ellens (2008b: 1) puts it, the widespread stories about Jesus's miracles must have been true; otherwise, they would be "significant numbers of voices raised to counter the claims of the biblical stories." However, contrary to Ellens's assertion, critics were plentiful. Ellens is either oblivious or has chosen to ignore the shameful fact that the early Christians systematically destroyed all the works that contained "significant numbers of voices raised to counter the claims of the biblical stories." Christians were not only plagiarists, they also made up ludicrous stories, altered texts at will, and were avid book burners. The works of critics such as Celsus and Porphyry discussed below are two of the many volumes containing forceful criticisms and voices of opposition that were destroyed by the intolerant and zealous Christians.

## Jesus as Sorcerer and Magician: Arguments from the Greek Philosopher Celsus and the Early Christian Apologist Origen of Alexandria

The prevalent image of Jesus among non-Christians during the first century was that he practiced sorcery (see Bonner 1943,1927; Conner 2006: 115–60: Hull 1974; Janowitz 2001: 3, 17, 23). The implication is that the source of his powers was demonic rather than divine. The gospels repeatedly discuss this accusation. An opponent of the early Christians, the Greek philosopher Celsus (ca. 185), who studied the Jesus cult and wrote a scathing treatise about it called *On the True Doctrine*, detailed the charge of sorcery as well as raising many other questions (Smith 2014: 79–86). The original work was sadly destroyed by zealous Christians who systematically obliterated all such books, including Porphyry's anti-Christian masterpiece *The Philosophy from Oracles* and his book *Against the Christians* when their religion triumphed (Hoffmann 1987: 29). However, excerpts of Celsus's treatise are to be found in the book *Contra Celsus* (ca. 248), which was a refutation of Celsus by the Christian apologist and preeminent theologian of early Christianity, Origen of Alexandria. Origen inadvertently preserved large parts of Celsus's narrative by quoting sections of it in the context of his invective. Historians have thus been able to restore much of Celsus's original text.

Celsus was an eclectic thinker who studied different schools of thought, such as Platonism and Stoicism, and had considerable knowledge of history and the religious beliefs of many cultures (Hoffmann 1987: 29–20). He was also thoroughly familiar with the Hebrew Bible, the gospels, and other Christian sources. The noted historian of early Christianity Raymond Hoffmann (1987: 37) points out Celsus's remarkable observation about the apologetic purpose of the gospels, that is, as missionary propaganda literature, not sacred biography. Hoffman considers Celsus as the forerunner among the New Testament demythologizers that included Porphyry, Voltaire, Thomas Paine, David Friedrich Strauss, Arthur Drews, and Rudolf Bultmann.

The historian Charles Freeman (2009: 170), who considers Celsus as a conservative and not a particularly sophisticated thinker, is not very balanced and overlooks the Greek philosopher's powerful and penetrating insights as a Bible demythologizer. Celsus raised various indictments against the Christian religion at a high philosophical level that necessitated well-reasoned rebuttals. As noted before, Origen used close to a quarter of a million words in his effort to refute Celsus's arguments (Doherty 2005: 209).

The philosopher Paul Kurtz (2013: 24) correctly notes that Celsus was a skeptic who relied upon reason during his analyses. Celsus (1987: 54–55) expressed this as follows:

> One ought first to follow reason as a guide before accepting any belief, since anyone who believes without testing a doctrine is certain to be deceived. We have plenty of examples in our own time: the sniveling beggers of Cybele, the soothsayers, the worshippers of Mithras and Sabzaius those gullible believers in apparitions of Hecate [the Greek goddess of magic and witchcraft], and assorted other gods.

Celsus (1830: 2) compared the Christians to such cultists:

> Men who irrationally assent to anything, resemble those who are delighted with jugglers and enchanters. For as most of these are depraved characters, who deceive the vulgar, and persuade them to assent to whatever they please, this also takes place with the Christians. Some of these are not willing either to give or receive a reason for what they believe; but are accustomed to say, "Do not investigate, but believe, your faith will save you. For the wisdom of the world is bad."

Celsus said that Jesus conducted his paranormal demonstrations to support his claims that he was a god using magic tricks he learned from sorcerers in Egypt, rather than through divine powers. In his words,

> Jesus, who, through poverty being obliged to serve as a hireling in Egypt, learnt there certain [magical] arts for which the Egyptians are famous. Afterwards, returning from thence, he thought so highly of himself, on account of the possession of these [magical] arts, as to proclaim himself to be a God. (Celsus 1830: 5–6)

Celsus thus relegated Jesus to the ranks of the plentiful lowly everyday magicians, miracle-mongers, charlatans, prophets, exorcists, and corpse reanimators of the time operating throughout the Mediterranean coastlines. The problem he posed for contemporary Christian apologists was that the miraculous feats of these lowly magicians were indeed identical to those rendered by their Messiah (Smith 2014: 99, 115).

Lucian of Samosata, a second-century Syrian-born Roman naturalist and critic of the paranormal, described the repertoire of these tricksters and charlatans. He observed that their artifices included walking on water, the ability to appear and disappear, clairvoyance, exorcism of demons, prophecy, producing banquets out of thin air, healing the sick, and raising the dead. Here is how Lucian (1905: 205) described the performance of one of these conjurers:

> His patients are the sort who throw fits at the new moon, rolling their eyes and foaming at the mouth. Yet he always manages to cure them, and send them home perfectly sane, charging a large fee for his services. When he finds them lying on the ground, the first question he asks them is: "What are doing there?" The patient makes no reply, but the devil explains, either in Greek or some foreign language, who it is, where it comes from, and how it goes into the man. Then [the magician] starts swearing at the devil and if necessary, threatening it until it goes away.

Lucian could very well be describing one of Jesus's performances. Compare his account to what the Gospel of Mark (1: 21–28) says about Jesus:

> Now there was a man in their synagogue with an unclean spirit. And he cried out, saying, "Let *us* alone! What have we to do with You, Jesus of Nazareth? Did You come to destroy us? I know who You are—the Holy One of God!"

> But Jesus rebuked him, saying, "Be quiet, and come out of him!" And when the unclean spirit had convulsed him and cried out with a loud voice, he came out of him. Then they were all amazed, so that they questioned among themselves, saying, "What is this? What new doctrine *is* this? For with authority He commands even the unclean spirits, and they obey Him." And immediately His fame spread throughout all the region around Galilee.

During the past several decades numerous practitioners have emerged in the United States, undertaking so-called exorcism ministries, replicating the procedures of Lucian's charlatans and Jesus, and shamelessly preying on gullible and distraught believers who require actual psychiatric help (see Cuneo 2001). This is yet another example of how the paranormalism in the Bible continues to influence present-day practitioners and self-styled messiahs and ambassadors from heaven.

Regarding Jesus's miracles in general, Celsus (1830: 8) raised the following question:

> Let us grant that these [wondrous] things were performed by [Jesus]; but they are common with the works of enchanters, who promise to effect more wonderful deeds than these, and also with what those who have been taught by the Egyptians to perform in the middle of the forum for a few oboli [small denomination coins]; such as expelling dæmons from men, dissipating diseases by a puff, evocating the souls of heroes, exhibiting sumptuous suppers, and tables covered with food, which have no reality. These magicians also represent animals as moving, which are not in reality animals, but merely appear to the imagination to be such.

For the skeptical Celsus (1830: 8), the implications of this concerning Jesus's claims of divinity were all too clear:

> Is it fit, therefore, that we should believe these men to be the sons of God because they worked these wonders? Or ought we not rather say, that these are the arts of depraved and unhappy men?

Some authors of the gospels went to some lengths to set Jesus apart from other exorcists, prophets, miracle workers, and healers of the day. As Cotter (1999: 177) points out, Matthew and Luke delete from their texts the exorcism stories of Jesus and his utterances of foreign phrases (i.e., magical incantations) that appear in the Gospel of Mark because they resemble the recitations of the ordinary sorcerers and magicians of the time. However, in the earlier tradition, there was no distinction between such magical actions (Conner 2006: 143). A central and recurring feature of the gospel writers' literary repertoire is the retro-correcting of their Jesus stories. Such tactics, of course, are to be expected because the gospels were propaganda tracts, not historical biographies as modern critical scholarship has conclusively demonstrated. Celsus who, as noted, may be given the distinction of being one of the earliest Bible demythologizers was well aware of this. In his words, "But let us not omit this: the writings of the disciples contain only those fact about Jesus that put a flattering face on the events of his life" (Celsus 1987: 62).

Origen and other later Christian apologists conceded that the miracles of Jesus were indeed remarkably like other magicians and enchanters. They tried as best as they could to explain the facts away. Ultimately, their rebuttal was to firmly aver that Jesus's miracles were real, while those of the other magicians (*goēteia*, meaning sorcery in Greek) were mere appearances. Unlike the others, they insisted, Jesus did not achieve his miracles through trickery, incantations, or invocation of demons. He did not perform for money or to provide an empty spectacle. Instead, Jesus's magic was to instill the message of God upon those awed by the marvels (Smith 2014: 114). Such arguments fail because Jesus and the ordinary magicians used their conjurations for personal gain, the sorcerers wanting money and Jesus desiring aggrandizement by being recognized as the foretold Messiah of the Jews (cf., Helms 2006: 86). In his book *Arcana Mundi: Magic and the Occult in the Greek and Roman World* (2006), Georg Luck provides a similar excuse that Jesus's miracles were distinct. Luck (2006: 63, 64) writes that Jesus's miacles may have appeared to be similar to the other miracle workers because he expelled demons, healed the sick, prophecized, and reanimated the dead. Indeed, other magicians may have viewed him as a colleague. However, he adds, this does not mean that he was a magician because of the nature of his mission.

These are paltry defenses because the parallels are too striking and compelling for anyone but fervent believers to justify the conclusion that one set of magic tricks is genuine and unique but its identical counterpart is not. Celsus raised this very issue 2,000 years ago. Moreover, he observed that others, such as the disciples of Jesus who did not claim to be the sons of God, also performed identical miracles and hence should be classified as "very powerful fellow magicians." As the theologian Ernest Barnes (1948: 84) pointed out, it is difficult to put Jesus's miracles into a special category because they were on par with those performed by his wonder-working apostles, who could also cast out demons and cure the sick.

## Jesus's Miraculous Works Compared to the Deeds of Miracle Workers Today

Thus, at this stage, we must ask: How do the miracles of the Son of God, the preeminent paranormalist of Western culture, stand up against those performed by paranormalists and miracle workers today? Oddly, Jesus's repertoire is identical to those of today's paranormal showmen. His healings are indistinguishable from the stunts performed by evangelical preachers, exorcists, and healers (Tobin 2009: 387). Surprisingly, the religionist Keener (2011: 133) maintains that such feats by present-day evangelical preachers duplicate and hence bestow credibility upon or validate the miracles of the Bible, not realizing that his observation undermines the case. This is because deceptions are deceptions regardless of time or place.

As Tobin (2009: 388) points out, these tricks work because "as long as the audience is receptive and gullible almost anything can be interpreted as a healing." In my work with practitioners who use comparable procedures, it became evident that any plausible therapeutic procedure can be effective in the case of certain psychosomatic maladies (Sidky 2010). These "miraculous cures" are never miraculous. Brazen trickery and deception are rampant across cultures and through space and time (cf., Randi 1987: 104–4, 112–23).

Like our present-day shamans, evangelical preachers, and psychic healers, Jesus succeeded by exploiting the expectations, fears, psychological vulnerabilities, false hopes, gullibility, and ignorance of his audiences. These were uneducated folk steeped in boundless credulity and superstition who lived in a world governed by magic and who could easily be swayed by charismatic individuals with a good tall tale (Cotter 1999; Shapiro 2016: 121). Present-day examples patently demonstrate how quickly people are duped by pretended miracle workers, which sheds light on the success of Jesus and his miracle-mongering counterparts in the ancient world in baffling their audiences most of the time. As the skeptic and conjuror James Randi (1982a: 62) has shown regarding faith healers in our own time, "people will accept and rationalize almost any pronouncement by someone believed to be an authority with mystical powers."

The gospels describe approximately 40 miracles performed by Jesus (Cotter 1999: 54–56, 119–25, 165–66, 269–72, 223–24). These include healing of the sick, three events during which Jesus resurrected dead people, and various other conjurations. Many of these miracle stories were likely fictional accounts added to the gospel narratives decades later for effect by the evangelical spin doctors. As Tobin (2009: 391) has shown, the report of Jesus healing the leper, in Mark 1:40–44, Matthew 8:1–2, and Luke 5:12–13, is probably fictional. According to the Gospel of Mark 1:40–44, a man with leprosy came and begged Jesus to make him clean. Jesus touched the ailing man and immediately leprosy left him. The reason why this story is not credible is that in Galilee, a Jewish province where this incident is situated, lepers were forbidden to live or come near the towns. Only those certified by a priest to be healed were allowed near the settlements. Thus, if any purported lepers were wandering around for Jesus to encounter, they were no longer sick and what transpired was not a miracle but a purification ritual (Craveri 1967: 108–9).

Among Jesus's corpse reanimations was the raising of the daughter of Jairus. In Mark 5:22–24 the girl is at the point of death, in Luke 8:41–42 the girl is also at the point of death, but in Matthew 9:18–19 the girl is already dead. This tale is nearly identical to that of the prophet Elisha raising a dead child found in 2 Kings 4:20–37, in the Old Testament. There is strong evidence that all the resurrection accounts in the gospels plagiarize this earlier story (Helms 2006: 88; Tobin 2009: 393). Funk and members of the Jesus Seminar (1998: 82–83) also reached a similar conclusion.

The second resurrection story is to be found in Luke but not in Mark or Matthew. In this story, Jesus and his disciples are in the midst of a crowd outside the city of Nain, in Galilee. Here Jesus raised the deceased son of a widow while the body was being borne out of the city gates in a coffin. Jesus "touched the open coffin, and those who carried *him* stood still. And He said, 'Young man, I say to you, arise.' So he who was dead sat up and began to speak." The crowd was in awe and proclaimed that "God has visited His people" (Luke 7:11–17). Comparative analysis by Helms (2006: 87–90) and Tobin (2009: 393) shows that this tale is fictional and is an imitation of the story of the raising of another widow's son by the prophet Elijah (1 Kings 17:7–24). Funk and members of the Jesus Seminar (1998: 289) have reached a similar conclusion. A further blow to the historicity of this story is that archaeological excavations show that the town of Nain never had walls and hence would not have had a gate (Tobin 2009: 396).

The most remarkable and perhaps Jesus's most dramatic miracle of this type was the reanimation of Lazarus, the brother of Martha and Mary, described in the Gospel of John. Lazarus had been dead for four days with his body in a state of decomposition when Jesus arrived at the scene. The story goes that Jesus came to the tomb, which was sealed with a stone. He ordered that the stone be moved, but Martha objected saying there will be a stench because Lazarus has been dead for four days. Jesus reassured here that a miracle would occur. After the tomb was opened he cried out: " 'Lazarus, come forth!' And he who had died came out bound hand and foot with graveclothes, and his face was wrapped with a cloth" (John 11:17–44).

Kurtz (2013: 146) suggests that if this event indeed happened, it is very likely that Lazarus, who is described as Jesus's friend, helped stage the miracle to bolster Jesus's reputation as the Son of God. I say if it happened because the story only appears in the Gospel of John. Luke 10:38–42 describes Martha and Mary as Jesus's good friends but does not mention that they had a brother who was brought back to life. It makes no sense for this evangelist to have omitted this spectacular miracle had he known about it. The more probable explanation is that the Lazarus story was a later fabrication by the author of the Gospel of John who used the story of the raising of Jairus's daughter, as well as embellishing borrowed elements from Egyptian or Greco-Roman myths about other god-men who also raised the dead on various occasions (Helms 2006: 89; Kurtz 2013: 110, 146).

The literary critic Randel Helms (2006: 89–90) shows that the Lazarus tale is a variant of a story in the no-longer-extant "Secret Gospel of Mark" (also known as The Mar Saba Fragment). The relevant part of this lost book appears in a letter written by Clement of Alexandria to a person named Theodore around 200 CE. The historian and biblical scholar Morton Smith discovered this text in 1958. The account in the Gospel of John, however, includes different details. Helms shows that John drew upon the same tradition employed in the Secret Gospel of Mark, namely the Book of Kings, but the source of the variant details is Egypt, where the story in Secret Mark originated. Those details come from the myth of the resurrection of Osiris by Horus. The Egyptian term for Osiris is Asar, and in Hebrew, Lazarus is *El-azar* (Helms 2006: 89–90). Whatever the case may be concerning the specifics of the various miracle tales, what is certain is that tales about Jesus's miracles were carefully crafted to establish the divine nature of Jesus's mission (John 11:41–42).

## The Many Raisers of the Dead: The Banality of Resurrection Events in the Ancient World

Even if the resurrection stories in the New Testament are historical, that is, that Jesus did indeed perform such feats before audiences, bringing back the dead was not a unique exploit in the ancient world. It is therefore impossible to comprehend how Christian writers can assert that the resurrection of Jesus was a singular event in human history. Reanimating corpses was, in fact, an ordinary conjurer's trick. Apollonius of Tyana, a contemporary of Jesus, who was also of divine origin, born of a virgin, died, rose from the dead, and then ascended to heaven, is said to have brought back to life a bride who died on her wedding day (Philostratus 1912: 457). This story is identical to Jesus raising the daughter of Jairus.

In other words, the raising of the dead from the grave was part of the repertoire of many of the self-styled miracle workers of the time, not just that of Jesus. Moreover, being the Son of God was not a requirement to achieve such a wondrous feat. Even Jesus's disciple Peter manages to perform this trick (Acts 9:36–42). The self-styled apostle Saul of Tarsus, or Paul, was also able to bring people back from the dead (Acts 20:7–12). In what way is the action of reanimating a corpse by Jesus different from those performed by Apollonius of Tyana, by his own disciples, or by the Apostle Paul? It is not! Apologists argue, however, that these alleged miracles by pagan magicians were similar, but Jesus's feats were genuine. Alternatively, the claim is that ancient anti-Christian propagandists contrived such stories, which were modeled after the biblical tales, to offer an alternative to Jesus for their audiences (e.g., Keener 2011: 40, 51). This is not a convincing argument to which I shall return in Chapter 14.

A rather embarrassing question that arises is, Was Jesus's own resurrection, if it in truth happened, achieved in the same way? Is it not a bit suspicious that members of a cult known for the illusion of bringing dead people back to life are also the ones closely linked to the greatest resurrection miracle story of all time, Jesus returning from the grave?

It is also important to note that Jesus did not perform his paranormal tricks anywhere and on demand. He outrightly refused such requests on several occasions (Matthew 13:53–58). Why would the Son of God, whose powers came from the highest source, need people to have faith in order to perform miracles? Only ordinary conjurers depend on believing audiences to achieve their stunts successfully. The implication is that perhaps Jesus was indeed a miracle worker of the latter kind.

Like today's wonder-workers, Jesus had to establish the necessary conditions beforehand. He had shills or decoys and used "advanced men" (Luke 10:1–2) who were directed to go to the towns Jesus intended to visit ahead of time to set up the needed conditions and gather necessary information (Kurtz 2013: 144). Larue (1990: 211) calls attention to Jesus's 70-person team who went, two by two, to the communities he was about to visit in the same way Billy Graham's squads arrived beforehand and made all the necessary arrangement to ensure the evangelist had a compliant and sympathetic crowd. After his advance men provided the gathered intelligence, Jesus would then reveal private details of peoples' lives to the astonishment of all (John 4:8–30). During my fieldwork, I found that this type of advance work and intelligence gathering is also the basis of the success of shamans, mediums, oracles, and god-men. Such information is then used to baffle gullible subjects, rendering them susceptible to manipulation.

The televangelist Peter Popoff, who operated during the 1980s, is a notorious contemporary example of this type of con-artistry. Popoff had members of his audience fill out cards with their personal information, such as ailments, home address, and so forth before they entered the rented auditoriums where he conducted his mass healings. While on stage, Popoff obtained this information from his wife using an earpiece and a radio transmitter. He would then disclose the details of people's lives and the nature of their maladies, claiming he received the information from God. The skeptic James Randi (1987: 147) was able to intercept these radio transmissions and exposed this disgraceful swindler's trickery.

After looking at the miracles described in the gospels, it appears that none of Jesus's magical feats were unique or unprecedented. The French historian Charles Guignebert (1958: 194) pointed this out long ago that the miracles performed by Jesus "were in no way original." Exorcising demons, healing lunatics, curing the sick, and even the resurrection of the dead were what was culturally expected of miracle workers in general. The gospels of Mark and Matthew confirm the fact that other similar miracle workers were operating in the area and tried to differentiate these ordinary conjurers from Jesus. Mark 13:22 states that false messiahs and false prophets will appear and deceive the people with their wonders. In Matthew 24:24, Jesus himself warned his disciples to be wary of other miracles workers: "there will arise false Christs and false prophets" who will lead the faithful, even the chosen ones astray with their marvels.

Celsus (1830: 14), with his impeccable logic and sharp pagan cynicism, pointed out this inconsistency and elaborated upon its implications:

> O light and truth, which clearly proclaims in its own words, as you write, that other men, and these depraved and enchanters, will come among you, possessing similar miraculous powers! Christ also feigns that a certain being, whom he denominates Satan, will be the source of these nefarious characters: so that Christ himself does not deny that these arts possess nothing divine, and acknowledges that they are the works of depraved men. At the same time [...] he discloses both the arts of others and his own. Is it not, therefore, a miserable thing, to consider, from the performance of the same deeds, this man to be a God, but others to be nothing more than enchanters? [...] Indeed, Christ confesses that these arts are not indications of a divine nature, but of certain impostors, and perfectly wicked characters.

Many suspicions and doubts thus arise about biblical miracles in general. So what made Jesus's conjurations different from those of his fellow illusionists and magicians? Was the difference in "Jesus' life and teaching," as Luck (2006: 63) maintains? The answer is probably not. These are merely rationalizations by a true believer. What the other conjurers lacked was very competent propagandists, spin doctors, public relations specialists, and apologists, such as the gospel writers and the leaders of the Church who managed to elevate Jesus's tricks to a class above all others. The most significant miracle of Christianity, one could argue, was not Jesus's paranormal tricks. As we have seen, there were plenty of others who performed the same stunts. Even Jesus's resurrection itself does not qualify. Resurrections were common events in those days, and there was a profusion of corpse reanimators. The real miracle was the ingenious way early Christian propagandists were able to pass off an ordinary conjurer with delusions of grandeur, and one whose prophecies about the imminent establishment of the Kingdom of God were decisive failures, as the Messiah, savior of humanity, and Son of God.

## Present-Day Miracle-Working Messiahs and Jesus's Miracles: A Comparative Look

For millennia charlatans and religious fanatics have used the procedures and tactics described here to dupe gullible followers and superstitious crowds. Contemporary self-styled messiahs and paranormal showmen have replicated many of Jesus's miracles, and some have even surpassed them. In one such case, the self-styled god-man, whose identity I shall reveal below, was convinced of his divinity, said he spoke to God directly, and his followers proclaimed him to be "God almighty himself" (Chidester 1988: 5; Kinsolving 1979a; Sidky 2015: 232). Like Jesus, this "ambassador from heaven" also had an apocalyptic message. He proclaimed that following the predicted imminent end times, he would emerge as ruler, not as the King of the Jews but as the president of the United States, to end inequality, oppression, and usher in a new utopia on earth (Mills 1979: 205–6, 218). Like Jesus, this megalomaniacal self-proclaimed prophet also had delusions of grandeur, demanded unconditional personal devotion from his piteous followers (see Matthew 10:37–38), and cursed and rebuked all dissenters (see Matthew 7:23).

His purported paranormal powers, which he also used as a recruitment aid, were numerous. These included clairvoyance, sending telepathic messages, and teleporting people from place to place. He too was able to feed a multitude with magically materialized banquets, in this case not fish and loaves of bread but Kentucky Fried Chicken! This god-man could also heal the sick, communicate with the spirits of the departed, and, best of all, bring the dead back to life with a mere touch (Mills 1979: 162–63, 219, 265). In the sphere of resurrections of the dead, he surpassed Jesus. As one of his disciples put it, he brought back "more than 40 persons [...] people stiff as a board, tongues hanging out, eyes set, skin graying, and all vital signs absent" (Kinsolving 1979b).

In this case, we have the sordid details and know exactly how the putative miraculous deeds were accomplished. Like Jesus, this bogus showman used shills in his healing sessions and had his own advance men who conducted background research on subjects ahead of a public demonstration. One of their tactics was to rummage through people's garbage to learn what they ate, drank, which medicines they used based on discarded pill bottles, and obtain other information from tossed-out letters, receipts, and magazines (Mills 1979: 124, 130). The god-man would then reveal the private details of people's lives during public performances to everyone's astonishment.

Also, he would instruct people on his staff to sit among the audience and pretend to miraculously recover from some feigned malady, such as a broken arm in a fake cast. As for the cases of the dead magically brought back to life, these were accomplished through the use of powerful drugs that produced the appearance of death, "tongues hanging out, eyes set, all vital signs absent" (Mills 1979: 13, 256–60). Our contemporary god-man managed to pull off these stunts by exploiting the vulnerabilities, expectations, false hopes, fears, superstitions, and gullibilities of his hapless audiences just like other miracle-working quacks and hacks across space and time. Here is yet another example of how easily people are bamboozled by an individual thought to be an authority with supernatural powers (cf., Randi 1987: 62).

The megalomaniacal god-man I have described was Jim Jones, founder of the Peoples Temple. One might argue that this is an unfair comparison because Jones merely copied Jesus's prototypical miraculous feats. However, Jesus did the same thing by modeling his procedure after those of his miracle-working counterparts and the exploits of the other alleged messiahs described in the Jewish Scriptures.

Jones ascended to heaven (?) on November 18, 1979, with over 900 of his followers after he compelled them to imbibe a concoction made from the soft drink Flavor-Aid laced with cyanide and tranquilizers (Sidky 2015: 234). This is the origin of the phrase "drinking the Kool-Aid (sic)" to refer to the uncritical acceptance of false ideas. This Messiah's utopian egalitarian socialist community, the foretold heaven on earth, thus came to a woeful and horrifying end in the steamy jungles of Guyana where the suicides took place. This tragic event represents the most massive single case of American civilian deaths until the 9/11 attacks in 2001, the acts of a different sort of religious fanatic. One wonders how these deaths would have been portrayed if Jones had the same kind of skilled and ingenious propagandists, public relations specialists, and spin doctors that sold the Jesus myth to the world. Jones too could easily have been portrayed as a god-man martyr who ascended to heaven with his devout worshippers, rather than the perverted sexual deviant and dangerously disturbed maniac and mass murderer that he was. Here again, the parallels are too close to justify the conclusion that this Messiah was a fraud (which he was), while the one who died 2,000 years ago was the genuine thing just because antiquity has bestowed an aura of sacredness upon his story.

The final questions that arise are, If Jesus was divine, with the limitless powers of God at his fingertips, why didn't he produce miracles of an entirely different order, instead of duplicating what other wonder-workers and magicians of his time had been doing for centuries without God's help? Why could he accomplish what any ordinary conjured could do but no more? Why didn't he regrow people's amputated limbs? Why just prosaic adrenaline-rush placebo-based healings and no more? The healing ceremonies of many of the shamans I have studied are more impressive than the ones described in the gospels. As far as I know, none of these shamans are the sons of God or claim genealogical connections with any other paranormal beings.

The final question is, Why was Jesus's miraculous powers operative only under specific circumstances? His failure to perform on demand and inability to accomplish mighty deeds before the people of his hometown of Nazareth, who told him to depart, reveals the limitations of an ordinary magician who is only able to perform by capitalizing on the element of surprise, the unfamiliarity of his audience, and with considerable prior preparation. As Humphrey (1999: 98) points out, a common question put to Jesus was why do you behave like a sorcerer if you are not one? Or why can you do miraculous deed here but not there? Thus, the genuine paranormal phenomena for which Jesus's miracles set the paradigmatic standards were not authentic. Even the preeminent paranormal trickster of Western culture failed because paranormal powers are not real. They have never been real.

# Chapter Fourteen

# JESUS'S EMPTY TOMB, MISSING BODY, AND RETURN FROM THE DEAD: SOURCES FOR THE PARANORMAL TALE

*A religionist may be an enthusiast, and imagine he sees what has no reality: he may know his narrative to be false, and yet persevere in it, with the best intentions in the world, for the sake of promoting so holy a cause.*

—David Hume, *Enquiries Concerning the Human Understanding* (1748)

*Looking at it historically, as an outward event, the resurrection of Jesus has not the very slightest foundation. Rarely has an incredible fact been worse attested, or one so ill-attested been more incredible in itself. [...] Taken historically, i.e., comparing the immense effect of this belief with its absolute baselessness, the story of the resurrection of Jesus can only be called a world-wide deception.*

—David Friedrich Strauss, *The Old Faith and the New* (1873)

*It is not difficult to account for the credit that was given to the story of Jesus Christ being the son of God. [...] Almost all the extraordinary men that lived under the heathen mythology were reputed to be the sons of some of their gods. [...] the story, was conformable to the opinions that then prevailed among the people called Gentiles [...] and it was those people only that believed it.*

—Thomas Paine, *The Age of Reason* (1794)

*And when we say also that the Word, who is the first-birth of God, was produced without sexual union, and that He, Jesus Christ, our Teacher, was crucified and died, and rose again, and ascended into heaven, we propound nothing different from what you believe regarding those whom you esteem sons of Jupiter.*

—Justin Martyr, *First Apology* (155–57 CE)

We now turn to the most significant paranormal event in Christianity, the resurrection of Jesus. Again, the reason for this discussion is the necessity to critically assess the "evidence base" and "positive theistic arguments" that religionists have proposed as a better alternative to science and the scientific perspective. The classical scholar Reginald Macan (1877: 6) called the resurrection "the miracle of miracles." The significance of this extraordinary event is stated emphatically by the self-styled apostle, Saul of Tarsus, or Paul:

> If there is no resurrection of the dead, then not even Christ has been raised. And if Christ has not been raised, our preaching is useless and so is your faith. (1 Corinthians 15:13–14)

"The dogma of the Resurrection," according to Craveri (1967: 438), "marks the beginning of *real* Christianity," or the development of the cult of Christ, which went beyond the efforts of a radical rabbi attempting to augment traditional Jewish religion. What's more, Jesus's return from the dead is of crucial emotional significance to the believers past and present. As the theologian Ernest Barnes (1948: 165) puts it, the bodily resurrection of Jesus and Christian sentimentality are inextricably linked so that for believers the mere suggestion of abandoning it is excruciating.

## The Apologists' Perspective

For present-day believers, the anchor of the Christian religion as a whole is the singular paranormal event of the bodily resurrection of Jesus. The New Testament scholar Hugh Anderson (1964: 186) calls it "constitutive for the community's faith and worship, its discipleship, and mission to the world." For the apologist Terry Miethe (2003: xv), "The Christian faith—and its claim to be the truth—exists only if Jesus rose from the dead." For such believers, the literal physical restoration of Jesus to life after physical death is the basis of Christianity's miraculous standing. This event, believers assert, explains why after the crucifixion, the personnel of the Jesus cult risked everything to proclaim that Jesus rose from the dead and the rapid spread of Christianity.

The apologist Gary Habermas (2003: 19–20) is confident that there is "strong historical evidence" that Jesus got up and walked out of the grave and maintains that scholars who deal with this topic agree on the essential historical facts. These include: (1) that Jesus died on the cross; (2) was buried; (3) the disciples lost faith; (4) Jesus's body was put in a tomb later found vacant. However, contrary to what Habermas says, there is considerable disagreement among historians and philosophers over even the basic facts. These include the details of Jesus's life, the period in which he lived, the length of his ministry, the date of the crucifixion, the veracity of the Passion narratives, whether Jesus's body was buried or tossed aside, the existence of an empty tomb, and what ensued afterward. Indeed, there is disagreement on nearly everything apart from the bare fact that a man was nailed to a cross or perhaps even a tree or a pole (Evans 1977: 28; Kahl 1971: 103; Trilling 1969: 64; Wilson 1984: 142).

What gave rise to the belief in this paradigmatic paranormal phenomenon of the Western culture, that an executed man came back to life through a divine miracle? There are two interconnected traditions. The first relates the mysterious disappearance of Jesus's body from his tomb, that is, the empty tomb story. The second involves reports of Jesus appearing to his disciples after he was killed and buried.

## The Empty Tomb Story, Its Sources, Documentation, and Creative Fiction Writing

We shall begin with the first tradition, the story of the empty tomb. The postmortem appearances are the topic of the following chapter. Several questions require answers: How did the story of Jesus's return from the dead get written? When and where does the earliest narrative about this event first appear? What were the sources for the story? Are the stories reliable?

Descriptions of Jesus's burial and the disappearance of his body appear in the Synoptic Gospels (Mark, Luke, and Matthew) and the Gospel of John. Meticulous scholarship shows that the Gospel of Mark, once thought to be a condensed version of the Gospel of Matthew, is the first of the four texts to be written (Erham 2016: 242–43). The earliest versions of this text date to about 70 CE (Tobin 209: 252–56; Wells 1996: xxi). Luke and Matthew repeat the same stories found in Mark, listing them in the same order, sometimes even using the same words, which suggests that these texts came after Mark (Ehrman 2016: 59; Philipse 2014: 172). These two gospels also seem to have another source for the sayings of Jesus not found in Mark. Some scholars posit that they draw upon a no-longer-extant account referred to as "Q," from the German word *Quelle*, or source (Ehrman 2016: 60). Some disagreement exists over the chronological order of Luke and Matthew. They may have been written at the same time because their authors appear to be unaware of each other. Altogether, these three texts are referred to as the Synoptics or Synoptic Gospels, meaning "seem together" (Goodacre 2001: 13–32).

The Gospel of John appears last. It departs from the others on numerous points, plays fast and loose with the source materials, has a different chronology of Jesus's ministry, portrays him as a non-Jew (John 8:43), and is considered the least historically reliable of the four texts (Goodacre 2001: 13–32; Tobin 2009: 276–79). However, John draws on the Synoptics for the passion story, which is the main concern in this chapter. The New Testament scholar, theologian, and historian of early Christianity, Dale Allison (2005: 301), however, seems to think that John's use of the passion narrative in the Synoptics is uncertain.

Complicating matters further is evidence that Mark's passion story is his literary creation with nearly every detail of the story having parallels down to specifics in the Septuagint, or the Greek Old Testament, which was the earliest Greek translation of the Hebrew Scriptures (Carnley 1987: 47; Crossan 1976; Kirby 2005: 233: Spong 1995: 226). In other words, the basis of the whole narrative is not an articulated oral tradition but only snippets of received tradition that Mark seems to have first woven together on paper using the Septuagint to fill in the missing details (Helms 2006: 92–99; Funk 1996: 238). Such use of the Septuagint, that is, the Scriptures, is indeed evident even in the earliest document that refers to the resurrection, which is Paul's first letter to the Corinthians 15:3–8, which dates to around 50–60 CE. Paul emphatically says,

> that Christ died for our sins according to the Scriptures [i.e., the Septuagint], that he was buried, that he was raised on the third day according to the Scriptures, and that he appeared to Cephas [Peter], and then to the Twelve [disciples].

The contributors to Werner Kelber's volume *The Passion in Mark: Studies on Mark 14–16* (1976) reach a similar conclusion regarding the use of the Greek Old Testament by Mark and the early Christians. What we have is not "history remembered" but a story created out of the "bare and brutal facts of crucifixion" woven together according to the Jewish Scriptures (Crossan 1998: 568). In his book *The Bible Against Itself*, Randel Helms (2006: 92–99) reaches a similar conclusion. If all of this is correct, then the entire tale of Jesus's burial and resurrection (the Easter story) found in Mark is highly fictionalized with no corroboration.

As Doherty (2005: 241) points out, New Testament scholarship over the last two centuries has shown that the texts of the gospels Matthew and Luke are not independent accounts but duplicate of the material in the Gospel of Mark. Matthew copies nearly 90 percent of Mark, and Luke more than 50 percent. Moreover, the passion narratives in these two books are almost identical to the text in Mark. It appears that the authors of Matthew and Luke were ignorant of the circumstance of Jesus's death—the event which brought salvation to the world and on which Christianity is anchored—until they read the Gospel of Mark (Doherty 2005: 241). Along the same lines, the New Testament scholar and historian of early Christianity John Crossan (1998: 521) states that there could not have been an independent tradition of the passion narrative. Everyone copies directly or indirectly from Mark. If the story existed early on as history and was widely known among the Christians, he asks, then why did the evangelists not copy from it, rather than base their accounts on Mark? (Crossan (1998: 521). It is therefore untrue to assert as some true believers do (e.g., Craig 1998: 257–57) that the four gospels provide mutually corroborating testimonials (Dunn 1985: 66) or that they represent independent and historically accurate transcripts of the same events. The reason adherents hold this idea is because they are unable to treat this material objectively despite their pretensions of being engaged in historical scholarship, as discussed in Chapter 12.

What this means is that the evidentiary basis for Jesus's resurrection on which the Christian faith rests is even weaker than previously thought (cf., Kirby 2005: 237). As Doherty (2005: 244) sums it up, the four canonical gospels do not comprise independent corroborative accounts of the events at the heart of the Christian faith. There is simply one account, one story, and one sequence of events that contains the alleged central events of Christianity (Doherty 2005: 244). Thus, it appears that in the case of the resurrection of Jesus, we may not even have any genuine eyewitness accounts of a miracle to weigh against Hume's criteria for assessing miraculous claims.

The parallels between the resurrection story and the Roswell myth are remarkable. Both were purported occurrences for which there was insufficient information to make any determinations about an actual event. Such circumstances create space for wishful thinkers and other interested parties to interject wholly conjectural possibilities, rumors, and hearsay. The socio-psychological mechanisms of how such stories, memes, or X-claims develop, the way they grab hold of people's minds and spread across populations, move from community to community, and are passed on through generations are well known. In the case of Roswell, we have speculations and imputations of an extraterrestrial spacecraft with actual aliens aboard crashing with no witnesses to the event as well as claims about a grand governmental cover-up. In the case of the resurrection, there was a complete lacuna of information about the disposition of the body and whereabouts of a grave and speculations and rumors about a dead man who came back to life and walked away when no witnesses were present.

Another similarity is that for both events we have to rely on the recollections of purported on-the-scene reporters whose testimonials have come down to us in the form of second- and third-hand anecdotal accounts that were circulating for years and collected many decades after the alleged events are said to have occurred (see Chapter 7). Here again, what we know about the processes that alter, distort, and even create entirely false memories and the massive reliability problems associated with anecdotal materials that render such information highly unreliable if not implausible.

Before examing the resurrection story further, it is crucial to point out that modern New Testament scholars who are not votaries do not take it for granted that these narratives are history (Price 2010b: 209–10). The mistake made by the eighteenth- and early nineteenth-century "rationalists" who inaugurated the modern critical scholarship of the gospels and who provided naturalistic explanations for the resurrection event was to make such a dispensation (Patterson 1998: 28–32). In other words, they "conceded too much" when dealing with the story by granting that parts of it were historical (Watson 1987: 369). It is not merely a question, for instance, that the Joseph of Arimathea sequence of the tale, or the women visiting the tomb segment of the script, are historical and only the finale, "the resurrection," is legendary. There is no reason to assume that any part of this narrative is factual from a historical perspective (Price 2011: 220). What follows, therefore, is merely to show the flaws in the gospel narratives, the historicity of these stories are to be rejected entirely.

The detailed narrative of the resurrection of Jesus and the empty tomb first appears in the Gospel of Mark. Again, it is significant to point out that for 2,000 years Christians have believed that their faith originated in the events of the passion story related in Mark and reworked in the subsequent gospels (Doherty 2005: 240). The relevant part of the story for the present discussion, which the New Testament scholar Stephen Patterson (1998: 200) aptly calls "literary theater," relates how Jesus and his 70 or so disciples entered Jerusalem with high hopes and bravado, enthralled with apocalyptic expectations and great messianic enthusiasm. If Jesus rode into the city on an ass (Mark 11:1–11), he must have thought that he was fulfilling the prophecy of Zechariah (9:9). However, we have good reason to doubt that this was the case because the early Christians scoured the Septuagint for passages and lifted them out of context to make prophetic statements about Jesus's activities long after Jesus was dead and buried (Helms 2006: 92–99; 1988: 63, 131).

The text in Mark suggests that members of the Jesus cult who accompanied their rabbi to Jerusalem believed that he was about to transform society, end the Roman occupation, restore the 12 tribes of Israel, and rule as their king (Philipse 2014: 179). Jesus's promise to them was that they would "sit on the twelve thrones, judging the twelve tribes of Israel" and that they would receive "a hundred times as much and will inherit eternal life" in the Kingdom of God (Matthew 19:27–9). Things, however, did no go as expected. Instead of a successful outcome and realization of what was promised, Jesus was seized by the local Jewish authorities, probably the Temple guards where he caused a commotion (Mark 11:15–19), and brought before the Sanhedrin, the Jewish council. Members of the council construed the prisoner as a seditious eschatological prophet and unanimously convicted him of blasphemy (Mark 14:12–65), a crime punishable by death (Lüdemann 1995:131). The Sanhedrin then handed Jesus over to the Romans, who also tried him and found him guilty. The man was humiliated, scourged like a common criminal, and put to a shameful death on the cross alongside two highway brigands (Funk 1998: 121–22, 133, 145–46, 152).

The crucifixion was an unthinkable catastrophe for the cultists who had staked their hopes and desires, indeed their entire lives, on Jesus's triumph a the Messiah. Horrified, dumbfounded, and fearing for their own lives, the disciples deserted their master, scattered, and fled (Mark 14:50) from Jerusalem back to Galilee (Funk 1998: 466–67). According to theologian Herman Hendrickx (1978: 15), "The men left for Galilee after the tragedy of the day of Preparation, and there is no indication that they left with any knowledge of an empty tomb." To the Jews, as the classical scholar Reginald Macan (1877: 81) put it, "the death of Jesus on the cross was [...] the divine judgment upon him as an imposter [and] blasphemer." All this amounts to a sad tale of false prophecies, failed disciples, betrayal, abandonment, and disgrace. These were terrible things, the correction of which would require that the authors of the gospels who wrote a couple of generations after the events engage in reverse-engineering or retro-correcting of the narrative.

The reaction of faithless and cowardly cultists to the apprehension and execution of Jesus and their later skepticism toward the postmortem sightings are substantial evidence that the calamity that befell their hapless master was utterly and shockingly unexpected. Luke (24:21) captures this with two of the disciples saying, "but we had hoped he was the one who was going to redeem Israel." Had all those terrible events of that Easter been foretold and if the prophecy had been integral to the beliefs of the cultists, they would not have reacted in this fashion. Also, the women would not have visited the tomb intending to anoint the corpse if they did not think that their rabbi was dead, and the disciples would not have been surprised that the tomb was found empty.

As Macan (1877: 93–94) stated long ago, the disciples could not have known about the prophecy; otherwise, they would not have been so unprepared when Jesus was executed and not have so completely lost heart and faith. Instead, the suffering and death of their rabbi, which was allegedly foretold to them, would simply have corroborated his supernatural powers and divine mission and their faith. They would also not have been surprised by an empty tomb, if one even existed, would not have doubted the resurrection, or disbelieve when Jesus appeared to them. He adds that: "If the Apostles little expected the death of their master, still less did they expect his Resurrection and he cannot have foretold it as he is represented to have" (Macan 1877: 93–94).

Similarly, the courageous and implacable Bible demythologizer David Friedrich Strauss (1902: 635) observed that the disciples had no foreknowledge of the predictions of death and resurrection and that the evangelists put these words in Jesus's mouth long after the fact. The technical theological term for this is *vaticinium ex eventu* [hindsight bias] (Bultmann 1965: 129–30). In other words, the argument that it was the disciple's faith before the crucifixion that produced the resurrection belief, as Allison (2005: 209–10) maintains, is entirely implausible. That belief could not have been a continuation of "pre-Easter faith" but rather a consequence of the crucifixion and the ensuing events.

Confronting the evangelists who wrote the gospels was a significant dilemma, that is, how to explain Jesus's unanticipated and ignoble death and the betrayal by his disciples who fled upon his arrest and still preserve a dignified picture (Mark 14:50). Their solution was to reverse-engineer a story to make it appear that the betrayal, crucifixion, and death of Jesus were known ahead of time as part of a prophecy foretold long before the events came to pass (Mark 14:28; Luke 24:7, 46). The story in the Gospel of Mark shows how the early Christians retrojected and recast the unexpected calamitous failure by spinning a tale in which a shameful death as a crucified criminal rather than being a disqualification, in fact, confirmed Jesus as the Messiah. As is discussed in Chapter 16, such circumstances are not unique in the annals of the history of religion. There are many instances when disappointed followers of a failed messiah have done precisely the same thing.

Celsus (1987: 64) was well aware of the tendencies of the Christians to rewrite and change their accounts as necessary:

> It is clear to me that the writings of the Christians are a lie, and [their] fables have not been well constructed to conceal this monstrous fiction. [Their] interpreters, as if they had just come out of a tavern, are onto the inconsistencies and pen in hand, alter the original writings three, four, and several more times over in order to be able to deny the contradictions in the face of criticism.

Creative storytelling was an essential element in Judaism with incredible tales spun around the lives of known historical actors as illustrated by Midrashic and Haggadic literature (Crossley 2005: 179). The professor of Bible James Crossley (2005: 179) points out that it should not be surprising to anyone that something similar happened in the gospel traditions. As he puts it, looking at the Jewish and pagan contexts of Christianity, it is to be expected that the gospel writers would have followed the standard practice of their Jewish and pagan counterparts by making up stories. The narratives themselves indicate as much. Thus, as Crossley says, a high degree of skepticism is necessary when we find in Luke 24:11–12; John 20:6–8 that Peter is at the empty tomb when Mark clearly states that the women told no one. It is the same when the women in Matthew 28:8–9 suddenly relate the news that they saw Jesus to the disciples, but Mark says they remained silent (Crossley 2005: 181).

Similarly, doubt is needed regarding the historicity of the narrative in Matthew (28:16–20) that puts the early Church's mission statement for the Gentiles in the words of the physically risen Jesus on a mountain. Also, some suspicion must be raised when in the theology of Luke (24:6–7) the Markan promise that Jesus will return to Galilee (Mark 16:7) is replaced by two dazzling men who locate all the appearances and the ascension in Jerusalem. It is evident, Crossley adds, that the tradition of Mark has been monumentally embellished to address contemporary needs by making the physical resurrection the central Christian belief. All of this makes sense in light of the Jewish tradition of storytelling and creative rewriting of the narratives (Crossley's 2005: 181).

Thus, out of what was a fiasco, the author of the Gospel of Mark and the gospel writers who penned their works after him fabricated an entirely new kind of Messiah, one who suffers and dies to bring salvation to humankind and is vindicated by God raising him from the dead (cf., Ehrman 2016: 249–51). To do this the early Christians, who were Torah-abiding Jews, turned to their holy texts, namely the Septuagint, eventually to be called the Old Testament in contrast to the New Testament that they created for themselves (Crossan 1995: 2; Larue 1990: 12). As theologian Paul Van Buren (1998: 26) points out, it is not necessary to think that the disciples retreated to the study hall inside a synagogue to carefully scrutinize the texts. They were likely illiterate. However, they knew the contents of the Torah because many times they had heard them.

To accomplish this objective, the cultists searched their memories of the Jewish Scriptures, recalling suitable passages, and used them to assemble a passion narrative after the fact to explain what happened in the present. However, the prophecies in these texts are so general and vague as to fit almost any case. And as Celsus (1830: 11) pointed out long ago, "What is asserted by the Jewish prophets may be much more probably adapted to ten thousand other persons than to Jesus." This is how the early Christians recast their stories to present the events in Jesus's life as the fulfillment of the prophecies in the Jewish religious literature.

The literary critic Randel Helms (1988: 18, 63, 131) points out that, in the hands of the early Christians, the Old Testament became a book about Jesus. The passages were dissected, taken out of context, and decoded as if they were prophecies about the activities of Jesus. Thus, Helms (1988: 131) adds, "the story of Jesus came into being as a mirror of the Old Testament; the Gospels closed the self-reflective circle: Old Testament-New Testament."

Helms (2006: 93) goes on to show how, to fill in the missing details of the crucifixion, including the division of Jesus's clothes by the Roman soldiers, the jeering and taunting by the passer-bys, the drink consisting of vinegar offered to the dying man, and Jesus's last words, the gospel writers used the Septuagint "as a script." The literary theorist Northrop Frye (1982: 78) describes this process as a kind of circular argument. The gospel stories are declared to be genuine because they confirm Old Testament prophecies. Those prophecies are pronounced to be true because the gospel stories confirm them. He adds that what is offered as evidence flung back and forth between the testaments like a tennis ball. No other evidence is on offer. Thus, the Old Testament and the New Testament comprise "a double mirror, each reflecting the other but neither the outside world" (Frye 1982: 78). Some of the main difficulties in Christian theology arise from the inconsistencies of the effort by the early believers to create in this fashion a plausible tale after the fact.

Along the same lines, the theologian John Spong (1995: 226) points out, "the details of the story of the crucifixion were actually written with Hebrew Scriptures open and under the primary influence of Psalms 22 and Isaiah 53." Moreover, the historian of Christianity R. Joseph Hoffmann (1996: xiii) observes in this regard that the central historical event of the gospel tradition, the death and resurrection of Jesus, is devoid of historical details and is like a liturgical drama created out of the Psalms and prophetic texts. As Spong (1995: 58) adds, the gospel writers had very little historical details to draw upon and many blanks to fill in the portrait of Jesus's life. They solved this problem by simply searching the Hebrew Scriptures to complete the missing details and portraying Jesus's carrier as the fulfillment of God's promises to his chosen people. In other words, Spong (1995: 58) adds, "Mark, the first Gospel, was Christian Midrash [working an ancient theme into a new or present context] at its best, and this Gospel set the style for all the other Gospels." Crossan (1994: 163, 1998: 568) calls this "prophecy historicized" in contrast to "history remembered," or an account of what occurred in fact.

Mark's narrative also attempts to explain away other puzzling facts, such as why, if Jesus was the Son of God, he could not gain immediate and widespread popular support by suggesting that he kept his messianic mission a secret. Hence, wherever someone realized that Jesus is the Messiah, he told them to reveal his identity to anyone (Erhman 2016: 60–61). William Werde explored this theme in his book *The Messianic Secret* (1901). Thus, Mark is as theological as the other gospels (Ehrman 2016: 61). Allison (2005: 321) is incorrect in asserting that Mark does not provide theological reflections on the resurrection and that this is evidence of historical content. As discussed in Chapter 12, the Gospel of Mark and the gospels written after it are missionary propaganda tracts of the cult of Christ, not historical biographies. The people who wrote these texts were zealous evangelical spin doctors, who carefully crafted their works to persuade readers that Jesus was the risen Son of God (Gorham 1908: 13, 16; Hoffmann 1984: 7; Parsons 2005: 440). Present-day apologists such as Alison and others are taking advantage of the naïveté of their audiences when they make spurious statements regarding the historical accuracy of these narratives (Price 2011: 219).

## The Burial Story and Fate of Jesus's Body

We know that Jesus died alone because, as Mark 14:50 says, "They all forsook him and fled." If Jesus's followers deserted him, how did anyone know the manner of his death or what happened to his body? Also, under ordinary circumstances, the corpses of people crucified by the Romans were left on the cross as an object-lesson and deterrence to others to be devoured by birds and wild animals (Hengel 1977: 87–88; Strauss 1902: 790). Crossan (1995: 187–88) suggests that this was the exact fate of Jesus's body (see also Brown 1994: 1207–8; Sloyan 1995: 16). The faithful have naturally been horrified by such a suggestion. However, the alternative looks no better. Criminals put to death by the Jewish court were given dishonorable burials in a public graveyard designated for criminals according to Rabbinic law (Lowder 2005: 266). The graves of such hapless folk would have been marked by a pile of loose stones, without any inscriptions. In some cases, chalk mixed with water was poured over the spot to indicate ritual uncleanliness, warning people to keep away (Komarnitsky 2014a: 27).

Jewish religious law stipulated that mourners could not attend dishonorable burials. So no one acquainted with Jesus would have been present during the disposal of his body had there been a burial. Also, if any of the disciples had, in fact, been hiding somewhere in Jerusalem, as some claim (Allison 2005: 330; Gardner-Smith 1926: 144; Wedderburn 1999: 58–60), they would have surely avoided public humiliation by appearing in public or attending the burial of a false messiah (Komarnitsky 2014a: 29). More importantly, visiting the grave would have exposed the fearful disciples, who were potential wanted men, to arrest as public threats by the Romans or the Jewish authorities who, as the Gospel of Peter 12:50 says, "were inflamed with wrath." What this implies is that if Jesus's body was not left to decompose on the cross, it was buried dishonorably in a pit. The theologian Alfred Loisy (1962: 85) made this observation years before Crossan, namely that the standard procedure was for the bodies of executed criminals to be buried in a common grave unless the family secured special permission to bury it themselves. However, in the case of Jesus's body, no one interceded. Much later, when the need arose to dignify the circumstances somehow and provide an honorable burial, "tradition imagined for the part a person of consideration alike for his social standing and character," that is, Joseph of Arimathea is conjured up out of nowhere (Loisy 1962: 85). It is therefore highly unlikely that Jesus's followers, family members, or sympathizers, if any, were present or even knew the location of the grave or disposition of his body.

There is some independent evidence in texts outside the New Testament that suggest that the Jews who had Jesus crucified were also the ones who removed him from the cross and dishonorably interred him in the ground (Kirby 2005: 246–48). In the Gospel of James 5, Jesus says:

> Or do you not know that you have not yet been mistreated and have not yet been accused unjustly, nor have you yet been shut up in prison, nor have you yet been condemned lawlessly, nor have you yet been crucified without reason, nor have you yet been buried shamefully, as I was myself, by the evil one?

The Gospel of Peter 6:21 relates: "And then the Jews drew the nails from the hands of the Lord and laid him on the earth." We can be certain of one thing, as the New Testament scholar Gerd Lüdemann (1995: 20) points out, "there are indications that Mark was confronted with the tradition of dishonorable burial and reinterpreted this."

### *Inconsistencies in the Gospel of Mark*

The story that follows in the Gospel of Mark is full of improbabilities and contradictions. These arise out of the author's efforts to explain away Jesus's horrifying end, the failure of the disciples, rectify the tradition of dishonorable burial, and, above all else, to definitively establish that Jesus rose from the grave in his physical body. A physical reanimation may have become necessary at this historical juncture, as biblical scholar Michael Goulder (1996: 55–59) points out, to settle a controversy that had emerged among the Christians regarding whether Jesus exited from the tomb as a spirit or with the same body that was tied and nailed to the cross.

One group of Christians known as the Docetists claimed that Jesus was a paranormal or phantasmal being, without a flesh-and-blood body (González 2005: 46–47). Alternatively, some Docetists believed that Christ was a paranormal being who had occupied the physique of the flesh-and-blood Jesus and returned to heaven the moment Jesus died (Ehrman 2011: 53–54; 2005: 16; Gorham 1908: 221–22; Mansel 1875).

The religious studies professor Bart Ehrman (2014: 168–69) notes that the narrative about the discovery of an empty tomb was necessary for the claim that Jesus was physically raised. Some Christians questioned the bodily resurrection, and this may have been an intense and ongoing dispute among the early Christian communities from the very start. He adds that the books that became the New Testament, in contrast to the many that were excluded, emphatically claimed that Jesus arose in his physical body. In other words, the empty tomb story addresses the dissenters as well as validating for the faithful that the resurrection was not of a spirit but of a body (Ehrman 2014: 168–69).

Writing about the discovery of a tomb that should have contained a body but did not was a dramatic way to underscore that a physical reanimation had occurred (Goulder 1996: 57). Establishing this was crucial to the central premise of the Christian faith that had developed by the time that the resurrection was of the body not of the spirit and therefore not to be dismissed as a ghost story. To accomplish this, a tomb for Jesus had to be written in the script, as well as friends to put his body there, and others to find the location vacant. We are, in other words, dealing with fiction (Loisy 1962: 85).

It is for the same reasons that the reported postmortem sighting of Jesus, which in the original reports are undoubtedly visionary experiences, to be discussed in the next chapter, are rewritten in the gospels as physical encounters. Put simply, the Christian evangelists changed the story. In the gospels (texts written long after Paul's death), the initial claim by Paul that Jesus's spirit was taken to heaven and provided with a new celestial body, a form in which he appeared to several of his acolytes as visions (1 Corinthians 15:42–50), is transformed into physical encounters with a flesh-and-blood human being. We can trace the transformation of the story from the account in Mark (which ends at verse 16:8), where there is a suggestion of a future postmortem appearance in Galilee, into actual encounters with a physically risen corpse in Matthew 28:9, 10; Luke 24:36, 39; and John 20:19–20, 26. That these were visionary experiences is indicated by the fact that Jesus entered through locked doors and appeared suddenly amid the disciples, who at first thought they saw a ghost. The later insertion of verses 9–19 at the end of Mark that relate postmortem appearances of Jesus to Mary Magdalene and the disciples had the same objective. The meaning and significance of the postmortem Jesus apparitions are examined in greater detail in Chapter 15.

The errors and inconsistencies are evident when we look at the actual narrative of Jesus's burial in Mark 15:40–47. The story goes that upon Jesus's death on the cross, a pious Jew named Joseph of Arimathea decided to bury him. Joseph is said to be a respected member of the Sanhedrin, the council that unanimously condemned Jesus to death. He wanted to observe God's law that the body of an executed person should not remain on the cross and must be interred the same day before sunset. This injunction is stated in Deuteronomy 21:22–23: "If someone guilty of a capital offense is put to death and [his] body is exposed on a pole […] [be] sure to bury it that same day, because anyone who is hung on a pole is under God's curse. You must not desecrate the land the Lord your God is giving you as an inheritance" [by leaving the body hanging overnight].

Loisy (1962: 86) makes an important observation: "Joseph of Arimathea was the male figure indispensable for the decency of burial and boldly selected as a member of the Sanhedrin." Mark relates that Joseph makes a personal plea to Pontius Pilate, the Roman governor of Judea who ordered the crucifixion, for permission to remove Jesus's corpse from the cross.

Joseph's identity is unknown despite numerous conjectures. There is no textual or archaeological evidence to indicate the location of a village or town called Arimathea (Brown 1994: 1213 n. 17; Goldin 1948; Kirby 2005: 237). Moreover, there is no indication that Paul, our earliest source, knew anything about this Joseph of Arimathea or the details of the burial described in Mark (Ehrman 2014: 142, 152). This character is written into the script by Mark to advance a plotline that a friendly person gave Jesus an honorable burial and, as already noted, to establish the existence of a tomb to later be discovered empty (Crossan 1995: 172–73; Doherty 2005: 257; Tobin 2009: 537).

Surprisingly, religionists Raymond Brown (1994: 1240) and Willliam Lyons (2004: 49) suggest that the fact that Joseph is from an unidentifiable location of Arimathea attests to his historicity. However, the efforts to establish that Joseph was a historical personage are not very convincing (e.g., O'Collins and Kendall 1994a). Contra to Brown and Lyons, an unidentifiable location does not prove historicity but the opposite. It makes perfect sense to create a fictional place as the home for a nonexistent character such as Joseph if one wishes to avoid disconfirmation.

Similarly, spurious is Lyon's (2004: 48–49) suggestion that it makes no sense for Mark to have utilized a pious Jew as the person burying Jesus unless it had historical foundations. To the contrary, using such a person to lend credibility to the narrative makes perfect sense. The author of Mark 15:39 uses the same tactic when he has a Roman centurion rather than a disciple or an ordinary spectator make the realization and declare Jesus's divinity: "And when the centurion, who stood there in front of Jesus, saw how he died, he said, 'Surely this man was the Son of God!'" All of this, it must be kept in mind, is imaginary because none of the disciples or the evangelists who penned the gospels were present to record the circumstances of Jesus's suffering on the cross or the final moments of life.

Returning to the narrative, Mark relates that Joseph does not ask Pilate to release the bodies of all three crucified men, just that of Jesus. This exception is puzzling because the stated objective is to dispose of all corpses out of piety to ensure ritual purity during the Sabbath. One possibility could be that the two other hapless men were still alive at the time Joseph made the request since Jesus's death was unexpectedly quick (Lowder 2005: 265). The passage does not make sense, however, because John 19:31–33 says the Jewish leaders who were in a hurry to have the bodies taken down because of the approaching Sabbath asked Pilate to have the legs of condemned men broken, a method used to accelerate death, which the soldiers did in the case of the two criminals. However, when they approached Jesus, "he was already dead, and they did not break his legs" (John 19:31–33).

What this means is that the Jews, in fact, had to deal with the disposal of three cadavers. Hence, it is all the more likely that Jesus's corpse was deposited along with the other two in a common grave for criminals (cf., Crossan 1998: 555). The author of Mark deliberately left out the simultaneous burial of the three men to convey the impression that Jesus received a dignified burial. More importantly, if the story stated that Joseph buried all three men, there could be no empty tomb (Crossan 1998: 555). Apologists claim that Joseph left the fate of the corpses of the highwaymen to the Romans. However, this statement is implausible if there was concern about observing God's law. If the Romans were going to bury the executed prisoners as part of their routine in any case, there was no need for Joseph to intervene. Altogether, these inconsistencies further suggest that the story of burial by Joseph of Arimathea is a fiction created by Mark. As Crossan (1998: 555) concludes, there is no pre-Markan tradition for this tale. Lyon's (2005) critique of Crosson's view on this matter is entirely unconvincing.

Returning to the storyline, upon hearing Joseph's request, Pilate orders his centurion to confirm the death and then permits him to retrieve the corpse:

> Pilate was surprised to hear that he was already dead. Summoning the centurion, he asked him if Jesus had already died. When he learned from the centurion that it was so, he gave the body to Joseph. (Mark 15:44–45)

Jesus's death is thus definitively established in the passage. This part of the story has been carefully worded to refute anti-Christian polemic at the time of the writing of this text that Jesus did not die on the cross but was in a coma and was later revived (Lüdemann 1995: 19). According to professor of theology Francis Watson (1987: 369), the strange emphatic and repetitive language in this segment of the narrative suggests that the author was intentionally making a point that Jesus was indeed dead. Similarly, Loisy (1962: 86) says that the passage where the centurion tells Pilate about Jesus's death was intended to address a controversy between the Jews and Christians that "the body had been carried away before death, neither party knowing more than the other how the matter had really gone." This is yet another instance where the near-total absence of any information makes room for interjecting rumors, hearsay, speculations, and conspiracies. These are just the sort of circumstances for the development of paranormal explanations and hypotheses.

There is no need to posit that an enthusiastic and creative redactor inserted these verses later on for apologetic purposes as a "double witness of Pilate and the centurion" that Jesus was indeed dead and that the resurrection was not a resuscitation from a coma (Brown 1994: 1219). Strauss (1902: 700) observed that doubts that Jesus had not died on the cross might have been in circulation early in the Christian period, and the passage in Mark was intended to dispel those doubts. These views, as already noted, were expressed explicitly later by doctrinal Docetists (Allison 2005: 204, n. 20). Such beliefs are probably the reason why years after the events John (19:31–34) appends the additional fictional detail of the Roman soldier piercing Jesus's side with a spear, copied directly from Zechariah 2:10 in the Old Testament, to signify his unequivocal death.

Next comes the description of the burial. With sunset approaching on the eve of the Sabbath during the Passover, Joseph has his servants hurridly take Jesus's body down from the cross, buys strips of linen and anointing oils at his own expense, and hastily places the corpse in a nearby tomb. The texts distinctly specify strips of fabric, not a single large cloth as in the case of the bogus Shroud of Turin. These details form essential elements of Mark's fictional tale. The purchase of the linen implies that the pieces of cloth were clean, which is another attempt to make the burial a dignified occasion (Lüdemann 1995: 20). Hasty burial presupposes the incompletion of the ritual preparation of the body, which sets up the reason why the women have to return to the tomb and find it empty.

It is puzzling that there is no indication of cooperation between Joseph and Jesus's female followers who purportedly watched the crucifixion and burial from afar, given the short amount of time left to complete all the necessary ritual tasks before nightfall (Kirby 2005: 242–45). It is also inexplicable why the women, who presumably saw the tomb sealed with a massive stone, went there alone on the third day without asking Joseph or his people for permission or help to unseal the tomb.

Even if a Joseph character did exist, it is baffling why a pious Sanhedrinist who took part in sentencing Jesus to death—the vote was unanimous (Mark 14:65)—went through the trouble of personally disposing of the body of a convicted blasphemer. In the later gospels, the evangelists attempt to rectify this glaring inconsistency by declaring that Joseph was a secret disciple of Jesus (John 19:38). However, all of this makes even less sense. As Craveri (1967: 420) observed, the gospel writers were inattentive to their fictitious elaborations because at the very instance when the disciples are fearful of being implicated and are fleeing for their lives, "they introduce this eleventh-hour convert" who dares risking eviction from the Sanhedrin and from his own social circles to "perform an act of mercy toward the cadaver of a rebel whom everyone had deserted" (Craveri 1967: 420).

The third burial tradition in the New Testament, in the Book of Acts, which says that the same enemies who had Jesus crucified also buried him, goes against the assertion that friends and sympathizers did the job (cf., Spong 1995: 224). According to Acts 13:28–30,

> Though they found no proper ground for a death sentence, they [the Jewish authorities in Jerusalem] asked Pilate to have him executed. When they had carried out all that was written about him, they took him down from the cross and laid him in a tomb.

McGrath (2008: 72) suggests that the plural "they laid him" either refers to Joseph's servants who did the deed or to the fact that the burial was at the behest of the Sanhedrin. However, this is reading more in this passage than is warranted by the text.

### *Honorable or Ignominious Burial?*

There is another troubling issue. It is puzzling why Pilate permitted Jesus to receive an honorable burial because this would not only suggest an unjust execution but would also legitimize Jesus's sedition and create a martyr. Such an action would have constituted an unnecessary headache for the Roman governor (Kirby 2005: 242–45). Moreover, from what is known, Pilate was a violent, murderous, and malicious governor who would not have shown mercy toward his subjects or display respect for Jewish sensitivities (Ehrman 2014: 160–63). He was certainly not a man to break tradition and policy if asked by a Jewish council member for the body of a crucified criminal. Indeed, the Jewish historian Josephus and the philosopher Philo describe Pilate as a man devoid of kindness who was detestably cruel toward his subjects (Wells 1996: 70). Also, later on, Pilate is removed from office because of his excessive brutality and needless cruelty, even according to Roman imperial standards (Crossan 1995: 157–58).

Religionists argue that in some cases exceptions were made, and certain families received the bodies of their crucified kin for a decent burial. This, however, as Ehrman (2014) says, was a favor reserved only for elite Jewish families, and Jesus's family had no high connections in Jerusalem. Moreover, a Roman governor would only make such an exception to honor the emperor's birthday. Jesus's crucifixion occurred during the Jewish Passover. None of these conditions for releasing the body apply to Jesus's circumstances. Nor was there a reason to return the body to placate the Jewish crowd because earlier in the narrative they had sealed Jesus's fate by asking Pilate to release Barabbas in his place allegedly according to the custom of *privilegium paschal*, or amnesty to a single person during the Passover (Mark 15:6; John 18:39–40). This crowd, in the words of the gospel writers themselves, had turned against Jesus and did not require placating. What this means is that Jesus's body was not handed over to anyone and probably remained on the cross.

An essential part of the Roman punishment for ignominious crimes was to leave the bodies of crucified victims to decompose on the cross for scavengers to eat as an object-lesson for others (Ehrman 2014: 160–61). The historian of religion Martin Hengel states in his book *Crucifixion in the Ancient World and the Folly of the Message of the Cross* (1977):

> Crucifixion was aggravated further by the fact that quite often its victims were never buried. It was a stereotyped picture that the crucified victim served as food for wild beasts and birds of prey. In this way, his humiliation was complete. (Hengel 1977: 87)

Crossan (1993: 142) calls attention to the aspect of the crucifixion that many people overlook: "the carrion crow and the scavenger dog who respectively croak above and growl below the dead or dying body." Ultimately, what remained of the cadaver would be tossed into a common grave to decompose beyond recognition. None of the available sources state otherwise. Thus, Crossan's (1995: 187–88) suggestion about the fate of Jesus's remains is very plausible. While there is a possibility that an exception was made in the case of Jesus, according to Ehrman (2014: 160), there is also the fact that the Christian raconteurs who related the tale had very compelling reasons to say that this is what happened because without interment there would be no tomb to be discovered vacant.

Apologists cite the archaeological discovery in 1968 of a single heel bone of a man named Yehochanan with a crucifixion nail through it in an ossuary (limestone bone box) within a family tomb in Giv'at ha-Mivtar, in Jerusalem, dating from the first century (Davis 2002; Hass 1970; Zias 1985). This suggests that the body of this crucified victim was returned to his family. For some, this burial implies that the same may have been true for Jesus's body. However, religionists have inflated the significance of this single example (e.g., Brown 1994: 1210; Magness 2007: 6–7). If the Romans did frequently return the bodies, then, as Crossan (1995: 168) asks, where are the burial remains of the many thousands of others crucified by the Romans during the first century?

Of course, religionists' post hoc explanations for the absence of the remains of other crucifixion victims are plentiful. One states that crucifixion nails were highly prized as magical charms and would have been extracted for that purpose before the interment of the victims. The implication is that the burial of crucified individuals minus the nails was a routine occurrence. The same would have been the case for the individual from Giv'at ha-Mivtar, the argument goes, had the nail not been stuck in a knot in a piece of olive-wood placed between the nail's head and the heel bone to prevent the condemned from tearing his foot free. But if the nails were prized so highly surely the person wanting the object would have exerted the necessary force and effort to retrieve this particular magical nail. This explanation is bogus. The more plausible scenario is that this archaeological case was an exception. Nothing more can be assumed as we do not know the social and political circumstances that resulted in the return of this body to the family.

Mark's narrative contains additional discrepancies. The story continues with Joseph putting Jesus's body in a rock-hewn tomb with a round blocking stone rolled into position to seal it. The great stone rolled into place at the entrance in the story is no doubt intended to enhance the mystery of the tomb being found open and empty and implies supernatural intervention (Loisy 1962: 86). But here the gospel writer makes a critical blunder because this design for blocking stones appears in the archaeological record after 70 CE, the time of the writing of the Gospel of Mark. Before then, the stones used were square-shaped and impossible to roll (Kloner 2007: 10–11). This error indicates that the author of Mark was retrojecting what he knew about tombs in his own time to describe Jesus's fictional resting place (Kirby 2005: 242).

Further indications that we are reading a fictional account or literary theatre is how over time the character of Joseph of Arimathea acquires additional embellishments. He transforms from a "respected" Sahhedrinist in Mark 15:43, "who was himself waiting for the kingdom of God," to one "who had himself become a disciple of Jesus" [...] "but secretly because he feared the Jewish leaders" in Matthew 27:57 and John 19:38. The Gospel of John 19:30 also introduces the character of Nicodemus, a "Pharisee" and "member of the Jewish ruling council" who earlier "had visited Jesus at night," to talk about his message (John 3:1–2). It is Nicodemus who brings a massive amount of embalming spices and to prepare the body for burial.

### *The Transforming Nature of Jesus's Tomb*

The nature of the tomb itself transforms in the same way. In Mark, it is merely a rock-hewn tomb (modeled after the passage in Isaiah 22:16, 23:16). In Matthew 27:60, it becomes Joseph's future tomb. In John 20:15 and the Gospel of Peter 6:24, the tomb is given distinction by being located in "a garden." In Matthew 27:60, Luke 23:53, and John 19:14 it is described as "a new tomb," thereby eliminating the possibility that Jesus ends in a common grave for criminals (Lüdemann 1995: 21). All of this strongly indicates that we are reading a pious fiction.

Many scholars who are not votaries have now concluded that the story of the burial in a tomb is a later invention by the evangelists who wrote the gospels. They transform Jesus's ignominious death, betrayal, and abandonment by the disciples, who scattered and hid not knowing or caring about their master's body or the location of his grave, and the dishonorable disposal of his remains at the hands of the Jews who had him crucified him. Crossan's reflections on this are, "I find [here] a trajectory of hope but not history. Behind that hope lies, at worse, the horror of a body left on the cross as carrion, or, at best a body consigned like others to 'a lime pit.'" In the place of this horrible reality, the gospels supply a royal entombment of Jesus by a faithful but hitherto unknown devotee. Along the same lines, Spong (1994: 240–41) says that the phrase "they all forsook him and fled" means that Jesus died alone, executed as a criminal, and his remains were probably unceremoniously buried in a common unmarked grave in an unknown location. The story of Joseph of Arimathea, Spong (1995: 225) concurs, was invented to mask over the pain of the disciples that they had no clue about the disposition of their teacher's body. Lüdemann (1995: 23–24) grants a bit more stating that it was probably the Jews who buried Jesus, a man named Joseph of Arimathea may have been in charge of the burial detail, but it is unlikely that he was a disciple or a friend of the deceased (cf., Brown 1994: 1240). He adds that neither the disciples nor Jesus's next of kin bothered about his body and did not know its final disposition.

To recap, as Crossan (1995: 186–87) suggests, either the Roman soldiers placed the body in a shallow grave under a layer of lime and dirt, or it was left on the cross to decompose. In his words, this means "lime, at best, and the dogs again, at worst." Crossan (1995: 187) concludes that the burial stories are not historical memories but "are hope and hyperbole expended into apologetics and polemics."

It must be noted that those infected with the religion meme cannot be objective about this evidence, which comprises various X-claims. The believers' only concern is to somehow preserve their faith by forwarding various paltry rationalizations for literally accepting Mark's entire plotline. One such effort is the assertion that Christians did not need to script in a dignified burial for their Messiah since they took and even glorified an equally shameful fact, death as a common criminal on the cross (Allison 2005: 345). Therefore the story of the honorable burial must be historical. This misses a significant point. The crucifixion was a public event and thus ruled out any outlandish literary embellishment to recast it as anything other than what it was, a horrible and shameful demise. The burial, however, was a private affair, an event for which there was no direct information, and offered opportunities to embellish and improvise in the manner we find. Here again, the parallels with how the Roswell myth got started are remarkable.

Another spurious reason on offer for accepting Mark's narrative in totality is that the Joseph of Arimathea sequence of the script is said to contain no fantastic elements and is therefore historical rather than legendary (Allison 2005: 356). This view ignores the fact the Joseph sequence is part of a larger narrative that is blatantly paranormal, that is, a supernaturally disappearing reanimated corpse. This assertion is akin to stating that the opening scene of the movie *The Wizard of Oz* depicting Dorothy's family does not contain any fantastic or paranormal elements, such as witches and flying monkeys, and the scene must be historically accurate.

Finally, another assertion is that honorable burial is mentioned in all four canonical gospels and must, therefore, be historical (Allison 2005: 354). The problematic assumption here is that we are working with four independent sources, which, as already discussed, is not the case (see Chapter 12). Indeed, the theologian John A. T. Robinson goes so far as to make the preposterous statement that the burial scene in the gospels is "one of the most firmly grounded facts in Jesus' life" (cited in Allison

2005: 354). Regarding this, the expert on oral narratives Jan Vansina (1985: 159) makes a highly relevant point:

> We cannot assume that the testimony of two different informants from the same community or even the same society is really independent. This is very important. In history, proof is given only when two independent sources confirm the same event or situation, but […] it is not possible to do this with oral tradition wherever a corpus exists and information flows are unstemmed (i.e., in most cases). Feedback and contamination is the norm. […] No one will consider the three synoptic Gospels as independent sources, even though they have different authors […] they stemmed from one single oral milieu, from one corpus in one community. Once this is realized, it is easy to see that it also applies to John, the fourth Gospel.

What we have is the copying and reworking of the content of one uncorroborated source, the Gospel of Mark. This source is itself a missionary and apologetic propaganda tract, not a historical text for use to make statements of fact. The other texts do not draw on additional external sources.

### *The Missing Body and the Vacant Sepulcher*

Returning to Mark's narrative, the story of Jesus's burial sets up the scenario for his physical resurrection as inferred by the discovery of the missing body and a message from a mysterious boy in a white robe. Mark 16:1–8, which provides the earliest tale of Jesus rising physically from the dead, leaving behind an empty tomb, relates that "on the first day of the week" immediately after sunrise, Mary Magdalene and some other ladies took spices to anoint Jesus's body. On the way, they deliberated how they would unroll the large stone blocking the tomb's entrance. However, when they reach the site, they see that the stone has already been rolled away. Inside the tomb, they discover a young man in a white robe who tells them not to be afraid and says: "You are looking for Jesus the Nazarene, who was crucified. He has risen! He is not here. See the place where they laid him. But go, tell his disciples and Peter, 'He is going ahead of you into Galilee. There you will see him, just as he told you.'" The narrative ends abruptly in verse 16:8 as follows: "Trembling and bewildered, the women went out and fled from the tomb. They said nothing to anyone because they were afraid."

Mark uses the phrase "the first day of the week" instead of the more common "on the third day" motif, as in 1 Corinthians 15:4, "raised on the third day according to the Scriptures." The idea that the resurrection occurred on the third day after death is copied directly from Hosea 6:2 in the Septuagint. The phrase "the first day of the week" is a Hebraic form commonly employed by Greek-speaking Jews in Hellenistic times (Lowder 2005: 279). It does not imply an older Aramaic antecedent that can be used to establish a link between the story and the first disciples, as apologists claim (e.g., Craig 1994: 275) in their efforts to validate the historicity of Mark's fictional narrative. The youth's white robe probably denotes his status as a paranormal being, a character that in the later gospels is transformed into an angelic being, or beings, wearing white garb (Spong 1995: 60–61).

The evangelists writing later found Mark's strategy problematic because it did not definitively resolve the issue of how the Jesus cultists found out that their rabbi had come back from the dead. For this reason, they changed their accounts. However, the literary twist on the part of the author of Mark is a significant move. As Lüdemann (2004: 87) points out, the suggestion that the women did not tell anyone was a way to explain why no one had heard of the empty tomb story until Mark related it circa 70 CE. Similarly, Goulder (1996: 57–58) says that Mark sought to address skepticism among the Jewish Christians familiar with 1 Corinthians 15:12 who would ask why no one had heard of this tale in over 40 years. Ending the story with the silence of the frightened women was the explanation, that is, "the foolish women were too afraid to tell anyone." Lowder (2005: 284) and Price (2003: 333) make the same argument. As to the quandary of how the message reached the disciples, Mark simply retrojected the same communication coming from Jesus himself earlier in 14:28: "But after I have risen, I will go ahead of you into Galilee."

In contrast to these views, Allison (2005: 304) provides a somewhat far-fetched interpretation of the phrase "they said nothing to anyone" to mean that they said nothing to anyone aside from the disciples. Reginald Fuller (1971: 53) objects to such reasons pointing out that interpreting the women's silence in these terms is too modern and rationalistic. The evangelists, he adds, were not concerned with inconsistent evidence in contrast to modern historical critics, which support the very point Goulder and like-minded scholars are making, namely that the gospels are not historical tracts and it is imprudent to approach them as such.

At a later date, more reverse-engineering was done by some other inspired evangelist to insert 12 additional verses 9–20 to the end of Mark 14, referred to as "pseudo-Mark." In this passage, the women tell the disciples that Jesus has risen: "When Jesus rose early on the first day of the week, he appeared first to Mary Magdalene, out of whom he had driven seven demons. She went and told those who had been with him and who were mourning and weeping. When they heard that Jesus was alive and that she had seen him, they did not believe it." The text goes on with a description of the various other appearances to the disciples who are finally convinced that the Lord has risen.

"Pseudo-Mark" is simply a summary of the material found in the other three gospels that were written later, which are themselves reworkings of Mark's original resurrection story. In this ingenious feat of reverse-engineering, the new expanded material is tacked back on to the original text (cf., Ehrman 2011: 243). The additional verses merely reinforce the physical resurrection story based on Mark's original narrative. Here the evangelists also have Jesus preaching "the gospel," the Church's post-resurrection announcement contrived long after the events that Jesus died for the sins of the world and is the risen Son of God.

In the subsequent gospels, new details are added to establish further that the resurrection was a physical event. In Matthew 28:9–10, the women grovel before a physically manifested Jesus and touch his feet. In Luke 24:15–49, Jesus appears before his acolytes in person, breaks bread with them, and they can touch him, establishing that this was a corporeal manifestation and not a vision or a ghost. Finally, and remarkably, John 20:14–29 confirms the physical resurrection by having a skeptical Thomas place his fingers in the wounds on Jesus's body. A skeptic changing his mind is an effective rhetorical device (Gorham 1908: 179) that is also frequently used by present-day proponents of the paranormal, that is, "I did not believe in Bigfoot or UFOs until I saw these with my own eyes." The evangelists are also trying to convey a message to all religious doubters, namely that the faithful do not need proof (Goguel 1953: 50). Thus, John 20:29 states: "Then Jesus told him, 'Because you have seen me, you have believed; blessed are those who have not seen and yet have believed.'"

## Seven Non-Paranormal Explanations for the Empty Tomb

Over the years, various scholars, especially the eighteenth- and early nineteenth-century rationalists, who analyzed the empty tomb story have offered several alternative, non-paranormal scenarios to explain the missing body. It must be noted, however, that such efforts are pointless from the start because the entire burial and empty tomb narrative is a fiction. Nevertheless, a brief examination is necessary for the sake of comprehensiveness.

Allison (2005: 200–13) has listed the following proposals:

(1) The Jews stole the body and then spread rumors that Jesus's disciples absconded with the corpse (Bostock 1994). Alternatively, the gardener working on the property where the tomb was located moved Jesus's body to prevent crowds of venerators from trampling on his vegetable patch. The historian and philosopher Richard Carrier (2005b: 351) calls this character the "annoyed vindictive gardener-turned-bodysnatcher." There is a hint of this in John 20:13: "They have taken my Lord away," [Mary Magdalan] said, "and I don't know where they have put him." John 20:15 says "Thinking he [Jesus] was the gardener, she said, 'Sir, if you have carried him away, tell me where you have put him, and I will get him.'" Later Jewish tradition expands upon this to assert that Mary went to the wrong tomb and that the entire resurrection belief was merely due to an erroneous deduction (Price 1989), that is, the foundation of the Christian faith is a mistaken assumption.

(2) The body was moved by the same people who put it there, or "the relocation hypothesis." This perspective necessitates that we accept the assertions that the Romans released the body, Joseph was an actual person, a rushed burial occurred, there was a nearby rock-hewn tomb, and Peter came out of hiding or turned back from his flight to Galilee to investigate the vacant sepulcher, and so forth (cf., Lowder 2005: 264–66). None of this is admissible.

According to this explanation, Mark relates that Joseph of Arimathea temporarily placed the body in the tomb as an emergency measure because time was running out with the approaching sunset that Friday. Mark's 16:2 statement that the women arrived early, "just after sunrise," is intended to rule out the possibility of someone claiming that earlier Joseph retrieved the body for burial elsewhere, as an explanation for the vacant tomb (Komarnitsky 2014a: 39–41). However, Joseph could very well have retrieved, transported, and buried the body in another place as soon as it was possible. In such a scenario, Lowder (2005: 267, 272) suggests that the body could have been shifted

Saturday night and dishonorably buried in the criminal's graveyard outside the walls of Jerusalem. That information was not shared and hence the discovery of the empty tomb that generated rumors, hearsay, and conjectures, giving birth to the resurrection story (Carrier 2001: 386–87; Holtzmann 1904: 499; Klausner 1925: 357; Price 2011: 227).

Joseph did not tell anyone either because he did not care or he wanted to keep his actions secret had he acted without the blessings of the Sanhedrin. Alternatively, he may have merely kept quiet in support of the Christian cause (Allison 2005: 334). Or Joseph may have moved back to his hometown or died soon after the events described. He is not heard from again and is absent from Acts and never mentioned in the Epistles (Carrier 2005c: 386–87). Lowder (2005: 268, 274) maintains that the relocation hypothesis is sufficient to explain the empty tomb. However, as already noted, this line of reasoning is unnecessary because the burial narrative, including the character of Joseph of Arimathea, the rock-hewn tomb, and the discovery by the women are all fictional.

(3) The body was stolen by unknown agents. Body snatching was a significant problem at that time and place (de Zulueta 1932). If Jesus's burial happened late Friday and the discovery of the empty sepulcher occurred Sunday morning, the thieves would have had two entire nights to accomplish their gruesome task. It is possible that criminals stole the corpse for some undetermined reason (Whittaker 1970), or it was taken by necromancers to obtain the highly prized magical body parts of a crucified holy man (Carrier 2001, 2005b: 349–50; Luck 2006: 167, 212–17). If one were to accept the historicity of the empty tomb story, then the presence of various unknown individuals at the tomb raises suspicions. Gorham (1908: 169) queried, "Who were these men?" He called attention to the numerous suspicious signs of human agency "of unknown visitants," sometimes describes as "angels," sometimes "men" that may have removed the body (Gorham 1908: 169). An intriguing possibility here is that the women who visited the tomb, in reality, encountered the body snatchers pretending to be angels or messengers and bamboozled them.

(4) Jesus did not die on the cross but lost consciousness and was subsequently revived (Cheek 1959; Davis and Davis 1991; Derrett 1982; Price 2011: 222–26; Schonfield 1965; Thiry 1813: 253, 257–58; see O'Collins and Kendall 1994b). Another term for this is the *Scheintod* ("seeming death") or the swoon hypothesis. According to Price (2011: 223), that Jesus did not die on the cross is hinted at by Pilate's surprise at how quickly the man had succumbed (Mark 15:44–45), as already noted, and asked a centurion to verify the matter before granting Joseph permission to take charge of the body. Jesus's "as-yet unexplained premature death" may be one significant clue. The other clue, Price maintains, is the "build up devoted to giving Jesus a drink [that] is surprising if there will not prove to have been a payoff." The relevant verses are Mark 15:36–37:

> Someone ran, filled a sponge with wine vinegar, put it on a staff, and offered it to Jesus to drink. "Now leave him alone. Let's see if Elijah comes to take him down," he said. With a loud cry, Jesus breathed his last.

The implication here is that supporters gave Jesus wine/vinegar laced with a drug to feign his death so that he could be taken from the cross and later revived (McGarth 2008: 67; Strauss 1902: 843–44; see Schonfield 1965). Price finds the application of the liquid at the very moment Jesus passed out most peculiar. It follows that the seemingly dead Jesus is revived in the cold tomb or his accomplices resuscitate him, and he departs to some unknown destination (Paulus 1828). However, we have already discussed the evangelicals plagiarized this detail from the Septuagint. There is, therefore, no reason to think that there is a grain of truth in any of this material.

Price (2011: 224) calls attention to the similarities between Mark 15:43–46, which relates how Joseph of Arimathea boldly asks Pilate for Jesus's body, and the following account by the Jewish historian Josephus bar-Matthias:

> And when I was sent by Titus Caesar with Cerealins, and a thousand horsemen, to a certain village called Thecoa, in order to know whether it was a place fit for a camp, as I came back, I saw many captives crucified, and remembered three of them as my former acquaintances. I was very sorry at this in my mind, and went with tears in my eyes to Titus, and told him of them; so he immediately commanded them to be taken down, and to have the greatest care taken of them, in order to their recovery; yet two of them died under the physician's hands, while the third recovered. (*The Life and Works of* Flavius Josephus, 1996: 72)

That a crucifixion victim could survive his injuries if taken off the cross relatively soon confirms the "seeming death" hypothesis rather than ruling it out, contra to what apologists assert (McGrath 2008: 67; see Strauss 1902: 843).

Apologists eagerly quote David Friedrich Strauss saying that the idea of survival should be rejected because the trauma of crucifixion would have made it impossible for Jesus to appear to his disciples as the resurrected Lord (e.g., Yamauchi 1974a, 1974b). A statement of this nature from a skeptic such as Strauss is considered all the more potent in supporting their case that a genuine resurrection must have taken place. What Strauss (1902: 844) really said was,

> Truly it is difficult to perceive how it can hence be shown probable that Jesus, who when taken from the cross showed all the signs of death, should have come to life entirely of himself, without the application of medical skill.

But, Strauss (1902: 844) added: "According to a certain opinion, however, these two conditions some remains of conscious life, and careful medical treatment were not wanting in the case of Jesus."

Thus, Christian apologist Habermas (2003: 21) is being deceptive when he avers that Strauss delivered the death blow to the swoon theory. It is nothing of the sort. Moreover, as Price (2011: 222) points out, "the seeming death hypothesis" merely suggests that Jesus cheated death, not that he was immediately functional and set about preaching to his acolytes. Indeed, he adds, "the ensuing doting of his relieved disciples upon the recuperating savior would have fed the instinct to worship him."

Mark (15:44–45) and John (19:30–35) include details such as Pilate asking a centurion to verify the death and the spear thrust to the side to definitively establish that Jesus was dead before being removed from the cross, which suggests that the "seeming death hypothesis" was in circulation during their time (Lüdemann 1995: 19). As the religious scholar James McGrath (2008: 67) says, this appears to be the main intention in John 19:30–35. As Strauss (1902: 794) saw it, "This event is ordinarily regarded as the chief voucher for the reality of the death of Jesus, and in relation to it the proof to be drawn from the synoptists is held inadequate." However, this detail does not reflect what actually transpired; it is not history but is a line stolen from Zechariah 2:10 in the Old Testament because the writer of the Gospel of John needed to signify Jesus's unequivocal death.

(5) The disciples stole the body (Smith 2014: 74, 83). Matthew 28:11–15 mentions that the Jews accused the Christians of taking the corpse. Celsus also called attention to this possibility. Allison (2005: 208) observes, however, that the disciples were too frightened and vulnerable to dare undertake such a criminal act and manage to conceal their conspiracy. However, Carrier (2001: 306–7) points out that this does not rule out a single or a handful of disciples from among the more than 70 followers from carrying out the theft as an act of pious fraud to vindicate their master's reputation. Alternatively, it is possible that someone else committed the fraud. Research into UFO hoaxes and claims of the paranormal reveals that the individuals responsible for fraud are not always the ones who discover the faked event (Martin 1991: 96).

Finally, a sixth item to be considered that is not on Allison's list is the possibility that someone else hitherto not considered removed the body. The historian Charles Freeman presents this scenario to account for the empty tomb in his book *A New History of Early Christianity* (2009). He accepts as factual the central elements of the story in the gospels, the historicity of which has been disputed by other scholars. Again, these include the premise that Joseph of Arimathea buried Jesus in a tomb, that people knew the location of the burial place, that Pilate provided soldiers to guard the site to prevent the disciples from removing the body, and that the priests themselves oversaw the complete security of the site. This grants too much, a mistake also made by the eighteenth-century rationalists. The story of the Roman guards at the tomb is found only in the gospels of Matthew 27:62–66 and Peter *2:30–31 (*Cassels 1894: 9). The doubtful historicity of this particular element of the story is discussed later in this chapter.

However, for the moment, let us go along with Freeman's use of this information. According to Freeman (2009: 32), the reason for posting guards at the tomb is that the Jewish high priest Caiaphas, who was the chief architect of Jesus's demise, was fearful that the body might become the focal point for dissident worship. The mastermind in this theft scenario is, therefore, the high priest himself. According to Freeman, Caiaphas was at once motived to demonstrate his firm stance against disorder to the Romans and at the same time did not want to jeopardize his position with the Jews by causing more bloodshed by persecuting the disciples. To diffuse the situation and thwart the Jesus cultists, he bribed the Roman guards not to interfere, had the body removed, and left a message with a boy to tell the disciples that Jesus would reappear in Galilee. In Galilee, the cultists would be under the jurisdiction of Herod Antipas, and hence would become his problem, and what they believed about Jesus afterward really did not matter.

If Caiaphas were the mastermind behind the theft, then the task would have been accomplished by priests. It makes sense that the women described the figure or figures lurking about in or near the tomb as wearing white clothes, which matches the white linen robes worn by the junior members of the priesthood. Freeman finds further relevant clues in the Gospel of Peter. Verses 37–9 relate that two soldiers enter the open tomb and come out carrying a third man. Although the tale has acquired paranormal features, such as the two supporters having heads that extended to the sky and there is a talking cross following them, an actual story of two men removing the body may be at the core of this narrative. Thus, according to the circumstantial evidence, Freeman (2009: 34) observes, "Caiaphas put in place a plan which would defuse the Jesus movement, or at least transfer it to Galilee, without further bloodshed."

A seventh possibility is that the women simply went to the wrong tomb. New Testament scholar Kirsopp Lake (1907) proposed this idea by amending Mark 16:6 to read, "He is not here. See (pointing to the correct tomb) the place where they laid him."

### *Does Refuting Non-Paranormal Explanations Validate the Supernatural Hypothesis?*

Devotees have expended much energy diligently tearing down all such non-paranormal explanations. Sadly, these religionists operate under the false assumption that the refutation of naturalistic explanations by default validates their superstitions. For example, Habermas (2001: 96) writes, "The more thoroughly naturalistic theories are dismantled, the more solid data in favor of Jesus' resurrection is displayed." Such critical fatuity is remarkable. This religionist assumption regarding naturalistic explanations is false for several reasons. First, even if all the non-paranormal hypotheses are decisively refuted (none have been!), this does not validate an absurd and entirely implausible paranormal explanation that entails a reanimated corpse. Second, even if the reanimation of a cadaver could be proven, this does not mean that the Christian God was responsible. Nor would such an event establish that the Christian God exists or that Jesus was the Son of God (Martin 1991: 97).

Present-day writers claiming that the resurrection was real because the gospel narratives say the body was missing are bamboozled by a fable that has duped the faithful for 2,000 years. Moreover, as already pointed out, asserting the veracity of these texts by quoting the same material entails a crude form of circular reasoning or begging the question. Finally, this story is not historical, a point that requires emphasis. There was no tomb, and there was no cadaver to place in it (cf., Spong 1995: 228). The alternative explanations regarding the fate of the corpse reviewed above are all superfluous.

Allison (2005: 214) sees it differently and asks the following question: Can any of these options be deemed more probable than another? Allison, a religionist who surprisingly treats the evidence in a more balanced fashion than many of his fellow votaries, nevertheless opts for the literal resurrection of Jesus, or the supernatural explanation, as being the more plausible case. Other apologists hold similar views. Bishop Nicholas Wright (2003: 720) affirms his belief in the literal resurrection as the "best explanation" for the preponderance of the data. Such ideologues regularly claim that the hypothesis that God truly raised Jesus from the dead has greater explanatory scope compared to naturalistic explanations because it accounts both for the empty tomb and for the resurrection (Craig 1997; Wright 2003: 781). However, as Carrier (2005b: 354) points out, the criterion of explanatory scope alone is not sufficient to make one hypothesis more credible than another. Indeed, the "Ancient Aliens" hypothesis regarding the rise of civilizations on earth has greater explanatory scope than mainstream archaeological theories. Aside from paranormalists, UFO enthusiasts, and perhaps the individuals in charge of programming for the History Channel, few others would opt for extraterrestrials as the force behind human history, the development of cultural complexity, and the rise of the early civilizations.

Christian apologists opt for miracles. Miracle claims, however, are extraordinary claims that require extraordinary evidence, and no religionist has ever even come close to providing such evidence (see Chapter 8). The resurrection of Jesus is a miracle that defies probability and as Ehrman (2014: 165) has put it, "To say that an event that defies probability is more probable than something that is simply improbable is to fly in the face of anything that involves probability."Alternatively, as Gorham (1908: 75) put it,

> No testimony can establish such a miracle, because the probability that the universal law of death operates in a particular instance must always remain infinitely greater than the probability of any exception to it having occurred.

Understandably, there can be no other choice for the devout but to cling to the miraculous because their entire belief system depends on it, and they are unable to treat the evidence in an objective and balanced fashion. To reiterate, the defining feature of faith-based perspectives is the axiom "I wish to believe" rather than "What is the evidence?" All their efforts to show that they have carefully weighed the evidence is a mere pretense. Few will object if believers acknowledge that they have opted for faith over reason and evidence. This is everyone's right. Allison (2005: 331–32) to his credit does this, stating that for him materialistic explanations only encompass one part of reality and expresses his own faith that Jesus triumphed over death and let his follower know about it. This, of course, is a believer's perspective. However, ultimately, he acknowledges that the evidence is inconclusive. What is objectionable is when religionists dress up their superstitions in scholarly sounding jargon to resemble mainstream scholarship and make claims that they know the absolute, incontrovertible truth. These sorts of limping apologetics and tortuous sophistries are an assault on the sensibilities and intelligence of rational people.

Even if the empty tomb story is real, that is, that there was a corpse that disappeared, rather than the entire story comprising a fiction made up by the early evangelists, the rational conclusion is the same. Any of the dozens of non-paranormal alternatives on offer are more plausible given our background knowledge than the cadaver reanimation hypothesis. The dead (i.e., the genuinely deceased) only come back to life in George

Romero movies, not in the real world today or at any time in the history of humankind. Efforts by religionists such as Keener (2011: 227–40) to marshall evidence that resurrections of the dead are a common occurrence in the world today and hence the biblical events must have been genuine only makes them look naïve and stupid.

## Critically Assessing the Empty Tomb Story

Among the significant problems with the empty tomb narratives in the gospels is that they are at odds with each other in irreconcilable ways on nearly every detail (Ehrman 2009: 133). Ehrman (2014: 134) has summarized some of these. Concerning the discovery of the empty tomb, it is unclear who arrived first. Was it Mary Magdalene (John), Mary and another Mary (Matthew), Mary, another Mary, and Salome (Mark), or Mary, Mary, and Joanna, along with other ladies (Luke)? It is also unclear who they encountered. Matthew says it was an angel, Marks says a youth, and Luke says two men. Similarly, did the women keep silent about seeing Jesus (Mark, Matthew, and Luke), or did they immediately inform the disciples (John)? Did the follower see Jesus (Matthew, Luke, and John) or not? (Mark). Finally, where was Jesus seen, only in Galilee (Mark and Matthew) or in Jerusalem (Luke)?

The inconsistencies and mutual contradictions in these texts make their historicity highly suspect. Here we have to refer back to Hume (1902 [1748]: 112–13) who advises extreme caution in any matter of fact "when the witnesses contradict each other; when they are few, or of a doubtful character; when they have an interest in what they affirm." We have no eyewitnesses in this case, and our only sources are the individuals who wrote the gospels working with second- and third-hand information, meaning anecdotes in circulation for years, passed on from person to person and between communities before they were written down. They had no personal knowledge of the facts, lived decades apart from the events and far away from the locations they discussed, and did not even speak the same language as the alleged witnesses. Also, the authors of these texts not only contradict each other on significant points but were exceedingly credulous and as evangelists had plenty of interest in the tales they narrated. Religionists may vouch that such factors do not affect the quality of the evidence. However, as Gorham (1908: 76) queried long ago, "If testimony is not weakened by internal contradictions, credulity on the part of the witness, and the absence of corroboration, by what is it weakened?"

## The Problem of Apostle Paul's First Letter to the Corinthian Christians

Another reason to doubt the empty tomb story is Paul's first letter to the Corinthians (15:3–11), cited in part at the beginning of this chapter, which was written decades before the Gospel of Mark. Paul is the only New Testament writer to claim that he saw the risen Jesus personally. His account comes a few years after the crucifixion. There is not even a hint of the Easter story in what Paul writes (Hoover 2008: 82). The silence is a good indication that in his time there was no oral tradition circulating about an empty tomb (Anderson 1964: 192–95; Hoover 2008: 83; Kümmel 1973: 98–99). Indeed, there was no such authentic folk tradition in circulation until Mark contrived it out of bits and pieces of hearsay, conjecture, and his creative imagination.

The gospel narratives of the crucifixion provide another clue that the Easter story was a later invention rather than an eyewitness account of what happened. While all the gospels give very similar descriptions of the crucifixion, which was a public event, their resurrection stories differ so much that they are difficult if not impossible to harmonize (Hoover 2008: 84). Of significance is that Mark, the earliest of the canonical gospels, does not provide any appearance stories. All Mark says is that Jesus will appear at a future time.

Similarly, Q, the source of Jesus's sayings, imparts nothing about postmortem manifestations. This is puzzling because the appearance stories were too sensational to have remained a secret and hence to have been unknown to the author of Mark. Also, a physical appearance event was a way of addressing the suspicions of tomb robbing and body snatching generated by the story of a vacant sepulcher itself. It, therefore, makes no sense for Mark to have left the appearance stories out of his account if he had heard them. That such suspicions were in circulation and posed an ongoing problem for the later evangelists is evident by the fact that the author of the Gospel of Matthew inserts an entirely new element, namely Roman guards posted at the tomb, jettisoning the possibility of body snatching.

In his first letter to the Corinthians, Paul says that Jesus was "buried," not entombed, and provides the comprehensive list of postmortem sightings available to him. Paul asserts that he obtained this knowledge from believers who came before him. However, he says nothing about Joseph of Arimathea, Nicodemus, the women who found the tomb empty, angels descending from the sky, the corpses of reanimated saints rising from the graves, or the postmortem appearances of Jesus mentioned in the gospels in connection with the story (Doherty 2005: 71; Price 2005a: 422). It is odd that Paul is silent about these things in the context of a narrative intended to allay doubts by the Christians of Corinth regarding the reality of the resurrection, precisely when an empty tomb story and all the related details would have been crucial. Paul (1 Corinthians 15:42–44, 50) asserts as follows:

> The body that is sown is perishable, it is raised imperishable; it is sown in dishonor, it is raised in glory; it is sown in weakness, it is raised in power; it is sown a natural body, it is raised a spiritual body. [...] I declare to you, brothers and sisters, that flesh and blood cannot inherit the kingdom of God, nor does the perishable inherit the imperishable.

Here he clearly differentiates between a celestial and a terrestrial "flesh and blood body" and emphasizes that Jesus has not risen with his earthly body but with a celestial one (*sooma pneumatikon*), or the physical one metamorphosed into a spiritual body, and that he and others saw the resurrected Jesus in his celestial form (Philipse 2014: 5; Spong 1995: 50).

For Paul, there was no empty tomb, no missing corpse, no bodily rising, no physical appearances of a being who ate fish, offered his wounds for inspection, or levitated to the sky afterward (Spong 1995: 51). Thus, contrary to mendacious claims by apologists (e.g., Wright 2003: 317–22), Paul's account provides evidence that the empty tomb story was unknown before the gospel writers invented it decades later (Crossley 2005: 177). A reanimated cadaver is crucial solely to present-day literalizing fundamentalists and evangelical Christians who fear that minus a physically resurrected body there is no Easter and without Easter, there is no Christianity. In Paul's time, the need to make the resurrection a physical one had not yet arisen. The religionist assertion that Paul knew about the empty tomb but did not mention it because it was an indisputable fact (Wright 2003: 321) is hardly credible and is an embarrassing misrepresentation.

### *Attempts to Harmonize Paul's Statement with the Gospel Accounts*

The length to which the faithful have gone to make Paul's statement harmonize with the gospels is lamentable. They maintain that merely stating that Jesus was "buried" and "raised" is, in fact, saying that a corpse walked out of a tomb and hence Paul had no reason to further elaborate upon the empty tomb story (Allison 2005: 315). Religionist Herbert Rose (1938: 140) says something similar, asserting that the belief that the resurrection has taken place denotes that a physical body has come out of a grave, and hence an empty tomb is implied. However, Allison (2005: 311) ultimately does acknowledge that even if Paul knew about the empty tomb, the fact of the matter is that he does not mention it. Hence, he adds, we should not use 1 Corinthians 15 for or against the empty tomb story.

Allison's stance is not very convincing because Paul also fails to mention various other facts that should be in his letter. To reiterate, these included Joseph of Arimathea, Nicodemus, the female corpse anointer, Mary's encounter with the risen Jesus, angels swooping down from above, supernatural earthquakes, zombified saints roaming the streets of Jerusalem, the disciples' inspection of the tomb, or any of the postmortem Jesus sightings mentioned in the gospels. These are all details tied to the empty tomb story that would have been relevant to the case Paul was trying to make before the Corinthian Christians. He did not mention any of these things because he did not know about them. Moreover, there is also the significant fact to bear in mind that the empty tomb was not part of Paul's gospel, and he categorically did not preach it (Bater 1969: 53). Why wouldn't he preach it if he knew it? What this suggests is that we are dealing with two independently evolved traditions. The first is encapsulated in Paul's account, and the second one is the empty tomb story of the Gospel of Mark. These separate traditions later merge into a single creed in the gospels of Matthew and Luke (Ehrman 2014: 143).

As noted earlier, the legend of the empty tomb appears in response to the intra-ecclesiastical controversy regarding the nature of the resurrection. It may have also been a rejoinder to the opposition Christians encountered as they began to spread their message, first among the Jews and later among pagan gentiles (Pagels 1979: xiii–xxxvi, 3–27; Goulder 1996: 58; Parsons 2005: 434). As Hick (1993: 44) puts it, this was an aspect of "the growing and developing church [having] to explain its beliefs to the Greek-speaking Mediterranean world, and at the same time to itself, in acceptable philosophical terms." Similarly, Philipse (2014: 181) observes that Mark's empty tomb and bodily rising are indications of the Hellenization or Romanization of Christianity during the late first and early second centuries (see also De Jong 1989: 43–45; Funk et al. 1998: 533).

## The Similarities of the Resurrection Narrative and the Stories of Other Sons of God in the Greco-Roman World

A skeptic would ask: If the incarnation of God as a human being was an unprecedented event of cosmic significance, as Christians aver, then why does the whole tale closely resemble the many stories of the other dying-rising "sons of God" apotheosis narratives circulating at the time? The answer is simple—the Christians copied the well-known god-man stories or memes that were part of the cultural repertoire of the Greco-Roman world. For instance, the cynical Celsus (1987: 67) observed: "Clearly, the Christians have used the myths of Danae [...] or the Auge and the Antiope in fabricating the story of Jesus' virgin birth." Danae was the daughter of the king of Argos, who was impregnated by Zeus in the form of golden rain and gave birth to the hero Perseus. Auge was the virgin priestess of Athena, who was impregnated by the god-man and divine hero Heracles and gave birth to the hero Telephus who later became the king of Mysia, in Asia Minor. Antiope became pregnant by Zeus and gave birth to Amphion, the legendary builder of Thebes.

These types of stories were a common and widespread tradition of the time (Carrier 2011: 59). Thomas Paine (1880 [1794]: 4) perspicaciously commented on the prevalence of god-men stories in pagan mythology and how they were used to fashion the Jesus story for the consumption of potential converts in the Greco-Roman world, making the story "conformable to the opinions that then prevailed among the people called Gentiles." In other words, the evangelists who wrote the gospels modified their story to fit the model of Greco-Roman heroes familiar to their targeted pagan audiences outside the Middle East. This makes it challenging to fathom comments by apologists such as Keener (2011: 51) that the gospels were not Hellenized.

However, in a sense, this was the vulgarization of what during the time of Paul was a spiritual narrative through the introduction of a reanimated corpse, or a walking dead man, into the tale to provide a narrative suited for a non-Jewish, pagan audience elsewhere in the Roman world. Christian propagandists, to put it succinctly, were merely exploiting the already familiar dying-and-rising god-man apotheosis stories of the audiences they were trying to convert (cf., De Jong 1989: 43–45). The details of these stories are remarkably similar to the Christian fable. The pagan god-man apotheosis stories center upon a divine personage or a God incarnate, born of a virgin, who has great wisdom and magical powers to heal the sick. This divine personage is crucified or martyred by corrupt officials, miraculously rises from death, leaves behind an empty tomb, ascends to the realm of the gods to rule from above, and is after that worshipped as a god (Bolt 1996; Brodie 2004; Collins 1997; Price 2005b: 14–15).

One of these god-men was Apollonius of Tyana, discussed in Chapter 13. The theologian Ferdinand Christian Baur (1832) attempted to refute the case of Apollonius by arguing that it was fiction concocted by the pagans to discredit the New Testament. His apologetic argument is not very persuasive. Keener (2011: 40–69) makes the same assertion demonstrating that not much has changed in the repertoire of Christian apologetics. Moreover, there were many other god-men like Apollonius, who are identical to the character of Jesus. These include Romulus, Hercules, Aeneas, Asclepius, Attis, Empedocles, and even the Osiris, the Egyptian god of the afterlife.

Present-day apologists adamantly deny that the Christian copied the resurrection motif from the pagan god-men narratives by presenting the specious arguments that the Hellenistic mystery religions plagiarized these from Christianity (Eddy and Boyd 2007: 91–132). Edwin Yamauchi (1974a, 1974b), a former colleague in the history department at my university, states explicitly, for example, that the mystery religions borrowed these themes from early Christianity. Jonathan Smith (1987: 143–45) also forwards a similar idea. Price (2000: 90–95) has soundly demolished all such arguments. Contrary to such spurious apologetics, there is plenty of evidence indicating that dying-and-rising god-men cults predated Christianity, which rules out any possibility of the earlier forms being copies of the later one (Mettinger 2001).

Allison (2005: 308, 311) uses another tactic. He acknowledges that humans have made up stories about missing bodies and also that they have written fictional stories. He also notes the striking parallels between the legends of the resurrected heroes with empty tombs and the tale of Jesus's vacant sepulcher in Mark, but goes on to say that while copying and fiction writing is possible, this does not mean that this is what happened. But, it also could very easily mean that this is precisely what happened. He forgets that the early Christians excelled at forging stories and fiction writing, and they resorted to this strategy whenever and wherever it suited them (see Chapter 12). To cite Celsus (1987: 64) once again, the Christians "pen in hand, alter the original writings three, four, and several more times over."

An important point to remember as well is that early Christian polemicists were well aware of the close parallels between the Greco-Roman dying-and-rising god-men narratives and the story of Jesus. Why didn't they deny these parallel? Why didn't they claim that the Greco-Roman traditions have stolen elements from Christianity? The answer is simply that these tales were too well-known for such a strategy to work. As the second-century Christian apologist Justin Martyr put it while proselytizing to the pagans,

> And by declaring the Logos, the First-begotten of God, our Master Jesus Christ, to be born of a Virgin without any human mixture, and to be crucified and dead, and to have risen again and ascended into heaven, we say no more in this than what you say of those whom you style the sons of Jove [Jupiter]. (*The First Apology of Justin Martyr*, chapter 28, 1889: 29)

Justin drew numerous parallels between Christ and the pagan gods:

> But now if we say that the Logos of God is properly the begotten of God [...] you have your Mercury in worship under the title of the Word and Messenger of God. As to the objection of our Jesus being crucified, I say that suffering was common to all the aforementioned sons of Jove, but only they suffered another kind of death; so that Christ does not seem at all inferior to them upon the score of the difference of His suffering [...] As to His being born of a Virgin, you have your Perseus to balance that; as to His curing the lame and the paralytic, and

> such as were cripples from their birth, this is little more than what you say of your Æsculapius [the hero, god of medicine, and son of Apollo]. (*The First Apology of Justin Martyr*, chapter 30, 1889: 30–31)

Justin added:

> For you need not be told what a parcel of sons the writers most in vogue among you assign to Jove; there is Mercury, Jove's interpreter, in imitation of the Logos, in worship among you, and your grand teacher; there is Æsculapius, the physician smitten by a bolt of thunder, and after that ascending into heaven; there is Bacchus [Dionysus among the Greeks, the Roman deity of wine and agriculture, who was the offspring of Jupiter and Semele, the princess of Thebes], torn to pieces; and Hercules, burnt to get rid of his pains; there are Pollux and Castor, the sons of Jove by Leda, and Perseus by Danne [Danae], and the mortal Bellerophon [the Greek hero who slew the monster Chimaera], who fell from his Pegasus; not to mention Ariadne [the daughter of King Minos of Crete, who was a son of Zeus], and others like her, translated into constellations, according to your writers. Moreover, I would fain know why you always deify the departed emperors, and have a fellow at hand to make an affidavit that he saw Caesar mount to heaven from the funeral pile? Nor can I think there is any need of repeating to such knowing persons the extravagances recorded of every son of Jove, only to put you in mind that they are recorded for the better corrupting […] young students in the arts of debauchery. […] These are the stratagems of wicked spirits. (*The First Apology of Justin Martyr*, chapter 29, 1889: 29–30)

Thus, rather than deny the similarities between the stories, as present-day literalists do through embarrassing special pleading, the early Christians tried to explain them away. Thus, Justin said that pagan stories were the work of evil spirits or devils who knew about Jesus's resurrection from the prophecies in advance and planted false stories beforehand through some time-traveling magic to make people think that Christian beliefs were plagiarized (Price 2010: 281, 2000: 91). As Justin put it,

> Upon hearing [the] prophetic words, the devils set up Bacchus for the son of Jove […] they proclaimed Bellerophon, a mere man of man, to have ascended up to heaven upon his horse Pegasus. Moreover, finding by another prophet […] that He was to be born of a virgin, and ascend to heaven by Himself, they forged a Perseus to mimic Him in this also. And when they saw Him described by the prophecies, "Rejoicing as a giant to run his course," they preached up the giant Hercules running over the whole earth. And again, perceiving by the prophets that He was to cure all sorts of diseases, and to raise the dead, they palmed their Æsculapius upon the world to ape Him in this also. (*The First Apology of Justin Martyr*, chapter 71, 1889: 67)

Finally, Justin's main rejoinder, a familiar tactic among apologists, was that while the pagan gods had many of the characteristics that the Christians ascribed to Jesus, the pagan gods were false:

> Jesus alone is properly the Son of God, as being the Logos, and First-begotten, and Power of God, and by His counsel was made a man, and taught these doctrines for the conversion and

> restoration of mankind [...] before Whose coming in our flesh these same evil spirits, by their instruments, the poets, dressed up fables to represent these things as already past and over, on purpose to defeat the good designs of His coming; just such another pack of scandalous wicked lies they have at present invented to render Christians odious. (*The First Apology of Justin Martyr*, chapter 31, 1889: 31)

To reiterate, the reason Justin and the other early apologists did not deny the similarities between the Jesus legend and the earlier mythology was that these tales were too well-known. So they adopted the "it is the work of Satan" tactic to explain it away. Today's literalists are being duplicitous or are engaging in pious fraud when they deny that any such parallels exist or that pagan mythology borrowed such tales from Christian lore (e.g., Eddy and Boyd 2007: 91–132; Yamauchi 1974a, 1974b).

As noted, Celsus (1830: 15), pointed out the similarities between the dying-and-rising god-men narratives and the story of Jesus and considered them all to be fictitious. More importantly, Celsus (1830: 30) was well aware of how the many religious charlatans or self-appointed ambassadors from heaven in his day often used such stories to dupe the gullible:

> Each of these likewise is readily accustomed to say, "I am God, or the son of God, or a divine spirit. But I came because the world will soon be destroyed, and you, O men! on account of your iniquities will perish. I wish, however, to save you, and you shall again see me, returning with a celestial army. Blessed is he who now worships me; but I will cast all those who do not, into eternal fire, together with the cities and regions to which they belong. Those men also that do not now know the punishments which are reserved for them, shall afterwards repent and lament in vain: but those who believe in me I will forever save" Extending to the multitude these insane and perfectly obscure assertions, the meaning of which no intelligent man is able to discover,—for they are unintelligible and a mere nothing,—they afford an occasion to the stupid and to jugglers of giving to them whatever interpretation they please.

Celsus (1830: 15) also stressed the significant inconsistency already mentioned, pointing out that while the Christians declared that all other dying and rising god-man stories are legends, they claimed that their resurrection story is true. In his words,

> but how many others have employed such-like prodigies [dying and rising from the grave], in order by a fabulous narration to effect what they wished; persuading stupid auditors to believe in these miracles? Zamolxis among the Scythians, who was a slave of Pythagoras, used this artifice; Pythagoras also himself, in Italy; and in Egypt, Rhampsinitus. For it is related of the latter that he played at dice with Ceres in Hades, and that he brought back with him as a gift from her a golden towel. Similar artifices were likewise employed by Orpheus among the Odryssians; by Protesilaus among the Thessalians; and by Hercules and Theseus [a founding hero for the Athenians] in Tænarus [Corinth].

Zamolxis was a divine being who was formerly a human, also known as Gebeleizis, as mentioned by Herodotus. Pythagoras was an ancient Ionian Greek philosopher that legends claimed was a supernatural being and wonder-worker who descended to the underworld and returned. Rhampsinitus possibly refers to Ramses III, also mentioned by Herodotus. Orpheus was a Greek hero, the son of the muse Calliope, who had supernatural musical skills. Protesilaus was a venerated hero who appears in Homer's Iliad. Finally, Theseus was a founding hero for the Athenians.

But, Celsus (1830: 15) perceptively called attention to a crucial point:

> This, however, is to be considered—whether anyone who in reality died, ever rose again in the same body: unless you think that the narrations of others are fables, but that your catastrophe of the drama will be found to be either elegant or probable, respecting what was said by him who expired on the cross.

Along the same lines, Price (2008) asks, why is it that only in the case of Jesus, a myth becomes fact? And Crossley (2005: 181) queries why the pagan and Jewish texts are deemed fictitious, but Christian stories are genuine? Of course, it is only the true believers who accept the reality of this archaic narrative on faith, rather than any evidence, that would make such an assertion.

## The Role of Women in the Vacant Tomb Story as Evidence of Historicity of the Empty Tomb Story

Another issue modern-day Christian apologists have fixated upon to validate their supernaturalism is the role of women in Mark's narrative. This element of the story is deemed crucial evidence for the historicity of the narrative because of the inferior social position of women means that they were not qualified to serve as legal witnesses. If the tale is fictional, then females would not have been written in as the ones to discover the vacant sepulcher as this would have weakened the argument (Licona 2010: 349–54; Craig 1998: 259). Yamauchi (1974a, 1974b) similarly restates this apologist assertion that the events must be historical otherwise the gospel writers would not have given a significant role to lowly women as the discoverers of the empty tomb because they were unacceptable as witnesses. Allison (2005: 327–29), who also maintains this view, says that this is the most recent robust argument put forth for the historicity of the empty tomb tale. For Allison, the involvement of the women means that the core of the narrative is historic. What other reasons could there be, Allison queries, for Mark to not use Peter, John, or some other authoritative males as the ones who made the monumental discovery?

This sounds plausible, but it is not for several reasons. First, as Ehrman (2014: 166–67) points out, we are not dealing with a Jewish court of law but with a story about a man's burial. Second, the core of the story may have, in fact, come from women who were the storytellers and chief mourners. Women had a notably significant role in Jesus's ministry, and it makes sense that Mark refers to them (Crossely 2005: 184). Women also had leadership roles in the early Christian communities. Evidence for this comes from the letter written by Pliny the Younger, the Roman governor of Bithynia et Pontus (the Roman province on the Black Sea coast of modern-day Turkey) to Emperor Trajan. Pliny states that while trying suspected Christians, the highest ranking members of the church he was able to interrogate were women (*Epistles*10.96; Carrington 2011: 429).

Third, elsewhere the New Testament emphasizes women's crucial role in Christianity; this includes the actions of Elizabeth, the mother of John the Baptist, who acknowledged Mary as the Mother of God, and Anna, who blessed the baby Jesus at the temple (Watt 2001: 94). Therefore, it is perfectly reasonable for women to have a central place in Mark's fable. Also, women were allowed to give evidence if male witnesses were not available (Lowder 2005: 283). Mark indeed finds no need to defend the prominence of women in his narrative. Also, as pointed out earlier, Mark makes the discoverers of the tomb to be women to provide a plausible reason why his tale was not known previously.

Fourth, it must not be overlooked that preparing bodies for burial, serving as principal lamenters, and checking on deceased relatives after interment were the responsibilities of women. These, as the Gospel of Peter 12:50 says, are things "what women are wont to do for their beloved of them who die." The role of women as chief lamenters is clear from what Mary Magdalene says in Peter 12:52: "Although on the day he was crucified we could not weep and beat our breasts, we should now perform these rites at his tomb." Inserting men into the script as the first to go to the tomb to prepare the body was contrary to local cultural conventions and would have all the hallmarks of deception.

Fifth, we know that the disciples had scattered in terror, either fleeing back to Galilee (Hendrickx 1978: 15) or hiding somewhere in Jerusalem "for fear of the Jews" (Allison 2005: 332). They were sought by the Romans and the Jews who, as the Gospel of Peter 12:50 says, "were inflamed with wrath." In either case, they were potential wanted men, a fact that did not change between Friday when Jesus was executed and buried and Sunday when the discovery of the alleged vacant tomb occurs. Scripting male disciples doing what the women did in the story would seem deceptive. Thus, Mark's use of female protagonists does in no way prove the historicity of the fictional empty tomb. Ultimately, however, the message about Jesus rising from the dead does, in fact, come from a *man*, the angel dressed in white who provides all the authority Mark required (Crossely 2005: 184).

By playing up the role of women as unreliable witnesses to suggest historicity for the tale, today's apologists are retrojecting their own shameful cultural male chauvinistic biases into the argument. For Mark, Jesus's principal female and male followers were equally important (Crossan 1998: 557). As noted, women, especially Mary Magdalene, had considerable prominence in the Jesus movement and were especially close to him and the principal disciples. It is not surprising that Mark portrays her as the chief mourner. After the disciples fled, it was Mary, because she was close to Jesus, who is written into the story as the most believable character to go to the burial place. However, she did not find an empty tomb but discovered the stark reality that no one could identify the location of the common grave. Spong (1995: 229) thinks that Mary's plaintive cry, "They have taken away my Lord, and I do not know where they have laid him" (John 20:13) represents one of a few single brute facts around which Mark and the other gospel writers developed their empty tomb story.

### The Absence of an Exhumed Body as Evidence of Historicity of the Empty Tomb Story

Another argument, a rather morbid and inane one, put forth by fervent believers is that if the empty tomb were not a historical reality, the Jewish or Roman authorities would have squelched assertions about Jesus's resurrection by having his corpse exhumed and put on public display (Barclay 1996: 22). In other words, the apostles would not have dared to preach that Jesus had risen from the grave unless they, along with everyone else, knew that the tomb was unoccupied (Bode 1970: 162–63; Craig 2003: 193–94; Cranfield 1990). Otherwise, all their opponents had to do was point a finger to Jesus's burial site (Pannenberg 1996: 69).

The exhumation argument that present-day apologists still keep circulating was addressed long ago by writers such as Macan (1877: 106). Those who raise this issue assume that first-century Palestinians thought the same way as people do in our time. The notion of resurrection was part of the then current "apocalyptic language of exaltation" and did not entail reanimated cadavers crawling out of graves and sauntering in the streets. According to the Gospel of Mark (6:16), Herod Antipas believed that Jesus was John the Baptist returned from the dead. However, there is no evidence that Antipas had John's corpse exhumed to verify his suspicions (Macan 1877: 106). As Hoover (2008: 112) observes, "In first-century Palestine, belief in a resurrection did not depend on cemetery records and could not be shaken by exhumations or autopsies."

Also mistaken is the suggestion that the disciples had no basis for formulating the concept of resurrection and that only Jesus walking out of the tomb could have led to this conclusion. Herod unquestionably thought Jesus was John the Baptist resurrected. He did not believe this could be another preacher but jumped to the paranormal conclusion. So, this was not a hitherto unimagined concept (Gorham 1908: 117–18). Alternatively, the skeptical philosopher and Enlightenment writer Paul-Henri Thiry (Baron d'Holbach) (1813: 257) observed that the disciples came up with the idea of the resurrection from the fact that "their master having, during his life, raised other from the dead, had after his own death raised himself by virtue of his omnipotence." Raising the dead, we might recall, was part of the repertoire of the many magicians and sorcerers of the day.

Moreover, as Strauss (1902: 851) pointed out, an empty tomb was not necessary for the disciples to conceive of the idea of Jesus's reanimation. The disciples we might recall had fled to Galilee, where they did not need to shut their doors "for fear of the Jewish leaders" (John 20:19–23). There they acquired breathing room, regrouped, and restored their faith in Jesus that had temporarily faltered. In Galilee, "where no body lay in the grave to contradict the bold suppositions," they formed the idea that Jesus had risen (Strauss 1902: 851). This conviction elevated their courage, and they set forth to proclaim it in the metropolis, whereby this time a body could no longer be produced to refute their claim if that was ever a possibility.

Finally, while apologists place great emphasis on the bold proselytization of the disciples, most of which occurred to Galilee, there is little evidence that their preaching to the Palestinian Jews was an astounding success (Watson 1987: 371). So it is unlikely that at this stage, their evangelization would have demanded a response by digging up someone's bones.

As Watson (1987: 370) cogently points out, the assertion about the public display of a corpse is based on four presuppositions: (1) that the Jews and the general public knew precisely where the grave was located; (2) that the Galilean missionaries who came back to Jerusalem were outstandingly successful; (3) that Caiaphas and his colleagues had an urgent need to refute the proclamations of the Jesus cultists about their risen rabbi;

(4) that the biblical narratives about Jesus's burials are accurate. There are no grounds for accepting any of these suppositions.

Why did not Caiaphas order the morbid task of displaying the rotting corpse for public viewing? Simple because there was no reason to enter into a public debate with what at the time was an insignificant, irreligious sect made up of vulgar, illiterate peasants and hallucinating sociopaths who for the most part went unnoticed (Wells 1996: 39; Wilken 1984: xviii). The Roman writers Pliny and Tacitus described the Christians as "loathed" purveyors of "a perverse and extravagant superstition" who share "a hatred of the human race" (Wells 1996: 41–42). And as the theologian and scholar of early Christianity and ancient Judaism John Meier states, for the Jewish and Roman writers of the first and second centuries CE, the Christians were an insignificant and marginal lot. Meier (1991: 7–8) even refers to Jesus as a "marginal Jew," a man who from the Jewish perspective had died "accursed by God" (Deuteronomy 21:23).

Christians were one among many groups of fanatics from the hinterlands who periodically appeared in the streets of Jerusalem to cause trouble (Parsons 2005: 451). As the philosopher Jeffrey Lowder (2005: 288) has put it, there was as much interest in refuting the claims of these imperceptible undesirables during the first century as twentieth-century skeptics had in refuting the bizarre assertions of members of the Heaven's Gate cult. Also, why enter into a public debate when persecution of the deviants is an option, which is precisely what happened later on when Jesus's followers became too much of a nuisance.

Furthermore, the suggestion about corpse exhumation is absurd because even if the authorities were compelled to provide a cadaver, it would have made no difference. This is because Jesus's followers did not begin public proclamations of the resurrection until at least 50 days after the crucifixion. By that time the body (if locating it was even possible) would have decomposed beyond recognition, making identification impossible without dental records and modern forensic science (Lowder 2005: 283–84; Macan 1877: 106; Price 2005:422; Strauss 1873, I: 743; Thrall 1979: 201). Moreover, even if a body were produced and put on display and somehow identified, the disciples would have resorted to the same specious arguments and special pleading used by present-day religionists and purveyors of paranormal beliefs and simply denied that the corpse was that of Jesus. We must remember that no amount of evidence is sufficient to change the true believers' conviction about the veracity of their superstitious beliefs.

## Body Snatching as Evidence of Historicity of the Empty Tomb Story

Another assertion regarding the historicity of the tale of a vacant sepulcher is to cite the passages in Matthew that talks about guards at the tomb and the subsequent discovery of the empty tomb by the women (this also occurs in the Gospel of Peter 8–14). Matthew is a writer known for flagrant inventions who also gave us the bizarre story of zombie saints invading Jerusalem. According to Matthew 27:62–66,

> The next day, the one after Preparation Day, the chief priests and the Pharisees went to Pilate. "Sir," they said, "we remember that while he was still alive that deceiver said, 'After three

> days I will rise again.' So give the order for the tomb to be made secure until the third day. Otherwise, his disciples may come and steal the body and tell the people that he has been raised from the dead. This last deception will be worse than the first." "Take a guard," Pilate answered. "Go, make the tomb as secure as you know how." So they went and made the tomb secure by putting a seal on the stone and posting the guard.

This meeting, "the next day" after the Day of Preparation, takes place on Saturday, the Jewish Sabbath. It is improbable that "the chief priests and the Pharisees" would meet with Pilate on a Sabbath day, which is another clue that the narrative is a fabrication (Tobin 2009: 538). Matthew 28:1–10 adds,

> After the Sabbath, at dawn on the first day of the week, Mary Magdalene and the other Mary went to look at the tomb. There was a violent earthquake, for an angel of the Lord came down from heaven and, going to the tomb, rolled back the stone and sat on it. His appearance was like lightning, and his clothes were white as snow. The guards were so afraid of him that they shook and became like dead men. The angel said to the women, "Do not be afraid, for I know that you are looking for Jesus, who was crucified. He is not here; he has risen, just as he said. Come and see the place where he lay. Then go quickly and tell his disciples: 'He has risen from the dead and is going ahead of you into Galilee. There you will see him.' Now I have told you." So the women hurried away from the tomb, afraid yet filled with joy, and ran to tell his disciples. Suddenly Jesus met them. "Greetings," he said. They came to him, clasped his feet and worshiped him. Then Jesus said to them, "Do not be afraid. Go and tell my brothers to go to Galilee; there they will see me."

Here, Matthew's paranormal interjections continue with yet another earthquake and a dazzling angel descending from the heavens. The writer of this gospel has invented these details that appear nowhere else out of thin air, including the angel, the Roman guards, and the groveling females.

The fabrications continue further as Matthew 28:11–15 describes the actions of the guards and a conspiracy by the Jewish priests:

> While the women were on their way, some of the guards went into the city and reported to the chief priest everything that had happened. When the chief priests had met with the elders and devised a plan, they gave the soldiers a large sum of money, telling them, "You are to say, 'His disciples came during the night and stole him away while we were asleep.' If this report gets to the governor, we will satisfy him and keep you out of trouble." So the soldiers took the money and did as they were instructed. And this story has been widely circulated among the Jews to this very day.

Price (2000: 338) fittingly refers to this whole scenario as an outrageous farce. The assertion here is that the Jews falsified the story that the disciples stole the body from the tomb to cover up the actual resurrection. Thiry (1813: 265) addressed this problematic argument long ago, noting how strange it was that the Jewish elders who were moved by the prodigy were convinced of Jesus paranormal powers and realized that he had come back from the dead, did not immediately "recognize Jesus as the Messiah, and [...] unite with him in laboring to deliver their country from the yoke of idolaters." Instead, they conspired to hide this miracle of God, namely the appearance of long-awaited Savior of the Jews.

The farcicality of the story is also evident in the fact that Matthew is asking us to believe that Pilate, not a man to be sympathetic toward the Jews, would agree to their requests to post sentries at the tomb. Cavari (1967: 420) refers to this as "an episode whose incongruousness and *naïveté* clearly demonstrate its falsity." Furthermore, Matthew wants us to think that the Jewish priests could convince the Roman guards of their ability to placate the vengeful and ill-tempered Pilate's wrath toward them for sleeping on the job (Tobin 2009: 539), a crime minimally punishable by severe flogging.

True believers take these passages literally and claim that they constitute concrete historical data and independent confirmation coming from the Jewish enemies of the Christians that the tomb was empty (Craig 1995: 152; Wright 2003: 636–40). Every feature of this narrative suggests, however, that the guarded tomb motif is not historical. Only Matthew (and the non-canonical Gospel of Peter) covers it; it is at odds with the other gospels and is an effort to unequivocally counter a rumor going around in Matthew's own time that the disciples absconded with their master's body (McGrath 2008: 85).

However, there is a more significant problem in the religionist case. At the time of the crucifixion and burial of Jesus, none of the disciples knew that their master would rise from the dead. The idea that the entire tragedy was foretold to them and was part of a grand plan is a later invention (cf., Strauss 1902: 807). These claims were scripted in the gospels long after the fact by the evangelists. This is why the disciples abandoned Jesus at the time of his arrest (Mark 14:50), were utterly unprepared for the horrifying events that culminated in the crucifixion, and did not believe the women that Jesus has risen (Mark 16:11–13) (cf., Wells 1996: 122). Yet, Matthew relates the Jewish leaders knew that Jesus had foretold that after three days he would rise again. The difficulty with this is that if the disciples did not know about Jesus's predictions, then neither did the Jewish authorities. Therefore, the tale about the chief priest and Pharisees knowing what the disciples did not know at the time and asking Pilate for guards is pure post hoc fiction. Indeed, Celsus (1987: 62) called attention to this long ago, and many New Testament scholars have arrived at the same conclusion (Funk and Hoover 1993: 36, 75, 83, 94, 212, 255, 312, 397, 406; Strauss 1902: 805).

Finally, the apologists' assertions fail because there are no records of grave-robbing or body snatching allegations by the Jews against the Christians at the time of Jesus's death (Allison 2005: 312; Lowder 2005: 291). Also, the date of the polemic is uncertain and, if true, was probably generated in response to Mark's empty tomb story, around 70 CE and later (McGrath 2008: 85). By that time, Jerusalem had been sacked, the body long since decomposed, and the location of a tomb, if there ever was one, was forgotten. So, there was no way for anyone to check any tomb. Finally, as already noted, it is very likely that the Jewish polemic itself was a Christian literary invention to address doubts that were occurring among converts regarding the veracity of Jesus's physical resurrection (Lowder 2005: 291; Parsons 2005: 443; Strauss 1902: 809; Wells 1996: 113).

## Historicity Based on the Absence of Secondary Burial and Veneration of Jesus's Tomb

Another argument for the historicity of the empty tomb is "that there never was a question of anyone performing a secondary burial for Jesus" (Wright 2003: 707–8). This task, if there is truth to any part of this story, would have fallen upon Joseph of Arimathea. He would have had to gather the bones and deposit them elsewhere. The timing of this event would have been after the disciples had already declared their master risen from the dead. However, this is implausible, as Crossley (2005: 185) points out. There is no evidence that Joseph existed or, if he did, what happened to him in the period immediately after he allegedly placed Jesus's body in a tomb. More importantly, as Crossley (2005: 185) observes, if Joseph went to rebury Jesus's remains and found the sepulcher vacant (i.e., confirmation of the prophecy about the Messiah), why is there no evidence that Joseph and his associates converted to Christianity?

Finally, believers argue that the empty tomb story must be true because there is no evidence that Christians venerated the grave site (Dunn 2003: 837–38; Harris 1983: 40). They insist that no one venerated the grave "because it *was* empty" (Gurdry 2000: 114, n. 10). Remarkably, these apologists are contradicting the very theological precept they are trying to establish, namely that the miracle of Christianity requires that the tomb must be empty. In other words, for the Christians, the significant event was the cosmic miracle of resurrection, which entails and indeed *necessitates* that there would be no corpse at the location. Why would they venerate the grave of a non-resurrected rabbi and false Messiah? Thus, had believers known the site of the tomb they would undoubtedly have gone there to absorb the paranormal ambience of the holy locale where this spectacular magical event or miracle transpired. In other words, the site itself would have been considered sacred, like the two alleged empty burial sites of Jesus in Jerusalem (Gordon Calvery discovered during the sixteenth century, and the location of the Holy Sepulcher found during the fourth century) that today attracts thousands of worshippers (cf., Carnley 1987: 58).

Also, it is implausible for Paul not to have visited Jesus's tomb and written about it had he known where it was during his two weeks stay in Jerusalem a few years after the crucifixion to meet Peter, the leader of the Christian community (Hoover 2008: 82). However, for Paul, the whereabouts of a grave would have been irrelevant, to begin with, because his theology was anchored on a spiritual resurrection, and an immediate translation of the spirit to Heaven at the moment of death, not on the idea of a walking corpse.

Moreover, as the skeptic Earl Doherty (2005: 75) asks, if the tomb's location was known, why is there no mention of it in hundreds of years of Christian writing? The biblical scholar John Barclay (1996: 22–23) has pointed out that the argument that no one venerated the grave because it was empty does not work because the absence of a body does not preclude veneration. Otherwise, today there would be no worshippers at the alleged grave site, the empty Holy Sepulchre in Jerusalem. Instead, believers have been flocking to this place in large numbers ever since its "discovery" in 326 CE. For Barclay, the lack of veneration lends support to the premise that the whereabouts of Jesus's burial place were unknown.

True believers, however, maintain that the site of Jesus's tomb was known all along, just that people did not worship there. Given the above discussion, this makes no sense. Brown's (1994: 1281–83) assertion, for example, that the memory of the location of Jesus's tomb was retained over the centuries until Emperor Constantine had a church built on the spot goes beyond what the evidence can certify (cf., Taylor 1998). The fact that no one attended a supposed burial site for Jesus for 300 years is a strong indication that the location was unknown for the reasons discussed in this chapter. Constantine built the Church of the Holy Sepulcher for symbolic purposes. It occupies an imaginary site selected based on an alleged vision or "divine revelation" on the part of an enthusiastic cleric (Guignebert 1958: 493).

The philosopher Michel Onfray (2011: 115) calls the sepulcher an invention of St. Helena, Constantine's mother. This paranormally detected site also conveniently yielded a chip from the original cross, the actual crown of thorns the Romans placed on Jesus's head, and the lance that pierced his side (Tobin 2009: 544). There was, however, no burial garment resembling the Turin relic among this assemblage of counterfeit holy relics. The presence of such articles in Jesus's grave is implausible. It required that we believe that the people burying Jesus, who did not even have the time to complete their task before sundown, as the gospels relate, had time to gather the crown of thorns, secure the spear from the Roman guard who was willing to part with an official piece of military equipment, as well as taking a chip of the cross? All of these attests to the bogus nature of this claim.

As Ernest Barnes observes in his book *The Rise of Christianity* (1948), it is difficult to establish the authenticity of these grave sites. The discovery is first discussed in 326 CE in Eusebius's *Life of Constantine* (iii. 25–6), probably written in 338 CE. This writer, we may recall, was a notorious forger and fabricator of false tales. He relates that Emperor Constantine constructed a house of prayer over the site. Barnes (1948: 163) also notes that this location was not determined according to any local tradition or folk memory but decided upon based on a religionist's "vision of the Savior!"

There is nothing unusual about this set of circumstances. I encountered a similar case in the context of field research involving the grave site of Ali, the fourth Caliph of Islam. Ali's tomb is in the city of Najaf in Iraq. However, there is another grave site for Ali in the city of Mazar-i-Sharif (grave of the honorable one) in northern Afghanistan. People there are convinced that this is Ali's actual burial site. Every year thousands of people converge on this site on the Islamic New Year's Day. The tomb is known for its miraculous healing effects, and there are many stories of crippled persons being able to walk again, and the blind magically regaining their sight. This holy local was also discovered when some religionist had a vision or dream.

What seems to have happened in the case of Jesus's grave is another well-known anthropological occurrence, which is for one religion to co-opt the holy places of the faith it has supplanted. A good example is when the Spaniards built their Cathedral of the Assumption of the Most Blessed Virgin Mary into Heaven on top of the main Aztec Temple (Templo Mayor) in their capital city of Tenochtitlan, which is today Mexico City. During fieldwork in Central Asia, I came across numerous per-Islamic holy sites that are now the locations of Muslim sacred shrines. A similar thing has happened in the context of Hinduism, Bon, and Buddhism as well. The places identified as the sites of Jesus's burial were initially pagan shrines (Barnes 1948: 163–64).

The noted German theologian Joachim Jeremias made the following observation: "The 'rediscovery' of the tomb of Jesus in 326 has nothing to do with his real place of burial and is a pious legend" (cited in Lüdemann 1995: 139, n. 21). Moreover, as McGrath (2008: 93) acknowledges, "at present, there is no way to know for certain whether this is the actual site of the tomb." Regarding the whereabouts of Jesus's grave, Lüdemann (1995: 20) says that no one, not even members of the earliest Christian community, knew the location of the site. Given the importance of the tombs of saints at the time, had the location of Jesus's tomb been known, the early Christians would have venerated it, and the tradition would have been preserved. These comprise the final bits of evidence in support of the conclusion that the empty tomb and appearance stories are a later fictional embellishment and that the Christians at the time had no idea about the location of their Messiah's grave (Carnley 1987: 58).

In this chapter, we have examined aspects of the Christian evidence, which is the basis of the religionist assault on science and anthropology. Such an investigation has become necessary solely because by proposing that their supernatural view of the world is a superior explanatory framework in comparison to science, religionists have put up their theistic premises for scientific and anthropological scrutiny per the tradition of systematic skepticism. As discussed here, the results of such an inquiry do not bode well for the credibility of the Christian evidence base on offer as the basis of a more genuine and authentic investigatory paradigm.

# Chapter Fifteen

# THE POST-RESURRECTION APPEARANCES IN THE NEW TESTAMENT

*If this Jesus were trying to convince anyone of his powers, then surely he ought to have appeared first to the Jews who mistreated him—and to his accusers—indeed to everyone, everywhere. [...] When he was punished, everyone saw; yet risen from the tomb, almost no one.*

—Celsus, *On the True Doctrine* (circa 185 CE)

*The story of Jesus Christ appearing after he was dead is the story of an apparition, such as timid imaginations can always create in vision, and credulity believe. Stories of this kind had been told of the assassination of Julius Caesar, not many years before; and they generally have their origin in violent deaths, or in the execution of innocent persons.*

—Thomas Paine, *The Age of Reason* (1795)

*Why did [Jesus] not show conclusively, before hostile witnesses, the reality of his triumph over death [...] thus proving the divinity of his mission, and of saving future generations from infinite difficulties and perplexities? [...] If the object of Jesus was the salvation of the world, why should he have concealed from the world the divine ratification of his claims?*

—Charles Gorham, *The First Easter Dawn* (1908)

*It is difficult to avoid the conclusion that we are in the domain of religious romance, not of religious history.*

—Ernest William Barnes, *The Rise of Christianity* (1948)

There are no actual witnesses to the greatest miracles of Christianity, namely that a risen Jesus walked out of the tomb in which his lifeless body had been placed. These events are a product of imagination. The belief that he rose from the dead originates from reports by his disciples that they had seen visions of their rabbi alive after his execution. For this reason, the ancient historian Robin Lane Fox (1986: 379) states that early Christianity was "born from visionary experience." Accounts of this event, however, were not recorded by the disciples or anyone else at the time and come down as second- and third-hand reports by others of what these individuals may have experienced.

Adding to these difficulties, as Ehrman (2014: 135) has summed it up, is the fact that these reports contain contradictions and are at variance with each other in numerous crucial details (see below). Yet, this is what religionists consider as irrefutable proof and "eyewitness testimony" that Jesus "literally" came back from the dead (Habermas 2003: 22–27). This event is central to what the theistic philosopher Alvin Plantinga has proposed as evidence of God's action in the world and the basis of a better alternative to science and its epistemological and philosophical foundations. The skeptical assessment of this claim continues in this chapter.

## The Earliest Resurrection Story

The oldest report of someone claiming that they saw Jesus's apparition occurs in Paul's (Saul of Tarsus) first letter to the Corinthians (15:3–8), which dates to around 50–60 CE:

> For what I received I passed on to you as of first importance: that Christ died for our sins according to the Scriptures [i.e., the Septuagint], that he was buried, that he was raised on the third day according to the Scriptures, and that he appeared to Cephas [Peter], and then to the Twelve [disciples]. After that, he appeared to more than five hundred of the brothers and sisters at the same time, most of whom are still living, though some have fallen asleep [died]. Then he appeared to James, then to all the apostles, and last of all he appeared to me also, as to one abnormally born.

The immediate question to ask is, Where did Paul obtain this information? Aside from his own visionary experience, which is problematic as we shall see, what we have is a second- or third-hand report of other people's alleged visions or sightings of the risen Jesus. Paul's narrative as a whole is very vague. Also, there are no explicit accounts of the apparition sighting by Peter apart from the one in conjunction with the "Twelve" (Lüdemann 2004: 72, 81). And Paul does not say which James saw Jesus—there were three men named James among the Christians, the brother of Jesus, the brother of John, and the son of Alphaeus (Gorham 1908: 34). It was probably James, the brother of Jesus, but the text is unclear.

The Greek word Paul uses is *ophthe*, which translates to "he was seen" and does not indicate an actual bodily appearance, that is, that Jesus was there "in person" (Guignebert 1958: 522–23). This is the case with Paul's own religious experience, as is related in Acts 22:6–11. The passage states that Paul was on the road to Damascus when a bright light flashed from above that temporarily blinded him. He fell to the ground and heard a voice that said: "Saul! Saul! Why do you persecute me?" When Paul asked who was speaking, the voice replied: "I am Jesus of Nazareth, whom you are persecuting." Those with Paul saw the light but did not hear the voice. In Acts 9:7–9, the story is different, with Paul's companions hearing only a noise. Then when Paul asked what he was supposed to do, the voice replied: "'Get up, and go into Damascus. There you will be told all that you have been assigned to do.'"

Religious experiences, we might recall from Chapter 9, represent a nonpublic, subjective encounter with a supernatural being that only the percipient can see or hear (something commonly associated with various psychological maladies). Here, to identify the voice as that of God necessitates that others hear and recognize it as the voice of such an entity. But this did not happen. Moreover, this scenario is impossible because God is immaterial, has no vocal cords, and hence no audible voice. Thus, this is not an of-God experience but a purported experience of something allegedly produced by God (Philipse 2014: 328). As such, the degree of paranormal significance believers attribute to Paul's Damascus road religious experience or hallucination is unwarranted given the evidence.

It is also important to remember that this account was written by someone else (Luke) of what happened. Paul himself refers to his experience briefly in Galatians 1:12–16, where he relates that he did not receive his religious wisdom from any man but through a revelation from Jesus Christ. He adds that once he was a persecutor of the church of God but was transformed into a believer when God revealed "his Son" to him so that he might preach the word "among the Gentiles." Paul also makes references to his visionary experiences in 1 Corinthians 9:1 and 15:8. Luke, the author of Acts, describes it in Acts 9, 22, and 26. Paul's seeming autobiographical description of an ascent to heaven in 2 Corinthians 12:1–10, which reveals his propensity for deliriums, is not an encounter with the apparition of Jesus and is not relevant in the context of this discussion.

What is portrayed in these narratives is a vision, not a meeting with Jesus in person (Tobin 2009: 557). Thomas Paine (1880 [1795]: 136) thought that the story on the road to Damascus involved lightning striking Paul, which does not entail a miracle and would probably account for the flash of light and loud noise and his loss of sight and inability to eat or drink for three days.

As for Paul's reference to the 500 adherents who saw the risen Lord, it is vital to keep in mind that he says nothing concrete about the people involved or says precisely what they saw. Was it a full-body apparition? Was the appearance in the form of bright light, as in the case of his own encounter on the road? Did they see Jesus or merely feel his presence? Did the apparition speak? Did he introduce himself? If so, did he use Aramaic, Hebrew, or maybe even Greek? Was Peter there? Were any of the other apostles present? Paul provides no such information. Also, where was Jesus during this event? On a podium? On a hillside? How far away was he from the crowd? How did the spectators recognize or identify him? Such information is lacking. These gaps in the narrative and uncertainty about this event open up space for interjecting paranormal conjectures and explanations.

Another significant point is that Paul does not differentiate between his vision and the ones experienced by Peter, the 12 disciples, or the appearance before the 500 brothers and sisters (Armstrong 1983: 55). In other words, he treats all of them as visionary experiences on par with each other rather than some events being visionary and others being actual encounters with Jesus in the flesh. In the case of Paul and the early Christians differentiating between a visionary and actual appearance was not of concern. In was much later, with the writing of the Gospel of Mark around 70 CE, and the gospels that came after, that it became necessary to stress that the appearances were physical and not merely visions. This is why the evangelists at this time invented the empty tomb story, as related in the previous chapter.

## The Significance of the Appearance before the 500 Witnesses

Religious polemicists place decisive significance on one specific detail in Paul's story of the postmortem Jesus sighting by the 500, namely his assertion that many of the witnesses were still alive at the time and hence it was possible to consult them. A further contention is that Paul could not have made such a statement and challenged his audience to check the veracity of the claim if what he said was untrue (Kreeft and Tacelli 1994: 186–87). This is not a compelling argument. First, it is unlikely that the Corinthian Christians had the means or inclination to travel from Greece to Palestine to check the claim. If Paul had powerful and resourceful enemies who wished to refute his claims and would have investigated the matter, as apologists say, why would they take the trouble to go to Palestine to check the facts, and so forth, rather than resort to direct action against him?

Second, Paul does not say who these people were, or where and how to find them. Absent from the story are essential details regarding time, place, and circumstances, and there are no other clues about their identities or addresses. Moreover, Paul does not say he was one of the 500 (Gorham 1908: 34). Clearly, he is recounting a second-, third-, or even a fourth-hand account. So Paul was on perfectly safe grounds in making such rhetorical remarks about living witnesses who would corroborate his tale (Parsons 2005: 438).

There are several other reasons to doubt this story. First, the New Testament sources that contain appearance stories, the gospels of Matthew, Luke, John, and Acts of the Apostles, say nothing about Jesus appearing before "five hundred of the brothers and sisters at the same time." Why not? The respective evangelists who wrote these accounts would have surely recorded this extraordinary and astonishing case had they known of it (Parsons 2005: 437). Second, as Gorham (1908: 33) queried, how is it possible that soon after the death of Jesus there were 500 individuals in existence who could be called "brethren" to gather in Jerusalem? And Loisy (1962: 88) noted that it is highly unlikely that Jesus had an opportunity to teach in Jerusalem long enough to recruit many followers.

According to Maurice Goguel (1953: 43), some have suggested that Paul is referring to the coming of the Holy Spirit at the Pentecost described in Acts 2:1–4 when the worshippers saw "tongues of fire" and they were filled with the Holy Spirit and spoke in tongues. Others disagree with this suggestion (Conzelmann 1987: 16). The event on the day of Pentecost appears to be a case of groupthink and socio-psychological contagion, described in Chapter 7, processes which become operational when enthusiastic people with similar beliefs and attitudes congregate in one place. In such religiously charged situations, some may undergo anomalous experiences, and others who have no such experience will go along with whatever the claim is so as not to undermine their own worthiness. Still others will be caught up in the exuberance of the situation and come to believe that they are indeed experiencing something paranormal. Such circumstances are on record in the context of modern-day Marian apparitions discussed in the chapter on religious experiences.

However, in the Pentecost event, there is no report of anyone seeing an apparition of Jesus, or hearing his voice. Instead, there are visions of flames and speaking in tongues, and it is unlikely that this was the occasion referred to in Paul's story of the mass vision. Alternatively, if he is referring to this event, then Paul is deceptive that it involved Jesus appearing before 500 witnesses. Or Paul could have been referring to an ecstatic worship experience that an early Christian group might have interpreted in a general sense as an appearance of the risen Jesus (Patterson 1998: 236). Again, the socio-psychological mechanisms at work would be ones similar to those documented during Marian apparitions. These could not have been physical manifestations of a reanimated corpse in a public setting.

The theologian Ernest Barnes (1948: 173) dismissed the reference to the appearance of the 500 as non-historical and a later redaction. Otherwise, he adds, this incredible bit of evidence would have been the centerpiece of Christian apologetics. However, there are no mention of this event in any other source. From this, he concluded that this story was invented after Paul's time. Barnes is generous by attributing this tale to the work of some later religious enthusiast rather than deception on the part of Paul, who is given deference because he is an important Christian saint.

However, the main question is, How could such an astonishing and very public event have taken place without anyone else rendering testimony about it? If the story of the physical appearance before 500 did indeed occur, it would have constituted a momentous event and the most substantial proof available to the Christians to validate their beliefs (Martin 1991: 90). Lüdemann (1994: 101) notes how very improbable it is for such a mass sighting to have happened without leaving a trace. Also, as Paine (1880 [1795]: 126) reminds us, the only source for the story of the 500 witnesses is Paul. It is the testimony of one individual about an event that allegedly took place before Paul's conversion.

Additionally, 500 people claiming that they saw an executed man alive would have drawn the attention of the authorities as well as historians and scholars across the region. However, there is no mention of this incident in the gospels, the other New Testament texts, or in the works of pagan and Jewish writers of the time. This is Paul's potentially most verifiable claim, yet there is not a shred of evidence for it anywhere (Goguel 1953: 43; Lüdemann 2004: 73–74). The fact that he uses this story suggests a pious lie, and it undermines his credulity as a witness in this and all other matters as well (cf., Martin 1991: 90).

Here we would do well to recall Hume's observation regarding the religionist tendency to distort information and espouse falsehoods. Hume's (1902 [1748]: 125–26) remarks, which I shall cite again, seem to apply to Paul's case in an uncanny manner, whose conversion to Christianity elevated him to a leading authority figure:

> But what greater temptation than to appear a missionary, a prophet, an ambassador from heaven? Who would not encounter many dangers and difficulties, in order to attain so sublime a character? Or if, by the help of vanity and a heated imagination, a man has first made a convert of himself, and entered seriously into the delusion; whoever scruples to make use of pious frauds, in support of so holy and meritorious a cause?

Believers' construal of Paul as a holy man and a revered saint prevents them from considering the likelihood that we are looking at a self-styled representative of Jesus, a character like Peregrine, the con artist who joined the church to exploit the credulous Christians for personal gain. It is not just that we only have Paul's word for this event involving the 500 witnesses; there is also the fact that he is operating as an evangelist, spin doctor, and propagandist. He, therefore, has every reason in his role as a self-appointed "ambassador from heaven" to resort to pious lies for what he believed was a meritorious and most holy cause, that of keeping the wayward Corinthian converts from defecting.

For the same reason, Paul's own Jesus experience carries little weight. Yet, apologists attribute exceptional credibility to Paul's paranormal encounter because it led him to convert from a skeptic and persecutor of Christians to a believer. However, there is nothing extraordinary about this. Lots of non-believers have converted, and some have even gone on to become religious fanatics like this apostle. Conversion, therefore, does not add more weight to Paul's testimony because at the time he wrote it, he was already a fervent devotee (Martin 1991: 84).

## Post-Resurrection Encounters in the New Testament Texts: Problems and Discrepancies

Turning to the principal accounts of the post-resurrection Jesus encounters found in the New Testament, it is significant that the Gospel of Mark, which was written circa 70 CE and is the earliest of the Synoptic Gospels, does not provide any such narrative. Mark ends with a young man (angel?) at the tomb telling the women to inform the disciples that Jesus will meet them in Galilee. The shocked and bewildered women then flee and say "nothing to anyone because they were afraid" (Mark 16:7–8). At a later date, additional verses (16:9–20), referred to as "pseudo-Mark," were added by an unknown but creative redactor that recapitulates the descriptions of the encounters with the risen Jesus found in the gospels written after Mark.

Matthew 28:8–10, which dates circa 90 CE, tells us that the women meet and touch Jesus in person. Here it is Jesus himself who relays the message to the ladies: "Do not be afraid. Go and tell my brothers to go to Galilee; there they will see me." In Luke 24:13–35, written about 85–90 CE, it is not the women in Mark and Matthew but two followers who first encounter the risen Jesus on the road to Emmaus near Jerusalem, although they do not recognize him. Luke 24:36–43 also describes Jesus appearing to and asking his follower to touch his body and eating food: "Touch me and see; a ghost does not have flesh and bones, as you see I have."

These accounts pose problems because they contradict Jesus's own directive for the disciples to go to Galilee, as recorded in Mark. Luke 24:33–34 also mentions Jesus appearing to Peter. Aside from Paul's letter, this is the only other reference regarding a personal appearance to Peter, no explicit tradition of this appearance has survived in the New Testament (Perrin 1977: 62). The biblical scholar William Walker (1969:164, n. 32) suggests that traces of the narrative of the appearance to Peter are hinted at in the following passage in Mark 16:7: "But go, tell his disciples and Peter, He is going ahead of you into Galilee. There you will see him, just as he told you." In the account in John 20:11–18, written circa 90–100 CE, the first person who encounters Jesus is Mary Magdalene. He tells her to relay the message to the disciple: "I am ascending to my Father and your Father, to my God and your God.'" Mary Magdalene then tells the followers: "I have seen the Lord!" John 20:19–23 also relates how Jesus materialized before his followers. The story goes that the disciples were cowering behind locked doors in fear of the Jewish authorities. Then Jesus appeared, greeted his students, and displayed the wounds on his hands and side.

John 20:24–25 also relates that Jesus asked Thomas the doubter to touch his wounds as a tangible demonstration that he was not a ghost: "Put your finger here; see my hands. Reach out your hand and put it into my side. Stop doubting and believe." Thomas said to him, "My Lord and my God!" As stated in the previous chapter, the inclusion of "doubters," such as Thomas, in this narrative is an apologetic maneuver to counter criticisms that the disciples were too gullible or that they had merely seen the ghost of their beloved master (Fox 1986: 378; Goguel 1953: 47). Crossley (2005: 182) raises an important point that if Thomas indeed had such an awe-inspiring experience, then everyone should have been talking about it. Instead, we have to wait until the Gospel of John is written circa 90–100 CE to hear of this astonishing encounter, which is a very good indication that this is a later theological embellishment. The biblical scholar Norman Perrin (1977: 66–67) refers to this as "an apologetic legend of corporality of Jesus" intended to prove that Jesus had risen not as a disembodied spiritual being or appeared as a ghost but that he could be seen, touched, and so on. It is, as noted before, the vulgarization of a spiritual tale for propaganda and proselytizing purposes.

John 21:1–14 also narrates the appearance of Jesus to his followers by the Sea of Tiberias when he eats breakfast with them. This passage requires little commentary because the appearance by the sea is believed to also be a later fictional addition (Fox 1986: 378–79). Initially, as Perrin (1977: 361) points out, this gospel ended with the following verses:

> Jesus performed many other signs in the presence of his disciples, which are not recorded in this book. But these are written that you may believe that Jesus is the Messiah, the Son of God, and that by believing you may have life in his name. (John 20:30–31)

The Acts of the Apostles1:3–9, written around 80–90 CE, has Jesus appearing to the disciples in Jerusalem for more than a month, which again contradicts the other texts that have appearances occur only in Galilee (Lüdemann 2004: 139; Strauss 1902: 820–28). Moreover, this passage conflicts with Matthew as well, who has the duration of the apparitions lasting only a few days (the amount of time needed to travel from Jerusalem to Galilee). It is also contrary to the Gospel of John that has Jesus appearing on the evening of the resurrection and eight days later in Jerusalem. In Acts 3–9, written by the author of Luke, the appearances and ascension occur in a single day, on Easter Sunday (Craveri 1967: 428; Strauss 1902: 821; Tobin 2009: 553). Mark and Matthew state that the first appearances were in Galilee. There are no references to the Jerusalem sightings in the other accounts. Thus, Gorham (1908: 92) observed, it was wholly incomprehensible that the disciples saw Jesus in Jerusalem when Mark and Matthew say that they had to go to Galilee to see their master.

We should recall that upon Jesus's arrest, the disciples fled back to their native Galilee. For this reason, many scholars believe that the earliest apparitions occurred in Galilee (Barclay 1996:25; Komarnitsky 2014a: 58; Lüdemann 1994: 174). The accounts of Jesus apparitions in Jerusalem are fictitious. In this regard, Craveri (1967: 428) observes that because the gospel texts do not agree on the place and duration of the apparitions, it is very probable that none of these accounts are historical. Strauss (1902: 826, 852–53) suggested that the first appearances occurred in Galilee, but over time another tradition developed that expediently put the apparitions in Jerusalem, the location of Jesus's death and the seat of the first Christian church. Crossley (2005: 182) similarly finds the passages in Luke-Acts that locate all the purported occurrences in Jerusalem while eliminating the possibility of a Galilean appearance in contradiction to Mark 16:7 to be theological embellishments.

The New Testament sources reviewed here, therefore, differ from one another in crucial details, such as where these appearances took place, their frequency, duration, as well as the identities of the first percipients (Tobin 2009: 553). Another critical evidentiary problem is that all of these narratives comprise second-, third-, or even fourth-hand accounts provided by others about the experiences of Jesus's followers. Moreover, these reports were further altered to suit the apologetic agendas of the evangelists who wrote the gospels (Parsons 2005: 438). For this reason, these sources are not disinterested, mutually independent, or impartial (Philipse 2014: 172). From a strictly Humean perspective, we must dismiss any matter of fact when witnesses contradict each other, are few, and have an interest in what they affirm, which are all criteria applicable in the case of the resurrection stories (Hume 1902 [1748]: 112). This is solely a question of evidence regardless of whether a miracle is or is not involved.

In this respect, the accounts of Jesus's appearances contrast sharply with the narratives we have regarding his crucifixion and death, where there is a degree of concurrence in the texts. Thus, as the biblical scholar Roy Hoover (2000: 135–36) observes, based on what we know about how gospel writers went about their task and the many inconsistencies in their Easter stories, we can surmise that the appearance stories were inventions long after the accounts of the appearances described by Paul. The evangelists fabricate the appearance stories to make the resurrection "believable to popular religious imagination" (Hoover 2000: 135–36). The evangelists were inventing stories, and this explains the contradictions and inconsistencies in their narratives. Barnes (1948: 170), having reviewed these materials, observes: "it is difficult to avoid the conclusion that we are in the domain of religious romance, not of religious history." To reemphasize an earlier point, the fact that Mark, the earliest of the gospels, does not mention any of the appearance stories that occur in the other gospels further suggests that the tales of a physically resurrected Jesus are expedient subsequent legendary embellishments and do not encapsulate any actual temporal events (Parsons 2005: 439).

The problems discussed can be summarized as follows. First, the accounts are inconsistent and contradict one another on critical points. Second, all of the alleged eyewitnesses of the post-resurrection appearances are suspect. These were intensely involved followers or friends of Jesus and not objective or impartial observers. They had lots of motives to exaggerate and fabricate stories. Third, the individuals present at the purported time of Jesus's rising did not leave any first-hand accounts. All the information comes from unknown second-, third-, or fourth-hand renditions by others of anecdotes about what was reported. Therefore, the credibility and trustworthiness of these secondary and tertiary reporters are highly doubtful. There is also the substantial amount of fiction writing involved. But this should not come as a surprise because the writers of the relevant New Testament texts had every motive to fabricate and narrate false stories, amend, alter, and distort the information to further their objective of creating new converts. These texts were solely meant to be instruments of preaching (Martin 1991: 78). As the

New Testament scholar Reginald Fuller (1971: 172–73) observes, the gospels were not meant to tell us what happened but were "vehicles for proclamation." Similarly, Perrin (1977: 78) says that none of the gospels contain historical information and are the works of evangelists, not historians.

## The Post-Resurrection Appearances and the Case for the Paranormal

For the sake of argument, let us assume that some individuals did, in reality, see the apparition of Jesus after the crucifixion. A few may have, as discussed below. The question is, Does the way these experiences unfolded offer proof of God or the supernatural at work? Not really. If this event was to be a demonstration of Jesus's godly powers and proof that death is overcome (Romans 6:9), that good has triumphed over evil, and sins have been expiated, then why did he not convey these messages in a spectacular way, such as magically vanishing from the cross to the amazement of all? Why bother with being nailed and pierced, having his body carried away, undergoing a hasty burial, and waiting three days to come back from the dead with no eyewitnesses to record this pivotal event?

Moreover, what is even more mystifying is that after his resurrection, Jesus appears in private to a mere handful of people in a remote location over a very short period. These few who claimed to have seen the risen Lord were uneducated, superstitious, and gullible individuals of highly dubious character, mental stability, and reputation who constituted the worst kind of witnesses there could be to this cosmically significant event. This is poor public relations planning and advertising on the part of the all-knowing deity purportedly orchestrating this event to convey a message of salvation to humankind.

## The Problematic Secretive Nature of the Postmortem Appearances

Thomas Paine (1880 [1795]: 127) also puzzled over the secretive nature of the postmortem appearances. If God wanted to demonstrate his awesome powers, then the appearances should have taken place in the plain light of day before mass audiences. He adds that an event made to convince the world should have been seen by everyone instead of a handful of dubious characters who became proxies for the rest of humanity who are called upon to believe.

The Greek philosopher Celsus (1987: 68) drew attention to another inconsistency:

> If this Jesus were trying to convince anyone of his powers, then surely he ought to have appeared first to the Jews who mistreated him—and to his accusers—indeed to everyone, everywhere.

Alternatively, Celsus (1830: 14) asked,

> Is it to be believed that [Jesus], when he was alive, openly announced to all men what he was; but when it became requisite that he should procure a strong belief of his resurrection from the dead, he should only show himself secretly to one woman and to his associates?

In other words, Celsus (1987: 68) was also particularly puzzled by the fact that Jesus's crucifixion was seen by many, but no one saw him rise from the grave.

Given that in his teachings Jesus did not articulate a divinely ordained scheme for the redemption of humanity before his death, the only other way of proving that the message of redemption came from him was to appear before the entire world after rising from the grave. As Gorham (1908: 140–41) queries, why did he not demonstrate the reality of his triumph over death to hostile witnesses, thereby proving the divine nature of his mission and unburdening future generations from infinite perplexities?

We must remember that the resurrected Jesus had even greater paranormal powers than before, such as flight (Luke 25:51, Acts 1:9–11), teleportation (Luke 24:31–37), and the ability to walk through solid objects and locked doors (John 20:19–23). Why did he not use these powers to demonstrate his triumph over death and evil in an impossible to dismiss fashion? He could have done this by appearing in front of the Jewish high priest Caiaphas, the chief architect of his calamity, or called upon the Sanhedrin that judged him. Alternatively, he could have materialized before Pilate, who condemned him, show up before the crowds in Jerusalem who forsook him, and even manifest in the presence of the Roman emperor and the Senate (Carrier 2010: 308–9). Any of these scenarios would have surely been indisputable proof of God's plan. However, none of this happened. What we have is a poorly planned and poorly executed presentation, which is inconsistent with the handiwork of an all-knowing, all-powerful, and capable deity. It is utterly baffling, therefore, to read Habermas's (2003: 39) absurd declaration that the resurrection is consistent with God's attributes and that there is a general line of argument from the existence of God to the resurrection.

Christian apologists such as Swinburne (2003: 172) forward feeble justifications asserting that God would not have made his objectives too apparent because that would lead to a loss of human freedom of choice. If this theological claim has merits and there are indeed circumstances when God not revealing too much may serve some divine purpose, this was certainly not one such occasion because the entire event was meant to incontrovertibly convey a message of salvation to the world. Also, why would a God that is infinitely good and benevolent, according to theistic definitions, who took the trouble of self-incarnating, suffering the agonies of death by crucifixion—basically sacrificing himself to himself—and rising from the dead for the redemption of humankind transmit his message so ineffectively? Why deny feeble humans, with whom God wishes to empathize using such an "indisputable miracle and sacrifice" the full force of the message openly and clearly? As the handiwork of an all-knowing, all-powerful being, none of this makes any sense at all (Carrier 2010: 308–9). Other feeble apologetic claims include Origen's assertion that Jesus avoided appearing to the judges who condemned him or to his enemies so that they would not be smitten with blindness, or that such an appearance would not actually convince anyone (Strauss 1902: 845–46).

Another question is why Jesus's tormentors and executioners did not suffer divine wrath for their deeds? Celsus (1987: 65) was particularly bewildered by this and queried why the Christian God did not make these malefactors agonize in the same way that Pentheus the King of Thebes suffered by going mad and being torn to pieces by animals for failing to recognize Dionysus as a God. Then there is the perplexing fact that Jesus's apparition did not confer upon the percipients otherwise unobtainable knowledge. Nowhere does the risen Jesus, now a reanimated paranormal entity privy to the databases in Heaven, impart messages or new expertise from the beyond that could not be known or conceived of by the local community at that particular historical juncture (Philipse 2014: 328). There are no fresh theological precepts, no novel ideas from the beyond, and no ground-breaking practical knowledge of any sort. Also, there are no weighty doctrinal discussions between the risen God-man and his eager disciples. Mandates to the disciples to preach the message or facilitating their better understanding of the scriptures do not qualify as new knowledge. Jesus's appearances are the only notable feature of these alleged paranormal encounters.

Also, none of the individuals who allegedly saw the risen Jesus took the opportunity to have unanswered questions resolved about such things as life after death, the happenings in the Kingdom of Heaven, the hour of his rising, or even how the risen one was faring in his transformed paranormal state. All of this is very odd as these are what one would expect the disciples to want to know had they indeed encountered their reanimated master whom they loved. The one question that was asked, as the professor of oriental laws J. Duncan Derrett (2005: 398) points out, is mentioned in Acts 1:6–7 and is curtly brushed off: "it is not for you to know times of seasons." After that, no one sees Jesus again. A further problem arises here. If the message of salvation was so vital that imparting it required that Jesus the man suffer terrible tortures and die a dishonorable death by being nailed to a cross, why were there no follow-up visitations to spread the good news to mass audiences, across generations, up to the present? Why did the appearances terminate? Hallucinations act this way, but this is not how divine god-men act.

Finally, if any of the apparition encounters were historical events, and we have plenty of reasons to doubt that most of them were, then they constitute religious experiences. In these instances, as is the case with the examples found in the extensive literature on religious experiences, the outcome is once again mundane and banal aphorisms easily imagined by anyone without recourse to paranormal resources and heavenly databases.

Thus, the most persuasive evidence against the assertion that a risen Jesus appeared to the disciples as a mind-independent, physically real entity is the pattern mentioned above of how, when, and before whom the apparition presented itself and what it did and did not do. All of these circumstances are inconsistent with the idea that this was a miraculous event engineered by God to transmit a central divine message of salvation to all of humanity. What we have is a ghost story and rumors coming from a small group of ignorant, gullible, superstitious, and delusional hallucinators. This is an X-claim. Where information about an event is sparse and contradictory, where all the facts and details are obscure, where rumor and hearsay abound, discursive space occurs for interjecting paranormal hypotheses and supernatural explanations. This is what UFO believers and conspiracy theorists did in the case of Roswell, and this is what the followers of Jesus did in the case of the resurrection.

## Can the Evidence of Apparitions and the Empty Tomb Taken Together Make a Case for the Paranormal?

Those who aver that Jesus physically rose up from the grave are espousing a paranormal hypothesis. A claim such as this carries a heavy burden of proof because such an event has never transpired anywhere at any time and space. In a laborious effort to offer a convincing argument for the resurrection, Wright (2003: 686–87) says that the postmortem visions by themselves would not have sufficed to generate early Christian beliefs. Alone, he says, such experiences would have been treated as hallucinations. For this writer, it was the postmortem visions and the existence of the empty tomb *taken together* that are the decisive combination that explains the development of a new fanatical devotion among the disciples, their willingness to die for their beliefs, and the rapid spread of Christianity. This view of the transformation of the disillusioned Jesus cultists into missionaries is referred to as the "beaten-men argument" (Goulder 1996: 54).

For Wright and other religionists, the only explanation for the rise and success of Christianity is a physical corpse reanimation (Wright 2003: 717; Yamauchi 1974a: 663, 1974b). Wright asserts further that the successful spread of Christianity is the ultimate proof of the historical truth of the miracle upon which it is based. This, however, is a misleading statement. What Wright fails to consider is that the highly credulous Jesus cultists lived in a very different time and place, a world governed by magic, where there was no clear demarcation between sorcery and religion, and "appearances" were part of the accepted cultural pattern (Fox 1986: 117). Moreover, strange paranormal happenings were routine events in the lives of these people. This was a time and place teeming with miracle workers, prophets, oracles, and many corpse reanimators (Cotter 1999; Shapiro 2016: 123). Thus, the superstitious cultists did not need an empty tomb to convince them of the veridicality of what they saw.

For Habermas (2003: 21–29) the case for a corpse reanimation is supported by other unassailable "evidences." The most important items in his list are: (1) the empty tomb; (2) transformation of the disciples into bold witnesses willing to die for their beliefs, that is, religious fanaticism; (3) that the Jewish enemies of the Christians could not disprove the resurrection even though they had the means and motives, such as producing a decomposing corpse; (4) conversion of skeptics such as Paul and James, the brother of Jesus; (5) the Shroud of Turin.

For Wright and Habermas to rely so heavily on the empty tomb story is an unwise strategy that undermines their case from the start. As discussed in Chapter 14, the tale was an expedient fiction invented long after the fact to address the theological and propaganda needs of the early Christians at the time the Gospel of Mark was written and afterward. What happened to Jesus's body is unknown. This conclusion is not a "pure invention of modern scholarship without the slightest evidence," as the true believer Wolfhart Pannenberg (1996: 69) confidently states but is based on overwhelming evidence as already discussed in the previous chapter.

Similarly, making a case for the historicity of the resurrection as a mind-independent fact on the basis of the transformation of the disciples into energetic proselytizers willing to die for their beliefs, that is, using "the beaten-men argument," as both of these writers do, overlooks the grotesque fact that no religion has a monopoly on fanaticism. Indeed, as the philosopher and historian Ernest Renan (1866: 13) put it long ago, other religions possess "as many resigned martyrs" as Christianity. Fanatics of all sorts have been willing to die for their beliefs, including Hindus, Jews, Muslim *jihadis*, Mormons, suicide bombers, communists, anarchists, Kamikaze pilots, and so on (cf., Martin 1991: 91). The fact that fanatics hold radical ideas does not make what they believe factual. Indeed, this argument, as Gorham (1908: 107) puts it, "may be held to justify the divine origin of every faith under the sun, good, bad, or indifferent, from the monotheism of the Jew to the cosmogony of the Fiji Islander."

Also, the cultists were put to death because they were deemed to be a political nuisance by the Jewish and the Roman authorities not because they believed in the resurrection of Jesus (Kent 1999: 91). If belief in the resurrection was the issue, then the high priest in Jerusalem should have persecuted the Pharisees and the Essenes as well who also had beliefs in the resurrection of the dead (cf. Wilson 2008: 140). Moreover, it is unclear just exactly how many early Christians actually died for their beliefs at this time.

That James, the brother of Jesus, became a follower after his brother's death, an event also frequently mentioned as proof of a physical resurrection (Yamauchi 1974b), is similarly an unconvincing argument. Among the early Christians, Jesus's appearances were a means of asserting religious authority, which is why these events always involved the leading figures in the Christian cult in Jerusalem. Lüdemann (2004: 72) suggests that Peter's rise to leadership was because he was the first to see a vision of the risen Jesus. There were public relations rewards and payoffs to be reaped from such stories. Descriptions of the appearance to James occur in a fragment of the Gospel of the Hebrews. However, this is a highly problematic text. First, it makes James a member of Jesus's entourage before the crucifixion, which is false. James was not a follower of Jesus while he was alive and thought that his brother was insane (Mark 3:21). Second, it says that James, rather than Peter, was the first witness to the apparition of Jesus, which is also untrue. This text must be understood in terms of the internal political struggles within the early Christian community that resulted in James replacing Peter as leader of the Christians in Jerusalem (Lüdemann 2004: 81).

The Gospel of the Hebrews is late and is intended to glorify James among his admirers as the victor in the political struggle by making him the first and supreme witness of the risen Lord (Pratscher 1987: 47). As such, it cannot be treated as historical. It is not improbable for someone like James aspiring to a position of prominence to claim that he saw Jesus for the big payoff even if he had no such experience (Funk et al., 1998: 484–85, 492; Walker 1969: 164). But even if there had been a genuine vision to James, using this as proof that a dead man came back to life and had supper with his brother has virtually no evidentiary value. There is also the fact that all the individuals involved in these events were prolific hallucinators prone to all sorts of delusions. Also, the fact that James later assumed leadership of the early Christian community was because he was a member of Jesus's family, not because of his claim that he had the honor of being the first witness of the risen Christ (Lüdemann 1994: 94).

As for Paul's own experience, we encounter credibility issues. His use of the dubious story of Jesus appearing before the 500 undermines his reliability. Indeed, as already stated, this raises suspicions about everything else he says (Martin 1991: 92). However, even if Paul had a genuine conversion experience and heard Jesus's voice on the road to Damascus, this means very little. Lots of people have conversion experiences in vastly different belief systems. The biblical studies scholar Michael Goulder (1996: 49) describes an almost identical experience by Susan Atkins, a convicted member of the murderous Charles Manson cult. Also, that a non-believer becomes a fanatic believer says nothing about the truth of those beliefs. There were fanatic converts in the Heaven's Gate cult, Aum Shinrikyô, Peoples Temple, and the Branch Davidians, who zealously believed in all sorts of false ideas and were willing to die for their beliefs (see Sidky 2015: 225–41). Such conversion experiences mean nothing. Paul's conversion experience has zero evidential value as proof that Jesus physically rose from the dead.

Finally, for Habermas to include the Shroud of Turin as proof, which is an indisputable forgery, discussed in Chapter 7, is indicative of how desperate apologists are for anything to vindicate their superstitions. Overall, it is impossible to provide shoddier "evidences" for the resurrection than what is on offer.

## Apparitions of Jesus: Miraculous Visions or Hallucinations?

Christian apologists such as Habermas (2003: 20–21, 50–51) and the historian Edwin Yamauchi (1974a, 1974b) believe that there are no naturalistic explanations for the miracle of the resurrection. In this case, what is under discussion is a "violation miracles" in contrast to a "coincidence miracles," as discussed in Chapter 8. They thus offer several objections to the non-paranormal hypothesis that the post-resurrection appearances were hallucinatory phenomena. To put it in other words, these writers are asserting the empirical veridicality of the unreal real or X-claims. However, we should consider the fact that there are also no naturalistic explanations for Santa Claus and his levitating reindeer. However, science can render a determination as to whether or not believing in such entities is justified. It does this first by weighing the probability of the truth of the testimony relative to the likelihood of the event. The claim here is that a deceased person came back to life and appeared in person to others, which has never happened anywhere and at any time. The low probability of a fantastic or extraordinary claim such as this taking into consideration what we already know about how the world operates is grounds for skepticism. The other way of assessing the plausibility of this paranormal postulate is to look for alternative hypotheses that are more consistent with other empirical explanations and observations. The existence of more plausible parsimonious alternative and empirically grounded explanations is always ample reason to justify skepticism toward any paranormal claim on offer.

## Religionist Objections to the Hallucination Hypothesis

Religionists Peter Kreeft and Ronald Tacelli provide what they think is a comprehensive set of apologist objections to the hallucination hypothesis in their book *Handbook of Christian Apologetics* (1994). For this reason, what these writers have to say is examined in some detail here. Habermas's and Yamauchi's objections are addressed in this context as well. Like these two true believers, Kreeft and Tacelli believe that the appearances were mind-independent encounters with the risen Jesus in his physical body (Kreeft and Tacelli 1994: 175–98). They, therefore, begin with the highly questionable assumption that the resurrection narratives in the gospels are entirely reliable historical accounts of actual events. Only devout believers can overlook in this way the historical development and contradictory nature of the resurrection narratives that disagree over such basic facts as to who saw Jesus, where, and when.

Let us look at the case point by point. First, Kreeft and Tacelli (1994: 186–87) maintain that hallucinations are private events, while the gospels report that Jesus appeared to several people at the same time. Habermas (2003: 50–51) offers the same argument regarding the nature of hallucinations. The assertion that many persons cannot have a simultaneous vision is a worn-out and utterly false apologist rejoinder that has been around for a long time, as Gorham (1908: 129) pointed out over a century ago. Yamauchi (1974a, 1974b) perpetuates the same misconceptions arguing that hallucinations only affect single individuals, only once or infrequently, and in private. Moreover, he adds that the gospel appearances occurred under a variety of conditions and hence militate against hallucinations. Regrettably, Yamauchi also mentions the problematic case of the 500 as evidence of a physical appearance on the assumption that group hallucinations do not take place.

These writers seem to be utterly ignorant of the large body of scientific research from the fields of anomalistic, experimental, and cognitive psychology and the neurosciences relating to thinking and perception and the well-known socio-psychological phenomenon of collective delusions (see Bartholomew 2001; Bartholomew and Goode 2000; Brugger 2001: 201; Evans 1984: 76; Green and McCreery 1975: 1; Holt et al. 2012: 125–26; Irwin and Watt 2007: 192–93). In reality, hallucinations frequently occur under a variety of conditions. Also, group hallucinations are very common, as discussed in Chapter 9, and are similar to the situation of the so-called 500 visionaries, if we have any justification not to rule out that tale as a legendary fabrication.

Yamauchi also incorrectly maintains that only drugs and extreme physical deprivation induce hallucinations, conditions which he says do not apply to the disciples. However, as already discussed, the extensive scientific literature on hallucinations indicates that numerous factors produce such experiences, such as temporal lobe epilepsy, isolation, a decrease in external stimuli, extreme stress, sensory overload, hypoxia, hyperventilating, hypoglycemia, high fever, severe pain, and malfunctions of the sleep–wake system. Specifically, bereavement, traumatic stress, and fear frequently induce hallucinations, conditions precisely applicable to the grieving and frightened disciples who fled back to Galilee "for fear of the Jews" who were "inflamed with wrath," as the gospels say. These writers are not addressing all the relevant evidence. Habermas, for instance, only refers to eighteenth- and nineteenth-century "rationalist" sources when discussing "naturalistic theories," perhaps so that he can bypass the masses of modern scientific data on hallucinations and group delusions that demolish his supernatural thesis.

Based on these series of erroneous assumptions about hallucinatory experiences, Yamauchi and other religionists conclude that the cases of the epiphanies of Jesus were "a unique eschatological event," something "earth-shaking" caused by God that goes "beyond ordinary experience" (Lillie 1965: 125; Ramsey 1946: 40; Tenney 1963: 133). This relegates the phenomenon outside the confines of history, culture, time, and space. It becomes something extraordinary and a weighty burden of proof shifts to the persons who make such a claim. Yet, apologists, whose sole explanation is that these events are real because the sacred texts say so, are begging the question and are unable to bear this burden.

The next argument presented is the character of the witnesses, who are said to be "simple, honest, moral people with firsthand knowledge of the facts," or "qualified and skeptical witnesses," whose testimony should receive full weight (Kreeft and Tacelli 1994: 187). This claim is fallacious. It would be difficult to find a more abysmal group of witnesses than the individuals described in the gospels. As noted, they were ignorant, uneducated, highly superstitious, and fantasy-prone individuals who routinely fell into trances, spoke in tongues, became spirit possessed, and heard voices. The critical thinking or skeptical inquiry was entirely alien to these perfidious zealots. Also, the gospels attest to their treachery and moral cowardice in betraying and denying their rabbi, the man who trusted them. Again, we certainly do not have honest and "qualified skeptical witnesses," contra to what Kreeft and Tacelli assert. We must also bear in mind that none of these alleged honest and qualified witnesses left any first-hand accounts. What we know about the visionary events have come down to us from second-, third-, and maybe even fourth-hand tales related in the form of anecdotes by others long after the events are said to have taken place.

Another assertion Kreeft and Tacelli (1994: 187) make is that the risen Jesus stayed with the disciples for 40 days in Jerusalem, as indicated in Acts: 3–9, therefore the experiences could not have been hallucinations. Any critical assessment of the sources will reveal that all the appearances happened in Galilee, where Peter and the other disciples fled (Lüdemann 1995: 132, 171, 174). The Jerusalem story is a later invention. Acts of the Apostles is the work of the same evangelist who wrote the Gospel of Luke. In the latter text, he says that Jesus's appearance and ascension took place in one day, on Easter Sunday, yet in Acts, he has Jesus lingering for more than a month (Parsons 2005: 441). Which is it? How trustworthy is this author who provides contradictory accounts of the same event? Lack of critical acumen and a canon-mentality prevents present-day apologists from making an honest appraisal of the sources and severely damages their case.

The next point made is that what the disciples experienced could not have been hallucinations because hallucinations only happen once, except to the insane (Kreeft and Tacelli 1994: 187). This is another inaccurate statement. As discussed in Chapter 9, there is substantial scientific evidence that a significant proportion of the nonclinical population, which comprise well-adjusted individuals not "insane people," experience repeated hallucinations over long periods of time (Aleman and Larøi 2009: 83; David 2004:111; Johns and van Os 2001; Peters 2010:127; Rees 1977: 38; Shuchter 1986: 3).

Kreeft and Tacelli (1994: 187) also believe that hallucinations stem from what one already knows, and hence, apparitions cannot display unanticipated behaviors, but the risen Jesus did act unexpectedly. Here as well, these writers are wrong. The only unexpected behavior by Jesus's apparition to be found in these narratives was walking through walls and appearing and disappearing, in other words behaving just like a ghost or hallucination. Also, one only needs to think about the number of surprising dreams people have, during which all sorts of unexpected events transpire. Dreams also stem from what we already know (cf., Parsons 2005: 442).

Another argument is that what members of the Jesus cult saw could not have been hallucinatory because Jesus dispelled their skepticism by eating and had them touch his wounds. In other words, overwhelming physical evidence convinced the initially doubtful disciples. There are several problems with this assertion. First, as already noted, the cultists needed no convincing about the veridicality of their visions. These were superstitious folk and phantoms and paranormal appearances were a part of their cultural reality. Second, because Kreeft and Tacelli have not critically assessed the sources, or are displaying the usual dishonesty of Christian apologists, they fail to realize that the story of Jesus eating food and being touched was a later "apologetic legend of corporality of Jesus." It was invented years later to refute challenges by critics that the disciples were a gullible lot spreading ghost stories (Perrin 1977: 66–67). A legend of a corporeal Jesus was not necessary until the time the Gospel of Mark was written and afterward. Hence, Paul is silent on the matter.

A third point to consider is that the inclusion of doubters in these narratives was a way of countering the accusation of gullibility (Fox 1986: 378). As Gorham (1908: 179) pointed out, there is nothing more convincing that the conversion of a doubter. The "artificial air" of this account, he adds, is a strong indication that this is a legend. This is a familiar rhetorical tactic used by believers in all sorts of paranormal things to demonstrate their trustworthiness by declaring initial skepticism and stressing that only overwhelming evidence compelled them to change their minds (Parsons 2005: 443). Also, Thomas's declaration, "My Lord and my God," which articulates a theory of the deity of Jesus that appeared much later, is further support that the story is a subsequent embellishment.

Remarkably, Yamauchi cites novelist Clive Staples Lewis's (1996) spurious assertion that because on several occasions, such as the incident on the road to Emmaus, the disciples did not immediately recognize Jesus, therefore, the event could not have been a hallucination. If these stories are not legendary embellishments—and we have lots of reasons to think they are—these could have easily been cases of mistaken identity and wishful thinking. How many times have you thought you had seen someone you know in a public place only to find out you were mistaken? Lots of people have. Think about the numerous sighting of Elvis Presley (Lacy 2006) or the doppelgänger of Paul McCartney. Also, bereaved and traumatized individuals often report seeing their deceased loved ones among crowds and in other circumstances (Shuchter 1986: 119). Moreover, because apologists such as Yamauchi deny that Christians borrowed from the pagan savior myths, they miss the fact the Emmaus apparition story (Luke 24:13–31) that C. S. Lewis cites is, in fact, a version of the Asclepius god-man story. It entails a dejected couple on the way home meeting a stranger—the savior incognito—who explains the circumstances, reveals his identity, and then disappears (Price 2007).

Kreeft and Tacelli next suggest that the appearances were not hallucinations because Jesus had extended and profound conversations with the percipients. This is another questionable statement. The psychiatric and psychological literature provides ample examples of individuals talking to apparitions and having two-way conversations. This is especially true in cases of bereavement, which describes the emotional state of the disciples after the violent killing of their rabbi. These individuals were also highly perturbed because they had no idea about the fate of Jesus's remains (cf., Aleman and Larøi 2009: 67; French and Stone 2014: 99; Kent 1999: 31–32; Rees 1977: 38; Shuchter 1986: 3).

As to the nature of the interactions between the apparition of Jesus and the disciples, Kreeft and Tacelli are being deceptive. Nowhere in the gospels or Acts are there any profound exchanges taking place between the cultists and their paranormal master (Parsons 2005: 444). Indeed, as noted before, the appearances are the only noteworthy feature of these encounters.

Finally, as to be expected, Kreeft and Tacelli also appeal to the story of the empty tomb, which is a standard item in the apologists' repertoire. They argue that the disciples were convinced of the veridicality of their encounters with the risen Jesus because the tomb was empty. They go on to yet again repeat the worn-out argument that had there been a body in the tomb the Jewish opponents of the Christians would have inevitably produced it to refute the claim that Jesus had risen from the dead. The problematic nature of this contention has already been addressed in the context of the empty tomb story in Chapter 14.

Kreeft and Tacelli avow that hallucinations could perhaps account for the post-resurrection appearances but not for the empty tomb, the rolled-away stone, and the absence of a body. For them, only the fact of Jesus coming back to life after physical death can explain all of these factors taken together (Kreeft and Tacelli 1994: 188). Sadly, the empty tomb is a fable, and the case presented is therefore wholly unconvincing. As an aside, these apologists also fail to consider that the rolled-away stone element in the story is problematic because the risen Jesus who was now endowed with paranormal powers to walk through locked doors and solid objects (John 20:24–25), which he did to meet his disciples, had no need to have the blocking stone moved to exit the tomb. He could simply pass through the stone sealing the tomb. The massive blocking stone is a literary invention intended to add to the astonishing nature of the event.

Thus, we may conclude, as Parsons (2005: 448–49) has, that the assertion that the post-resurrection appearances of Jesus are explicable only by an actual physical return from the grave is untenable according to the known historical and psychological evidence. It is the religionist paranormal thesis, not naturalistic theories that are refuted by the evidence, contra Habermas (2003: 22) and his associates.

## The Post-Resurrection Appearances as a Collective Delusion

Theological fiction-writing and embellishments have transformed the appearance stories in the gospels to such an extent that utterly removes them from any actual historical context. But let us assume that a few members of the Jesus cult genuinely had visions of their executed rabbi. Is this all that surprising or unexpected as to require an extraordinary or paranormal explanation? The answer is no. As Goguel (1953: 75) observed, such experiences "are not isolated phenomena in religious history." Indeed, they are not unique phenomena in human experience in general. The shamans with whom I worked had visions of dead people all the time. I also know of many ordinary people who have had visions of their dead relatives, experiences that address deep psychological needs of the survivors. These occurrences have little value in supporting paranormal conclusions.

As discussed in Chapter 6, our theory of mind compels us to experience the world as full of animate agents and to assume an intentional stance toward such entities. The intentional stance is such a fundamental aspect of human cognition that it is difficult to shut it down even when it is no longer appropriate. Thus, when someone close to us dies or is killed, we continue taking the intentional stance toward them, although they are no longer physically present. Instead of deleting the file containing the memory of deceased loved ones, humans transform them into "virtual persons" and continue to experience their presence as ghosts, which are manifestations conjured up by the troubled mind-set of the living kinfolk (Dennett 2006: 112–13). The particular disciples who had post-mortem visions of Jesus very likely perceived a virtual person, not a flesh-and-blood entity.

People have reported encounters with such virtual persons across space and time for thousands of years often in connection with religious phenomena (Aleman and Larøi 2009: 9–10; Leudar and Thomas 2000: 1–13; McCarthy-Jones 2012). Indeed, the subjective perception of apparitions is a near-universal event (Aleman and Larøi 2009: 10; Irwin and Watt 2007: 192; Zusne and Jones 1989: 225). Ghosts and apparitions are X-claims generated by human cognitive biases. These are brain-based hallucinatory occurrences for which there is overwhelming scientific evidence (Saver and Rabin 1997: 498). As discussed in the chapter on religious experiences, terms such as "vision," "revelations," and "sense of presence," often used to describe these types of occurrences, are merely dignified descriptors or theological ornamentations attaching cosmic significance to hallucinations (Beyerstein 2007: 300; Zusne and Jones 1989: 114). These experiences have enough of a sense of reality to be mistaken for veridical perceptions (Aleman and Larøi 2009: 23). Contra to the apologetic assertion, as iterated by Barclay (1996: 26), there is nothing particularly strange for the disciples to "interpret their visions as a *resurrected* Jesus." The prevailing cultural beliefs were that such visionary experiences were of paranormal origin and significance. How and why the cultists invented the idea that Jesus had come back to life without the necessity of there being a reanimated corpse is discussed later in this chapter.

A single person can perceive apparitions, or a group of people may experience them at the same time (Evans 1984: 76; Green and McCreery 1975: 1; Holt et al. 2012: 125–26; Irwin and Watt 2007: 192–93). Shared visions do not mean that they are veridical mind-independent phenomena but that they are cases of collective delusions involving perceptual contagion, examples of which are plentiful in the psychiatric literature (Brugger 2001: 201). It is impossible to deny the reality of mass hallucinations and perceptual contagion, as Habermas (2003: 25–26) does, without distorting the evidence and utterly ignoring the relevant scientific data.

The socio-psychological mechanisms of such phenomena are fully understood, as discussed in the previous chapter (see Bartholomew 2001; Bartholomew and Goode 2000). As the neurologist Oliver Sacks (2012: 244) observes, "a deeply superstitious and delusional atmosphere can […] foster hallucinations arising from extreme emotional states and these can affect entire communities." These bizarre incidents attest to the remarkable force of wishful thinking, human insecurities, psychological needs, and gullibility. Hines (2003: 383) characterizes these episodes as a collective delusion or mass hysteria during which a group of people, small as the occupants of a building or as large as a regional population, are convinced that they have experienced an inexplicable paranormal event. Many contemporary examples of this are on record. Specific recent instances of collective delusions involving a single initial report followed by a barrage of others include the massive numbers of UFO sightings reported after a preliminary account on June 24, 1947 by the pilot Kenneth Arnold (Peebles 1994; Sidky 2015: 111–13). Another notorious example is the myth of the Roswell UFO crash that developed long after the fact, which has many parallels with the resurrection event, as discussed in Chapters 7 and 14.

During the 1950s there were a series of "contactees," individuals who reported personal encounters with the extraterrestrial UFO pilots and received important messages from them for the benefit of humankind. These narratives are surprisingly reminiscent of the plot of the 1951 movie *The Day the Earth Stood Still*, and other films, which were probably precipitating factors (Sidky 2015: 114). There was also the rash of alien abduction reports that followed a first kidnapping story by Betty and Barney Hill on September 19, 1961, that continues today (Clancy 2005; Matheson 1998). The "satanic ritual abuse" scare, or "the satanic panic," in the United States during the 1980s and 1990s is yet another example of such a mass delusion (Bottoms and Davis 1997; Lanning 1992; Sidky 2015: 84–88; Victor 1993). A more recent version of this delusion is the so-called Pizza Gate conspiracy, in which some were led to believe that high officials in the Democratic Party were involved in a child prostitution ring and human trafficking using a local pizza restaurant in Washington, DC. This delusion played a role in the 2016 US presidential election. There is no objective evidence for any of these events despite intensive investigations by scientists, government officials, and law enforcement agencies. Large numbers of people were nevertheless convinced that such things indeed happen. In the case of the Pizza Gate affair, one believer even took matters into his own hands and tried to rescue the children. On December 4, 2016, this individual attacked the restaurant with a military assault rifle.

## Jesus and Sasquatch

Goulder (1996: 52–54) has examined the similarities between the collective apparition sightings in first-century Palestine and a case involving a succession of Sasquatch (Bigfoot) sightings reported during three months in the autumn of 1977, in a Native American community in South Dakota (Stewart 1989). What precipitated the Bigfoot event was a preliminary report by a young man seeing "a big, dark-brown thing" emerging from a distant tree line. Another youngster provided a second account involving "a big hairy man" who jumped out of the bushes. The inspiration for these reports was a recent showing of a B-grade movie called *Sasquatch*. A rash of additional stories followed these two preliminary reports by people claiming that they too had seen the creature (Stewart 1989: 295). The Sasquatch meme had gotten a hold of the community. Media coverage, sensational reporting, confusion, and all the rest followed.

Goulder highlights several sociological dynamics involved in both cases. First, there has to be a close-knit community isolated from the wider skeptical world among which the rumor can quickly spread. These circumstances apply to the people in South Dakota and the members of the Jesus cult in first-century Galilee. Second, the existence of structural strain is needed, such as anxiety due to the presence of ambiguous information regarding the reports and the presence of poorly educated individuals. These features apply to both the Native Americans in South Dakota and the followers of Jesus (Goulder 1996: 53; Stewart 1989: 293). The latter group was under considerable strain and anxiety "for fear of the Jews," who "were inflamed with wrath," as already noted.

Third, there has to be a cultural mechanism for the growth and spread of the generalized belief. The Sasquatch legend was part of preexisting Native American cultural lore. Among the members of the Jesus cult, resurrection and messianic beliefs were part of their cultural lore. There was also their conviction that the advent of God's kingdom was at hand and will be accompanied by the rising of the dead. Fourth, there have to be precipitating factors. These were the reports by the two young men and the Bigfoot movie in South Dakota. For the disciples, it was Jesus's execution, the uncertain whereabouts of his body, fear of being implicated in Jesus's crimes, and Peter's vision of the apparition of their rabbi.

Fifth, the community must mobilize. In South Dakota law enforcement was harnessed, there were town meetings, and some even entertained the idea of digging pits to trap and tranquilize the monster. The nascent Christians also mobilized by meeting in frequent prayer sessions and debated what to do. Sixth, there has to be a payoff or social rewards for the sightings. Those who saw Bigfoot became the center of attention, the talk of the community, lived in the limelight, and gained prestige, at least temporarily (Stewart 1989: 292). Individuals who saw the apparition of Jesus gained prominence in the eyes of their group members. For example, as already stated, Peter rose to a position of leadership because he saw the apparition of slain Jesus. The event also reassured him that despite the crucifixion, Jesus was right after all and that his belief in the Lord was vindicated (Goulder 1996: 54).

Another attribute of the South Dakota Sasquatch event with a bearing on the Jesus sightings that Goulder does not mention is that descriptions of the creature progressively grew more detailed with each additional sighting incorporating information from the previous accounts. As sociologist James Stewart (1989: 297) points out, from vague early reports, the sightings increasingly acquired remarkable details, going from a big, dark human-like creature to an eight feet tall monster covered with thick black fur approximating an ape-like beast. In the full versions of the reports, the beast's face was described as simian-like, with arms long enough to reach its knees, moving like a monkey, and emitting a terrible odor comparable to the smell of rotten eggs (Stewart 1989: 297). The Jesus sightings similarly become more and more detailed and elaborate, transforming with time from the vague account of a spiritual being provided by Paul to a fully embodied person who ate food and had his followers touch his wounds (Luke 24 and John 20).

## Grief Hallucinations and the Rise of Christianity

As discussed in the previous chapter, where we have more plausible and parsimonious alternate and empirically grounded explanations, there are ample reasons to justify skepticism toward any paranormal claim on offer. One such explanation for the case at hand is the force of grief hallucinations on human emotions and perceptions. Seeing the apparition of deceased loved ones, which may be heard, touched, and felt is relatively common during bereavement (Aleman and Larøi 2009: 67; Ehrman 2009: 178; French and Stone 2014: 99). As Sacks (2012: ix) points out, such visions "can mimic perception in every respect, starting with the way they are projected into the external world."

These experiences are often visual and auditory, with a small proportion of cases being exclusively acoustic (Irwin and Watt 2007: 195). Apparitions may appear and disappear and pass through walls and locked door (Evans 1984: 85–86). These are precisely the types of events or experiences described in the gospels. For example, Luke 24:13–35 relates: "Then their eyes were opened, and they recognized [Jesus], and he disappeared from their sight." And John 20:24–25 says: "Though the doors were locked, Jesus came and stood among them and said, 'Peace be with you!' Then he said to Thomas, 'Put your finger here; see my hands.'" Assuming for the moment that these accounts reflect actual events, the fact that these cultists had such an experience is not unusual given their grief and because phantasms were an accepted part of their cultural reality.

As mental constructs, apparitional encounters always reflect the percipient's cultural background and life experiences. Thus, Christians see Jesus or Mary, Buddhists see Buddha, and Hindus have visions of Shiva, the shamans I worked with regularly saw members of the local pantheon, and these entities always speak the language percipients understand (cf., Flew 1989: 313; Stenger's 1990: 107). No extraordinary or previously unknown or unknowable information is ever attained during these encounters to suggest the involvement of some super-intelligent paranormal source beyond the human brain and the local culture. Thus, the post-resurrection appearances of Jesus belong to a broader and well-known category of anomalous phenomena recorded across space and time. The visions were not in any way exceptional, extraordinary, paranormal, or miraculous, despite assertions by literalists and believers wish.

Interestingly, the fact that people frequently see the apparitions of their departed loved ones was noted long ago by Celsus and Thomas Paine, who referred to what researchers now frame in terms of the psychology of grief. In his rancorous pagan wisdom, Celsus (1830: 16) made the following observation regarding postmortem Jesus sightings:

> But who was it that saw this? A furious woman [i.e., Mary Magdalene who was a demonic], as you acknowledge, or some other of the same magical sect; or one who was under the delusion of dreams, and who voluntarily subjected himself to fallacious phantasms—a thing which happens to myriads of the human race. Or, which is more probable, those who pretended to see this were such as wished to astonish others by this prodigy, and, through a false narration of this kind, to give assistance to the frauds of other impostors.

Celsus is, in effect, saying that the Christian faith arose from hallucinations, collective delusions, rumors, hearsay, and a strong dose of pious fraud. The implications of the hallucination hypothesis are far-reaching, and this explains why Christian apologists have exerted great efforts to refute it. They have to.

Paine (1880 [1795]: 129–30) came to the same conclusion that the postmortem Jesus sightings were merely hallucinations of the sort that happen among those in profound grief in association with an execution or violent death, pointing out the similarities between these stories and tales about people seeing the ghost of Julius Caesar after his assassination. As part of this psychological explanation Paine added that once a ghost story is launched, it takes a life of its own, and soon variants that contradict each other appear as well. This is why the accounts of these events in the gospels diverge in important ways. Furthermore, the paranormal element of the stories about Jesus, such as his sudden materialization, ability to pass through locked doors, and disappearing from sight, all suggest that this was a phantasm (Paine 1880 [1795]: 130). Paine also added that the gospel writers did not think all the details of their storyline through because they say that when Jesus arose, he left his clothes behind, but they forgot to supply other clothes for him in which to appear later.

Such stories about the ghosts of those slain were aspects of the local cultural beliefs along with beliefs about angelic appearances, demonic possession, and casting out of devils. For such stories to circulate about the death of Jesus, Paine noted, is no surprise. However, he concluded that unless an adequate explanation for the many contradictions in the different accounts is offered, they are all to be treated as "downright impositions, lies, and forgeries, without even the apology of credulity" (Paine 1880 [1795]: 134–35). Theologian Jack Kent credits the German theologian Christian Hermann Weisse (1838) as being the first scholar to propose a psychological approach to the resurrection (Kent 1999: 1–2; Schweitzer 2005:130–136). However, the credit should go to Celsus and Paine.

## Do Present-Day Psychiatric Findings on Grief Apply to First-Century People?

The question to ask at this stage is, Could the apparitions of Jesus seen by the disciples have been hallucinations caused by grief or bereavement? Before attempting to answer this, we have to decide whether it is appropriate to use contemporary psychological and psychiatric findings to try and understand the mind-sets of first-century peasants from Galilee. Did they experience grief and sorrow over the death of a loved one in the same way as contemporary people? Did they cry? Did they feel anger? Did they have feelings of survivor guilt? The answer to these questions depends on whether we see all humans as sharing a common psychobiological heritage or whether we adhere the idea of a radical plurality of cultures and human behavior espoused by the postmodernist skeptics, that is, deny universal human experiences.

Religionist professor of Scripture John Pilch dismisses all scientific medical and psychological approaches to the postmortem appearances of Jesus as "positivistic" (a pejorative term akin to scientism) and suggests that Western science is "monocultural" and inappropriate for the understanding of non-Western cultures. He has adopted the familiar banal and failed postmodern anti-science perspective that once flourished in academic circles in the West and still lingers in some quarters where they have bolstered supernatural and paranormal nonsense (Sidky 2018). However, to make his case, Pilch (1998: 57–58) has no problems drawing upon ideas from neo-shamanic and New Age literature (e.g., Goodman 1990), which are also products of Western culture, to posit a paranormal hypothesis that altered states of consciousness provide access to an actual mind-independent "alternate reality," or access to a real supernatural domain. Here, he says holy personages live on as a reward for their righteousness. These deceased holy ones can contact mortals through visions, visitational dreams, or apparitional appearances that are veridical. The con artist Helena Blavatsky, the chief proponent of Theosophy, espoused similar bogus stories about obtaining messages from hidden masters in occult places or dimensions that is now a crucial element of New Age thinking in Western cultures.

Pilch goes on to suggest that the post-resurrection appearances of Jesus were therefore real, his companions truly saw him but not physically in his shattered body, as other Christian apologists affirm but in an "alternate reality." Pilch has thus harnessed anthropological research on altered states of consciousness, particularly the work of my early mentor the late Erika Bourguignon (1974, 1979), in support of his supernatural/paranormal hypothesis. This argument fails because there is no evidence that altered states of consciousness enable access to a mind-independent alternate reality or supernatural realm. My work with shamans and mediums who are adept at entering altered states of consciousness to heal patients or divine the future has revealed nothing to suggest an opposite conclusion.

The relativist perspective is problematic because it excludes the possibility of generalizing about the human condition (Parkes et al. 2015a: 13). Without the effort to discover such uniformities or regularities in human experience the anthropological enterprise is transformed into merely an exercise in the production of disconnected descriptive accounts with little or no theoretical significance (see Sidky 2007a). However, relativists do not encompass or speak for all anthropologists.

Anthropologists who do not subscribe to the problematic relativist stance have shown that generalizations based on cultural universals about human behavior across space and time are not only possible but are crucial to our understanding of the human condition (see Brown 1991). Certain aspects of grief are physiological rather than being culturally specific, such as weeping (with some exceptions), sadness, anguish, guilt, anger, idealizing and recollecting the deceased (Allison 2005: 365), the sense of presence, and seeing apparitions of the dead. Cross-cultural comparisons show that beliefs in apparitions or ghosts and communication with them are near universal, if not ubiquitous across cultures (Rosenblatt 1976: 51–52). Such research has also shown that the ghosts people see are most often those of their close loved ones. As W. Dewi Rees (1977: 41) points out, hallucinations of departed loved ones occur irrespective of gender, race, creed, or domicile, are not abnormal, and tend to diminish with time. Moreover, "the finding of a relationship between hallucination and grief has also been replicated across cultures," as pointed out by Slade and Bentall (1988: 88).

There are other commonalities in how humans cope with grief and loss associated with death. First, humans nearly everywhere rely upon explanatory religious precepts and guidelines for coming to terms with death. Second, people in all cultures see death as a transition, use myths to make sense of mortality, and depend on fellow humans for sympathy and support (Parkes et al. 2015b: 7–8). The sense of sorrow, fear, guilt, anger, anxiety and their associated physical expressions seem to be part of our shared human heritage and are virtually ubiquitous (Brown 1991: 70; Parkes et al. 2015b: 7–8; Klass 1999: 153). As Rosenblatt et al. (1976: 23) point out, emotional reactions such as crying, anger, or fear are all part of being human.

Yes, there are cross-cultural variations in mourning behaviors (Irish et al. 1993), and cultural meaning plays a vital role in how humans cope with loss (Klass 1999: 163). However, a great deal of the differences is related to the rituals and practices aimed at transcending death rather than the fundamental emotional responses expressed (Klein and Alexander 2003: 265–66). Hence consistent general themes and resemblances exist across cultures to the extent that we can rely on anthropological and psychological findings to try and understand the reactions of Jesus cultists to the death of their rabbi.

## The Circumstances of Jesus's Death and the Socio-Psychological Dynamics of the Disciples

Jesus was the type of charismatic individual that always appears at the center of apocalyptic and millenarian cults familiar to anthropologists and historians. Such persons exercise considerable psychological influence over their followers who often become heavily invested emotionally and wager everything in their messianic leader's promises of glory. The socio-psychological dynamics of such circumstances are highly significant. The followers of Jesus comprised a small group of believers, disengaged from broader society, who had risked all by abandoning their jobs, homes, families, and friends to become followers (Lüdemann 1994: 99). They were, therefore, psychologically heavily dependent upon their leader.

These were the characteristics of the group that entered Jerusalem with high expectations. Hope turned into a calamity for the disciples with the violent death of their leader. Fearing for their own lives, the disciples renounced their faith in Jesus whose mortifying death exposed him in their minds at that time as a false messiah, scattered, and fled back to their homes in Galilee. In shock and deep despair over their shattered hopes and expectations, and mourning for their master, they were left pondering how to make sense of the tragedy and horror that befell them. These are all universal human responses to events of this kind. Bereavement associated with the murder of a loved one, as this was, is often associated with very intense emotional reactions of anger, bewilderment, traumatic stress, denial, and guilt.

Moreover, the disciples had to come to terms with the absence of the deceased's body. This is a particularly important point. The corpse represents tangible evidence that death has taken place. Viewing it dispels all doubts as to its appearance, serves as a final confirmation of the death, and provides the bereaved an opportunity to express regrets, take away a keepsake, such as a lock of hair, or leave one behind, and to say farewell (Klein and Alexander 2003: 266–67). Observing the body provides closures. The disciples were denied all of this because Jesus's body was disposed of by others in some unknown location. These factors thus precluded appropriate burial rites honoring the dead and comforting the mourners, which are two crucial commandments in Jewish tradition regarding death (Levine 2006: 98). For the cultists, there was no sense of closure that happens upon seeing the mortal remains of a loved one and knowing their proper ultimate disposition. These conditions would have been especially emotionally painful and disturbing. Such factors alone, as the cognitive scientist Ilkka Pyysiäinen (2007: 59) points out, could have resulted in the disciples' memories of their teacher to become deindividuated, leading to sightings of the apparition of the risen Lord.

In the weeks after the crucifixion, the cultists struggled with sadness, confusion, hopelessness, doubts, self-reproachment, denial, and survivor guilt for abandoning Jesus to a lonely death at the hands of his enemies. Survivor guilt commonly occurs in circumstances that involve wars, accidents, major tragedies, and especially when a loved one dies violently, but others are spared (Shuchter 1986–35). It is also very likely that the disciples felt an overwhelming need for forgiveness because of their betrayal and desertion (Allison 2005: 370; Lüdemann 1994: 95–100).

At this stage, two concurrent processes came into play: (1) grief hallucinations; (2) the psychological process involved in coming to terms with the disconfirmation of deeply held beliefs. Here I shall examine the role of grief hallucinations in the formulation of resurrection ideas. How committed true believers cope with disconfirmation of intensely held beliefs and prophecies is the topic of the next chapter.

## The Psychology of Grief and the Origins of the Resurrection Story

The literature on the psychology of grief reveals that the bereaved frequently undergo recurring series of hallucinatory encounters involving the departed loved ones (Kent 1999: 27–28). As theologian Jack Kent points out in his book *The Psychological Origins of the Resurrection Myth* (1999), grieving people sometimes try to hang on to the deceased psychologically and experience feeling their presence, hearing their voices, being touched by them, and seeing their apparitions. Contemporary grief literature considers these hallucinations as a normal part of the grieving and coping process (Kent 1999: 31–32). The reason for this is that in the minds of the bereaved the deceased's program is not erased, but instead, the dead individual is recast as a "virtual person," with whom the living can continue to interact as they did before. The same cognitive mechanisms are involved here that generate other X-claims, such as sensing ghosts and other non-corporeal intentional entities we think we detect in our surroundings.

Grief hallucinations are exceptionally compelling. As Sacks (2012: 233) points out, "Bereavement hallucinations, deeply tied to emotional needs and feelings, tend to be unforgettable." The psychiatrist and expert on bereavement Stephen Shuchter (1986: 116, 118–19) points out that human attachment bonds are powerful and deep and often mere physical death cannot erase them. Psychologically, the newly bereaved are driven to retrieve the loved one who has died. For this reason, most people during the early weeks and months of their grief believe that they have seen, heard, touched, smelled, or felt the presence of the dead person. In other words, internal psychological forces, along with cultural beliefs about spiritual survival, ensure that the emotional relationships with the deceased continue. Even for those who are aware that they are hallucinating, the experience seems very real (Shuchter 1986: 118). For the disciples seeing visions of their dead rabbi would have reinforced their convictions that he had survived death because God vindicates the righteous.

Wright (2003: 690) asserts, however, that people in the ancient world knew the difference between visions and events that happened in the "real world." In other words, if apparitions of Jesus were merely hallucinations, the disciples would have known this fact. Moreover, he adds that postmortem hallucinations of deceased loved ones at other times have not resulted in the belief in resurrected dead people (Wright 2003: 690). What he means is that the disciples would not have become convinced that the Lord has risen if Jesus had not actually visited them in person. Wright overlooks the fact that history is full of instances of unexpected occurrences. Also, there are many other cases where the followers of dead prophets and messiahs become convinced that their leaders live on, as discussed in the next chapter.

We must also take into consideration that the individuals described in the New Testament were consummate visionaries who attributed anything contrary to ordinary experience to heavenly or paranormal sources. This fact was noted by scholars long ago. As Gorham (1908: 86) observed, for those who do not understand the origins of their vision, the hallucination appears powerfully real, and it is difficult to differentiate between what is illusionary and what is not. Similarly, Macan (1877: 74, 140) pointed out that the visions were treated as mind-independent and objectively real because the followers of Jesus were believers in miracles, supernatural interventions in the natural course of things, heavenly warnings through dreams, angelic visitations, theophanies, and revelations.

As a deeply committed believer, Wright is compelled to treat in this fashion tales that are otherwise "of extremely dubious historical worth" (Crossley (2005: 176). He has no other options. Wright's contention that people in the ancient world could separate vision and events in the real world is more hyperbole. Some could; others could not. The idea that a vision can serve as evidence of a real encounter finds support in Paul's statements in 1 Corinthians 15, which does not entail eating or touching (Crossley 2005: 178). There are plenty of other examples across space and time. During the Middle Ages, people took hypnogogic and hypnopompic hallucinations as physical attacks by tangible rapacious demonic beings called *incubi* and *succubi* that visited at night and engaged in sexual intercourse with them. They could not tell hallucinations apart from a real event. Present-day alien abductees experiencing the same type of hallucinations believe that they have been the victims of actual abductions by extraterrestrial visitors (see Hines 2003: 277–81). Indeed, their accounts are so compelling as to persuade the late Harvard University psychiatrist John Mack (1997) that alien encounters are real (unless he made this claim for publicity purposes to generate book sales).

The shamans I have worked with, while able to distinguish the natural from the supernatural realms, treat the paranormal beings they encounter during their ecstatic states as actual entities that exist in the real world and can and do impinge upon earthly human affairs in tangible ways. I have also encountered lots of people in lots of cultures who believe that their dead relatives somehow live on and can interact with them because they had visions of those individuals. Hope and wishful thinking are as limitless as the human imagination.

Moreover, there is considerable ethnographic evidence that people in many cultures interpret apparitions as veridical. There are even instances when present-day university-trained, Western-educated anthropologists have taken hallucinatory phenomena as mind-independent occurrences, including one researcher who reported that he observed a corpse come back to life and dance to the rhythm of drumbeats, as discussed in Chapter 7.

People's cultural background and life experiences have a bearing on the contents of hallucinations, as already noted. Hence people in Newfoundland suffering from hallucinations due to sleep paralyses believe themselves to be the victims of nocturnal assaults by a creature known as the "Old Hag" (Hufford 1982), while some in the United States experiencing the same type of phantasms conclude that they have been assaulted or kidnapped by beings from other planets and star systems (Adler 2011: 31–35). It is for this reason that the disciples did not see apparitions of Jupiter, Ahura Mazda, Marduk, or Osiris but saw their teacher.

The disciples' Jewish background beliefs that wrongful deaths are vindicated by God factored in on the contents of their hallucinations (cf., Crossley 2005: 175). Thus, if they were inclined to think that God would exculpate Jesus in this way, then there is no reason why they would not have interpreted their grief hallucinations as evidence that Jesus has risen from the dead in a modified resurrected body. Paul expressed this very point in his first letter to the Corinthians.

Evidence from cognitive psychology, discussed in Chapter 6, also has a direct bearing on this question. As cognitive scientist István Czachesz (2007: 53) points out, the fact that the disciples thought that Jesus was still alive is an aspect of the human predisposition to detect agency in the environment, and the theory of mind accounts for their inclination to attribute thoughts and intentions to perceive agents. These common human cognitive predispositions make it easy to conceive of dead people in the form of paranormal agents who can move about, enter into conversation, and interact with the living. The result is the development of a cognitively resonating and seductive X-claim that the dead live on in a nonmaterial form.

If the accounts are not legendary, the fact that they describe Jesus in modified resurrected form who could appear and disappear and walk through locked doors (Luke 24:31; John 20:19), that is, violate ontological expectations, is consistent with the cognitive theory of counterintuitiveness of religious beliefs (Boyer 2001). As also discussed in Chapter 6, paranormal agent ideas that are part of religious beliefs around the world involve attributes that violate specific ontological categories. Agent concepts that lack this attribute are less appealing and harder to remember and less likely to be transmitted. Such ideas are also less alluring and less memorable if they have too many fantastic attributes. Paranormal agent concepts that have only a single or just a few violations of expectations seem more memorable than overly preposterous ones. For this reason, the conception of Jesus in 1 Corinthians 15 and the canonical gospels had a greater chance of being remembered and transmitted in comparison to the more complex construals of Jesus associated with Docetism, that Jesus had two forms with multiple violations of expectations (Czachesz 2008: 104).

Given what is known about the psychological, psychiatric, and cognitive dimensions of hallucinations, the constructive nature of perception and memory, the various cognitive biases, psychological contagion, mass delusions, and the force of grief hallucinations, it was not necessary for all the Jesus cultists to see a corporeal Jesus in order to conclude that he had risen. It is very likely that one or a small number of these individuals experienced grief hallucinations because such apparitions are always perceived by those closest to the deceased. Scholars generally concur that Peter was the likely candidate to have been the first percipient of Jesus's apparition (Barclay 1996: 25). The likelihood of this being the case is the fact, as Guignebert (1958: 522) observes, that Peter was the earliest of Jesus's disciples and foremost in matters of affection and confidence.

In addition to these circumstances, Peter was psychologically vulnerable because he had to cope with the overwhelming disconfirmation of his deep convictions by the execution of a man that he ardently believed was the Savior. He also bore a heavy burden of guilt for his betrayal of Jesus (Mark 14:66–72). Another clue is that Paul (1 Corinthians 25:5) names Peter as the disciple who first saw the risen Jesus. Also, Luke 24:34 says, "The Lord has risen indeed and hath appeared to Simon [Peter]." As already noted, the reason that Peter rose to a position of leadership of the Christians in Jerusalem may have been because he was the first to see Jesus's apparition (Lüdemann (2004:72). The women are interjected into this story much later with the development of the empty tomb legend "in relation to creedal considerations unconnected with historical facts" (Guignebert 1958: 522).

## The Possibility of Resurrection Beliefs without a Resurrected Body

Christian literalists are adamant that without Jesus's bodily appearance, Peter and the disciples could never have conceived of the idea of a resurrected Messiah. In other words, without a walking corpse, beliefs, and visions alone could not have produced the reinvigorated faith of the disciples after the demise of their master. A corollary to this is the assumption that the success of a movement substantiates the miraculous nature of that movement, as already noted. The New Testament scholar Bishop Ulrich Wilckens (1968: 61) clearly states this apologist position as follows:

> It is quite impossible that the disciples of Jesus should have reacted to the catastrophe of his death by the conviction suddenly dawning on them that he had been raised from the dead—which had never previously been asserted in Israel of any mortal.

This is a standard apologist retort to justify treating the resurrection as a miraculous event (i.e., a violation miracle, as discussed in Chapter 8), an occurrence somehow apart from historical and cultural contexts. In other words, it allows these ideologues to dismiss historical and cultural factors and substitute supernaturalism and superstition in their place. However, as already noted, we could make this argument for practically every religion on the planet (Gorham 1908: 107). Moreover, this is an old worn-out debate. Indeed, Macan (1877: 23) outlined its flaws many years ago by stating the premise that "the effects of a belief are a proof of its truth" is a common but mistaken idea. In other words, he suggests that Christianity, which has had a significant effect on history, is anchored in the doctrine of resurrection, therefore the resurrection must have been an actual event. Macan correctly added, "even if the premises were true, the conclusion that follows from them is not."

Furthermore, the assertion that the only reason the disciples came to believe that their rabbi had returned from the dead was "by tangible and indisputable proofs such as would satisfy impartial investigators in the scientific age" is highly problematic (Loisy 1962: 92). The noted theologian and biblical scholar Alfred Loisy (1962: 92) rejected this assertion pointing out that the first believers were the sort of people who had no interests in such proofs. Their preexisting faith made it impossible for them to believe that death was the end of their teacher and that therefore he had risen. They were not the least bit concerned about "how" this event came about. Such doubts arose, he adds, when the Christian evangelists began to spread the word among non-Jewish people.

Religionists overlook another vital fact that history is replete with examples of all kinds of beliefs, benign and evil, that have had major transforming powers independently of their foundations in reality or the involvement of supernatural forces (Watson 1987: 366). In the words of the New Testament scholar Francis Watson (1987: 366), it is erroneous to treat the surprising reaction of Jesus's followers to his demise as a miracle because historically "surprising things happen from time to time without requiring one to infer divine intervention as their cause."

Moreover, there were numerous beliefs in the cultural milieu of first-century Palestine that would have inspired this belief. Wilckens's assertion that the idea of someone being raised from the dead "had never previously been asserted in Israel of any mortal" is pure religionist hyperbole. The circumstances of Jesus's unjust execution as a malefactor could alone have generated the idea that he would somehow be exonerated. The foundations for this were the preexisting beliefs spelled out in the Jewish Scriptures that God vindicates the righteousness (2 Maccabees 7). Hence, such an unjust fate required a reversal and conversion into triumph, which was accomplished by believing that death was but a step for a higher life in heaven (Gorham 1908: 228). These early proclamations that Jesus had risen from the dead, biblical scholar Stephen Patterson (1998: 237) observes, were not based on anything other than the conviction that God would vindicate Jesus who was so unjustly put to death. This was part of the ancient Jewish beliefs about resurrection in a "martyrological context." Experiencing a reanimated corpse or finding a vacant tomb was not necessary. The disciples would have made the same claim even if they knew that Jesus's body was still in a grave. Patterson (1998: 237) adds that "the origin of Christian claims about the resurrection of Jesus was the conviction among his followers that he had been right about God." Such an eventuality was simply an indication that the deceased had entered heaven (De Jong 1989: 34, 36, 38; Philipse 2014: 180).

True believers also neglect to mention that beliefs in resurrection were, in fact, widespread during the first century in Palestine, perhaps except for the Sadducees. Such ideas were inextricably linked to the expectation of a new epoch of God and the vindication of his chosen people, an event expected to occur on earth, rather than in a spiritual world (Dein 2012: 123). Beliefs about the dead coming back to life occur in the various Old

Testament verses, for example, "The Lord brings death and makes alive; he brings down to the grave and raises up" (1 Samuel 2:6) and many other passages, such as 2 Kings 13:21; Ezekiel 37:9–12; 1 Samuel 2:6; Job 19:26; Isaiah 26:19; Daniel 12:1–4. Also, there was the idea that the major prophets were taken up bodily to heaven as the vindication of their righteousness, as in the case of Enoch and Elijah. Moses too was said to have been raised to heaven in this manner. The assumption into heaven was the reward for supreme moral virtue and piety. Thus, to reiterate, the assertion that the idea of resurrection was entirely unique is untrue and constitutes one more of a series of apologetic misrepresentations.

The skeptic Kris Komarnitsky (2014a: 63–80) has pointed out that the Jewish belief in a general resurrection at the end of time would have inspired the idea of the resurrection of the dead among the early Christians. Moreover, there were the beliefs within the broader Greco-Roman culture about the various heroes raised in spiritual form or bodily to the domain of the gods, as in the case of Herakles, Aeneas, and Romulus, among others. Patterson (1998: 222) writes in this regard that in the broader Hellenistic world, speaking of heroic figures as having ascended and dwelling with the gods was the reward and vindication for an exemplary life. Such beliefs would have influenced the Hellenized Jewish world during the first century and undoubtedly "influenced the formulation of early Christian claims about Jesus" (Patterson 1998: 222). Apologists continue to claim that the gospels were not Hellenized (Keener 2019: 51), forgetting the syncretic nature of Christianity, which integrates various religious and cultural elements.

There is no question that these narratives had a significant impact on the resurrection belief as it was carried outside the Middle East, as discussed in Chapter 14. Christian apologist today adamantly refuse to acknowledge the impact of these pagan apotheosis stories (Price 2007) because they believe the event that precipitated their religion was a violation miracle. Such a stance is merely an article of faith and has no evidentiary justification.

Another claim by believers is that if Jesus had not appeared in person, his death would have nullified any claims that he was the Messiah because there were no Jewish precedents for a Messiah who died a failure before completing his mission, that is, bringing redemption to Israel (Wright 2003: 562, 700). In the absence of such a miracle, believers assume that the Jesus movement would have become extinct. In support of this assertion, they mention the first- and second-century Jewish Messianic movements, such as the ones led by Simon bar Giora (died 70 CE) and Simon bar Kokhba (died 135 CE), that fell apart after their deaths in battle.

As Komarnitsky (2014a: 72–73) points out, however, these cases could not be rationalized because they were military movements that suffered defeat in battle. Here, as Crossley (2005: 172) puts it, we must consider the historical particularities of these events. Simon bar Giora and Simon bar Kokhba were military figures who promised military victories and their deaths nullified their claims. This is because both their military failures and their deaths would require justification. The case of Jesus was different, and the analogy with such violent figures is not an appropriate one (Crossley 2005: 172). This is because it was possible to rationalize the death of a nonmilitary messiah by shifting his functions—at least for the first round—from the visible to the invisible world (Barger 2008: 157–58) on the basis of the conjecture that he would complete his mission later upon being resurrected from the dead (Komarnitsky 2014a: 74). Such rationalization is no longer open to empirical disconfirmation and enables the messiah's followers to maintain their faith without further risks of failures or disconfirmation, at least for some time. Loisy's (1962: 100) comments are relevant here: "Removed to the invisible world, the object of their faith was beyond the reach of the accidents which might otherwise have shaken belief."

As for the assertion that other messianic groups ended with the death of their founder, but the Jesus movement did not, and therefore we are confronted with a miraculous event (Wright 2003: 700), Philipse (2014: 181) questions whether the hypothesis of Jesus's physical resurrection is really the most plausible explanation for the persistence of the cult. There are plenty of historical cases where the death of a messianic figure has, in fact, triggered the "backfire effect" leading to a doubling down on beliefs, galvanizing the group, and contributing to its persistence and even proliferation. As Loisy (1962: 91) observed, the movement started by the quasi-messianic figure John the Baptist, "a prophet of the end of the age with a mission subordinate to that of no other prophet, and not even that of the Messiah," survived his violent death "and his followers did not believe that he had perished in the grave." Another example is Shia Islam, which is describable as a messianic martyrdom cult that flourished after the death of its leader Hussein in Karbala, Iraq, in 680 CE.

Also, several other more recent religious movements have survived the demise of their founding figures, including Sabbatian and Lubavitch messianism to be discussed in the next chapter. Thus, professor of the New Testament Pieter Craffert (1989: 334) is on the mark that Christian apologists operate on the erroneous assumption that followers of a religious movement will automatically abandon their beliefs when they encounter a significant disconfirmation. Some do, others do not. From this, they conclude the reason the disciples of Jesus did not renounce the belief that Jesus actually and miraculously appeared to them after his death. Such a paranormal postulate, however, is based on a faulty assumption contradicted by what anthropological, sociological, and historical evidence shows about the behavior of staunch members of messianic or apocalyptic cults, as the examples provided in the next chapter will show.

Another argument forwarded against the idea that the disciples could have spontaneously conceived of the idea of a resurrected Messiah was the Jewish belief that the resurrection of individuals would not occur before the mass resurrection at the end of time (Wright 2003: 636). However, the gospels themselves suggest that the idea of such a rising of the dead was, in fact, conceivable (Price 2007). Again, there is the example of Herod in Mark 6:14–16, who thought Jesus was John the Baptist resurrected: "But when Herod heard this, he said, 'John, whom I beheaded, has been raised from the dead.'" This indicates that the notion of a person coming back to life was not an inconceivable concept that required the discovery of an empty tomb or a corpse walking out of a grave (Komarnitsky 2014a: 76). A similar idea occurs in the Gospel of Matthew (27:51–53) where we find the bizarre account of the reanimated saints pouring out of their graves onto the streets of Jerusalem, discussed in Chapter 12: "and the graves were opened; and many bodies of the saints who had fallen asleep were raised." Also, as discussed in Chapter 13, the many magicians and sorcerers operating during the first century routinely raised the dead as part of their magical repertoire. The idea of the resurrection of the dead was, therefore, neither rare nor infrequent.

Present-day defenders of the bodily resurrection scenario go to extremes in their efforts to explain away these instances of individual resurrections sometimes verging on the absurd. Wright (2003: 636), for example, dismisses the risen saints described in Matthew as an odd exception to the rule. The examples from Hellenistic culture are rejected as isolated exceptions and the cases of Enoch, Elijah, and Moses as "inexplicable exceptions" (Wright 2003: 28, n. 67, 94–95, 413). But for such ideologues, the belief in the resurrection of Jesus could not have been yet another exception. Such special pleading and deception become compulsory when theology and superstitious beliefs become substitutes for historical evidence.

Finally, there were plenty of other ideas the disciples of Jesus could draw upon to rationalize his resurrection and translation to heaven after death. First, we must take the specific circumstances of Jesus and his disciples when they arrived in Jerusalem on that fateful occasion. As Loisy (1962: 91) points out, during the final days, Jesus and his followers expected that the Great Event was at hand, that their master would become the foretold Messiah, and that they would enter "alive and glorified, into the felicity of the Kingdom." Ulrich Wilckens (1977: 125) makes a relevant observation that in Judaism, "the resurrection was expected in connection with the Final Days of Judgment." If in the minds of the disciples present in Jerusalem at the time that the Kingdom of God was at hand, and the resurrection of the righteous was imminent, it was unmistakable that Jesus, as its prophet and founder, would be "raised in advance of the resurrection of his followers, so soon to come" (Loisy 1962: 91).

## The Relationship between the Postmortem Visions and the Earliest Resurrection Beliefs

With the abundance of ideas available to the disciples within their cultural milieu that easily lend themselves to conceptualizing that Jesus was in some sense still alive, we can return the postmortem visions and how they generated the resurrection beliefs. According to Loisy (1962: 98–99) the vision, whatever its contents, was sudden and provided the answer to "the riddle of the crucifixion," that death was not the end, Jesus was alive in the presence of God, and was on the verge of returning as the Christ to establish the Kingdom. Similarly, Goguel (1953: 75) pointed out that the appearances served to unquestionably establish the belief in the resurrection and rendered the visionaries more conscious of what they already presupposed from a psychological perspective.

It was not on the "third day," or the Sunday after the Sabbath that the visionary phenomena transpired. The return trip to Galilee where the event took place involved a journey of several days. As the philosopher Christian Weisse surmised in his book *A Critical and Philosophical Study of the Gospel History* (1838), the first visions of Jesus and his "glorified body" occurred far from Jerusalem, away from the grave. It happened in Galilee, as the genuine ending of Mark says, and "bringing that spiritual corporeity into any kind of relationship with the dead body of the Crucified was not on the minds of the disciples" (in Schweitzer 2005: 130).

Similarly, Loisy (1962: 100) wrote: "We may assume that Peter had his vision in the days immediately following his return to Capernaum [his village along the edge of the

Sea of Galilee], days filled with the thought of his lost Master." Thus, it was sometime after the return that the anguished, mourning, and guilt-ridden Peter saw and heard Jesus in a vision (Lüdemann 1994: 174). This is a classic case of grief hallucination. As Peter imagined it, Jesus was not dead. God had vindicated him. The Lord had risen! Everything was now under a new light (Macan 1877: 81). The disciple's faith and their religious fervor and cultural background made them interpret the appearances as mind-independent events (Gorham 1908: 78–79). Peter's sins against his master were in that instance washed away, as Lüdemann (1995: 32) observes and, with it, the overwhelming guilt of his betrayal. After that, Jesus's crucifixion became linked with the forgiveness of sin (Lüdemann 1994: 176). Repentance and forgiveness of sins as the necessary preliminaries for the soon to come Kingdom of God came to dominate the thoughts of the disciples (Macan 1877: 80). Allison (2005: 369) points out that this may account for the emphasis that the early church placed upon the ideas of sin and forgiveness. The realization that God had exalted Jesus most unexpectedly now rectified the tragedy. But beyond that, this was evidence of the conquest of death. The prophecy was true after all, a general resurrection of the dead was about to commence (1 Corinthians 15:20), and the Kingdom of God and all the rest were at hand.

Peter's vision turned out to be contagious, and others also saw the risen Jesus (Loisy 1962: 100). The psychological mechanisms of this phenomenon are well known, as discussed in Chapter 7. Peter was thus able to gather the scattered brethren and regroup, imparting his own confidence to them. There were no mass sightings of Jesus by crowds of 500 people that apologists claim is definitive proof that a dead man came back to life and was God (Kreeft and Tacelli 1994: 187). Peter's vision of Jesus provided the pattern for the hallucinations among the other disciples (Lüdemann 1994: 96). There is nothing miraculous or paranormal about any of these circumstances. Such phenomena recur in many religious contexts that are well known to anthropologists and historians. Anthropological examples include the rash of visions among believers that succeeded an initial one by the messianic figures associated with the Melanesian cargo cult religions and the visions of the members of the Ghost Dance movement that came after the revelation to the prophet Wovoka (Sidky 2015: 200–211). There are plenty of other examples as well. The same processes were at work during the Sasquatch sightings in South Dakota, the mass sightings of UFOs across the United States since the 1940s, and the cases of the messianic figures discussed in the next chapter.

Group dynamics, as analyzed in Chapter 7, provided the basis for others to experience visions of the risen Lord themselves. These include the phenomena of groupthink, emotional contagion, top-down processing (the influence of existing beliefs on perception), and folie à deux (the transmission of delusional beliefs and hallucinations from one individual to another). Renan (1866: 21–22) cogently detailed this process long ago. He observed that circumstances that generate ecstasy, visions, and apparitions are contagious, as indicated by the history of all major religious crises. In a gathering of a group of enthusiastic people sharing the same beliefs, it suffices that one individual affirms that he or she sees or hears something supernatural and others will have the same experience. In this excitement, no one will be excluded nor will any admit that he or she has not been graced in this manner. Those who see nothing will attribute the failure to their own shortcomings and remain silent, wishing not to disrupt the collective joy. Consequently, when an apparition is seen during such meetings, the result is that everyone will see it or accept that it has been seen. The disciples, Renan (1866: 21–22) adds, were simple uneducated folk who believed in phantoms and imagined that miracles surrounded them. Among such people beliefs in marvelous things spread and are propagated in extraordinary ways. Hence, once the idea of the resurrected Jesus was circulated, the result was numerous visions and apparitions.

## The Visions as Understood by the Disciples

It is important to emphasize just how the disciples construed the visions of their master. Guignebert (1958: 527) noted that the visions did not mean that they thought Jesus had emerged from the tomb, but rather that he has been "glorified," was still alive in the presence of God in heaven waiting with the "Most High" for the time of the advent of the Kingdom. Their conclusion was not: "he rose again in the body," or as "he came out from the tomb," but "God has exalted and glorified him until the time appointed for his return" (Guignebert 1958: 528). Paul espoused this perspective, as Lüdemann (1994: 177) points out, according to which "Jesus entered God's presence directly at the moment of this death; he was exalted directly from the cross to God."

Christ did not eat, spend 40 days with his disciples, let people touch his wounds, and so forth. These are all fictional events concocted later and entail the vulgarization of a spiritual narrative. The belief that Jesus had been exalted and went to heaven at the instance of his death derived from preexisting beliefs contained in the Jewish religious texts and reinforced by the psychological phenomenon of grief hallucinations. Much later, the gospel writers responding to the theological needs of their time inserted a walking corpse into the narrative to emphasize that Christianity was not based on a ghost story as their enemies alluded.

Grief hallucinations are most intense during the weeks and months following the death (Kent 1999: 38; Sacks 2012: 233). The visions continue until the percipients come to terms with the loss. In the case of the followers of Jesus, the hallucinations ended when they answered the question: "Brethren, what shall we do?" (Acts 2:37), reinterpreted everything that had transpired, convinced themselves that the death, crucifixion, and resurrection were foretold as part of God's plan for the salvation of humanity, and decided to spread the good news, or *the gospel*, to everyone else (Kent 1999: 48).

The disciples thus became "apostles." From this point forward, the validation of their own beliefs depended on convincing as many others as possible to accept those beliefs as well, that is, making new converts. These are universal themes associated with apocalyptic groups that encounter disconfirmation of their prophecies, as the examples in the next chapter will show. The sudden start and end of the Jesus apparitions during a relatively short time closely fits the pattern of grief hallucinations. This also fits the profile of episodes of collective delusions, which involve an initial report, followed by other stories, and then rapid termination (Allison 2005: 205).

It was the grief hallucinations of the one or a few individuals that were part of the primitive tradition upon which the authors of the gospels later drew upon to write their elaborate fictional post-resurrection appearance stories, including the motif of burial by friends and the discovery of an empty tomb. Putting it plainly, the evangelists took a spiritual concept and transformed it into a story about a reanimated corpse that walks out of a grave through magical resuscitation. It is this vulgarized rendition that today's literalists are peddling. The metamorphosis of these narratives can be traced from Paul's first letter to the Corinthians to the Gospel of John. The new theological view thus expounded involved the replacement of the teachings of the historical Jesus, who was merely a radical Jewish rabbi, with a cosmic view of God incarnate in Jesus, which made sense in the context of the Greco-Roman world (Kent 1999: 36). Thus, the theological and thoroughly fictionalized resurrection narratives proffered in the gospels written many years later no longer had anything to do with the original grief-hallucinations that lay at the foundation of the resurrection idea. The new perspective is encapsulated in John 20:30–31, which says: "Jesus is the Messiah, the Son of God, and that by believing you may have life in his name."

An entirely different type of religionist rejoinder to the undeniable involvement of visionary appearances in the origins of Christianity is that the visions of Peter, Paul, and the others may be of significance to psychologists, but they are irrelevant to theologians and that the Christian faith is not grounded in the psyches of Peter and the first disciples (Fischer 1980: 88–91). Allison (2005: 207) believes that with this tactic religionists have settled the issue. For stanch believers, God is involved in "the reality of historical processes" and "can bring about what exceeds the limitations of our human knowledge" (Penennenberg 1996: 71). This is the omni-explanatory "everything is due to the action of God" hypothesis to which religionists frequently resort, as discussed in Chapters 3 and 6. It construes the resurrection an eschatological event "beyond ordinary experience," outside history, in other words, a violation miracle involving direct supernatural intervention into physical reality (cf., Watson 1987: 368). However, evidence for violation miracles in any context is altogether absent (see Chapter 8). Moreover, there is overwhelming anthropological and historical evidence to demonstrate that nothing about humans is outside of history, culture, or ordinary experience in any place or time. To say otherwise is fantasy and hyperbole.

The trite paranormal stance adopted by religionists has no place in the domain of critical historical or anthropological research and does not advance our understanding in any way. As noted before, this stance grants the apologists the freedom to replace historical, anthropological, and psychological evidence with their own superstitious beliefs. It dignifies credulity as a method and is an apologetic maneuver in which "theology is claimed in solemn exaggeration as the better history" (Lüdemann 1994: 180). The simple fact is that the psyche of consummate visionaries such as Peter and the members of the Jesus cult had a great deal to do with the development of this religion. Even Paul's vision on the road has a significant role in these events (see below).

Believers, however, cannot admit such a possibility. As the theologian Friedrich Schleiermacher (1963: 420) puts it, not to accept the literal truth of the resurrection suggests that

> the disciples were deceived and took an inward experience for an outward one [thus attributing] such weakness of intellect that not only is their whole testimony to Christ thereby

> rendered unreliable, but also Christ, in choosing for himself such witnesses, cannot have known what is in men.

This is a remarkable case of denying the evidence, whereas, in fact, those are the exact characteristics of the followers of Jesus. Did not Jesus choose his disciples? Did they not betray him? Did they not deny him? Did they not flee for their lives rather than risk themselves to stay with him in the hour of need? Did they not desert his corpse to the malefactors who killed him? Did not Jesus himself constantly rebuke them for their stupidity and ignorance?

## The Significance of Paul's Visionary Experience

How does Paul's visionary experience fit into the picture? He describes his experience in Galatians 1:12–16, as already noted. He also refers to his visions in 1 Corinthians 9:1 and 15:8. The author of Luke describes Paul's hallucination in Acts 9, 22, and 26. Paul did not know Jesus, so his experience on the road to Damascus was not a case of grief hallucination. Providing that we are not dealing with a pious fraud, which is a good possibility, the best way to describe what happened is that Paul had a "conversion vision" involving an auditory and visual hallucination of a bright light that often express an unresolved psychological conflict or deep-seated guilt (Goulder 1996: 50; Kent 1999: 50). Alternatively, Paul's hallucination may have involved an episode of temporal lobe epilepsy, as suggested by Landsborough (1987), discussed in Chapter 10. It is even possible that he was struck by lightning as Thomas Paine surmised.

Paul asserted that his message came directly from the mystical Christ, not via any human agency (Galatians 1:15–17). For this reason, there seems to be a disconnect between Paul's theological message and that of the still Torah-observant Christians in Jerusalem under the leadership of Peter and later James, the brother of Jesus. Paul's movement was a non-Torah-observant one, and his message was formulated specifically for "the Gentiles." It was in Paul's theological imagination that Jesus, a radical Jewish rabbi, is transformed into a mystical being, Christ the Son of God that eventually came to dominate Christian thought. This idea powerfully resonated with the targeted non-Jewish audiences already familiar with stories of other god-men, the sons of Jupiter, that were a deep-rooted part of their culture.

In his book *How Jesus Became Christian* (2008), the religious studies scholar Barrie Wilson builds a case that one should differentiate between the Jesus organization in Jerusalem and Paul's Christ movement. These were not two branches of the same movement. Paul's enterprise, Wilson argues, was not a logical outgrowth of Jesus's mission but was a parallel development focused on Christ as a divine being, the Son of God. The rift between the two religious movements is so vast that it has led some scholars to posit that Christ was a mystical being and a historical Jesus did not exist (e.g., Carrier 2014; Doherty 2005, 2009; Wells 1996).

Paul's efforts as an evangelist who spread the word among the Gentiles was successful because he promised life eternal and all the perks of Judaism without any of its taboos and ritual requirements (Wilson 2008: 136, 140–41). This is one of the reasons why his theology was so successful outside the Middle East. The Torah-observant and geographically confined Jesus movement, however, was massively impacted by political developments inside Palestine. The anti-Roman violence in Israel in the 60s crippled the Christians in Jerusalem, and after the Romans destroyed the city in 70 CE, the Christians there scattered (Wilson 2008: 135–36). Josephus describes these violent events in the fourth book of his *Jewish Wars* (2017), written around 75 CE. Thus, the churches that survived were the ones Paul had established outside Palestine. So it was Paul's conversion vision of a mystical Christ, rather than anyone seeing a flesh-and-bones Jesus, that turned out to be the most decisive factor in the development of the Christian faith (Kent 1999: 85, 92). In sum, there is extensive evidence that the resurrection narratives in the gospels are not historical. There is also overwhelming evidence that the resurrection was not a unique eschatological event or a historical reality. Apologists are guilty of what no legitimate historians would ever do, that is, to sacrifice their own critical reasoning and to swallow wholesale the fables contained in texts of highly dubious historical utility (cf., Craffert 1989: 335).

This perspective entails considerable doses of credulity and deception. As Watson (1987: 367) observes, to say that only a miraculous physical resurrection of Jesus can explain the belief of his followers is "mere rhetoric and hyperbole." That the disciples came to this conclusion may surprise us and may even seem inexplicable, he adds, but this is only an indication of our ignorance of the circumstances. To infer divine intervention is a "god-of-the-gaps argument" that always fails. Moreover, the events in question are only surprising to those who assume that adherents of a religious movement will abandon their extant beliefs in the face of a major setback, such as the death of their leader. This, however, is an erroneous assumption because while such a stumbling block may result in some members dropping out or some groups to disperse, there are innumerable other cases when such a crisis had not resulted in comprehensive apostasy but a doubling down on the beliefs. This is achieved by reinterpreting the beliefs "in the light of the crisis and of the crisis in the light of the beliefs," articulating an entirely new reality while still retaining elements of the old doctrines (Watson 1987: 367). Several contemporary examples of this phenomenon are discussed in the next chapter. At this stage, it is difficult not to concur with Strauss's (1873: 82–83) conclusion that from a historical perspective, as an objective event, the resurrection of Jesus has no evidentiary foundations. In his words, "comparing the immense effect of this belief with its absolute baselessness, the story of the resurrection of Jesus can only be called a world-wide deception."

Christian apologetic tracts are deeply flawed because their authors are unable to examine the evidence impartially. All of this does not bode well for the epistemological status of Plantinga's "Augustinian science" in which God plays a direct interventionist role in the world offered as a better framework for understanding the world and universe over the scientific perspective. This evidence base is highly flawed, problematic, and unpersuasive.

# Chapter Sixteen

# COPING WITH FAILED PROPHESY: A SOCIO-PSYCHOLOGICAL EXPLANATION FOR THE RISE OF CHRISTIANITY

*I've had to go a long way. I've given up just about everything. I've cut every tie: I've burned every bridge. I've turned my back on the world. I can't afford to doubt. I have to believe. And there isn't any other truth.*

—Dr. Armstrong, a disappointed Sananda cult member (1956)

*Suppose an individual believes something with his whole heart; suppose further that he has a commitment to this belief, that he has taken irrevocable actions because of it; finally, suppose that he is presented with evidence, unequivocal and undeniable evidence, that his belief is wrong: what will happen? The individual will frequently emerge, not only unshaken, but even more convinced of the truth of his beliefs than ever before. Indeed, he may even show a new fervor about convincing and converting other people to his view.*

—Leon Festinger et al., *When Prophecy Fails* (1956)

*Hardly had the report arrived from Aleppo that Elijah had appeared in the Old Synagogue there, and Elijah walked streets of Smyrna. Dozens, even hundreds, had seen him: he was the anonymous beggar asking for alms, as well as the as the invisible guest, at every banquet.*

—Gershom Scholem, *Sabbatai Ṣevi* (1973)

*The stunning speed with which this belief has spread in the absence of a scintilla of evidence should capture the attention of all historians who have struggled to explain and reconstruct the development of early Christian beliefs in the resurrection and the empty tomb.*

—David Berger, *The Rebbe, the Messiah and the Scandal of Orthodox Indifference* (2008)

As discussed in the previous chapter, two concurrent processes came into play to generate the resurrection beliefs of the early Christians: (1) grief hallucinations; (2) the psychological process involved in coming to terms with the disconfirmation of deeply held beliefs. In this chapter, I shall look specifically at how the Jesus cultists came to terms with their shattered dreams and disappointment after the unexpected execution of their rabbi and how these efforts contributed to the development of Christianity.

Seeing the apparition of Jesus was a powerful force that convinced the cultists what they already anticipated based on their background beliefs that their teacher had been glorified and ascended to heaven to remain with the Most High but would shortly after that return to inaugurate the Kingdom of God on earth. However, the belief that "the Lord has risen" alone does not fully explain why these cultists took up proselytization and become missionaries. The second concurrent factor was socio-psychological and relates to how staunch believers come to terms with the disconfirmation of deeply held convictions to which they have committed everything.

Jesus's followers were members of an apocalyptic cult who believed that their master, a radical Jewish rabbi who predicted the End Time, would transform society, end the Roman occupation, restore the twelve tribes of Israel, and rule as King. Many of these devotees were deeply committed believers who abandoned their jobs, homes, families, and friends to follow Jesus (Philipse 2014: 179). In turn, Jesus promised that his followers would receive immense rewards for leaving their homes, families, and fields for his sake: [you] "will also sit on twelve thrones, judging the twelve tribes of Israel" [...] [and] will receive a hundred times as much and will inherit eternal life" (Matthew 19:27–29).

It is possible that Jesus's follower believed that his prophecies would come to pass precisely at the time when they were with their master in Jerusalem at the Passover (Watson 1987: 367). However, instead of the anticipated glorious events occurring, Jesus was arrested and killed. The disciples thus had to confront an overwhelming disconfirmation of their deeply held beliefs. Had God forsaken them? Had they made a terrible mistake in placing their trust in Jesus? Were their detractors right all along that Jesus was a false Messiah? There was also the overwhelming grief that overcame them. As Mark 16:10 says, "they mourned and wept." Social psychologists refer to such a dramatic inconsistency between expectations and experience as a state of cognitive dissonance.

## The Relevance of the Theory of Cognitive Dissonance and Its Critics

The theory of cognitive dissonance is the brainchild of the American social psychologist Leon Festinger (Festinger et al. 1956; Festinger 1957). It was a pioneering premise that brought the issue of dissonance reduction to the attention of social scientists. The classic case study is by Festinger, Riecken, and Schachter called *When Prophecy Fails* (1956). It involved an apocalyptic UFO cult whose eschatological beliefs were highly reminiscent of the followers of Jesus. The paranormal source for the beliefs of this cult was an extraterrestrial being named Sananda. It is from this entity that Marian Keech (the pseudonym used for Dorothy Martin), the prophet of the cult, obtained her information and instructions. Sananda later revealed himself as "the contemporary identity of the historical Jesus—his new name having been adopted with the beginning of the 'new cycle' or age of light" (Festinger et al. 1956: 36).

In this chapter, I shall explore the relevance of the socio-psychological phenomenon of cognitive dissonance as it relates to the behavior of the disciples of Jesus. Here I am indebted to Kris Komarnitsky's (2014a) remarkable work who has the credit of providing the most recent and cogent case that the belief in the resurrection was a response to cognitive dissonance among the disciples after Jesus's execution (for earlier works, see Gager 1974; Jackson 1975; Wernick 1975).

Before discussing the specifics of Festinger's theory, it is necessary to dispel several specious rejoinders by Christian apologists regarding this compelling rival secular explanation of the evidence (Coyne 2015: 123; Philipse 2014: 181). One of the chief modern-day defenders of the historicity of Jesus's bodily resurrection, Wright feels obliged to refute the postulate that cognitive dissonance played a part in transforming the beliefs of the failed and disappointed Jesus cult members into a face-saving denial by rationalizing a dead Messiah. Wright (2003: 698) states confidently that this theory is deeply flawed and expresses surprise to find serious scholars who speak of it in "deferential terms."

The reason Wright and his colleagues adopt this position is that it offers a non-supernatural explanation that calls into question the validity of the Christian faith as a miraculous phenomenon as understood by literalists. However, is such an assessment of the theory of cognitive dissonance cogent or compelling? The answer is a resounding no. As is usual of such committed religionists, Wright is so biased by his "canon mentality" that he is incapable of admitting any other possibilities. Furthermore, as discussed in the previous chapters, religionists refuse to be swayed by evidence. They have no other options. Thus, as Price (2007) points out, Wright "suicidally mentions this theory, only to dismiss it, as usual, with no serious attempt at refutation." So, once again, bluster and bluff are used to bludgeon readers into believing that the superstitions being peddling are "the truth." It is as if pronouncing an idea with which one disagrees to be wrong alone suffices as a refutation. For example, Wright asserts that Festinger's analysis is invalid because the sociologists who infiltrated the group altered the conditions and impacted the behavior of the individuals in the study. However, he provides no evidence that this was the case. Thus, as the philosopher Philipse (2014: 181) observes, to sustain such an argument, Wright must first establish that this is indeed the case before dismissing the theory. Wright has not done that.

Others have characterized early Christianity as a sectarian or social revolutionary movement rather than a millenarian one (Esler 1996; Horsley 1993; Watson 2007). Some researchers have dismissed the relevance of the theory by arguing that Christianity developed over a long period while the Festinger study entails a case involving a relatively brief interval (Richter 1984). Still others have said that the followers of Jesus misunderstood his teachings about the imminence of the millennium and question whether it is possible to comprehend the missionary project of the Christians in terms of cognitive dissonance.

It may be correct to say that the sparse nature of the evidence is amenable to different interpretations. However, the time scale issue raised by Richter is not entirely valid. First, the theory may have been inspired by a temporally limited event, the UFO cult of Sananda; however, there are numerous other very similar historical and anthropological cases involving both longer and shorter periods that support the cognitive dissonance perspective. Also, the idea that the followers of Jesus had not understood his teaching about the millennium is nonsensical. The millenarian dimension was, in fact, the singular invention of the early Christians themselves because of the contradictory nature of the events facing them, that is, a dead Messiah instead of the restoration of Israel. It was millenarianism that spurred their missionary zeal.

The assertion that millenarianism was not involved in the case of the rise of Christianity is made because it was only from the time of the Pentecost that the Jesus cultists undertook long-term missionary work, which was a strategy based on the conclusion that making the End Time happen required that they spread the gospel truths. The disciples sought to resolve their cognitive dissonance through this strategy of missionization (Tidball 1985). In other words, if cognitive dissonance does not characterize what happened after the Pentecost when the zealous Jesus cultists decided what to do, it is because undertaking missionary work was how they resolved their dilemma and answered the question: "Brethren, what shall we do?" (Acts 2:37). Instead of refuting the theory, this suggests that cognitive dissonance was indeed one of the major forces in the rise of Christianity. Other groups, such as the Lubavitch, a case discussed later in this chapter, employed a similar strategy for the same purpose. Such efforts are in perfect alignment with Festinger's findings. The same impetus, it should be noted, continues to fuel Christian evangelism today, namely that missionary work and conversions are necessary to prepare for the end of history (Percy 2001: 29). These proselytizers believe that Jesus's return is dependent on their global success in spreading the word. Given the numerous comparable historical and anthropological examples, the perspective of cognitive dissonance is a highly plausible approach to understanding what happened in the early stages of Christianity.

Moreover, there are good reasons why scholars refer to the theory in "deferential terms." As psychologist Joel Cooper (2007: 6) has put it, the theory of cognitive dissonance is "one of the best-known and prolifically documented theories in social psychology." Moreover, the numerous millennialism studies engendered by this theory have become "an international field of research" (Landes 1999: 736). While aspects of this theory have been modified and expanded during the 50 years since its initial proposal, as is the case with many other innovative ideas, many continue to consider it as a viable theoretical perspective for the analysis of human behavior (Beauvois and Joule 1996; Beauvois and Joule 1999; Cooper 1999; Harmon-Jones and Mills 1999; Mahnke and Morrison 1997; Morvan and O'Connor 2017).

The basic premise of this theory is that when people deeply hold two or more inconsistent beliefs (cognitions) a state of cognitive dissonance arises, which they experience as an uncomfortable tension that must be reduced by altering aspects of the belief or finding supporting rationalizations for continuing to maintain those beliefs. For example, a general form of cognitive dissonance is to be found in the cultural context in the United States, as Coyne (2015: 97) points out, where people who live in a society that has benefited tremendously from science still cling on to superstitious, pseudoscientific and religious fables by contriving a variety of rationalizations to maintain both sets of beliefs.

The degree of cognitive dissonance depends on the degree of discrepancy between such conflicting sets of beliefs. The higher the incongruity, the higher the motives to reduce it (Cooper 2007: 7). To do this, humans will invent stories to obscure the incompatibilities, change their behavior, or strive to convince others about the truth of their beliefs (Philipse 2014: 179). Believers may employ one or all of these strategies. This aspect of the theory sheds considerable light on the behavior of members of many millenarian and messianic cults that have appeared throughout human history, including the activities of the disciples of Jesus.

In its classic expression, the theory closely fits the case of Jesus's followers who were without question members of an eschatological or apocalyptic cult (Perrin 2012; Loftus 2010; Madigan and Levenson 2008: 9–23), contra the evangelical Tidall's (1985) assertions. It is this specific application of the theory that is of concern to us. Here is how Festinger (1956: 3) and his colleagues summarized the process of cognitive dissonance:

> Suppose an individual believes something with his whole heart; suppose further that he has a commitment to this belief, that he has taken irrevocable actions because of it; finally, suppose that he is presented with evidence, unequivocal and undeniable evidence, that his belief is wrong: what will happen? The individual will frequently emerge, not only unshaken, but even more convinced of the truth of his beliefs than ever before. Indeed, he may even show a new fervor about convincing and converting other people to his view.

Such reactions to disconfirming evidence of deeply held beliefs occur under the following five conditions:

1. A belief must be held with deep conviction, and it must have some relevance to action, that is, to what the believer does or how he behaves.
2. The person holding the belief must have committed himself to it; that is, for the sake of his belief, he must have taken some decisive action that is difficult to undo. In general, the more important such activities are, and the more difficult they are to undo, the greater is the individual's commitment to the belief.
3. The belief must be sufficiently specific and sufficiently concerned with the real world so that events may unequivocally refute the belief.
4. Such undeniable disconfirmation must occur and be recognized by the individual holding the belief.
5. The individual believer must have social support. It is unlikely that one isolated believer could withstand the kind of disconfirming evidence we have specified. If, however, the believer is a member of a group of convinced persons who can support one another, we would expect the belief to be maintained and the believers to attempt to proselyte or to persuade nonmembers that the belief is correct (Festinger et al. 1956: 4).

Some further clarifications are necessary before proceeding with this discussion. Critics assert that this perspective is problematic because failed prophecies do not always lead to proselytization and that there are alternative ways of dealing with prophetic disconfirmation (Melton 1985; Stone 2000; Zygmunt 1972). These conditions, however, are not incompatible with the original formulation of the theory. The theory posits that when inconsistencies between deeply held beliefs and actual empirical experience arise, they produce an uncomfortable tension, and people will attempt to deal with what is perceived to be a terrible and unacceptable reality creatively using various strategies.

The responses, however, will vary among different group members and between separate groups as a whole across time and space. Not everyone is equally committed to their group's beliefs, and they will react to disconfirmation differently rather than being at the mercy of some powerful, all-encompassing determinative social force that they cannot comprehend, contra Dein (2001: 385). Some may abandon their beliefs and drop out.

Indeed, even in the case of the original study by Festinger and his associates, following the failure of the prophecy, two committed individuals abandoned their beliefs and left the cult permanently. Perhaps a similar sentiment is captured in Luke (24:21) where we hear two disappointed disciples of Jesus bemoaning: "but we had hoped he was the one who was going to redeem Israel." Others may respond by altering aspects of their belief, adding new ones to preexisting tenets, or various combinations of these approaches.

Cognitive dissonance theory specifies several preconditions that require emphasis. First, the group must subscribe to a set of beliefs that is subject to clear empirical disconfirmation. Not all groups espouse such views. Festinger et al. (1956: 4) underscored that the theoretical parameters apply only to movements that specify a date or an interval of time for the predicted events to occur as well as describe in detail what is to happen. Some messianic or millenarian cults subscribe to complex cosmologies in which prediction is not central. They may instead espouse "explanatory millennialism," where such beliefs have a rhetorical function to explain undesirable contemporary existential circumstances (Dein 2012: 10–11). Present-day millennialists are aware of the fallout of disconfirmations and deliberately avoid making prophecies that are falsifiable (Thompson 2005). These circumstances do not invalidate the phenomenon of cognitive dissonance and efforts to rationalize failed prophecies as posited by Festinger, contra Melton (1985).

Second, group members must be so heavily invested in a set of beliefs that they cannot easily abandon them. Not all groups across space and time possess this characteristic. Such investments vary even among members of particular assemblages of believers. Third, to reduce cognitive dissonance believers will resort to one or several approaches, such as collaborative storytelling and mutual support to restore threatened social bonds, adjusting their core tenets, adding novel doctrines, or increasing proselytization based on the idea that convincing others and increasing the numbers of believers determines the truth of their beliefs. The fact that multiple strategies may be employed to reduce dissonance does not undermine Festinger's theory, contra Zygmunt (1972) and Melton (1985). Fourth, rationalizations in response to cognitive dissonance do not occur in every single instance, which is why after an initial major disconfirmation of their prophecy some religious sects and cults have disintegrated and disappeared (Komarnitsky 2014b).

However, *under certain specified conditions,* response to cognitive dissonance due to the disconfirmation of prophecy can *sometimes* result in the development of radically new beliefs with stunning sociocultural consequences. Thus, whether or not proselytization follows in every instance does not detract from the theory's validity, contra Dawson (1999), Hardyck and Braden (1962), and Stone (2000). Moreover, there are a substantial number of historical cases where disconfirmation has indeed resulted in radically new beliefs followed by vigorous proselytization. These include the Jesus cult, the Montanists, the Anabaptists, the Sabbatians, and the Millerites, discussed by Festinger et al. (1956).

What also factors in this process of addressing disconfirming evidence of cherished beliefs are various cognitive biases, such as groupthink, memory conformity, evidence distortion, and the confirmation bias and the backfire effect. A discussion of how powerfully these biases impact what people believe and how they sustain those beliefs is the topic of Chapter 7. Dissonance reduction may very well be an inbuilt human cognitive attribute. Although not explicitly stated, Festinger's theory implies the operation of these psychological factors.

For these reasons, humans have demonstrated a remarkable tendency through time and space to be able to justify in extraordinary ways nearly any cherished but patently false beliefs. As Komarnitsky (2014b) has put it, "people can sometimes come up with ingenious and complex explanations to make sense of a disconnect between deeply held beliefs and the harsh reality of events." Similarly, historian of religion Hugh Jackson (1975: 425) notes that we have plenty of historical evidence "of just how creative a deeply felt faith can be."

In certain circumstances, such face-saving rationalizations and creative post hoc explanations to reduce cognitive dissonance have resulted in the formulation of entirely new sets of beliefs never before encountered. In the case of the members of the Jesus cult, this novel idea was the presumption that a Messiah who has died before completing his mission has become the embodiment of God and will return from the dead to perform his assignment during a subsequent round of activities. This development among the early Christians was such a departure from its broader strict monotheistic Jewish religious and cultural contexts as to lead some scholars to conclude that the rise of Christianity and the veneration of Jesus were extraordinary and puzzling historical phenomena unique unto themselves, without exact historical or cultural analogies or counterparts anywhere. As such, they argue, the rise of Christianity is inexplicable according to conventional historical forces. Hence the paranormal fantasy of a reanimated corpse, or a violation miracle, is offered as the only possible explanation for these circumstances. These, however, are ruminations by true believers who have already accepted the miraculous origins of their religion on faith.

## Was the Rise of Christianity a Violation Miracle?

The New Testament scholar Larry Hurtado espouses such a perspective in his book *How on Earth Did Jesus Become God?* (2005). He stops just short of adopting the passé religionist stance that the rise of Christianity was a singular eschatological event and a case of God directly intervening in human history (Hurtado 2005: 20–30). Nevertheless, he implies that Christianity is an extraordinary phenomenon and hence "special" among all the other faiths. However, let us not forget that believers of all religions make such grandiose claims about the sublime nature and extraordinary cosmic significance of their faiths. As the philosopher David Hume (1902 [1748]: 121) noted in his essay "Of Miracles" (1748), all religions make such cosmic claims and use such declarations as evidence of the truth of their supernatural beliefs.

The apparent sudden manifestations of unique innovations out of seemingly incompatible religious contexts are not uncommon, consider for instance the creation of monotheistic beliefs by the pharaoh Akhenaten (Amenhotep IV) circa 1350 BCE in polytheistic Egypt (Hoffmeier 2015: 211–65). There is also the example of monotheistic Islam that arose in the context of polytheistic Arabian culture during the seventh century. Other cases included the UFO religions that appeared in the Christian United States during the twentieth century (see Sidky 2015: 111–22). As the discussion below will show, the rise of Christianity is comparable to the emergence of many other religions that have developed in antagonistic cultural contexts and is explicable in terms of similar sociocultural and historical forces, the process of cognitive dissonance reduction being among them.

Returning to Jesus's disciples, the core personnel of the cult, who had turned their backs on the world, gave up their occupations, abandoned their families, homes, and possessions, were so deeply committed that they could not admit they were wrong or discard their beliefs and resume their old lives. The words of one of the members of the cult Festinger and his colleagues studied in 1956 could very well have been those of Peter or one of the other key disciples:

> I've had to go a long way. I've given up just about everything. I've cut every tie: I've burned every bridge. I've turned my back on the world. I can't afford to doubt. I have to believe. And there isn't any other truth. […] I've taken an awful beating in the last few months, just an awful beating. But I do know who I am and I know what I've got to do. […] I won't doubt even if we have to make an announcement to the press tomorrow and admit we were wrong. You're having your period of doubt now, but hang on, boy, hang on. This is a tough time but we know that the boys upstairs are taking care of us. They've given us their promise. These are tough times and the way is not easy. We all have to take a beating. I've taken a terrific one, but I have no doubt. (Festinger et al. 1956: 168)

These were probably the sort of dilemmas the disciples of Jesus had to face. The incredulous Reimarus (1879: 89) called attention to the social and economic predicament of the disciples. Returning to their old lives and occupations, he observes, was not an option. It would mean poverty and disgrace. This is because they had become habituated to not working and because they had foolishly followed a false prophet.

Given these factors, the disciples would have been experiencing a painful psychological conflict. They had made such a significant investment in Jesus's eschatological promises that they could not abandon their beliefs. Some, no doubt, did drop out. Others, however, chose to cope with the shock of disconfirmation by regrouping, seeking mutual support, engaging in collaborative storytelling, doubling down on their beliefs, and generating a rationalization for the failed prophecy and a way to move forward (cf., Philipse 2014: 180). These factors are all classic stuff of Festinger's theory of cognitive dissonance.

## How Millenarians Reconfigure Their Beliefs to Avert Empirical Disconfirmation

It is important to stress again that some millenarian groups do not advance prophecies that are open to disconfirmation, that is, they articulate their core beliefs in such a way as to be unfalsifiable. The existence of such cases does not refute the theory of cognitive dissonance. However, there are groups, such as the Jesus cult, whose members are committed to a prophecy that is open to disconfirmation (cf., Jackson 1975: 418). In such a case, the rationalizing of a major disconfirmation involves reconfiguring the central claims in the form of new postulates that are immune to falsification. An unfalsifiable explanation deflects failure. As Watson (1987: 368) has cogently pointed out, the follower of Jesus reinterpreted their original beliefs: their "old hopes in the light of the crucifixion, and the crucifixion in light of the old hopes." He adds, hence it is untrue to assert that the disciple's resurrection beliefs are explicable only if a corpse magically came back to life. Moreover, there are alternate and more plausible explanations for what happened. This very possibility invalidates "the naïve and exaggerated claim that the disciples' faith was so remarkable that only a genuine resurrection of Jesus can account for it" (Watson 1987: 368).

Once such a resynthesis of beliefs has taken place, it is possible to maintain them for some time without further risks of empirical disconfirmation. Hence the promise of an empirically verifiable event, such as the claim that Jesus will appear in person on such and such a date in this or that location that fails to occur, is replaced with a non-empirically verifiable one. This was the assertion that the Second Coming has taken place invisibly in heaven, or that it will happen at an as yet to be determined time.

As an exemplar, Festinger (1956: 11–23) and his associates described the Millerites, a nineteenth-century millenarian group in the United States, whose visionary leaders predicted the specific date (1843 and then 1844) for the Second Coming of Jesus based on the Book of Daniel (8:13–14). The first designated date came and went with no signs of the Messiah. Their first reaction was to attribute the failure to a calculation error and determined a new date. The second prediction failed as well and came to be known as "Great Disappointment." Remarkably, the Millerites did not disband after this major disconfirmation, contra Melton (1985), but reinterpreted their theology. One post hoc rationalization was that the Second Coming had indeed occurred but in heaven rather than on earth. Millerites eventually transformed into the Advent Christian Church (1861), the much larger Seventh-day Adventist Church (1863), which today has millions of followers, as well as several smaller Adventist groups (Doniger 1999: 738; Kirsch 2006: 184–86; Newport 2001). Seventh-day Adventists addressed the failure of prophecy by embarking upon a worldwide missionizing program to gain new converts. I even encountered one of their mission outposts on Rapa Nui (Easter Island), which is one of the remotest locations on this planet.

## "Not of This World": Ways Millenarians Cope with Prophetic Failures due to the Passage of Time

Such rationalizations work at least for a while because the passage of time will expose all prophecies to refutation. None of Jesus's prophecies came to pass. The implications of this did not escape Celsus (1830: 9, 11) who asked: "How can we think him to be a God, who [...] performed, as we learn, nothing that was promised?" The early Christians did not abandon their beliefs in light of these failures but attempted to rationalize them. Aside from the defeat and death of a Messiah who was expected to restore Israel gloriously, the other major disconfirmation with which they had to contend was the non-occurrence of the predicted Second Coming or the Parousia.

As the historian and expert in millennialism Richard Landes (1999: 728) observes, as in the case of all apocalyptic movements, the passing of time posed a significant difficulty for the early Christians as it dawned upon them that the Second Coming was not at hand.

Those that did not revert to Judaism contended with the delay of the Parousia through community rituals, such as the Eucharist or the recitation of Revelation, in anticipation of the great event, offering a "foretaste of the coming world" (Landes 1999: 728). They also set a new timeline during which the end would not come until the faithful complete the task assigned by God to spread the Gospel all over the world. This is an important observation that addresses the apologist argument that cognitive dissonance theory may explain how new reconfigured beliefs may arise but does not specify how those beliefs are *sustained*. In the Christian context, the ritualization of communal practices, the two primary ones being Baptism and the Eucharist, functioned to bolster and perpetuate such beliefs (see Hurtado 2005: 28; Johnson 1998: 70–79, 137–63).

The Christian reconfiguration of their beliefs involved the non-falsifiable explanation that Jesus's kingdom was "not of this world" (Landes 1999: 729). Various ingenious methods of calculating and calibrating time were proposed as well in which one day is thousands of years long, providing an easy solution that time yet remains before the millennium. Along the same lines, another tactic was to "de-apocalypicize" Christianity (Dein 2012: 129; Landes 1999: 728–29). This version appears in the Gospel of John 14:1–3, where the assurance of eternal life in heaven replaces the promise of the coming Kingdom of God on earth: "You believe in God; believe also in me. My Father's house has many rooms [...] I am going there to [...] prepare a place for you, I will come back and take you to be with me that you also may be where I am."

The earliest Christian theologian of import to explicitly reject millenarianism was Origen who asserted that the establishment of the Kingdom would not occur in time or space but in the souls of the faithful (Cohn 1970: 29; Watt 2001: 91). Thus, with no indication of a return by Jesus or the materialization of any Godly kingdoms, Christian apologists have been "moving the goal posts" ever since in the same manner as the members of other failed millenarian cults continue to do so (Loftus 2010: 333).

Another criticism of Festinger's theory is that it imposes the notion of falsifiability that may be meaningful in terms of the scientific worldview upon groups that may not operate according to such premises (O'Leary 2000). This reflects the influence of the solipsistic, and unproductive anti-science postmodernist perspective that infected academia during the 1980s (see Sidky 2018). Another problem pointed out by critics is that the theory ignores the emic view of the believers and hence they call for a relativistic stance that emphasizes meaning and interpretive or hermeneutical approaches (Spilka et al. 2003). These criticisms are not compelling for several reasons. First, the proposed alternative perspectives merely offer subjective story-telling as a substitute for theory without any explanatory power. Second, as discussed in Chapter 1, no one is so well-placed to grasp the insider's point of view. Also, believers do not have privileged access to the reasons for their own beliefs. Scientific anthropologists have demonstrated that the emic perspective alone seldom provides adequate anthropological explanations. Third, such perspectives deny the reality of universal human experience. Finally, they unjustifiably dignify the irrationalism of true believers and the pathetic recurring travesty of millenarianism and messianic movements that have marred human history resulting in the deaths of millions of people.

I call these a travesty because no prophecy has ever succeeded in any place or time and the outcome of movements inspired by such pronouncements has often been staggering violence and destructiveness. The Jewish apocalyptic revolts against the Romans ended with the deaths of hundreds of thousands of people in battle or by gruesome mass crucifixions by the Romans. Similar horrific results occurred in Europe during the Middle Ages (Cohen 1970). In more recent history, the mystical visions of Hong Xiuquan, a blend of Buddhist and Christian millennialism, resulted in the Taiping Rebellion in nineteenth-century China that led to the deaths of 20 to 35 million people (see Hunt 2001). During the twentieth century, there were the genocidal Nazis and their so-called *Tausendjähriges Reich*, or the "Thousand-Year Reich," steeped with millennialism and conspiracy thinking that resulted in the scapegoating and systematic murder of millions of people in death camps and the fields of combat (cf., Landes 1999: 737). There are sadly many more such religiously inspired horrors. On a smaller scale, there are the doomsday suicide cults during the twentieth century, including the UFO millenarian group Heaven's Gate, the apocalyptic Order of the Solar Temple, whose members anticipated the Second Coming of Christ as "the Solar God-king," Peoples Temple, the Branch Davidians, and the murderous Aum Shinrikyô cult (Blach and Tylor 2002; Hall and Schuyler 1997; Lewis 2000; Moore 2009; Reader 2001).

Millennialism, as Landes (1999: 737) has put it, has the power to "fire the imagination and elicit passions" that can arouse vast numbers of people into extraordinary creativity, self-sacrifice, and destructiveness and "may be one of the most protean social and religious forces" in human history. It is deeply rooted in wishful thinking and the eternal hope or quest for a chimerical utopia. Despite the numbers of failed prophecies, many spectacular implosions, untold violence, the countless occasions when alleged messiahs have failed to appear, the repeated instances when justice on earth and the Kingdom of God have not materialized, and the inevitable disasters and mass murders, such irrationalism continues to reoccur. There is nothing praiseworthy to dignify here.

## What Recent Historical Parallels Can Tell Us about the Early Christians

The theory of cognitive dissonance does indeed explain the surprising behavioral responses by members of certain religious groups following major prophecy failures. Numerous historical examples fit all of the parameters of the theory. Two cases of Jewish millenarian movements will be examined here, one from the seventeenth century and the other from the twentieth century: Sabbatian Messianism and Lubavitch Messianism. These examples display many parallels with the Jesus movement and shed considerable light on the events in first-century Palestine. In all three cases, creative eschatological hermeneutics have given dead Messiahs a second chance and the believers a road map to move forward.

### *Sabbatian Messianism*

The Sabbatian movement developed around a seventeenth-century charismatic Sephardic Jewish rabbi named Sabbatai Ṣevi. His life and the activities of his followers are described by the noted scholar of Jewish mysticism Gershom Scholem in his massive book *Sabbatai*

*Ṣevi: The Mystical Messiah* (1973). Sabbatai was born in 1626, in Smyrna, a city located on the Aegean coast of Anatolia (now part of Turkey), then a territory of the Ottoman Empire. In 1665 he was convinced of his messianic status by Nathan of Gaza, an ecstatic visionary who claimed to be the risen Elijah. Nathan declared that Sabbatai was the expected Messiah who would restore the glory of Israel and subsequently became Sabbatai's lieutenant. It seems that the long-awaited miraculous event had finally come to pass, and the Messiah had arrived! The news quickly spread among Jewish communities inside the Ottoman Empire and throughout Europe, in Italy, Holland, Germany, and Poland.

A striking phenomenon at this stage that is highly relevant to our discussion was the rapid growth of mythical beliefs and miracle tales around the proclaimed savior in a manner very similar to the stories that developed and spread about the crucified Jesus, a process referred to as *legendization* (Komarnitsky 2014a: 198). Almost immediately, and at a faster rate than in the case of Jesus, incredible fables began circulation about Sabbatai. They detailed marvels and paranormal happenings described are astonishing and reveal the power of human imagination, wishful thinking, psychological needs, and the depths people go in staking their hopes and desires in what on any other less fervent occasion they would declare absurdities. As Scholem (1973: 265–66) observed, legends about the Messiah appeared and diffused so quickly that by the autumn of 1665, they surpassed the known facts. There were reports of angelic voices emanating from a fiery cloud along with rumors that the Messiah was on the verge of finding the hidden blemish-free red heifer indicating the fulfillment of the prophecy regarding the End Times. Other stories related that at his command all Christian churches, including the one in Aleppo, had been swallowed by the earth.

Other stories related that massive rocks from heaven had battered the Church of the Sepulcher, darkness had engulfed the Gentiles, and their places of worship in different parts of Palestine had been destroyed by massive hailstones, fire, and brimstone. The Jews, however, were unaffected. The believers were thus caught up in a whirlwind of legends, miracles, and revelations. Scholem (1973: 266) adds that transition from mere "factual reality to the transfigured reality of legend" was swift and "collective enthusiasm" quickly placed an aura of sacredness upon these happenings. Komarnitsky (2014a: 198) makes an insightful comment that the legendization associated with Sabbatai occurred so rapidly and in such a remarkable way because there was already a foundation for the legends in the several-thousand-year-old Jewish messianic lore found in the Old Testament and other literature.

The rapid development of legends around Sabbatai is worth remembering when assessing apologetic claims that the length of time between the crucifixion of Jesus and the writing of the earliest gospel was too short for legend and myth to obscure the historical basis of the narratives (Komarnitsky 2014a: 188–89). The ancient historian Adrian Nicholas Sherwin-White turned Christian apologist made this argument in his book *Roman Society and Roman Law in the New Testament* (1963). Predictably, Sherwin-White's work suffers from the same canon mentality as those of other believers writing on the subject. As the historian Peter Brunt (1995: 467) points out in his biographical summary of Sherwin-White's life for the British Academy, he was "a practicing Church-man, and this may explain his unconvincing adventures into apologetics."

Sherwin-White claimed that "two generations [roughly 70 years] are too short a span to allow the mythical tendency to prevail over the hard historic core of the oral tradition" relating to Jesus (Sherwin-White 1963: 190). It is worth noting that the German theologian Julius Müller (1844: 29) had stated something very similar in the previous century in an attempt to refute the work of his detested contemporary, the Bible critic David Friedrich Strauss.

Based on the assumption that there was not enough time for the development of legendary materials, Sherwin-White posited that the Synoptic Gospels were historically reliable and described their authors "quite generally as primitive historians." Contemporary true believers, such as Lee Strobel (1998: 264), author of the journalistic book *The Case for Christ*, cite Sherwin-White's claim to assert that the gospel narratives comprise a reliable historical record. However, as already discussed, the historicity of these narratives is highly questionable (Bater 1969: 51–52; Botha 1989: 46, 55; Watson 1987: 366). Or to put it bluntly, the gospels are propaganda literature, not historical records (Crossan 1994: 163, 1998: 568; Kelber 1976; Price 2010b: 209–10; Spong 1995: 228; Strauss 1873 82–83). These texts were instruments of preaching to gain converts, and their authors were evangelists, apologists, and spin doctors, not historians (Blunt 1995, 1964: 210; Fuller 1971: 78; Martin 1991: 78; Perrin 1977: 78). David Friedrich Strauss's (1860: 68–69) brilliant response to this assertion is worth repeating:

> A frequently raised objection remains [...] namely, that the space of about thirty years, from the death of Jesus to the destruction of Jerusalem, during which the greater part of the narratives must have been formed [...] is much too short to admit of the rise of so rich a collection of myths. But [...] the greater part of these myths did not arise during that period, for their first foundation was laid in the legends of the Old Testament. [...] So that for the period between the formation of the first Christian community and the writing of the Gospels, there remains to be effected only the transference of Messianic legends, almost all ready formed, to Jesus, with some alterations to adapt them to Christian opinions, and to the individual character and circumstances of Jesus; only a very small proportion of myths having to be formed entirely new.

I have already examined in the previous chapter how the early Christians converted the Old Testament into a text about Jesus using passages out of context to fill in the missing details about what happened to Jesus, the fate of his corpse, and the true nature of his message (Helms 1988: 18, 63, 131, 2006: 92–99; Funk 1996: 238). Thus, as in the case of Sabbatai Ṣevi, the early Christian stories about Jesus were also founded upon the preexisting extensive and ancient groundwork of messianic legends in the Septuagint, or the Greek Old Testament (see Chapter 12).

As already discussed, Christian polemicists have made enormous efforts to convince themselves and others that there is a large amount of reliable historical information about the life, death, and resurrection of Jesus. In this connection, journalist Strobel (1998: 73–91) discusses the ideas of the historian Edwin Yamauchi, an enthusiastic man of faith who shares the canon mentality of other apologists regarding the absolute truth of the gospels. Like other religionists, Yamauchi considers Jesus to be a divine paranormal being and sees the resurrection as a unique eschatological happening involving divine intervention into history. Yamauchi surprisingly cites Josephus and Tacitus as providing especially valuable information regarding Jesus and the resurrection because they were unsympathetic sources. Unfortunately, as reviewed in Chapter 12, both of these sources are incredibly problematic and do not help the apologists' case in any way. Such stanch believers have meticulously dissected the relevant passages by Josephus and Tacitus, analyzing each word, phrase, and punctuation mark in hopes of uncovering "proof" that these writers were talking about Jesus. No such proof has yet been offered. Why does it require so much effort to glean the most trivial bits of information as evidence for such a pivotal miracle? After all, religionists claim that Jesus is the Light of the World, so should not the evidence for such an awesome figure be as bright as the sun? It should, but it is not.

Returning to our discussion of the Messiah from Smyrna, another similarity between Sabbatai Ṣevi and Jesus was the nature of the paranormal claims circulating among their followers. In both instances, various socio-psychological mechanisms contributed to mass hallucinations and paranormal experiences, such as social contagion, groupthink, top-down processing, and *folie à deux*. In the case of Sabbatai's followers, the reported miracles, and prophecies, and vision became infectious. It sufficed for one among the believer to experience a supernatural manifestation, and soon others claimed to see or feel it as well (Scholem 1973: 417).

In the year 1666, in the midst of the wild enthusiasm, "massive repentance, spiritual regeneration, visions, and miracles" engendered by the news of the Messiah's arrival, Sabbatai set off to Constantinople, where he would depose the Sultan, free his people, and bring about the Kingdom of God (Craffert 1989: 344). However, something bizarre happened. The Turks arrested Sabbatai on a charge of sedition. The Sultan gave the Messiah the option of converting to Islam or execution. Sabbatai opted to convert for which he earned a substantial pension and an appointment as the Sultan's doorkeeper (Scholem 1973: 678–81). He died in exile 10 years later.

What transpired next is remarkable. As Scholem (1973: 792–93) notes, the messiah's apostasy caught his followers and enemies by complete surprise. An apostate Messiah was an unparalleled phenomenon for which there were no precedents in Jewish literary tradition. Of interest to this discussion is how the Sabbatians rationalized and transformed this shocking and seemingly irresolvable set of circumstances that went against everything they believed into a positive affirmation of their faith. The similarities between these circumstances and how the followers of Jesus dealt with his death are striking. Rather than Sabbatai's dumbfounded devotees abandoning their faith and melting away because of their Messiah's disgraceful behavior, some did precisely what the theory of cognitive dissonance predicts. They developed an entirely new theology that made it possible to cope with the agonizing inconsistency through rationalization.

In many cases, at this juncture, a new charismatic figure may emerge to undertake the reformulation of the beliefs. In this case, it was the self-appointed ambassador from heaven Nathan of Gaza. As in the case of Peter and other foremost disciples, a compelling vision from God explained the Messiah's apostasy and revealed the needed secrets to press onward, spurring Nathan in his role as the new sect leader (Scholem 1973: 203–5). Like the disciples of Jesus, Nathan reconfigured the traditional Jewish doctrine of the Messiah to accommodate the embarrassing circumstances confronting Sabbatai's followers.

It was the development of such alternative doctrines that rapidly took shape in the years after the apostasy that enabled the movement to survive (Scholem 1973: 793, 795). As in many other cases in the history of religion, Scholem (1973: 795) adds, two factors were involved: deeply held convictions whose truths were independent of rational reflection; and the need to somehow rationalize the shocking contradiction between faith and historical reality. The outcome was the birth of an entirely innovative Sabbatian theology. The paramount author of the new doctrine was Nathan of Gaza.

Like the Torah-observant disciples of Jesus, the followers of Sabbatai turned to the Jewish Scriptures. They also scrutinized rabbinic Haggadah and kabbalistic texts to make sense of the bewildering events that had transpired. Not surprisingly they found exactly what they were looking for, namely all sorts of allusions to Sabbatai Ṣevi and his apostasy. What this entailed, of course, was a great deal of reading between the lines, interpretation, and twisting of passages, a talent for which, as Scholem (1973: 803) observes, "the Jews forever have had such an uncontested reputation." Sabbatai's followers went about their task by scouring the sacred texts, rabbinic aphorisms, paradoxical sayings in the kabbalistic literature, and other Jewish writings selecting verses, pieces of verses, and snippets of texts. The hitherto unnoticed implications of these verses were teased out in a way as to create material never before encountered in Jewish literature. This was not mere "exegetical nonsense," as some historians have portrayed it, Scholem (1973: 802–3) adds, but the creation of an original ideology capable of coping with the contradictions in the life and career of their Redeemer.

The new theology elucidated the appalling apostasy as a planned and necessary strategy to defeat evil, thereby creating an utterly original doctrine that from the perspective of traditional Judaism would be considered deviant and heretical. As Scholem (1973: 800) explains, Nathan and his acolytes stressed that unlike all the other saints and prophets who had stayed above the dangers of the *qelippah*, or the realm of evil and demons, this Messiah had taken the descent into the depths of hell ("the terrible *descensus ad inferos*"). He did this so that "He may do His work, strange is His work, and bring to pass His act, strange is his Act" [Isaiah 28:21] (Scholem 1973: 800).

The Messiah's apostasy thus acquired cosmic significance by radically recasting orthodox conceptions of the relationship between the forces of good and evil. This effort illustrates the powers of human imagination and wishful thinking and the extremes to which people venture to make sense of and rationalize what does not make sense and is entirely implausible, which are all in line with the theory of cognitive dissonance. The new Sabbatian theology, Scholem (1973: 800) observes, postulated that for the Messiah to accomplish his mission, the holiness embodied in him had to descend into impurity, with the good assuming the form of evil. To expunge evil required total identification with it. This would give the appearance that evil has been empowered but would, in fact, finally defeat it from within. The parallels with what the disciples of Jesus did are undeniable. Through the same sort of "interpreting, hairsplitting, and twisting texts," they concocted the idea of a Messiah who dies only to come back at some later date to finish his mission.

Another resemblance between the two groups was the reaction of Sabbatai's followers to the death of their unconventional Messiah. When Sabbatai died in 1676, his followers did not consider it a "real death" but a kabbalistic mystery. The Sabbatian legend that developed around the Messiah's demise placed him in a cave that he specially prepared for his passing. However, when his brother entered the grotto, he found it empty and wrote: "neither Our Lord nor anything else was in the cave, but it was full of light" (Scholem 1973: 920). In other words, the Messiah was not really dead but had become hidden or entered into a state of occultation. Thus, here too, we find an "empty tomb" story. Historians generally agree that the resemblances are not due to Christian influence on these seventeenth-century Jews, many of whom lived in Muslim countries, but due to comparable circumstances faced by the early Christians and the Sabbatians (Berger 2008: 157).

The way the Sabbatians addressed a seemingly irresolvable inconsistency confronting them is therefore highly reminiscent of what the disciples of Jesus did with their novel conception of resurrection that cast a failed Messiah as a victorious one. Apostasy in one case and death in the other came to stand for the opposite of their conventional meanings and significance. As Scholem (1973: 795) notes, both movements were the products of the twin factors of faith and rationalizations that entailed explaining the unprecedented circumstances of their respective Saviors. The disciples of Jesus accomplished this through the idea of the resurrection and the expectation of his triumphant return as Savior and Judge. Scholem (1973: 795) added,

> Both Christianity and the Sabbatian movement took at their point of departure the ancient Jewish paradox of the Suffering Servant which, however, they stressed with such radicalism that they practically stood it on its head. Both movements gave rise to a mystical faith centered on a definite historical event, and drawing its strength from the paradoxical character of this event.

### *Lubavitch Messianism: Implications for Early Christianity*

The second case that also bears remarkable parallels with early Christianity is the messianic movement that started in the 1990s among a group of Hasidic Jews called the Lubavitch, or Chabad (Marcus 2000: 382). This movement is examined by the Orthodox Jewish scholar and outspoken Lubavitch critic David Berger in his book *The Rebbe, the Messiah, and the Scandal of Orthodox Indifference* (2008). Simon Dein offers an anthropological assessment of Lubavitch messianism in his book *Lubavitcher Messianism: What Really Happens When Prophecy Fails?* (2012). The historian of Jewish mysticism Elliot Wolfson provides a historical treatment in his book *Open Secret: Postmessianic Messianism and Mystical Revision of Menaḥem Mendel Schneerson* (2009).

Lubavitch is the name of the town in Ukraine where the movement began, and Chabad is an acronym for "wisdom, understanding, and knowledge" (Marcus 2000: 381). Since the late 1940s, the main Lubavitch center has been New York, but there are approximately 200,000 followers around the world. The Lubavitch refer to their spiritual leader as "Rebbe" (from the Yiddish word "rabbi"), a personage thought capable of prophecy, who can perform miracles and act as a link between believers and God. According to

Jewish teachings, the concept of messiah or *Moshiach* ("the anointed") and the task of waiting for his arrival are basic tenets and an obligation for the faithful. Hassidic doctrine holds further that a potential messiah is born in every generation, but the disclosure of his identity and his inauguration depends on whether the time of redemption has arrived. Of course, this provides a convenient excuse to explain why such a person has failed to appear at any given historical period.

At the start of the 1990s, some members of Lubavitch began to openly proclaim that the last Rebbe, a man named Menaḥem Mendel Schneerson, was the long-awaited Messiah who would redeem the world and usher the End of Time. They based their case for messianic status on Schneerson's attributes as a highly educated man of great wisdom and perception known for his religious and secular scholarship, piety, powers of prophecy, and the ability to work miracles (Dein 2012: 55). Several books containing stories about the Rebbe's miraculous deeds were published (Gotfryd 2000: 58–59; Touger and Touger 1993–1994), which are similar to the miracle stories about Jesus in the gospels (Marcus 2000: 386). The Rebbe's own published works, referred to as "good news" (i.e., gospel) or "news of the redemption," were printed and disseminated widely on the assumption that facilitating the spread of the news around the world would bring the end of days even faster, beliefs that are analogous to those in the gospels of Mark 13:10 and Matthew 24:10 (Marcus 2000: 386).

While Schneerson did not personally say he was the Messiah, he made no efforts to hinder his followers from making such proclamations about him. Thus, as Marcus (2000: 393) points out, like Jesus who did nothing to stop the crowd from acclaiming him the Messiah as he entered Jerusalem (Mark 11:1–10), Schneerson's silence was a tacit acceptance of the acclamation. Followers published several books on Schneerson's messianic status and undertook an intensive Messiah campaign. At this time, messianic enthusiasm was high in the Lubavitch communities, and Schneerson's followers expected that he would imminently disclose his true identity and announce the coming of the Redemption (Dein 2012: 55). At the same time, the Rebbe himself proclaimed the impending arrival of the Moshiach in a tacit manner similar to Jesus's dialogues about the Son of Man (Marcus 2000: 394; on the son of man concept, see Walker 1972).

Then a significant and unexpected setback occurred. In March 1992, Schneerson suffered a stroke that left him speechless and paralyzed on the right side of his body. Remarkably, the reaction of his followers was to downplay the stroke as "mild" and offer post hoc rationalizations for the Rebbe's illness derived from the Scriptures, such as Isaiah 53 ("a man of suffering, and familiar with pain … surely he took up our pain and bore our suffering"). Such passages made it evident that the Rebbe himself had elected to become sick to take on "the suffering of the Jewish people," and the stroke was a necessary step before he could reveal himself as the redeemer (Dein 2012: 56). Meanwhile, the Lubavitchers sought to restore his health magically by holding daily meetings and reciting Psalms. The critical point is that the Rebbe's incapacity and inability to talk did not deter his followers from their messianic expectations that he would disclose his identity as the savior at any moment. Still, Schneerson did nothing to dissuade his followers from their beliefs.

In March 1994, the Rebbe suffered another stroke, went into a coma, and was put on a ventilator. News reports indicated that Schneerson was "brain dead," but his followers remained steadfast. They explained the latest calamity as an indicator that "we are on the threshold of the Messianic era" (Dein 2012: 395). Followers held additional and more intense prayer meetings to hasten his recovery. These efforts, however, were unsuccessful. The Rebbe never regained consciousness and died on June 12, 1994. Again, something incredible ensued. The response of Rebbe's followers at this point closely parallels the reaction of the disciples of Jesus to the death of their rabbi. Marcus (2000: 394) observes the most remarkable similarity between Chabad messianism and the early Christians was the reaction of the disciples to the death of Jesus and the response of the Rebbe's followers to his death in 1994. In both cases, the death of the ostensible Messiahs before they could accomplish their missions hurled the believers into an acute state of cognitive dissonance. In both cases, the respective believers resolved this incongruity through rationalizations and the reinterpretation of their beliefs.

Schneerson's funeral in Queens, New York, attracted thousands and was a curious affair. Some wailed and sobbed. Some began to shout, "the Revelation will come," expecting until the moment of burial for the Rebbe to rise from his casket and proclaim himself as Moshiach. Other sang and danced and averred that Schneerson's Resurrection and Redemption would follow. Arnie Gotfryd (2000: 100), a Lubavitcher believer and enthusiast, described the funeral as follows:

> Some were crying hysterically, some were simply stunned, some felt betrayed, almost everyone was miserably sad. Strangely, many were feasting, singing and dancing, and yet they too were sad. They were certain that any second, the hoax would end and the Rebbe would get up and lead us to the redemption right then and there.

To cope with the cognitive dissonance caused by this calamity, the believers adamantly claimed that the Rebbe was not actually dead (Dein 2010: 553–4, Marcus 2000: 396).

The idea of a dead Messiah developed by the Rebbe's followers departs so radically from the orthodox Jewish perspective as to bewilder mainstream believers. Berger (2008: 13), a devout Orthodox Jew, described his reaction as "bewilderment" and feeling as if he had entered "a Jewish Twilight Zone" where all conventions were on hold. He adds that a movement of "a posthumously false messianism" is so alien to Judaism that mainstream believers could not imagine such circumstance even for an instant. As in the case of the followers of Sabbatai Şevi, there is no evidence that this belief developed under the influence of Christianity (cf. Dein 2012: 133). The Lubavitcher belief in the resurrected Messiah was the product of a similar "interpreting, hairsplitting, and twisting texts," or creative eschatological hermeneutics.

The acceptance of Schneerson's resurrection rapidly spread through Lubavitch communities around the world, attracting a significant number of additional believers. Berger (2008: 25, n. 9) makes an important observation about the parallels to the rise of Christianity:

> The stunning speed with which this belief has spread in the absence of a scintilla of evidence should capture the attention of all historians who have struggled to explain and reconstruct the development of early Christian beliefs in the resurrection and the empty tomb.

Some Lubavitcher said the Messiah, now the embodiment of God, was in a state of occultation in some paranormal realm, as did the followers of Sabbatai Şevi and Jesus. Others said he has been risen from the dead non-corporeally and is supernaturally more potent than ever before and that the faithful could keenly feel his spiritual presence (Marcus 2000: 396–97). Marcus (2000: 398) draws parallels between this and the experiences of the post-resurrection Christians. As in the case of Jesus, death before accomplishing his messianic mission did not disqualify the Rebbe from the status of the Messiah. Also, like the disciples of Jesus in first-century Palestine, his followers were convinced that soon the Risen One would reappear to complete the works he started during his lifetime. As Marcus (2000: 400–1) observes, this shared apocalyptic vision offered "a reality so topsy-turvy that death has been transformed into a revelation of life," and this constitutes one of the numerous profound parallels between Chabad messianism and early Christianity.

As in the case of Jesus's disciples, after a brief initial state of confusion about how to proceed, the Lubavitchers assumed the task of facilitating the coming redemption by doubling their global outreach efforts and undertaking extensive proselytization, as predicted by Festinger's theory. Thus, while the Messiah tarries in some posited supernatural realm in a state of occultation, his followers have assumed the task of spreading the good news (i.e., gospel) to prepare for and hasten the arrival of the promised Kingdom. Dein and Dawson (2008) note that the Rebbe's death has resulted in a remarkable process of reaffirmation and has powerfully energized the movement that has continued to grow ever since. There is no question that most of Lubavitch Hasidim have complete faith in the return of the Rebbe as the Messiah and are willing to wait for the joyous occasion as long as it is necessary. The Lubavitch, except for Sabbatianism, comprise the largest and most enduring messianic movement in Jewish history since ancient times. As in the case of Sabbatianism and Christianity, the Lubavitch movement has also survived the death of its Messiah.

Lubavitch messianism provides crucial insights into how similar processes could have led the early Christians to conclude that Jesus was not dead and had been risen and would return to accomplish the tasks he began during his lifetime. It also shows the extemporaneous evolution of entirely novel theological precepts that depart radically from the Judaic Messiah concepts from which they derived. Like the followers of the Rebbe, the early Christians reached a similar conclusion without a shred of evidence.

Despite the bluff and bluster of Christian apologists such as Wright, Craig, Habermas, and Yamauchi, who parrot each other's aphorisms, the beliefs about a dead Messiah who returns from the grave could easily crystallize without a reanimated corpse or the discovery of an empty grave or vacant sepulcher. In other words, the formulation of resurrection beliefs does not require that a dead man walked out of a crypt. Creative eschatological hermeneutics and post hoc rationalizations provide all that is necessary. The Lubavitch case is highly significant because, as Komarnitsky (2014a: 57) perceptively points out, if twentieth-century Jews fully aware that their Messiah is dead and buried are able to rationalize that he had undertaken the suffering of the Jews and would come back from the dead, then it is not at all difficult to understand how some first-century Jews, who did not know the whereabouts of their executed Messiah "rationalize that he died for their sins and had already resurrected from the dead."

Based on his analysis of Lubavitch messianism Berger (2008: 156–57) makes several relevant observations about the case of Jesus and his followers in first-century Palestine. The crucifixion, he points out, was a terrible psychological blow to the disciples of Jesus. The Messiah was supposed to restore Israel, not die. Some of the Jews who had followed Jesus probably accepted the sad conclusion made necessary by his death that they had made a mistake and dropped out. The redemption was yet to come, and they had to wait. For others, however, the belief was too powerful and facing the truth too painful. There simply had to be an explanation to resolve the paradox of a crucified Messiah. The answer was, first, the postulate that Jesus had come back to life. Second, the Bible was scoured for evidence to show that a Messiah would be killed without bringing redemption. Third, a second round of activities was posited, when the Messiah would return and complete his mission. Finally, an explanation was needed for the Messiah's failure on the first round, which was that the initial mission was not the redemption of Israel, something that had not occurred, but the atonement of original sin as a form of inner redemption (Berger 2008: 156–57).

The parallels between Sabbatian and Lubavitch messianism and Christianity are undeniable. Arguments by apologists and believers about the extraordinary, miraculous, and unique nature of their Messiah are highly implausible. For example, Wright (2003: 718) asserts that the premise that Jesus came back to life "possesses unrivaled power to explain the historical data at the heart of early Christianity." He adds that "the historian, of whatever persuasion, has no option but to affirm both the empty tomb and the 'meetings' with Jesus as historical events: they took place as real events" (Wright 2003: 709). Such statements are simply untrue. Here it is again necessary to point out that these are assertions by a profoundly committed religionist, who is unable to be objective, has already accepted the truth of Christianity on faith, and is under the false impression that the New Testament sources contain incontrovertible historical evidence. The believer has no other options. However, nothing is further from what is the case, as we have seen. It is deplorable that such writers, Church-men and evangelicals, misrepresent their ventures into unpersuasive apologetics as historical research and scholarship. As a final comment, Wright and like-minded ideologues are recapitulating the exact ideas formulated by the archaic mentality of ignorant and superstitious Middle Eastern peasants who died 2,000 years ago. It is astonishing that in all that time Christian theology has failed to produce a better story than what is on offer.

# Chapter Seventeen

# CONCLUSIONS: WHY RELIGIOUS AND PARANORMAL BELIEFS PERSIST AND THEIR DANGERS

*As long as people believe in absurdities, they will continue to commit atrocities.*

—Voltaire, *Questions sur les miracles* (1765)

*Baloney, bamboozles, careless thinking, flimflam, and wishes disguised as facts are not restricted to parlor magic and ambiguous advice on matters of the heart. Unfortunately, they ripple through mainstream political, social, religious, and economic issues in every nation.*

—Carl Sagan, *The Demon-Haunted World* (1995)

*The simple fact of the matter is that every religious belief in every culture in the world is demonstrably untrue. Regardless of whether the religious practices are organized communally or ecclesiastically, regardless of whether they are mediated by shamans or priests, regardless of whether the intent is manipulative or supplicative … all such practices are founded upon nonfalsifiable or falsified beliefs concerning the paranormal.*

—James Lett, Science, Religion, and Anthropology (1997)

Most rational people reject supernatural claims by the founders of recently developed religions, sects, and cults such as Mormonism, the Christian Science Church, Scientology, Peoples Temple, Order of the Solar Temple, and Heavens Gate because details about how those belief systems originated are well-known. These religions, like all others, also claim supernatural origins, cosmic significance, as well as espousing mysteries and miracles. However, the deceitful character and motives of the creators of these dogmas are well-known. For this reason, aside from the indoctrinated, few others will accept their supernatural truth claims and cosmic significance. Yet, the assertions and tenets of these recently created religions are no different and no less implausible than those associated with the older, established faiths. These also claim celestial significance and promote beliefs in divine appearances, talking fiery bushes, seas parting, people transmuted into globs of salt, serpents that hold conversations and engage in conspiracies, global deluges, angelic visitations, virgin births, the dead coming back to life, and other miraculous and supernatural happenings.

Why are these beliefs not treated with skepticism in the same way as Scientology, Mormonism, and the others mentioned? A significant reason is that these religions have been around for thousands of years and no contemporary eyewitnesses were present when they were formulated (Coyne 2015: 83). As the philosopher and skeptic Paul Kurtz (2013: 165) observed in this regard, people venerate antiquity that tends to lend these religions an aura of believability. Moreover, these faiths have extensive institutional and infrastructural support that bolsters and propagates their respective X-claims.

Furthermore, none of these religions provide any means whereby a person can assess or validate their central tenets. Instead, each one possesses various measures to safeguard their truth claims from any validation, testing, and disconfirmation. Critics and disbelievers are subject to threats, intimidation, and even the death penalty. All religions have such inbuilt defense mechanisms that render their truth claims and divine status immune from critical appraisal. To question is forbidden and sacrilegious. And believers are taught that the mysteries of faith transcend meager human intellect and rational faculties and so it is pointless even to ask questions or try to comprehend.

If these defenses are insufficient to squelch doubts, then there is the diabolical lie, that is, that anyone who questions or criticizes our sacred dogma is Satan or one of his minions bent on leading the righteous astray. Dennett (2006: 207–8) characterizes this as "an all-purpose loyalty-enforcer paranoia in a pill" guaranteed to silence the critics. Let us also not forget the ghastly sentence of perpetual combustion in the depths of some fiery, demon-infested locale that is pronounced upon those who question, doubt, or disbelieve. Incineration in hell represents, as the philosopher Keith Parsons (2011: 253–54) puts it, "an eternal glorification of vindictiveness." It ensures that believers will remain obedient and submissive. This perverse doctrine is, in Parson's words, the supreme appeal to force that warns the faithful to obey the precepts on offer or suffer penalties too horrendous to imagine.

Thus, the X-claims upon which these belief systems are anchored have persisted over time and humanity remains shackled to superstitions inherited from a benighted time of ignorance, cruelty, and violence. But adherence to such beliefs has had very high costs. The reason is that whenever and wherever people imagine that the only requirement for them to justify their actions is to believe the truth of their supernatural propositions without evidence, they become capable of all sorts of holy horrors, examples of which stain every page of human history (cf., Harris 2004: 85).

Critical thinkers have long observed that religion rather than being a divine miracle is a contrivance of devious ideologues to terrify and enslave humankind and monopolize power and profit. Those indoctrinated in such belief systems or are infected with the meme for religion have no desire to examine their faiths critically. Rarely is open-minded exploration and comparison with other belief systems ever entertained, which is why otherwise reasonable and intelligent individuals view religion as something independent of facts. Religion teaches that its precepts are cosmic and do not require evidence in the way that is considered necessary for assertions and claims in other areas of life. Theologians, religious demagogues, and other such specialists reinforce these assumptions. Thus, believers are kept spellbound with specious arguments, theological casuistry, mystification, obfuscations, absurdities, and falsehoods.

The result has been a bizarre and peculiar phenomenon, namely, that highly implausible and nonsensical anachronistic beliefs that were aspects of ancient and defunct understandings of the world and universe have been retained, while the broader worldviews to which these beliefs belonged were discarded long ago. Hence, most rational people today do not believe that seeds grow into plants by magic, spit and mud can cure blindness, lightning, tsunamis, hurricanes are divine punishment for sinful behavior, or that demons cause disease. Yet, these same individuals accept a wide range of equally preposterous supernatural postulates or X-claims inherited from the past. These include the premise that humans share the world with invisible paranormal beings, such as ghosts, demons, and devils, miracles, the idea of life after death, the possibility of communication between dead people and the living, spirit possession, and the resurrection of the dead. There is also the belief in an invisible Super Being out there, or up there, who is particularly interested in humans and continuously monitors every aspect of people's behavior, down to what they eat, what they wear, the length of their hair, and so forth.

Another reason for the persistence of these supernatural beliefs is that a majority of the faithful acquire their ideas as part of their upbringing or enculturation. In other words, they are indoctrinated instead of adopting their beliefs through reason, argumentation, and comparison. As discussed in Chapter 1, this process entails hijacking an evolutionary feature of our species, which is for the young to accept the authority of their elders that once enhanced survival among early human populations. Children were taught to adopt the ideas and trust the experiences of adults obviating the need for them to start from scratch and engage in dangerous trial-and-error approaches to various tasks that others in their groups had already discovered and mastered. Religious indoctrination specialists and enforcers realized long ago the importance and necessity of instilling their tenets in the minds of the very young as soon as possible. As the sixteenth-century Jesuit missionary Francis Xavier put it, "Give me the children until they are seven, and anyone may have them afterward."

For this reason, religionists seek to control educational systems or provide their own alternative systems. Hence, the enormous efforts behind Bible colleges, seminaries, monasteries, *madrassas*, religious homeschooling, creation museums, and Ark and Bible amusement parks. These comprise incredibly effective ways of fostering X-claims and instilling all sorts of superstitious beliefs in the receptive minds of children before they have developed any critical analytical skills.

Above all, religion incites intolerance, prejudice, misogyny, gender apartheid, racism, and violence toward others. The love, compassion, and God's mercy endlessly preached never extends to outsiders and nonbelievers. History demonstrates this terrible dark side of faith-based beliefs. Devotees everywhere are taught that people of other faiths should be denigrated, suppressed, or even exterminated. God or the gods above seem to always sanction this type of violence against other human beings as moral deeds of the highest caliber. Hence the enthusiastic way in which believers have time and again engaged in crusades, *jihads*, inquisitions, beheadings, burning people alive, torture, mutilation, and unlimited vehemence toward apostates and nonbelievers.

What is ironic is that these acts are invariably committed in the name of some compassionate, merciful, and loving God. For these reasons, great atrocities have been committed by purported moral and ethical religious people across space and throughout time. Also included here are the so-called religions of peace, such as Buddhism. Pious cruelty, abuse, violence, and homicide, as we have seen, are an in-built aspect of all religions. All religious dogmas, to state it differently, contain subroutines for violent behavior that spring into action under particular circumstances with ghastly consequences.

Finally, whatever solace religion pervades is always in the form of some future reward in a conjectured paranormal realm after death. Immediate solutions to the adversities of life are never provided. Otherwise, we would not be living in the kind of world in which we live that is rife with suffering, inequities, and cruelties.

Today, religious beliefs have become one of the most formidable and threatening forces in the world. It seems that we have entered a new "age of faith" and a time of reinvigorated fundamentalisms and dogmatic beliefs along with all of the horrors and cruelties that come with such faith-based belief systems.

In the twenty-first century, not only has uncompromising religious fundamentalism become a renewed political threat to human life, liberty, property, and cultural resources but also emboldened purveyors of supernaturalism, paranormalists, home-grown ayatollahs, and religious fundamentalists are now touting their beliefs as superior explanatory frameworks and more authentic investigatory paradigms in comparison to science and rationality. However, as I have discussed, by issuing this challenge and crossing over into the domain of science, advocates of these modes of thought have made their own central epistemological and ontological premises legitimate subjects for critical scrutiny and skeptical analysis. In this study I have attempted to put the entire range of supernatural and paranormal ideas to such systematic skeptical assessment using textual analysis, historical records, anthropological findings, the principles of evolutionary and cognitive psychology, prior probabilities, the presence or absence of disconfirming evidence, and the availability of non-supernatural explanations that accord with empirical evidence. The results of this inquiry have not been very flattering concerning the veracity and credibility of the perspectives espoused by the purveyors of paranormal and supernatural modes of thought.

In this book, we have also seen that supernatural and related paranormal beliefs, and the belief in God or the gods, in particular, are attributes of our evolved cognitive systems that appeared for adaptive reasons during humanity's early career on this planet. These include our hyperactive agency detection module, the theory of mind, and various related cognitive dispositions. These are the mechanisms that render X-claims alluring to the point of hijacking our cognitive apparatus and switching off all rational ideation and critical faculties. The paranormal and supernatural beings with which humans have remained enthralled are cognitive illusions that distort how we think about ourselves, the world, and the universe, indeed all of objective reality. History is replete with the awful repercussions of such distorted thinking. The evolutionary chimera that there is an awe-inspiring and fearsome punishing moral overseer, an invisible Super-Agent watching us from on high, kept early *Homo sapiens* cowering in fear and compelled them to behave appropriately in the context of increasingly larger, more extensive, and complex social groups. For this reason, this cognitive fantasy embedded inside human heads turned out to be a convenient and powerful tool of social control later on with the emergence of hierarchical societies. Ruling elites and demagogues in the ancient complex societies and their priestly classes who usurped all things religious employed the illusion of a paranormal overseer to monopolize and maintain their power and privilege.

In our time, religion continues to serve this purpose. Thus, people have remained shackled to archaic fantasies and superstitions. It is probably the case, as evolutionary psychologist Jesse Bering (2013: 200–201) points out, that entirely expunging or deprogramming God from our heads may never be possible. However, recognizing this illusion for what it genuinely represents offers us some choices. The first is to continue as our evolutionary antecedents did during humanity's childhood and credulously submit to our cognitive illusions and hold on to archaic myths and anachronistic precepts. That option has led humans time after time to engage in unimaginable horrors and atrocities against others of their kind to appease their purported angry, vindictive, jealous gods who paradoxically need puny humans to defend their reputations. Or we can liberate our minds and psyches from such ancient, obsolete, and often pernicious fantasies. As Bering (2013: 201) puts it,

> Do we keep blindly serving our genes and continue falling for this spectacular evolutionary ruse of a caring God, or do we peek behind the curtain and say, "Aha! That's not God, that's just Nature up to her dirty little tricks!"

Can humanity move beyond childhood and refuse to remain shackled to this archaic illusion and the credulities that our ancestors invented to sustain it? Can people give up their addiction to X-claims? I hope so. Given the circumstance confronting everyone today in this globally connected planet, it is certainly time for humans to rise above their childish superstitions. Whether they will is unclear.

Finally, what can we say about the merits of an "Augustinian science," which holds that "God periodically adjusts the orbits of the planets," "has created life specially," and has "intelligently designed certain features of the natural world," as a better alternative to science? Based on the assessment of the best theistic arguments, the answer is not much. The theistic perspective, Augustinian science, or whatever other labels one wishes to employ, comprise a set of X-claims. All such claims have been demystified, disconfirmed, and debunked by the neurosciences, evolutionary and cognitive psychology, and scientific anthropology.

# REFERENCES


Abel, Reuben. 1976. *Man Is the Measure: A Cordial Invitation to the Central Problems of Philosophy*. New York: The Free Press.

Al-Ghazālī. 2000. *The Incoherence of the Philosophers*. Provo, UT: Brigham Young University Press.

———. 2005. "Al-Ghazālī, Rescuer from Error." In *Medieval Islamic Philosophical Writings*, edited by Muhammad Ali Khalidi, 59–98. Cambridge: Cambridge University Press.

Alcock, James. 1981. *Parapsychology: Science or Magic*. London: Pergamon.

———. 1985. "Parapsychology as a 'Spiritual Science.'" In *A Skeptic's Handbook of Parapsychology*, edited by Paul Kurtz, 537–68. Buffalo, NY: Prometheus Books.

———. 1990. *Science and Supernature: A Critical Appraisal of Parapsychology*. Buffalo, NY: Prometheus Books.

———. 2003. "Give the Null Hypothesis a Chance." In *Psi Wars: Getting to Grips with the Paranormal*, edited by James Alcock, Jean Burns, and Anthony Freeman, 29–50. Charlottesville, VA: Imprint Academic.

Alder, Shelly. 2011. *Sleep Paralysis: Nightmares, Nocebos, and the Mind-Body Connection*. New Brunswick, NJ: Rutgers University Press.

Aleman, André, and Frank Larøi. 2009. *Hallucinations: The Science of Idiosyncratic Perception*. Washington, DC: American Psychological Association.

Allison, Dale. 2005. *Resurrecting Jesus: The Earliest Christian Tradition and Its Interpreters*. New York: T&T Clark.

Alper, Mathew. 2008. *The God Part of the Brain: A Scientific Interpretation of Human Spirituality and God*. Naperville, IL: Sourcebooks.

Ambasciano, Leonardo. 2018. *An Unnatural History of Religions: Academia, Post-Truth, and the Quest for Scientific Knowledge*. London: Bloomsbury.

American Society for Psychical Research. 1907. *Proceedings of the American Society for Psychical Research*, vol. 1. Boston, MA: H.B. Turner.

Anderson, Hugh. 1964. *Jesus and Christian Origins: A Commentary on Modern Viewpoints*. New York: Oxford University Press.

Andrae, Tor. 1960. *Mohammed: The Man and His Faith*. New York: Harper and Row.

Archer, Gleason. 1982. *New International Encyclopedia of Bible Difficulties*. Grand Rapids, MI: Zondervan.

Armstrong, Karen. 1983. *The First Christians: St. Paul's Impact on Christianity*. New York: Macmillan.

———. 2014. *Fields of Blood: Religion and the History of Violence*. New York: Anchor Books.

Arnold, Ludwig. 1990. "Altered States of Consciousness." In *Altered States of Consciousness*, edited by Charles Tart, 18–33. San Francisco: Harper.

Atran, Scott. 2002. *In Gods We Trust: The Evolutionary Landscape of Religion*. Oxford: Oxford University Press.

Atran, Scott, and Joseph Henrich. 2010. "The Evolution of Religion: How Cognitive By-Products, Adaptive Learning Heuristics, Ritual Displays, and Group Competition Generate Deep Commitments to Prosocial Religion." *Biological Theory* 5: 18–30.

Atran, Scott, and Ara Norenzayan. 2004. "Religion's Evolutionary Landscape: Counterintuition, Commitment, Compassion, Communion." *Behavioral and Brain Sciences* 27: 713–70.

Augustine, Keith. 2015. Near-Death Experiences are Hallucinations. In *The Myth of an Afterlife: The Case against Life after Death*, edited by Michael Martin and Keith Augustine, 529–69. Lanham, MD: Rowman and Littlefield.

Augustine, Keith, and Yonatan Fishman. 2015. "The Dualist's Dilemma: The High Cost of Reconciling Neuroscience with a Soul." In *The Myth of an Afterlife: The Case against Life after Death*, edited by Michael Martin and Keith Augustine, 203–92. Lanham, MD: Rowman and Littlefield.

Ayala, Francisco. 2007. *Darwin's Gift to Science and Religion*. Washington, DC: Joseph Henry Press.

———. 2016. *Evolution, Explanation, Ethics, and Aesthetics: Toward a Philosophy of Biology*. London: Academic Press.

Bacon, Francis. [1620]. 1902. *Novum Organum*, or True Directions Concerning the Interpretation *of Nature*, edited by Joseph Devey. New York: P.F. Collier. Accessed September 1, 2018. https://oll.libertyfund.org/titles/1432.

Bader, Christopher, Joseph Baker, and Carson Mencken. 2017. *Paranormal America: Ghost Encounters, UFO Sightings, Bigfoot Hunts, and Other Curiosities in Religion and Culture*. New York: New York University Press.

Bailey, Frederick George. 1991. *The Prevalence of Deceit*. Ithaca, NY: Cornell University Press.

Baker, Robert. 1997a. "No Aliens, No Abductions: Just Regressive Hypnosis, Waking Dreams, and Anthropomorphism." In *The UFO Invasion: The Roswell Incident, Alien Abductions, and Government Coverups*, edited by Kendrick Frazier, Barry Karr, and Joe Nickell, 249–65. Amherst, NY: Prometheus Books.

———. 1997b. "The Aliens among Us: Hypnotic Regression Revisited." In *The UFO Invasion: The Roswell Incident, Alien Abductions, and Government Coverups*, edited by Kendrick Frazier, Barry Karr, and Joe Nickell, 210–27. Amherst, NY: Prometheus Books.

Balch, Robert, and David Taylor. 2002. "Making Sense of the Heaven's Gate Suicides." In *Cults, Religion, and Violence*, edited by David Bromley and J. Gordon Melton, 209–28. Cambridge: Cambridge University Press.

Ball, Walter. 1895. *A Short Account of the History of Mathematics*. London: Macmillan.

Barclay, John. 1996. "The Resurrection in Contemporary New Testament Scholarship." In *Resurrection Reconsidered*, edited by Gavin D' Costa, 13–30. Oxford: One World Publication.

Barker, Dan. 2016. *God: The Most Unpleasant Character in all Fiction*. New York: Sterling.

Barnes, Ernest William. 1948. *The Rise of Christianity*. London: Longmans, Green.

Barrett, Justin. 2004. *Why Would Anyone Believe in God?* Walnut Creek, CA: AltaMira.

———. 2009. "Cognitive Science, Religion, and Theology." In *The Believing Primate: Scientific, Philosophical, and Theological Reflections on the Origins of Religion*, edited by Jeffrey Schloss and Michael Murray, 76–99. New York: Oxford University Press.

———. 2011. *Cognitive Science, Religion, and Theology: From Human Minds to Divine Minds*. West Conshohocken, PA: Templeton Press.

Barrow, John, and Frank Tipler. 1988. *The Anthropic Cosmological Principle*. Oxford: Oxford University Press.

Bartlett, Rober. 2008. *The Natural and Supernatural in the Middle Ages*. Cambridge: Cambridge University Press.

———. 2013. *Why Can the Dead Do Such Great Things: Saints and Worshippers from the Martyrs to the Reformation*. Princeton, NJ: Princeton University Press.

Bartholomew, Robert. 2001. *Little Green Men, Meowing Nuns, and Head-Hunting Panics: A Study of Mass Psychogenic Illness and Social Delusion*. London: McFarland.

Bartholomew, Robert, and Erich Goode. 2000. "Mass Delusions and Hysterias: Highlights from the Past Millennium." In *Scientific Perspectives on Pseudoscience and the Paranormal: Readings for General Psychology*, edited by Timothy Lawson, 301–14. Upper Saddle River, NJ: Prentice Hall.

Basinger, David. 1984. "Miracles as Violations: Some Clarifications." *The Southern Journal of Philosophy* 22: 1–7.

Bater, R. Robert. 1969. "Toward a More Biblical View of the Resurrection." *Interpretation* 23, no. 1: 47–65.

Batson C. Daniel. 1976. "Religion as Prosocial: Agent or Double Agent?" *Journal for the Scientific Study of Religion* 15: 29–45.

Bauckham, Richard. 2006. *Jesus and the Eyewitnesses: The Gospels as Eyewitness Testimony*. Grand Rapids, MI: Eerdmans.

Bauer, Joseph. 1997. "A Surgeon's View of the 'Alien Autopsy.'" In *The UFO Invasion: The Roswell Incident, Alien Abductions, and Government Coverups*, edited by Kendrick Frazier, Barry Karr, and Joe Nickell, 154–60. Amherst, NY: Prometheus Books.

Baur, Ferdinand Christian. 1832. *Apollonius Von Tyana Und Christus, Oder, Das Verhältniss Des Pythagoreismus Zum Christenthum: Ein Beitrag Zur Religionsgeschichte Der Ersten Jahrhunderte Nach Christus* [Apollonius of Tyana and Christ, or, The Relation of Pythagorism to Christianity: A Contribution to the Religious History of the First Centuries After Christ]. Tübingen: L.F. Fues.

Beauvois, Jean-Léon, and Robert-Vincent Joule. 1996. *A Radical Dissonance Theory*. London: Taylor & Francis.

———. 1999. "A Radical Point of View on Dissonance Theory." In *Cognitive Dissonance: Progress on a Pivotal Theory in Social Psychology*, edited by Eddie Harmon-Jones and Judson Mills, 43–70. Washington, DC: American Psychological Association. http://dx.doi.org/10.1037/10318-003.

Begley, Sharon. 1997. "Seek and Ye Shall Find," *Newsweek*, July 20, 1997, 66–67.

Behe, Michael. 1996. *Darwin's Black Box: The Biochemical Challenge to Evolution*. New York: The Free Press.

———. 2001. "Reply to My Critics: A Response to Reviews of Darwin's Black Box: The Biochemical Challenge to Evolution." *Biology and Philosophy* 16: 685–709.

Beloff, John. 1977. "Historical Overview." In *Handbook of Parapsychology*, edited by Benjamin Wolman, Laura Dale, Gertrude Schmeidler, and Montague Ullman, 3–24. New York: Van Nostrand Reinhold.

Bennett, Jeffrey. 2012. *When the Sun Dances: Myth, Miracles, and Modernity in Early Twentieth-Century Portugal*. Charlottesville, VA: University of Virginia Press.

Benson, Herbert, Jeffery Dusek, and Jane Sherwood. 2006. "Study of the Therapeutic Effects of Intercessory Prayer (STEP) in Cardiac Bypass Patients: A Multicenter Randomizations Trial of Uncertainty and Certainty of Receiving Intercessory Prayer." *American Heart Journal* 151: 934–42.

Bentall, Richard. 2000. "Hallucinatory Experiences." In *Varieties of Anomalous Experience: Examining the Scientific Evidence*, edited by Etzel Cardeña, Steven Lynn, and Stanley Krippner, 85–120. Washington, DC: American Psychological Association.

Berger, David. 2008. *The Rebbe, the Messiah and the Scandal of Orthodox Indifference*. London: The Littman Library of Jewish Civilization.

Bering, Jesse. 2013. *The God Instinct: Psychology of Souls, Destiny, and the Meaning of Life*. London: Nicholas Breadlye.

Berlitz, Charles, and William Moore. 1980. *The Roswell Incident*. New York: Berkley Books.

Bernard, Russell. 1995. *Research Methods in Anthropology: Qualitative and Quantitative Approaches*. Walnut Creek, CA: AltaMira.

Berry, Colin. 2019. "Sindonology's 10 Biggest Mistakes." Accessed June 18, 2019. https://shroudofturinwithoutallthehype.wordpress.com/2019/04/04/sindonologys-10-biggest-mistakes/#more-11415.

Best, Robert. 1999. *Noah's Ark and the Ziusudra Epic: Sumerian Origins of the Flood Myth*. Fort Myers, FL: Enlil Press.

Beyerstein, Barry. 2007. "The Neurology of the Weird: Brain States and Anomalous Experience." In *Tall Tales about the Mind and Brain: Separating Fact from Fiction*, edited by Sergio Sala, 314–35. Oxford: Oxford University Press.

Bielo, James. 2015. *Anthropology of Religion: The Basics*. New York: Routledge.

———. 2018. *Ark Encounter: The Making of a Creationist Theme Park*. New York: New York University Press.

Bivins, Jason. 2008. *Religion of Fear: The Politics of Horror in Conservative Evangelicalism*. New York: Oxford University Press.

Blackmore, Susan. 1993 *Dying to Live: Near-Death Experiences*. Amherst, NY: Prometheus Books.

———. 1998. "Abducted by Aliens or Sleep Paralysis?" *Skeptical Inquirer* 22: 23–28.

———. 1999. *The Meme Machine*. Oxford: Oxford University Press.

Blavatsky, Helena Petrovna. [1888]. 1993. *The Secret Doctrine*. Wheaton, IL: Quest Books.

Bloom, Paul. 2004. *Descartes' Baby: How the Science of Child Development Explains What Makes Us Human*. New York: Basic Books.

———. 2009. "Religious Belief as an Evolutionary Accident." In *The Believing Primate: Scientific, Philosophical, and Theological Reflections on the Origins of Religion*, edited by Jeffrey Schloss and Michael Murray, 118–27. New York: Oxford University Press.

———. 2012. "Religion, Morality, Evolution." *Annual Review of Psychology* 63: 179–99.

Blunt, Peter. 1964. "A Historian of Rome on the New Testament." *The Oxford Magazine* 4, no. 13: 209–10.

———. 1995. "Lectures and Memoirs." *Proceedings of the British Academy* 87: 462–67.

Bode, Edward. 1970. *The First Easter Morning: The Gospel Accounts of the Women's Visit to the Tomb of Jesus*. Rome: Biblical Institute.

Bolt, Peter. 1996. "Mark 16:1–8: The Empty Tomb of a Hero?" *Tyndale Bulletin* 47: 27–38.

Bondi, Hermann. 2003. "Uniting the World—Or Dividing It: Which Outlook Is Truly Universal, Which Parochial in the Extreme?" In *Science and Religion: Are They Compatible?* edited by Paul Kurtz, Barry Karr, and Ranjit Sandhu, 145–48. Amherst, NY: Prometheus Books.

Bonner, Campbell. 1927. "Traces of Thaumaturgic Technique in the Miracles." *Harvard Theological Review* 20: 171–81.

———. 1943. "The Technique of Exorcism." *Harvard Theological Review* 36: 39–49.

Borrini, Matteo, and Luigi Garlaschelli. 2018. "A BPA Approach to the Shroud of Turin." *American Academy of Forensic Sciences*. Accessed October 6, 2018. https://onlinelibrary.wiley.com/doi/epdf/10.1111/1556-4029.13867.

Bostock, Gerald. 1994. "Do We Need an Empty Tomb." *Expository Times* 105: 201–4.

Botha, Pieter. 1989. "The Historical Domitian: Illustrating Some Problems of Historiography." *Neotestamentica* 23, no. 1: 45–59.

Bottoms, Bette, and Suzanne Davis. 1997. "The Creation of Satanic Ritual Abuse." *Journal of Social and Clinical Psychology* 16, no. 13: 112–32.

Boudry, Maarten, and Johan Braeckman. 2011. "Immunizing Strategies and Epistemic Defense Mechanisms." *Philosophia* 39, no. 1: 145–61.

Boudry, Maarten, Stefaan Blancke, and Johan Braeckman. 2010. "How Not to Attack Intelligent Design Creationism: Philosophical Misconceptions about Methodological Naturalism." *Foundations of Science* 22: 921–49.

Bourguignon, Erika. 1974 *Culture and the Varieties of Consciousness*. Addison-Wesley Module in Anthropology. No. 47. Reading, MA: Addison-Wesley.

———. 1979. *Psychological Anthropology: An Introduction to Human Nature and Cultural Difference*. New York: Holt, Rinehart, and Winston.

Boyer, Pascal. 2001. *Religion Explained: The Evolutionary Origins of Religious Thought*. New York: Basic Books.

———. 2007. Hume's Chief Objection to Natural Theology. *Religious Studies*, 43, no. 3: 249–70. http://www.jstor.org/stable/20006373.

Bradley, M. C. 2001. "The Fine-tuning Argument." *Religious Studies* 37, no. 4: 451–66.

Bradley, Raymond. 2015. *God's Gravediggers: Why No Deity Exists*. Aberdeen, UK: Ockham.

Brain, Marshall. 2014. *How "God" Works; A Logical Inquiry on Faith*. New York: Sterling.

Braithwaite, Jason. 2008. "Toward a Cognitive Neuroscience of the Dying Brain." *Skeptic* 21, no. 20: 8–16.

Brandon, Ruth. 1983. *The Spiritualists: The Passion for the Occult in the Nineteenth and Twentieth Centuries.* New York: Alfred Knopf.

Brauer, Mathew, and Daniel Brumbaugh. 2001. "Biology Remystified: The Scientific Claims of the New Creationists." In *Intelligent Design Creationism and Its Critics: Philosophical, Theological, and Scientific Perspectives*, edited by Robert Pennock, 289–334. Cambridge, MA: MIT Press.

Bridgstock, Martin. 2009. *Beyond Belief: Skepticism, Science and the Paranormal.* Cambridge: Cambridge University Press.

Brodie, Richard. 2009. *Virus of the Mind: The New Science of the Meme and How It Can Help You.* London: Hay House.

Brodie, Thomas. 2004. *The Birthing of the New Testament: The Intertextual Development of the New Testament Writings.* Sheffield: Sheffield Pheonix Press.

Bronowski, Jacob. 1973. *The Ascent of Man.* Boston: Little Brown.

Brown, Donald. 1991. *Human Universals.* New York: McGraw-Hill.

Brown, Mick. 1994. *The Death of the Messiah: From Gethsemane to the Grave: A Commentary on the Passion Narratives in the Four Gospels.* New York: Doubleday.

———. 2016. "Did Mother Teresa Really Perform Miracles?" *The Telegraph*, September 2, 2016. Accessed January 3, 2019. https://www.telegraph.co.uk/news/0/did-mother-teresa-really-perform-miracles/.

Brown, Raymond. 1972. *The Virginal Conception and Bodily Resurrection of Jesus.* New York: Paulist Press.

Brugger, Peter. 2001. "From Haunted Brain to Haunted Science: A Cognitive Neuroscience View of the Paranormal." In *Hauntings and Poltergeists: Multidisciplinary Perspectives*," edited by James Houran and Rense Lange, 195–213. Jefferson, NC: MacFarland.

Brunt, Peter. 1995. "1994 Lectures and Memoirs." *Proceedings of the British Academy* 87: 455–70.

Bultmann, Rudolf. 1965 *Theology in the New Testament.* London: SCM Press.

———. 1978. "New Testament Mythology." In *Main Currents of Western Thought: Readings in Western European Intellectual History from the Middle Ages to the Present*, edited by Franklin Le Van Baumer, 668–70. New Haven, CT: Yale University Press.

Burckhardt, Jacob. 1949. *The Age of Constantine the Great.* New York: Pantheon Books.

Bushman, Richard Lyman. 2008. *Mormonism: A Very Short Introduction.* Oxford: Oxford University Press.

Cairns-Smith, Alexander Graham.1986. *Seven Clues to the Origins of Life: A Scientific Detective Story.* Cambridge: Cambridge University Press.

Card, Jeb. 2018. *Spooky Archaeology: Myth and the Science of the Past.* Albuquerque: University of New Mexico Press.

Cardeña, Etzel, Steven Lynn, and Stanley Krippner. 2000. "Introduction: Anomalous Experience in Perspective." In *Varieties of Anomalous Experience: Examining the Scientific Evidence*, edited by Etzel Cardeña, Steven Lynn, and Stanley Krippner, 3–22. Washington, DC: American Psychological Association.

Carnley, Peter. 1987. *The Structure of Resurrection Beliefs.* New York: Oxford University Press.

Carrier, Richard. 2001. "The Guarded Tomb of Jesus and Daniel in the Lion's Den: An Argument for the Plausibility of Theft." *Journal of Higher Criticism* 8: 304–18.

———. 2005a. *Sense and Goodness without God: A Defense of Metaphysical Naturalism.* USA: Author House.

———. 2005b. "The Plausibility of Theft." In *the Empty Tomb: Jesus Beyond the Grave*, edited by Robert Price and Jeffrey Lowder, 349–68. Amherst, NY: Prometheus Books.

———. 2005c. "The Burial of Jesus in Light of Jewish Law." In *The Empty Tomb: Jesus Beyond the Grave*, edited by Robert Price and Jeffrey Lowder, 369–92. Amherst, NY: Prometheus Books.

———. 2006a. "Why I Don't Buy the Resurrection Story: The Rubicon Analogy." Accessed September 1, 2018. https://infidels.org/library/modern/richard_carrier/resurrection/rubicon.html.

———. 2006b. "Why I Don't Buy the Resurrection Story: The Main Argument." Accessed September 1, 2018. https://infidels.org/library/modern/richard_carrier/resurrection/rubicon.html.

———. 2010. "Why the Resurrection Is Unbelievable." In *The Christian Delusion: Why Faith Fails*, edited by John Loftus, 291–315. Amherst, NY: Prometheus Books.

———. 2011. "Christianity's Success Was Not Incredible." In *The End of Christianity*, edited by John Loftus, 53–74. Amherst, NY: Prometheus Books.

———. 2012. *Proving History: Bayes's Theorem and the Quest for the Historical Jesus*. Amherst, NY: Prometheus Books.

———. 2014a. *On the Historicity of Jesus: Why We Might Have Reason for Doubt*. Sheffield, UK: Sheffield Phoenix Press.

———. 2014b. "The Prospect of a Christian Interpolation in Tacitus, Annals 15.44." *Vigiliae Christianae* 68, no. 3: 264–83.

Carlino, Elvio, Liberato De Caro, Cinzia Giannini, and Giulio Fanti. "Atomic Resolution Studies Detect New Biologic Evidences on the *Turin Shroud*." 2017. PLoS ONE 12, no. 6: e0180487. Accessed Mach 1, 2019. https://doi.org/10.1371/journal.pone.0180487 pmid:28666007.

Caroll, Robert. 2003. *The Skeptic's Dictionary: A Collection of Strange Beliefs, Amusing Deceptions, and Dangerous Delusions*. Hoboken, NJ: John Wiley.

———. 2007. "Anecdotal (testimonial) Evidence." *Skepdic*. Accessed January 8, 2019. http://skepdic.com/testimon.html.

———. 2015. "The Anthropic Principle." Accessed January 18, 2019. http://skepdic.com/anthropic.html.

Carrington, Philip. 2011. *The Early Christian Church*, vol. 1. Cambridge: Cambridge University Press.

Carter, Jacob, and Emily Berman, Anita Desikan, Charise Johnson, and Gretchen Goldman. 2109. *The State of Science in the Trump Era: Damage Done, Lessons Learned, and a Path to Progress*. Washington, DC: Center for Science and Democracy.

Cartmill, Matt. 1998. "Oppressed by Evolution." *Discover* 19, no. 3: 78–83.

Cassels, Walter. 1894. *The Gospel According to Peter*. London: Longmans, Green.

Castaneda, Carlos. 1968. *The Teachings of Don Juan: A Yaqui Way of Knowledge*. Berkeley, CA: University of California Press.

Catalano, John. 2004. "Some Published Works on Biochemical Evolution." Accessed March 11, 2018. http://www.talkorigins.org/faqs/behe/publish.html.

Celsus. 1830. "The Arguments of Celsus against the Christians." In *Arguments of Celsus, Porphyry, and the Emperor Julian against the Christians*. Translated by Thomas Taylor. London: Rodd. Accessed July 17, 2018. https://www.gutenberg.org/files/37696/37696-h/37696-h.htm.

———. 1987. *On the True Doctrine: A Discourse against the Christians*. Translated by R. Joseph Hoffmann. New York: Oxford University Press.

Chapman University. 2018. "Chapman University Survey of American Fears 2018." Accessed November 22, 2018. https://www.chapman.edu/wilkinson/research-centers/babbie-center/survey-american-fears.aspx.

Cheek, John. 1959. "The Historicity of the Markan Resurrection Narrative." *Journal of Bible and Religion* 27: 191–200.

Chevalier, Ulysse. 1903. *Autour des origines du suaire de Lirey avec documents inédits* [On the Origins of the Shroud of Lirey with Unpublished Documents]. Paris, France: Picard. Accessed July 4, 2018. https://archive.org/details/autourdesorigine00chev/page/n5.

Chibnall, J. T, J. M. Jeral, and M. A. Cerullo. 2001. "Experiments on Distant Intercessory Prayer: God, Science, and the Lesson of Massah." *Archives of Internal Medicine* 161: 2529–36.

Chidester, David. 1988. *Salvation and Suicide: An Interpretation of Jim Jones, Peoples Temple, and Jonestown*. Bloomington: Indiana University Press.

Clancy, Susan. 2005. *Abducted: How People Come to Believe They Were Kidnapped by Aliens*. Cambridge, MA: Harvard University Press.

Claridge, Gordon. 2010. "Spiritual Experience: Healthy Psychoticism?" In *Psychosis and Spirituality: Consolidating the New Paradigm*, edited by Isabel Clarke, 77–88. Oxford: Wiley-Blackwell.

Clarke, Arthur C. 2003. "Credo." In *Science and Religion: Are They Compatible?*, edited by Paul Kurtz, Barry Karr, and Ranjit Sandhu, 181–87. Amherst, NY: Prometheus Books.

Clarke, Isabel. 2010. "Psychosis and Spirituality: The Discontinuity Model." In *Psychosis and Spirituality: Consolidating the New Paradigm*, edited by Isabel Clarke, 101–14. Oxford: Wiley-Blackwell.

Clifford, William K. 1999. *The Ethics of Belief and Other Essays*. Amherst, NY: Prometheus Books.

Cohn, Norman. 1970. *The Pursuit of the Millennium: Revolutionary Millenarians and Mystical Anarchists of the Middle Ages*. Oxford: Oxford University Press.

Coker, Rory. 2001. "Distinguishing Science and Pseudoscience." Austin Society to Oppose Pseudoscience Fact Sheet. Austin, Texas. Accessed August 19, 2009. https://hep.physics.utoronto.ca/~orr/wwwroot/JPH441/Pseudoscience.pdf.

Cole, John. 1983. "Reply to Meacham." *Current Anthropology* 24, no. 3: 297.

Collins, Adela. 1997. "Apotheosis and Resurrection." In *The New Testament and Hellenistic Judaism*, edited by Peder Borger and Søren Giversen, 88–100. Peabody, MA: Hendrickson.

Comings, David. 2008. *Did Man Create God? Is Your Spiritual Brain at Peace with Your Thinking Brain?* Durante, CA: Hope Press.

Conference of Catholic Bishops. 2016. *Catechism of the Catholic Church* (2nd ed.). Washington, DC: United States Conference of Catholic Bishops. Accessed October 6, 2018. http://ccc.usccb.org/flipbooks/catechism/index.html#IV.

Conner, Robert. 2006. *Jesus the Sorcerer, Exorcist, and Prophet of the Apocalypse*. Oxford: Mandrake.

Conzelmann, Hans. 1987. *Acts of the Apostles: A Commentary on the Acts of the Apostles*. Philadelphia, PA: Fortress Press.

Cooper, Joel. 1999 "Unwanted Consequences and the Self: In Search of the Motivation for Dissonance Reduction." In *Cognitive Dissonance: Progress on a Pivotal Theory in Social Psychology*, edited by Eddie Harmon-Jones and Judson Mills, 149–73. Washington, DC: American Psychological Association. Accessed September 1, 2018. http://dx.doi.org/10.1037/10318-007.

———. 2007. *Cognitive Dissonance: Fifty Years of a Classic Theory*. Los Angeles: Sage.

Cook, C. M., and Michael Persinger. 1997. "Experimental Induction of the 'Sensed Presence' in Normal Subjects and an Exceptional Subject." *Perceptual Motor Skills* 85: 683–93.

Cook, John Granger. 2000. *The Interpretation of the New Testament in Greco-Roman Paganism: Studies and Texts in Antiquity and Christianity*. Tübingen: Mohr Siebeck,

Cordry, Benjamin. 2006. "Theism and the Philosophy of Nature." *Religious Studies* 42: 273–90.

Cosmides, Leda, and John Tooby. 2000. "Consider the Source: The Evolution of Adaptations for Decoupling and Metarepresentation." In *Metarepresentations: A Multidisciplinary Perspective*, edited by Dan Sperber, 53–114. New York: Oxford University Press.

Cotter, Wendy. 1999. *Miracles in the Greco-Roman Antiquity: A Sourcebook for the Study of New Testament Miracle Stories*. New York: Routledge.

Coyne, Jerry. 2009. *Why Evolution Is True*. New York: Penguin Books.

———. 2015. *Faith Versus Fact: Why Science and Religion are Incompatible*. New York: Penguin Books.

Cowie, Catherine, and Keith Rust, Earl Ford, Mark Eberhardt, Danita Byrd-Holt, Chaoyang Li, Desmond Williams, Edward Gregg, Kathleen Bainbridge, Sharon Saydah, Linda Geiss. 2009. "Full Accounting of Diabetes and Pre-Diabetes in the U.S. Population in 1988–1994 and 2005–2006." *Diabetes Care* 32, no. 2: 287–94.

Craffert, Pieter. 1989. "The Origins of Resurrection Faith: The Challenge of a Social Scientific Approach." *Neotestamentica* 23, no. 2: 331–48.

Craig, William. 1979. *The Kalām Cosmological Argument*. London: McMillan Press.

———. 1981. *The Son Rises: Historical Evidence for the Resurrection of Jesus*. Chicago, IL: Moody.

———. 1994. *Reasonable Faith: Truth and Apologetics*. Wheaton, IL: Crossway.

———. 1995. "Did Jesus Rise from the Dead?" In *Jesus Under Fire: Modern Scholarship Reinvents the Historical Jesus*, edited by Michael Wilkins and J. P. Moreland, 147–82. Grand Rapids, MI: Zondervan.

———. 1997. "The Empty Tomb of Jesus." In *Defense of Miracles: A Comprehensive Case for God's Action in History*, edited by R. Douglas Geivett and Gary Habermas, 247–61. Downers Grove, IL: InterVarsity Press.

———. 1998. "John Dominic Crossan and the Resurrection." In *The Resurrection: An Interdisciplinary Symposium on the Resurrection of Jesus*, edited by Stephen Davis, Daniel Kendall, and Gerald O' Collins, 249–71. Oxford: Oxford University Press.

———. 2003. "The Empty Tomb." In *Gospel Perspectives: Studies of History and Tradition in the Four Gospels*, edited by R. T. France and David Wenham, 173–200. Eugene, OR: Wipf and Stock.

Cranfield, C. B. E. 1990. "The Resurrection of Jesus Christ." *Expository Times* 101: 167–72.

Crapo, Richley. 2003. *Anthropology of Religion: Unity and Diversity of Religions*. Boston: McGraw-Hill.

Craveri, Marcello. 1967. *The Life of Jesus*. New York: Grove Press.

Crislip, Mark. 2008. "Near Death Experiences and the Medical Literature." *Skeptic* 14, no. 2: 14–15.

Crossan, John.1976. "The Empty Tomb and Absent Lord." In *The Passion in Mark: Studies on Mark 14–16*, edited by Werner Kelber, 134–52. Philadelphia, PA: Fortress.

———.1994. *Jesus: A Revolutionary Biography*. New York: HarperOne.

———.1995. *Who Killed Jesus? Exposing the Roots of Anti-Semitism in the Gospel Story of the Death of Jesus*. New York: HarperOne.

———. 1998. *The Birth of Christianity: Discovering What Happened in the Years after the Execution of Jesus*. New York: HarperSanFrancisco.

Crossley, James. 2005. "Against the Historical Plausibility of the Empty Tomb Story and the Bodily Resurrection of Jesus: A Response to N. T. Wright." *Journal for the Study of the Historical Jesus* 3, no. 3: 171–86.

Cuneo, Michael. 2001. *American Exorcism: Expelling Demons in the Land of Plenty*. New York: Doubleday.

Curry, Patrick. 2010. *Divination: Perspectives for a New Millennium*. Burlington, VT: Ashgate.

Czachesz, István. 2007. "Early Christian Views on Jesus' Resurrection: Toward a Cognitive Psychological Interpretation." *Nederlands Theologisch Tijdschrift* 61, no. 1: 47–59.

———. 2008. "The Promise of the Cognitive Science of Religion for Biblical Studies." *CSSR Bulletin* 37, no. 4: 102–5.

———. 2012. *The Grotesque Body in Early Christian Discourse: Hell, Scatology, and Metamorphosis*. Sheffield: Equinox.

———. 2017. *Cognitive Science and the New Testament: A New Approach to Early Christian Research*. Oxford: Oxford University Press.

Daegling, David. 2005. *Bigfoot Exposed: An Anthropologist Examines America's Enduring Legend*. Walnut Creek, CA: Altamira Press.

Dalley, Stephanie. 2000. *Myths from Mesopotamia: Creation, the Flood, Gilgamesh, and Others*. Oxford: Oxford University Press.

Damon, Paul, D. J. Donahue, B. H. Gore, A. L. Hatheway, A. J. T. Jull, T. W. Linick, et al. 1989. "Radiocarbon dating of the Shroud of Turin." *Nature* 337, no. 6208: 611–15.

Darwin, Charles.1859. *On the Origin of Species*. London: John Murray.

———. 1887. *Life and Letters of Charles Darwin*, vol. 1. New York: D. Appleton.

Dash, Mike. 2000. *Borderland: The Ultimate Exploration of the Unknown*. New York: Dell.

David, Anthony. 2004 . "The Cognitive Neuropsychiatry of Auditory Verbal Hallucinations: An Overview." *Cognitive Neuropsychiatry* 9, nos. 1/2: 107–23.

Davis, Edward. 1991. "A Whale of a Tale: Fundamentalist Fish Stories." *Perspectives on Science and Christian Faith* 43: 224–37.

Davis, John. 2002. "Bones, Burials and Biblical History: The Results of Burial Excavation." *Bible and Spade* 15: 81–84.

Davis, Margaret, and Trevor Davis. 1991. "Resurrection or Resuscitation?" *Journal of the Royal College of Physicians of London* 25, no. 2: 167–70.

Davis, Paul. 1992. *The Mind of God: Science and the Search for Ultimate Meaning*. New York: Simon and Schuster.

Dawkins, Richard. 1976. *The Selfish Gene*. Oxford: Oxford University Press.

———. 1982. *The Extended Phenotype*. San Francisco, CA: Freeman.

———. 1991. "Viruses of the Mind." Accessed September 18, 2017. https://www.inf.fu-berlin.de/lehre/pmo/eng/Dawkins-MindViruses.pdf.

———. 1996. *The Blind Watchmaker: The Evidence of Evolution Reveals a Universe Without Design*. New York: W. W. Norton.

———. 1997. "Obscurantism to the Rescue." *Quarterly Review of Biology* 72: 397–99.

———. 1999. Foreword to *The Meme Machine*, by Susan Blackmore, vii–xvii. Oxford: Oxford University Press.

———. 2000. *Unweaving the Rainbow: Science, Delusion, and the Appetite for Wonder*. New York: Houghton Mifflin.

———. 2003. *A Devil's Chaplain: Reflections on Hope, Lies, Science, and Love*. New York: Houghton Mifflin.

———. 2006. *The God Delusion*. New York: Houghton Mifflin.

———. 2016. Foreword to *God: The Most Unpleasant Character in All Fiction*, by Dan Barker, viii–ix. New York: Sterling.

Dawson, Lorne. 1999. "When Prophecy Fails and Faith Persists: A Theoretical Overview." *Nova Religio: The Journal of Alternative and Emergent Religions* 3, no. 1: 60–82.

De Jonge, Henk Jan. 1989. "Ontstaan en ontwikkelmg van het geloof in Jezus' opstanding" [The Origin and Development of the Belief in Jesus' Resurrection]. In *Waarlijk opgestaan! Een discussie over de opstanding van Jezus Christus* [Truly Stood Up!: A Discussion about the Resurrection of Jesus Christ], edited by Henk de Jonge and Frederik Gennep, 31–50. Baarn, The Netherlands: Ten Have.

De Marchi, John. 1952. *The Immaculate Heart*: The True Story of Our Lady of Fatima. New York: Farrar, Straus, and Young.

———. 1956. *True Story of Fatima*. St. Paul, Minnesota: Catechetical Guild Educational Society.

De Mille, Richard. 1976. *Castaneda's Journey: The Power of an Allegory*. Lincoln, NE: University.com.

———. 1990. *The Don Juan Papers: Further Castaneda Controversies*. Belmont, CA: Wadsworth.

De Wesselow, Thomas. 2012. *The Sign: The Shroud of Turin and the Secret of Resurrection*. New York: Penguin.

Dein, Simon. 2001. "What Really Happens When Prophecy Fails: The Case of Lubavitch." *Sociology of Religion* 62, no. 3: 383–401.

———. 2010. "A Messiah from the Dead: Cultural Performance in Lubavitcher Messianism." *Social Compass* 57, no. 4: 537–54.

———. 2012. *Lubavitcher Messianism: What Really Happens When Prophecy Fails?* London: Bloomsbury.

Dein, Simon, and Lorne Dawson. 2008. "The 'Scandal' of the Lubavitch Rebbe: Messianism as a Response to Failed Prophecy." *Journal of Contemporary Religion* 23, no. 2: 163–80.

Dembski, William. 2003. "Skepticism's Prospect for Unseating Intelligent Design." In *Science and Religion: Are They Compatible?*, edited by Paul Kurtz, Barry Karr, and Ranjit Sandhu, 89–97. Amherst, NY: Prometheus Books.

Dennett, Daniel. 1991. *Consciousness Explained*. New York: Little, Brown.

———. 1995. *Darwin's Dangerous Idea: Evolution and the Meaning of Life*. New York: Simon and Schuster.

———. 1999. "Foreward to *Leaps of Faith: Science, Miracles, and the Search for Paranormal Consolation*, by Nicholas Humphrey," ix–xi. New York: Copernicus.

———. 2006. *Breaking the Spell: Religion as a Natural Phenomenon*. New York: Penguin Books.

Derrett, J. Duncan. 1982. *The Anastasis: The Resurrection of Jesus as a Historical Event*. Warwickshire, UK: Drinkwater.

———. 2005. "Financial Aspects of the Resurrection." In *The Empty Tomb: Jesus Beyond the Grave*, edited by Robert Price and Jeffrey Lowder, 393–410. Amherst, NY: Prometheus Books.

Dever, William. 1990. *Recent Archaeological Discoveries and Biblical Research*. Seattle: University of Washington Press.

Diaconis, Persi, and Frederick Mosteller. 1989. "Methods of Studying Coincidence." *Journal of the American Association: Applications & Case Studies* 84: 853–61.

Dobzhansky, Theodosius. 1967. *The Biology of Ultimate Concern*. New York: New American Library.

Doherty, Earl. 2005. *The Jesus Puzzle: Did Christianity Begin with a Mythical Christ?* Ottawa: Age of Reason.

———. 2009. *Jesus: Neither God nor Man: The Case for a Mythical Jesus*. Ottawa: Canadian Humanist Press.

Doniger, Wendy. 1999. "Miller, William." In *Merriam-Webster's Encyclopedia of World Religions*, edited by Wendy Doniger, 738. Springfield, MA: Merriam-Webster, Incorporated.

Donner, Fred. 2008. "The Qur'ān in Recent Scholarship: Challenges and Desiderata." In *The Qur'ān in Its Historical Context*, edited by Gabriel Said Reynolds, 29–50. New York: Routledge.

Drange, Theodore. 1998. *Nonbelief and Evil: Two Arguments for the Nonexistence of God*. Amherst, NY: Prometheus Books.

Draper, Paul. 2002. "Irreducible Complexity and Darwinian Gradualism: A Reply to Michael J. Behe." *Faith and Philosophy* 19: 3–12.

Drosnin, Michael. 1997. *The Bible Code*. New York: Simon and Schuster.

———. 2002. *Bible Code II: The Countdown*. New York: Viking.

———. 2010. *Bible Code III: Saving the World*. London: Weidenfeld and Nicolson.

Drummond, Henry. 1896. *The Lowell Lectures on the Ascent of Man*. London: Hodder and Stoughton.

Dunbar, Robin. 2003. "The Social Brain: Mind, Language, and Society in Evolutionary Perspective." *Annual Review of Anthropology* 32: 163–81.

———. 2004. *The Human Story: A New History of Mankind's Evolution*. London: Faber and Faber.

Dunn, James. 1985. *The Evidence for Jesus: The Impact of Scholarship on Our Understanding of How Christianity Began*. London: SCM.

———. 2003. *Jesus Remembered*, vol. 1. Grand Rapids, MI: Eerdmans.

Durkheim, Émile. [1912] 1961. *The Elementary Forms of the Religious Life*. New York: Collier Books.

Earman, John. 1987. "The Sap Also Rises: A Critical Examination of the Anthropic Principle." *American Philosophical Quarterly* 24, no. 4: 307–17.

Eddy, Paul, and Gregory Boyd. 2007. *The Jesus Legend: A Case for the Historical Reliability of the Synoptic Jesus*. Tradition. Grand Rapids, MI: Baker.

Edis, Taner. 1998. "Taking Creation Seriously: Are Skeptics Answering Creationists Effectively?" *Skeptic* 6: 2–56.

———. 2008. *Science and Nonbelief*. Amherst, NY: Prometheus Books.

Edwards, David. 2017. *Caravan of Martyrs: Sacrifice and Suicide Bombing in Afghanistan*. Oakland, CA: University of California Press.

Ehrman, Bart. 2005. *Lost Christianities: The Battles for Scripture and the Faiths We Never Knew*. Oxford: Oxford University Press.

———. 2009. *Jesus, Interrupted: Revealing the Hidden Contradictions in the Bible (and Why We Don't Know About Them)*. New York: HarperOne.

———. 2011. *Forged: Writing in the Name of God—Why the Bible's Authors Are Not Who We Think They Are*. New York: HarperOne.

———. 2014. *How Jesus Became God: The Exaltation of a Jewish Preacher from Galilee*. New Work: HarperOne.

———. 2016. *Jesus before the Gospels: How the Earliest Christians Remembered, Changed, and Invented Their Stories of the Savior*. New York: HarperOne.

Eisler, Robert. 1931. *The Messiah, Jesus, and John the Baptist: According to Flavius Josephus' Recently Rediscovered "Capture of Jerusalem" and other Jewish and Christian Sources*. New York: Dial Press.

Elbert, Jerome. 2003. "Does the Soul Exist? From the Mythological Soul to the Conscious Brain." In *Science and Religion: Are They Compatible?*, edited by Paul Kurtz, Barry Karr, and Ranjit Sandhu, 243–55. Amherst, NY: Prometheus Books.

Eliade, Mircea. 1963a. *Myth and Reality*. New York: Harper and Row.

———. 1963b. *Patterns in Comparative Religion.* Cleveland: Meridian Books.
———.1969. *The Quest.* Chicago, IL: University of Chicago Press.
Ellens, J. Harold. 2008a. "God and Science." In *Miracles: God, Science, and Psychology in the Paranormal,* vol. 2: *Religious and Spiritual Events,* edited by J. Harold Ellens, 1–16. Westport, CT: Praeger.
———. 2008b. Biblical Miracles and Psychological Process; Jesus as Psychotherapists." In *Miracles: God, Science, and Psychology in the Paranormal,* vol. 1: *Religious and Spiritual Events,* edited by J. Harold Ellens, 1–14. Westport, CT: Praeger.
Eller, Jack. 2009. *Introducing Anthropology of Religion: Culture to the Ultimate.* New York: Routledge.
Ellwood, Robert. 1995. "UFO Religious Movements." In *America's Alternative Religions,* edited by Timothy Miller, 393–400. New York: State University of New York Press.
Emery, C. Eugene, Jr. 1995 "'Alien Autopsy' Show and Tell: Long on Tell, Short on Show." *Skeptical Inquirer* 19: 15–16, 55.
———. 1997. "Top-Secret Balloon Project Looms over TV Movie on the Roswell Incident." In *The UFO Invasion: The Roswell Incident, Alien Abductions, and Government Coverups,* edited by Kendrick Frazier, Barry Karr, and Joe Nickell, 94–97. Amherst, NY: Prometheus Books.
Esler, Philip. 1996. *Community and Gospel in Luke-Acts: The Social and Political Motivations of Lucan Theology.* Cambridge: Cambridge University Press.
Espinoza, John. 2013. *The Biblical God Does Not Exist: Argument and Evidence.* No Publisher.
Evans, Christopher. 1977. *Explorations in Theology,* vol. 2. London: SCM Press.
Evans, Hilary. 1984. *Visions, Apparitions, and Alien Visitors: A Comparative Study of the Entity Enigma, from Ancient Astronauts to Modern UFOnauts.* Northamptonshire: The Aquarian Press.
Evans-Pritchard, Edward. 1965. *Theories of Primitive Religion.* Oxford: Clarendon Press.
Everitt, Nicholas. 2004. *The Non-Existence of God.* New York: Routledge.
Eyghen, Hans Van. 2019. "Are Design Beliefs Safe?" *Studia Humana* 1, no. 8: 75–83.
Fagan, Garret, and Chris Hale. 2001. "The New Atlantis and the Dangers of Pseudohistory." *Skeptic* 9, no. 1: 78–87.
Feldman, Louis. 1984. *Josephus and Modern Scholarship.* Berlin: De Gruyter.
Fenwick, Peter. 2001. "The Neurophysiology of Spirituality and Mysticism: Recent Developments." In *Psychosis and Spirituality: Consolidating the New Paradigm,* edited by Isabel Clarke, 9–18. Oxford: Wiley-Blackwell.
Festinger, Leon. 1957. *A Theory of Cognitive Dissonance.* Evanston, IL: Row, Peterson.
Festinger, Leon, Henry Riecken, and Stanley Schachter. 1956. *When Prophecy Fails.* Minneapolis: University of Minnesota Press.
Feynman, Richard. 1992. "Richard Feynman." In *Superstrings: A Theory of Everything?,* edited by P. Davies and Julian Brown, 92–210. Cambridge: Cambridge University Press.
Fingelkurts, Alexander, and Andrew Fingelkurts. 2009. "Is Our Brain Hardwired to Produce God, or is our Brain Hardwired to Perceive God? A Systematic Review of the Role of the Brain in Mediating Religious Experience." *Cognitive Processing* 10: 293–326.
Finkelstein, Israel, and Neil Silberman. 2001. *The Bible Unearthed: Archaeology's New Vision of Ancient Israel and the Origin of Its Sacred Texts.* New York: Free Press.
Fischer, Karl Martin. 1980. *Das Ostergeschehen* [The Easter Event]. Göttingen: Vandenhoeck & Ruprecht.
Fisher, Ronald. 1937. *The Design of Experiments.* London: Oliver & Boyd, Gail.
Fishman, Yonata. 2009. "Can Science Test Supernatural Worldviews?" *Science and Education* 18: 813–37.
Fishman, Yonata, and Maarten Boudry. 2013. "Does Science Presuppose Naturalism (or Anything at All)?" *Science and Education* 22: 921–49.
Fitzgerald, David. 2010. *Nailed: Ten Christian Myths That Show Jesus Never Existed at All.* USA: Lulu.
Flew, Antony. 1989. "The Problem of Evidencing the Improbable, and the Impossible." In *Exploring the Paranormal: Perspectives on Belief and Experience,* edited by George Zollschan, John Schumaker, and Greg Walsh, 313–27. Bridgeport, UK: Prism.

Fogelin, Robert. 2003. *A Defense of Hume on Miracles*. Princeton, NJ: Princeton University Press.

Fontana, David. 2003. *Psychology, Religion, and Spirituality*. Oxford; Blackwell.

Forrest, Barbara. 2002. "The Newest Evolution of Creationism." *Natural History* 11, no. 3: 80.

Forrest, Barbara, and Paul Gross. 2004. *Creationism's Trojan Horse: The Wedge of Intelligent Design*. Oxford: Oxford University Press.

Fox, Robin Lane.1986. *Pagans and Christians*. San Francisco, CA: Harper and Row.

Frankenberry, Nancy, and Hans Penner. 1999. "Clifford Geertz's Long-Lasting Moods, Motivations, and Metaphysical Conceptions." *The Journal of Religion* 79, no. 4: 617–40.

Frazer, James. [1918]. 1988. *Folklore in the Old Testament: Studies in Comparative Religion, Legend, and Law*. New York: Avenel Books.

Freud, Sigmund. [1927]. 1961. *The Future of an Illusion*, edited by James Strachey. London: Hogarth Press.

Freeman, Charles. 2009. *A New History of Early Christianity*. New Haven, CT: Yale University Press.

———. 2011. *Holy Bones, Holy Dust: How Relics Shaped the History of the Medieval World*. New Haven, CT: Yale University Press.

———. 2012. "The Shroud of Turin and the Image of Edessa: A Misguided Journey." Accessed November 6, 2018. http://www.llanoestacado.org/freeinquiry/skeptic/shroud/articles/freeman_shroud_edessa_misguided_journey/.

Freke, Timothy, and Peter Gandy. 1999. *The Jesus Mysteries: Was the "Original Jesus" a Pagan God*. New York: Harmony Books.

French, Christopher. 2001a. "Why I Study Anomalistic Psychology." *The Psychologist* 14: 356–57.

———. 2001b. *Paranormal Perception: A Critical Examination*. The Institute for Cultural Research. Monograph Series 42: 1–24.

French, Christopher, and Julia Santomauro. 2007. "Something Wicked This Way Comes: Cases and Interpretations of Sleep Paralysis." In *Tall Tales about the Mind and Brain: Separating Fact from Fiction*, edited by Sergio Sala, 380–400. Oxford: Oxford University Press.

French, Christopher, and Anna Stone. 2014. *Anomalistic Psychology: Exploring Paranormal Belief and Experience*. New York: Palgrave Macmillan.

French, Christopher, and Krissy Wilson. 2003. "Fantastic Memories: The Relevance of Research into Eyewitness Testimony and False Memories for Reports of Anomalous Experiences." *Journal of Consciousness Studies* 10: 153–74.

———. 2006. "Incredible Memories—How Accurate are Reports of Anomalous Events?" *European Journal of Parapsychology* 212: 166–81.

Frye, Northrop.1982. *The Great Code: The Bible and Literature*. New York: Harcourt Brace.

Fuller, Reginald. 1971. *The Formation of the Resurrection Narratives*. New York: Macmillan.

Funk, Robert (and the Jesus Seminar). 1996. *Honest to Jesus: Jesus for a New Millenium*. New York: HarperCollins.

———. 1998. *The Acts of Jesus: What Did Jesus Really Do?* New York: HarperCollins.

Funk, Robert, and Roy Hoover (and the Jesus Seminar). 1993. *The Five Gospels: What Did Jesus Really Say?* New York: HarperCollins.

Futuyma, Douglas. 1982. *Science on Trial: The Case for Evolution*. New York: Pantheon Books.

Gager, John. 1975. *Kingdom and Community: The Social World of Early Christianity*. Englewood Cliffs, NJ: Prentice Hall.

Galton, Francis. 1872. "Statistical Inquiries into the Efficacy of Prayer." *Fortnightly Review* 12: 125–35.

Gardner, Martin. 1957. *Fads and Fallacies in the Name of Science*. New York: Dover.

———. 1989. *Science: Good, Bad, and Bogus*. Buffalo, NY: Prometheus Books.

Gardner-Smith, Percival. 1926. *The Narratives of the Resurrection: A Critical Study*. London: Methuen.

Gaskin, John. 1976. "The Design Argument: Hume's Critique of Poor Reason." *Religious Studies* 12, no. 3: 331–45.

Gauch, Hugh. 2009. "Science, Worldviews, and Education." *Science and Education* 18: 667–95.

Geertz, Clifford. 1973. *The Interpretation of Cultures*. New York: Basic Books.
Geivett, Douglas. 1997. "The Evidential Value of Miracles." In *Defense of Miracles: A Comprehensive Case for God's Action in History*, edited by Douglas Geivett and Gary Habermas, 178–98. Downers Grove, IL: InterVarsity Press.
Gennaro, Rocco, and Yonatan Fishman. 2015. "The Argument from Brain Damage Vindicated." In *The Myth of an Afterlife: The Case against Life after Death*, edited by Michael Martin and Keith Augustine, 105–33. Lanham, MD: Rowman and Littlefield.
Gildenberg, Bernard, and David Thomas. 1998. "Case Closed: Reflections on the 1997 Air Force Report." *Skeptical Inquirer* 22: 31–36.
Gilovich, Thomas. 1991. *How We Know What Isn't so: The Fallibility of Human Reason in Everyday Life*. New York: The Free Press.
Gillooly, Robert. 1990. *All about Adam and Eve: How We Came to Believe in Gods, Demons, Miracles, and Magical Rites*. Amherst, NY: Prometheus Books.
Ginges, Jeremy, Ian Hansen, and Ara Norenzayan. 2009. "Religion and Support for Suicide Attacks." *Psychological Science* 20, no. 2: 224–30.
Glass-Coffin, Bonnie. 2010. "Anthropology, Shamanism, and Alternative Ways of Knowing- Being in the World: One Anthropologist's Journey of Discovery and Transformation." *Anthropology and Humanism* 35, no. 2: 204–17.
Glass-Coffin, Bonnie, and Kiiskeentum. 2010. "The Future of a Discipline: Considering the Ontological/Methodological Future of the Anthropology of Consciousness, Part IV: Ontological Relativism or Ontological Relevance: An Essay in Honor of Michael Harner." *Anthropology of Consciousness* 23, no. 2: 113–26.
Glassner, Barry. 1999. *The Culture of Fear: Why Americans Are Afraid of the Wrong Things*. New York: Basic Books.
Goldin, Hyman. 1948. *The Case of the Nazarene Reopened*. New York: Exposition Press.
Goguel, Maurice. 1953. *The Birth of Christianity*. London: George Allen & Unwin.
Goldschmidt, Walter. 1968. Foreward to *The Teachings of Don Juan: A Yaqui Way of Knowledge*, by Carlos Castaneda, xxi-xxii. Berkeley: University of California Press.
González, Justo. 2005. *Essential Theological Terms*. Louisville, KY: Westminster John Knox Press.
Goodacre, Mark. 2001. *The Synoptic Problem: A Way through the Maze*. London: Continuum Books.
Goode, Erich. 2012. *The Paranormal: Who Believes, Why They Believe, and Why It Matter*. Amherst, NY: Prometheus Books.
Goodman, Felicitas. 1990. *Where the Spirits Ride the Wind: Trance Journeys and other Ecstatic Experiences*. Bloomington: Indiana University Press.
Goodrick-Clarke, Nicholas. 2005. *The Occult Roots of Nazism: Secret Aryan Cults and Their Influence on Nazi Ideology: The Ariosophists of Austria and Germany, 1890–1935*. New York: I.B. Tauris.
Gorham, Charles. 1908. *The First Easter Dawn: An Inquiry into the Evidence for the Resurrection of Jesus*. London: Watts.
Gosse, Philip Henry. 1857. *Creation (Omphalos): An Attempt to Untie the Geological Knot*. London: J. Van Voorst.
Gotfryd, Arnie. 2000. *Living in the Age of Moshiach*. New York: Mendelsohn Press.
Goulet, Jean-Guy, and Bruce Miller. 2007. "Embodied Knowledge: Steps toward a Radical Anthropology of Cross-Cultural Encounters." In *Extraordinary Anthropology: Transformations in the Field*, edited by Jean-Guy Goulet and Bruce Miller, 1–14. Lincoln: University of Nebraska Press.
Goulet, Jean-Guy, and David Young. 1994. "Theoretical and Methodological Issues." In *Being Changed: Anthropology of Extraordinary Experience*, edited by Jean-Guy Goulet and David Young, 298–335. Orchard Park, NY: Broadview.
Gould, Stephen. 1999. *Rock of Ages: Science and Religion in the Fullness of Life*. New York: Ballantine Books.
Gould, Stephen Jay, and Richard Lewontin. 1979. "The Spandrels of San Marco and the Panglossian Paradigm: A Critique of the Adaptationist Programme." *Proceedings of the Royal Society of London. Series B, Biological Sciences* 205, no. 1161: 581–98.

Goulder, Michael. 1996. "Baseless Fabric of a Vision." In *Resurrection Reconsidered*, edited by Gavin D' Costa, 48–61. Oxford: One World Publication.

Graham, Jesse, and Jonathan Haidt. 2010. "Beyond Beliefs: Religions Bind Individuals into Moral Communities." *Personality and Social Psychology Review* 14, no. 1: 140–50.

Gray, Kurt, and Daniel Wegner. 2010. "Blaming God for our Pain: Human Suffering and the Divine Mind." *Personality and Social Psychology Review* 14, no. 1: 7–16.

Green, Celia, and Charles McCreery. 1975. *Apparitions*. London: Hamish Hamilton.

Griffel, Frank. 2016. "Al-Ghazali." In *The Stanford Encyclopedia of Philosophy*, edited by Edward Zalta. Accessed September 6, 2018. https://plato.stanford.edu/archives/win2016/entries/al-ghazali.

Grindal, Bruce. 1983. "Into the Heart of Sisala Experience: Witnessing Death Divination." *Journal of Anthropological Research* 39, no. 1: 60–80.

Grove, Harry. 1996. *Relic, Icon or Hoax? Carbon Dating the Turin Shroud*. London: Institute of Physics.

Grünbaum, Adolf. 2001. "A New Critique of Theological Interpretations of Physical Cosmology." *British Journal of Philosophy* 51: 1–43.

Guignebert, Charles. 1958. *Jesus*. New York: University Books.

Gundry, Robert. 2000. "Trimming the Debate." In *Jesus' Resurrection, Fact or Figment?: A Debate Between William Lane Craig and Gerd Lüdemann*, edited by Paul Copan and Ronald Tacelli, 104–23. Downers Grove, IL: Intervarsity Press.

Guthrie, Stewart. 1980. "A Cognitive Theory of Religion." *Current Anthropology* 21, no. 2: 181–203.

———. 1993. *Faces in the Clouds: A New Theory of Religion*. Oxford: Oxford University Press.

———. 1997a. "Anthropomorphism: A Definition and a Theory." In *Anthropomorphism, Anecdotes, and Animals*, edited by Robert Mitchell, Nicholas Thompson, and H. Lyn Miles, 50–58. Albany, NY: State University of New York Press.

———. 1997b. "The Origin of an Illusion." In *Handbook of the Anthropology of Religion*, edited by Stephen Glazier, 489–504. Westport, CT: Greenwood Press.

———. 2001. "Why Gods? A Cognitive Theory." In *Religion in Mind: Cognitive Perspectives on Religious Belief, Ritual, and Experience*, edited by Jensine Andresen, 94–112. Cambridge: Cambridge University Press.

———. 2007. "Anthropology and Anthropomorphism in Religion." In *Religion, Anthropology, and Cognitive Science*, edited by Harvey Whitehouse and James Laidlaw, 37–62. Durham, NC: Carolina Academic Press.

———. 2008. "Spiritual Beings: A Darwinian, Cognitive Account. In *The Evolution of Religion: Studies, Theories, and Critiques*, edited by Joseph Bulbulia, Richard Sosis, Erica Harris, Russell Genet, Cheryl Genet, and Karen Wyman, 239–45. Santa Margarita, CA: Collins Foundation Press.

Haas, Nicu. 1970. "Anthropological Observations on the Skeletal Remains from Giv'at ha-Mivtar." *Israel Exploration Journal* 20: 38–59.

Habermas, Gary. 2001. "The Late Twentieth-Century Resurgence of Naturalistic Responses to Jesus' Resurrection." *Trinity Journal* 22: 179–96.

———. 2003. "Affirmative Statement." In *Did Jesus Rise from the Dead?: The Resurrection Debate*, edited by Gary Habermas, Antony Flew, and Terry Miethe, 15–32. Eugene, OR: Wipf and Stock.

Haldane, John. 1927. *Possible Worlds*. London: Harper.

Hall, Deborah, David Matz, and Wendy Wood. 2010. "Why Don't We Practice what we Preach? A Meta-Analytic Review of Religious Racism." *Personality and Social Psychology Review* 14, no. 1: 126–39.

Hall, John, and Philip Schuyler. 1997 . "The Mystical Apocalypse of the Solar Temple." In *Millennium, Messiahs, and Mayhem*, edited by Thomas Robbins and Susan Palmer, 285–312. New York: Routledge.

Hamnett, Ian. 1973. "Sociology of Religion and Sociology of Error." *Religion* 3: 1–12.

Hanson, Norwood. 1971. *What I Do Not Believe, and Other Essays*. Dordrecht, Holland: D. Reidel.

Hardyck, Jane, and Marcia Braden. 1962. "Prophecy Fails Again: A Report of a Failure to Replicate." *Journal of Abnormal and Social Psychology* 65, no. 2: 137–41.

Harmon-Jones, Eddie, and Judson Mills. 1999. "An Introduction to Cognitive Dissonance Theory and an Overview of Current Perspectives on the Theory." In *Cognitive Dissonance: Progress on a Pivotal Theory in Social Psychology*, edited by Eddie Harmon-Jones and Judson Mills, 3–21. Washington, DC: American Psychological Association. Accessed September 1, 2018. http://dx.doi.org/10.1037/10318-001.

Harris, Marvin. 1971. *Culture, Man, and Nature: An Introduction to General Anthropology*. New York: Thomas Y. Crowell.

———. 1977. *Cannibals and Kings: The Origins of Cultures*. New York: Random House.

———. 1979. *Cultural Materialism: The Struggle for a Science of Culture*. New York: Random House.

———. 1987. *Why Nothing Works: The Anthropology of Daily Life*. New York: Simon & Schuster.

———. 1989. *Our Kind: Who We Are, Where We Came from, Where We Are Going*. New York: Harper and Row.

———. 1994. "Cultural Materialism Is Alive and Well and Won't Go Away until Something Better Comes Along." In *Assessing Cultural Anthropology*, edited by Robert Borofsky, 62–76. New York: McGraw-Hill.

Harris, Murray. 1983. *Raised Immortal: Resurrection and Immortality in the New Testament*. Grand Rapids, MI: Eerdmans.

Harris Poll. 2009. What People Do and Do Not Believe in. Accessed September 1, 2018. https://theharrispoll.com/ wp-content/uploads/2017/12/Harris_Poll_2009_12_15.pdf.

Harris, Sam. 2004. *The End of Faith: Religion, Terror, and the Future of Reason*. New York: W.W. Norton.

Harris, William, and William Isley. 2002. "Massah and Mechanisms." *Archives of Internal Medicine* 162: 1420.

Harvey, Nicholas Peter. 1989. "Frames of Reference for the Resurrection." *Scottish Journal of Theology* 42, no. 3: 335–39.

Haught, James 1990 *Holy Horrors: An Illustrated History of Religious Murder and Madness*. Amherst, NY: Prometheus Books.

Hay, David. 1990. *Religious Experience Today: Studying the Facts*. London: Mowbray.

Heath, Chip, and Dan Heath. 2007. *Made to Stick: Why Some Ideas Take Hold and Others Come Unstuck*. London: Arrow Books.

Hellweg, Joseph, Joshua Englehardt, and Jesse Miller. 2015. "Raising the Dead: Altered States, Anthropology, and the Heart of Sisala Experience." *Anthropology and Humanism* 40, no. 2: 206–24.

Helms, Randel. 1988. *Gospel Fictions*. Amherst, NY: Prometheus Books.

———. 1997. *Who Wrote the Gospels?* Altadena, CA: Millennium Press.

———. 2006. *The Bible against Itself: Why the Bible Seems to Contradict Itself*. Altadena, CA: Millennium Press.

Hendrickx, Herman. 1978. *The Resurrection Narratives of the Synoptic Gospels*. London: Chapman.

Hengel, Martin. 1977. *Crucifixion in the Ancient World and the Folly of the Message of the Cross*. Philadelphia, PA: Fortress.

Herzer, Catherine. 2001. *Literacy in Roman Palestine*. Tübingen: Mohr Siebeck.

Hick, John. 1993. *The Metaphor of God Incarnate: Christology in a Pluralistic Age*. Louisville, KY: Westminster/John Knox Press.

Hines, Terence. 2003. *Pseudoscience and the Paranormal*. Amherst, NY: Prometheus Books.

Hinton, Devon, David Hufford, and Laurence Kirmayer. 2005. "Culture and Sleep Paralysis." *Transcultural Psychiatry* 41, no. 1: 5–10.

Hitchens, Christopher. 2007. *God Is Not Great: How Religion Poisons Everything*. New York: Twelve Hachette Book Group.

Hoffmann, R. Joseph. 1984. *Jesus Outside the Gospels*. Buffalo, NY: Prometheus Books.

———. 1987. "General Introduction." In *Celsus on the True Doctrine: A Discourse Against the Christians*, translated by R. Joseph Hoffmann, 5–49. New York: Oxford University Press.

———. 1996. Foreword to *The Jesus Legend*, by George Wells, vii–xiii. Peru, IL: Carus.
Hoffmeier, James. 2015. *Akhenaten and the Origins of Monotheism*. Oxford: Oxford University Press.
Holden, Janice, Bruce Greyson, and Debbie James. Eds. 2009. *The Handbook of Near-Death Experiences: Thirty Years of Investigation*. Santa Barbara, CA: Praeger.
Holt, Nicola, Christine Simmonds-Moore, David Luke, and Christopher French. 2012. *Anomalistic Psychology*. Basingstoke: Palgrave Macmillan.
Holton, Gerald. 1992. "How to Think about the 'Anti-Science' Phenomena." *Public Understanding of Science* 1: 103–28.
Holtzmann, Oskar. 1904. *The Life of Jesus*. London: Adam & Charles Black.
Hood, Bruce. 2009. *Supersense: From Superstition to Religion—the Brain Science of Belief*. London: Constable and Robinson.
Hoover, Roy. 2000. "A Contest between Orthodoxy and Veracity." In *Jesus' Resurrection: Fact or Figment?: A Debate Between William Lane Craig & Gerd Lüdemann*, edited by Paul Copan and Ronald Tacelli, 124–46. Downers Grove, IL: Intervarsity Press.
———. 2008. "Was Jesus' Resurrection a Historical Event?" In *The Resurrection of Jesus: A Sourcebook*, edited by Bernard Scott, 75–92. Santa Rosa, CA: Polbridge Press.
Horsfall, Sara. 2000. "The Experiences of Marian Apparitions and the Mary Cult." *The Social Science Journal* 37, no. 3: 375–84.
Horsley, Richard. 1993. *Jesus and the Spiral of Violence: Popular Jewish Resistance in Roman Palestine*. Minneapolis, MN: Augsburg Fortress.
Horton, Robin. 1960. "A Definition of Religion, and Its Uses." *The Journal of the Royal Anthropological Institute of Britain and Ireland* 90, no. 2: 201–26.
Houdini, Harry. 1924. *Houdini: A Magician among the Spirits*. New York: Harper.
Houran, James, and Michael Thalbourne. 2001. "Further Study and Speculation on the Psychology of "Entity Encounter Experiences." *Journal of the Society for Psychical Research* 65: 26–37.
Howson, Colin, and Peter Urbach. 2006. *Scientific Reasoning: The Bayesian Approach*. Peru, IL: Open Court.
Hubbard, Timothy. 2002. "Some Correspondences and Similarities between Shamanism and Cognitive Science: Interconnectedness, Extension of Meaning, and Attribution of Mental States." *Anthropology of Consciousness* 13, no. 2: 24–45.
Hufford, David. 1982. *The Terror That Comes in the Night: An Experience-Centered Study of Supernatural Assault Traditions*. Philadelphia: University of Pennsylvania Press.
Hull, John. 1974. *Hellenistic Magic and the Synoptic Tradition*. Naperville, IL: A. R. Allenson.
Humber, Thomas. 1978. *The Sacred Shroud*. New York: Pocket Books.
Hume, David. [1779]. 1980. *Dialogues Concerning Natural Religion*, 2nd ed. London. Accessed September 1, 2018.https://archive.org/details/dialoguesconcern1779hume/page/n3.
———. [1757]. 1889. *The Natural History of Religion*. London: A. and H. Bradlaugh Bonner. Accessed September 1, 2018. https://archive.org/details/dialoguesconcern1779hume/page/n3.
———. [1748]. 1902. *Enquiries Concerning the Human Understanding and Concerning the Principles of Morals*. Oxford: Clarendon Press. Accessed September 1, 2018. https://oll.libertyfund.org/titles/341.
———. [1758]. 1987. Essay IX. In *Essays Moral, Political, Literary*, by David Hume. Indianapolis, IN: Liberty Fund. Accessed September 1, 2018. http://lf-oll.s3.amazonaws.com/titles/704/0059_Bk.pdf.
Humphrey, Nicholas. 1999. *Leaps of Faith: Science, Miracles, and the Search for Supernatural Consolation*. New York: Copernicus.
Hunt, Stephen. 2001. "The Revolutionary Dimension of Millenarianism: The Case of the T'aiping Rebellion." In *Christian Millenarianism: From the Early Church to Waco*, edited by Stephen Hunt, 116–30. Bloomington: Indiana University Press.

Hunter, Jack. 2012. "Anthropology and the Paranormal." In *Paranthropology: Anthropological Approaches to the Paranormal*, edited by Jack Hunter, 21–42. Bristol, UK: Paranthropology.
———. 2018. *Engaging the Anomalous: Collected Essays on Anthropology, the Paranormal, Mediumship and Extraordinary Experience*. Hove, UK: White Crow Productions.
Hurtado, Larry. 2005. *How on Earth Did Jesus Become God?: Historical Questions about Earliest Devotion to Jesus*. Grand Rapids, MI: Willam Erdmans.
Hutton, Ronald. 1999. *The Triumph of the Moon: A History of Modern Pagan Witchcraft*. Oxford: Oxford University Press.
Hyman, Ray. 1985. "A Critical Historical Overview of Parapsychology." In *A Skeptic's Handbook of Parapsychology*, edited by Paul Kurtz, 3–96. Buffalo, NY: Prometheus Books.
Ibn Rushd (Averroes). 2005. "Ibn Rushd, The Incoherence of Incoherence." In *Medieval Islamic Philosophical Writings*, edited by Muhammad Ali Khalidi, 155–80. Cambridge: Cambridge University Press.
Ingersoll, Robert. 1907. *Lectures of Col. R. G. Ingersoll*. Chicago: Rhodes and McClure.
Irish, Donald, Kathleen Lundquist, and Vivian Nelsen. Eds. 1993. *Ethnic Variations in Dying, Death and Grief: Diversity in Universality*. New York: Routledge.
Irwin, Harvey. 2009. *The Psychology of Paranormal Belief: A Researcher's Handbook*. Hertfordshire, UK: University of Hertfordshire Press.
Irwin, Harvey, and Caroline Watt. 2007. *An Introduction to Parapsychology*. London: McFarland.
Isaak, Mark. 2002. "A Philosophical Premise of Naturalism?" Accessed October 15, 2018. http://www.talkdesign.org/faqs/naturalism.html.
Jackson, Hugh. 1975. "The Resurrection Belief of the Earliest Church: A Response to the Failure of Prophecy." *Journal of Religion* 55, no. 4: 415–25.
James, William. 1902. *The Varieties of Religious Experience: A Study of Human Nature*. New York: Longmans and Green.
———. 1909. "The Confidences of a 'Psychical Researcher.'" *The American Magazine* 68, no. 6: 580–89.
———. 1987. *William James: Writings 1902–1910*. New York: The Library of America.
Janin, Hunt. 2005. *The Pursuit of Learning in the Islamic World, 610–2003*. Jefferson, NC: McFarland.
Janowitz, Naomi. 2001. *Magic in the Roman World: Pagans, Jews, and Christians*. London: Routledge.
Jansen, Karl. 1997. "The Ketamine Model of the Near-Death Experience: A Central Role for the N-Methyl-D-Aspartate Receptor." *Journal of Near-Death Studies* 16: 5–26.
Jaynes, Julian. 1976. *The Origin of Consciousness in the Breakdown of the Bicameral Mind*. Boston: Houghton Mifflin.
Jillette, Penn. 2014a. *God, No!: Signs You May Already Be an Atheist and Other Magical Tales*. New York: Simon & Schuster.
———. 2014b. *Every Day is an Atheist Holiday!*. London: Penguin Books.
Johns, Louise, and Jim van Os. 2001. "The Continuity of Psychotic Experiences in the General Population." *Clinical Psychology Review* 21: 1125–41.
Johnson, David. 1999. *Hume, Holism, and Miracles*. Ithaca, NY: Cornell University Press.
Johnson, Dominic, and Jesse Bering. 2006. "Hand of God, Mind of Man: Punishment and the Evolution of Cooperation." In *The Believing Primate: Scientific, Philosophical, and Theological Reflections on the Origins of Religion*, edited by Jeffrey Schloss and Michael Murray, 26–43. New York: Oxford University Press.
Johnson, Luke. 1998. *Religious Experience in Earliest Christianity: A Missing Dimension in New Testament Study*. Minneapolis, MN: Fortress Press.
Johnson, Raynor. 1963. *A Religious Outlook for Modern Man*. London: Hodder and Stoughton.
Josephus, Flavius. 1996. *The Life and Works of Flavius Josephus: The Learned and Authentic Jewish Historian and Celebrated Warrior*. Translated by William Whiston. Albany, Oregon: Sage Software. https://archive.org/details/TheLifeAndWorksOfFlaviusJosephus.

———. 2007. *Josephus: The Complete Works*. Grand Rapids, MI: Christian Classics Ethereal Library. Accessed October 15, 2018. http://adventist.org.uk/__data/assets/pdf_file/0012/61122/Josephus-Complete-Works.pdf.

———. 2017. *The Jewish War*. Oxford: Oxford University Press.

Justin (Martyr), John Kaye, and William Reeves. 1889. *The First Apology of Justin Martyr, Addressed to the Emperor Antoninus Pius; Prefaced by Some Account of the Writings and Opinions of Justin Martyr.* Ancient and Modern Library of Theological Literature, 25. London: Griffith, Farran, Okeden & Welsh. Accessed March 19, 2018. https://archive.org/details/firstapologyofju00just/page/n5.

Kahl, Joachim. 1971. *The Misery of Christianity*. New York: Pelican Books.

Kahneman, Daniel. 2011. *Thinking, Fast and Slow*. New York: Farrar, Straus and Giroux.

Kakutani, Michiko. 2018. *The Death of Truth: Notes on Falsehood in the Age of Trump*. New York: Tim Duggan Books.

Kane, Margaret. 1985. "Spiritualism Exposed: Margaret Fox Kane Confesses Fraud." In *A Skeptic's Handbook of Parapsychology*, edited by Paul Kurtz, 225–34. Buffalo, NY: Prometheus Books.

Keener, Craig. 2011. *Miracles: The Credibility of the New Testament Accounts*. 2 Vols. Grand Rapids, MI: Baker.

Kelber, Werner. ed. 1976. *The Passion in Mark: Studies on Mark 14–16*. Philadelphia, PA: Fortress Press.

Kelemen, Deborah. 1999. "The Scope of Teleological Thinking in Preschool Children." *Cognition* 70: 241–72. Accessed October 15, 2018. https://www.bu.edu/cdl/files/2013/08/1999_Kelemen_Scope.pdf.

Kelemen, Deborah, and Evelyn Rosset. 2009. "The Human Function Compunction: Teleological Explanation in Adults." *Cognition* 111, no. 1: 138–43. Accessed October 15, 2018. https://doi.org/10.1016/j.cognition.2009.01.001.

Kelly, Ivan. 1998. "Why Astrology Doesn't Work." *Psychological Reports* 82, no. 2: 527–46.

Kent, Jack. 1999. *The Psychological Origins of the Resurrection Myth*. London: Open Gate Press.

Keyhoe, Donald Edward. 1953. *Flying Saucers from Outer Space*. New York: Holt.

Keynes, John Maynard. 1947. "Newton, the Man." In *Proceedings of the Royal Society Newton Tercentenary Celebrations, 15–19 July 1946*, 22–34. Cambridge: Cambridge University Press.

Kimball, Charles. 2008. *When Religion Becomes Evil: Five Warning Signs*. San Francisco, CA: HarperSanFrancisco.

———. 2011. *When Religion Becomes Lethal: The Explosive Mix of Politics and Religion in Judaism, Christianity, and Islam*. San Francisco, CA: Jossey-Bass.

Kinsolving, Lester. 1979a. "Healing Prophet Hailed as God." Jonestown Apologists Article Archive. Accessed September 19, 2018. https://jonestown.sdsu.edu/?page_id=14083.

———. 1979b. "The Prophet Who Raises the Dead." Jonestown Apologists Article Archive. Accessed September 19, 2018. https://jonestown.sdsu.edu/?page_id=14082.

Kirby, Peter. 2005. "The Case against the Empty Tomb." In *The Empty Tomb: Jesus Beyond the Grave*, edited by Robert Price and Jeffrey Lowder, 233–60. Amherst, NY: Prometheus Books.

Kirsch, Jonathan. 2006. *A History of the End of the World: How the Most Controversial Book in the Bible Changed the Course of Western Civilization*. New York: HarperSanFrancisco.

Klass, Dennis. 1999. "Developing a Cross-Cultural Model of Grief: The State of the Field." *OMEGA—Journal of Death and Dying* 39, no. 3: 153–78.

Klausner, Joseph. 1925. *Jesus of Nazareth: His Life, Times, and Teaching*. New York: Macmillan.

Klausner, William. 1994. "Going Native." *Anthropology Today* 10, no. 3: 18–19.

Klotz, Irving. 1980. "The N-Ray Affair." *Scientific American* 242, no. 5: 168–75.

Klein, Susan, and David Alexander. 2003. "Good Grief: A Medical Challenge." *Trauma* 5, no. 4: 261–71.

Kloner, Amos. 2007. "Did a Rolling Stone Close Jesus' Tomb?" In *The Burial of Jesus*, edited by Kathleen Miller, Sara Murphy, Steven Feldman, and Susan Laden, 9–13. Washington, DC: Biblical Archaeology Society.

Komarnitsky, Kris. 2014a. *Doubting Jesus' Resurrection: What Happened in the Black Box?* Draper, UT: Stone Arrow Books.

———. 2014b. "Cognitive Dissonance and the Resurrection of Jesus." *The Fourth R* 27, September/October. Accessed October 15, 2018. https://www.westarinstitute.org/resources/the-fourth-r/cognitive-dissonance-resurrection-jesus/.

Konner, Joan. 2007. *The Atheist's Bible: An Illustrious Collection of Irreverent Thoughts.* New York: Harper Collins.

Konner, Melvin. 2019. *Believers: Faith in Human Nature.* New York: W.W. Norton.

Koss-Chioino, Joan. 2010. "Introduction: Do Spirits Exist?" *Anthropology and Humanism* 35, no. 2: 131–41.

Kramer, Samuel. 1981. *History Begins at Sumer: Thirty-Nine Firsts in Recorded History.* Philadelphia: University of Pennsylvania Press.

Kreeft, Peter, and Ronald Tacelli. 1994. *Handbook of Christian Apologetics: Hundreds of Answers to Crucial Questions.* Downers Grove IL: Intervarsity Press.

Kroll, Jerome, and Bernard Bachrach. 1982. "Visions and Psychopathology in the Middle Ages." *Journal of Nervous and Mental Disease* 170: 41–49.

Krucoff, Mitchell, S. W. Crater, D. Gallup, J. C. Blankenship, M. Cuffe, M. Guarneri, R. A. Krieger, V. R. Kshettry, K. Morris, M. Oz, A. Pichard, M. H. Sketch, H. G., Koenig, D. Mark D, and K. L. Lee. 2005. "Music, Imagery, Touch, and Prayer as Adjuncts to Interventional Cardiac Care: The Monitoring and Actualization of Noetic Training (MANTRA) II Randomised Study." *The Lancet* 366: 211–17.

Kruse, Kevin. 2015. *One Nation Under God: How Corporate America Invented Christian America.* New York: Basic Books.

Kuijsten, Marcel. ed. 2008. *Reflections on the Dawn of Consciousness: Julian Jaynes's Bicameral Mind Theory Revisited.* Henderson, NV: Julian Jaynes Society.

Kümmel, Werner. 1973. *The Theology of the New Testament: According to Its Major Witnesses: Jesus-Paul-John.* Nashville: Abingdon Press.

Küng, Hans. 1984. *On Being Christian.* New York: Doubleday.

Kurlander, Eric. 2017. *Hitler's Monsters: A Supernatural History of the Third Reich.* New Haven, CT: Yale University Press.

Kurtz, Paul. 1985a. "Is Parapsychology Science?" In *A Skeptic's Handbook of Parapsychology*, edited by Paul Kurtz, 503–18. Buffalo, NY: Prometheus Books.

———. 1985b. "Spiritualists, Mediums, and Psychics: Some Evidence of Fraud." In *A Skeptic's Handbook of Parapsychology*, edited by Paul Kurtz, 177–223. Buffalo, NY: Prometheus Books.

———. 2003a. "Why Do People Believe or Disbelieve?" In *Science and Religion: Are They Compatible?*, edited by Paul Kurtz, Barry Karr, and Ranjit Sandhu, 275–89. Amherst, NY: Prometheus Books.

———. 2003b. "Examining Claims of the 'Paranatural:' Life after Death." In *Science and Religion: Are They Compatible?*, edited by Paul Kurtz, Barry Karr, and Ranjit Sandhu, 217–27. Amherst, NY: Prometheus Books.

———. 2013. *The Transcendental Temptation: A Critique of Religion and the Paranormal.* Amherst, NY: Prometheus Books.

Kuznar, Lawrence. 2008. *Reclaiming a Scientific Anthropology*. Walnut Creek, CO: AltaMira.

Labriolle, Pierre de. 1930. *Porphyre et le Christianisme* [Porphyry and Christianity]. Paris: J. Gamber.

———. 1935. *La Réaction Païenne. Étude Sur La Polémique Antichrétienne* [The Pagan Reaction. Study on the Antichristian Polemic]. Durand: Paris.

Lacy, Patrick. 2006. *Elvis Decoded: A Fan's Guide to Deciphering the Myths and Misinformation.* Bloomington, IN: AuthorHouse.

Lagemann, Robert. 1977. "New Light on Old Rays: N Rays." *American Journal of Physics* 45, no. 3: 281–84.

Lake, Kirsopp. 1907. *Historical Evidence for the Resurrection of Jesus Christ.* Trieste Publishing. Accessed October 15, 2018. https://triestepublishing.com.

Lambert, Wilfred G., and Alan R. Millard. 1969. *Atra-Hasīs: The Babylonian Story of the Flood.* Oxford, Clarendon Press.

Landes, Richard. 1999. "Millennialism." In *Merriam-Webster's Encyclopedia of World Religions*, edited by Wendy Doniger, 772–37. Springfield, MA: Merriam-Webster, Incorporated.

Landsborough, D. 1987. "St. Paul and Temporal Lobe Epilepsy." *Journal of Neurology, Neurosurgery, and Psychiatry* 50: 659–64.

Lanning, Kenneth. 1992. "A Law Enforcement Perspective on Allegations of Ritual Abuse." In *Out of Darkness: Exploring Satanism and Ritual Abuse*, edited by David Sakheim and Susan Devine, 109–46. New York: Lexington.

Larue, Gerald. 1990. *The Supernatural, the Occult, and the Bible.* Buffalo, NY: Prometheus Books.

Laurentin, René. 1990 . *The Apparition of the Blessed Virgin Mary Today.* Dublin: Veritas.

Law, Stephen. 2016. "The X-claim Argument Against Religious Belief." *Religious Studies* 54: 15–35.

Leahy, Thomas, and Grace Evans. 1983. *Psychology's Occult Doubles: Psychology and the Problem of Pseudoscience.* Chicago, IL: Nelson-Hall.

Lehmann, Arthur, and James Myers. 2001. *Magic, Witchcraft, and Religion: An Anthropological Study of the Supernatural.* Mountain View, CA: Mayfield.

Lester, David. 2015. "Is There Life after Death?: A Review of the Supporting Evidence." In *The Myth of an Afterlife: The Case against Life after Death*, edited by Michael Martin and Keith Augustine, 631–49. Lanham, MD: Rowman and Littlefield.

Lett, James. 1987. *The Human Enterprise: A Critical Introduction to Anthropological Theory.* Boulder, CO: Westview.

———. 1997a. "Science, Religion, and Anthropology." In *Anthropology of Religion: A Handbook*, edited by Stephen Glazier, 103–20. Westport, CT: Praeger.

———. 1997b. *Science, Reason, and Anthropology: The Principles of Rational Inquiry.* Lanham, MD: Roman and Littlefield.

Leudar, Ivan, and Philip Thomas. 2000. *Voices of Reason, Voices of Insanity.* London: Routledge.

Levine, Ellen. 2006. "Jewish Views and Custom on Death." In *Death and Bereavement across Cultures*, edited by Colin Parkes, Pittu Laungani, and Bill Young, 98–130. New York: Routledge.

Lewontin, Richard. 1997. "Billions and Billions of Demons." *New York Review of Books* 44, no. 1: 28–32.

Lewis, Clive Staples. 1996. *Miracles: A Preliminary Study.* New York: HarperCollins.

Lewis, James. 2000. *UFOs and Popular Culture: An Encyclopedia of Contemporary Myth.* Santa Barbara, CA: ABC-CLIO.

Licon, Jimmy. 2015. "The Fine-Tuning Argument and the Problem of Poor Design." *Philosophia* 43: 411–26.

Licona, Michael. 2010. *The Resurrection: A New Historiographical Approach.* Downers Grove, IL: Intervarsity Press.

Lilienfeld, Scott. 2005 . "The 10 Commandments of Helping Students Distinguish Science from Pseudoscience." *Observer* 18:39–40, 49–51. Accessed September 16, 2018. https://www.psychologicalscience.org/observer/the-10-commandments-of-helping-students-distinguish-science-from-pseudoscience-in-psychology.

Lillie, William. 1965. "The Empty Tomb and the Resurrection." In *Historicity and Chronology in the New Testament*, edited by Dennis, Nineham, Allan Barr, A. R. C.Leaney, C. S.Mann, H. E. W. Turner, George Ogg, A. N. Sherwin-White, W. Lillie, A. M. Ramsey, R. R. Williams, 100–45. London: SPCK.

Liu, Renyi, and Howard Ochman. 2007. "Stepwise Formation of the Bacterial System." *Proceedings of the National Academy of Sciences of the United States of America* 104, no. 17: 7116–121.

Loftus, Elizabeth. 1993. "The Reality of Repressed Memories." *American Psychologist* 48: 518–37.

Loftus, John. 2010. "At Best Jesus Was a Failed Apocalyptic Prophet." In *The Christian Delusion: Why Faith Fails*, edited by John Loftus, 316–43. Amherst, NY: Prometheus Books.

———. 2011. "Christianity is Wildly Improbable." In *The End of Christianity*, edited by John Loftus, 75–104. Amherst, NY: Prometheus Books.

Loisy, Alfred. 1962. *The Birth of the Christian Religion*. New Hyde Park, NY: University Books.

Long, Joseph. ed. 1977. *Extrasensory Ecology: Parapsychology and Anthropology*. Metuchen, NJ: Scarecrow Press.

Lowder, Jeffrey. 2005. "Historical Evidence and the Empty Tomb: A Reply to William Lane Craig." In *The Empty Tomb: Jesus Beyond the Grave*, edited by Robert Price and Jeffrey Lowder, 261–305. Amherst, NY: Prometheus Books.

Lucian of Samosata 1905. "The Death of Peregrine." In *The Works of Lucian of Samosata*, vol. 4. Translated by H. W. Fowler and F. G. Fowler, 79–94. Oxford: Clarendon Press. Accessed May 11, 2018. http://www.gutenberg.org/files/47242/47242-h/47242-h.htm#Page_79.

Luck, Georg. 2006. *Arcana Mundi: Magic and the Occult in the Greek and Roman World*. Baltimore, MD: Johns Hopkins University Press.

Lüdemann, Gerd. 1994. *The Resurrection of Jesus: History, Experience, Theology*. Minneapolis, MN: Fortress Press.

———. 1995. *What Really Happened to Jesus: A Historical Approach to the Resurrection*. Louisville, KY: Westminster John Knox Press.

———. 2004. *The Resurrection of Christ: A Historical Inquiry*. Amherst, NY: Prometheus Books.

Lyell, Charles. 1830–32. *Principles of Geology: Being an Attempt to Explain the Former Changes of the Earth's Surface, by Reference to Causes Now in Operation*. London: John Murray.

Lynch, Aaron. 1996. *Thought Contagion: How Belief Spreads through Society*. New York: Basic Books.

Lyons, William. 2004. "On the Life and Death of Joseph of Arimathea." *Journal for the Study of the Historical Jesus* 2, no. 1: 29–53.

Macan, Reginald. 1877. *The Resurrection of Christ: An Essay in Three Chapters*. London: William & Norgate.

Mack, John. 1997. *Abduction: Human Encounters with Aliens*. New York: Ballantine Books.

Mackay, Charles. 1842. *Memoirs of Extraordinary Popular Delusions and the Madness of* Crowds. London: Robson, Levey, and Franklyn.

Mackie, John. 1982. *The Miracle of Theism: Arguments for and against the Existence of God. Oxford:* Oxford University Press.

———. 2013. *The Miracle of Theism: Arguments for and against the Existence of God*. Oxford: Clarendon Press.

Madigan, Kevin, and John Levenson. 2008. *Resurrection: The Power of God for Christians and Jews*. New Haven, CT: Yale University Press.

Magness, Jodi. 2007. "What did Jesus' Tomb Look Like?" In *The Burial of Jesus*, edited by Kathleen Miller, Sara Murphy, Steven Feldman, and Susan Laden, 1–8. Washington, DC: Biblical Archaeology Society.

Mahner, Martin. 2012 . "The Role of Metaphysical Naturalism in Science." *Science and Education* 21: 1437–59.

Mahnke, Barbara, and Vanessa Morrison. 1997. "Coping with Cognitive Dissonance in a Baha'i Sect." In *Millennium, Messiahs, and Mayhem*, edited by Thomas Robbins and Susan Palmer, 73–92. New York: Routledge.

Malinowski, Bronislaw. 1955. *Magic, Science and Religion and Other Essays*. New York: Doubleday.

Mansel, Henry. 1875. *The Gnostic Heresies of the First and Second Centuries*. London: John Murray.

Marcus, Joel. 2000. "The Once and Future Messiah in Early Christianity and Chabad." *New Testament Studies* 46: 381–401.

Martin, Michael. 1990. *Atheism: A Philosophical Justification*. Philadelphia, PA: Temple University Press.

———. 1991. *The Case against Christianity*. Philadelphia, PA: Temple University Press.

Martin, Michael, and Keith Augustine. Eds.2015. *The Myth of an Afterlife: The Case against Life after Death*. Lanham, MD: Rowman and Littlefield.

Martin, Luther, and Donald Weibe. 2012. "Religious Studies as a Scientific Discipline: The Persistence of a Delusion." *Journal of the American Academy of Religion* 80, no. 3: 587–97.

Martin, Luther, and Donald Weibe. eds. 2016. *Conversations and Controversies in the Scientific Study of Religion: Collaborative and Co-authored Essays*. Leiden: Brill.

Masters, Kevin, and Glen Spielmans. 2007. "Prayer and Health: Review, Meta-Analysis, and Research Agenda." *Journal of Behavioural Medicine* 30: 329–38.

Matheson, Terry. 1998. *Alien Abductions: Creating a Modern Phenomenon*. Amherst, NY: Prometheus Books.

Mcafee, David. 2011. *Disproving Christianity: Refuting the World's Most Followed Religion*. UK: Dangerous Little Books.

———. 2017. *No Sacred Cows: Investigating Myths, Cults, and the Supernatural*. Durham, NC: Pitchstone.

McCarthy-Jones, Simon. 2012. *Hearing Voices: The Histories, Causes, and Meanings of Auditory Verbal Hallucinations*. Cambridge: Cambridge University Press.

McConnell, Robert. 1982. *Parapsychology and Self-deception in Science*. Pittsburgh: R. A. McConnell.

McCrone, Walter. 1986. "Shroud Image the Work of an Artist." In *Science Confronts the Paranormal*, edited by Kendrick Frazier, 344–48. Amherst, NY: Prometheus Books.

———. 1999. *Judgment Day for the Shroud of Turin*. Buffalo, NY: Prometheus Books.

McDowell, Josh. 1973. *Evidence That Demands a Verdict*. San Bernardino, CA: Here's Life.

McGrath, James. 2008. *The Burial of Jesus: History and Faith*. Englewood, CO: Patheos Press.

McKay, Brendan. 1997. "Assassinations Foretold in Moby Dick!" Accessed September 1, 2018. http://users.cecs.anu.edu.au/~bdm/dilugim/moby.html.

McKay, Brendan, Dror Bar-Natan, Maya Bar-Hillel, and Gil Kalai. 1999. "Solving the Bible Code Puzzle." *Statistical Evidence* 14: 150–73.

McShea, Daniel. 1991. "Complexity and Evolution: What Everybody Knows." *Biology and Philosophy* 6: 303–24.

McCutcheon, Russell. 1997. "A Default of Critical Intelligence? The Scholar of Religion as Public Intellectual." *Journal of the American Academy of Religion* 65, no. 2: 443–68.

———. 2001. *Critics Not Caretakers: Redescribing the Public Study of Religion*. Albany, NY: State University of New York Press.

McIntyre, Lee. 2018. *Post-Truth*. Cambridge, MA: MIT Press.

McTernan, Oliver. 2003. *Violence in God's Name: Religion in an Age of Conflict*. Maryknoll, NY: Orbis Books.

Mead, Margaret. 1977. "An Anthropological Approach to Different Types of Communication and the Importance of Differences in Human Temperaments." In *Extrasensory Ecology: Parapsychology and Anthropology*, edited by Joseph Long, 47–50. Metuchen, NJ: Scarecrow Press.

Meldrum, Jeff. 2006. *Sasquatch: Legend Meets Science*. New York: Tom Doherty.

Melton, J. Gordon. 1985. "Spiritualization and Reaffirmation: What Really Happens when Prophecy Fails." *American Studies* 26, no. 2: 17–29.

Merrill Tenney. 1963. *The Reality of the Resurrection*. New York: Harper & Row.

Metzger, Bruce. 1987. *The Canon of the New Testament: Its Origin, Development, and Significance*. Oxford: Clarendon Press.

Mooney, Chris, and Sheril Kirshenbaum. 2009. *Unscientific America: How Scientific Illiteracy Threatens our Future*. New York: Basic Books.

Moore, Rebecca. 2009. *Understanding Jonestown and Peoples Temple*. Westport, CT: Praeger.

Meacham, William. 1983. "The Authentication of the Turin Shroud: An Issue in Archaeological Epistemology." *Current Anthropology* 24, no. 3: 283–311.

Medvedev, Zhores. 1969. *The Rise and Fall of T. D. Lysenko*. New York: Columbia University Press.

Meier, John. 1991. *A Marginal Jew: Rethinking Historical Jesus*, vol. 1. New York: Doubleday.

Mettinger, Tryggve. 2001. *Riddle of Resurrection: "Dying and Rising Gods" in the Ancient Near East*. Stockholm: Almqvist & Wiksell International.

Miethe, Terry. 2003. "Introduction." In *Did Jesus Rise from the Dead? The Resurrection Debate*, edited by Gary Habermas, Anthony Flew, and Terry Miethe, xiv–xxii. Eugene, OR: Wipf & Stock.

Mill, John Stuart. 1874. *Three Essays on Religion: Nature, the Utility of Religion, and Theism.* London: Longmans, Bader, and Dyer.

Miller, Kenneth. 2006. "The Flagellum Unspun: The Collapse of 'Irreducible Complexity.'" In *Debating Design: From Darwin to DNA*, edited by William Dembski and Michael Ruse, 81–97. Cambridge: Cambridge University Press.

Mills, Jeannie. 1979. *Six Years with God: Life Inside Rev. Jim Jones's Peoples Temple.* New York: A & W.

Moody, Raymond. 1975. *Life after Life.* New York: Bantam Books.

Morris, Brian. 2006. *Religion and Anthropology: A Critical Introduction.* Cambridge: Cambridge University Press.

Morvan, Camille, and Alexander O'Connor. 2017. *A Theory of Cognitive Dissonance.* London: Macat International.

Mueller, Marvin. 1983. "Reply to Meacham." *Current Anthropology* 24, no. 3: 299.

———. 1986. "The Shroud of Turin: A Critical Appraisal." In *Science Confronts the Paranormal*, edited by Kendrick Frazier, 324–43. Amherst, NY: Prometheus Books.

Müller, Julius. 1844. *The Theory of Myths, in Its Application to the Gospel History, Examined and Confuted.* London: Chapman.

Murdock, George. 1980. *Theories of Illness: A World Survey.* New York: Columbia University Press.

Murphy, Martin, and Maxine Margolis. 1995. "An Introduction to Cultural Materialism." In *Science, Materialism, and the Study of Culture*, edited by Martin Murphy and Maxine Margolis, 1–4. Gainesville: University Press of Florida.

Murray, Michael. 2009. "Scientific Explanations of Religion and the Justification of Religious Belief." In *The Believing Primate: Scientific, Philosophical, and Theological Reflections on the Origins of Religion*, edited by Jeffrey Schloss and Michael Murray, 168–78. New York: Oxford University Press.

Musella, David. 2006. "Alien Autopsy Hoax Revealed–Again." *Skeptical Inquirer* 30: 9, 11.

Nagel, Ernest. 1997. "Philosophical Concepts of Atheism." In *Critiques of God: Making the Case against Belief in God*, edited by Peter Angeles, 3–18. Amherst, NY: Prometheus Books.

National Academy of Science. 1998. *Teaching about Evolution and the Nature of Science.* Washington, DC: National Academy Press.

Narveson, Jan. 2003. "God by Design?" In *God and Design: The Teleological Argument and Modern Science*, edited by Neil Manson, 88–105. New York: Routledge.

National Academy of Sciences. 1998. *Teaching about Evolution and the Nature of Science.* Appendix C. USA: National Academies Press.

Newman, Hannah. 2005. "Blavatsky, Helena P. (1831–1891)." *Antisemitism: A Historical Encyclopedia of Prejudice and Persecution*, edited by Richard S. Levy, 72–73. Santa Barbara: ABC-CLIO.

Newport, Kenneth. 2001. "The Heavenly Millennium of Seventh-Day Adventism." In *Christian Millenarianism: From the Early Church to Waco*, edited by Stephen Hunt, 131–48. Bloomington: Indiana University Press.

Nickell, Joe. 1995. "'Alien Autopsy' Hoax." *Skeptical Inquirer* 19: 17–19.

———. 1997. "A Study of Fantasy Proneness in the Thirteen Cases of Alleged Encounters in John Mack's Abduction." In *The UFO Invasion: The Roswell Incident, Alien Abductions, and Government Coverups*, edited by Kendrick Frazier, Barry Karr, and Joe Nickell, 237–44. Amherst, NY: Prometheus Books.

———. 1998a. *Looking for a Miracle: Weeping Icons, Relics, Stigmata, Visions, and Healing Cures.* Amherst, NY: Prometheus Books.

———. 1998b. *Inquest on the Shroud of Turin.* Amherst, NY: Prometheus Books.

———. 2003. "Science versus Shroud Science." In *Science and Religion: Are They Compatible?*, edited by Paul Kurtz, Barry Karr, and Ranjit Sandhu, 263–72. Amherst, NY: Prometheus Books.

———. 2007. *Relics of the Christ.* Lexington: University of Kentucky Press.

———. 2013. *The Science of Miracles: Investigating the Incredible.* Amherst, NY: Prometheus Books.

Nielsen, Kai. 2001. *Naturalism and Religion.* Amherst, NY: Prometheus Books.

Noll, Mark. 1994. *The Scandal of the Evangelical Mind.* Grand Rapids, MI: William Eerdmans.

Norenzayan, Ara. 2013. *Big Gods: How Religion Transformed Cooperation and Conflict.* Princeton, NJ: Princeton University Press.

Norenzayan, Ara, and Scott Atran. 2004. "Cognitive and Emotional Processes in Cultural Transmission of Natural and Nonnatural Beliefs." In *The Psychological Foundations of Culture*, edited by Mark Schaller and Christian Crandall, 149–69. Mahwah, NJ: Lawrence Erlbaum Associates.

Nye, Bill, and Kenneth Ham. 2014. "The Bill Nye and Ken Ham Debate: Is Creation a Viable Model of Origins?" (February 4, 2014). Accessed January 11, 2019. https://www.youtube.com/watch?v=z6kgvhG3AkI.

Nye, Malory. 2008. *Religion: The Basics.* London: Routledge.

Nye, Mary. 1980. "N-rays: An Episode in the History and Psychology of Science." *Historical Studies in the Physical Sciences* 11, no. 1: 125–56.

O'Collins, and Daniel Kendall. 1994a. "Did Joseph of Arimathea Exist?" *Biblica* 75, no. 2: 235–41.

———. 1994b. "On Reissuing Venturini." *Gregorianum* 75, no. 2: 241–65.

O' Leary, Stephen. 2000. "When Prophecy Fails and When It Succeeds: Apocalyptic Prediction and the Re-entry into Ordinary Time." *Apocalyptic Time: Studies in the History of Religions*, edited by Albert Baumgartner, 341–62. Leiden: Brill.

Olson, Ken. 1999. "Eusebius and the Testimonium Flavianum." *Catholic Biblical Quarterly* 61: 305–22.

———. 2013. "A Eusebian Reading of the *Testimonium Flavianum.*" In *Eusebius of Caesarea: Tradition and Innovations* (Hellenic Studies Series 60), edited by Johnson, Aaron, and Jeremy Schott. Washington, DC: Center for Hellenic Studies. Accessed August 1, 2018. https://chs.harvard.edu/CHS/article/display/5871.5-a-eusebian-reading-of-the-testimonium-flavianum-ken-olson#noteref_n.52.

Onfray, Michel. 2011. *Atheist Manifesto: The Case against Christianity, Judaism, and Islam.* New York: Arcade.

Oppy, Graham. 2002. "Arguing about the Kalam Cosmological Argument." *Philo* 5, no. 1: 34–61.

———. 2006. *Arguing about Gods* Cambridge: Cambridge University Press.

———. 2018. *Naturalism and Religion: A Contemporary Philosophical Investigation.* New York: Routledge.

Orenstein, Alan. 2002. "Religion and Paranormal Belief." *Journal for the Scientific Study of Religion* 41, no. 2: 301–11.

Orr, David. 2003. "Medicine Cured 'Miracle' Woman—Not Mother Teresa, Say Doctors." *The Telegraph*, May 10, 2003. Accessed August 1, 2018. https://www.telegraph.co.uk/news/0/did-mother-teresa-really-perform-miracles/.

Osis, Karlis, and Erlendur Haraldsson.1977. "Deathbed Observations by Physicians and Nurses: A Cross-Cultural Survey." *Journal of American Society for Physical Research* 71: 237–59.

Otto, Rudolf. 1923. *The Idea of the Holy: An Inquiry into the Non-Rational Factor in the Idea of the Divine and Its Relation to the Rational.* Oxford: Oxford University Press.

Otto, Shawn. 2016. *The War on Science: Who Is Waging It, Why It Matters, What We Can Do about It.* Minneapolis, MN: Milkweed.

Overall, Christine. 2003a. "Miracles as Evidence against the Existence of God." In *The Impossibility of God*, edited by Michael Martin and Ricki Monnier, 147–53. Amherst, NY: Prometheus Books.

———. 2003b. "Miracles and God: A Reply to Robert A. H. Larmer." In *The Impossibility of God*, edited by Michael Martin and Ricki Monnier, 154–66. Amherst, NY: Prometheus Books.

Pagels, Elaine. 1979. *The Gnostic Gospels.* New York: Vintage.

Paine, Thomas. 1776. "The Forester Letter, March 28." Accessed September 1, 2018. http://www.thomaspaine.org/essays/american-revolution/the-forester-s-letters.html.

———. 1778. *The American Crisis.* Accessed September 30, 2017. http://www.ushistory.org/paine/crisis/c-05.htm.

———. 1797a. "Prosecution of the Age of Reason: A Letter to Mr. Erskine. September." Accessed September 30, 2017. http://www.thomaspaine.org/essays/religion/prosecution-of-the-age-of-reason.html.

———. 1797b. "Age of Reason Letters: An Answer to a Friend. Paris, May 12." Accessed January 11, 2018. http://thomaspaine.org/essays/religion/age-of-reason-letters.html.

———. 1797c. *Letter to the Honourable Thomas Erskine on the Prosecution of Thomas Williams for Publishing the Age of Reason.* Paris: The Author.

———. 1835. *The Theological Works of Thomas Paine.* New York: George E. Evans.

———. 1858. *The Works of Thomas Paine: Hero of the American Revolution.* Philadelphia, PA: Moss Brothers.

———. 1880. *The Age of Reason: An Investigation of True and Fabulous Theology.* London: Freethought Publishing Company (Part I [1794], Part II [1795], Part III [1807]). Accessed January 11, 2018. https://openlibrary.org/works/OL60357W/The_Age_of_Reason.

———. 1892. *The Life of Thomas Paine: With a History of His Literary, Political, and Religious Career in America, France, and England,* vol. 2. New York: G. P. Putnam.

———. 1908. *The Writings of Thomas Paine,* vol. 4. New York: G. P. Putnam.

Paley, William. 1802. *Natural Theology, or Evidences of the Existence and Attributes of the Deity, Collected from the Appearance of Nature.* Philadephia: John Morgan.

Pallen, Mark, and Nicholas Matzke. 2006. "From *The Origin of Species* to the Origin of Bacterial Flagella." *Nature Reviews Microbiology* 4: 784–90.

Pandian, Jacob. 2003. "The Dangerous Quest for Cooperation between Science and Religion." In *Science and Religion: Are They Compatible?,* edited by Paul Kurtz, 161–69. Amherst, NY: Prometheus Books.

Pandian, Kevin. 2002. "Waiting for the Watchmaker." *Science* 295, no. 5564: 2373–74.

Pannenberg, Wolfhart. 1964. *Grundzüge der Christologie.* Güterslo: Gütersloher Verl.-Haus Mohn.

———. 1996. "History and the Reality of the Resurrection." In *Resurrection Reconsidered,* edited by Gavin D' Costa, 62–72. Oxford: One World.

Papineau, David. 2015. "There Is No Trace of Any Soul Linked to the Body." In *The Myth of an Afterlife: The Case against Life after Death,* edited by Michael Martin and Keith Augustine, 369–76. Lanham, MD: Rowman and Littlefield.

Parkes, Collin, Pittu Laungani, and William Young. 2015a. "Culture and Religion." In *Death and Bereavement across Cultures,* edited by Collin Parkes, Laungani Pittu, and Bill Young, 9–20. London: Routledge.

———. 2015b. "Introduction." In *Death and Bereavement across* Cultures, edited by Collin Parkes, Laungani Pittu, and Bill Young, 3–8. London: Routledge.

Parsons, Keith. 1989. *God and the Burden of Proof: Plantinga, Swinburne, and the Analytic Defense of Theism.* Buffalo, NY: Prometheus Books.

———. 2005. "Peter Kreeft and Ronald Tacelli on the Hallucination Theory." In *the Empty Tomb: Jesus beyond the Grave,* edited by Robert Price and Jeffrey Lowder, 443–52. Amherst, NY: Prometheus Books.

———. 2011. "Hell: Christianity's Most Damnable Doctrine." In *The End of Christianity,* edited by John Loftus, 233–54. Amherst, NY: Prometheus Books.

Pascal, Blaise. 1958. *Pascal's Pensées.* New York: E. P. Dutton. http://www.gutenberg.org/files/18269/18269-h/18269-h.htm#p_894.

Paul, Gregory. 2005. "Cross-National Correlations of Quantifiable Societal Health with Popular Religiosity and Secularism in the Prosperous Democracies." *Journal of Religion and Society* 7: 1–17.

Paulus, Heinrich.1828. *Das Leben Jesu als Grundlage einer reinen Geschichte des Urchristentums.* Heidelberg: C. F. Winter.

Patterson, Stephen. 1998. *The God of Jesus: The Historical Jesus and the Search for Meaning.* Harrisburg, PA: Trinity Press International.

Peebles, Curtis. 1994. *Watch the Skies: A Chronicle of the Flying Saucer Myth.* Washington: Smithsonian Institution Press.

Pennock, Robert. 1999. *Tower of Babel: The Evidence against the New Creationism.* Cambridge, MA: MIT Press.

Percy, Martyn. 2001. "Whose Time Is It Anyway? Evangelicals, the Millennium, and Millenarianism." In *Christian Millenarianism: From the Early Church to Waco*, edited by Stephen Hunt, 26–38. Bloomington: Indiana University Press.

Perrin, Norman. 1977. *The Resurrection According to Matthew, Mark, and Luke*. Philadelphia, PA: Fortress Press.

———. 2012. *The Kingdom of God in the Teaching of Jesus*. London: SMC Press.

Persinger, Michael. 1993. "Paranormal and Religious Beliefs May Be Mediated Differentially by Subcortical and Cortical Phenomenological Processes of the Temporal (Limbic) Lobes." *Perceptual and Motor Skills* 76: 247–51.

———. 2008. Foreword to Reflections on the Dawn of Consciousness: Julian Jaynes's Bicameral Mind Theory Revisited. Henderson, NV: Julian Jaynes Society, edited by Marcel Kuijsten, vii-x. Henderson, NV: Julian Jaynes Society.

Persinger, Michael, and Katherine Makarec. 1987. "Temporal Lobe Epileptic Signs and Correlative Behaviors Displayed by Normal Populations." *Journal of General Psychology* 114: 179–95.

Peters, Emmanuelle. 2010. "Are Delusions on a Continuum? The Case of Religious and Delusional Beliefs." In *Psychosis and Spirituality: Consolidating the New Paradigm*, edited by Isabel Clarke, 127–38. Oxford: Wiley-Blackwell.

Pettitt, Paul. 2011. *The Palaeolithic Origins of Human Burial*. London: Routledge.

Pew Forum on Religion and Public Life. 2008. U.S. Religious Landscape Survey: Religious Beliefs and Practices. Accessed October 15, 2018. https://www.pewforum.org/2008/06/01/u-s-religious-landscape-survey-religious-beliefs-and-practices/.

Philipse, Herman. 2014. *God in the Age of Science? A Critique of Religious Reason*. Oxford: Oxford University Press.

Philostratus. 1912. *The Life of Apollonius of Tyana*. Translated by F. C. Conybeare. London: William Heinemann.

Pigliucci, Massimo. 2003. "Design Yes, Intelligent No: A Critique of Intelligent-Design Theory of Neocreationism." In *Science and Religion: Are They Compatible?*, edited by Paul Kurtz, Barry Karr, and Ranjit Sandhu, 99–110. Amherst, NY: Prometheus Books.

Pilch, John. 1998. "Appearances of the Risen Jesus in Cultural Context: Experiences of Alternate Reality." *Biblical Theology Bulletin: Journal of Bible and Culture* 28, no. 2: 52–60.

Pinker, Steven. 2006. "The Evolutionary Psychology of Religion." In *Where Gods and Science Meet: How Brain and Evolutionary Studies Alter Our Understanding of Religion*, vol. 1, edited by Patrick McNamara, 1–9. Westport, CT: Praeger.

———. 2018. *Enlightenment Now: The Case for Reason, Science, Humanism, and Progress*. New York: Viking.

Plantinga, Alvin. 1991. "When Faith and Reason Clash: Evolution and the Bible." *Christian Scholar's Review* 21: 8–32.

———. 1993. *Warrant and Proper Function*. Oxford: Oxford University Press.

———. 2000. *Warranted Christian Belief*. New York: Oxford University Press.

———. 2001. "Methodological Naturalism?" In *Intelligent Design, Creationism and Its Critics*, edited by Robert Pennock, 339–61. Cambridge, MA: MIT Press.

———. 2009. "Games Scientists Play." In *The Believing Primate: Scientific, Philosophical, and Theological Reflections on the Origins of Religion*, edited by Jeffrey Schloss and Michael Murray, 139–67. New York: Oxford University Press.

———. 2011. *Where the Conflict Really Lies: Religion and Naturalism*. Oxford: Oxford University Press.

PLoS ONE Editors. 2018. Retraction: Atomic Resolution Studies Detect New Biologic Evidences on the *Turin Shroud*. *PLoS ONE* 13, no. 7. Accessed April 1, 2019. https://doi.org/10.1371/journal.pone.0201272.

Pratscher, Wilhelm. 1987. *Der Herrenbruder Jakobus und die Jakobustradition*. Göttingen: Vandenhoeck & Ruprecht.

Price, Robert. 1989. "Jesus' Burial in a Garden: The Strange Growth of the Tradition." *Religious Traditions* 12: 17–30.

———. 2000. *Deconstructing Jesus*. Amherst, NY: Prometheus Books.

———. 2003. *The Incredible Shrinking Son of Man: How Reliable Is the Gospel Tradition?* Amherst, NY: Prometheus Books.
———. 2005a. "By This Time He Stinketh: The Attempt of William Craig to Exhume Jesus." In *the Empty Tomb: Jesus Beyond the Grave*, edited by Robert Price and Jeffrey Lowder, 411–31. Amherst, NY: Prometheus Books.
———. 2005b. "Introduction: The Second Life of Jesus." In *The Empty Tomb: Jesus Beyond the Grave*, edited by Robert Price and Jeffrey Lowder, 9–18. Amherst, NY: Prometheus Books.
———. 2007. Review of *The Resurrection of the Son of God*, edited by N.T. Wright. Accessed May 11, 2010. http://www.robertmprice.mindvendor.com/rev_ntwrong.htm.
———. 2008. "Brand X Easters." In *The Resurrection of Jesus: A Sourcebook*, edited by Bernard Scott, 49–59. Santa Rosa, CA: Polbridge.
———. 2010a. "Jesus: Myth and Method." In *The Christian Delusion: Why Faith Fails*, edited by John Loftus, 273–90. Amherst, NY: Prometheus Books.
———. 2010b. *The Case against the Case for Christ: A New Testament Scholar Refutes the Reverend Lee Strobel.* Crawford, NJ: American Atheist.
———. 2011. "Explaining the Resurrection without Recourse to Miracle." In *The End of Christianity*, edited by John Loftus, 219–32. Amherst, NY: Prometheus Books.
Proud, Louis. 2009. *Dark Intrusions: An Investigation into the Paranormal Nature of Sleep Paralysis*. San Antonio, TX: Anomalist Books.
Pyysiäinen, Ilkka. 2004. *Magic, Miracles, and Religion: A Scientist's Perspective*. Walnut Creek, CA: AltaMira.
———. 2007. "The Mystery of the Stolen Body: Exploring Christian Origins." In *Explaining Christian Origins and Early Judaism: Contributions from Cognitive and Social Science*, edited by Luomanen, Petri, Ilkka Pyysiäinen, and Risto Uro, 57–72. Atlanta, GA: SBL Press.
———. 2008. "Enduring Fascination of Miracles." In *Miracles: God, Science, and Psychology*, vol. 2, edited by Harold Ellens, 17–26. Westport, CT: Praeger.
Radin, Dean. 1997. *The Conscious Universe: The Scientific Truth of Psychic Phenomena*. New York: Harper Collins.
———. 2006. *Entangled Minds: Extrasensory Experiences in a Quantum Reality*. New York: Paraview.
Ramsey, Michael. 1946. *The Resurrection of Christ: An Essay in Biblical Theology*. London: Geoffrey Bles.
Randi, James. 1976. *Houdini, His Life and Art*. New York: Grosset and Dunlap.
———. 1982a . *Flim-Flam: Psychics, ESP, Unicorns and other Delusions.* Amherst, NY: Prometheus Books.
———. 1982b. *The Truth about Uri Geller*. Amherst, NY: Prometheus Books.
———. 1985. "The Role of Conjurers in Psi Research." In *A Skeptic's Handbook of Parapsychology*, edited by Paul Kurtz, 339–50. Buffalo, NY: Prometheus Books.
———.1987. *The Faith Healers.* Amherst, NY: Prometheus Books.
Randle, Kevin, and Don Schmitt. 1994. *The Truth about the UFO Crash at Roswell.* New York: M. Evans.
Rathje, William.1992. *Rubbish: The Archaeology of Garbage*. New York: HarperCollins.
Ratzsch, Del. 2003. "Perceiving Design." In *God and Design: The Teleological Argument and Modern Science*, edited by Neil Manson, 125–45. New York: Routledge.
Ratzsch, Del, and Koperski, Jeffrey. 2016. Teleological Arguments for God's Existence. *The Stanford Encyclopedia of Philosophy.* Accessed April 1, 2019. https://plato.stanford.edu/archives/win2016/entries/teleological-arguments/.
Ray, Darrel. 2009. *The God Virus: How Religion Infects Our Lives and Culture*. Bonner Springs, KS: IPC Press.
Rea, Michael. 2004. *World without Design: The Ontological Consequence of Naturalism*. Oxford: Oxford University Press.
Read, Graham. 1988. *The Psychology of Anomalous Experience*. Buffalo, NY: Prometheus Books.
Reader, Ian. 2001. "Violent Millennialism with a Christian Touch: Syncretic Themes in Millennial Perspective of Aum Shinrikyô." In *Christian Millenarianism: From the Early Church to Waco*, edited by Stephen Hunt, 239–54. Bloomington: Indiana University Press.

Redman, Judith. 2010. "How Accurate are Eyewitnesses? Bauckham and Eyewitnesses." *Journal of Biblical Literature* 129: 177–97.

Reece, Gregory. 2006. *Elvis Religion: The Cult of the King*. New York: I.B. Tauris.

Rees, Martin. 2001. *Just Six Numbers: The Deep Forces That Shape the Universe*. New York: Basic Books.

Rees, W. Dewi. 1977. "The Hallucinations of Widowhood." *British Medical Journal* 4, no. 5778: 37–38, 39–41.

Regal, Brian. 2009. *Pseudoscience: A Critical Encyclopedia*. Santa Barbara, CA: ABC-CLIO.

———. 2011. *Searching for Sasquatch: Crackpots, Eggheads, and Cryptozoology*. New York: Palgrave Macmillan.

Reimarus, Hermann. 1879. *Fragments from Reimarus: Brief Critical Remarks on the Object of Jesus and His Disciples as Seen in the New Testament*. London: Williams and Norgate.

Renan, Ernest. 1866. *The Apostles*. New York: Carleton.

Rhine, Joseph. 1953. *The New World of the Mind*. New York. William Morrow.

———. 1954. "The Science of Nonphysical Nature." *Journal of Philosophy* 51, no. 25: 801–10.

———. 1972. "Parapsychology and Man." *Journal of Parapsychology* 36: 101–21.

———. 1977. "History of Experimental Studies." In *Handbook of Parapsychology*, edited by Benjamin Wolman, Laura Dale, Gertrude Schmeidler, and Montague Ullman, 25–47. New York: Van Nostrand Reinhold.

Rhine, Joseph, and Joseph Pratt. 1957. *Parapsychology: Frontier Science of the Mind*. Springfield, IL: Charles C. Thomas.

Rice, Tom. 2003. "Believe it or Not: Religious and Paranormal Beliefs in the United States." *Journal for the Scientific Study of Religion* 42, no. 1: 95–106.

Richards, Robert. 2013. *Was Hitler a Darwinian? Disputed Questions in the History of Evolutionary Theory*. Chicago, IL: University of Chicago Press.

Richter, Philip. 1984. "Recent Sociological Approaches to the Study of the New Testament." *Religion* 14, no. 1: 77–90.

Ring, Kenneth. 1980. *Life and Death: A Scientific Investigation of the near-Death Experience*. New York: Coward, McCann, and Geoghegan.

Rogo, Douglas. 1982. *Miracles: A Parascientific Inquiry into Wondrous Phenomena*. New York: Dial Press.

Rose, Herbert. 1938. "Herakles and the Gospels." *Harvard Theological Review* 31: 113–42.

Rosenblatt, Paul, Patricia Walsh, and Douglas Jackson. 1976. *Grief and Mourning in Cross- Cultural Perspective*. New York: Human Relations Area Files Press.

Ross, Eric.1980. "Introduction." In *Beyond the Myths of Culture: Essays in Cultural Materialism*, edited by Eric Ross, xix–xvi. New York: Academic Press.

Roughgarden, Joan. 2006a. *Evolution and Christian Faith: Reflections of an Evolutionary Biologist*. Washington, DC: Island Press.

———. 2006b. Beyond Belief: Science, Reason, Religion & Survival Symposium, session 3 (November 5–7, 2006). Accessed December 17, 2018. https://www.youtube.com/watch?v=kbkOJr8klhA.

Roy, Rustum. 2005. "Scientism and Technology as Religions." *Zygon* 40, no. 4: 835–44.

Ruse, Michael. 2001. Methodological Naturalism under Attack. In *Intelligent Design Creationism and Its Critics: Philosophical, Theological, and Scientific Perspectives*, edited by Robert Pennock, 363–85. Cambridge, MA: MIT Press.

———. 2006. "The Argument from Design." In *Debating Design: From Darwin to DNA*, edited by William Dembski and Michael Ruse, 13–31. Cambridge: Cambridge University Press.

———. 2011. *Science and Spirituality: Making Room for Faith in the Age of Science*. Cambridge: Cambridge University Press.

Russell, Bertrand. 1957. *Why I Am Not a Christian: And Other Essays on Religion and Related Subjects*. New York: Simon and Schuster.

———. 2004. *Sceptical Essays*. London: Routledge.

Sacks, Oliver. 2012. *Hallucinations*. New York: Vintage Books.

Sagan, Carl. 1980. "Encyclopaedia Galactica." *Cosmos* (episode 12. 01:24 minutes, first aired December 14, 1980 on PBS). Accessed March 5, 2018. https://www.youtube.com/watch?v=Bxdsh6RjnQI.

———. 1993. *Broca's Brain: Reflections on the Romance of Science*. New York: Ballantine Books.

———. 1995. *The Demon-Haunted World: Science as a Candle in the Dark*. New York: Random House.

———. 2001. "The Burden of Skepticism." In *Magic, Witchcraft, and Religion: An Anthropological Study of the Supernatural*, edited by Arthur Lehman and James Myers, 389–94. Mountain View, CA: Mayfield.

———. 2006. *The Varieties of Scientific Experience: A Personal View of the Search for God*. New York: Penguin Books.

Saler, Benson. 1977. "Supernatural as a Western Concept." *Ethos* 5: 31–53.

Saler, Benson, Charles Ziegler, and Charles Moore. 1997. *UFO Crash at Roswell: The Genesis of a Modern Myth*. Washington: Smithsonian Institution Press.

Sandmel, Samuel. 1965. *We Jews and Jesus: Exploring Theological Differences for Mutual Understanding*. New York: Oxford University Press.

Sarkar, Sahotra. 2007. *Doubting Darwin? Creationist Designs on Evolution*. Oxford: Blackwell.

Saver, Jeffrey, and John Rabin. 1997. "The Neural Substrates of Religious Experience." *Journal of Neuropsychiatry and Clinical Neuroscience* 9: 498–510.

Schacter, Daniel. ed. 1995. *Memory Distortion: How Minds, Brains, and Societies Reconstruct the Past*. Cambridge, MA: Harvard University Press.

Schafersman, Steven. 1983. "Reply to Meacham." *Current Anthropology* 24, no. 3: 301–2.

———. 1998. "Unraveling the Shroud of Turin." *Approfondimento Sindone*, Year II, vol. 2, 29–48. Accessed January 11, 2018. http://sindone.weebly.com/schafersman.html.

Schellenberg, John. 2006. *Divine Hiddenness and Human Reason*. Ithaca, NY: Cornell University Press.

Schleiermacher, Friedrich. 1963. *The Christian Faith*. New York: Harper & Row.

Schloss, Jeffrey. 2009. "Introduction: Evolutionary Theories of Religion: Science Unfettered or Naturalism Run Wild?" In *The Believing Primate: Scientific, Philosophical, and Theological Reflections on the Origins of Religion*, edited by Jeffrey Schloss and Michael Murray, 1–25. New York: Oxford University Press.

Scholem, Gershom. 1973. *Sabbatai Ṣevi: The Mystical Messiah*. Princeton, NJ: Princeton University Press.

Schonfield, Hugh. 1965. *The Passover Plot: New Light on the History of Jesus*. New York: B. Geis Associates.

Schick, Theodore, and Lewis Vaughn. 2014. *How to Think about Weird Things: Critical Thinking for a New Age*. New York: McGraw Hill.

Schmidt, Wilhelm. 1926–55. *Der Ursprung der Gottesidee: eine historisch-kritische und positive Studie* [The Origin of the Idea of God: A Historical-critical and Positive Study]. 12 vols. Münster: Aschendorff.

Schweitzer, Albert. 2005. *The Quest of the Historical Jesus*. Mineola, NY: Dover.

Scriven, Michael. 1966. *Primary Philosophy*. New York: McGraw-Hill.

Scott, Eugenie. 1999. "'The 'Science and Religion Movement:' An Opportunity for Improved Public Understanding of Science?" *Skeptical Inquirer* 23: 29–31.

———. 2001. "My Favorite Pseudoscience." In *Skeptical Odysseys: Personal Accounts by the World's Leading Paranormal Inquirers*, edited by Paul Kurtz, 245–56. Amherst, NY: Prometheus Books.

———. 2008. "Science and Religion, Methodology and Humanism." Accessed January 11, 2018. https://ncse.com/religion/science-religion-methodology-humanism.

Segal, Robert. 1980. "The Social Sciences and the Truth of Religious Belief." *Journal of the American Academy of Religion* 48, no. 3: 403–13.

———. 1983. "In Defense of Reductionism." *Journal of the American Academy of Religion* 51, no. 1: 97–124.

Shaffer, Ryan. 2013. "Blasphemy, Free Speech, and Rationalism: An Interview with Sanal Edamaruku." *The Humanist* (February 15). Accessed January 30, 2018. https://thehumanist.com/march-april-2013/blasphemy-free-speech-and-rationalisman-interview-withsanal-edamaruku/.

Shapiro, Larry. 2016. *The Miracle Myth: Why Belief in the Resurrection and the Supernatural is Unjustified.* New York: Columbia University Press.

Shanks, Niall. 2006. *God, the Devil, and Darwin: A Critique of Intelligent Design Theory.* Oxford: Oxford University Press.

Shea, William. 1984. *The Naturalists and the Supernatural: Studies in Horizon and an American Philosophy of Religion.* Macon, GA: Mercer University Press.

Sheehan, Thomas. 2008. "How Did Easter Originally Happen?" In *The Resurrection of Jesus: A Sourcebook*, edited by Bernard Scott, 105–15. Santa Rosa, CA: Polbridge Press.

Sher, Leo. 2000. "Neuroimaging, Auditory Hallucinations, and the Bicameral Mind." *Journal of Psychiatry and Neuroscience* 25, no. 3: 239–40.

Shermer, Michael. 2002. *Why People Believe Weird Things.* New York: St. Martin's Press.

———. 2011. *The Believing Brain: From Ghosts and Gods to Politics and Conspiracies—How We Construct Beliefs and Reinforce Them as Truths.* New York: St. Martin's Press.

Sherwin-White, Adrian Nicholas. 1963. *Roman Society and Roman Law in the New Testament: The Sarum Lectures 1960–1961.* Oxford: Oxford University Press.

Shotwell, David. 2003. "From the Anthropic Principle to the Supernatural." In *Science and Religion: Are They Compatible?*, edited by Paul Kurtz, Barry Karr, and Ranjit Sandhu, 47–49. Amherst, NY: Prometheus Books.

Shuchter, Stephen. 1986. *Dimensions of Grief: Adjusting to the Death of a Spouse.* San Francisco, CA: Jossey-Bass.

Sidky, H. 1997. *Witchcraft, Lycanthropy, Drugs, and Disease: An Anthropological Study of the European Witch-Hunts.* New York: Peter Lang.

———. 2004 *Perspectives on Culture: A Critical Introduction to Theory in Cultural Anthropology.* Upper Saddle River, NJ: Prentice Hall.

———. 2006. "Afghanistan." In *Peoples and Cultures of Asia*, edited by Raymond Scupin, 14–102. Upper Saddle River, NJ: Prentice Hall.

———. 2007a. "Cultural Materialism, Scientific Anthropology, Epistemology, and "Narrative Ethnographies of the Particular." In *Studying Societies and Cultures: Marvin Harris's Cultural Materialism and its Legacy*, edited by Lawrence Kuznar and Stephen Sanderson, 66–77. Boulder, CO: Paradigm.

———. 2007b. "War, Changing Patterns of Warfare, State Collapse, and Transnational Violence in Afghanistan: 1978–2001." *Modern Asian Studies* 41, no. 4: 849–88.

———. 2008. *Haunted by the Archaic Shaman: Himalayan Jhakris and the Discourse on Shamanism.* Lanham, MD: Lexington Books.

———. 2010. "A Shaman's Cure: The Relationship between Altered States of Consciousness and Shamanic Healing." *Anthropology of Consciousness* 20, no. 2: 171–97.

———. 2011. "The State Oracle of Tibet, Spirit Possession and Shamanism." *Numen* 58: 71–99.

———. 2015. *Religion: An Anthropological Perspective.* New York: Peter Lang.

———. 2017a . Review of *Caravan of Martyrs: Sacrifice and Suicide Bombing in Afghanistan*, by David Edwards. *Journal of International and Global Studies* 9, no. 1: 129–32.

———. 2017b. *The Origins of Shamanism, Spirit Beliefs, and Religiosity: A Cognitive Anthropological Perspective.* Lanham, MD: Lexington Books.

———. 2018. "The War on Science, Anti-Intellectualism, and 'Alternative Ways of Knowing' in 21st-Century America." *Skeptical Inquirer* 42: 38–43.

Sidky, H., Janardan Subedi, and James Hamill. 2002. *Halfway to the Mountain: The Jirels of Eastern Nepal.* Kathmandu, Nepal: Tribhuvan University Press.

Simons, Ronald, and Charles Hughes, eds. 1985. *The Culture-Bound Syndromes: Folk Illnesses of Psychiatric and Anthropological Interest.* Dordrecht, Holland: D. Reidel.

Slade, Peter, and Richard Bentall. 1988. *Sensory Deception: A Scientific Analysis of Hallucination.* Baltimore: John Hopkins University Press.

Slakey, Francis. 1993. "When the Lights of Reason Go Out." *New Scientist* 11 September. Accessed January 23, 2018. https://www.newscientist.com/article/mg13918905-000- forum-when-the-lights-of-reason-go-out-francis-slakey-ponders-the-faces-of-fantasy-and-new-age-scientists.

Slezak, Peter. 1996. Review of *The Mind of God: Science and the Search for Ultimate Meaning*, by Paul Davis. *Science and Education* 5: 201–12.

———. 2012. Review of *Science and Spirituality: Making Room for Faith in the Age of Science*, by Michael Ruse. *Science and Education* 21: 403–13.

Sloyan, Gerard. 1995. *The Crucifixion of Jesus: History, Myth Faith.* Minneapolis, MN: Fortress Press.

Smart, Ninian. 1989 *The World's Religions.* Englewood Cliffs, NJ: Prentice Hall.

———. 1996. *Dimensions of the Sacred: An Anatomy of the World's Beliefs.* London: HarperCollins.

Smith, James. 2015. "Science as Cultural Performance: Leveling the Playing Field in the Theology and Science Conversation." In *Scientism: The New Orthodoxy*, edited by Richard Williams and Daniel Robinson, 177–91. New York: Bloomsbury.

Smith, Jonathan C. 2010. *Pseudoscience and Extraordinary Claims of the Paranormal.* West Sussex, UK: Wiley-Blackwell.

Smith, Jonathan Z. 1987. "Dying and Rising Gods." In *The Encyclopedia of Religion*, vol. 4, edited by Mircea Eliade, 521–27. New York: Macmillan.

Smith, Kelly. 2001. "Appealing to Ignorance behind the Cloak of Ambiguity." In *Intelligent Design Creationism and Its Critics: Philosophical, Theological, and Scientific Perspectives*, edited by Robert Pennock, 705–35. Cambridge, MA: MIT Press.

Smith, Morton. 1968. "Historical Method in the Study of Religion." *History and Theory* 8: 8–16.

———. 2014. *Jesus the Magician.* San Francisco, CA: Red Wheel/Weiser.

Smith, Philip. 2002. "The Effects of Prayer: Scientific Study." *Archives of Internal Medicine* 162b, no. 12: 1420.

Smith, Quentin. 1992. "Anthropic Coincidences, Evil and the Disconfirmation of Theism." *Religious Studies* 28: 347–50.

Sober, Elliott. 2006. "The Design Argument." In *Debating Design: From Darwin to DNA*, edited by William Dembski and Michael Ruse, 98–129. Cambridge: Cambridge University Press.

Society for Psychical Research. 1883. *Proceedings of the Society for Psychical Research*, vol. 1 (parts 1–4). London: Trubner.

Soifer, Valerii. 1994. *Lysenko and the Tragedy of Soviet Science.* New Brunswick, NJ: Rutgers University Press.

Sosis, Richard, and Candace Alcorta. 2004. "Is Religion Adaptive?" *Behavioral and Brain Sciences* 27: 749–50.

Spanos, Nicolas, Stacey McNulty, Susan DuBreuil, Martha Pires, and Melissa Faith. 1995. "The Frequency and Correlates of Sleep Paralysis in a University Sample." *Journal of Research in Personality* 29, no. 3: 285–305.

Sparks, Glenn. 2001. "The Relationship between Paranormal Beliefs and Religious Beliefs." *Skeptical Inquirer* 25: 50–56.

Sperber, Dan. 2000. "Metarepresentations in an Evolutionary Perspective." In *Metarpresentations: A Multidisciplinary Perspective*, edited by Dan Sperber, 117–37. Oxford: Oxford University Press.

Spiegelberg, Herbert. 1951. "Supernaturalism or Naturalism: A Study in Meaning and Verifiability." *Philosophy of Science* 18, no. 4: 339–68.

Spilka, Bernard, Ralph Hood, Bruce Hunsberger, and Richard Gorsuch. 2003. *The Psychology of Religion: An Empirical Approach.* New York: Guilford Press.

Spiro, Melford. 1966. "Religion: Problems of Definition and Explanation." In *Anthropological Approaches to the Study of Religion*, edited by Michael Banton, 85–126. London: Tavistock.

———. 1982. "Collective Representations and Mental Representations in Religious Symbol Systems." In *On Symbols in Anthropology: Essays in Honor of Harry Hoijer*, vol. 2, edited by

James Fernandez, Melford Spiro, and Melton Singer, 45–72. Los Angeles: University of California Press.

Spong, John. 1995. *Resurrection: Myth or Reality: A Bishop's Search for the Origins of Christianity*. San Francisco, CA: HarperCollins.

Stark, Rodney. 1984. "The Rise of a New World Faith." *Review of Religious Research* 26: 18–27.

———. 1996. *The Rise of Christianity: How the Obscure Marginal Jesus Movement Became the Dominant Religious Force in the Western World in a Few Centuries*. Princeton, NJ: Princeton University Press.

———. 1999. "A Theory of Revelations." *Journal for the Scientific Study of Religion* 38: 287–306.

Stark, Rodney, and Roger Finke. 2000. *Acts of Faith: Explaining the Human Side of Religion*. Berkeley, CA: University of California Press.

Stenger, Victor. 1990. *Physics and Psychics: The Search for a World Beyond the Senses*. Buffalo, NY: Prometheus Books.

———. 2003. *Has Science Found God? The Latest Results in the Search for Purpose in the Universe*. Amherst, NY: Prometheus Books.

———. 2008. *God: The Failed Hypothesis: How Science Shows That God Does Not Exist*. Amherst, NY: Prometheus Books.

———.2007. *God: The Failed Hypothesis: How Science Shows That God Does Not Exist*. Amherst, NY: Prometheus Books.

———. 2012. *God and the Folly of Faith: The Incompatibility of Science and Religion*. Amherst, NY: Prometheus Books.

Stevenson, Kenneth, and Gary Habermas. 1981. *Verdict on the Shroud: Evidence for the Death and Resurrection of Jesus*. Ann Arbor, MI: Servant Books.

Stewart, James. 1989. "Sasquatch Sightings in South Dakota: An Analysis of an Episode of Collective Delusion." In *Exploring the Paranormal: Perspectives on Belief and Experience*, edited by George Zollschan, John Schumaker, and Greg Walsh, 287–304. Bridgeport, UK: Prism.

Stewart-Williams, Steve. 2015. "Foreword: On the Origins of Afterlife Beliefs by Means of Memetic Selection." In *The Myth of an Afterlife: The Case against Life after Death*, edited by Michael Martin and Keith Augustine, xiii–xxv. Lanham, MD: Rowman and Littlefield.

Stokes, Trey. 1996. "How to Make an 'Alien' for 'Autopsy.'" *Skeptical Inquirer* 20: 19–23.

Stoller, Paul, and Cheryl Olkes. 1989. *In Sorcery's Shadow: A Memoir of Apprenticeship among the Songhay of Niger*. Chicago, IL: University of Chicago Press.

Stone, Jon, ed. 2000. *Expecting Armageddon: Essential Readings in Failed Prophecy*. London: Routledge.

Strauss, David Friedrich. 1860. *The Life of Jesus Critically Examined*, vol. 1. New York: Calvin Blanchard.

———. 1873. *The Old Faith and New*. New York: Holt.

———. 1902. *The Life of Jesus Critically Examined*, vol. 2. London: Swan Sonnenschein.

Stringer, Chris. 2012. *Lone Survivors: How We Came to Be the Only Humans on Earth*. New York: St. Martin's Press.

Strobel, Lee 1998 *The Case for Christ: A Journalist's Personal Investigation of the Evidence for Jesus*. Michigan: Zondervan.

Swinburne, Richard. 1992. *Revelation: From Metaphor to Analogy*. Oxford: Oxford University Press.

———. 2003. *The Resurrection of God Incarnate*. Oxford: Oxford University Press.

———. 2004. *The Existence of God*. Oxford: Oxford University Press.

Szasz, Thomas. 1996. *The Meaning of Mind: Language, Morality, and Neuroscience*. Westport, CT: Praeger.

Tabor, James. 2007. *The Jesus Dynasty: The Hidden History of Jesus, His Royal Family, and the Birth of Christianity*. New York: Simon and Schuster.

Tacitus. 1869. *The Annals of Tacitus*. Translated by Alfred John Church and William Jackson Brodribb. London: Macmillan. http://classics.mit.edu/Tacitus/annals.mb.txt.

Taliaferro, Charles. 2009. "Explaining Religious Experience." In *The Believing Primate: Scientific, Philosophical, and Theological Reflections on the Origins of Religion*, edited by Jeffrey Schloss and Michael Murray, 201–14. New York: Oxford University Press.

Tart, Charles. 2009. *The End of Materialism: How Evidence of the Paranormal Is Bringing Science and Spirit Together*. Oakland, CA: Harbinger.

Tattersall, Ian. 2012. *Masters of the Planet: The Search for Our Human Origins*. New York: St. Martin's Griffin.

Tattersall, Ian, and Peter Névraumont. 2018. *Hoax: A History of Deception: 5,000 Years of Fakes, Forgeries, and Fallacies*. New York: Black Dog and Leventhal.

Taylor, David. 1992. *Mark's Gospel as Literature and History*. Crawley, UK: Ferry House Books.

Taylor, Joan. 1998. "Golgotha: A Reconsideration of the Evidence for the Sites of Jesus' Crucifixion and Burial." *New Testament Studies* 44: 180–203.

Thalbourne, Michael, and Peter Delin. 1994. "A Common Thread Underlying the Belief in the Paranormal, Mystical Experience and Psychopathology." *Journal of Parapsychology* 58: 3–38.

Thomas, Dave. 1997a. "The Roswell Incident and Project Mogul." In *The UFO Invasion: The Roswell Incident, Alien Abductions, and Government Coverups*, edited by Kendrick Frazier, Barry Karr, and Joe Nickell, 114–22. Amherst, NY: Prometheus Books.

———. 1997b. "Hidden Messages and the Bible Code." *Skeptical Inquirer* 21: 30–36.

———. 1998. "Tolstoy Predicts Bull's Sixth Championship (in Code of Course)." *Skeptical Inquirer* 22: 16–17.

———. 2001. "Beyond the Bible Code: Hidden Messages Everywhere!" In *Skeptical Odysseys: Personal Accounts by the World's Leading Paranormal Inquirers*, edited by Paul Kurtz, 388–402. Amherst, NY: Prometheus Books.

Thompson, Keith. 1991. *Angels and Aliens: UFOs and the Mythic Imagination*. Reading, MA: Addison-Wesley.

Thompson, Michael, and Gregory Smulewicz-Zucker. 2018. *Anti-Science and the Assault on Democracy: Defending Reason in a Free Society*. Amherst, NY: Prometheus Books.

Thompson, Damien. 2005. *Waiting for Antichrist: Charisma and Apocalypse in a Pentecostal Church*. Oxford: Oxford University Press.

Thouless, Robert. 1942. "The Present Position of Experimental Research into Telepathy and Related Phenomena." *Proceedings for the Society of Psychical Research* 42: 1–19.

———. 1977. "Implications for Religious Studies." In *Advances in Parapsychological Research*, vol. 1, edited by Stanely Krippner, 175–90. New York: Plenum.

Thiry, Paul (Baron d'Holbach). 1813. *Ecce Homo! or A Critical Enquiry into the History of Jesus Christ*. London: D. I. Eton.

Thrall, Margaret. 1979. "Resurrection Traditions and Christian Apologetics." *Thomist* 43: 197–216.

Thurston, Herbert. 1903. "The Holy Shroud and the Verdict of History" *The Month* 101 (January and February): 17–29. Accessed October 2, 2018. http://priory-of-sion.com/biblios/links/memorandum.html.

Tidball, Derek. 1985. *The Social Context of the New Testament: A Sociological Analysis*. Grand Rapids, MI: Zondervan.

Tillich, Paul. 1957. *Dynamics of Faith*. New York: Harper and Row.

Tobin, Paul. 2009. *The Rejection of Pascal's Wager: A Skeptic's Guide to the Bible and the Historical Jesus*. Bedfordshire, UK: Authors OnLine.

Tolbert, Natalie. 2010. "The Polarities of Consciousness." In *Psychosis and Spirituality: Consolidating the New Paradigm*, edited by Isabel Clarke, 37–48. Oxford: Wiley-Blackwell.

Tomasello, Michael. 1999. *The Cultural Origins of Human Cognition*. Cambridge, MA: Harvard University Press.

Tor, Andræ. 1960. *Mohammed, the Man and His Faith*. New York, Harper.

Touger, Eliyahu, and Malaka Touger. 1993–94. *To Know and to Care: An Anthology of Chassidic Stories about the Lubavitcher Rebbe Shlita, Rabbi Menachem M. Schneerson*. 2 Vols. New York: Sichos in English.

Tremlin, Todd. 2006. *Minds and Gods: The Cognitive Foundations of Religion*. Oxford: Oxford University Press.

Trilling, Wolfgang. 1969. *Fragen zur Geschichtlichkeit Jesu*. Leipzig: St. Benno Verlag.

Truzzi, Marcello. 1978. "On the Extraordinary: An Attempt at Clarification." *Zetetic Scholar* 1, no. 1: 11–19.

———. 1996. "Pseudoscience." In *The Encyclopedia of the Paranormal*, edited by Gordon Stein, 560–75. Amherst, NY: Prometheus Books.

Tumin, Melvin, and Arnold Feldman. 1955. "The Miracle at Sabana Grande." *Public Opinion Quarterly* 19: 124–39.

Turner, Edith. 1998. *Experiencing Ritual: A New Interpretation of African Healing*. Philadelphia: University of Pennsylvania Press.

Tylor, Edward. 1929. *Primitive Culture: Researches into the Development of Mythology, Philosophy, Religion, Language, Art, and Custom*, vol. 2. London: John Murray.

Tyson, Neil Degrasse. 2003. "Holy Wars: An Astrophysicist Ponders the God Question." In *Science and Religion: Are They Compatible?*, edited by Paul Kurtz, Barry Karr, and Ranjit Sandhu, 73–87. Amherst, NY: Prometheus Books.

———. 2012. "The Intellectual Collapse of Islam." Accessed December 12, 2017. https://www.youtube.com/watch?v=Fl1nJC3lvFs.

Van Buren, Paul. 1998. *According to the Scriptures: The Origins of the Gospel and of the Church's Old Testament*. Grand Rapids, MI: Eerdmans.

Van de Castle, Robert. 1977. "Parapsychology and Anthropology." In *Handbook of Parapsychology*, edited by Benjamin Wolmann, Laura Dale, Gertrude Schmeidler, and Montague Ullman, 667–86. New York: Van Nostrand Reinhold.

———. 2012. Foreword. In *Paranthropology: Anthropological Approaches to the Paranormal*, edited by Jack Hunter, 15–19. Bristol, UK: Paranthropology.

Van Flandern, Tom. 2002. "Mysterious Mars." Accessed October 1, 2018. https://www.youtube.com/watch?v=zgzkjsMmRZg.

Van Inwagen, Peter. 1993. "Genesis and Evolution." In *Reasoned Faith: Essays in Philosophical Theology in Honor of Norman Kretzmann*, edited by Eleonore Stump, 93–127. Ithaca: Cornell University Press.

———. 2009. "Explaining Belief in the Supernatural: Some Thoughts on Paul Bloom's Religious Belief as an Evolutionary Accident." In *The Believing Primate: Scientific, Philosophical, and Theological Reflections on the Origins of Religion*, edited by Jeffrey Schloss and Michael Murray, 128–38. New York: Oxford University Press.

Van Lommel, Ruud van Wees, Vincent Meyers, and Ingrid Elfferich. 2001. "Near-death Experience in Survivors of Cardiac Arrest: A Prospective Study in the Netherlands." *The Lancet* 358, no. 9298: 2039–45.

Vansina, Jan. 1985. *Oral Tradition as History*. Madison: University of Wisconsin Press.

Varghese, Roy. 2003. Preface in *Did Jesus Rise from the Dead? The Resurrection Debate*, edited by Gary Habermas, Anthony Flew, and Terry Miethe, ix–xiii. Eugene, OR: Wipf & Stock.

Velmans, Max. 2000. *Understanding Consciousness*. London: Routledge.

Victor, Jeffrey. 1993. *Satanic Panic: The Creation of a Contemporary Legend*. Chicago: Open Court.

Voltaire (Francois Maria Arouet). [1759]. 1918. *Candide*. New York: Boni and Liveright. Accessed January 30, 2018. https://archive.org/stream/candide19942gut/19942.txt.

———. [1764]. 1901. *Philosophical Dictionary*, vol. 5. Translated by William F. Fleming. London: E. DuMont. Accessed January 6, 2018. https://oll.libertyfund.org/titles/voltaire-the-works-of-voltaire-vol-v-philosophical-dictionary-part-3.

———. 2017. *The Best Voltaire Quotes*. James Alexander. Crombie Jardine.

Walker, William. 1969. "Post-crucifixion Appearances and Christian Origins." *Journal of Biblical Literature* 88, no. 2: 157–65.

———. 1972. "The Origin of the Son of Man Concept as Applied to Jesus." *Journal of Biblical Literature* 91, no. 4: 483–90.

Wallace, Anthony. 1966. *Religion: An Anthropological View*. New York: Random House.

Warburton, William. 1841. *A Selection from Unpublished Papers of the Right Reverend William Warburton.* London: John Boyer Nichols.

Warraq, Ibn. ed. 2000. *The Quest for the Historical Muhammad.* Amherst, NY: Prometheus Books.

Warraq, Ibn.1998. "Introduction." In *The Origins of the Koran: Classic Essays on Islam's Holy Book,* edited by Ibn Warraq, 9–35. Amherst, NY: Prometheus Books.

Watkins, John. 2008. *Hearing Voices: A Common Human Experience.* Melbourne: Michelle Anderson.

Watson, Francis. 1987. "Historical Evidence and the Resurrection of Jesus." *Theology* 90, no. 737: 365–72.

———. 2007 . *Paul, Judaism and the Gentiles: Beyond the New Perspectives.* Grand Rapids, MI: Eerdmans.

Watt, Caroline, and Richard Wiseman. 2009. Foreword to *The Psychology of Paranormal Belief: A Researcher's Handbook,* by Irwin Harvey, xvii–xviii. Hertfordshire, UK: University of Hertfordshire Press.

Watt, Diane. 2001. Medieval Millenarianism and Prophecy. In *Christian Millenarianism: From the Early Church to Waco,* edited by Stephen Hunt, 88–97. Bloomington: Indiana University Press.

Watt, Montgomery. 1961. *Muhammad: Prophet and Statesman.* Oxford: Oxford University Press.

Watt, William. 1963. *Muslim Intellectual: A Study of al-Ghazali.* Edinburgh: Edinburgh University Press.

Wedderburn, Alexander. 1999. *Beyond Resurrection.* London: Hendrickson.

Weinberg, Steven. 1993 *Dreams of a Final Theory: The Scientist's Search for the Ultimate Laws of Nature.* New York: Vintage Books.

———. 1999. "A Designer Universe?" *New York Review of Books,* October 1999: 46–48.

Weisberg, Barbara. 2005. *Talking to the Dead: Kate and Maggie Fox and the Rise of Spiritualism.* New York: HarperOne.

Weisse, Christian Hermann. 1838. *Die evangelische Geschichte: kritisch und philosophisch bearbeitet.* Leipzig: Breitkopf und Härtel.

Weisman, David. 2015. "Dissolution into Death." In *The Myth of an Afterlife: The Case against Life after Death,* edited by Michael Martin and Keith Augustine. 83–104. Lanham, MD: Rowman and Littlefield.

Wells, George Albert. 1979. *The Jesus of the Early Christians.* London: Pemberton Books.

———. 1996. *The Jesus Legend.* Peru, IL: Carus.

Werde, William. 1983. *The Messianic Secret.* Minneapolis, MN: Fortress Press.

Wernick, Uri. 1975. "Frustrated Beliefs and Early Christianity: A Psychological Inquiry into the Gospels of the New Testament." *Numen* 22: 96–130.

Wesselman, Henry. 1996. *Spiritwalker: Messages from the Future.* New York: *Bantam Books.*

Whealey, Alice. 2007. "Josephus, Eusebius of Caesarea, and the *Testimonium Flavianum.*" In *Josephus und das Neue Testament,* edited by Christfried Böttrich and Jenz Herzer, 73–116. Tübingen: Mohr Siebeck.

Whinnery, James. 1979. "Techniques for Simulating G-Induced Tunnel Vision." *Aviation and Space Environmental Medicine* 50: 1076.

———. 1997. "Psychophysiologic Correlates of Unconsciousness and Near-Death Experiences." *Journal of Near-Death Studies* 15, no. 4231–58.

Whinnery, James, and Angela Whinnery. 1990. "Acceleration-Induced Loss of Consciousness: A Review of 500 Episodes." *Archives of Neurology* 47: 764–76.

White, Michael. 1998. *Isaac Newton: The Last Sorcerer.* New York: Basic Books.

Whitehouse, Harvey. 2004. *Modes of Religiosity: A Cognitive Theory of Religious Transmission.* Walnut Creek, CA: AltaMira.

———. 2007. "The Evolution and History of Religion." In *Holistic Anthropology: Emergence and Convergence,* edited by David Parkin and Stanley Ulijaszek, 212–33. New York: Berghahn Books.

———. 2008. "Cognitive Evolution and Religion; Cognition and Religious Evolution." In *The Evolution of Religion: Studies, Theories, and Critiques,* edited by Joseph Bulbulia, Richard Sosis, Erica Harris, Russell Genet, Cheryl Genet, and Karen Wyman, 31–41. Santa Margarita, CA: Collins Foundation Press.

Whitehead, Alfred. 1974. *Religion in the Making*. New York: New American Library.

Whittaker, David. 1970. "What Happened to the Body of Jesus?" *Expository Times* 81: 307–10.

Wiebe, Donald. 1984a. "Beyond the Sceptic and the Devotee: Reductionism in the Scientific Study of Religion." *Journal of the American Academy of Religion* 52, no. 1: 157–65.

———. 1984b. "The Failure of Nerve in the Academic Study of Religion." *Studies in Religion* 13, no. 4: 401–22.

Wilckens, Ulrich. 1968. "The Tradition-history of the Resurrection of Jesus." In *The Significance of the Message of the Resurrection for Faith in Jesus Christ*, edited by Dorothea Barton and R. Wilson, 51–76. London: SCM Press.

———. 1977. *Resurrection: Biblical Testimony to the Resurrection: An Historical Examination and Explanation*. Edinburgh: The Saint Andrew Press.

Wilken, Robert. 1984. *The Christians as the Romans Saw Them*. New Haven, CT: Yale University Press.

Williams, Michael. 2001. *Problems of Knowledge: A Critical Introduction to Epistemology*. Oxford: Oxford University Press.

Williams, Richard, and Daniel Robinson. eds. 2015. *Scientism: The New Orthodoxy*. New York: Bloomsbury.

Wilson, Barrie. 2008. *How Jesus Became Christian*. New York: St. Martin's Griffin.

Wilson, Ian. 1984. *Jesus: The Evidence*. San Francisco. CA: Harper and Row.

———. 2011. *The Shroud: The 2000-Year-Old Mystery Solved*. New York: Bantam.

Wilson, Krissy, and Christopher French. 2006. "The Relationship between Susceptibility to False Memories, Dissociativity, and Paranormal Belief and Experience." *Personality and Individual Differences* 41: 1493–502.

Winzeler, Robert. 2008. *Anthropology and Religion: What We Know, Think, and Question*. Lanham, MD: AltaMira.

Wiseman, Richard. 2010. "Heads I Win, Tails You Lose: How Some Parapsychologists Nullify Null Results and What to Do about It." In *Debating Psychic Experience: Human Potential or Human Illusion*, edited by Stanley Krippner and Harris Friedman, 169–78. Santa Barbara, CA: Praeger.

Wiseman, Richard, and Emma Greening. 2005. "It's Still Bending: Verbal Suggestion and Alleged Psychokinetic Ability." *British Journal of Psychology* 96: 115–27.

Woerlee, Gerald. 2003. *Mortal Minds: The Biology of Near-Death Experiences*. Amherst, NY: Prometheus Press.

Wolfson, Elliot. 2009. *Open Secret: Postmessianic Messianism and Mystical Revision of Menaḥem Mendel Schneerson*. New York: Columbia University Press.

Wood, Robert.1904. "The N-Rays." *Nature* 70: 530–31.

Worrall, John. 1997. "Is the Idea of Scientific Explanation Unduly Anthropocentric? The Lessons of the Anthropic Principle." *LSE – CPNSS: Discussion Paper*, Series 25–96: 1–20. London: London School of Economics Staff.

Wright, Nicholas Thomas. 2003. *The Resurrection of the Son of God*. Minneapolis, MN: Fortress Press.

Wulff, David. 2000. "Mystical Experiences. "In *Varieties of Anomalous Experience: Examining the Scientific Evidence*, edited by Etzel Cardeña, Steven Lynn, and Stanley Krippner, 397–440. Washington, DC: American Psychological Association.

Yamauchi, Edwin.1974a. "Easter-myth, Hallucination, or History? Part 1." *Christianity Today* 15: 660–63.

———. 1974b. "Easter-myth, Hallucination, or History? Part 2." *Christianity Today* 29: 728–32.

Ziegler, Charles. 1997. "Mythogeneis: Historical Development of the Roswell Narrative." In *UFO Crash at Roswell: The Genesis of a Modern Myth*, edited by Benson Saler, Charles Ziegler, and Charles Moore, 1–29. Washington: Smithsonian Institution Press.

Zusne, Leonard. 1985. "Magical Thinking and Parapsychology." In *A Skeptic's Handbook of Parapsychology*, edited by Paul Kurtz, 685–700. Buffalo, NY: Prometheus Books.

Zusne, Leonard, and Warren Jones. 1989. *Anomalistic Psychology: A Study of Magical Thinking*. Hillsdale, NJ: Lawrence Erlbaum Associates.

Zias, Joseph, and Eliezer Sekeles. 1985. "The Crucified Man from Giv'at ha-Mitvar: A Reappraisal." *Israel Exploration Journal* 35: 22–27.

Zuckerman, Phil. 2008 . *Society Without God: What the Least Religious Nations Can Tell Us about Contentment*. New York: New York University Press.

Zulueta, F. de. 1932. "Violation of Sepulture in Palestine at the Beginning of the Christian Era." *Journal of Roman Studies* 22: 184–97.

Zygmunt, Joseph. 1972. "When Prophecies Fail: A Theoretical Perspective on the Comparative Evidence." *American Behavioral Scientist* 16, no. 2: 1552–3381.

# INDEX

www.ingramcontent.com/pod-product-compliance
Ingram Content Group UK Ltd.
Pitfield, Milton Keynes, MK11 3LW, UK
UKHW041830100926
8556IPUK00002B/99

9 781785 27162